The Political Economy of Covid-19

This comprehensive book brings together research published during 2021 analysing the impact of the Covid-19 pandemic on the economy – on output and employment, on inequality, and on public policy responses.

The Covid-19 pandemic has been the greatest public health crisis for a century – since the 'Spanish Flu' pandemic of 1919. The economic impact has been equally seismic. While it is too early to measure the full economic cost – since much of this will continue to accumulate for some time to come – it will certainly be one of the greatest global economic shocks of the past century.

Some chapters in this edited volume report on specific countries, while some take a comparative look between countries, and others analyse the impact upon the global economy. Even before the Covid-19 pandemic, there had been calls for a 'great reset' in face of the climate crisis, the increased income and wealth inequality, and the need to avoid further global financial crisis. With the devastating Covid-19 pandemic – a harbinger for further such pandemics – there is an even greater need for a reset, and for the reset to be that much greater.

The chapters in this book were originally published as special issues in the journal *International Review of Applied Economics.*

Jonathan Michie is Professor of Innovation and Knowledge Exchange at the University of Oxford, where he is also President of Kellogg College. He is the managing editor of the *International Review of Applied Economics*, and Chair of the Universities Association for Lifelong Learning.

Maura Sheehan is Professor of International Management at Edinburgh Napier University. She is Associate Editor of the *International Review of Applied Economics* and Editor in Chief of the *Journal of Organisational Effectiveness: People and Performance* (JOEPP).

The Political Economy of Covid-19

Covid-19, Inequality and Government Responses

Edited by
Jonathan Michie and Maura Sheehan

LONDON AND NEW YORK

First published 2023
by Routledge
4 Park Square, Milton Park, Abingdon, Oxon OX14 4RN

and by Routledge
605 Third Avenue, New York, NY 10158

Routledge is an imprint of the Taylor & Francis Group, an informa business

British Library Cataloguing in Publication Data
A catalogue record for this book is available from the British Library

ISBN13: 978-1-032-30957-6 (hbk)
ISBN13: 978-1-032-30959-0 (pbk)
ISBN13: 978-1-003-30744-0 (ebk)

DOI: 10.4324/9781003307440

Typeset in Minion Pro
by Newgen Publishing UK

Publisher's Note
The publisher accepts responsibility for any inconsistencies that may have arisen during the conversion of this book from journal articles to book chapters, namely the inclusion of journal terminology.

Disclaimer
Every effort has been made to contact copyright holders for their permission to reprint material in this book. The publishers would be grateful to hear from any copyright holder who is not here acknowledged and will undertake to rectify any errors or omissions in future editions of this book.

Contents

Citation Information

The chapters in this book were originally published in the *International Review of Applied Economics*, volume 35, issue 02 and 06 (2021). When citing this material, please use the original page numbering for each article, as follows:

Introduction

Building back better?
Jonathan Michie and Maura Sheehan
International Review of Applied Economics, volume 35, issue 2 (2021), pp. 111–116

Chapter 1

Organizational participation in post-covid society – its contributions and enabling conditions
John Child
International Review of Applied Economics, volume 35, issue 2 (2021), pp. 117–146

Chapter 2

The psychological consequences of COVID-19 lockdowns
Kien Le and My Nguyen
International Review of Applied Economics, volume 35, issue 2 (2021), pp. 147–163

Chapter 3

COVID-19: effectiveness of socioeconomic factors in containing the spread and mortality
Joshua Ping Ang, Fang Dong and Jason Patalinghug
International Review of Applied Economics, volume 35, issue 2 (2021), pp. 164–187

Chapter 4

Is there a shift contagion among stock markets during the COVID-19 crisis? Further insights from TYDL causality test
Amine Ben Amar, Néjib Hachicha and Nihel Halouani
International Review of Applied Economics, volume 35, issue 2 (2021), pp. 188–209

Chapter 5

Health risk and the efficient market hypothesis in the time of COVID-19
Evangelos Vasileiou, Aristeidis Samitas, Maria Karagiannaki and Jagadish Dandu
International Review of Applied Economics, volume 35, issue 2 (2021), pp. 210–223

Chapter 6

Behavioral finance and market efficiency in the time of the COVID-19 pandemic: does fear drive the market?
Evangelos Vasileiou
International Review of Applied Economics, volume 35, issue 2 (2021), pp. 224–241

Chapter 7

Analysis of containment measures and economic policies arising from COVID-19 in the European Union
Javier Cifuentes-Faura
International Review of Applied Economics, volume 35, issue 2 (2021), pp. 242–255

Chapter 8

Covid 19: Ramifications for progress towards the sustainable development goals (SDGs) in Nigeria
O'Raye Dicta Ogisi and Toritseju Begho
International Review of Applied Economics, volume 35, issue 2 (2021), pp. 256–268

Chapter 9

The political risk factors of COVID-19
J. Eduardo Vera-Valdés
International Review of Applied Economics, volume 35, issue 2 (2021), pp. 269–287

Chapter 10

A green new deal and debt sustainability for the post COVID-19 world
Juan Rafael Ruiz and Patricia Stupariu
International Review of Applied Economics, volume 35, issue 2 (2021), pp. 288–307

Chapter 11

COVID-19 and the Chinese economy: impacts, policy responses and implications
Kerry Liu
International Review of Applied Economics, volume 35, issue 2 (2021), pp. 308–330

Chapter 12

The 'Great Reset' to tackle Covid-19 and other crises
Jonathan Michie and Maura Sheehan
International Review of Applied Economics, volume 35, issue 6 (2021), pp. 793–795

Chapter 13

The Covid-19 pandemic and economic stimulus in India: has it been a hostage of macro-economic complications?
Himadri Shekhar Chakrabarty, Partha Ray and Parthapratim Pal
International Review of Applied Economics, volume 35, issue 6 (2021), pp. 796–812

Chapter 14

Accounting for global value chains: rising global inequality in the wake of COVID-19?
Christa D. Court, João-Pedro Ferreira, Geoffrey J.D. Hewings and Michael L. Lahr
International Review of Applied Economics, volume 35, issue 6 (2021), pp. 813–831

Chapter 15

Impact of pandemics on income inequality: lessons from the past
Pinaki Das, Santanu Bisai and Sudeshna Ghosh
International Review of Applied Economics, volume 35, issue 6 (2021), pp. 832–850

Chapter 16

The Korean government's public health responses to the COVID-19 epidemic through the lens of industrial policy
Hee-Young Shin
International Review of Applied Economics, volume 35, issue 6 (2021), pp. 851–869

Chapter 17

The impact of COVID-19 on the Indian economy
Deepak Kumar Behera, Maryam Sabreen and Deepika Sharma
International Review of Applied Economics, volume 35, issue 6 (2021), pp. 870–885

Chapter 18

An empirical analysis of COVID-19 response: comparison of US with the G7
Mahua Barari, Srikanta Kundu and Saibal Mitra
International Review of Applied Economics, volume 35, issue 6 (2021), pp. 886–903

Notes on Contributors

Amine Ben Amar, UIR, RBS College of Management, Morocco.

Joshua Ping Ang, Department of Business, Rogers State University, OK, USA.

Mahua Barari, Department of Economics, Missouri State University, Springfield, MO, USA.

Toritseju Begho, Rural Economy Environment and Society, Scotland's Rural College (SRUC), Edinburgh, UK.

Deepak Kumar Behera, Department of Humanities and Social Science, National Institute of Technology Patna, Patna, Bihar, India.

Santanu Bisai, Department of Economics, Sidho Kanho Birsha University, Purulia, India.

Himadri Shekhar Chakrabarty, Economics Group, IIM Calcutta, Kolkata, India.

John Child, Birmingham Business School, University of Birmingham, Birmingham, UK.

Javier Cifuentes-Faura, University of Murcia, Murcia, Spain.

Christa D. Court, Food and Resource Economics Department, University of Florida, Gainesville, FL, USA.

Jagadish Dandu, College of Business, Zayed University, Dubai, UAE.

Pinaki Das, Department of Economics, Vidyasagar University, Midnapur, India.

Fang Dong, Department of Economics, Providence College, Providence, RI, USA.

João-Pedro Ferreira, Food and Resource Economics Department, University of Florida, Gainesville, FL, USA.

Sudeshna Ghosh, Department of Economics, Scottish Church College, Kolkata, India.

Néjib Hachicha, FSEGS, University of Sfax, Sfax, Tunisia.

Nihel Halouani, ISAAS, University of Sfax, Sfax, Tunisia.

Geoffrey J.D. Hewings, Regional Economics Applications Laboratory, University of Illinois at Urbana-Champaign, IL, USA.

Maria Karagiannaki, School of Social Sciences, Hellenic Open University, Patras, Greece.

Srikanta Kundu, Department of Economics, Centre for Development Studies, Trivandrum, India.

Michael L. Lahr, Edward J. Bloustein School of Planning & Public Policy, Rutgers, The State University of New Jersey, New Brunswick, NJ, USA.

Kien Le, The Faculty of Economics and Public Management, Ho Chi Minh City Open University, Ho Chi Minh City, Vietnam.

Kerry Liu, China Studies Centre, University of Sydney, Australia.

Jonathan Michie, University of Oxford, Kellogg College, Oxford, UK.

Saibal Mitra, Department of Physics, Astronomy and Material Science, Missouri State University, Springfield, MO, USA.

My Nguyen, The Faculty of Economics and Public Management, Ho Chi Minh City Open University, Ho Chi Minh City, Vietnam.

O'Raye Dicta Ogisi, Department of Agricultural Economics and Extension, Faculty of Agriculture, Delta State, University, Asaba Campus, Asaba, Nigeria.

Parthapratim Pal, Economics Group, IIM Calcutta, Kolkata, India.

Jason Patalinghug, Department of Economics, Southern Connecticut State University, New Haven, CT, USA.

Partha Ray, Economics Group, IIM Calcutta, Kolkata, India.

Juan Rafael Ruiz, Department is Applied Economics, Universidad Complutense de Madrid, Madrid, Spain.

Maryam Sabreen, Department of Humanities and Social Science, National Institute of Technology Patna, Patna, Bihar, India.

Aristeidis Samitas, College of Business, Zayed University, Abu Dhabi, UAE.

Deepika Sharma, Department of Humanities and Social Science, National Institute of Technology Patna, Patna, Bihar, India.

Maura Sheehan, Professor of International Management, Edinburgh Napier University, Edinburgh, UK.

Hee-Young Shin, Department of Economics, Wright State University, Dayton, OH, USA.

Patricia Stupariu, Instituto Complutense de Estudios Internacionales (ICEI), Complutense University of Madrid, Madrid, Spain.

Evangelos Vasileiou, Department of Financial and Management Engineering, University of the Aegean - School of Engineering, Chios, Greece.

J. Eduardo Vera-Valdés, Department of Mathematical Sciences, Aalborg University, Aalborg East, Denmark.

Introduction: Building back better?

Jonathan Michie and Maura Sheehan

ABSTRACT
A global health and economic crisis was created by the spread of Covid-19 across the world during the course of 2020 and into 2021. This Special Issue of the *International Review of Applied Economics* brings together papers analysing various aspects of this twin crisis. The crisis led to massive intervention by governments, both to tackle the health crisis - through lock-downs; social distancing measures; test, trace and isolate programmes; and to develop and then provide vaccinations - and to offset the economic damage created by the lock-downs, the fall in travel and trade, and so forth. Several of the papers take up the challenge of how we might 'build back better'. The leading expert on organisational studies and organisational behaviour John Child notes that while the Covid-19 pandemic intensified many of the economic and social problems that societies were already facing, the public response to the crisis points to a constructive way forward, including people participating in collective activities to contribute to addressing the common challenge, arguing that "it is timely to widen participation in organisational decision-making as an approach to addressing many of the problems which will continue to be with us post-Covid, and which indeed the pandemic has exacerbated". These further challenges include inequality, and the climate crisis. Both could be tackled through a global Green New Deal.

1. Introduction

The Covid-19 pandemic spread rapidly across the globe during the course of 2020, and continues into 2021 – with new variants most notably in the UK, South Africa and Brazil – on a scale and with a severity not seen since the devastating Spanish flu of 1918–20. We are in a human, economic, environmental and social crisis. Action will continue to be needed for some time, including by governments and other public authorities – within as well as across countries and their regions – to deal not only with the crisis itself but also with its aftermath, to enable economies and societies to recover, and to make our economies and societies more resilient and sustainable for the future. Creating this resilience includes addressing the inequalities in society which have made some communities more vulnerable than others – as witnessed both within and between countries.[1]

The magnitude of the crisis requires very different types of government response compared to the *laissez faire* attitudes promoted since the 1980s. The response to the 2007–2008 international financial crisis and the resultant global recession of 2009 was inadequate, leaving largely unreformed the system of international financial speculation, underlying inequalities and industrial scale tax avoidance and evasion. Since then, in many countries a decade of austerity had left critical public institutions under-funded and insufficiently prepared to deal with the Covid-19 crisis. But with governments forced to act dramatically and intervene extensively, the crisis presents an opportunity to bring about a fundamental shift in the political landscape, so that more sustainable and equitable economic and social policies might become the new norm.

This Special Issue brings together contributions from economists, economic sociologists, financial and health economists, management scientists, policy analysts and other social scientists. They offer critical insight into the causes, effects and opportunities around the Covid-19 crisis – with several of the papers reporting research into the impact of the Covid-19 crisis in developing and emerging economies, and upon vulnerable and disadvantaged individuals and communities.

2. The papers

In 'Organizational participation in post-covid society – its contributions and enabling conditions', the leading expert on organisational studies and organisational behaviour John Child notes that while the Covid-19 pandemic intensified many of the economic and social problems that societies were already facing, the public response to the crisis points to a constructive way forward. This includes people participating in collective activities to contribute to addressing the common challenge. The paper argues that 'it is timely to widen participation in organisational decision-making as an approach to addressing many of the problems which will continue to be with us post-Covid, and which indeed the pandemic has exacerbated.' John Child develops a framework for defining and classifying the principal forms of organisational participation, considers how these may contribute to economic and social improvement, and discusses the practical policy implications.

The Covid-19 crisis led to governments across the globe imposing lockdowns of their populations to seek to reduce the spread of the virus. In 'The Psychological Consequences of Covid-19 Lockdowns', Kien Le and My Nguyen analyse the various adverse psychological outcomes with which these lockdowns were associated, and how these outcomes – such as anxiety and depression – may be attributed in turn to concerns over food, housing, and employment security. They also report that 'African Americans and women were especially susceptible to these adverse repercussions of the lockdowns', and argue that 'lockdowns should be accompanied by policies aimed at preventing these repercussions, of exacerbating inequality and impacting on mental health'. This contribution demonstrates how the most marginalised in economies and societies have been the most disproportionately impacted psychologically by the pandemic.

In 'Covid-19: Effectiveness of Socioeconomic Factors in Containing the Spread and Mortality', Joshua Ang, Fang Dong and Jason Patalinghug report the results of evaluating the socioeconomic factors in containing the spread of Covid-19 and its mortality, across eighty countries. As one might expect, having had previous coronavirus outbreaks helps, creating the benefit of institutional learning and memory. But the fact of 'globalisation' does not mean that such learning is then spread uniformly across the globe – it does remain embedded to some degree in the localities where that learning occurred. One of the social factors that appears to play a positive role is better education in science.

Amine Ben Amar, Nejib Hachicha and Nihel Halouani ask 'Is there a Shift Contagion Among Stock Markets During the Covid-19 Crisis?', and find that while 'the Chinese stock index had no influence on the rest of the studied stock market indices during the Covid-19 crisis', the European stock index did influence market sentiment more widely. In addition, while there was an initial impact on equity markets from the Covid-19 crisis, policy interventions did seem to have helped in providing reassurance, and thereby mitigating, at least in the short-medium term, the spread of such financial stress.

In 'Health Risk and the Efficient Market Hypothesis in the time of Covid-19', Evangelos Vasileiou, Aristeidis Samitas, Maria Karagiannaki and Jagadish Dandu report that the stock markets did not always incorporate all the available information, in many cases evaluating the available news only slowly, and in certain time periods having a reaction that seemed both irrational and inefficient. The paper's findings of health risks being underestimated, and of slow responses, suggest that a behavioural view may be more appropriate than a 'financial economics' approach. In a second paper, 'Behavioural Finance and Market Efficiency in the Time of the Covid-19 Pandemic: does Fear Drive the Market?', Evangelos Vasileiou examines the US stock markets during the Covid-19 outbreak, finding that 'during some periods the health risk was significantly underestimated and/or ignored'.

Javier Cifuentes-Faura presents an 'Analysis of Containment Measures and Economic Policies Arising from Covid-19 in the European Union', finding that those countries that acted early were less affected. The paper also discusses possible policies that might be developed at the European Union level in response to the Covid-19 crisis. The paper argues that coordinated EU wide monetary and fiscal policies have significant potential to mitigate and truncate the duration of the adverse social and economic impacts of Covid-19.

In 'Covid-19: Ramifications for progress towards the sustainable development goals (SDGs) in Nigeria', Toritseju Begho and O'Raye Ogisi analyse data from 954 farm households in Nigeria, finding a significant threat from the Covid-19 crisis on farm household food security. The paper argues that Covid-19 poses a threat to the attainment of SDGs 1, 2, 3 and 8, namely 'no poverty', 'zero hunger', 'good health and wellbeing', and 'decent work and economic growth'. The paper concludes that beyond the urgent need for financial and food assistance, 'government would need to mitigate the impact of Covid-19 through targeted social protection programs and policies to ensure that the country gets back on track to achieve the SDGs'.

In 'The Political Risk Factors of Covid-19', J. Eduardo Vera-Valdés analyses how the number of Covid-19 cases and deaths relate to 23 explanatory variables covering health, political, and economic factors across 94 countries, finding that: 'A higher level of trust in medical personnel is associated with fewer cases, while a higher level of trust in the government is associated with fewer deaths due to Covid-19', and 'hospital beds per thousand inhabitants are a statistically significant factor in reducing the number of deaths'.

Covid-19 first emerged in China, and that country has thus had the longest record of seeking to deal with the crisis in terms both of measures that seek to stop the spread of the disease, and in taking actions to counteract the damaging economic impact of lockdowns, social distancing and other such measures. These policy responses and their implications are analysed by Kerry Liu in 'Covid-19 and the Chinese Economy: Impacts, Policy Responses and Implications'. Given the role of the Chinese economy internationally, there is clearly a danger of an economic downturn in that country exacerbating economic problems elsewhere, and so the fact that to date the mitigating measures do seem to have prevented the sort of downturn that might otherwise have been expected is good news. However, the paper also considers the extent to which the costs of these measures themselves will have to be paid for – in various ways – in the future. And this of course is an issue that all governments will be facing.

Finally, Juan Rafael Ruiz and Patricia Stupariu look at precisely this issue – of how the world's economies might best 'build back better' – in 'A Green New Deal and debt sustainability for the post Covid-19 world', which explores the design and impact on public finances of a global investment plan directed at supporting post-Covid-19 reconstruction efforts by investing in climate change mitigation. This chimes nicely with the January 2021 meetings of the World Economic Forum – the gathering that is usually held at Davos, but this year will be both virtual and global, with 'gatherings' planned in cities across the globe. This 'global' format was chosen precisely to emphasise the fact that we face global challenges – including Covid-19 and the threat of further such pandemics, and the climate crisis – which demand global solutions, although for a critique, see https://theconversation.com/davos-2021-to-achieve-a-great-reset-we-cant-count-on-the-same-old-globalists-to-lead-the-way-153508.

3. Conclusion

The 'capitalism unleashed' variety of globalisation that has been promoted since the 1980s has produced and exacerbated a range of economic, social and environmental crises – from increased inequalities, to the climate crisis, to the 2007–2009 international financial crisis and global recession.[2] In relation to the Covid-19 crisis – and the likelihood of further such pandemics in the future – a fundamental issue is what role is played by the drive for unending growth on a planet with limited resources.[3] Unlike other pandemics and famines, Covid-19 struck both developed and developing countries, regardless of economic, political and social systems, making it in some ways a 'leveller' but also placing a spotlight on the inequalities and injustices across these systems. Government responses to the pandemic also illustrates widening and deepening global political polarisation.

There is widespread agreement on the need to 'build back better' from the Covid-19 crisis. This needs to segue into tackling the climate crisis. So, one major task is to develop a more socially, economically and environmentally sustainable form of globalisation – with stricter regulation of speculative financial flows and illegal tax evasion, and collaboration around a Global Green New Deal.[4]

As John Child's paper argues, we also need reform at the corporate and organisational level. Our own research on employee participation and engagement found consistently the sort of positive results described by John Child, with improved corporate performance and organisational outcomes.[5] Management practices that promote these policies and practices – of participation and engagement – can be encouraged and embedded when the corporate ownership itself is mutual, with ownership stakes in the hands of its employees, customers or other stakeholders such as the local community.[6]

So, while the papers in this volume point to various failures of the current socio-economic system that may have exacerbated the spread of the virus (Joshua Ang, Fang Dong and Jason Patalinghug), and to the damage done by the covid-19 crisis to individuals and communities (Kien Le and My Nguyen), they also report findings that show that we can build back better (Javier Cifuentes-Faura; Juan Rafael Ruiz and Patricia Stupariu). J. Eduardo Vera-Valdés's findings on the importance of trust links back to the arguments in John Child's paper, regarding the benefits of engaging people in the world of work, which also apply more generally within communities and across society. Joshua Ang, Fang Dong and Jason Patalinghug find that education in science played a positive role in reducing the spread of the infection and in mortality rates, and education could also play a crucial role in building back better – education in communities, at work, and throughout life.[7]

In response to our call for papers that analyse the political economy of the covid-19 crisis, and how we can build back better globally, we received a large number of outstanding contributions, the first batch of which are published in this Special Issue, with many more currently being revised in response to referees' reports – so we look forward to publishing a follow-up Special Issue in due course. Further papers are still welcome. One thing is certain, that we need this research and analysis, both to inform public policy, and also to refresh our approach to economic theory, to make it more realistic and relevant.[8] We need to build back better – society, economies, and economics.

Notes

1. See for example United Nations (2020).
2. 'Capitalism unleashed' was the term coined by Andrew Glyn (2006) to describe the current era of deregulated free-market globalisation.
3. On the 'rapacious consumption' of the global north pushing farming and other economic activity globally into the likes of the Brazilian rainforest, creating new opportunities for viruses to be transmitted, see Spinney (2020).
4. As argued in detail by, for example, Michie (2017), Pettifor (2019) and Pollin (forthcoming).
5. See for example Michie and Sheehan (2003), which reports and discusses a number of our published research papers on this topic, of progressive management practices around employee participation and engagement on the one hand, and positive corporate performance and organisational outcomes on the other.
6. For a discussion of which, see for example the July 2020 *International Review of Applied Economics* issue on 'Alternative Corporate Forms in the Global South', 35:4.
7. When Britain was considering how to 'build back better' from the social and economic ravages of World War One, their Ministry of Reconstruction saw adult education and lifelong learning as playing a key role – for the participation of citizens in debating the big issues facing society, for dealing with the new industries and technologies on the horizon, and for the health of democracy. See The Centenary Commission on Adult Education (2019), which also sets out an agenda for adult education and lifelong learning in today's world – available free of charge at www.CentenaryCommission.org. The House of Commons Education Committee (2020) argues that this agenda is all the more important for the post-covid world – see https://wonkhe.com/blogs/government-could-support-lifelong-learning-or-just-launch-initiatives/.

8. On which, see amongst others Promoting Economic Pluralism – http://economicpluralism.org – and their journal The Mint Magazine, www.themintmagazine.com.

Disclosure statement

No potential conflict of interest was reported by the authors.

References

Glyn, A. 2006. *Capitalism Unleashed: Finance, Globalization, and Welfare*. Oxford: Oxford University Press.

House of Commons Education Committee. 2020. *A Plan for an Adult Skills and Lifelong Learning Revolution*. 19 December. London: House of Commons.

Michie, J., and M. Sheehan. 2003. "Labour 'Flexibility' – Securing Management's Right to Manage Badly?" *In Systems of Production: Markets, Organisations and Performance*, edited by B. Burchell, S. Deakin, J. Michie, and J. Rubery, 178–191. In Routledge.

Michie, J. 2017. *Advanced Introduction to Globalisation*. Cheltenham: Edward Elgar.

Pettifor, A. 2019. *The Case for the Green New Deal*. London & New York: Verso.

Pollin, R. forthcoming. "The Industrial Policy Requirements for a Global Climate Stabilization Project." *International Review of Applied Economics* forthcoming [published online].

Spinney, L. 2020. "The Colonialist Thinking that Skews Our View of Deforestation." *The Guardian Journal*, December 22, 1–2.

The Centenary Commission on Adult Education. 2019. "'A Permanent National Necessity . . . ' – Adult Education and Lifelong Learning for 21st Century Britain." www.CentenaryCommission.org

United Nations. 2020. *Everyone Included: Social Impact of COVID-19*. UN: Department of Economic and Social Affairs Social Inclusion.

Part I

Causes, Effects and Impact of the COVID-19 Crisis

Organizational participation in post-covid society: its contributions and enabling conditions

John Child

ABSTRACT

The Covid-19 pandemic has intensified the economic and social problems that societies face today. At the same time, the public response to the crisis points to a constructive way forward. It has brought people together and unleashed a desire to contribute in many ways, some small and others spectacular. It has demonstrated how opportunities for people to participate in collective activities both psychologically and behaviorally can achieve remarkable results, especially when addressing a common danger. This paper argues that it is timely to widen participation in organizational decision-making as an approach to addressing many of the problems which will continue to be with us post-Covid, and which indeed the pandemic has exacerbated. In order to arrive at practical policy options, it proceeds through the following stages. The first is to establish a working definition of organizational participation and to develop a framework for classifying its principal forms. This framework serves to identify the more advanced and consequential forms of participation, and is then used to structure an evidence-based review of how they can constructively contribute to economic and social improvement. The final part of the paper reviews conditions bearing on the practical implementation of participation and which serve to clarify practical policy implications.

1. Introduction

The Covid-19 pandemic has intensified the economic and social problems that societies face today.[1] Economies have suffered deep recessions, recovery from which will require a renewed competitive vigour sustained by rising productivity and innovation. The uneven impact of the pandemic on different socio-economic and ethnic groups has added to inequalities between them and is likely to reignite already acute social tensions once the immediate health crisis has eased. While these challenges were present before the pandemic, it has served to deepen them.

At the same time, the public response to the crisis points to a constructive way forward. As history shows, times of crisis tend to bring forth community action (Kuecker, Mulligan, and Nadarajah 2011). Despite its uneven social impact, a recognition that the pandemic is a shared threat has strengthened our sense of community (Alberti, 2020). It has brought people together and unleashed a desire to contribute in many ways, some small and others spectacular. It has demonstrated how opportunities for people to participate in collective activities both psychologically and behaviorally can achieve remarkable results, especially when addressing a common danger. As one commentator put it, the pandemic has brought to light society's latent social capital (Haldane 2020), and demonstrated the value of broadly-based participation and involvement.

So while the coronavirus crisis itself is expected to be time-limited, it has created a propitious opportunity to reflect on how a more effective system of social collaboration could enable us to work together more effectively in addressing other challenges of a more enduring nature. Before the pandemic, economic and social organization had already reached a critical point in countries like the USA and UK which were pursuing the neo-liberal free-market variant of capitalism. The economic viability and social legitimacy of this system is now in doubt. On the economic side there is a toxic cocktail of marked inequality, stagnating productivity, and organizational inefficiency. These are significant negatives in the context of technological disruption and growing global competitiveness where business must more than ever be innovative and resilient. On the social side, there are large differences in levels of opportunity and wellbeing among different generational, regional and social class categories, and those in authority are widely distrusted. Adding to this dystopian scene are underlying trends that pose existential threats to the population at large, namely environmental degradation and climate change, which decision-makers are failing to address with sufficient urgency. This is generating deep anxieties, especially among the younger generation who are leading the demand that the public should have a greater say in deciding appropriate policy responses. Fuelling the wave of social protests that have escalated in recent years is a widespread feeling that those who are heading business and governmental hierarchies are not listening to the concerns of ordinary people and are behaving in a self-serving and anti-social manner (Child 2019).

The thesis informing this paper is that greater participation in organizational decision-making could, at the very least, mitigate these fundamental economic and social problems, and help to restore confidence in leadership. The general unease is generating rising pressures for the reform of business and its governance, including from some large investors (Edgecliffe-Johnson 2019). The legitimacy of corporations, and of many other institutions, is being called into question. In the post-covid 'new normal', it is unlikely that the present system of hierarchically based business and governmental decision-making will be able to assuage public concerns and retain social legitimacy unless it undergoes radical change. One way to restore this legitimacy and re-establish trust is through making decision-making more transparent and accessible. This means that it is timely to identify the options for achieving greater participation, to demonstrate their potential benefits and to examine the conditions for their efficacy. It is important to collate and bring to attention the evidence on these matters in view of the strenuous resistance that elites have mounted to any significant advances in participation.[2]

The potential economic and social contribution offered by a broadening of participation in decision-making provides the rationale for the present paper. Its focus is on decision-making in and by organizations in view of their overwhelming role in modern societies. This is a well-worn subject, but it deserves re-visiting for two principal reasons. The first is the considerable body of evidence we shall review that indicates the significant economic and social contribution that organizational participation can make. The second reason for revisiting the subject stems from this contribution, namely there is a need to identify the factors that help to make participation work in practice.

The argument informing this paper is therefore that it is timely to apply participative solutions to many of our contemporary problems which will continue to be with us post-Covid, and which indeed the pandemic has exacerbated. In order to arrive at practical policy options, it proceeds through the following stages. The first is to establish a working definition of organizational participation and to develop a framework for classifying its principal forms. This framework serves to identify the more advanced and consequential forms of participation, and is then used to organize an evidence-based review of how they can constructively contribute to economic and social improvement. The final part of the paper reviews conditions bearing on the practical implementation of participation and which serve to clarify practical policy implications.

2. Participation – definition

Given its contemporary significance, it is not surprising that the number of papers and reports produced on organizational participation has increased substantially in recent years, and that a new academic journal has been established focusing on the subject.[3] Nevertheless, despite the growing attention participation is receiving, it continues to suffer from definitional ambiguities as well as from uncertainty about the conditions that are propitious for it to flourish. If greater organizational participation is to offer a constructive way forward in present socio-economic conditions, it is essential to achieve greater clarity about what it is and what makes it possible.

Agreement is lacking on the definition and scope of participation (Busck, Knudsen, and Lind 2010: 288; Litwin and Eaton 2018, 307). The lack of agreement reflects the different perspectives brought to bear on the subject by a wide range of disciplines: political science and sociology, economics, industrial relations, labor process theory, organizational design, organizational behavior, HRM, and corporate governance (Budd, Gollan, and Wilkinson 2010). Different perspectives in turn reveal a variety of social and economic aims that are attached to particular forms of participation. Broadly, they divide into aims that align with employee and/or other stakeholder interests and those related to organizational or managerial interests.[4] The former include supporting stakeholder rights and reflecting their interests (through governance provisions such as representation on boards, co-determination); ensuring a fairer distribution of rewards (e.g. collective bargaining, employee ownership, representation on remuneration committees); and counteracting abuses of hierarchical power (e.g., works councils, protection of whistleblowers). The latter include co-opting employees into the objectives and culture of the organization (e.g., joint consultation); improving productivity and economizing on middle management (e.g., self-managing teams, employee involvement); and promoting innovation (e.g., employee-driven innovation – EDI).

The question arises whether to focus attention on participation in organizational ownership or on participation in decision-making. Employee ownership is an important and continuing theme in discussions of organizational participation. However, while ownership normally provides the right to share in financial surpluses, it does not necessarily convey rights to share in decision-making (e.g. through voting). The same limitation applies to schemes for profit and gain-sharing and it is doubtful whether normally they effectively engage employees in decision making (Marchington 2005). Long's (1978) finding that worker participation in decision-making has much stronger positive effects on key job attitudes than does individual employee share ownership suggests the greater significance of sharing in decision-making. As Archer (2010, 605) has observed, 'while it may be possible in certain circumstances to use worker ownership as a vehicle to achieve worker self-government, it is the system of government and not the system of ownership that defines an economic democracy.' Decision-making is therefore a more appropriate criterion for analyzing organizational participation. It allows different methods of participation to be assessed in terms of the possibilities they afford for workers (and potentially other stakeholders) to make decisions, or share in their making, or influence them in other ways.

Nevertheless, without a broadening of ownership there is the danger that provisions for participation in decision-making will be transitory. If participation is only sustained by the belief and commitment of an organization's leadership, there is the real danger that it can erode if and when the leader moves on, either due to retirement or replacement. In other words, if employees and possibly other stakeholders do not possess the legal right to a voice in decision-making that is provided by ownership, that voice can be transitory. The case for participation in ownership therefore does not rest so much on its motivational consequences, or on the extent to which it actually promotes a lively engagement in the decision-making process, but rather on its role in ensuring that the right to participate in decision-making is sustained over time.[5] Another consideration is that employee shareholding often contributes positively to company performance. A review of 32 studies conducted in the USA and some other countries found both favorable and neutral results on the relationship between employee ownership schemes and overall firm performance, but there were very few negative findings (Kruse, 2002). The adoption of employee stock ownership plans on average led to a productivity improvement of 4–5% in the year of their adoption, with this higher productivity level being maintained in subsequent years.

3. Forms of organizational participation

The wide range of perspectives on participation in organizational decision-making is matched by a correspondingly large variety of forms that it can take. While this diversity is enriching, it can obscure the fundamental contrasts between modes of participation and the choices they present. There is value therefore in utilizing an analytical framework that categorizes broad alternatives. Such a framework can offer a basis for systematic comparison and at the same time can help to organize evidence on the contextual factors at different levels that are likely to support or constrain the development of participation.

A categorization of organizational participation needs to proceed from a recognition of the multi-dimensionality of the concept. Bernstein (1976, 492) distinguished three constituent dimensions of worker participation in decision-making: '(1) the degree of control employees enjoy over any particular decision; (2) the issues over which that control is exercised; and (3) the organizational level at which their control is exercised.' He identified eight levels of ascending control. Wilkinson et al. (2010) subsequently expressed these degrees of control as an 'escalator of participation' rising from information through communication, consultation, co-determination, to control. Bernstein

(1976) identified 16 issues over which control may be exercised, ranging from those limited to the worker's own work, through organizational decisions including determination of conditions of employment and investments, to those concerning company goals such as division of profits and raising capital.

Wilkinson et al. (2010, 11) added a fourth dimension to those that Bernstein had identified – the form of participation. Their analysis identified four constituent dimensions of participation: *degree* (ranging from being informed to being in control); *form* (indirect vs direct); *level* (work task to corporate); and *range* (just trivial issues vs. whole range of issues including strategic).[6] While these dimensions of participation are defined with reference to workers, most could apply also to the participation of other stakeholder groups including consumers, pension scheme trustees, and long-term shareholders (Sikka et al., 2018).[7]

The dimensions of organizational participation can configure in different combinations. In practice, this potential complexity is reduced by the likelihood that some dimensions of participation will normally be associated with each other. For example, the potential range of issues over which there is some participation is likely to increase with the organizational level involved. The form of participation is also likely to vary with organizational level. In organizations above a certain size, participation in 'top' decision-making relevant to the whole organization will necessarily involve representatives chosen by members at lower levels – i.e. its form will be indirect in nature. Thirdly, a higher degree of control is likely to result in a greater range of issues entering into discussion. In other words, the more that workers or their representatives can influence the decision agenda, the less trivial (the wider the range of) issues that are likely to be discussed.

With these considerations in mind, for ease of analysis we utilize a simplified classification of participation based on two key dimensions – organizational level and the degree of control. Although in a large organization, there are intermediate levels such as divisions and departments, for the sake of simplicity our classification shown in Table 1 just distinguishes between the whole organization and the immediate work group or unit. The former refers to issues affecting a firm or other organization as a whole. Group refers to the face-to-face level of workplace relations characterized by a workgroup or team, or by a relatively small department. Normally, employees and other stakeholders participate indirectly in decisions at the

Table 1. The main forms of organizational participation – A simplified classification.

	Degree of member control	
Focal level	Extends to policy-making and implementation	Extends to implementation only
Whole organization	**Co-determination** This form includes worker (and/or stakeholder) control and ownership. Its scope includes decisions on organizational policies and procedures to hold managers to account.	**Joint consultation** Involves consultation rather than making or sharing in decisions. Usually aims to increase employee involvement (and potentially productivity) through discussion and strengthening consensus with management. Collective bargaining confined to pay and conditions of employment also falls into this category.
Group	**Workplace self-management** This form only provides control over issues located at lower levels of the organization. However, in small organizations workplace self-management approximates to co-determination.	**Employee involvement** Limited participation at the work group/team level within an essentially unchanged managerial system. Usually focused on productivity improvement and health, safety and welfare issues.

Adapted from Child (1969, 89)

whole organization level through representatives, whereas at the group level all members can participate directly. In a very small organization, the two levels tend to converge. The other factor, degree of control, distinguishes between (1) arrangements that permit participants to share in, or even determine, policies and objectives as well as ways to implement and achieve them and (2) arrangements that only permit participation in discussions on implementation and problem solving. The former introduce a degree of organizational democracy, whereas the latter 'conserves' managerial prerogatives. This classification identifies four broad categories which are now discussed in turn: co-determination, joint consultation, workplace self-management, and employee involvement. Because they are more advanced forms of shared decision-making, we shall devote most attention to co-determination and workplace self-management.

3.1. Co-determination

Co-determination includes several arrangements such as employee representation on company boards, works councils, and employee participation in executive remuneration committees. It also embraces the governance systems associated with employee ownership and most co-operatives. The idea that employees (and potentially other stakeholders) should control or at least jointly determine the decision-making of their organizations and share in their surpluses has a long history. It draws from a number of academic and political traditions. One tradition is that of industrial democracy, achieved either through direct control of enterprises or through the power of external unions. Nineteenth century anarchists, most notably Proudhon, advocated the ownership and direct control of enterprises by workers through democratically-organized workers' associations or cooperatives. These would be based on non-hierarchical forms of self-management (Proudhon 1970). British social reformers, notably Sidney and Beatrice Webb, argued that industrial democracy could be best achieved through trade unions representing workers' interests through collective bargaining (Webb and Webb 1897). Another strand of thinking on industrial democracy which originated in the UK – Guild Socialism – harked back to the middle ages in advocating workers' control of industry through the medium of trade-related guilds, as opposed to relying on the mediation of the state or trade unions (Cole 1920).

Many advocates of collective ownership in the form of cooperatives also maintain that one of its significant benefits lies in the rights to control the policies and conduct of the whole organization that can be attached to such ownership.[8] These rights can be exercised directly through assemblies in smaller organizations or through representatives in larger ones. The expectation is that common interest based on shared ownership will enable whole organization decisions to be made on the basis of consensus (Rothschild 2016; Rothschild and Whitt 1986). However, cooperatives can be beset by problems such as workers' limited knowledge of market conditions, a conflict of interest between the original members and later joiners, and the temptation for members to sell out for a sometimes large personal profit. Many do not survive (Markey, Balnave, and Patmore 2010).

It is estimated that in the United States, about 32 million employees participate in an employee ownership plan, controlling approximately 8% of corporate equity (National Center for Employee Ownership 2019). In the UK, the employee owned sector accounts for over £30 billion in annual turnover (Employee Ownership Association 2018). A number of other countries have introduced tax advantages to encourage employee share ownership, though it remains relatively marginal compared to the dominant privately-owned corporate sector. Moreover, many such plans limit the percentage of a company's stock that can be acquired by employees which means that they do not confer any meaningful participation in the governance or management of the firm. By contrast, some ownership trusts such as that operating in the John Lewis Partnership are accompanied by a structure for partner representation at different levels of the company, including the board (Salaman and Storey 2016).

Today, stimulated by the growing public criticism of corporate behavior, the argument that a shareholder-value model of corporate purpose should be replaced by a stakeholder model has gained traction. This change in purpose is typically framed by leading executives and those academics close to them in terms of a shift away from producing profits for the benefit largely of shareholders towards 'profitable solutions' that benefit society as a whole (e.g. British Academy 2018; Centre for Responsible Business 2019). It relies primarily on a change of heart among corporate owners and senior executives, and tends to discount the potential role of participative mechanisms that permit representatives of wider interests actually to have a voice in corporate governance.

A contrasting view is advanced by those who argue that wider participation in corporate decision-making is in fact essential for achieving progress towards a more socially acceptable capitalism. This alternative view is cogently argued by Sikka and his colleagues in a report commissioned by the UK Labour Party (2018) which focuses on corporate governance. The report points to the short-termism that has characterized many UK companies manifested by a higher proportion of company earnings paid in dividends and a lower proportion allocated to investment, compared to their competitors in other European countries. In addition, it draws attention to the extreme levels of inequality that have evolved between top and bottom levels of pay, and the way that hostile takeovers and corporate collapses have harmed the interests of employees and other stakeholders. The report cites evidence from experience in other European countries that a 'direct representation of employees on both unitary and two-tier boards has helped to improve corporate performance and success for the benefit of all stakeholders' (p. 32). It argues that a shift in corporate orientation away from the short-term interests of 'speculative shareholders' requires a reform of corporate governance through legislation to ensure the representation on company boards of employees, consumers, pension scheme members and long-term shareholders so as to introduce different perspectives on corporate decisions. Along with other recent contributions,[9] the report articulates the case for a fuller measure of co-determination in contemporary capitalism, working primarily through a reconstitution of company board membership.

3.2. Joint consultation

Non-union employee representation [NER] is the distinctive approach within this second category of organizational participation. Its scope extends to issues that apply to whole organizations or establishments, but it excludes any discussion, let alone decision-making, concerning matters of fundamental policy or purpose. Rather, joint consultation is confined to information-sharing and discussion of policy implementation, problem solving or productivity improvement. In the UK, the characteristic form of NER has historically been effected through what are often called Joint Consultative Committees.[10] While it is normally treated as a separate (indeed antithetical) process, collective bargaining on behalf of workers by unions is akin to joint consultation insofar as it is a representative system and its scope is confined to terms and conditions of employment, rather than including broader policy issues.

Joint consultation in the UK had its origins in the early 20th century and has historically had a mixed relationship with collective bargaining. The idea behind it was to promote discussion and sharing of information of matters of mutual interest to employers and workers through joint councils consisting of managerial and worker representatives. At certain times, such as after World War I in the light of the 1917 Whitley Report, such councils were seen as complementary to collective bargaining with unions. However, there has been a long-running concern that joint consultation may weaken union organization by establishing a rival form of worker representation initiated by management to promote the interest of the company potentially at the expense of workers (Patmore 2013). Kaufman and Taras (2010, 270) suggest that in practice, non-union employee representation 'is a tangled web consisting of many different threads of values and perspectives', which involve contrasting stances towards unionization. In recent years, in a period of declining union membership and power, especially in the private sector, some employers have taken the initiative to substitute in-company forms of communication and representation in place of working with trade unions. Interest in joint consultation has accordingly revived as one of the managerially-led means of promoting employee engagement (Barry et al. 2018).

3.3. Workplace self-management

This category comprises schemes to create workgroup control through direct participation in group and team decisions. They focus on the self-management of work through the decentralization of authority to individuals and teams, who nevertheless are guided by the organization's overall purpose and strategy. In larger firms, workplace self-management is removed organizationally from the level at which major policy decisions are normally taken, whereas in small firms it tends to merge into co-determination. Worker cooperatives and firms in which entrepreneurs are committed to a high level of worker autonomy are two examples of this genre of participation, although each proceeds from a quite different ownership foundation.

Worker cooperatives embody the legacy of direct participatory democracy in contrast to the exercise of membership voice through representatives (Rothschild and Whitt 1986; Michie, Blasi, and Borzaga 2017). However, as is well recognized, direct democracy is only feasible within relatively small organizational units. While there are a few notable exceptions, such as the John Lewis Partnership in the UK and the Mondragon Corporation in Spain's Basque country, most worker cooperatives are quite small in terms of employment. However, John Lewis has the advantage of comprising shops which are individually relatively small, while Mondragon, conscious of the size constraint on meaningful participation, introduced a rule that when any one of its member cooperatives grows too large it has to split into smaller cooperatives all of which remain members of the network. In line with the size distribution of firms in many countries, the great majority of cooperatives have under 20 members (Pérotin 2015). This small size makes it possible for owner-members to participate directly both in the making of policy decisions for the organization as a whole, such as the distribution of the cooperative's surplus, as well as in operational decisions concerning matters such as the specialization of members' roles and their working methods. In principle, at least, cooperatives enable organizational democracy to go hand-in-hand with employee workplace autonomy, although the degree of organizational democracy actually achieved will depend on members' motivations to engage in it.

The second example of workplace self-management is found in firms whose leaders have a personal belief in its appropriateness. Lee and Edmondson (2017) instance a number of firms that have moved away from the traditional managerial hierarchy and given employees extensive autonomy to manage themselves. Of the examples they cite, the one that appears to have taken workplace self-management furthest is Valve, a moderately large (approximately 360 employees in 2016) maker of computer games. Valve was founded in 1996 by two former Microsoft employees. Officially, employees in Valve have full authority to select the games on which they wish to work and this determines which games the company develops. Activities and decisions that are fully decentralized at Valve to employees or self-organizing project teams include the execution of work, responsibility for monitoring and managing work, work allocation to individuals, work roles and workgroup design. Additionally, employees share in decisions concerning individual performance monitoring and the firm's strategy. Major decisions reserved to executives include hiring and firing, and periodic strategic decisions such as deciding whether to enter new markets (Lee and Edmondson 2017: Appendix A).

A hazard facing both co-determination and workplace self-management arrangements is that of 'degeneration' from their founding ideals. The degeneration thesis maintains that under pressure from external forces such as market competition as well as from the impact of internal forces such as the overshadowing of collective interests by those of individuals, worker cooperatives and other democratic firms will inevitably adopt the same structures and practices as capitalist firms (Storey, Basterretxea, and Salaman 2014; Langmead 2017). Degeneration in various forms has been noted among worker cooperatives (e.g. Craig and Pencavel 1992; Cornforth 1995) and in so-called self-managing firms such as Valve (Spicer 2018). One internal process of degeneration is the emergence of informal hierarchies and power structures that monopolize decision-making behind the scenes despite management's claims that there is transparency and participation.[11] An absence of formal rules on employees' rights and procedures to protect them can open the door to favoritism and the exploitation of individual staff. So despite the democratic credentials of workplace self-management, it is often precarious and in reality may amount to little more than freedom from certain management controls rather than offering a meaningful share in management decision-making.

3.4. Employee involvement

Employee involvement falls into the human relations tradition and is characterized by opportunities for employees to take part in discussions, but not necessarily decisions, that affect their job and work. It is 'direct' in nature insofar as it features unmediated interaction between employees and managers and/or employers. It aims to meet two objectives. The first is to harness employees' potential by engaging them in a process of contributing ideas for operational improvements and by enhancing their motivation to increase productivity. The second objective is to improve the experience of individuals at work through measures that increase their sense of control and sense of worth in the organization. This experiential and subjective aspect of direct participation is often referred to as 'employee engagement' (Truss et al. 2013). Keywords frequently used to identify employee involvement include autonomy, empowerment, involvement, participatory management and self-direction (Lee and Edmondson 2017).

A strand of employee involvement is intended to enable employees to contribute to an organization's innovation. 'Employee-driven innovation' [EDI] focuses on innovative ideas and practices that employees can contribute over and above their primary job responsibilities. A growing number of workers today enjoy high levels of trained expertise, combined with the benefits of practical experience. Their knowledge is often embedded in work teams, which are therefore a relevant medium for its articulation and transfer to the organization. As Høyrup (2010, 149) has summarized: 'Basically, employee-driven innovation takes the form of a bottom-up process, but it needs to be supported, recognized and organized, for example, in the form of participation in innovation processes and high-involvement innovation in the firm.'

4. The contributions of participation in post-covid society

We have given more attention to co-determination and workplace self-management because they are the most advanced and potentially consequential forms of participation. They allow for significant contributions to organizational decision making by workers and, in the case of co-determination, other stakeholders. By comparison, the other forms run the risk of only offering 'pseudo' participation. Co-determination and workplace self-management serve somewhat different purposes, but they are essentially complimentary. Successful experience with participation at the workgroup level can engender enthusiasm and develop skills which stand constituents and representatives in good stead for engaging in representative participation at the whole organization level. Moreover, effective representation at a higher level needs to be informed by the outcome of discussions and problem solving 'at the coal-face'. Also the right to take part in policy formation, for instance through representation on company boards, could prove futile in the absence of employee involvement at lower levels helping to ensure that higher level decisions are actually carried out. When combined, co-determination and workplace self-management promise to alleviate the social and economic challenges of contemporary societies that we identified at the beginning of this paper. This section reviews evidence supporting this assertion, first in respect of the economic challenge and then in respect of the social challenge.

4.1. Economic contributions of organizational participation

The economic contributions of advanced participation relate particularly to productivity, innovation and the effectiveness of managing.

4.2. Productivity

Productivity is the principal determinant of our collective standards of living. In developed economies the rate of productivity growth has been declining since the 2008 financial crisis. It actually fell in absolute terms in both the UK and USA during some quarters of 2019. Economists identify among possible causes of low productivity growth a slow-down of investment in plant and infrastructure, inadequate innovation, defensive worker behavior in face of employment insecurity, and the concentration of employment growth in low-productivity sectors (McKibbin and Triggs 2019).

The possibility that limited organizational participation may also be constraining productivity improvement is not often considered by economists, despite the assumption of mainstream industrial relations theory that effective organizational participation should enhance productivity (Van den Berg et al. 2013). There are several reasons underlying this assumption. One is motivational. Active participation by employees or their representatives in the formulation of both policy and operational decision is likely to engender among them greater shared understanding and acceptance of organizational goals. Rights to participation give workers more control over their job security and working conditions, and this should motivate them to stay loyal to their organization and commit additional effort to its success. A second reason is that participation can be competence-enhancing and so benefit productivity. The presence of participation schemes encourages companies to train their employees to be able to contribute to decision-making constructively, and their sharing in decision-making also provides opportunities for personal learning. A third consideration is that participation can improve organizational functioning. The participation of workers in problem-solving offers a channel for them to contribute their experience and training to finding solutions to operational and organizational problems.

The claim that both co-determination and workplace self-management can enhance productivity is not refuted by available evidence. Employee representation on company boards and works councils are characteristic co-determination arrangements. Most available evidence points to positive effects on labour productivity, but mixed results for other indicators such as profitability (FitzRoy and Kraft 2005; Müller & Stegmaier, 2016). Zwick (2004, 724) cites studies which conclude that the presence of works councils is usually associated with higher productivity 'because the exchange of private information is valuable, because consultation offers new solutions to production problems, and because co-determination encourages workers to take a longer-run view of the prospects of the firm'. The interpretation of research findings is, however, complicated by the fact that some studies have assessed firm performance rather than productivity per se. For instance, a comparative multi-country study using 2009 data from European Union member countries produced mixed and unexpected findings between different countries for the relationship between employee workplace representation through 'information and consultation bodies' (such as works councils and joint consultative committees) and firm performance in private sector firms (Van den Berg et al. 2013). Another complication is that factors such as firm size, managerial attitudes, age of the participation scheme, and stage in the business cycle appear to moderate the effects of co-determination (Hübler, 2015; Kleinknecht, 2015). For instance, schemes for employee participation can help to bridge the hierarchical distance that arises between top management and the workforce in larger firms, and they do appear to have more positive performance effects in larger units (Addison & Belfield, 2001). A favorable managerial attitude towards participation also tends to increase its positive contribution to firm performance (Van den Berg et al. 2013). Jirjahn, Mohrenweiser, and Backes-Gellner (2011) found that in Germany the age of works councils was associated with higher productivity suggesting a positive experience effect. Overall, despite the presence of mixed results, the weight of evidence is that co-determination tends to have positive effects on productivity so long as various supporting factors, such as a favourable managerial attitude, are in place.

Workplace self-management entails the decentralization of authority to individuals and teams. In small organizations like most worker cooperatives, self-management may extend to decision-making on organizational policy as a whole and hence overlap with co-determination. Many examples of successful self-managed teams have been reported by various authors (e.g. Laloux, 2014; Senor and Singer, 2009; Wellins, Byham, and Dixon 1994). A common theme is that teams have been able to undertake decision-making and tasks previously carried out by middle-level executives. In this way, self-management enhances the overall productivity of an organization by enabling the elimination of one or more layers in their organizations' hierarchies (Child 2019). There is evidence that it can also have positive motivational effects that improve productivity and a willingness to work flexibly. For instance, Evans and Davis (2005) concluded from a review that High Performance Work Systems, of which workplace participation is a major component, have positive effects on productivity through improving ties between groups, encouraging workers to define their work roles proactively, increasing mutual understanding, and strengthening positive worker attitudes. Zwick (2004) concluded from a large-scale panel study of German establishments that teamwork, autonomous work groups and the reduction of hierarchies provided establishments with an average productivity increase of 28% over four years, and that the presence of works councils enhanced these productivity effects of shop-floor self-management. Wood (2015) drawing from his research on the UK's 2004 and 2011 Workplace Employment Relations Surveys, concluded that employee involvement through both co-determination and self-management has positive effects on productivity across the whole economy, private and public, manufacturing and services.

Many issues concerning the performance consequences of organizational participation require further investigation, one of them being the effect of the relationship between co-determination (indirect) and self-management (direct) participation arrangements. In principle, they are mutually supportive – indirect participation should help to create a consensus over and organization's goals and objectives, while direct participation provides an opportunity for mutual group discussion on their achievement, dealing with issues that affect productivity, staff turnover, and welfare. Problems may arise, however, if there is a disconnect between the two levels of participation. For instance, it has been found that when an effective system of direct participation is already in place, employees may regard the presence of indirect arrangements as unnecessary or even counter-productive with negative performance consequences (Litwin and Eaton 2018).

4.3. Innovation

Innovation has significant productivity-enhancing potential. It is also the driver of technological disruption, motivated by the competitive advantage that innovation-based product and service differentiation can offer (Christensen 1997). Innovation relies heavily on the exchange of tacit knowledge especially at the early exploratory stage of the process. This can be hindered by the way that conventional hierarchy and bureaucracy encourage conformity and inhibition among employees (Parker 2012).

As indicated by Burns and Stalker's (1961) pioneering research and amply confirmed since, it is highly functional for innovation to encourage employees with ideas and specialist knowledge to take the initiative in communicating information and ideas freely both upwards and between different specialities. This behavior is consistent with a strong culture of participation and the organizational practices that accompany it. It is the rationale behind the concept of employee-driven innovation, discussed earlier, which can have strategic consequences and become a quite far-reaching form of participation (Kesting et al. 2016). Innovation is therefore likely to benefit from both co-determination and workplace self-management. Contrary to oft-heard criticisms of co-determination, research conducted in German companies found no evidence that it slows down technological progress and reduces innovation (Kraft, Stank, and Dewenter 2011).

Commentators have coined the term 'new economy' to denote the current phase of capitalism in which innovation has become a key competitive factor (Jones 2003). Various forms of AI and digitalization now provide the dynamic for technological disruption (Schwab 2017). New technologies are disrupting conventional strategies, modes of organization and sector boundaries. Harnessing their potential places a premium on the possession of superior knowledge and on the contributions made by generally young 'knowledge workers' who have the competencies to create and apply such knowledge. Millennial (Generation Y) staff working in high tech sectors are likely to be university graduates with distinctive views about responsible corporate conduct, as well as on modes of working. They are less inclined to accept without question the authority of managers who may well have inferior expertise and be pursuing policies they regard as socially irresponsible (Pinzaru et al. 2016; Hirsh et al., 2018). However, rather than relying on traditional formal representative mechanisms for expressing their voice, they employ social media. Social media today enable a rapid and large-scale mobilization of protest, as has been evident in employee dissent against management policies in major high-tech companies such as Amazon, Google and Microsoft (Greene 2020). This is in effect a form of co-determination insofar as it provides a voice on corporate goals (particularly their ethics) by employees many of whom already enjoy a considerable level of workplace self-management. The opportunity to participate in these ways appears to be becoming a necessity for the retention and motivation of valuable knowledge workers who 'are emboldened by the knowledge that their skills are in short supply [and] are used to debating online freely ... [and who] can also rally their networks to make it harder for organisations to hire' (Jacobs 2018, 14).

4.4. *Effectiveness of managing*

Consistent with the conditions that encourage innovation, a third economic contribution that both co-determination and workplace self-management offer lies in the way they can increase managerial effectiveness. Participation can help reduce managerial hierarchies through the delegation and distribution of decision-making to non-managerial personnel. These hierarchies impose a direct financial burden on organizations through the additional administrative overhead incurred in a proliferation of vertical levels. This burden is inflated by high levels of executive pay accompanied by substantial office and support costs (Child 2019).

Practices associated with active participation, including the wide circulation of information and meaningful discussions across hierarchical boundaries help to offset the negative effects of managerial hierarchy. The divisive and distorting effects of hierarchy on internal organizational communications are well documented (Milliken, Morrison, and Hewlin 2003). Hierarchical levels within organizations have consistently been found to inhibit and/or distort essential upward communication (Young, Anderson, and Stewart 2015). They are conducive to misunderstanding, poor motivation, mistrust of management, and the withholding of information; all of which are likely to have negative consequences for performance.

Active participation by employees and other stakeholders can also constrain managerial excess and hubris, which are legitimated by the ideology of managerialism (Deetz 1992; Locke and Spender 2011). Managerialism privileges managers' authority and exclusiveness, which in turn has often been used to conceal self-serving behavior (Westphal and Zajac 2013). It also tends to restrict opportunities for the managed to exercise their talents and achieve personal development. When governed by systems that do not admit of significant sharing of information, let alone meaningful participation in decision making, managerially-dominated hierarchies deny people the opportunity to grow personally through progressively assuming greater levels of responsibility (Scott 1985). This antithesis of participation not only restricts opportunities for employees to contribute new ideas into the innovation process; at the same time it denies them the chance to build their personal capabilities – their personal capital – in an era when younger generations are generally better educated and motivated to do so. Hamel (2011) has asked whether managers really add value; participation can prevent them from destroying value.

4.4.1. *Assessment of economic contributions*

In the light of available evidence, the concern that organizational participation jeopardizes economic performance appears to be largely unfounded. While participation may have some apparent downsides such as extending the time required for decision-making, exposing underlying conflicts, and challenges to managerial behavior, reported experience suggests that their consequence could well be an improvement in organizational policies, processes and relationships deriving from more open discussion, higher trust and improved motivation. It also needs to be borne in mind that the implementation of organizational participation takes time and effort, and is conditional upon various supporting factors identified in the next main section. Nevertheless, the overall effect of participation on economic performance is generally positive rather than negative, especially when it is carefully designed and adequately supported by management in respect of, for example, training for the participants in matters such as in reading financial accounts (Heller et al. 1998). Thus Litwin & Eaton (2018, 308) conclude that 'to date, the most careful empirical studies have shown that worker participation, however labelled, when operationalized in a manner that makes sense to the actors in the workplace context in which it is being studied, benefits organizational performance.'

4.5. Social contributions of organizational participation

The case for greater participation in organizational decision-making also rests on the need to address increasingly acute social divisions. A combination of technological disruption with a centralization of hierarchical power in business and politics has contributed to rising economic inequality and insecurity that in turn is provoking high levels of stress and serious social tensions (Vergolini 2011; Alvaredo et al. 2018). The Economist (2020, 71) noted 'the growing gap between a political system that promises equality and an economic one that leads to inequality' As a consequence, there is a widespread demand for a more socially acceptable form of capitalism that will help reduce inequality in society, both of voice and of reward. The burgeoning of collective protest, organized with the aid of social media, is adding force to this demand. The material and psychological costs of extreme inequality have come to be widely recognized, as well as its sources (Wilkinson and Pickett 2018). A significant contributor to the problem is the hierarchical differentiation of power and voice embedded within large and powerful organizations. This encourages and sustains inequalities of income and wealth, a lack of transparency, and a breakdown of trust in leaders. The indirect and direct participation of lower-level members in organizational decision-making can go some way to offsetting these hierarchical dysfunctions (Child 2019).

Societies today operate largely through commercial and public organizations. A broadening of participation in their decision-making processes promises a constructive way of addressing the challenges just mentioned. The greater participation of ordinary people in the making of organizational decisions, including those on the distribution of rewards, offers a lever to reduce inequalities and a basis for enhancing transparency and trust. A great deal also hangs on who has access to decisions on technological disruption – about how new powerful technologies are to be used. The choice here lies between using technologies to control and exploit populations in the interests of the powerful, or using them to enrich peoples' lives including the reinforcement of their voice through digitalized social media. A key insight emerging from research is that the extent to which new technological potentialities are applied to the benefit of workers and other stakeholders depends crucially on their ability to take part in decisions on these matters (Child and Loveridge 1990).

Co-determination is necessary to address the inequalities of wealth and power in society through bringing a plurality of voices to bear on decisions that determine the distribution of economic rewards. It offers access to the process whereby decisions are made on the rewards paid to senior executives, and which tends to be self-serving when made behind closed doors (Westphal and Zajac 2013). This could be achieved, for example, through having representatives of employees and other stakeholders on companies' remuneration committees. Co-determination would provide the necessary structural support for the change in corporate purpose that some business leaders and scholars have called for (e.g. British Academy 2019; Henderson and Temple-West 2019), introducing into Anglo-Saxon 'liberal market' economies an approach that by and large works well in 'coordinated market economies' (Hall and Soskice 2001). Although there are some examples of employer-initiated co-determination in the UK and USA, they are rare. Cross-country comparisons indicate that legislation is a necessary condition for this form of participation to be widely introduced and maintained as of right.

While co-determination provides the more powerful means of mitigating significant asymmetries of income and power, workplace self-management can make a valuable contribution to achieving a fairer and more satisfying working environment. Engaging employees in local decision-making and sharing information transparently with them normally has positive social outcomes such as enhancing job satisfaction and strengthening trust in management. It also puts employees in a better position to monitor the behavior of managers higher up the hierarchy and to expose failings and misconduct. Several empirical studies report that self-management and other forms of workplace participation tend to increase employees' sense of control, job satisfaction, and motivation (e.g., Cordery, Mueller, and Smith 1991; Kirkman and Rosen 1999). By way of qualification, other research suggests that peer control in self-managed teams may for some people lead over time to stress and even burnout (Lee and Edmondson 2017). Therefore, while workplace self-management can bring both personal and organizational benefits, it does not suit everyone in personal terms.

5. Enabling conditions for participation

The previous section has reviewed evidence on the contributions that participation in organizational decision-making can make toward ameliorating contemporary economic and social problems. Its generally positive consequences make it appropriate to consider the conditions that enable participation to be introduced and to work. Although the literature identifies a wide range of such conditions, and despite several attempts at their synthesis (e.g., Whyte and Blasi 1982; Dachler and Wilpert 1978; Wilkinson et al. 2010; Lee and Edmondson 2017), a systematic review of the factors bearing on the viability of organizational participation is still required. For however compelling the case for greater participation may be, it is not a straightforward matter to introduce it and make it work. Table 2 summarizes the range of conditions that tend to facilitate and support co-determination and workplace self-management.

Co-determination embodies the idea that employees (and potentially other stakeholder groups) should control, or at least jointly determine, the decision-making of their organizations and share in their surpluses. In formal terms at least, it imposes a substantial limitation on the power of business elites. As a result, co-determination has been opposed consistently by most employers and senior executives. The opposition of powerful vested interests is the most important barrier to the implementation of co-determination. It is particularly marked in the so-called 'liberal market' Anglo-Saxon countries. These countries, in contrast to the European social democracies, lack an embedded institutional tradition of the coordination and cooperation between major constituents in their societies which co-determination embodies (Hall and Soskice 2001). The Anglo-Saxon countries (Australia, Canada, New Zealand, USA, UK) are among the

Table 2. Enabling conditions for co-determination and workplace self-management.

Form of participation	Facilitating/supporting conditions	Key references
co-determination: ● Covers whole organization ● Extends to goals + means ● Formal ● Indirect. Encompasses control or joint determination of policy as well as issues of its implementation. Primarily based on worker participation but in principle can be extended to other stakeholder groups. Main arrangements: 1. Worker directors 2. Works councils 3. Worker cooperatives, trusts 4. Employee representation on executive remuneration committees	(1) Institutional support: enabling national legislation on workers' rights for both formal and informal participation, ownership, etc./national industrial relations system (2) National culture/prevailing ideology is democratic (3) Initiative and commitment of owners/entrepreneurs (4) Employee ownership, or share in ownership (5) Availability of non-equity capital (6) Unionization of the workforce if unions are coopted into the participation process (7) National and organizational infrastructure for developing relevant competencies (training) (8) High job security/core workforce (9) Educational level: professional/high competence workers (10) Previous experience of participation is positive for both employees and managers	Brown (1960) Dachler and Wilpert (1978) Diefenbach (2019) Gumbrell-McCormick and Hyman (2010) Krzywdzinski (2017) Michie, Blasi, and Borzaga (2017) Nuttall (2012) OECD (2017) Rothschild and Whitt (1986) Salaman and Storey (2016) Sikka et al. (2018) Van den Berg et al. (2013) Walker and de Bellecombe (1967)
Workplace self-management ● Group/team ● Extends to goals + means ● Can be informal ● Direct (Also includes small collectives) Employees can to a degree challenge managerial power. Encompasses control and co-determination at work group/workplace level.	(1) Leadership belief and commitment to a radical approach to less-hierarchical organizing (2) Small organizational or work unit size (3) High rate of change (4) Knowledge-based work/high skill workers (5) Growing number of millennial workers (6) Supportive structure (e.g role definitions in holacracy) (7) Mutual trust (8) High use of ICTs (9) Group incentive payment	Blasi, Freeman, and Kruse (2016) Lee and Edmondson (2017) Rothschild and Whitt (1986) Wilkinson and Dundon (2010)

15 OECD countries that do not have legal provisions for employee representation on company boards. This contrasts to the other 20 OECD members – continental European countries and Israel – that do (OECD 2017; Sikka 2018).

It is therefore reasonable to conclude that a necessary condition for the presence of co-determination is that it is enshrined in formal rights founded on *institutional support*, particularly in the form of legislation. Such legislation typically covers employee representation on company boards and the right of employees to form works councils. An increasing number of countries have also enacted legislation intended to protect whistle-blowers who potentially play an important role in monitoring the behavior of senior managers so as to expose any abuses of their hierarchical position (Child 2019). The right to monitor behavior adds an informal dimension to participation that complements its formal provisions (Diefenbach 2019).

Institutional support emerges most naturally from a socio-political *culture* and tradition that is both democratic and places a high value on inclusion and equality. Sagie and Aycan (2003) argue that a national culture combining low power-distance with a modest level of individualism will encourage co-determination. Without solid embeddedness in a supporting culture, purely legal provisions run the risk of being just formalistic and not having a significant impact on the actual relations between hierarchical power-holders and employee and other stakeholder groups (Krzywdzinski 2017). France, with its historical tradition of employer paternalism and militant unionism, is arguably an example of how a country's cultural inheritance can limit the constructive operation of co-determination despite the presence of a large number of legally mandated structures for representation both within organizations and through trade unions (ETUI, 2016). In the French state-defined system, trade unions may appoint worker representatives on company boards. However, company-based schemes for co-determination, especially those initiated by employers rather than by the state, have often been viewed with suspicion by trade unions as an attempt by employers to weaken workers' identification with labour organizations (Ackers 2010; Gall 2010). It is therefore likely that *a high level of unionization* reinforces co-determination only when unions are actively involved in the process.

As discussed earlier, co-determination can also be supported by the rights attaching to *employee shares in the ownership of companies* through the establishment of cooperatives, trusts and mutual organizations, and to a lesser degree through employee stock ownership plans (Michie, Blasi, and Borzaga 2017). Although these schemes may enjoy institutional support through associated legal and taxation provisions, their initiation and maintenance usually depends on the belief placed in them by employers (or by members in the case of cooperatives) rather than on legislation.

Employee ownership schemes other than cooperatives are typically initiated by the original owners. Two UK examples are the John Lewis Partnership and Richer Sounds, both in the retailing sector. The JLP is owned by its employees (partners) with their shares in trust. The Partnership was formed in 1929 at the initiative of Spedan Lewis, son of the founder, and was accompanied by a formal constitution setting out both benefits and a structure of representative democracy within the company. In May 2019 Julian Richer the founder of an outstandingly successful home entertainment retailer transferred 60% of the business to an Employee Owned Trust. Accompanying this transfer, a 'colleague advisory council' will be established 'to represent the concerns of employees'.

While, along with many employee ownership schemes, the Richer scheme falls short of transferring decision-making rights, they all illustrate that *initiative and support by owners and/or senior managers* is another factor that can facilitate co-determination and sustain it once established.

The Glacier Metal Company provides another British example of an employer initiative to establish a co-determination system. This was instigated by the then managing director, Wilfred Brown, advised by Elliott Jaques of the Tavistock Institute. In the Glacier case, participation was not predicated on worker ownership but rather on a managerial recognition of the latent power of the company's stakeholder groups. Brown wrote that because 'in the last analysis, each of the shareholding, customer and employee-representative systems can close down the company, the chief executive can take no action that is not at least tolerated by a consensus of opinion in each of the three systems' (1971, 160). He therefore introduced a formalization of the power dynamics within the company into representative and legislative systems, together with an appeals procedure. The representative system was intended to communicate ideas and sentiments that would not readily travel up the executive hierarchy, bearing in mind the well-known problems of upward communication within hierarchies. The legislative system was intended to secure broad agreement among power groups – shareholders, customers and employees – on proposals for change affecting the whole company that each of them might otherwise effectively oppose. The appeals procedure was intended to enable subordinates to appeal through a formal and open process against managerial decisions rather than allowing perceived unfairness to create festering resentments and tacit resistance.

Employer initiation of, and support for, co-determination is a relatively rare phenomenon. Even in Germany where co-determination is a norm, there can be opposition by owners to works councils, which have to be formed at the initiative of employees. A study found that when German firms are owner-managed, work councils are less likely to be formed and to survive even when they have positive economic effects (Jirjahn and Mohrenweiser 2016). Its authors suggest that 'owner-managers may oppose works councils because co-determination reduces the utility they gain from being the ultimate bosses within the establishment.' (p. 816).

Employee stock ownership schemes can preclude equity being held by non-members of the firm. Other co-determination arrangements, even without employee ownership, may discourage outside investors due to fears (or prejudice) attached to employee influence on decision-making. As Rothschild and Whitt note, 'fledging democratic enterprises may not even get off the ground because they cannot raise sufficient capital' (1986, 69). The success and growth of firms with co-determination therefore normally depends on a combination of debt financing and re-investment of surpluses. In these circumstances, the *ability of the firm to secure non-equity capital* is a necessary condition for its survival and a condition for this advanced form of participation to succeed (Nuttall 2012). National schemes to provide tax breaks and other financial assistance to worker-owned firms and cooperatives can play an important facilitating role.

Another initiative at both national and organization levels that enhances the ability and motivation of employees to engage in opportunities for participation is *the provision of relevant training*. Such training can offer technical understanding, such as the interpretation of company accounts, as well as providing a motivating psychological message that the employee is considered worthy of investment. In regard to the latter, research suggests that opportunities to take part in organizational-level training tends to increase employees' commitment to their organization in the sense of their psychological attachment to it (Dias and Silva 2016). An employer's investment in training is also likely to signal that the person's employment is secure. These features should enhance employees' willingness to make the time and effort to engage in opportunities for participation.

The factors identified so far are all aspects of the firm or the situation in which it is located. As just mentioned, one of them – the provision of training – links to a further factor, namely the ability and motivation of employees to engage actively in co-determination, and indeed other forms of participation, for their benefit as well as that of their organization. The propensity to participate depends on two factors – the willingness to participate and the ability to participate. Despite high hopes that provisions for employees to participate in the framing of decisions affecting them would excite their active interest, studies suggest that often their interest is limited to a general approval of participation in principle rather than a willingness to become actively involved in it (Walker and de Bellecombe 1967). In other words, while the presence of co-determination may tend to strengthen employees' commitment to their organization, this is limited to a general positive attitude. A reluctance to engage more actively may reflect a feeling that the co-determination of broad policy issues at the level of the whole organization is removed from the immediate concerns of workers in their workplace (Hespe and Wall 1976). It may also betray a lack of confidence among employees in their ability to express an opinion publicly, especially on matters where they lack specialist knowledge.

Studies indicate that *people having a higher occupational and social status* are more likely to have the confidence to articulate their opinions and take an active part in the process of contributing to and sharing in decision-making (Dalton 2017; Lichtenstein et al. 2004; Sheehy-Skeffington, J. & Rea, J. 2017). These are persons with a higher level of education and an ability to engage in advanced tasks that require the application of advanced knowledge. The younger 'millennial' generation combines these attributes more frequently than do their forebears, and an organization employing a high proportion of millennials may therefore be a promising setting for participation to take on a healthy life. Millennials come with different assumptions about how to work, which make them less inclined than their predecessors to accept conformity and the authority of managers who have less specialist expertise (Altman and Deal 2010). Their intensive use of social media has led to a new norm of direct interpersonal communication unhindered by distinctions of position and status, which contributes to a culture of direct engagement favourable to participation in decision-making.

Experience over time with a system of participation may also influence the extent to which employees are willing and able to engage actively in it. As with all experience, it can have negative as well as positive effects. Negative effects for employee participants could result from several factors such as a managerial domination of the process, its inability to resolve problems or to provide benefits for stakeholders, and a failure to provide representatives with adequate information and sufficient time for preparation. Managers may also become hostile to participation if they perceive it to waste time or ferment dissent. On the positive side of experience, there is a potential learning effect whereby representatives or direct participants come to appreciate over time the value of opportunities to participate and gain confidence in so doing. For example, Josip Obradović of Zagreb University informed the writer that his participant observation studies of Yugoslav self-management councils had shown how over time worker representatives gained confidence in speaking up in these meetings which initially were dominated by managers and engineers (see also Obradović and Dunn 1978). It was found that in Germany older works councils tended to have a less adversarial relationship with management, greater influence in decision-making, and to be associated with higher productivity, thus also pointing to a learning effect (Jirjahn, Mohrenweiser, and Backes-Gellner 2011). Positive outcomes are also likely to strengthen management's commitment to participation arrangements.

Co-determination is an indirect form of participation that generally operates through representatives of employees and potentially other stakeholders, particularly in larger organizations. Indirect arrangements become necessary when organizations exceed the *size* at which face-to-face meetings or assemblies are practicable. By contrast, workplace self-management is a direct mode of participation in which there is a two-way communication between employees and employers without the intermediation of representatives. Much of the communication may be informal, while formal provisions can include consultative committees, work group or team meetings, and local 'town-hall' assemblies of all members in a small organization. The feasibility of direct participation depends on the *smallness* of the participating group of people. Workplace self-management includes decision-making on organizational policies as well as on their operational implementation. This means that the whole organization must be quite small for everyone to be directly involved, and for workplace self-management to equate to co-determination. As Rothschild and Whitt note (1986, 91), 'the face-to-face relationships and directly democratic forms that characterize *the collectivist organization probably cannot be maintained if the organization grows beyond a certain size*' [italics in original].

With the exception of cooperatives that are initiated by their members, workplace self-management is normally *established by managements* who believe in the appropriateness of high employee engagement in contemporary conditions. They are consistent with less hierarchical forms of organizing achieved through structural changes to the authority boundaries between managers and workers as well as through behavioral changes in managerial style. Group-based participation can also be encouraged by a group-focused reward system. For instance, a study of the '100 Best Companies to Work For in America' found that employees in the firms using *group incentive pay* more extensively participate in decisions, as well as having greater information sharing, trusting supervisors more and reporting a more positive workplace culture than in other companies (Blasi, Freeman, and Kruse 2016).

Lee and Edmondson (2017) identify three trends that motivate workplace self-management. The first is the *increased pace of change* created by faster information flows and disruptive technologies which require a more rapid response based on employees taking more of their own decisions. The second is the *growth of knowledge-based work* which requires contributions from a wide range of people at all levels of an organization rather than relying just on managers. Such work also places a premium on the employment of high-skill and professional workers who are likely to want their opinions to be heard. The third trend is towards regarding work as a source of personal meaning, especially bearing in mind the *expectations held by the millennials* who have now entered the workforce.

Workplace self-management is informed by a belief that it can contribute positively to organizational performance and job satisfaction. It is legitimized by an assumption of

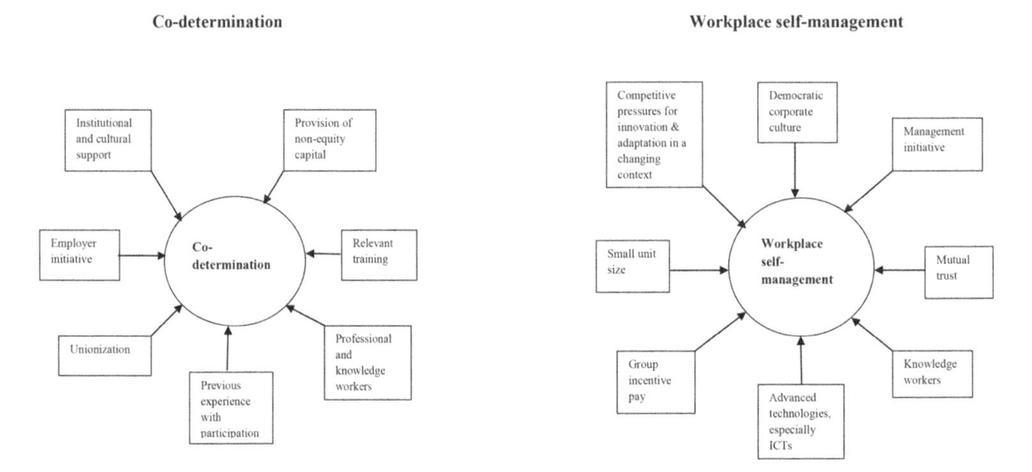

Figure 1. Enabling conditions for co-determination and workplace self-management.

shared interest and relies heavily on *mutual trust*. Fundamental requirements for such trust to develop are that fairness is demonstrated in the organization's behavior towards employees through avoiding threats to their personal security such as redundancy, and in equitable reward policies and transparent procedures for dealing with grievances and matters of discipline (Aryee et al. 2015). An additional factor is the way in which *ICT and social media* permit rapid access to, and sharing of information, which considerably aids the process of discussion and decision-making by groups and teams.

Workplace self-management faces two principal threats (Clegg 2019). The first lies in the danger of degeneration through the rise of an informal hierarchy in place of a formal one. When that happens, decisions continue to be made by an organizational elite behind the façade of democratic participation. This is 'mock participation', a quite familiar condition. The second threat lies in the inability of a system, in which employees (and potentially other stakeholders) share power with management and can veto its proposals, to cope with crises that expose a fundamental conflict of interest. A proposal to create job redundancies is a not uncommon example.

Figure 1 offers a graphical summary of the conditions that we have identified as being conducive to the presence and survival of co-determination and workplace self-management. Many of these conditions differ between the two forms, with an important contrast being that legislation is generally a necessary support for co-determination but not workplace self-management. Workplace self-management is more likely to derive from managerial initiative either emerging from experience with employee involvement that extends the boundaries of group decision-making over time (Wellins, Byham, and Dixon 1994) or from initiatives taken by idealistic entrepreneurs. Some of the enabling conditions for participation are macro (at the national level) such as legislation on workers' rights and national infrastructures that provide appropriate training for workers and/or their representatives. A low power-distance national culture may also favour participation. Other influences are located at the meso (organizational) level such as small work units, a highly qualified workforce, and a democratic corporate culture. Yet others are micro and include the personal commitment of organizational leaders to participation and a minimization of hierarchical behavior. An absence of these supporting factors impairs the prospects of participation.

6. Conclusion – implications for policy

The shock created by the Covid crisis provides an opportunity to reflect on how we might achieve a better society for the future – one that is not only productive but also more equal and harmonious. The public response to the emergency has clearly demonstrated the benefits that come from people personally participating and co-operating in community initiatives. This lesson can be taken into to the domains of work and organization. It is consistent with the already available evidence suggesting that a meaningful and substantial extension of participation in organizational decision-making could ease the severe economic and social challenges we face. These challenges were evident pre-Covid, but the pandemic has exacerbated them through the economic stress it has created and the uneven impact it has had on different parts of society.

We have argued that among the different forms of organizational participation, a combination of co-determination and workplace self-management is likely to have the most consequential effects. As summarized in Figure 1 the factors that support these forms of participation divide broadly into three categories:

(1) public policy provisions, including legislation on participative rights and access to non-equity capital;
(2) the enhancement of human capital to provide employees with professional and knowledge-related competencies, including schemes to train workers and stakeholder representatives in the competencies relevant to participating in decision-making;
(3) firm or micro-level factors, including idealistic entrepreneurs, smaller-sized work units, and managerial initiatives to devolve workplace decisions.

Each of these factors has a role to play in stimulating participation and enabling it to proceed to the stage when there is accumulated experience in applying it, so that its benefits become apparent, and the learning process reaches a point of generating a shared desire not only to continue with participation but to deepen it. The road to achieving mature and fruitful participatory processes may often be a rocky one, potentially beset by tensions between conflicting interests, but it is difficult to imagine a better method for building eventual consensus. Evidence on the present state of our organizations' health certainly does not suggest that their traditional hierarchical approach allowing for very limited participation is a viable alternative to solving our present social and economic challenges (Child 2019).

Legislation that provides rights to representation on company boards and assemblies representative of various interest groups is a sine qua non. In view of the strong opposition of many business leaders and executives, legislation is necessary for co-determination to become established in the first place and to be maintained as an established organizational practice. The instances in which enlightened employers have established co-determination are too rare to be able to rely on this factor. Moreover, the way that programmes aimed at corporate reform steer away from structural provisions embodying formal rights to stakeholder participation, and instead limit themselves to the declaration of a 'responsible' corporate purpose (e.g. British Academy 2019; Henderson and Temple-West 2019), indicate that co-determination will not emerge through a voluntary approach.

This paper has focused on participation within organizations and its potential contributions towards mitigating our current economic and social problems. However, the need for more extensive participation has ultimately to be placed within the broader context presented by the existential challenges that now face humankind – particularly climate change and environmental degradation. Their solution will require a wide measure of participation within society in order to mobilize a collective will that obliges political and business leaders to take the necessary corrective measures. An eight-country poll of over 1,000 people uncovered widespread resentment at politicians who were perceived not to be taking such action, with around half suggesting that politicians put the interests of big oil and gas corporations before those of local communities (Hope not Hate 2019).

A whole set of interest groups and organizations are necessarily involved in tackling climate change and environmental degradation, including companies, government departments, retraining agencies, schools, and community action groups. It is instructive that a leading expert has argued that the requisite consensus to achieve a transition to a low carbon economy which recognizes 'the massive social, economic and ecological costs associated with adapting to the climate emergency' can only be achieved through a 'compassionate transition' in which all stakeholders participate actively. One of the ways forward, in his opinion, 'will encompass many experiments with highly participatory just-transition commissions' (O'Riordan 2019: 8, 9).

In short, in the context of post-Covid society it is now more vital than ever to develop effective systems of participation at all levels of human organization. This is the only way that people's ingenuity and shared purpose can be harnessed constructively to tackle the extremely serious problems that we all face. It is incumbent on academics to investigate the conditions enabling this to occur and build on the initial insights provided by this paper.

Notes

1. I am grateful for comments offered on a previous draft by Alicia Clegg, Linda Hsieh, Joanna Karmowska, Ray Loveridge, Eugene McKenna, Jonathan Michie, and Nora Ramadan.
2. An example is the considerable opposition of business leaders to the proposal, mooted by the then UK prime minister, to oblige companies to appoint employee or consumer representatives to their boards. (Gordon, Oakley, and Pickard 2016).
3. See Jones (2018). The new journal is the *Journal of Participation and Employee Ownership*. Examples of recent reports in the UK are (Employee Ownership Association 2018). *The Ownership Dividend: The Economic Case for Employee Ownership*, https://employeeownership.co.uk/wp-content/uploads/The_Ownership_Dividend_The_economic_case_for_employee_ownership.pdf; (Sikka, P. et al., 2018). *A Better Future for Corporate Governance: Democratising Corporations for their Long-Term Success*, Review commissioned by the Labour Party. In the USA, attention has mainly focused on employee ownership through a growing number of ESOPs [Employee Stock Ownership Plans], rather than on participation in decision-making.
4. In this paper, we generally use the terms 'employee' and 'worker' interchangeably. However, an employee works under a formal contract of employment, whereas some categories of worker are subject to contingent work arrangements involving implicit contracts. Since all workers are subject to control by those employing them, the issue of their rights to participate in decisions affecting their interests remains relevant.

5. This point was made to me by Jonathan Michie in private correspondence. See also Michie, Blasi, and Borzaga (2017).
6. Other gradations of participation have been suggested. For example, Blumberg (1968: 71) identified 10 stages between a fully democratic and a purely nominal form of participation with respect to the scope of decision-making involved.
7. In the case of external stakeholders, the level of participation would normally be corporate/ whole organization.
8. Cooperatives are normally constituted to be both owned and run by their members, who share in the profits. When this paper refers to cooperatives, this is with 'worker cooperatives' in mind, in which enterprises are owned and managed by their workers. This category contrasts with 'producer cooperatives' where producers (often small farmers) create a cooperative with other producers to distribute and market their produce, and with 'consumer cooperatives' which are enterprises owned and operated by consumers (often retail outlets).
9. For example, Driver and Thompson (2018).
10. In the USA, equivalents are often called Productivity Committees or Plant Advisory Councils, whereas in Canada common terms are Joint Industrial Council and Employee-Management Advisory Committee (Kaufman and Taras 2010).
11. A rich description of this process is reported in the case study *Going Flat: Pursuit of a Democratic Organization Structure*. Darden Business Publishing. Reference no. UVA-OB-1041, 2012.

Disclosure statement

No potential conflict of interest was reported by the author(s).

References

Ackers, P. 2010. "An Industrial Relations Perspective on Employee Participation." In *The Oxford Handbook of Participation in Organizations*, edited by A. Wilkinson, P. J. Gollan, M. Marchington, and D. Lewin, 52–75. Oxford: Oxford University Press.

Alberti, F. B. 2020. "Coronavirus Is Revitalising the Concept of Community for the 21st Century." *The Conversation*, 29 April, https://theconversation.com/coronavirus-is-revitalising-the-concept-of-community-for-the-21st-century-135750

Altman, D. G., and J. J. Deal, eds. 2010. "Special Issue on Millennials and the World of Work: What You Didn't Know You Didn't Know." *Journal of Business and Psychology* 25: 2.

Alvaredo, F., L. Chancel, T. Piketty, E. Saez, and G. Zucman. 2018. *World Inequality Report 2018*. Cambridge, MA: Harvard University Press.

Archer, R. 2010. "Freedom, Democracy and Capitalism: Ethics and Employee Participation." In *The Oxford Handbook of Participation in Organizations*, edited by A. Wilkinson, P. J. Gollan, M. Marchington, and D. Lewin, 590–608. Oxford: Oxford University Press.

Aryee, S., F. O. Walumbwa, R. Mondejar, and C. W. L. Chu. 2015. "Accounting for the Influence of Overall Justice on Job Performance: Integrating Self-determination and Social Exchange Theories." *Journal of Management Studies* 52 (2): 231–252. doi:10.1111/joms.12067.

Barry, M., A. Bryson, R. Gomez, B. Kaufman, G. Lomas, and A. Wilkinson 2018. "The "Good Workplace": The Role of Joint Consultative Committees, Unions and HR Policies in Employee Ratings of Workplaces in Britain." London: University College Institute of Education, Department of Quantitative Social Science, Working Paper No. 18-08, October.

Bernstein, P. 1976. "Necessary Elements for Effective Worker Participation in Decision Making." *Journal of Economic Issues* 10 (2): 490–522. doi:10.1080/00213624.1976.11503358.

Blasi, J., R. Freeman, and D. Kruse. 2016. "Do Broad-based Employee Ownership, Profit Sharing and Stock Options Help the Best Firms Do Even Better?" *British Journal of Industrial Relations* 54 (1): 55–82. doi:10.1111/bjir.12135.

British Academy. 2018. *Reforming Business for the 21st Century: A Framework for the Future of the Corporation.* London: British Academy.

British Academy. 2019. *Principles for Purposeful Business.* London: British Academy.

Brown, W. 1971. *Organization.* London: Heinemann.

Budd, J. W., P. J. Gollan, and A. Wilkinson. 2010. "New Approaches to Employee Voice and Participation in Organizations." *Human Relations* 63 (3): 303–310. doi:10.1177/0018726709348938.

Burns, T., and G. M. Stalker. 1961. *The Management of Innovation.* London: Tavistock.

Busck, O., H. Knudsen, and J. Lind. 2010. "The Transformation of Employee Participation: Consequences for the Work Environment." *Economic and Industrial Democracy* 31 (3): 285–305. doi:10.1177/0143831X09351212.

Centre for Responsible Business, University of Birmingham 2019. *Annual Report 2018-19.* https://www.birmingham.ac.uk/Documents/college-social-sciences/business/research/responsible-business/Annual-Report-2019.pdf

Child, J. 1969. *The Business Enterprise in Modern Industrial Society.* London: Collier-Macmillan.

Child, J. 2019. *Hierarchy.* London: Routledge.

Child, J., and R. Loveridge. 1990. *New Technology in European Services.* Oxford: Blackwell.

Christensen, C. 1997. *The Innovator's Dilemma: When New Technologies Cause Great Firms to Fail.* Boston, MA: Harvard Business Review Press.

Clegg, A. 2019. "Boss-less Business Is No Workers' Paradise." *Financial Times,* 19 September, https://www.ft.com/content/34a86220-d639-11e9-8d46-8def889b4137

Cole, G. D. H. 1920. *Self-government in Industry.* London: Bell.

Cordery, J. L., W. S. Mueller, and L. M. Smith. 1991. "Attitudinal and Behavioral Effects of Autonomous Group Working: A Longitudinal Field Study." *Academy of Management Journal* 34 (2): 464–476.

Cornforth, C. 1995. "Patterns of Cooperative Management: Beyond the Degeneration Thesis." *Economic and Industrial Democracy* 16 (4): 487–523. doi:10.1177/0143831X95164002.

Craig, B., and J. Pencavel. 1992. "The Behavior of Worker Cooperatives: The Plywood Companies of the Pacific Northwest." *American Economic Review* 82 (5): 1083–1105.

Dachler, H. P., and B. Wilpert. 1978. "Conceptual Dimensions and Boundaries of Participation in Organizations: A Critical Evaluation." *Administrative Science Quarterly* 23 (1): 1–39. doi:10.2307/2392432.

Dalton, R. J. 2017. *The Participation Gap: Social Status and Political Inequality.* Oxford: Oxford University Press.

Deetz, S. A. 1992. *Democracy in an Age of Corporate Colonization.* Albany, NY: SUNY Press.

Dias, A., and R. Silva. 2016. "Organizational Training and Organizational Commitment: A Literature Review and Conceptual Development." *International Journal of Innovative Science, Engineering & Technology* 3 (1): 387–399.

Diefenbach, T. 2019. "Why Michels' 'Iron Law of Oligarchy' Is Not an Iron Law – And How Democratic Organizations Can Stay 'Oligarchy Free'." *Organization Studies* 40 (4): 545–562. doi:10.1177/0170840617751007.

Driver, C., and G. Thompson, eds.. 2018. *Corporate Governance in Contention.* Oxford: Oxford University Press.

The Economist 2020. "Too Much of a Good Thing. Review of Garett Jones." *10% Less Democracy,* 15 February: 71–72.

Edgecliffe-Johnson, A. 2019. "Beyond the Bottom Line: Should Business Put Purpose before Profit?." Financial Times. January 4. https://www.ft.com/content/a84647f8-0d0b-11e9-a3aa-118c761d2745

Employee Ownership Association. 2018. *The Ownership Dividend: The Economic Case for Employee Ownership.* Brough: Yorkshire. https://employeeownership.co.uk/wp-content/uploads/The_Ownership_Dividend_The_economic_case_for_employee_ownership.pdf

ETUI [European Trade Union Institute]. 2016. "National Industrial Relations: France." Brussels. https://www.worker-participation.eu/National-Industrial-Relations/Countries/France/Workplace-Representation

Evans, W. R., and W. D. Davis. 2005. "High-performance Work Systems and Organizational Performance: The Mediating Role of Internal Social Structure." *Journal of Management* 31 (5): 758–775. doi:10.1177/0149206305279370.

FitzRoy, F., and K. Kraft. 2005. "Co-determination, Efficiency and Productivity." *British Journal of Industrial Relations* 43 (2): 233–247. doi:10.1111/j.1467-8543.2005.00353.x.

Gall, G. 2010. "Labour Union Responses to Participation in Employing Organizations." In *The Oxford Handbook of Participation in Organizations*, edited by A. Wilkinson, P. J. Gollan, M. Marchington, and D. Lewin, 361–382. Oxford: Oxford University Press.

Gordon, S., D. Oakley, and J. Pickard 2016. "Theresa May Faces Fight over Plans to Reform Business. Opposition Grows to Putting Workers on Boards and Rules on Executive Pay." *Financial Times*, September 29. https://www.ft.com/content/99e5084e-862f-11e6-a29c-6e7d9515ad15

Greene, J., 2020. "Amazon Employees Launch Mass Defiance of Company Communications Policy in Support of Colleagues." *Washington Post*, January 28. https://www.washingtonpost.com/technology/2020/01/26/amazon-employees-plan-mass-defiance-company-communications-policy-support-colleagues/

Gumbrell-McCormick, R., and R. Hyman. 2010. "Works Councils: The European Model of Industrial Democracy?" In *The Oxford Handbook of Participation in Organizations*, edited by A. Wilkinson, P. J. Gollan, M. Marchington, and D. Lewin, 286–314. Oxford: Oxford University Press.

Haldane, A. 2020. "Reweaving the Social Fabric after the Crisis." *Financial Times*, 24 April, https://www.ft.com/content/fbb1ef1c-7ff8-11ea-b0fb-13524ae1056b?desktop=true&segmentId=d8d3e364-5197-20eb-17cf-2437841d178a

Hall, P. A., and D. Soskice, eds.. 2001. *Varieties of Capitalism: The Institutional Foundations of Comparative Advantage*. Oxford: Oxford University Press.

Hamel, G. 2011. "First, Let's Fire All the Managers." *Harvard Business Review* 89 (12): 48–60.

Heller, F., E. Pusic, G. Strauss, and B. Wilpert. 1998. *Organizational Participation: Myth and Reality*. Oxford: Oxford University Press.

Henderson, R., and P. Temple-West 2019. "Group of US Corporate Leaders Ditches Shareholder-first Mantra." *Financial Times*, 19 August, https://www.ft.com/content/e21a9fac-c1f5-11e9-a8e9-296ca66511c9

Hespe, G., and T. Wall. 1976. "The Demand for Participation among Employees." *Human Relations* 29 (5): 411–428. doi:10.1177/001872677602900503.

Hirsch, J. & 17 co-authors 2018. "Millennials in the Workplace." Academy of Management Proceedings, https://doi.org/10.5465/AMBPP.2018.14547symposium

Hope not Hate 2019. *Climate Change Won't Just Cause Extreme Weather but Extreme Politics*. London: Hope not Hate ., https://www.hopenothate.org.uk/climate-change-wont-just-cause-extreme-weather-but-extreme-politics/

Høyrup, S. 2010. "Employee-driven Innovation and Workplace Learning: Basic Concepts, Approaches and Themes." *Transfer* 16 (2): 143–154. doi:10.1177/1024258910364102.

Jacobs, E. 2018. "Loud and Public: How Employees are Taking Silicon Valley to Task." *Financial Times*, November 5: 14.

Jirjahn, U., and J. Mohrenweiser. 2016. "Owner-managers and the Failure of Newly Adopted Works Councils." *British Journal of Industrial Relations* 54 (4): 815–845. doi:10.1111/bjir.12148.

Jirjahn, U., J. Mohrenweiser, and U. Backes-Gellner. 2011. "Works Councils and Learning: On the Dynamic Dimension of Codetermination." *Kyklos* 64 (3): 427–447. doi:10.1111/j.1467-6435.2011.00514.x.

Jones, D. C. 2003. *New Economy Handbook*. San Diego, CA: Academic Press.

Jones, D. C. 2018. "The Economics of Participation and Employee Ownership (PEO): An Assessment." *Journal of Participation and Employee Ownership* 1 (1): 4–37. doi:10.1108/JPEO-02-2018-0004.

Kaufman, B. E., and D. G. Taras. 2010. "Employee Participation through Non-union Forms of Employee Representation." In *The Oxford Handbook of Participation in Organizations*, edited by A. Wilkinson, P. J. Gollan, M. Marchington, and D. Lewin, 258–285. Oxford: Oxford University Press.

Kesting, P., L. J. Song, Z. Qin, and M. Krol. 2016. "The Role of Employee Participation in Generating and Commercialising Innovations: Insights from Chinese High-tech Firms." *International Journal of Human Resource Management* 27 (10): 1059–1081. doi:10.1080/09585192.2015.1060512.

Kirkman, B. L., and B. Rosen. 1999. "Beyond Self-management: Antecedents and Consequences of Team Empowerment." *Academy of Management Journal* 42 (1): 58–74.

Kraft, K., J. Stank, and R. Dewenter. 2011. "Co-determination and Innovation." *Cambridge Journal of Economics* 35 (1): 145–172. doi:10.1093/cje/bep080.

Krzywdzinski, M. 2017. "Accounting for Cross-country Differences in Employee Involvement Practices: Comparative Case Studies in Germany, Brazil and China." *British Journal of Industrial Relations* 55 (2): 321–346. doi:10.1111/bjir.12230.

Kuecker, G., M. Mulligan, and Y. Nadarajah. 2011. "Turning to Community in Times of Crisis: Globally Derived Insights on Local Community Formation." *Community Development Journal* 46 (2): 245–264. doi:10.1093/cdj/bsq002.

Langmead, K. 2017. "Challenging the Degeneration Thesis: The Role of Democracy in Worker Cooperatives?." *Journal of Entrepreneurial and Organizational Diversity* 5 (1): 79–98. doi:10.5947/jeod.2016.005.

Lee, M. Y., and A. C. Edmondson. 2017. "Self-managing Organizations: Exploring the Limits of Less-hierarchical Organizing." *Research in Organizational Behavior* 37: 35–58. doi:10.1016/j.riob.2017.10.002.

Lichtenstein, R., J. A. Alexander, J. F. McCarthy, and R. Wells. 2004. "Status Differences in Cross-functional Teams: Effects on Individual Member Participation, Job Satisfaction, and Intent to Quit." *Journal of Health and Social Behavior* 45 (3): 322–335. doi:10.1177/002214650404500306.

Litwin, A., and A. E. Eaton. 2018. "Complementary or Conflictual? Formal Participation, Informal Participation, and Organizational Performance." *Human Resource Management* 57 (1): 307–325. doi:10.1002/hrm.21835.

Locke, R. R., and J.-C. Spender. 2011. *Confronting Managerialism: How the Business Elite and Their Schools Threw Our Lives Out of Balance*. London: Zed Books.

Long, R. J. 1978. "The Relative Effects of Share Ownership Vs Control on Job Attitudes in an Employee Owned Company." *Human Relations* 31 (9): 753–763. doi:10.1177/001872677803100901.

Marchington, M. 2005. "Employee Involvement: Patterns and Explanations." In *Participation and Democracy at Work. Essays in Honour of Harvie Ramsay*, edited by B. Harley, J. Hyman, and P. Thompson, 38–54. Basingstoke: Palgrave Macmillan.

Markey, R., N. Balnave, and G. Patmore. 2010. "Worker Directors and Worker Ownership/cooperatives." In *The Oxford Handbook of Participation in Organizations*, edited by A. Wilkinson, P. J. Gollan, M. Marchington, and D. Lewin, 237–257. Oxford: Oxford University Press.

McKibbin, W. J., and A. Triggs 2019. "Stagnation Vs Singularity: The Global Implications of Alternative Productivity Growth Scenarios." CAMA Working Papers 2019-26, Centre for Applied Macroeconomic Analysis, Crawford School of Public Policy, The Australian National University.

Michie, J., J. R. Blasi, and C. Borzaga, eds. 2017. *The Oxford Handbook of Mutual, Co-operative and Co-owned Business*. Oxford: Oxford University Press.

Milliken, F. J., E. W. Morrison, and P. F. Hewlin. 2003. "An Exploratory Study of Employee Silence: Issues that Employees Don't Communicate Upward and Why." *Journal of Management Studies* 40 (6): 1453–1476. doi:10.1111/1467-6486.00387.
National Center for Employee Ownership 2019. "*ESOP (Employee Stock Ownership Plan) Facts*, Oakland, CA. https://www.esop.org
Nuttall, G. 2012. *Nuttall Review of Employee Ownership*. London: Department of Business Innovation & Skills.
O'Riordan, T. 2019. "A Compassionate Transition to Sustainability." *British Academy Review* 36. December: 5-10.
Obradović, J., and W. N. Dunn. 1978. *Worker's Self-management and Organizational Power in Yugoslavia*. Pittsburgh, PA: University of Pittsburgh Press.
OECD 2017. *Board-level Employee Representation*. http://www.oecd.org/employment/collective-bargaining.htm
Parker, M. 2012. "Super Flat: Culture, Hierarchy and Dimensions of Organizing." In *Reinventing Hierarchy and Bureaucracy: From the Bureau to Network Organizations*, edited by T. Diefenbach and R. Todnem, 229–247. Bingley: Emerald.
Patmore, G. 2013. "Unionism and Non-union Employee Representation: The Interwar Experience in Canada, Germany, the US and the UK." *Journal of Industrial Relations* 55 (4): 527–545. doi:10.1177/0022185613489398.
Pérotin, V. 2015. *What Do We Really Know about Worker Co-operatives?* Manchester: Cooperatives UK. accessed 18 December, 2019 https://www.uk.coop/sites/default/files/uploads/attachments/worker_co-op_report.pdf
Pinzaru, F., E.-M. Vatamanescu, A. Mitan, R. Savulescu, A. Vitelar, C. Noaghea, and M. Balan. 2016. "Millennials at Work: Investigating the Specificity of Generation Y versus Other Generations." *Management Dynamics in the Knowledge Economy* 4 (2): 173–192.
Proudhon, J.-P. 1970. *Selected Writings*, ed. S. Edwards. London: Macmillan.
Rothschild, J. 2016. "The Logic of a Co-operative Economy and Democracy 2.0: Recovering the Possibilities for Autonomy, Creativity, Solidarity, and Common Purpose." *The Sociological Quarterly* 57 (1): 7–35. doi:10.1111/tsq.12138.
Rothschild, J., and J. A. Whitt. 1986. *The Cooperative Workplace: Potentials and Dilemmas or Organizational Democracy and Participation*. Cambridge: Cambridge University Press.
Sagie, A., and Z. Aycan. 2003. "A Cross-cultural Analysis of Participative Decision-making in Organizations." *Human Relations* 56 (4): 453–473. doi:10.1177/0018726703056004003.
Salaman, G., and J. Storey. 2016. *A Better Way of Doing Business? Lesson from the John Lewis Partnership*. Oxford: Oxford University Press.
Schwab, K. 2017. *The Fourth Industrial Revolution*. New York: Crown Business.
Scott, W. G. 1985. "Organizational Revolution: An End to Managerial Orthodoxy." *Administration & Society* 17 (2): 149–170. doi:10.1177/009539978501700202.
Sheehy-Skeffington, J., and J. Rea. 2017. *How Poverty Affects People's Decision-making Processes*. York: Joseph Rowntree Foundation.
Sikka, P.; 12 others. 2018. *A Better Future for Corporate Governance: Democratising Corporations for Their Long-Term Success*. Review commissioned by the British Labour Party, London.
Spicer, A. 2018. "No Bosses, No Managers: The Truth behind the 'Flat Hierarchy' Facade." *The Guardian*, 30 July, https://www.theguardian.com/commentisfree/2018/jul/30/no-bosses-managers-flat-hierachy-workplace-tech-hollywood, accessed 12 December 2019.
Storey, J., I. Basterretxea, and G. Salaman. 2014. "Managing and Resisting 'Degeneration' in Employee-owned Businesses: A Comparative Study of Two Large Retailers in Spain and the United Kingdom." *Organization* 21 (5): 626–644. doi:10.1177/1350508414537624.
Truss, C., A. Shantz, E. Soane, K. Alfes, and R. Delbridge. 2013. "Employee Engagement, Organisational Performance and Individual Well-being: Exploring the Evidence, Developing the Theory." *International Journal of Human Resource Management* 24 (14): 2657–2669. doi:10.1080/09585192.2013.798921.
Van den Berg, A., Y. Grift, A. van Witteloostuijn, C. Boone, and O. Van der Brempt 2013. "The Effect of Employee Workplace Representation on Firm Performance: A Cross-country

Comparison within Europe." Tjalling C. Koopmans Research Institute Utrecht School of Economics Utrecht University, Discussion Paper Series 13-05, http://www.uu.nl/rebo/economie/discussionpapers
Vergolini, L. 2011. "Social Cohesion in Europe: How Do the Different Dimensions of Inequality Affect Social Cohesion?." *International Journal of Comparative Sociology* 52 (3): 197–214. doi:10.1177/0020715211405421.
Walker, K. F., and L. G. de Bellecombe. 1967. "Workers' Participation in Management: The Concept and Its Implementation." *International Institute for Labour Studies Bulletin* 2: 67–106. February.
Webb, S., and B. Webb. 1897. *Industrial Democracy*. London: Longmans, Green.
Wellins, R. S., W. C. Byham, and G. R. Dixon. 1994. *Inside Teams*. San Francisco: Jossey-Bass.
Westphal, J. D., and E. J. Zajac. 2013. "A Behavioral Theory of Corporate Governance: Explicating the Mechanisms of Socially Situated and Socially Constituted Agency." *Academy of Management Annals* 7 (1): 607–661. doi:10.5465/19416520.2013.783669.
Whyte, W. F., and J. Blasi. 1982. "Worker Ownership, Participation and Control: Toward a Theoretical Model." *Policy Sciences* 14 (2): 137–163. doi:10.1007/BF00137114.
Wilkinson, A., and T. Dundon. 2010. "Direct Employee Participation." In *The Oxford Handbook of Participation in Organizations*, edited by A. Wilkinson, P. J. Gollan, M. Marchington, and D. Lewin, 167–185. Oxford: Oxford University Press.
Wilkinson, A., P. J. Gollan, M. Marchington, and D. Lewin. 2010. "Conceptualizing Employee Participation in Organizations." In *The Oxford Handbook of Participation in Organizations*, edited by A. Wilkinson, P. J. Gollan, M. Marchington, and D. Lewin, 3–25. Oxford: Oxford University Press.
Wilkinson, R., and K. Pickett. 2018. *The Inner Level: How More Equal Societies Reduce Stress, Restore Sanity and Improve Everyone's Well-being*. London: Allen Lane.
Wood, S. J. 2015. *Increasing Workplace Productivity through Employee Involvement*. London: Involvement and Participation Association (IPA). https://www.ipa-involve.com/News/increasing-workplace-productivity-through-employee-involvement
Young, K., M. Anderson, and S. Stewart. 2015. "Hierarchical Microaggressions in Higher Education." *Journal of Diversity in Higher Education* 8 (1): 61–71. doi:10.1037/a0038464.
Zwick, T. 2004. "Employee Participation and Productivity." *Labour Economics* 11 (6): 715–740. doi:10.1016/j.labeco.2004.02.001.

The psychological consequences of COVID-19 lockdowns

Kien Le and My Nguyen

ABSTRACT
COVID-19 outbreak has resulted in the largest number of lockdowns worldwide in history. While lockdowns may reduce the spread of COVID-19, the downside costs of this approach could be dreadful. By exploiting the differential timing of lockdown implementation across the United States within a difference-in-differences framework, we find that the pandemic lockdowns are associated with a variety of adverse psychological outcomes, namely, anxiety, worry, disinterest, depression, and poor general health perception. Our mechanism analyses suggest that these detrimental impacts could be attributed to concerns towards food, housing, and employment security. We further show that African Americans and women are especially susceptible to the adverse repercussions of the lockdowns. The findings imply that lockdowns should be accompanied by policies aimed to prevent mental health burden and deepening inequality.

1. Introduction

The detrimental ramifications of the COVID-19 pandemic have been widely felt across the globe. As of November 2020, over a million people worldwide had died. The U.S. death toll is well over 200,000. Such a humanitarian crisis has resulted in the largest number of lockdowns worldwide in history. Governments across countries, in the hope of reducing the transmission of COVID-19, issued lockdown orders on a massive scale – requiring people to stay at home and business to shut down. Such responses have received significant attention of scholars and policymakers.[1] However, much of the focus has been placed on the direct consequences, and little attention has been given to the less discernible downside costs of lockdowns. Focusing on the latter under-explored area, this paper quantifies the psychological ramifications associated with the COVID-19 lockdowns in the U.S.

This paper makes three contributions to the research on the consequences of COVID-19. First, we focus on the less discernible but dreadful costs of the pandemic lockdowns. Specifically, we examine the consequences of lockdowns on a variety of psychological outcomes, such as anxiety, worry, disinterest, depression, and general health perception. Second, perhaps due to time and data constraints, many previous studies on COVID-19 related subjects are plagued with problems of endogeneity. To ensure the internal validity of our estimates, we exploit the differential timing of lockdown implementation across the U.S. states within a difference-in-differences framework. Finally, we conducted rigorous analyses of the potential pathways to the adverse ramifications of lockdowns, and the heterogeneous impacts of lockdowns for various racial and gender groups. Understanding these underlying mechanisms, and identifying vulnerable groups could be helpful in designing targeted programs to minimize the costs of lockdowns.

We utilize the Household Pulse Survey Public Use File which provides rich information on individual experiences during the Coronavirus pandemic. Within a difference-in-differences framework, our paper reaches the following findings. First, we uncover the adverse effects of COVID-19 lockdowns on psychological outcomes. Exposure to lockdowns makes individuals more likely to be worried, disinterested, and depressed on a daily basis by 0.5, 0.8, and 0.8 percentage points, respectively. Taking the fractions of those experiencing worry, disinterest, and depression in the lockdown unexposed group as our benchmark, these estimated impacts imply the average increases by 5%, 10%, and 10%, respectively. Our results also indicate that individuals under lockdowns are more likely to have poor general health perception by 0.2 percentage points, corresponding to an 8% increase relative to the fraction reporting poor general health in the unexposed group. The findings are in line with the vulnerable outcomes for individuals in a liberal market economy during economic hardships (Hall and Soskice 2001). Second, we discover multiple channels through which lockdowns affect psychological outcomes. The adverse consequences could be attributed to individual concerns towards food, housing, and employment security, consistent with the theoretical frameworks of Higginbottom, Barling, and Kelloway (1993) and Brenner (1990). Moreover, we detect heterogeneity in the impacts of lockdowns on mental health across racial and gender groups. Consonant with theories on racial and gender discrimination (Brewer, Conrad, and King 2002; Bjomholt and McKay 2014), we find that African American and female populations are especially vulnerable to the psychologically detrimental repercussions of lockdowns during the COVID-19 pandemic.

Our findings suggest that lockdowns should be supplemented with policies intended to alleviate the burdens on inequality and mental health. It is important to develop interventions that aim to ensure food, housing, and employment security since these are potential pathways to the psychological ramifications of lockdowns. Extra attention should be paid to vulnerable groups, such as African Americans and women, to avoid deepening racial and gender inequalities. It is also important to raise awareness about various sources of public support for psychological needs.

The paper proceeds as follows. Section 2 presents the literature review. Section 3 describes the data and outlines the empirical strategy. Section 4 reports our estimating results, potential mechanisms, and heterogeneity analyses. Section 5 provides the discussion, study limitations, and directions for future research. Section 6 concludes the study.

2. Literature review

Our empirical study quantifies the psychological ramifications associated with COVID-19 pandemic lockdowns in the context of the U.S. In particular, we seek answers to the following three questions. First, what are the consequences of lockdowns on individuals' mental health? Second, through which channels are these impacts transmitted? Third, do the psychologically devastating impacts differ by race and gender? We address the first question in Section 4.1, the second question in Section 4.2, and the third question in Section 4.3.

The first question arises from the theoretical framework by Hall and Soskice (2001). In particular, Hall and Soskice (2001) theorize that a liberal market economy such as the U.S is characterized by competitive market arrangements with minimal state interventions. Compared to coordinated market economies like Germany and Japan, liberal market economies offer less protection for employees such as labor unions or social welfare. In other words, employers' unilateral control over firms makes employees highly dependent on them for jobs and incomes, thus exposing employees to substantial financial vulnerability during crises. Therefore, employees in liberal market economies tend to bear heavier financial burdens than those in coordinated market economies as their jobs and incomes are less secured. A highly deregulated economic system also exposes individuals to substantial uncertainty since minimal state intervention means a weak social safety net. As a result, individuals in liberal market economies are more likely to struggle and have their mental health deteriorated during economic hardships. In this study, we quantify the impacts of economic hardships induced by COVID-19 pandemic lockdowns on individuals' mental health measured by a variety of psychological outcomes, including anxiety, worry, disinterest, depression, and general health perception.

Furthermore, the data allow us to answer the second question by exploring two factors that could explain why lockdowns can generate a significant psychological strain on individuals. The first factor is the financial burden, such as unemployment or reduced incomes, which might impede emotional functioning and worsen individuals' mental health (Higginbottom, Barling, and Kelloway 1993). The second factor is individuals' expectations being altered by the societal economic circumstance, thus creating distress (Brenner 1990). In particular, lockdowns might engender tremendous uncertainty and concerns about a worsening future status, which could potentially undermine mental health (Burgard, Brand, and House 2009). Regarding financial burdens, we look at individuals' actual food, housing, and employment conditions recently. As for pessimistic expectations, we explore individuals' expectations of their food, housing, and employment conditions in the next four weeks. To facilitate the discussion, we categorize the potential pathways into three major groups, namely, food security concerns, housing security concerns, and employment security concerns.

Finally, the third question comes from the theories on racial and gender discrimination which emphasize the oppression of African Americans and women in the U.S. economy. Brewer, Conrad, and King (2002) argue that capitalism generates racism to the extent that they are mutually reinforcing. In times of crises, Bjomholt and McKay (2014) contend that deep cuts in public expenditures along with pay and recruitment freezes disproportionately affect women. Given the enormous impacts of lockdowns on the economy, we expect that African Americans and women are particularly vulnerable. For example, they might receive unfair wage reduction or lay-off and unequal access to government supports or public facilities. All these circumstances are likely to further impair the psychological well-being of African Americans and women. Therefore, it is of interest to examine the heterogeneous impacts of lockdowns on mental health along the lines of race and gender.

Empirically, the paper is closely related to two strands of literature. The first strand focuses on the impacts of COVID-19 lockdowns. It is documented that lockdowns are effective nonpharmaceutical intervention measures to contain the spread of COVID-19 in the absence of the vaccine. For instance, large scale lockdowns implemented by the French government contribute to the declines in COVID-19 related hospitalizations and ICU admissions (Roux, Massonnaud, and Crepey 2020). Besides curtailing transmissions, lockdowns also lead to an improvement in air quality (Mahato, Pal, and Ghosh 2020). Nevertheless, lockdowns caused substantial disruptions to the economy such as depressing employment opportunities, consumer spending, and business revenues (Chetty et al. 2020; Coibion, Gorodnichenko, and Weber 2020). The second line of literature our study also fits into is the stressful impacts of quarantine during pandemics. Prior studies document that social isolation due to lockdowns generates a tremendously traumatic experience for both children and adults. For example, quarantined individuals during the SARS outbreak in Canada tend to report psychological distress and display depressive symptoms (Hawryluck et al. 2004; Reynolds et al. 2008). Individuals in quarantine during the H1N1 pandemic in the U.S. are inclined to exhibit posttraumatic stress disorder symptoms (Sprang and Silman 2013). The authors point out that parents of children with such symptoms are more likely to suffer from depression as well.

3. Data and empirical methodology

3.1. Data

In this study, we employ four currently available waves of the Household Pulse Survey Public Use File (HPS-PUF). The four waves correspond to the four survey weeks, including Week 1 from April 23 to May 5, Week 2 from May 7 to May 12, Week 3 from May 14 to May 19, and Week 4 from May 21 to May 26. The survey is conducted by United States Census Bureau in conjunction with other agencies, such as Bureau of Labor Statistics (BLS), National Center for Health Statistics (NCHS), Department of Agriculture Economic Research Service (ERS), National Center for Education Statistics (NCES), Department of Housing and Urban Development (HUD).

Reaching over 350,000 respondents across 51 states of the U.S (including DC), the survey seeks to provide meaningful insights into individual experiences during the Coronavirus pandemic. The average response rate is approximately 2.74% with a standard deviation of 0.56. Overall, Alaska has the highest response rate (5%) and Mississippi has the lowest response rate (1.9%). This is visually illustrated in Figure A1. The response rate is not very high because this is not face-to-face interview (respondents are contacted via phone or email due to the COVID-19 pandemic). Table A1 in the Appendix provides the response rates by state and survey week (the response rate data are taken from U.S. Census Bureau (2020)). It is worth noting that 7.79% of individuals in the survey sample are African American although African Americans account for 13.4% of the total U.S. population. According to Figure A1, all the five states with the lowest response rate (Mississippi, Louisiana, Arkansas, Alabama, Oklahoma) are the Deep South states with a high concentration of African Americans. Furthermore, 83% of respondents are white while the proportion of whites in the U.S. population is 76.3%.[2] In other words, whereas African Americans are underrepresented in the sample, whites are overrepresented. As shown later, African Americans are more heavily affected by pandemic lockdowns than whites (Section 4.3), making our estimates the lower bounds of the true effects because of the underrepresentation of the more vulnerable group.

Besides standard demographic characteristics (age, gender, race, marital status, etc.), our analysis also draws from the HPS-PUF four groups of outcomes, including (i) mental health, (ii) food security concerns, (iii) housing security concerns, and (iv) employment security concerns. Tables A2 and A3 in the Appendix detail summary statistics and variable construction. We briefly discuss our main outcome variables as below.

To reflect individuals' mental health, we construct five indicators, namely Poor General Health Perception, Anxiety Every Day, Worry Every Day, Disinterest Every Day, and Depression Every Day. These variables are based on respondents' answers to the questions about their current self-assessed state of health. The responses are placed into a five or four-point scale ranging from the best state to the worst state. We then compute these health variables as dummies taking the value of one if the response falls into the worst state, and zero otherwise. With the Cronbach's Alpha of 0.79, Poor General Health Perception, Anxiety Every Day, Worry Every Day, Disinterest Every Day, and Depression Every Day are good measures of the psychological well-being of individuals.

To capture concerns towards food security, we construct five one-zero variables, namely, Afford More Food, Get Out to Buy Food, Get Food Delivered, Food Availability, and Food Sufficiency Confidence. The first four indicators take the value of zero if the respondent agrees to the statements: (i) could not afford to buy more food, (ii) could not get out to buy food, (iii) could not get food delivered, and (iv) the stores did not have the food needed. The last indicator, Food Sufficiency Confidence, takes a value of one if the respondent is highly confident that he/she could afford food for the next four weeks, and zero otherwise.

The third and fourth groups of indicators focus on individuals' concerns towards housing and employment security. Housing concerns are measured by two one-zero variables, namely: (i) Last Payment on Time takes a value of one if the respondent paid last month's mortgage or rent on time, and (ii) Next Payment Confidence takes a value of one if the respondent is highly confident in his/her ability to pay the mortgage or rent next month. Employment concerns are represented by two one-zero indicators, including: (i) Recent Unemployment takes a value of one if there is a job loss in his/her household recently, and (ii) Expected Unemployment takes a value of one if the respondent expects a job loss in his/her household in the next four weeks.

Our main explanatory variable is an indicator for whether the lockdown is currently effective in the respondent's residence state at the time of survey. The date of implementation and the date of expiration of lockdowns are collected from the state government websites. Given these implementation and expiration dates as well as the time of survey, we can identify whether an individual is currently exposed to a lockdown. In particular, we consider an individual to be in the lockdown if he/she is interviewed after the lockdown being imposed and before the lockdown being lifted. Table A4 in the Appendix presents the timing of lockdowns across states and indicates whether the date of survey falls into the lockdown period. The value of one (zero) indicates that the survey was (was not) conducted during the lockdown period. The final row gives the fractions of states where lockdowns were still in place as of the survey week. For example, if the average is 0.58, the fraction of states where lockdowns were still effective is 58%.

3.2. Empirical methodology

To investigate the extent to which lockdowns affect individuals' mental well-being, we exploit the differential timing of implementation across states in a difference-in-differences (DiD) framework given by,

$$Y_{ist} = \beta_0 + \beta_1 LD_{ist} + \lambda_s + \theta_t + X_{ist}\Gamma + \varepsilon_{ist} \quad (1)$$

where the subscripts *i*, *s*, and *t* refers to the individual, state, and time of survey. The dependent variable Y_{ist} stands for various measures of mental well-being, including whether an individual thinks his/her general health is currently in poor condition (Poor General Health Perception), whether the individual experiences anxiety every day (Anxiety Every Day), whether the individual feels worried on a daily basis (Worry Every Day), whether the individual feels disinterested or detached every day (Disinterest Every Day), and whether the individual suffers from depression on a daily basis (Depression Every Day). Besides, in the mechanism analysis, Y_{ist} represents various mechanism variables reflecting concerns towards food, housing, and employment security. Concerns towards food security are captured by five indicators, namely, Afford More Food, Get Out to Buy Food, Get Food Delivered, Food Availability, and Food Sufficiency Confidence. Concerns towards housing security are reflected by two indicators, Last Payment on Time and Next Payment Confidence. Employment security concerns are measured by two indicators, Recent Unemployment, and Expected Unemployment.

Our main explanatory variable LD_{ist} is an indicator that takes the value of one if the lockdown is in place in the individual's state of residence at the time of survey, and zero otherwise. The terms λ_s and θ_t represent state and survey week fixed effects, respectively. The covariate *Xist* includes individual characteristics such as age, age squared, marital status, race, gender, occupational sector, and educational attainment. Finally, we denote by ε_{ist} the error term. Standard errors throughout the paper are clustered at the state-by-week level.

The coefficient of interest is β_1 which captures the impacts of lockdowns. In this setup, we compare the outcomes for individuals currently exposed to lockdowns with those no longer exposed to lockdowns within the same state, relative to the analogous differences for individuals whose states of residence implement the statewide lockdowns in a different time frame or never enforce such orders. In other words, our treatment group consists of individuals residing in states where lockdowns are still effective at the time of survey. Our control group comprises individuals residing in states which either never implement statewide lockdowns or their lockdown periods expire at the time of survey.

4. Results

4.1. Main results

We provide the estimated psychological impacts of lockdowns in Table 1. Each column is a separate regression and the column heading specifies the outcome variable. The reported coefficient is β_1 from the DiD specification in equation (1). We also display the results for the uncoded psychological measures in Table A5 in the Appendix. Overall,

Table 1. The Psychological Impact of Lockdowns: Main Results.

	Poor General Health Perception (1)	Anxiety Every Day (2)	Worry Every Day (3)	Disinterest Every Day (4)	Depression Every Day (5)
Lockdowns	0.002**	0.005	0.005**	0.008***	0.008***
	(0.001)	(0.004)	(0.002)	(0.003)	(0.002)
Controls					
Ind. Characteristics	✓	✓	✓	✓	✓
State & Week FE	✓	✓	✓	✓	✓
Observations	317,950	317,592	317,445	317,296	317,594

*p < 0.1, **p < 0.05, ***p < 0.01. Individual Characteristics include age, age-squared, marital status, race, gender, occupational sector, and educational attainment. Robust standard errors are clustered at the State-by-Week level.

we find that the implementation of lockdowns during the COVID-19 pandemic exerts a devastating mental burden on individuals.

First, those exposed to lockdowns report worse general health conditions. Evident from Column 1, experiencing lockdowns deteriorates the health outcomes of those affected by raising the probability of poor general health status by 0.2 percentage points. This represents an 8% increase relative to the fraction reporting poor general health in the control group (Table A2). Second, those exposed to lockdowns are also more likely to report mental problems. In particular, lockdowns tend to raise the incidence of daily anxiety although the coefficient in the anxiety regression falls short of conventional statistical significance (Column 2). Moving to Columns 3 through 5, we find that the effects of lockdowns are all positive and statistically distinguishable from zero. Exposure to lockdowns makes individuals more likely to be worried, disinterested, and depressed on a daily basis by 0.5, 0.8, and 0.8 percentage points, respectively. Taking the fractions of those experiencing worry, disinterest, and depression in the unexposed group as our benchmarks, these estimated impacts imply the average increases by 5%, 10%, and 10%, respectively.

4.2. Potential mechanisms

We proceed to explore potential channels through which the implementation of lockdowns inflicts psychological health risks for individuals. Given the available information from our data, we investigate three groups of mechanisms, including (i) food security concerns, (ii) housing security concerns, and (iii) employment security concerns. To analyze the extent to which these concerns transmit the impacts of lockdowns on mental well-being, we estimate the DiD model as in equation (1) but replace the mental well-being outcomes with mechanism variables indicating various measures of concerns. The estimating results are provided in Tables 2 and 3 . Each column presents a separate regression and the column heading specifies the outcome variable. The reported coefficient is β_1 from the DiD specification in equation (1).

4.2.1. Food security concerns

- We capture the financial burden regarding food security by four indicators, whether the individual can afford more food (Afford More Food), whether the individual can get out to buy food (Get Out to Buy Food), whether the individual can get food delivered to him/

Table 2. Potential Mechanism – Food Concerns.

	Afford More Food (1)	Get Out to Buy Food (2)	Get Food Delivered (3)	Food Availability (4)	Food Sufficiency Confidence (5)
Lockdowns	−0.005*	−0.003***	−0.002	−0.012***	−0.016***
	(0.003)	(0.001)	(0.001)	(0.004)	(0.004)
Controls					
Ind. Characteristics	✓	✓	✓	✓	✓
State & Week FE	✓	✓	✓	✓	✓
Observations	343,929	343,929	343,929	343,929	321,099

*p < 0.1, **p < 0.05, ***p < 0.01. Individual Characteristics include age, age-squared, marital status, race, gender, occupational sector, and educational attainment. Robust standard errors are clustered at the State-by-Week level.

her (Get Food Delivered), and whether the individual can get the food he/she wants from the store (Food Availability). The individual pessimistic expectation of food security is measured by an indicator for whether the individual is confident about his/her food sufficiency in the next four weeks (Food Sufficiency Confidence). Evident from Table 2, individuals under COVID-19 pandemic lockdowns are less likely to afford more food, to get out for food purchase, to have food delivered to their doors, and to obtain the food they want from local stores by 0.5, 0.3, 0.2, and 1.2 percentage points, respectively (Columns 1 through 4). All estimates except the one in the food delivery regression are statistically significant. Finally, exposure to lockdowns during the COVID-19 pandemic raises individuals' concerns over future food sufficiency. Specifically, individuals exposed to lockdowns are less likely to be confident about their food sufficiency in the next four weeks by 1.6 percentage points (Column 5). Taken together, Table 2 suggests that lockdowns could potentially worsen individuals' mental well-being through aggravating their concerns over food sufficiency.

4.2.2. Housing security concerns

- In the second group of channels, the financial burden related to housing security is reflected by whether the individual paid the mortgage or rent on time last month (Last Payment on Time). The pessimistic expectation of future housing security is captured by an indicator for whether the individual is confident of his/her ability to pay mortgage or rent next month (Next Payment Confidence). As shown in Columns 1 and 2 of Table 3, lockdowns tend to deteriorate individuals' ability to afford housing security. In

Table 3. Potential Mechanism – Housing and Employment Concerns.

	Housing Concerns		Employment Concerns	
	Last Payment on Time (1)	Next Payment Confidence (2)	Recent Unemployment (3)	Expected Unemployment (4)
Lockdowns	−0.006**	−0.017***	0.001	0.007*
	(0.003)	(0.004)	(0.004)	(0.004)
Controls				
Ind. Characteristics	✓	✓	✓	✓
State & Week FE	✓	✓	✓	✓
Observations	234,205	234,389	348,507	348,098

*p < 0.1, **p < 0.05, ***p < 0.01. Individual Characteristics include age, age-squared, marital status, race, gender, occupational sector, and educational attainment. Robust standard errors are clustered at the State-by-Week level.

particular, Column 1 suggests that individuals exposed to lockdowns are 0.6 percentage points less likely to report on-time payment for last month's mortgage or rent. According to Column 2, lockdowns also decrease individuals' confidence in their next mortgage or rent payment by 1.7 percentage points. The reporting estimates are all statistically distinguishable from zero. Collectively, the presenting results suggest that lockdowns could aggravate individuals' mental well-being through raising their concerns over housing security.

4.2.3. Employment security concerns

- Finally, the financial burden related to employment prospects is captured by an indicator for whether the individual reports a recent job loss in his/her household (Recent Unemployment). The individual's pessimistic expectation of future job prospects is reflected by whether the individual expects a job loss in his/her household next month (Expected Unemployment). Evident from Columns 3 and 4 of Table 3, lockdown exposure is negatively associated with job prospects. Those subject to lockdowns are more likely to report a recent incidence of joblessness in their households, although the estimate falls short of conventional statistical significant levels (Column 3). Exposure to lockdowns induces individuals to expect to have at least one member in their households to become unemployed in the next four weeks by 0.7 percentage points (Column 4). Besides food and housing security concerns, there is some evidence that concerns about employment security could be one of the potential channels transmitting the psychological consequences of lockdowns.

4.3. Heterogeneity analyses

In this section, we explore how the psychological impacts of lockdowns differ across racial and gender groups. The estimating results (i.e. β_1 coefficient from the DiD specification) are reported in Table 4. Heterogeneity analyses along the line of race and gender are presented in Panel A and B, respectively. Each column consists of four separate regressions where the column headings indicate the dependent variables. In Panel A, the upper row provides estimates for white individuals and the lower row includes estimates for African American individuals. In Panel B, the upper row presents estimates for men and the lower row provides estimates for women.

4.3.1. White and African American

- First, we examine whether there exist any heterogeneous impacts of lockdowns between white and African American individuals. Evident from Panel A, we find that African American individuals tend to suffer more severe consequences of lockdowns than their white counterparts. African American individuals experiencing lockdowns are 0.3 percentage points more likely to report poor general health conditions while the effect on whites is 0.2 percentage points (Column 1). Exposure to lockdowns raises the incidences of worry, disinterest, and depression among African American individuals by 1.3, 1.7, and 2.0 percentage points, respectively, whereas the impacts on whites are approximately 60% smaller in magnitude. These findings suggest that the African American community is especially vulnerable to lockdowns during the global pandemic, which could further perpetuate the racial gap in the U.S society. Given the underrepresentation of African

Table 4. The Psychological Impact of Lockdowns: Heterogeneity Analysis.

	Poor General Health Perception (1)	Anxiety Every Day (2)	Worry Every Day (3)	Disinterest Every Day (4)	Depression Every Day (5)
Panel A: Impact of Lockdowns by Race					
Lockdowns on White	0.002*	0.006	0.005**	0.007**	0.007***
	(0.001)	(0.004)	(0.002)	(0.003)	(0.002)
Observations	265,059	264,777	264,670	264,568	264,773
Lockdowns on African American	0.003	0.000	0.013*	0.017**	0.020**
	(0.005)	(0.009)	(0.008)	(0.008)	(0.009)
Observations	23,752	23,717	23,702	23,680	23,727
Panel B: Impact of Lockdowns by Gender					
Lockdowns on Male	−0.001	0.002	0.000	0.007**	0.004*
	(0.002)	(0.005)	(0.003)	(0.003)	(0.002)
Observations	130,603	130,428	130,351	130,292	130,422
Lockdowns on Female	0.004***	0.007	0.009***	0.009**	0.011***
	(0.001)	(0.005)	(0.003)	(0.003)	(0.003)
Observations	187,347	187,164	187,094	187,004	187,172
Controls					
Ind. Characteristics	✓	✓	✓	✓	✓
State & Week FE	✓	✓	✓	✓	✓

*p < 0.1, **p < 0.05, ***p < 0.01. Individual Characteristics include age, age-squared, marital status, race, gender, occupational sector, and educational attainment. Robust standard errors are clustered at the State-by-Week level.

Americans in the data (Section 3.1), our estimates might be the lower bounds of the true impacts of pandemic lockdowns, since a fraction of this disadvantaged population could be unreachable for surveys.

4.3.2. Male and female

- Next, we proceed to investigate whether men and women are differentially affected by lockdowns. As shown in Panel B, women tend to be more susceptible than men. Specifically, lockdowns raise the incidence of poor general health perception among women by 0.4 percentage points whereas the estimate for the men sample carries the opposite sign and is statistically indistinguishable from zero. Lockdowns make women more likely to be anxious, worried, disinterested, and depressed by 0.7, 0.9, 0.9, and 1.1 percentage points, respectively while the impacts on men are much weaker in both economic (22% to 125% smaller in magnitude) and statistical sense.

Taken together, the disproportionate adverse psychological consequences on African Americans and women suggest that they are especially vulnerable to lockdowns during the COVID-19 global pandemic. If no measures were taken to protect these populations, pandemic lockdowns could potentially perpetuate the racial and gender gaps in the U.S. society.

5. Discussion, limitation, and direction for future research

5.1. Discussion

Our main findings indicate that lockdowns are associated with a variety of mental health problems. In particular, individuals experiencing lockdowns are 0.5, 0.8, and 0.8 percentage points more likely to feel worried, disinterested, and depressed on a daily basis, respectively. They are also more likely to have poor general health perception by 0.2 percentage points. Our findings are in line with the theoretical framework by Hall and Soskice (2001) where individuals in a liberal and highly deregulated economic system are left in vulnerable states during economic hardships. Our mechanism analyses provide evidence that lockdowns could potentially worsen individuals' mental well-being through aggravating both their current conditions and future expectations of food, housing, and employment security. In this respect, our results are consonant with Higginbottom, Barling, and Kelloway (1993) and Brenner (1990) where a societal economic change can create distress by imposing financial burdens and generating pessimistic expectations, respectively. Furthermore, guided by theories on racial and gender discrimination (Brewer, Conrad, and King 2002; Bjomholt and McKay 2014), we conduct the heterogeneity analyses along the lines of race and gender. We find disproportionate negative psychological effects on African American individuals and women. Given substantial disadvantages already faced by African Americans and women, their psychological well-being might be more acutely impacted by lockdowns compared to other racial and gender groups. Empirically, our heterogeneity results are consistent with Fairlie, Couch, and Xu (2020) and Alon et al. (2020) who also detect worsening employment outcomes for the African American and female populations in response to the COVID-19 epidemic, respectively.

Given the psychological costs of COVID-19 pandemic lockdowns, interventions intended to alleviate mental health burden should be implemented in accompany with lockdowns. Policies should be directed toward ensuring food, housing, and employment security to mitigate the psychological strain. Extra attention should be directed toward disadvantaged groups, such as African Americans and women, to avoid deepening racial and gender inequalities. It is also important to raise awareness about various sources of public support for psychological needs. In the US, federal agencies such as the Substance Abuse and Mental Health Services Administration (SAMHSA), Health Resources and Services Administration (HRSA), and Centers for Medicare & Medicaid Services (CMS) can provide useful information on treatment services and mental health care providers. Agencies at the state and county level can offer details on mental health services within a particular administrative area. Besides, there are advocacy and professional organizations such as the National Alliance on Mental Illness (NAMI) and Mental Health America (MHA) devoted to addressing the needs of those with mental health problems and improving the overall psychological well-being of the public. These organizations are also helpful in locating mental health practitioners.

5.2. Limitations and directions for future research

Using the HPS-PUF which focuses on individual experiences during the COVID-19 pandemic, we investigate the extent to which lockdowns affect individuals' mental well-being in the context of the U.S. There remain three major limitations to our study. First, although the DiD model strengthens the internal validity of our results, the focus on one liberal market economy might compromise the external validity of our estimates. It could be difficult for the estimated psychological impacts of lockdowns presented in our paper to be generalized to coordinated market economies such as Germany and Japan where employees are better protected with stronger labor unions and more generous social welfare (Hall and Soskice 2001). Therefore, future studies on the relationship between lockdowns and mental health for individuals in coordinated market economies are needed. Second, due to data limitation, we are unable to analyze the role of public spending in mitigating the psychological repercussions of lockdowns. Future works might empirically examine this relationship. Finally, the study only covers financial burdens and pessimistic expectations over food, housing, employment as potential mechanisms through which lockdowns aggravate individuals' mental health while it is likely that other mechanisms are also at work. To effectively respond to future circumstances, it is necessary to have a comprehensive evaluation of all possible pathways to the psychological impacts of lockdowns.

6. Conclusion

This paper quantifies the psychological consequences associated with COVID-19 lockdowns in the U.S. Our study utilizes the Household Pulse Survey Public Use File which contains individual responses to survey questions on experiences during the pandemic. Our identification strategy exploits the differential timing of lockdown implementation across the U.S. states within a DiD framework. We uncover adverse impacts of the lockdowns on a variety of psychological outcomes – namely anxiety, worry, disinterest, depression, and general health perception. The results are in line with Hall and Soskice (2001) on the vulnerable states of individuals in a liberal and highly deregulated economic system during economic hardships. Exploring the potential pathways, we show that the negative consequences could be attributed to individuals' concerns towards food, housing, and employment security, which is consistent with Higginbottom, Barling, and Kelloway (1993) and Brenner (1990). Finally, guided by theories on racial and gender discrimination (Brewer, Conrad, and King 2002; Bjomholt and McKay 2014), we conduct the heterogeneity analyses along the lines of race and gender. We find that African American and female individuals are disproportionately affected by the pandemic lockdown.

Our findings suggest that lockdowns should be supplemented with policies to prevent deepening inequality and mental health burdens. This includes developing interventions that aim to ensure food, housing, and employment security – as these are potential channels through which lockdowns aggravate mental health problems. Extra attention should be directed toward vulnerable groups, such as African Americans and women, to avoid deepening racial and gender inequalities in the U.S society. It is also important to raise awareness about various sources of public support for psychological needs.

Notes

1. For example, lockdowns are shown to be associated with reductions in new COVID-19 cases and COVID-19 related deaths (Hellewell et al. 2020; Roux, Massonnaud, and Crepey 2020) as well as the improvement in air quality (Mahato, Pal, and Ghosh 2020). However, lockdowns also resulted in massive declines in consumer spending and employment (Coibion, Gorodnichenko, and Weber 2020).
2. www.census.gov/quickfacts/fact/table/US/RHI225219

Data availability statement

The data underlying this study can be obtained from the U.S. Census website: census.gov/programs-surveys/household-pulse-survey/datasets.html

Disclosure statement

No potential conflict of interest was reported by the author(s).

References

Alon, T. M., M. Doepke, J. Olmstead-Rumsey, and M. Tertilt 2020. "The Impact of COVID-19 on Gender Equality." Working Paper No. w26947. National Bureau of Economic Research.

Bjomholt, M., and A. McKay. 2014. *Advances in Feminist Economics in Times of Economic Crisis*. Bradford: Demeter Press.

Brenner, M. H. 1990. "Influence of the Economy on Mental Health and Psychophysiologic Illness: International Perspective." *Community Mental Health in New Zealand* 5: 210.

Brewer, R. M., C. A. Conrad, and M. C. King. 2002. "The Complexities and Potential of Theorizing Gender, Caste, Race, and Class." *Feminist Economics* 8 (2): 3–17. doi:10.1080/135457002 2000019038.

Burgard, S. A., J. E. Brand, and J. S. House. 2009. "Perceived Job Insecurity and Worker Health in the United States." *Social Science & Medicine* 69 (5): 777–785. doi:10.1016/j. socscimed.2009.06.029.

Chetty, R., J. N. Friedman, N. Hendren, and M. Stepner 2020. "How Did Covid-19 and Stabilization Policies Affect Spending and Employment? A New Real-time Economic Tracker Based on Private Sector Data." Working Paper No. w27431. National Bureau of Economic Research.

Coibion, O., Y. Gorodnichenko, and M. Weber 2020. "The Cost of the Covid-19 Crisis: Lockdowns, Macroeconomic Expectations, and Consumer Spending." Working Paper No. w27141. National Bureau of Economic Research.

Fairlie, R. W., K. Couch, and H. Xu 2020. "The Impacts of Covid-19 on Minority Unemployment: First Evidence from April 2020 CPS Microdata." Working Paper No. w27246. National Bureau of Economic Research.

Hall, P. A., and D. Soskice. 2001. *Varieties of Capitalism: The Institutional Foundations of Comparative Advantage*. UK: Oxford University Press.

Hawryluck, L., W. L. Gold, S. Robinson, S. Pogorski, S. Galea, and R. Styra. 2004. "SARS Control and Psychological Effects of Quarantine, Toronto, Canada." *Emerging Infectious Diseases* 10 (7): 1206. doi:10.3201/eid1007.030703.

Hellewell, J., S. Abbott, A. Gimma, N. I. Bosse, C. I. Jarvis, T. W. Russell, … S. Flasche. 2020. "Feasibility of Controlling COVID-19 Outbreaks by Isolation of Cases and Contacts." *The Lancet Global Health* 8: e488-e496. doi:10.1016/S2214-109X(20)30074-7.

Higginbottom, S. F., J. Barling, and E. K. Kelloway. 1993. "Linking Retirement Experiences and Marital Satisfaction: A Mediational Model." *Psychology and Aging* 8 (4): 508. doi:10.1037/0882-7974.8.4.508.

Mahato, S., S. Pal, and K. G. Ghosh. 2020. "Effect of Lockdown amid COVID-19 Pandemic on Air Quality of the Megacity Delhi, India." *Science of the Total Environment* 730: 139086. doi:10.1016/j.scitotenv.2020.139086.

Reynolds, D. L., J. R. Garay, S. L. Deamond, M. K. Moran, W. Gold, and R. Styra. 2008. "Understanding, Compliance and Psychological Impact of the SARS Quarantine Experience." *Epidemiology & Infection* 136 (7): 997–1007. doi:10.1017/S0950268807009156.

Roux, J., C. Massonnaud, and P. Crepey. 2020. "COVID-19: One-month Impact of the French Lockdown on the Epidemic Burden." *medRxiv*. doi:10.1101/2020.04.22.20075705.

Sprang, G., and M. Silman. 2013. "Posttraumatic Stress Disorder in Parents and Youth after Health-related Disasters." *Disaster Medicine and Public Health Preparedness* 7 (1): 105–110. doi:10.1017/dmp.2013.22.

U.S. Census Bureau. 2020. "Source of the Data and Accuracy of the Estimates for the 2020 Household Pulse Survey." https://www2.census.gov/programs-surveys/demo/technical-documentation/hhp/Source-and-Accuracy-Statement-May-21-May-26.pdf

Appendix

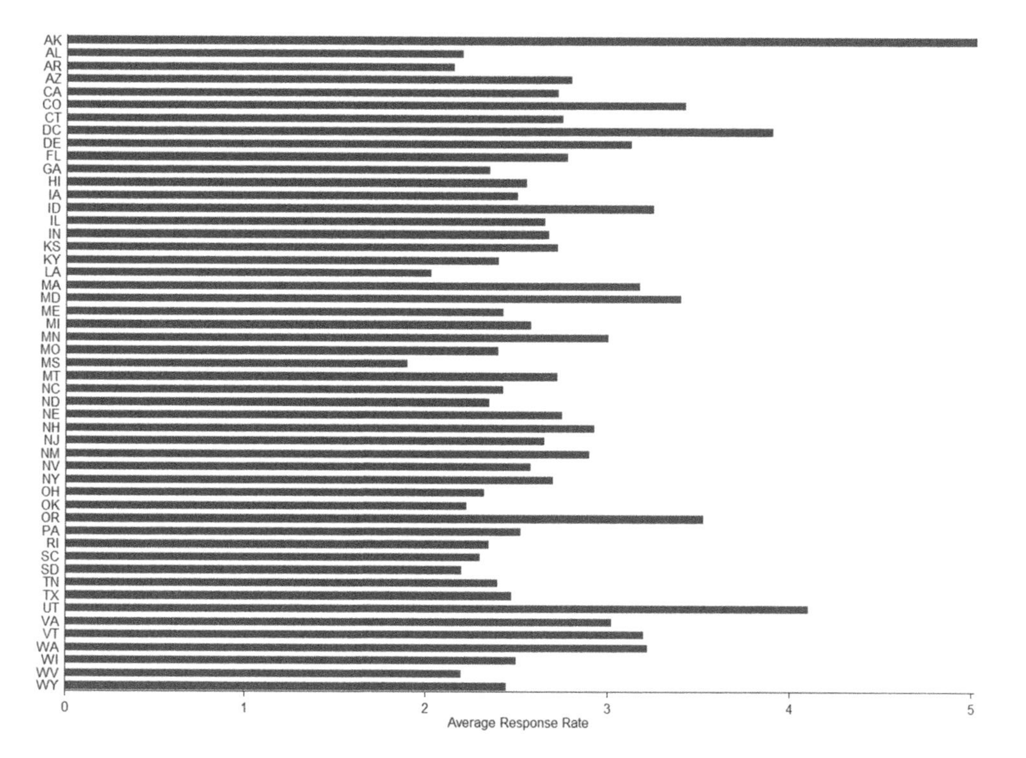

Figure A1. Average Response Rate by State. Note: The graph presents the average response rate for each state across four survey weeks. The data on response rate are taken from the U.S. Census Bureau (2020)

Table A1. Response Rate by State and Survey Week.

State	W1	W2	W3	W4	Average	State	W1	W2	W3	W4	Average
AL	3	1	2	2.8	2.2	MT	4.2	1.5	2.2	3	2.7
AK	8.4	2.7	3.8	5.2	5	NE	4.1	1.4	2.3	3.2	2.8
AZ	4.2	1.4	2.4	3.2	2.8	NV	3.7	1.3	2.3	3	2.6
AR	3	1.1	1.9	2.6	2.2	NH	4.6	1.7	2.3	3.1	2.9
CA	3.8	1.3	2.5	3.3	2.7	NJ	3.7	1.3	2.4	3.2	2.7
CO	4.9	1.8	3	4	3.4	NM	4.5	1.6	2.4	3.1	2.9
CT	3.5	1.3	2.5	3.7	2.8	NY	3.9	1.5	2.4	3	2.7
DE	4.5	1.7	2.7	3.6	3.1	NC	3.7	1.2	2.1	2.7	2.4
DC	5.6	2	3.3	4.7	3.9	ND	3.8	1.2	1.9	2.5	2.4
FL	3.7	1.3	2.2	3.9	2.8	OH	3.6	1.1	1.9	2.7	2.3
GA	3.6	1.2	2	2.6	2.4	OK	3.2	1.1	1.9	2.7	2.2
HI	3.2	1.3	2.4	3.3	2.6	OR	4.9	1.8	3.1	4.3	3.5
ID	5	1.7	2.7	3.6	3.3	PA	3.8	1.3	2.2	2.8	2.5
IL	3.6	1.3	2.4	3.3	2.7	RI	3.4	1.1	2.1	2.8	2.4
IN	3.7	1.3	2.4	3.3	2.7	SC	3.7	1.2	1.8	2.5	2.3
IA	3.7	1.3	2.2	2.8	2.5	SD	3.2	1	1.9	2.7	2.2
KS	3.6	1.3	2.5	3.5	2.7	TN	3.4	1.3	2.1	2.8	2.4
KY	3.7	1.2	2	2.7	2.4	TX	3.6	1.2	2.1	3	2.5
LA	2.9	0.9	1.8	2.5	2	UT	5.8	2.1	3.7	4.8	4.1
ME	4	1.4	1.9	2.4	2.4	VT	4.8	1.9	2.7	3.4	3.2
MD	4.8	1.7	4.6	2.5	3.4	VA	4.6	1.6	2.6	3.3	3
MA	4.3	1.7	2.9	3.8	3.2	WA	4.9	1.7	2.7	3.6	3.2
MI	3.9	1.4	2.2	2.8	2.6	WV	3.5	1.2	1.8	2.3	2.2
MN	4.2	1.5	2.7	3.6	3	WI	3.7	1.3	2.2	2.8	2.5
MS	2.9	1	1.6	2.1	1.9	WY	4	1.4	2.3	2.1	2.5
MO	3.6	1.1	2	2.9	2.4						

The table presents the response rate across states. W1, W2, W3, and W4 stand for Week 1 April 2023 – May 5), Week 2 (May 7 – May 12), Week 3 (May 14 – May 19), and Week 4 (May 21 – May 26) surveys, respectively. Average is the mean response rate over four weeks for each state. Source: U.S. Census Bureau (2020).

Table A2. Summary Statistics.

	Control			Treatmen			All		
	Mean (1)	SD (2)	Obs. (3)	Mean (4)	SD (5)	Obs. (6)	Mean (7)	SD 8)	Obs. (8)
Panel A: Control Variables									
Being White	0.85	0.357	183,971	0.806	0.395	166,614	0.829	0.376	350,585
Being African American	0.078	0.268	183,971	0.078	0.268	166,614	0.078	0.268	350,585
Being Other Races	0.072	0.259	183,971	0.116	0.32	166,614	0.093	0.29	350,585
Age	51.34	15.73	183,971	51.67	15.69	166,614	51.49	15.71	350,585
Being Married	0.587	0.492	183,971	0.562	0.496	166,614	0.575	0.494	350,585
Being Male	0.405	0.491	183,971	0.413	0.492	166,614	0.409	0.492	350,585
Went to College	0.85	0.357	183,971	0.868	0.338	166,614	0.859	0.348	350,585
Work for Government	0.104	0.305	183,971	0.101	0.301	166,614	0.102	0.303	350,585
Panel B: Outcome Variables									
Poor General Health Perception	0.025	0.157	166,224	0.023	0.149	151,726	0.024	0.153	317,950
Anxiety Every Day	0.141	0.348	166,037	0.153	0.36	151,555	0.147	0.354	317,592
Worry Every Day	0.097	0.296	165,961	0.101	0.301	151,484	0.099	0.298	317,445
Disinterest Every Day	0.076	0.265	165,915	0.078	0.269	151,381	0.077	0.267	317,296
Depression Every Day	0.076	0.266	166,055	0.078	0.268	151,539	0.077	0.267	317,594
Food Sufficiency Confidence	0.574	0.495	167,942	0.584	0.493	153,157	0.579	0.494	321,099
Afford More Food	0.882	0.323	180,446	0.894	0.308	163,483	0.887	0.316	343,929
Get out to Buy Food	0.968	0.176	180,446	0.963	0.19	163,483	0.965	0.183	343,929
Get Food Delivered	0.979	0.142	180,446	0.971	0.169	163,483	0.975	0.156	343,929
Food Availability	0.817	0.387	180,446	0.801	0.399	163,483	0.809	0.393	343,929
Next Payment Confidence	0.672	0.469	120,616	0.674	0.469	113,773	0.673	0.469	234,389
Last Payment on Time	0.895	0.306	120,505	0.898	0.303	113,700	0.896	0.305	234,205
Expected Unemployment	0.288	0.453	182,673	0.319	0.466	165,425	0.303	0.46	348,098
Recent Unemployment	0.622	0.485	182,887	0.597	0.491	165,620	0.61	0.488	348,507

Table A3. Outcome Variable Construction.

Question	Response	Coding
Would you say your health in general is:	1 = Excellent, 2 = Very good, 3 = Good, 4 = Fair, 5 = Poor	Poor General Health Perception equals to 1 if Response is 5
Over the last 7 days, how often have you been bothered by the following problems: (i) Feeling nervous, anxious, or on edge, (ii) Not being able to stop or control worrying, (iii) having little interest or pleasure in doing things, and (iv) feeling down, depressed, or hopeless.	1 = Not at all, 2 = Several days, 3 = More than half the days, 4 = Nearly every day	(i) Anxiety Every Day, (ii) Worry Every Day, (iii) Disinterest Every Day, and (iv) Depression Every Day equal to 1 if Response is 4
How confident are you that your household will be able to afford the kinds of food you need for the next four weeks?	1 = Not at all confident, 2 = Somewhat confident, 3 = Moderately confident, 4 = Very confident	Food Sufficiency Confidence equals to 1 if Response is 4
Why did you not have enough to eat? Choose all that apply: (i) Couldn't afford to buy more food, (ii) Couldn't get out to buy food, (iii) Couldn't get groceries or meals delivered to me, and (iv) The stores didn't have the food I wanted.	1 = Category marked	(i) Afford More Food, (ii) Get Out to Buy Food, (iii) Get Food Delivered, and (iv) Food Availability equals to 0 if Response is 1
How confident are you that your household will be able to pay your next rent or mort- gage payment on time?	1 = No confidence, 2 = Slight confidence, 3 = Moderate confidence, 4 = High confidence, 5 = Payment is/will be deferred	Next Payment Confidence equals to 1 if Response is 4
Did you pay your last months rent or mort- gage on time?	1 = Yes, 2 = No, 3 = Payment was deferred	Last Payment on Time equals to 1 if Response is 1
Do you expect that you or anyone in your household will experience a loss of employ- ment income in the next 4 weeks because of the coronavirus pandemic?	1 = Yes, 2 = No	Expected Unemployment equals to 1 if Response is 1
Have you, or has anyone in your household experienced a loss of employment income since 13 March 2020?	1 = Yes, 2 = No	Recent Unemployment equals to 1 if Response is 1

Table A4. Lockdowns by State and Week of Survey.

State	Start	End	W1	W2	W3	W4	State	Start	End	W1	W2	W3	W4
AL	Apr 04	Apr 30	0	0	0	0	MT	Mar 28	Apr 26	0	0	0	0
AK	Mar 28	Apr 24	0	0	0	0	NE	*No Lockdown*		0	0	0	0
AZ	Mar 31	May 15	1	1	0	0	NV	Apr 01	May 09	1	0	0	0
AR	*No Lockdown*		0	0	0	0	NH	Mar 27	*S.i.E*	1	1	1	1
CA	Mar 19	*S.i.E*	1	1	1	1	NJ	Mar 21	Jun 09	1	1	1	1
CO	Mar 26	Apr 26	0	0	0	0	NM	Mar 24	May 31	1	1	1	1
CT	Mar 23	May 20	1	1	1	0	NY	Mar 22	May 28	1	1	1	1
DE	Mar 24	May 31	1	1	1	1	NC	Mar 30	May 22	1	1	1	0
DC	Apr 01	May 29	1	1	1	1	ND	*No Lockdown*		0	0	0	0
FL	Apr 03	May 04	0	0	0	0	OH	Mar 23	May 29	1	1	1	1
GA	Apr 03	Apr 30	0	0	0	0	OK	*No Lockdown*		0	0	0	0
HI	Mar 25	May 31	1	1	1	1	OR	Mar 23	*S.i.E*	1	1	1	1
ID	Mar 25	Apr 30	0	0	0	0	PA	Apr 01	Jun 04	1	1	1	1
IL	Mar 21	May 29	1	1	1	1	RI	Apr 28	May 08	0	0	0	0
IN	Mar 24	May 04	0	0	0	0	SC	Apr 07	May 04	0	0	0	0
IA	*No Lockdown*		0	0	0	0	SD	*No Lockdown*		0	0	0	0
KS	Mar 30	May 03	0	0	0	0	TN	Mar 31	*S.i.E*	1	1	1	1
KY	Mar 26	*S.i.E*	1	1	1	1	TX	Apr 02	Apr 30	0	0	0	0
LA	Mar 23	May 15	1	1	0	0	UT	*No Lockdown*		0	0	0	0
ME	Apr 02	May 31	1	1	1	1	VT	Mar 25	May 15	1	1	0	0
MD	Mar 30	May 15	1	1	0	0	VA	Mar 30	Jun 10	1	1	1	1
MA	Mar 24	May 18	1	1	0	0	WA	Mar 23	May 31	1	1	1	1
MI	Mar 24	Jun 01	1	1	1	1	WV	Mar 24	May 03	0	0	0	0
MN	Mar 27	May 17	1	1	0	0	WI	Mar 25	May 13	1	1	0	0
MS	Apr 03	Apr 27	0	0	0	0	WY	*No Lockdown*		0	0	0	0
MO	Apr 06	May 03	0	0	0	0		**Average**		**0.58**	**0.57**	**0.43**	**0.39**

The table presents the timing of lockdowns across states. W1, W2, W3, and W4 stand for Week 1 (April 23 – May 5), Week 2 (May 7 – May 12), Week 3 (May 14 – May 19), and Week 4 (May 21 – May 26) surveys, respectively. They take the value of 1 if the survey was conducted during the lockdown period, and zero otherwise. S.i.E means the lockdown has not been lifted yet (still in effect).

Table A5. The Psychological Impact of Lockdowns – Uncoded Measures.

	Poor General Health Perception (1)	Anxiety Every Day (2)	Worry Every Day (3)	Disinterest Every Day (4)	Depression Every Day (5)
Lockdowns	0.015**	0.017	0.020**	0.026**	0.030***
	(0.006)	(0.011)	(0.009)	(0.012)	(0.010)
Controls					
Ind. Characteristics	✓	✓	✓	✓	✓
State & Week FE	✓	✓	✓	✓	✓
Observations	317,950	317,592	317,445	317,296	317,594

*p < 0.1, **p < 0.05, ***p < 0.01. Individual Characteristics include age, age-squared, marital status, race, gender, occupational sector, and educational attainment. Robust standard errors are clustered at the State-by-Week level.

COVID-19: effectiveness of socioeconomic factors in containing the spread and mortality

Joshua Ping Ang, Fang Dong and Jason Patalinghug

ABSTRACT

This paper presents a study on 80 countries that evaluates the socioeconomic factors in containing the spread and mortality of COVID-19. Our results show that the long-term social factors such as lower personal freedom, better education in science, and past coronavirus outbreak experience are more effective than the economic factors such as higher healthcare-associated factors per 1000 population and larger GDP. However, using GDP per capita as the instrumental variable, we also find that the richer countries with a high degree of personal freedom have a higher number of infection or death cases per million population because they would be less likely to adhere to and implement the policy of the movement restrictions to restrict their access to goods and services.

1. Introduction

Beginning in the 1960s, various types of human coronaviruses have been discovered. There have been several coronavirus outbreaks over the past two decades such as the Severe Acute Respiratory Syndrome (SARS) in 2002 and 2003, the Middle East Respiratory Syndrome (MERS) in 2012, and the Coronavirus Disease 2019 (COVID-19) in the present (Su et al. 2016). The spread of COVID-19 rises exponentially if left unaddressed (Berger, Herkenhoff, and Mongey 2020), result in high mortality. One of the approaches in containing the virus is movement restriction (social distancing, self-isolation, travel restrictions, etc.) because the virus spreads easily through close proximity contact with another human (Farooq and Hafeez 2020). One of the reasons for these restrictions being put in place is because of the fact that it takes about 14 days for a person showing mild symptoms to recover from the disease (Berger, Herkenhoff, and Mongey 2020). Most of the countries affected by the coronavirus have instituted restrictions in movement, with China being the first country to implement these restrictions – in December of 2019. Governments worldwide – including the U.S. government – have curtailed civil liberties in response to the coronavirus pandemic. The essential American right of free assembly, for example, has been restricted across much of the country (Merrefield 2020).

This paper contributes to the literature on COVID-19 studies from a socioeconomic perspective. Many papers have studied how government response such as movement restrictions can contain the virus spread and death (Baccini and Brodeur 2020; Bargain and Aminjonov 2020; Béland, Brodeur, and Wright 2020; Moser and Yared 2020; Yilmazkuday 2020; among others), but we join Bargain and Aminjonov (2020), Briscese et al. (2020), Chen, Frey, and Presidente (2020), Nay (2020), Litan and Lowy (2020), Nikolaev, Boudreaux, and Salahodjaev (2017), and Schwartz (2012) among others in considering how personal freedoms affect the spread of COVID-19 or vice versa. Motivated by Cutler and Lleras-Muney (2010), Lleras-Muney (2005), and Conti, Heckman, and Urzua (2010) on the important relationship between education and health, and by Leung et al. (2003), Tang and Wong (2004), Bawazir et al. (2018), Barr et al. (2008), Bish and Michie (2010), and Rosenberg et al. (2013) among others on the importance of science education, in processing facts and making decisions, we study how young adults' way of thinking mathematically and scientifically separately affect the spread of COVID-19 by using Programme for International Student Assessment (PISA) scores. The acquisition of knowledge in mathematics and science by young adults attained in secondary education is a part of the total social system. Following Amaral et al. (2019), Lorgelly and Adler (2020), and Qin et al. (2005), we examine how supplies of healthcare professionals and facilities affect a country's ability to handle a pandemic such as the COVID-19. Similar to Amaral et al. (2019), Gardner et al. (2018), Huang et al. (2020), and Teng et al. (2017), we also examine the size effect of an economy on containing the coronavirus. Noticing that past pandemic handling experience of a country can better prepare the country in the face of the COVID-19 pandemic (Chen, Frey, and Presidente 2020; Huang et al. 2020,; Schwartz and Yen 2017 among others), we also assess how the past experience of coronavirus (e.g., SARS and MERS) outbreaks can help a country contain the spread of COVID-19. Finally, the health effect of urbanization, which is one of the outcomes of industrialization, is studied (see Lai et al. 2004,; Neiderud 2015 among others).

This paper shows that countries with higher degrees of personal freedom are prone to have higher COVID-19 cases per million population; countries with higher PISA science scores but not higher PISA mathematics scores tend to lower the number of COVID-19 cases per million population; larger economies or economies with ample healthcare professionals and facilities tend to be able to contain the virus more successfully than smaller economies or economies that lack healthcare human capital and physical capital; countries that have experienced outbreaks of SARS and/or MERS tend to have lower cases of COVID-19 per million population; and countries with higher urbanization rates tend to have more cases per million population as people are highly likely to live and/or work in close proximity.

The rest of the paper is organized as follows. Section 2 provides a review of related literature, Section 3 provides an explanation of the data, Section 4 presents the model, Section 5 focuses on the Ordinary Least Squares (OLS) estimation. Section 6 focuses on the Two Stage Least Squares (2SLS) estimation and endogeneity assessment, Section 7 discusses the results within the wider literature, Section 8 provides policy recommendations, Section 9 points out the limitations of this study and directions for future research, and Section 10 provides the conclusion of this paper.

2. Literature review

2.1. Personal freedom

Bargain and Aminjonov (2020), Briscese et al. (2020), and Chen, Frey, and Presidente (2020) analyze the effect of democracy, trust and cohesion, compliance, and culture on the contagion and countries' responsiveness to COVID-19. Using data on human mobility and political trust at regional level in Europe, Bargain and Aminjonov (2020) examines whether the compliance to containment policies depends on the level of trust in policy makers prior to the crisis. They discovered that high-trust regions lower their nonessential movement significantly compared to low-trust areas, implying that personal freedom depends negatively on the level of trust in the government and by lowering the freedom of movement we can better contain the virus than otherwise. Briscese et al. (2020) shows how intentions to comply with the self-isolation restrictions introduced in Italy helped to mitigate the COVID-19 pandemic, implying the importance of sacrifice of personal freedom in containing the virus. Chen, Frey, and Presidente (2020) finds autocratic governments who imposed more stringent lockdowns and relied more on contact tracing have been more effective in reducing the movement of people to curb the spread of COVID-19. They also find that for the same policy stringency, countries with more obedient and collectivist cultural traits experienced larger declines in geographic mobility relative to their more individualistic counterparts. It is again proved that cutting personal freedom can be helpful for containing the virus, but the effectiveness may depend on other social traits like the culture structures. However, Ruger (2005) finds that China's political and cultural authoritarianism and a lack of civil liberties, political rights, and freedom of the press have dramatically and negatively impacted the population's health during China's famine of 1958–1961 and China's SARS epidemic in 2002–2003.

The downside with the implementation of movement restrictions or contact tracing to contain the virus requires the curtailing of personal freedoms, such as the rights to assembly and movement. Schwartz (2012) compares China's relatively effective response to the 2002–2003 SARS outbreak with Taiwan's relatively ineffective response, finds that China has an 'authoritarian advantage' where Taiwan lacks, and concludes that effective pandemic response depends on coercive government actions that may not be favorable by a more democratic country. Nay (2020) identifies three risks that could allow governments to use those surveillance tools as the norm beyond emergency situations. They are the risk of converting emergency measures into ordinary legislation, the risk of using emergency measures to strengthen surveillance politics, and the risk that citizens may change the value that they accord to freedom. Litan and Lowy (2020) states that most Americans agree on the need for movement restrictions and social distancing, but some Americans are anxious for the time when they can be fully reopened for the psychological and economic well-being of the country, implying that people may face a democratic dilemma, or what we loosely call a personal freedom dilemma.

In the study of Zika virus during 2015–2016, Teng et al. (2017) shows that the probability of Zika outbreaks decreases with GDP per capita. In the study of the potential impact of previous exposure to SARS or MERS on the control of the COVID-19 pandemic, Huang et al. (2020) uses GDP per capita as a control variable and finds a negative relationship between GDP per capita and the COVID-19 incidence rate. We propose to use GDP per capita as an instrumental variable for personal freedom to study the incidence of COVID-19. Our rationale is that with restrictions in movement, the expected utility of consumption is restricted since there are a lot of goods and services consumptions that require mobility or the freedom of movement, especially in rich countries. De Haan and Siermann (1998) conducts a robust check on the relationship between economic freedom and GDP per capita and finds that some indicators of economic freedom have a positive relationship with GDP per capita, but finds no relationship between the growth rate of real GDP per capita and the freedom of movement index. We hypothesize that the higher the GDP per capita, the higher the personal freedom, and the higher the COVID-19 cases per million population.

2.2. Program for international student assessment (PISA) mathematics and science scores

In the study of the relationship between health behaviors and education, Cutler and Lleras-Muney (2010) emphasizes and shows that better-educated people engage in more preventive and risk control behaviors. Lleras-Muney (2005) shows that education has a causal impact on mortality, implying that education policies could dramatically increase adult longevity. Conti, Heckman, and Urzua (2010) finds that education has an important causal effect in explaining differences in many adult outcomes and healthy behaviors. The selection of factors determined early in life such as family background characteristics, and cognitive, noncognitive, and health endowments developed by age 10, explains more than half of the observed difference by education in poor health, depression, and obesity.

Education in general also matters in adopting precautionary measures to protect against contagious disease such as SARS (Leung et al. 2003; Tang and Wong 2004), MERS (Bawazir et al. 2018), and pandemic influenza (Barr et al. 2008), see Bish and Michie (2010) for more information. However, we are interested in knowing the specific knowledge in education that matters, namely between mathematics and science. We assess the effect of education in mathematical and scientific knowledge separately among countries by using the PISA scores on the COVID-19 incidence. Public knowledge in science is important in shaping policy-making process for pandemic (Rosenberg et al. 2013). Establishing these social norms is part of a product of past education. The understandings of mathematics and science are important because it reflects the current skills to promote analytical thinking and ability to process scientific information on the pandemic. For example, the scientific facts that COVID-19 affects more elderly individuals than youth and the severity and death rate are also higher in elderly individuals than in youth (Yi et al. 2020) might lead young adults to believe that they would be less likely to take precautions and would be less willing to contain the coronavirus. We propose that having good analytical mathematics knowledge would enable the young adults to figure out their odd, hence less likely to take precautionary measures if the likelihood of severe impact on them is minimal. Without a strong knowledge in science among the young adults, they may discount the impact of their behavior by undermining the effects of this novel coronavirus on themselves and other people.

2.3. Healthcare-related factors

Healthcare-related resources of a country such as number of doctors per capita and number of hospital beds per capita indicate the capacity limit of the health services to be provided in response to COVID-19 relative to other countries. The healthcare systems have been overwhelmed and reached the capacity constraints on the number of critical care beds, the number of ventilators, and the tests for infections, which further strained due to the reduction of medical care to patients (Lorgelly and Adler 2020). In the study of spread patterns of microcephaly and zika virus in Brazil, Amaral et al. (2019) finds that microcephaly incidence in Brazil is significantly and positively related to access to primary care, population size and mobility index of the municipalities. On the other hand, microcephaly incidence shows a negative significant association with GDP and environmental index of the municipalities. In the study of SARS in China, Qin et al. (2005) shows that the poor living environment and inadequate health resources such as the medical facilities, health workers, and per capita public health expenditures contributed critically to the outbreak and mortality of SARS. We hypothesize that the more physicians and hospital beds per 1000 population, the lower the COVID-19 cases per million population.

2.4. Gross domestic product (GDP)

In the study of the risk factors which contributed to the geographic spread and local transmission of Zika during the 2015–2016 epidemic in the Americas, Gardner et al. (2018) finds that a lower regional GDP was the best predictor of Zika virus transmission, suggesting that Zika is primarily a disease of poverty. In the investigation of regional characteristics at the municipal level that can be associated with the incidence of microcephaly in Brazil in 2016, Amaral et al. (2019) shows that microcephaly incidence is significantly and negatively related to GDP. We choose to use GDP to check for countries with large economies that would have a greater ability to maneuver capital within the country to redirect resources to produce emergency goods temporarily during the pandemic. In other words, large nations with large GDP can maneuver their capital and capacity to reduce healthcare overload and contain the spread with cohesion efforts. For example, China constructed a COVID-19 hospital called Huoshenshan Hospital in Hubei Province, China in just 10 days (The Washington Post, February 3, 2020), Ford and GM were making tens of thousands of ventilators (The Washington Post, April 4, 2020), United States constructed several field hospitals, deployed navy ship to New York state (The Hill, March 18, 2020).

2.5. Past SARS and/or MERS experience

Countries that have had outbreaks of SARS and/or MERS should be able to better handle the pandemic because of better preparedness due to their past experience with an outbreak and because their governments are more willing to spend on public health for the future outbreak prevention. Chen, Frey, and Presidente (2020) uses a dummy variable to capture the past epidemic or pandemic experience and their results show that countries that experienced SARS or MERS, were more likely to implement more comprehensive testing policies. In the study of the potential impact of previous exposure to SARS or MERS on the control of the COVID-19 pandemic, Huang et al. (2020) finds that countries with previous exposure to SARS and/or MERS epidemics were significantly more likely to have lower incidence of COVID-19. Schwartz and Yen (2017) explains that the government of Taiwan has suffered and drawn lessons from its experiences with past pandemic outbreaks, from SARS through H7N9, H1N1, and dengue. As a result, the Taiwanese government adopted and adapted WHO recommendations, and thereby implementing 'best practices' in many aspects of pandemic preparedness and response. We choose to include past SARS and MERS cases per million population in our model to examine if past experience helps mitigate the coronavirus incidence rate.

2.6. Urbanization rate

We model with the urbanization rate as a proxy measure for population density, where urbanized areas are usually more densely populated than non-urbanized areas. Lai et al. (2004) applies cartographic and geostatistical methods in analyzing the patterns of disease spread during the 2003 SARS outbreak in Hong Kong using geographic information system (GIS) technology and showed that the urban population was at higher risk of contracting SARS. Neiderud (2015) reviews how urbanization affects the epidemiology of emerging infectious diseases and points out that urban population and the density of residents can meet the criteria for a new epidemic and create a public health disaster, if not taken seriously, especially in low-income developing countries where the urbanization rate is rapidly rising. So, urbanization rate gives an estimate of the population proportion who lives in a close proximity that affects the spread of a contagious virus.

3. Data

Our data is collected from different sources. Therefore, our estimation sample consists of cross-sections of countries with data from the European Center for Disease Control (ECDC) in 2020, Cato Institute 2017, World Health Organization (WHO) surveyed in 2006–2019, Organization for Economic Co-operation and Development (OECD) PISA 2006–2018, United Nations (UN), and the World Bank (WB) 2005–2019.

We use data from the ECDC to analyze the factors for the spread of COVID-19 pandemic. It has a large data providing information of each country which are affected by COVID-19 on the total cases, total death caused by the coronavirus, daily cases, and daily count of death in 2020. The number of 80[1] countries selected in the analysis are countries that have a record of, at least, 30 days after hitting the 10th reported case. We track the data of number of infection cases and death cases at 30 days and 60 days after the 10th case.[2] Given that the data for our estimation sample are from the specific interval of days, it is not affected by new daily reported cases. We choose the 10th cases because the exponential growth of spread is more evident when hitting the double-digit number of cases. Another reason that we choose to use the data at 30th and 60th day after the 10th case is to avoid accounting for the next wave that would occur in the later stage. To account for the effect of population, we use number of cases per million population.[3] Figure 1 presents the spread rate for the COVID-19 measured by infection cases

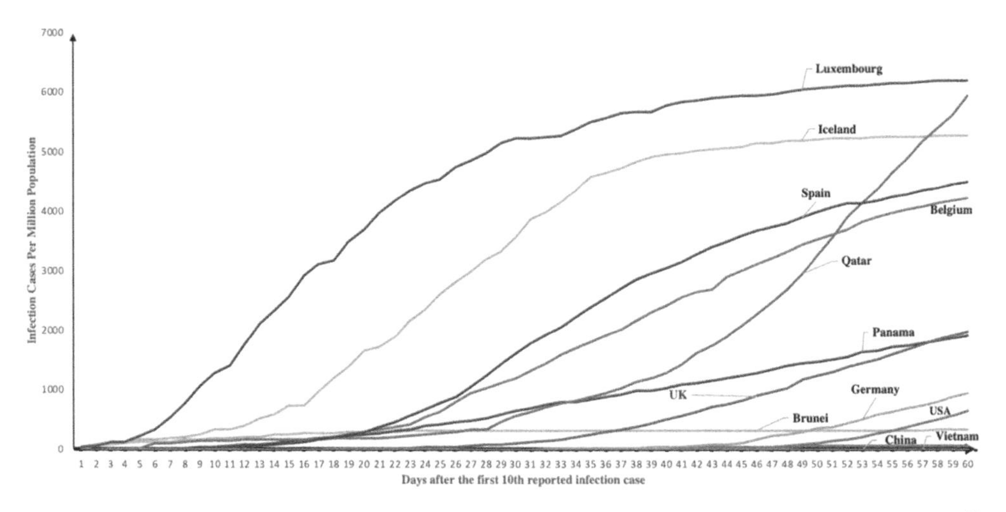

Figure 1. Number of COVID-19 cases per million population for selected countries after their 10th reported case.

per million population against the number of days after the 10th case is detected for a selected number of countries.

For the socioeconomic data, we use the 2017 Personal Freedom Index from Cato Human Freedom Index. This Index measures the legal protection and security (rule of law, security and safety), and specific personal freedom (movement, religion, association and assembly, information expression, relationship identity). It captures the degree of personal movement, rule of law, and information expression which is important to assess the right of individuals within a country to access services and consumption goods that would maximize their expected utility. When an idea of personal freedom is very high, it also implies that legal prospect of limiting the movement of those individuals would be harder. Figure 2 presents four scatterplots to indicate the associations between the number of infection cases per million population at 30 days and the personal freedom index; between the number of infection cases per million people at 60 days and the personal freedom index; between the number of death cases per million population at 30 days and the personal freedom index; and between the number of death cases per million people at 60 days and the personal freedom index.

We choose PISA scores that measure 15-year-old students' mathematics and science (and reading) literacy every three years across countries because it is a good sample to approximately measure the level of analytical thinking with the mathematics score and of scientific knowledge with the science score. We use the variable by average the PISA scores from 2006, 2009, 2012, 2015, and 2018 because it would be a good measure for whom those 15-year-old students are the young adults in 2020 aged from 17 until 29. We collect the PISA data from OECD.

We collect the data on the number of medical physicians (including medical generalists and specialists) per 1000 people[4] from 2014 to 2018 and the number of hospital beds per 1000 people from 2009 to 2015 from WHO's Global Health Workforce Statistics. Since the data on hospital beds and medical physicians of every country are not reported to or collected by WHO every year, we collected the data from WHO in 2020 that use the

Figure 2. The association between COVID-19 and Personal Freedom index.

value of the most recent year reported by each country. For example, for medical physician data, 2014 was the last year Azerbaijan and Kazakhstan reported their data to or collected by WHO. For example, for hospital bed data, 2009 was the last year the Netherlands reported their data to or collected by WHO. Hospital beds include in-patient beds available in public, private, general, and specialized medical centers for both acute and chronic care. With exception to Taiwan (Republic of China) and Hong Kong (SAR of

China), we supplemented the data on medical physicians and hospital beds from their government websites and the reports from PriceWaterhouseCoopers.

We use the nominal Gross Domestic Product (GDP) and the GDP per capita in 2019 with the data collected from the WB and OECD.

We collect the cumulative number of confirmed SARS from November 1, 2002 to August 7, 2003 and MERS from September 2012 to February 2020 cases of infection among human by country from WHO and the Food and Agriculture Organization of the UN (FAO). To account for the effect of population, we use the sum of past SARS and MERS cases per million[5] population.

Urbanization rate refers to the percentage of people living in urban areas by countries as defined by national statistical offices and the data are collected for 2018 from the United Nations Population Division (UN). With exception to Taiwan (Republic of China) and Hong Kong (SAR of China), we supplement the data on urbanization rate from their government websites and the reports from PriceWaterhouseCoopers.

For the 80 countries, the average number of cases per million population of COVID-19 at the 30 days after the 10th case is around 422 cases per million population with the highest value in Luxembourg (5398.8 cases per million population) and the lowest in Vietnam (0.18 cases per million population). The average mortality rate of COVID-19 at 30 days after the 10th case is around 11 cases per million population with the highest value in Luxembourg (108.6 cases per million population) and the lowest in Vietnam, Uruguay, Albania, Thailand, Singapore, Malaysia, and Germany (zero case per million population). For the 80 countries, at the 60 days after the 10th case, the average number of cases per million population of COVID-19 is around 1124 cases per million population with the highest value in Qatar (5398.8 cases per million population) and the lowest in USA (0.497 cases per million population). As for the average mortality rate of COVID-19 at the 60 days after the 10th case, it is around 57 cases per million population with the highest value in Belgium (679.8 cases per million population) and the lowest in Vietnam (zero case per million population). See Table AI in Appendix A for variable definitions and descriptive statistics, Table AII in Appendix A for data sources, compilation methods, and years collected, and Table AIII in Appendix A for the country list.

4. Model

In order to investigate the relationship between COVID-19 cases and the socioeconomic factors, we use the Ordinary Least Squares (OLS) estimation and the following is our baseline regression model:

$$\begin{aligned} covidcasesperpop_i = {} & \beta_0 + \beta_1 PersonalFreedom_i + \beta_2 PISAMath_i + \beta_3 PISAScience_i \\ & + \beta_4 Doctorpercapita_i + \beta_5 Hospitalpercapita_i + \beta_6 GDP_i \\ & + \beta_7 PastSARSMERS_i + \beta_8 UrbanizationRate_i + \varepsilon_i \qquad (1A) \end{aligned}$$

In Equation 1A, the subscript i stands for each country that contracted the virus. *covidcasesperpop* refers to the COVID-19 infection cases per million population at the 30th day. Relative to the baseline model, GDP is replaced by log of GDP to form our Equation 2A; *covidcasesperpop* is replaced by log of *covidcasesperpop* to constitute our

Equation 3A; and *covidcasesperpop* is replaced by log of *covidcasesperpop* and GDP is replaced by log of GDP to form our Equation 4A.

Following this pattern, we create Equations 1B, 2B, 3B, and 4B in which *covidcasesperpop* refers to the COVID-19 infection cases per million population at the 60th day. Similarly, when we define *covidcasesperpop* as COVID-19 death cases per million population at the 30th day, we have Equations 1 C, 2 C, 3 C, and 4 C. Lastly, we define *covidcasesperpop* as COVID-19 death cases per million population at the 60th day and we reach at our last set of equations, Equations 1D, 2D, 3D, and 4D.

PersonalFreedom is the variable for personal freedom in 2017. *PISAMath* is the 15-year -old student's PISA Mathematics score averaged over 2006, 2009, 2012, 2015, and 2018. *PISAScience* is the 15-year-old student's PISA Science score averaged over the same 5 years. *Doctorpercapita* is the number of medical physicians per 1000 population averaged from 2013 to 2018. *Hospitalpercapita* stands for the number of hospital beds per 1000 population averaged from 2009 to 2015. *GDP* is the Gross Domestic Products in 2019 measured in trillions of dollars. *PastSARSMERS* is the number of past SARS from November 1, 2002 to August 7, 2003 and MERS from September 2012 to February 2020 infection cases per million population. *UrbanizationRate* is the percent of total population in a country living in the urban areas in 2018.

We notice that higher personal freedom could contribute to more coronavirus spread and death, at the same time, the COVID-19 pandemic can constrain such civil liberties as personal freedom to move and the rights to assembly, making personal freedom to be endogenous. This paper is the first in the literature on the coronavirus to use instrumental variable (IV) regression method to study its spread. For our models, an instrumental variable (IV) considered is *GDPpercapita*, which is the nominal GDP per capita in 2019 and which would need to satisfy the following two requirements:

$$(i)cov(GDPpercapita, \varepsilon) = 0$$

$$(ii)cov(GDPpercapita, PersonalFreedom) \neq 0$$

For the first requirement, it is assumed that after controlling the independent variables, *GDPpercapita* has no separate effect on *covidcasesperpop*. For the second requirement, that is, GDP per capita and personal freedom must be correlated, it is discussed in the Literature Review.

We hypothesize that the following factors will lead to higher numbers of COVID-19 cases per million population (*covidcasesperpop*): higher personal freedom index scores (*PersonalFreedom*) using the GDP per capita as an IV, lower numbers of doctors per 1000 population (*Doctorpercapita*), lower numbers of hospital beds per 1000 population (*Hospitalpercapita*), and higher urbanization rates (*UrbanizationRate*). We also presume that countries that have had outbreaks of SARS or MERS (*PastSARSMERS*) will fare better because they have been through an outbreak before and will be better prepared. We assume that countries with higher PISA science scores (*PISAScience*) will lead to fewer cases because the citizens of these countries have a better ability to process and digest the information on the science and nature of the virus. However, we assume that countries with higher PISA math scores (*PISAMath*) will have more cases. This is because people who are skilled at mathematics may think in terms of the probability of contracting the disease. By looking at low probability certain groups may catch the coronavirus, these people may believe that the probability of them contracting the disease is low and thus they are going to be less likely to comply with social-distancing guidelines which are meant to contain the virus. Also, higher GDP (*GDP*) lowers the coronavirus cases because a larger country can maneuver its resources quickly to cope with the spread of coronavirus.

5. Results

In this section, we present the results from the Ordinary Least Squares (OLS) estimation method with robust standard errors that is applied to the regression equations from Equations 1A through 4D and we only interpret the statistically significant coefficients at the 1%, 5%, or 10%. Table 1 shows the estimation results for Equations 1A through 4B. For the infection cases per million population at the 30th day the labels are Equations 1A, 2A, 3A, and 4A, and at the 60th day the labels are 1B, 2B, 3B, and 4B, on the top of Table 1, where A stands for infection cases at the 30th day after the 10th reported case and B stands that at the 60th day after the 10th reported case, and where 1 stands for the baseline model, 2 replaces GDP in the baseline model by log GDP, 3 uses log of total infection cases per million population as the dependent variable, and finally, 4 uses both log GDP and log of total infection cases per million population.

The results from Equations 1A, 2A, 3A, and 4A show that countries with more personal freedom tend to have more coronavirus cases. Holding everything else

Table 1. Estimation results: total infection cases at 30-Day and 60-Day After the First 10th Case (with Robust Standard Errors).

	At 30th Day after the 10th Reported Case				At 60th Day after the 10th Reported Case			
	Equation 1A	Equation 2A	Equation 3A	Equation 4A	Equation 1B	Equation 2B	Equation 3B	Equation 4B
Personal Freedom	157**	135*	0.462**	0.401**	133	147	0.172	0.211
	(76.4)	(68.8)	(0.205)	(0.189)	(152.)	(156.)	(0.18)	(0.187)
PISA Math	15.8*	15.1*	0.0213	0.0203	20.7	21.5	0.0193	0.0219
	(8.53)	(7.83)	(0.0199)	(0.0186)	(13.3)	(13.1)	(0.0168)	(0.0168)
PISA Science	−15.1*	−13*	−0.0294	−0.0246	−18.2	−20	−0.0204	−0.0259
	(8.47)	(7.08)	(0.0211)	(0.0197)	(12.9)	(12.3)	(0.0178)	(0.0172)
Medical Physician per 1000 people	27.2	16.2	0.518	0.505	97.9	115	0.389*	0.444*
	(86.1)	(91.1)	(0.244)	(0.254)	(160.)	(164.)	(0.231)	(0.236)
Hospital Bed per 1000 people	−47.4	−48.8*	−0.0933	−0.0965	−96.6	−95.3	−0.0611	−0.0571
	(30.1)	(28.4)	(0.0947)	(0.0926)	(71.7)	(72.5)	(0.0907)	(0.0993)
GDP	−37**		−0.282***		−70.2***		−0.262***	
	(15.4)		(0.0668)		23.4		0.0841	
Past SARS MERS per million pop.	−5.46**	−5.63	−0.0121***	−0.0115***	−11***	−10.4***	−0.0111***	−0.00891**
	(2.42)	(2.5)	(0.00413)	(0.00414)	(3.47)	(3.54)	(0.0035)	(0.0036)
Urbanization Rate	10.1	12.8	0.0164	0.0277*	28.6*	28.8*	0.0254	0.0273*
	(7.47)	(8.47)	(0.0171)	(0.0162)	(15.4)	(16.7)	(0.0154)	(0.0148)
Log GDP		−117*		−0.533***		−30.3		−0.158
		(60.2)		(0.133)		(94.7)		(0.165)
Constant	−1612**	−2475**	3.05*	−0.0972	−2839**	−2652	2.93*	3.2*
	(802)	(1192)	(1.77)	(1.83)	(1393.)	(1660.)	(1.52)	(1.63)
Observations	80	80	80	80	80	80	80	80

*p**<0.1, *p***<0.05, *p****<0.01, standard errors in parentheses.

constant, a one unit increase in the personal freedom index is associated with an increase of 157 infection cases per million population in Equation 1A, increase of 135 cases in Equation 2A, increase of 46.2% in Equation 3A, and 40.1% increase in Equation 4A. Holding everything else constant, a one-point increase in the PISA science score (PISA mathematics score) is associated with a decrease of 15.1 (increase of 15.8) infection cases per million population in Equation 1A and a decrease of 13 (increase of 15.1) infection cases per million population in Equation 2A. Holding everything else constant, a one unit increase in the number of hospital beds per 1000 population is associated with a decrease of 48.8 infection cases per million population in Equation 2A. Holding everything else constant, a one trillion dollar increase in GDP is associated with a decrease of 37 infection cases per million population in Equation 1A and a decrease of 28.2% of infection cases per million population in Equation 3A. In Equations 2A and 4A, a one percent increase in GDP is associated with a decrease of 1.17 infection cases per million population and a decrease of 0.533% of infection cases per million population. Holding everything else constant, a one unit increase in the number of past SARS and MERS cases per million population is associated with a decrease of 5.46 COVID-19 infection cases per million population in Equation 1A, a decrease of 1.21% of COVID-19 infection cases per million population in Equation 3A, and a decrease of 1.15% in Equation 4A. Holding everything else constant, a one percentage point increase in the urbanization rate is associated with an increase of 2.77% of COVID-19 infection cases per million population in Equation 4A.

Table 1 also presents the corresponding estimation results for the infection cases per million population at 60th day after the 10th reported case, which are labelled as Equations 1B, 2B, 3B, and 4B in Table 1. Holding everything else constant, a one unit increase in the number of medical physicians per 1000 population is associated with an increase of 38.9% of COVID-19 infection cases per million population in Equation 3B, and this increase is 44.4% in Equation 4B. Holding everything else constant, a one trillion dollar increase in GDP is associated with a decrease of 70.2 COVID-19 infection cases per million population in Equation 1B and a decrease of 26.2% of COVID-19 infection cases per million population in Equation 3B. Holding everything else constant, a one unit increase in the number of past SARS and MERS cases per million population is associated with a decrease of 11 COVID-19 infection cases per million population, decrease of 10.4 cases in Equation 2B, decrease of 1.11% in Equation 3B, and decrease of 0.891% in Equation 4B. Holding everything else constant, a one percentage point increase in the urbanization rate is associated with an increase of 28.6 COVID-19 infection cases per million population in Equation 1B, an increase of 28.8 cases in Equation 2B, and an increase of 2.73% in Equation 4B.

Table 2 shows the OLS estimation results for Equations 1 to 4 for the death cases per million population at the 30th day labelled as Equations 1 C, 2 C, 3 C, and 4 C, and at the 60th day labelled as 1D, 2D, 3D, and 4D, on the top of Table 2, where C stands for the death cases per million population at the 30th day after the 10th reported case and D stands that at the 60th day after the 10th reported case, and where 1 stands for the baseline model, 2 replaces GDP in the baseline model by log GDP, 3 uses log of total death cases per million population as the dependent

Table 2. Estimation results: Total Death Cases at 30-Day and 60-Day After the First 10th Case (with Robust Standard Errors).

	At 30th Day after the 10th Reported Case				At 60th Day after the 10th Reported Case			
	Equation 1 C	Equation 2 C	Equation 3 C	Equation 4 C	Equation 1D	Equation 2D	Equation 3D	Equation 4D
Personal Freedom	4.37***	4.8***	0.382**	0.42**	20.8***	25.9***	0.553***	0.61***
	(1.65)	(1.66)	(0.164)	(0.169)	(6.57)	(7.79)	(0.154)	(0.153)
PISA Math	0.355*	0.373**	0.0134	0.015	1.29	1.49	−0.00187	0.000664
	(0.180)	(0.178)	(0.019)	(0.019)	(1.11)	(1.09)	(0.017)	(0.0171)
PISA Science	−0.334*	−0.382**	−0.0154	−0.0184	−0.945	−1.49	−0.0015	−0.00786
	(0.179)	(0.174)	(0.019)	(0.019)	(1.09)	(1.07)	(0.018)	(0.018)
Medical Physician per 1000 people	1.37	1.72	0.313	0.356	8.57	12.2	0.476	0.514
	(2.880)	(3.020)	(0.261)	(0.269)	(14.3)	(14.2)	(0.266)	(0.259)
Hospital Bed per 1000 people	−1.56	−1.53	−0.211**	−0.198**	−9.94*	−9.56*	−0.148	−0.142
	(1.050)	(1.030)	(0.091)	(0.094)	(5.59)	(5.58)	(0.099)	(0.104)
GDP	−0.513		−0.255***		−1.21		−0.00487	
	(0.389)		(0.036)		(2.69)		(0.035)	
Past SARS MERS per million pop.	−0.126	−0.115	−0.0114***	−0.00983**	−0.68*	−0.583	−0.0141***	−0.0132***
	(0.061)	(0.061)	(0.004)	(0.004)	(0.369)	(0.354)	(0.004)	(0.004)
Urbanization Rate	0.177	0.149	−0.0131	−0.0054	1.03	0.606	−0.00326	−0.00682
	(0.194)	(0.217)	(0.015)	(0.016)	(1.19)	(1.21)	(0.016)	(0.016)
Log GDP		0.946		−0.292**		16.6**		0.175*
		(1.790)		(0.138)		(7.57)		(0.102)
Constant	−40.5*	−28.1	0.434	−0.538	−314**	−149	−0.468	1.24
	(22.300)	(26.300)	(2.090)	(2.010)	(130.)	(120.)	(1.97)	(2.01)
Observations	80	80	74	74	80	80	79	79

p*<0.1, p**<0.05, p***<0.01, standard errors in parentheses.

variable, and finally, 4 uses both log GDP and log of total death cases per million population.

The results from Equations 1 C, 2 C, 3 C, and 4 C show that countries with more personal freedom tend to have more coronavirus deaths. Holding everything else constant, a one unit increase in the personal freedom index is associated with an increase of 4.37 death cases per million population in Equation 1 C, 4.8 cases in Equation 2 C, 38.2% in Equation 3 C, and 42% in Equation 4 C. Holding everything else constant, a one point increase in the PISA mathematics (PISA science) score is associated with an increase of 0.355 (a decrease of 0.334) death cases per million population in Equation 1 C and an increase of 0.373 (a decrease of 0.382) cases in Equation 2 C. As for the number of hospital beds per 1000 population, holding everything else constant, a one unit increase in the number of hospital beds per 1000 population is associated with a decrease of 21.1% of death cases per million population in Equation 3 C and it is a decrease of 19.8% in Equation 4 C. In Equation 3 C, a one trillion dollar increase in GDP is associated with a decrease of 25.5% of death cases per million population. In Equation 4 C, a one percent increase in GDP is associated with a decrease of 0.292% COVID-19 death cases per million population. In Equation 3 C, a one unit increase in the number of past SARS and MERS cases per million population is associated with a decrease of 1.14% of COVID-19 death cases per million population, and in Equation 4 C, the decrease is 0.983%. Overall, the results are consistent with what we found in Table 1.

Table 2 also presents the corresponding estimation results for the death cases per million population at 60th day after the 10th reported case, which are labelled as Equations 1D, 2D, 3D, and 4D in Table 2. Compared with the results for death cases per million population for the 30th day (i.e. Equations 1 C through 4 C), Equations 1D through 4D show that personal freedom, number of hospital beds per capita, log of GDP, and past SARS/MERS cases per million population continue to influence the death cases at the 60th day, indicating the robustness of the socioeconomic factors in its effect on death cases. Holding everything else constant, a one unit increase in the personal freedom index is associated with an increase of 20.8 death cases per million population in Equation 1D, of 25.9 cases in Equation 2D, increase of 55.3% in Equation 3D, and of 61% in Equation 4D. In Equation 1D, a one unit increase in the number of hospital beds per 1000 population is associated with a decrease of 9.94 COVID-19 death cases per million population. In Equation 2D, this decrease is 9.56 cases. A one percent increase in GDP is associated with an increase of 0.166 death cases per million population in Equation 2D. In Equation 4D, a one percent increase in GDP is associated with an increase of 0.175% of death cases per million population. A one unit increase in the number of past SARS and MERS cases per million population is associated with a decrease of 0.68 COVID-19 death cases per million population in Equation 1D. In Equation 3D, this decrease is 1.41%. In Equation 4D, this decrease is 1.32%.

6. Endogeneity assessment

We now use the Two Stage Least Squares (2SLS) estimation method to re-estimate our regression models, that is, from Equations 1A up to 4D. In this round of estimation, the personal freedom index is treated as an endogenous variable and GDP per capita is used as an instrumental variable. In our 2SLS estimations, both the Durbin χ^2 and Wu-Hausman F tests for endogeneity on the independent variable personal freedom index show large tests' statistics and small associated probability values in Table 3, indicating that the null hypothesis that personal freedom is an exogenous variable must be rejected. The 2SLS estimation results as well as the results for the endogeneity tests are summarized in Tables 3 and 4 for the number of infection cases per million population and for the number of death cases per million population as the dependent variable, respectively. The personal freedom index not only has a positive-estimated coefficient, but also is significant both statistically and numerically in all 8 columns/models from Equations 1A to 4B in Table 3.

Holding everything else constant, a one unit increase in the personal freedom index is associated with a large increase of 1855 infection cases per million population at the 30th day in Equation 1A, 1858 cases in Equation 2A, 226% in Equation 3A, and 221% in Equation 4A. Holding everything else constant, a one unit increase in the personal freedom index is associated with a large increase of 3383 infection cases per million population at the 60th day in Equation 1B, 3360 cases in Equation 2B, 203% in Equation 3B, and 194% in Equation 4B. These results are at least 10 times and 5 times as large as those without the IV estimation in the linear and log linear models in Section 5, respectively. Our understanding of the dramatic increase in the size of the personal freedom coefficients is due to the significance of GDP per capita in accounting for the impact of other unobserved factors on the spread and death of coronavirus. Holding

Table 3. IV regression results of total infection cases at 30-Day and 60-Day after the first 10th case: two-stage least squares with GDP per capita instrument.

	At 30th Day after the 10th Reported Case				At 60th Day after the 10th Reported Case			
	Equation 1A	Equation 2A	Equation 3A	Equation 4A	Equation 1B	Equation 2B	Equation 3B	Equation 4B
Personal Freedom	1855**	1858**	2.26**	2.21*	3383**	3360**	2.03*	1.94*
	(864)	(866)	(1.14)	(1.14)	(1648.)	(1623.)	(1.08)	(1.08)
PISA Science	−30.9	−32.3	−0.0462*	−0.0448	−48.5	−55.8	−0.0377	−0.0452*
	(20.6)	(21.4)	(0.0271)	(0.028)	(39.2)	(40.)	(0.0258)	(0.0265)
Observations	80	80	80	80	80	80	80	80
Pass Endog. Test	Yes	Yes	Yes	Yes	Yes	Yes	Yes	Yes
Durbin (Score)	27.828	29.7749	5.78924	5.9718	29.331	28.0357	8.93782	6.20469
Chi Sq. (1)	(p = 0.000)	(p = 0.000)	(p = 0.016)	(p = 0.015)	(p = 0.000)	(p = 0.000)	(p = 0.003)	(p = 0.013)
Wu-Hausman F(1,60)	37.3372	41.498	5.46075	5.64685	40.5211	37.7664	8.80423	5.88558
	(p = 0.000)	(p = 0.000)	(p = 0.022)	(p = 0.020)	(p = 0.000)	(p = 0.000)	(p = 0.004)	(p = 0.018)
F-Stat. Instruments First Stage	4.25592	4.33478	4.25592	4.33478	4.25592	4.3348	4.25592	4.33478
	(p = 0.043)	(p = 0.041)	(p = 0.043)	(p = 0.041)	(p = 0.043)	(p = 0.041)	(p = 0.043)	(p = 0.041)

p<0.1, *p*<0.05, *p*<0.01, standard errors in parentheses. All other control variables are included in the regression as before but not reporting the rest of the explanatory variables, which are all statistically insignificant, in this table.

Table 4. IV Regression Results of Total Death Cases at 30-Day and 60-Day After the First 10th Case: Two-Stage Least Squares with GDP Per Capita Instrument.

	At 30th Day after the 10th Reported Case				At 60th Day after the 10th Reported Case			
	Equation 1 C	Equation 2 C	Equation 3 C	Equation 4 C	Equation 1D	Equation 2D	Equation 3D	Equation 4D
Personal Freedom	26.4*	26.1*	1.95	1.93	58.5	55.6	2.0*	1.98**
	(14.3000)	(14.0000)	(1.3200)	(1.3600)	(52.9)	(50.6)	(1.04)	(1.01)
PISA Science	−0.54	−0.62*	−0.0294	−0.0332	−1.3	−1.82	−0.0243	−0.0315
	(0.3400)	(0.3450)	(0.0270)	(0.0279)	(1.26)	(1.25)	(0.0282)	(0.0282)
Observations	80	80	74	74	80	80	79	79
Pass Endog. Test	Yes	Yes	No	No	No	No	Yes	Yes
Durbin (Score)	5.32563	4.94407	2.90159	2.295	0.605349	0.395441	3.75877	3.75877
Chi Sq. (1)	(p = 0.021)	(p = 0.026)	(p = 0.089)	(p = 0.130)	(p = 0.437)	(p = 0.530)	(p = 0.053)	(p = 0.053)
Wu-Hausman F(1,60)	4.99226	4.61103	2.6119	2.04839	0.533719	0.34773	3.44698	3.44698
	(p = 0.029)	(p = 0.035)	(p = 0.111)	(p = 0.157)	(p = 0.468)	(p = 0.557)	(p = 0.068)	(p = 0.068)
F-Stat. Instruments First Stage	4.25592	4.33478	2.60809	2.53964	4.25592	4.33478	4.01747	4.01747
	(p = 0.043)	(p = 0.041)	(p = 0.111)	(p = 0.116)	(p = 0.043)	(p = 0.041)	(p = 0.049)	(p = 0.049)

p<0.1, *p***<0.05, *p****<0.01, standard errors in parentheses. All other control variables are included in the regression as before but not reporting the rest of the explanatory variables, which are all statistically insignificant, in this table.

everything else constant, a one-point increase in the PISA science score is associated with a decrease of 4.62% of infection cases per million population at the 30th day in Equation 3A. A one-point increase in the PISA science score is associated with a decrease of 4.52% of infection cases per million population at the 60th day in Equation 4B.

Similarly, after the 2SLS regression of the number of death cases per million population on the explanatory variables, both the Durbin χ^2 and Wu-Hausman F tests for endogeneity are performed on the suspected endogenous variable personal freedom. Table 4 presents the main regression and test results where the first four columns are for the death cases at the 30th day after the 10th reported death and the next four columns are for the death cases at the 60th day after the 10th reported death case. Like when we report Table 3, we suppressed to report the results for other explanatory variables in Table 4 because they are all statistically and individually insignificant. The null hypothesis that personal freedom is an exogenous variable is rejected only in columns 1, 2, 3, 7, and 8, that is, Equations 1 C, 2 C, 3 C, 3D and 4D. The personal freedom index, which is instrumented using GDP per capita, is still positive and statistically significant in Equations 1 C, 2 C, 3D, and 4D. Holding everything else constant, a one unit increase in the personal freedom index is associated with an increase of 26.4 COVID-19 death cases per million population at the 30th day in Equation 1 C. This increase is 26.1 in Equation 2 C. Holding everything else constant, a one unit increase in the personal freedom index is associated with an increase of 200% of COVID-19 death cases per million population at the 60th day in Equation 3D. This increase is 198% in Equation 4D. A one point increase in the PISA science score is associated with a decrease of 0.62 COVID-19 death cases per million population at the 30th day.

7. Discussion

Our results show that the lower the personal freedom, the lower the number of infection and death cases per million population – unlike the findings of Ruger (2005) that political and cultural authoritarianism and a lack of civil liberties, political rights, and freedom of the press have negatively impacted the population's health. We argue that some restrictions of civil liberties are necessary to contain the COVID-19. Our results are consistent with Baccini and Brodeur (2020), Bargain and Aminjonov (2020), Béland, Brodeur, and Wright (2020), Moser and Yared (2020), and Yilmazkuday (2020) which all showed that government responses such as movement restrictions can contain the virus spread and death levels.

With higher PISA scores in mathematics that reflects the mathematical knowledge of young adults in year 2020, they might comprehend their low contraction and mortality rate and would undermine their willingness to adhere to the movement restriction orders, and thus undermine the spread. From their economic perspective, their low opportunity cost from low perceived risk is an incentive for them not forgoing their higher net expected utility from consumption and freedom of movement. Such a way of thought contributes to the spread because the social contact among people would likely be unavoidable.

However, our estimation result reaffirms the importance of science education among the youth to enable them to process and accept the scientific information during an emergency crisis on a contagious disease. With the better education in science among the young adults, they would understand the science behind a contagious disease and be more likely to comply with the movement restriction orders. Given a strong background in science, it may also enable them to effectively filter the sensationalized information in news media. For example, people trust media information from public health officials rather than government politicians because of their belief in scientific experts (Baekkeskov and Rubin 2014) and policymakers should engage scientists and non-scientists alike in making good policy decisions (Rosenberg et al. 2013). This result of the importance of science knowledge is also consistent with the broader literature on the positive relationship between better education and good health (Cutler and Lleras-Muney 2010; Lleras-Muney 2005,; Conti, Heckman, and Urzua 2010).

Our results indicate that aggregate GDP have negative impacts on the number of coronavirus infection cases per million population in the first 30 and 60 days and on the death cases in the first 30 days, which are similar to Gardner et al. (2018) which finds that the higher the GDP the lower the Zika virus transmission and spread; and Teng et al. (2017) which finds that higher GDP can decrease the probability of Zika outbreaks.

For our results on the number of hospital beds per 1000 population, our finding is consistent with Smith and Fraser (2020) which shows the importance of maintaining and expanding our state-of-the-art public health laboratory capacity; continuing building a workforce of trusted, expert public health professionals; sustaining our capacity to rapidly respond to outbreaks at their source.

We capture the degree of severity of the past coronavirus pandemics and we find that it is negatively associated with the infection and mortality, which is similar to the findings in Chen, Frey, and Presidente (2020), Huang et al. (2020), and Schwartz and Yen (2017) that past experience of coronavirus outbreaks has a negative effect on future outbreaks.

For the last independent variable urbanization, our results show that the higher the urbanization rate, the higher the infection cases because the higher the percentage of a country's population lives in densely populated areas the higher the chance to catch the coronavirus. This result reaffirms the findings in Lai et al. (2004) and Neiderud (2015) that the density in population matters especially with containing the contagious diseases.

When we use GDP per capita of each country as the instrumental variable for the endogenous personal freedom variable, the effect of personal freedom variable is greatly magnified by at least ten-fold for infections and five-fold for mortality. This result is similarly consistent with Chodick and Weil (2020) that finds that COVID-19 had a greater toll in more developed nations. We argue that a well-established institution in rich countries supports and provides the laws and environment for its citizens to exercise more personal freedom. We can understand it from the supply side economics of personal freedom. On the one hand, a country can afford such an institution when it is developed and rich enough. On the other hand, the belief of high personal freedom maintained in the rich countries could not be shaken and should not be violated because of the prosperity it brought to be a rich country. Hence, the idea of having high personal freedom has become sacrosanct. So, high personal freedom maintained in the rich countries causes more infections indirectly because of such inviolable idea. This is reflected in some rich countries to be more reluctant to implement movement restriction orders and the people there may also be reluctant to follow an instruction that may seem to be violating their freedom, hence the higher number of cases in those countries. We can also understand from the demand side economics of personal freedom that the countries with more personal freedom, which is usually high in rich countries with more money per capita, need to spend to increase their expected utility. The movement restriction greatly limits the utility of individuals with the ability to spend in rich countries. People in these countries are more likely to defy restriction movement that would otherwise curtail the spread of the coronavirus. Also, business owners want to re-open their businesses sooner given that rich countries would have given them the rights to decide.

8. Policy Recommendations

For personal freedom, on the one hand, we suggest that it is necessary for all governments to restrict certain personal rights and to impose quarantine or isolation to limit freedom of movement as is justified by the scale and severity of the COVID-19 pandemic. On the other hand, governments should pay careful attention to human rights such as non-discrimination and human rights principles such as transparency and respect for human dignity because they can foster an effective response amidst the turmoil and disruption like the COVID-19 pandemic and limit the harms that can come from the imposition of overly broad and restrictive measures.

For PISA science and mathematics, in the long run, all countries must focus on the long-term social factors such as promoting a better education in science (besides for economic growth) to foster better understanding in science. When individuals attain better knowledge in science in high schools, it could lower the cost to process scientific information to understand and be able to follow the advice from the scientific community on the nature of a disease, thus adhere to the recommendations to reduce the spread and mortality. The education in science enables the processing of scientific information about a pandemic to be more effective and would be more positive on their response to the emergency public policy implemented by the government. Knowing that the people would understand the importance and severity of a pandemic scientifically, a government would more likely to implement drastic measures because people would be able to understand that those drastic measures would be the best approaches and the officials may not have to worry about their political cost. People tend more to be compliant to and to adhere to the emergency policy when they have a better scientific background from their education in science to comprehend the scientific evidence presented on the severity of a pandemic, even at the cost of their personal freedom. Countries also need to re-examine the importance of mathematics education that has not the same outcome as education in science.

9. Limitations and Future Research

Our model does not incorporate the effect of the governments' movement restrictions on the control of the spread of COVID-19 directly, a future research can be done to pursue in this direction along with the next wave of the spread to investigate a longer period since the 10th case.

The 80 countries selected for our study is mainly due to the data availability on the countries that have PISA scores. Future research can be done with more countries when data on other countries are available to assess the knowledge on science and mathematics.

For the data on hospital beds and medical physicians, we are limited with the data from the WHO because not all countries report them every year. The best approach for us is to use the most recent data being reported by each country that is published by WHO in 2020. We could not have the data for all countries from a particular year, otherwise there will be a lot of missing data. Further research can be done with more recent data and ideally reported by all countries for the year of 2019.

10. Conclusion

Our study shows how socioeconomic factors have their impacts on the infection and death cases per million population, and the results are accentuated when employing GDP per capita as the instrumental variable. Our key results can be summarized as follows. First, personal freedom has a dominating positive effect on both the number of infection cases and the number of death cases of COVID-19, implying that movement restraint orders are needed to control the spread of the coronavirus. Second, education in science matters in containing the spread of the coronavirus, implying the practical importance of scientific education early on as a cause of lower cases. Third, the countries with larger GDP, countries that have more healthcare facilities, and countries with experience in dealing with past epidemics or pandemics are usually better prepared to control the spread of COVID-19. This should provide an impetus for countries to pursue such preventative and preparation measures more seriously.

This paper highlights the effects of the socioeconomic characteristics in a society on containing the spread of COVID-19. It provides an important recommendation to governments of both large and small countries and for rich and poor countries that personal freedom needs to be curtailed in a timely way in the face of a critical public health crisis like the COVID-19 pandemic. For the long-term, policymakers should invest more in education on science. Understanding the science of a pandemic is important for the people to accept the emergency policies being implemented. Plus, policymakers would be more likely to make drastic measures knowing that the people would understand the importance of those measures scientifically even though these may affect their life and personal freedom.

Notes

1. The number of 80 countries selected was also due to the data on the countries that have PISA scores.
2. We track cases after the reported 10th case, or at least 10 cases being reported.
3. Per million population is the same as per capita multiplied by one million. It assists the interpretation of the coefficient in the results sections.
4. Per 1000 people is the same as per capita multiplied by 1000 people.
5. Per million people is the same as per capita multiplied by one million. It assists the interpretation of the coefficient in the results sections.

Disclosure statement

No potential conflict of interest was reported by the author(s).

References

Amaral, P., L. Resende de Carvalho, T. A. Hernandes Rocha, N. C. da Silva, and J. R. N. Vissoci. 2019. "Geospatial Modeling of Microcephaly and Zika Virus Spread Patterns in Brazil." *PLoS ONE* 14 (9): e0222668. doi:10.1371/journal.pone.0222668.

Baccini, L., and A. Brodeur. 2020. "Explaining Governors' Response to the COVID-19 Pandemic in the United States." IZA DP No. 13137. IZA Institute of Labor Economics. Accessed 22 July 2020. https://www.iza.org/publications/dp/13137/explaining-governors-response-to-the-covid-19-pandemic-in-the-united-states

Baekkeskov, E., and O. Rubin. 2014. "Why Pandemic Response Is Unique: Powerful Experts and Hands-off Political Leaders." *Disaster Prevention and Management* 23 (1): 81–93. doi:10.1108/DPM-05-2012-0060.

Bargain, O., and U. Aminjonov 2020. "Trust and Compliance to Public Health Policies in Times of COVID-19." Accessed 22 July 2020. IZA DP No. 13205. IZA Institute of Labor Economics. https://www.iza.org/publications/dp/13205/trust-and-compliance-to-public-health-policies-in-times-of-covid-19

Barr, M., B. Raphael, M. Taylor, G. Stevens, L. Jorm, M. Giffin, S. Lujic, et al. 2008. "Pandemic Influenza in Australia: Using Telephone Surveys to Measure Perceptions of Threat and Willingness to Comply." *BMC Infectious Diseases* 8: 117. doi:10.1186/1471-2334-8-117.

Bawazir, A., E. Al-Mazroo, H. Jradi, A. Ahmed, and M. Badri. 2018. "MERS-CoV Infection: Mind the Public Knowledge Gap." *Journal of Infection and Public Health* 11: :89–93. doi:10.1016/j.jiph.2017.05.003.

Béland, L.-P., A. Brodeur, and T. Wright 2020. "The Short-Term Economic Consequences of COVID-19: Exposure to Disease, Remote Work and Government Response." IZA DP No. 13159. Accessed 22 July 2020 https://www.iza.org/publications/dp/13159/the-short-term-economic-consequences-of-covid-19-exposure-to-disease-remote-work-and-government-response

Berger, D. W., K. F. Herkenhoff, and S. Mongey 2020. "An SEIR Infectious Disease Model with Testing and Conditional Quarantine." (Staff Report No. 597). Federal Reserve Bank of Minneapolis.Accessed 22 July 2020. https://www.minneapolisfed.org/research/staff-reports/an-seir-infectious-disease-model-with-testing-and-conditional-quarantine

Bish, A., and S. Michie. 2010. "Demographic and Attitudinal Determinants of Protective Behaviours during A Pandemic: A Review." *British Journal of Health Psychology* 15: 797–824. doi:10.1348/135910710X485826.

Briscese, G., N. Lacetera, M. Macis, and M. Tonin 2020. "Compliance with COVID-19 Social-Distancing Measures in Italy: The Role of Expectations and Duration." NBER Working Paper 26916. Accessed 22 July 2020. http://www.nber.org/papers/w26916

Chen, C., C. B. Frey, and G. Presidente 2020. "Democracy, Culture, and Contagion: Political Regimes and Countries Responsiveness to Covid19." Oxford Martin School, University of Oxford. Accessed 24 July 2020 https://www.oxfordmartin.ox.ac.uk/downloads/academic/Democracy-Culture-and-Contagion_May13.pdf

Chodick, G., and C. Weil. 2020. "COVID-19 Death Toll: The Role of the Nation's Economic Development." *medRxiv* 2020 (7): 18.20156778. doi:10.1101/2020.07.18.20156778.

Conti, G., J. Heckman, and S. Urzua. 2010. "The Education-Health Gradient." *American Economic Review: Papers & Proceedings* 100 (2) May: 234–238. doi:10.1257/aer.100.2.234.

Cutler, D. M., and A. Lleras-Muney. 2010. "Understanding Differences in Health Behaviors by Education." *Journal of Health Economics* 29 (1) January: 1–28. doi:10.1016/j.jhealeco.2009.10.003.

De Haan, J., and C. Siermann. 1998. "Further Evidence on the Relationship between Economic Freedom and Economic Growth." *Public Choice* 95 (3/4): 363–380. Accessed August 23 2020. http://www.jstor.org/stable/30025113

Farooq, M., and A. Hafeez 2020. "COVID-ResNet: A Deep Learning Framework for Screening of COVID19 from Radiographs." Unpublished manuscript. https://arxiv.org/ftp/arxiv/papers/2003/2003.14395.pdf

Gardner, L. M., A. Bóta, K. Gangavarapu, M. U. G. Kraemer, and N. D. Grubaugh. 2018. "Inferring the Risk Factors behind the Geographical Spread and Transmission of Zika in the Americas." *PLoS Neglected Tropical Diseases* 12 (1): e0006194. doi:10.1371/journal.pntd.0006194.

Huang, J., J. Y. Teoh, S. H. Wong, and M. C. S. Wong. 2020. "The Potential Impact of Previous Exposure to SARS or MERS on Control of the COVID-19 Pandemic." *European Journal of Epidemiology*. doi:10.1007/s10654-020-00674-9.

Lai, P. C., C. M. Wong, A. J. Hedley, S. V. Lo, P. Y. Leung, J. Kong, and G. M. Leung. 2004. "Understanding the Spatial Clustering of Severe Acute Respiratory Syndrome (SARS) in Hong Kong." *Environmental Health Perspectives*. 112 (15): 1550–1556. doi:10.1289/ehp.7117.

Leung, G. M., T. H. Lam, L. M. Ho, S. Y. Ho, B. H. Chan, I. O. Wong, and A. J. Hedley. 2003. "The Impact of Community Psychological Responses on Outbreak Control for Severe Acute Respiratory Syndrome in Hong Kong." *Journal of Epidemiology and Community Health* 57 (11): 857–863. doi:10.1136/jech.57.11.857.

Litan, R. E., and M. Lowy 2020. "Freedom and Privacy in the Time of Coronavirus." Brookings. Accessed July 22 2020. https://www.brookings.edu/research/freedom-and-privacy-in-the-time-of-coronavirus/

Lleras-Muney, A. 2005. "The Relationship between Education and Adult Mortality in the United States." *The Review of Economic Studies* 72 (1) January: 189–221. doi:10.1111/0034-6527.00329.

Lorgelly, P. K., and A. Adler. 2020. "Impact of a Global Pandemic on Health Technology Assessment." *Applied Health Economics and Health Policy* 18: 339–343. doi:10.1007/s40258-020-00590-9.

Merrefield, C. 2020. "Siphoning Civil Liberties in the Name of COVID-19: A Research Roundup." Journalist's Resource.Accessed 22 July 2020. https://journalistsresource.org/studies/government/civil-liberties-lockdown-covid-19-research/

Moser, C. A., and P. Yared 2020. "Pandemic Lockdown: The Role of Government Commitment." Social Science Research Network (SSRN) database. Accessed 22 July 2020. http://dx.doi.org/10.2139/ssrn.3581412

Nay, O. 2020. "Can a Virus Undermine Human Rights?" *Lancet Public Health* 5 (5): e238–e239. Accessed 22 July 2020. https://pubmed.ncbi.nlm.nih.gov/32325013/

Neiderud, C. J. 2015. "How Urbanization Affects the Epidemiology of Emerging Infectious Diseases." *Infection Ecology & Epidemiology* 5: 27060. doi:10.3402/iee.v5.27060.

Nikolaev, B., C. Boudreaux, and R. Salahodjaev. 2017. "Are Individualistic Societies Less Equal? Evidence from the Parasite Stress Theory of Values." *Journal of Economic Behavior & Organization* 138: 30–49. doi:10.1016/j.jebo.2017.04.001.

Qin, L., H. Jeng, Y. Rakue, and T. Mizota. 2005. "A Deficient Public Health System as A Contributing Cause of Severe Acute Respiratory Syndrome (SARS) Epidemic in Mainland China." *The Southeast Asian Journal of Tropical Medicine and Public Health* 36 (1): 213–216.

Rosenberg, A. A., M. Halpern, S. Shulman, C. Wexler, and P. Phartiyal. 2013. "Reinvigorating the Role of Science in Democracy."." *PLoS Biology* 11 (5): e1001553. doi:10.1371/journal.pbio.1001553.

Ruger, J. P. 2005. "Democracy and Health." *QJM: An International Journal of Medicine* 98 (4): 299–304. doi:10.1093/qjmed/hci042.

Schwartz, J. 2012. "Compensating for the 'Authoritarian Advantage' in Crisis Response: A Comparative Case Study of SARS Pandemic Responses in China and Taiwan." *Journal of Chinese Political Science* 17 (3): 313–331. doi:10.1007/s11366-012-9204-4.

Schwartz, J., and M. Y. Yen. 2017. "Toward a Collaborative Model of Pandemic Preparedness and Response: Taiwan's Changing Approach to Pandemics." *Journal of Microbiology, Immunology, and Infection* 50 (2): 125–132. doi:10.1016/j.jmii.2016.08.010.

Smith, N., and M. Fraser. 2020. "Straining the System: Novel Coronavirus (COVID-19) and Preparedness for Concomitant Disasters." *American Journal of Public Health* 110 (5): 648–649. doi:10.2105/AJPH.2020.305618. May 1.

Su, S., G. Wong, W. Shi, J. Liu, A. Lai, J. Zhou, W. Liu, Y. Bi, and G. F. Gao. 2016. "Epidemiology, Genetic Recombination, and Pathogenesis of Coronaviruses." *Trends in Microbiology* 24 (6): 490–502. doi:10.1016/j.tim.2016.03.003.

Tang, C. S., and C. Y. Wong. 2004. "Factors Influencing the Wearing of Facemasks to Prevent the Severe Acute Respiratory Syndrome among Adult Chinese in Hong Kong." *Preventive Medicine* 39 (6): 1187–1193. doi:10.1016/j.ypmed.2004.04.032.

Teng, Y., D. Bi, G. Xie, Y. Jin, Y. Huang, B. Lin, X. An, Y. Tong, and D. Feng. 2017. "Model-informed Risk Assessment for Zika Virus Outbreaks in the Asia-Pacific Regions." *The Journal of Infection* 74 (5): 484–491. doi:10.1016/j.jinf.2017.01.015.

The Hill. 2020. https://thehill.com/. March 18, 2020. The Washington Post. https://www.washingtonpost.com/ April 4, 2020.

Yi, Y., P. N. P. Lagniton, S. Ye, E. Li, and R. H. Xu. 2020. "COVID-19: What Has Been Learned and to Be Learned about the Novel Coronavirus Disease." *International Journal of Biological Sciences* 16 (10): 1753–1766. doi:10.7150/ijbs.45134.

Yilmazkuday, H. 2020. "Stay-at-Home Works to Fight against COVID-19: International Evidence from Google Mobility Data." SSRN Working Paper No. 3571708. doi:10.2139/ssrn.3571708.

Appendix A

Table AI. Variable definitions and summary statistics (observations = 80).

Variable	Definition	Mean	Std. Dev.
Dependent variables			
Infection at 30th day	Infection Cases Per Million Population at 30th day after the reported 10th cases	421.66	770.51
Death at 30th day	Death Cases Per Million Population at 30th day after the reported 10th cases	11.01	22.11
Infection at 60th day	Infection Cases Per Million Population at 60th day after the reported 10th cases	1124.24	1417.64
Death at 60th day	Death Cases Per Million Population at 60th day after the reported 10th cases	56.96	114.17
Explanatory variables			
Personal Freedom	Index: Most Free = 10 to Least Free = 0	7.75	1.33
PISA Science	Average PISA Science Score from 2006 to 2018	458.67	53.77
PISA Math	Average PISA Mathematics Score from 2006 to 2018	454.86	56.60
Medical physician	Number of medical physicians per 1000 population	2.76	1.12
Hospital bed	Number of hospital beds per 1000 population	4.20	2.48
GDP	Nominal GDP in 2019 (in trillions)	0.97	2.78
Urban Population	Percentage of people living in urban areas	74.14	14.82
Past SARS MERS	Sum of Past SARS and MERS pandemic cases per million population	5.10	27.43
Log GDP	Log of Nominal GDP in 2019	11.33	0.74
Instrument			
GDP per capita	The nominal GDP per capita in 2019	26,875.43	23,914.47

Table AII. Sample descriptions (observations = 80).

Variable	Data Compilation Method	Source	Year
Dependent variables			
Infection at 30th day	30th day after the reported 10th cases in 2020	ECDC	2020
Death at 30th day	30th day after the reported 10th cases in 2020	ECDC	2020
Infection at 60th day	60th day after the reported 10th cases in 2020	ECDC	2020
Death at 60th day	60th day after the reported 10th cases in 2020	ECDC	2020
Explanatory variables			
Personal Freedom	Latest reported in 2017 for all 80 countries	Cato Institute	2017
PISA Science	Simple Average PISA Science Score over the period 2006 to 2018 that were reported in a frequency of three years	OECD	2006, 2009, 2012, 2015, 2018
PISA Math	Simple Average PISA Science Score over the period 2006 to 2018 that were reported in a frequency of three years	OECD	2006, 2009, 2012, 2015, 2018
Medical physician	Use the value of the most recent year reported by the country	WHO†	2014–2018
Hospital bed	Use the value of the most recent year reported by the country	WHO†	2009–2015
GDP	Latest reported in 2019 for all 80 countries	WB, OECD	2019
Urban Population	Latest reported in 2018 for all 80 countries	UN†	2018
Past SARS MERS	Sum of all cases for past coronavirus for the whole period of data collected in 2002–2020	WHO, FAO	2002–2003* 2012–2020**
Log GDP	Latest reported in 2019 for all 80 countries	WB, OECD	2019
Instrument			
GDP per capita	Latest reported in 2019 for all 80 countries	WB, OECD	2019

*Time period for SARS-COV; **Time period for MERS-COV. †With exception to Taiwan (Republic of China) and Hong Kong (SAR of China), we supplemented the data on medical physician, hospital bed, and urbanization rate from their government websites and reports from PriceWaterhouseCoopers. ECDC stands for European Center for Disease Control, OECD for the Organization for Economic Co-operation and Development, WHO for the World Health Organization, WB for the World Bank, UN for the United Nations, and FAO for the Food and Agricultural Organization of UN.

Table AIII. List of the 80 countries used in this study.

Country Name	Country Name	Country Name	Country Name
Albania	Dominican Republic	Malaysia	Singapore
Algeria	Estonia	Malta	Slovakia
Argentina	Finland	Mexico	Slovenia
Australia	France	Moldova	Spain
Austria	Georgia	Montenegro	Sweden
Azerbaijan	Germany	Morocco	Switzerland
Belarus	Greece	Netherlands	Taiwan
Belgium	Hong Kong	New Zealand	Thailand
Bosnia and Herzegovina	Hungary	North Macedonia	Trinidad and Tobago
Brazil	Iceland	Norway	Tunisia
Brunei	Indonesia	Panama	Turkey
Bulgaria	Ireland	Peru	UAE
Canada	Israel	Philippines	UK
Chile	Italy	Poland	Ukraine
China	Japan	Portugal	Uruguay
Colombia	Jordan	Qatar	USA
Costa Rica	Kazakhstan	Romania	Vietnam
Croatia	Latvia	Russia	
Cyprus	Lebanon	S. Korea	
Czechia	Lithuania	Saudi Arabia	
Denmark	Luxembourg	Serbia	

Is there a shift contagion among stock markets during the COVID-19 crisis? Further insights from TYDL causality test

Amine Ben Amar, Néjib Hachicha and Nihel Halouani

ABSTRACT

Using the Toda-Yamamoto-Dolado-Lütkepohl measure of causality, namely the TYDL procedure, which is reliable whatever the variables' integration order, this study attempts to investigate the existence of *shift contagion* effect between a set of global, regional, country and US sectoral indices during the COVID-19 crisis. The empirical findings not only reveal that the Chinese stock index has no influence on the rest of the studied stock market indices during the COVID-19 crisis, but also that the European stock index seems to become the major node influencing the market sentiment and, therefore, the other indices during the crisis.

1. Introduction

Amongst the ten most likely risks cited by the World Economic Forum's *Global Risks Report 2020*, published on 15 January 2020, the risk of 'infectious diseases' was ranked tenth and considered quite unlikely. Two months after the publication of this report, the COVID-19 — a new strain of coronavirus from the SARS species — pandemic was present in most countries, changing the outlook unexpectedly and suggesting heavy human, economic and financial consequences (Elliot 2020). For example, in one week only, from 24th to 28th of February, global stock markets lost about US$6 trillion in terms of capitalization (Ozili and Arun 2020).

The COVID-19 outbreak effects on economic growth and financial markets are currently receiving increasing attention of economists and politicians. Some economists attempt to estimate the potential economic cost of this medical shock by comparing it to previous similar ones. According to Barro, Ursua, and Weng (2020), the so-called Spanish Flu pandemic, which travelled around the world in three waves (from 1918 to 1920), killed about 39 million people, representing 2% of the world's population, and reduced real per capita GDP by 6% on average in the 43 countries for which detailed data are available. A century after the Spanish flu, a new highly infectious—but not particularly deadly—disease, COVID-19, hit almost all the world's countries at the same time. According to available information, it started in China in December 2020. By mid-august, it had reached 188 countries and territories, with about twenty million people infected worldwide, 99% of them outside China[1]. Li et al. (2020) simulated the number of confirmed infections, deaths and cured persons for China, Italy, South Korea and Iran, with their simulations matching the observed data very well. At the same time, they realize forward-looking prediction of the evolution of the epidemic situation and, based on the main factors affecting the spread of the virus, they strongly recommend the implementation of social distancing policies in order to contain the epidemic. Current containment measures, aiming at flattening the epidemiological curve, are necessary from a public health point of view, but are likely to deepen the economic recession. In other words, even if the COVID-19 medical shock is transitory, the resulting economic damage could be persistent: '*the recession is a necessary public health measure*' (Baldwin and Weber Di Mauro 2020). By assuming that, relative to a baseline, containment measures reduce economic activity by 50% for one month and 25% for another month, after which the economy returns to the baseline, Gourinchas (2020) estimates that the decline in the annual US output growth could range between 6.5% and 10% in 2020 relative to 2019.[2] In the same vein, in March, the IMF announced that it expected for 2020 a global recession at least as severe as the financial crisis of 2007–08, followed by a recovery in 2021.

Ramelli and Wagner (2020a, 2020b) examine how stock prices reacted to the outbreak of COVID-19. Using the CAPM-adjusted returns (*i.e.* returns adjusted for a firm's exposure to the overall market) between January and early March 2020 for a selected subset of industries, the authors confirm that the sectors that are less impacted by the crisis are utilities, telecommunication services, healthcare, and to a lesser extent real estate and consumer goods. They find that, from 2 January to 6 March, US firms whose activity is exposed to China experienced 7.1% lower performance than comparable firms. The authors' results show that, from 23 February, the moment the epidemic exploded in Italy, investors' concerns have shifted to the financial characteristics of companies, *i.e.* corporate debt (leverage) and corporate liquidity (cash holding). Thus, the most liquid companies outperformed the most indebted companies.[3] These results suggest that investors are increasingly concerned about the possible financial constraints that companies will face if the COVID-19 crisis turns into a broader financial crisis. Based on logistic models of infectious disease, Alfaro et al. (2020) show that as the trajectory of COVID-19 infections become less uncertain, stock market volatility decreases, and vice versa. Gerding, Martin, and Nagler (2020) find that stock price reactions were more pronounced in countries having higher debt/GDP ratios. Using daily data on the 1579 stocks of both Hang Seng Index and Shanghai Stock Exchange Composite Index over the COVID-19 outbreak period (from January 10 to 16 March 2020), Al-Awadhi et al. (2020) highlight a negative and statistically significant relationship between stock returns and both the daily change in total confirmed cases and the daily change in total cases of death. This finding is consistent with earlier works that have examined how financial markets responded to previous epidemic diseases as the Severe Acute Respiratory Syndrome (SARS) outbreak (Chen, Jang, and Kim 2007; Chen et al. 2009) and the Ebola Virus Disease (EVD) outbreak (Ichev and Marinč 2018).

Even though a strand of the literature has recently examined the impact of the COVID-19 medical shock on financial markets, the way causal links among stock markets shifted from the pre-COVID-19 tranquil period to the COVID-19 crisis one remains unexplored. The goal of this paper is two-fold. First, using a Granger causality test procedure, it investigates the structure of causal links between a set of stock market indices before and during the COVID-19 crisis. Second, it uses a measure of causal intensity to highlight *shift contagion*,[4] *i.e.* differences in links between the considered stock market indices before and during the COVID-19 crisis (*cf.* Marais and Bates 2006).

The remainder of this paper is as follows: Section 2 presents the empirical strategy and the data. Section 3 reports our results. Section 4 concludes.

2. Methodology

2.1. Empirical strategy

This study uses the TYDL test, based on the works of Toda and Yamamoto (1995) and Dolado and Lütkepohl (1996), to examine the possible *shift contagion, i.e.* significant changes in causal links between a set of stock market indices before and during the COVID-19 crisis (*cf.* Marais and Bates 2006). This approach has no restrictions on the integration order of the variables, *i.e.* that variables can be integrated of order 0, 1 or 2, which is consistent with financial and economic data whose maximal integration order of financial and economic data is usually 1 or 2.

The TYDL procedure consists of two main steps. The first one identifies the order (p) of the VAR on which the causal analysis will be performed. This autoregression order (p) is the sum of the AR optimal order (k) of the VAR and the maximum order of integration (I_{max}) of the endogenous variables in the VAR model,[5] *i.e.* $p = k + I_{max}$. The Bayesian Information Criterion (BIC) is used to determine k (Schwarz 1978),[6] and, as in Marais and Bates (2006), the Phillips and Perron (1988) and the KPSS (Kwiatkowski et al. 1992) are employed to identify I_{max}. Consequently, the VAR(p), estimated in level by ordinary least squares,[7] depicts well the joined dynamics of both endogenous variable, regardless of their order of integration. The second step consists in testing the null hypothesis (H0) of Granger non-causality against the alternative hypothesis (H1) of Granger causality from standard Wald statistics (WS)[8] that only consider the first k matrices of coefficients.[9] The null hypothesis (H0) of non-causality is accepted (*i.e.* H1 is rejected) when the *p*-value of the WS is higher than the significance level α. However, the alternative hypothesis (H1) of causality is accepted when the *p*-value is lower than α.

Once H1 accepted, and as the data are in logarithm, Marais and Bates (2006) propose to extract the elasticity (e_{ZX}) of the caused variable (Z) related to the causal one (X) from the estimated parameters of the VAR(p) and use it as an indicator of the causal relation intensity.

For instance, lets $Z_t = (Z_t, X_t)'$ the vector of endogenous variables of dimension 2×1. The VAR(p) model can be written with the logarithmic transformation of X and Z as:

$$\begin{cases} Z_t = \sum_{i=1}^{k} \gamma_{1i} Z_{t-i} + \sum_{j=k+1}^{p} \gamma_{1j} Z_{t-j} + \sum_{i=1}^{k} \beta_{1i} X_{t-i} + \sum_{j=k+1}^{p} \beta_{1j} X_{t-j} + \varepsilon_{Zt} \\ X_t = \sum_{i=1}^{k} \gamma_{2i} Z_{t-i} + \sum_{j=k+1}^{p} \gamma_{2j} Z_{t-j} + \sum_{i=1}^{k} \beta_{2i} X_{t-i} + \sum_{j=k+1}^{p} \beta_{2j} X_{t-j} + \varepsilon_{Xt} \end{cases}$$

Upon the acceptance of causality from X to Z is identified from the TYDL, e_{ZX} is calculated from the first equation in the system as:

$$e_{ZX} = \frac{\sum_{i=1}^{k} \beta_{1i} + \sum_{j=k+1}^{p} \beta_{1j}}{1 - \sum_{i=1}^{k} \gamma_{1i} - \sum_{j=k+1}^{p} \gamma_{1j}}$$

This elasticity is a proxy of the causal relation magnitude between the two variables under study: the higher the level of the elasticity is, the more intense the causal relationship between both variables will be.

2.2. Data

Our data, collected from *https://us.spindices.com*, are daily observations of several global, regional, country and eleven US sectoral stock indices (*cf.* Table 1). To investigate the existence of *shift contagion* during the COVID-19 crisis, the causality is tested distinguishing a tranquil pre-crisis period (from 2 January 2019 to 30 December 2019) and a COVID-19 crisis period (from 31 December 2019 to 30 June 2020). This separation can be justified by the beginning of availability of data on COVID-19 by the European Center for Disease Prevention and Control (ECDC).[10] In addition, to assess the initial impact of the COVID-19 medical shock on financial markets, the COVID-19 crisis period is divided into two sub-periods: a first sub-period characterized by the collapse of the financial markets (Q1 2020), and a second sub-period characterized by the rebound in stock market values (Q2 2020). While events of the first COVID-19 crisis sub-period provide a snapshot of how market participants process information as disaster strikes, events of the second sub-period provide insight into the short-term effects on financial markets of policy interventions.

In order to interpret the relations between variables in terms of elasticity, a log-transformation of the data is chosen.

To visually diagnose the initial impact of the COVID-19 medical shock on financial markets, Figures 1 and 2 plot the relationships between Global total confirmed deaths and stock indices and between Global total confirmed cases and stock indices, respectively, between 31 December 2019 and 31 March 2020.[11] A simple visual inspection reveals that (i) all stock market indices reacted roughly similarly to the COVID-19 medical shock, (ii) the energy sector is the most affected, (iii) the IT sector is the less affected, (iv) the Chinese market is not the most affected by the crisis,[12] (v) market participants only started paying attention to the COVID-19 after 20 January,[13] (vi)

Table 1. List of stock indices.

Level	Indices		Level	Indices	
Global	S&P Global 1200	**SGL**	U.S. Sectoral	S&P 500 Utilities	**S5UTIL**
Regional	S&P Asia 50	**SPA50**		S&P 500 Energy	**SPN**
				S&P 500 Consumer Staples	**S5CONS**
	S&P Europe 350	**SPEURO**		S&P 500 Industrials	**S5INDU**
				S&P 500 Communication Services	**S5TELS**
Country	S&P 500	**SPX**		S&P 500 Consumer Discretionary	**S5COND**
				S&P 500 Financials	**SPF**
	S&P China 500	**SPC500**		S&P 500 Health Care	**S5HLTH**
				S&P 500 Information Technology	**S5INFT**
	S&P Japan 500	**SPJ500**		S&P Pharmaceuticals	**SPSIPH**
				S&P 500 Real Estate	**S5RE**

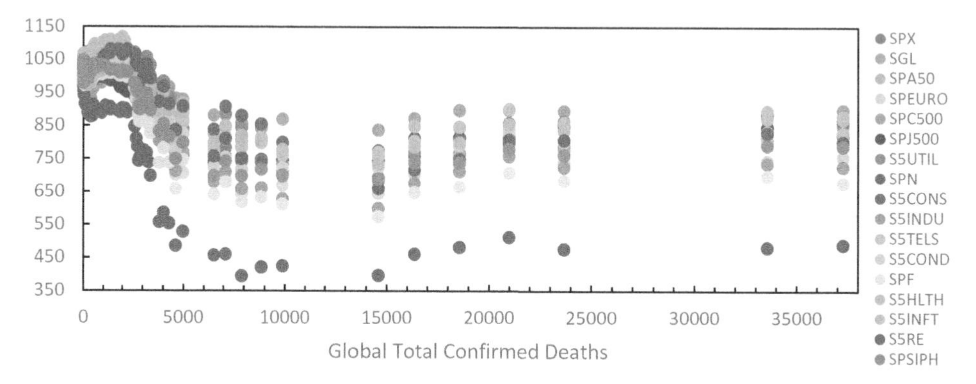

Figure 1. Total confirmed deaths vs stock indices. Source: Authors' elaboration based on ECDC and *https://us.spindices.com* online data (download 1 July 2020)

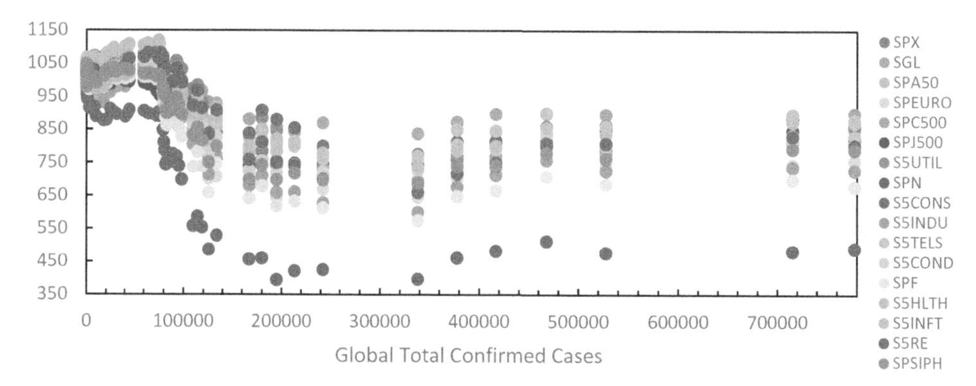

Figure 2. Total confirmed cases vs stock indices. Source: Authors' elaboration based on ECDC and *https://us.spindices.com* online data (download 1 July 2020)

market participants are more sensitive to information on the number of deaths than to information on the number of confirmed cases.

3. Results

Selected descriptive statistics of the log daily data are summarized in Table A1 (*cf.* the appendices). The integration order of series is almost equal to one and at most equal to two (*cf.* Table A1 in the appendices).[14] The results of the TYDL causality test and the measure of causal intensities are detailed in Tables B1–B3 in the appendices and summed up by Figures 3–5.[15]

During the tranquil period, SPX seems to have a major influence on the rest of the stock market indices around the world. Indeed, with the dominance of the US stock market, the causal structure during the tranquil period is widely expected.

Before discussing the results obtained for the crisis period, it is useful to examine how the studied indices evolved during this period. Figure 6 plots the evolution of the studied stock market indices over the crisis period (*i.e.* from 31 December 2019 to 30 June 2020). Interestingly, the most visible effect of the COVID-19 shock on the financial markets was

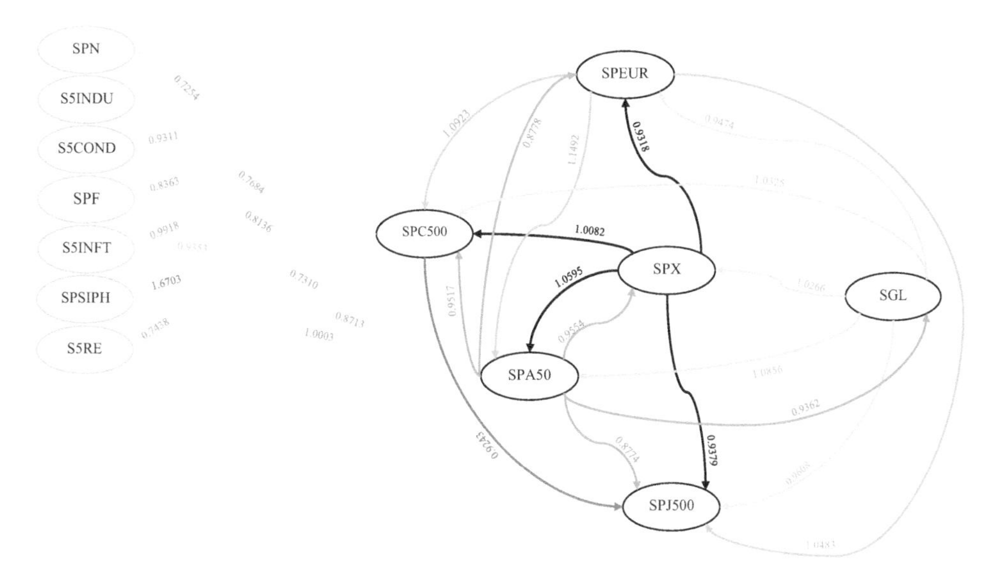

Figure 3. Causal links — tranquil period.

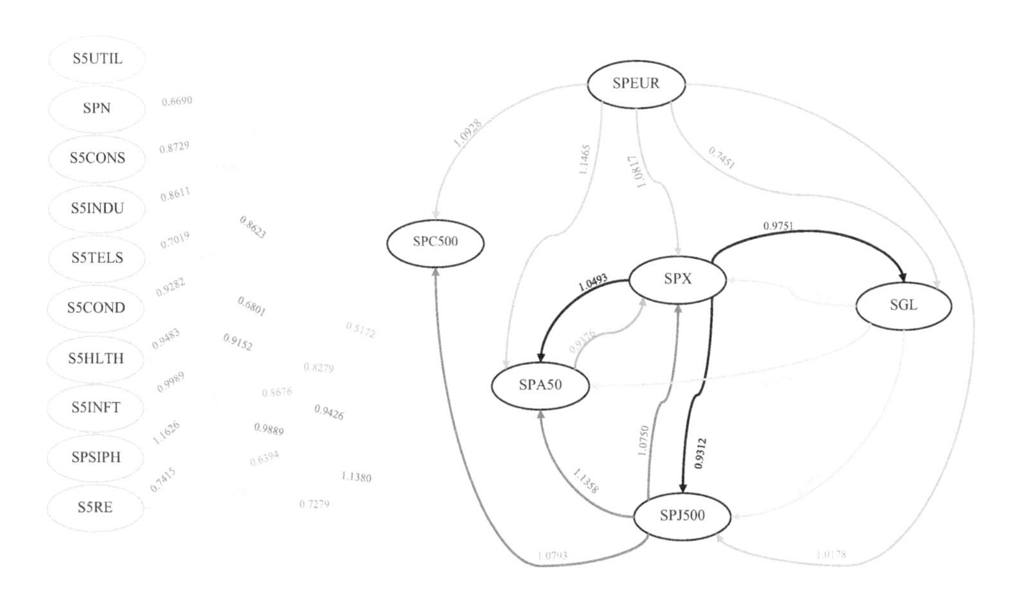

Figure 4. Causal links — COVID-19 crisis period (Quarter 1, 2020).

the effect on the European index (SPEUR), while the least visible outcome of this shock was the effect on the Chinese Index (SPC500). Regarding the US sectoral indices,[16] with a fall of around 60%, the energy sector (SPN) was by far the most affected US sector, followed by the financial (SPF) and industrial (S5INDU) sectors, which fell by 42% and 40% respectively.

The results of the TYDL causality test (*cf.* Tables B1–B3) show that all the elasticities are positive (*i.e.* $e_{ZX} > 0$) and suggest an increase in the number of causal links between the tranquil period and the COVID-19 crisis first sub-period (*i.e.* Q1 2020). Compared to

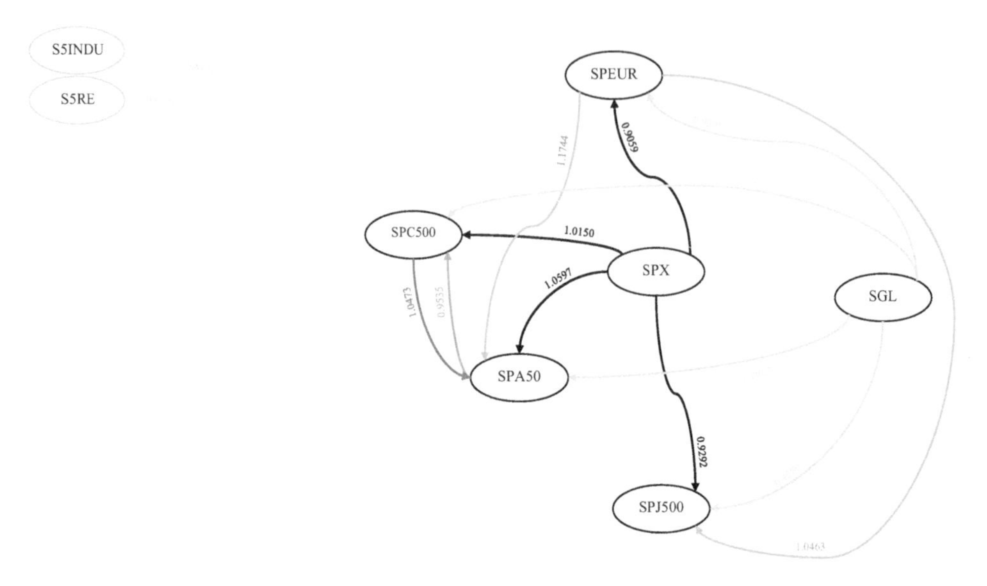

Figure 5. Causal links — COVID-19 crisis period (Quarter 2, 2020).

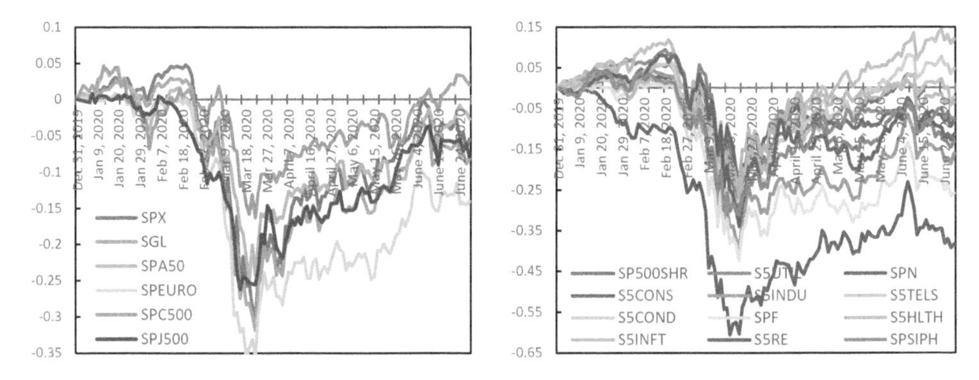

Figure 6. Relative winning and losing for the studied set of stock market indices. Source: Authors' elaboration based on *https://us.spindices.com* online data (download 1 July 2020)

the tranquil period, the crisis period is characterized by the presence of many linkages among stock markets. We count 30 effective causal relations identified by the TYDL test during the tranquil period and 42 during the crisis first sub-period (about 35% of them arise from SPEUR). The results not only reveal the emergence of new causal linkages among stock markets over the crisis first sub-period, but also a change in the causal structure between the two periods, reflecting *shift contagion* during the COVID-19 crisis period—*i.e.* the structure of causal relations during the tranquil period shifts during the COVID-19 crisis period.

This contagion can be summed up by four main points. Yet China is the 'ground-zero country', *i.e.* the origin of the COVID-19 medical shock, no causal relations arising from the Chinese index (SPC500) are identified. Indeed, the fall of the Chinese index (SPC500) during the crisis period has strangely not caused the fall of the other stock indices, regional and US sectoral indices.[17] Furthermore, the direction of the causality between SPEUR and

SPX, SPEUR and SGL, and SPC500 and SPJ500 are reversed. In addition, *shift contagion* has heavily hit most of the US sectoral indices. Moreover, the European stock index (SPEUR) seems to become the node that influences all the other studied indices during the crisis period. It highly causes: (**i**) SPX, which in turns influences SGL, SPJ500 and SPA50; (**ii**) SGL, which in turns influences SPX, SPJ500 and SPA50; (**iii**) SPJ500, which in turns influences SPX, SPA50 and SPC500; (**iv**) SPA50, which in turns influences SPX; (**v**) SPC500; (**vi**) all US sector indices except S5UTIL and SPF. This result suggests that the drop in the European stock market had a major effect on market sentiment.

Goldstein (1998) and Summers (2000) state that a shock in one country can result in a change in investors' perceptions of vulnerabilities and macroeconomic problems in other countries. Thus, how can we explain the fact that the markets have rather reacted to the European market and not to the Chinese market? The answer is given by Ramelli and Wagner (2020b) who examine three periods: 2 January 2020 to 17 January 2020 (incubation period),[18] 20 January 2020 to 21 February 2020 (outbreak period)[19] and 24 February 2020 to 20 March 2020 (Fever period).[20] According to these authors, market participants did not initially, *i.e.* during the incubation period, give too much importance to the COVID-19 medical shock and its potential consequences (Djalante et al. 2020).[21] Initially, the perception was that the COVID-19 outbreak would be contained within China only: the risk of leakage beyond China was not taken seriously enough (Ozili and Arun 2020). However, attention paid to this new disease increased considerably after 20 January, when the Chinese health authorities warned that the virus can be transmitted human-to-human, with each patient infecting two or three others on average. Thus, the virus got out of China and hit the entire planet through people movement and social interactions.[22] It should be noted that even the coronavirus search intensity in Google increased significantly after January 20, it spiked when the Fever period started (*cf.* Figure 7). Indeed, the events initiating the outbreak and fever periods, in particular, the facts that the COVID-19 is highly infectious and several European countries are becoming infected areas, shifted the attention of market participants. By the end of June, COVID-19 has spread throughout Europe, causing more than 2.61 million confirmed cases and 195,535 confirmed deaths. Most European countries imposed several strict containment measures, including lockdowns, restrictions on travel, schools shutting down and the

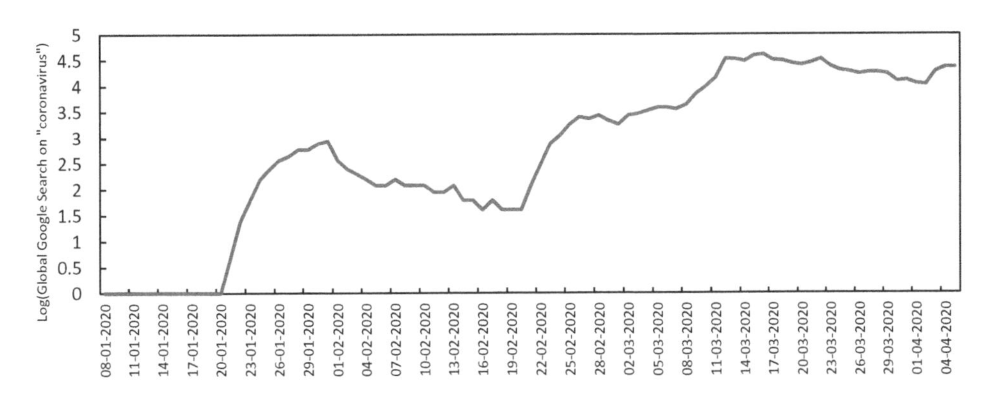

Figure 7. Global Google search on coronavirus. Note: The data are expressed in log.Source: *https://trends.google.com* (download 8 April 2020)

prohibition of large gatherings for an extended period.[23] As a result, the European Union GDP contracted by 2.5% (year-on-year) in the first quarter of 2020.

The speed and extent to which the COVID-19 has spread across Europe seem to have damaged the market sentiment about the resilience of the global economy, triggering the spread of the 'bad news' to all stock markets around the world by a domino effect. This explains why SPEUR and in a lesser extent SPX and SPJ500 were the most affected by the COVID-19 crisis.

Beyond the initial impact of the COVID-19 medical shock on financial markets (*i.e.* during the first quarter of 2020), some policy interventions helped to reassure market participants that the further spread of financial stress would be mitigated, which may explain, at least in part, the rebound in stock market values during the COVID-19 crisis second sub-period (*i.e.* Q2 2020) and the return of the hegemony of the US stock market (*cf.* Figure 5). Indeed, one of the goals of economic measures taken by Governments and Central Banks around the world is to offset the markets' response to the COVID-19 pandemic. Specifically, in the United States by the end of March 2020, the Corona Aid, Relief and Economy Security (CARES) Act, an estimated US$ 2.3 trillion relief bill, became law,[24] and on April 24, the Paycheck Protection Program and Health Care Enhancement Act, a US$ 484 billion bill providing additional funding for hospitals and COVID-19 testing, have been signed into law. Moreover, the Federal Reserve Board lowered the fund rate by 150 bp, reduced the discount window lending cost and announced new facilities aimed primarily at supporting the flow of credit to corporations and facilitating the issuance of commercial paper by corporations and municipal issuers. The easing of the Fed's monetary policy has led to a rapid increase in the monetary base and, consequently, a rise in stock market values (*cf.* Figure 8).[25]

In the European Union, more than 120 state aid measures have been implemented by the European Union to combat the COVID-19 human and economic effects. Key measures decided by the European Commission (EC) contain the pandemic and overcome its effects include: (i) enabling the European Stability Mechanism (ESM) to support health-related expenditure up to EUR 240 billion, (ii) providing guarantees to the European Investment Bank to support the financing of small and medium-sized enterprises and (iii) creating loan-based instrument for temporary Support to mitigate Unemployment Risks in Emergency (SURE). Furthermore, by activating the

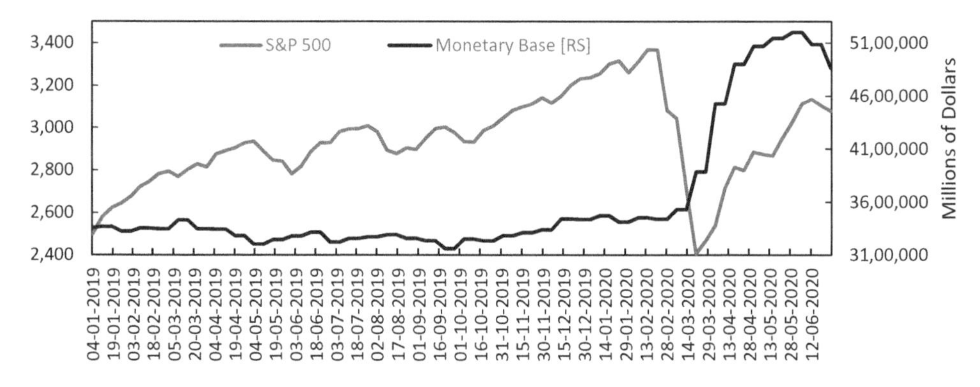

Figure 8. U.S. monetary base vs S&P 500. Source: FRED Economic Data (Download 2 July 2020)

general escape clause in the European Union fiscal rules, the EC has allowed EU member states to run deficits more than 3% of their GDP. Furthermore, 10 measures were authorized based on Article 107(2)(b) TFEU which enable state aid in the form of compensation for '*damage caused by natural disaster of exceptional occurrence*', such as COVID-19 (*cf.* Nicolaides 2020 for further details). At the time of publication of this paper, national liquidity measures amounted around EUR 2.9 trillion.

Regarding the European monetary policy, the ECB (i) decided to purchase additional assets with more favorable terms under the existing APP (Asset Purchase Program) and TLTRO-III (Targeted Longer-Term Refinancing Operation) programs, (ii) relaxed collateral standards for MRO (Main Refinancing Operations), LTRO (Long Term Refinancing Operations) and TLTRO (Targeted Longer-Term Refinancing Operations), (iii) broadened the range of eligible assets under the CSPP (Corporate Sector Purchase Program) and (iv) introduced new liquidity facilities: PELTRO (Pandemic Emergency Longer-Term Refinancing Operations) and PEPP (Pandemic Emergency Purchase Program).

On 18 June 2020, the 'banking package', which provides exceptional legislative amendments to the Capital Requirements Regulation, including more flexibility in the application of the accounting and prudential rules, was adopted by the European Parliament and the European Council to facilitate bank lending and thereby support the economy.

All these fiscal, financial and monetary measures in the United States and Europe have brought back a positive sentiment among market participants, allowing the various stock markets to regain their pre-crisis level and dynamics, and therefore explain the shift in the causal links observed during the second sub-period of the COVID-19 crisis, which seem to be converging towards the pre-crisis pattern.

4. Concluding remarks

It is widely recognized that, in normal times, developments in the US stock market exert a significant influence on most stock markets around the world. However, little attention has been paid to the impact of a global medical shock, such as the COVID-19 crisis, on the causal links among stock markets. Using the TYDL procedure and a measure of causal intensities, this paper fills this gap by providing a quantitative assessment of the existence of a change in the causal links among a set of stock market indices from the tranquil period to the COVID-19 crisis one. The results reveal a structural change in the links which signals the existence of *shift contagion* between the stock markets under consideration during the COVID-19 crisis. The emergence of new causal linkages over the crisis period highlights a shift in the transmission channels of shocks among these markets. Specifically, we find no causal relations from the Chinese index (SPC500) to the set of studied stock market indices during the crisis period. During the same period, the European market (SPEUR) seems to have a major influence on the other markets. The speed and extent to which the COVID-19 spread across European countries, especially Italy and Spain, seem to have damaged the market sentiment about the resilience of the global economy, causing the 'bad news' to spread to stock markets around the world. Beyond this initial impact of the COVID-

19 medical shock on financial markets, the results suggest that, during the second sub-period of the COVID-19 crisis, fiscal and monetary interventions seem to have helped financial markets to regain their pre-crisis pattern.

Although, to the best of our knowledge, ours is the first study that attempts to investigate the *shift contagion* over the COVID-19 crisis, there are, nevertheless, some limitations to the analysis: As only one indicator of contagion (stock markets indices) and a limited set of markets are studied, the causal structure is only partially identified. It would therefore be interesting for future studies to (i) expand this analysis by including more markets and other contagion indicators in order to get a more complete picture of how this crisis spread through stock markets, and (ii) investigate the channels through which key economic responses that Governments and Central Banks took to limit the human and economic damage of the COVID-19 pandemic were transmitted to the financial markets.

Notes

1. According to the regional data on the spread of the COVID-19 reported by the 205th World Health Organization's Situation Report, Americas had the highest number of confirmed cases (10 799 062 cases), followed by Europe (3 641 603 cases), South-East Asia (2 757 822 cases), the Eastern Mediterranean region (1 669 933 cases), Africa (909 547 cases) and the Western Pacific region (383 739 cases) as at 12 August 2020.
2. It should be noted that the U.S. GDP fell by about 4.5% during the 2008 subprime crisis.
3. These results have been confirmed by Fahlenbrach, Rageth, and Stulz (2020).
4. Marais and Bates (2006) define *shift contagion* as '*significant differences in cross-market links between tranquil and crisis periods*'. It should be noted that the *shift contagion* concept was first indicated in a study by Forbes and Rigobon (2001) to describe the increase in co-movements among markets after a shock.
5. Including the extra I_{max} lags in the VAR in level is necessary because it allows taking into account the potentially cointegrated characteristic of time series. Through estimation of VAR(p), there is a guarantee in the asymptotic χ^2 distribution of the Wald statistic.
6. Given the short observation period during the COVID-19 crisis (66 observations), k must be achieved from a criterion that does not over-parametrize the system to minimize the loss of power of the causality test (Saikkonen and Lutkepohl 1996).
7. This reduces the risks associated with possibly wrong identifying the order of integration of the series, or the presence of cointegration. Cf. Toda and Yamamoto (1995) for further details.
8. Interested readers are referred to Dolado and Lütkepohl (1996) for more details about the Wald test.
9. The two steps on which the TYDL procedure is based are valid only if $I_{max} \leq k$ (*cf.* Toda and Yamamoto 1995).
10. The first case was reported to the World Health Organization Country Office in China on 31 December 2019.
11. Figures covering the first two quarters (i.e. up to 30 June 2020) are available on request.
12. The Chinese stock market index (SPC500) seems to be relatively less affected than the U.S. (SPX), European (SPEUR), Japanese (SPJ500) and Asiatic (SPA50) stock markets indices, particularly after 20 January.
13. This finding is similar to that of Ramelli and Wagner (2020b).
14. The Phillips-Perron unit-root test and the KPSS stationarity test are not reproduced in this paper, but they are available upon request.

15. Table B4 in the appendices summarizes the results from the causality tests in both periods — the tranquil pre-COVID-19 period and the COVID-19 crisis period.
16. According to Ozili and Arun (2020), '*although the oil price war, in which Russia and Saudi Arabia were driving down oil price by increasing oil production, played a role in the fall in stock markets indices, the subsequent fall in stock market indices in March was mainly due to investors' flight to safety during the coronavirus pandemic*'.
17. Appendix C summarizes the main measures taken by the Chinese government to address the human and economic impact of the COVID-19 pandemic.
18. 2 January 2020 was the first trading day after the first cases of pneumonia detected in Wuhan City were reported to the World Health Organization Country Office in China on 31 December 2019.
19. After the first cases of human-to-human transmission have been confirmed, the World Health Organization published its first situation report concerning the novel coronavirus outbreak on January 20.
20. After registering its first deaths from corona virus, Italy decided to quarantine tens of thousands of people in Lombardy on 23 February.
21. The study of Djalante et al. (2020) is one of the first academic publications which analyzes the government and key organizations responses in Indonesia to COVID-19 propagation between January and March 2020. By using media content from government speeches and social and mass media platforms, they outline the gaps and the limitations of the responses to the corona virus spread.
22. When Wuhan was put under lockdown and airlines started to cancel flights at the end of January, it was already too late. Thousands of people had already left Wuhan to many countries around the world, and about 86% of all infected travelers went undetected (Li et al., 2020a).
23. As the numbers of new confirmed COVID-19 cases have moderated, some European countries have recently started easing containment measures. It should be noted that on 20 May 2020, the European Commission presented country-specific economic policy recommendations to all European Union member states, and called for a coordinated response to the COVID-19 medical shock (Cf. *https://ec.europa.eu/commission/presscorner/detail/en/IP_20_901*).
24. For more details on the CARES Act, see *https://www.congress.gov/bill/116th-congress/senate-bill/3548/text*.
25. See Lima et al. (2016) for more details on the impact of unconventional monetary policy on stock markets.

Disclosure statement

No potential conflict of interest was reported by the author(s).

ORCID

Amine Ben Amar http://orcid.org/0000-0002-5234-6420

References

Al-Awadhi, A. M., K. Al-Saifi, A. Al-Awadhi, and S. Alhamadi. 2020. "Death and Contagious Infectious Diseases: Impact of the COVID-19 Virus on Stock Market Returns." *Journal of Behavioral and Experimental Finance* 27: 100326. doi:10.1016/j.jbef.2020.100326.

Alfaro, L., A. Chari, A. N. Greenland, and P. K. Schott. 2020. "Aggregate and Firm-level Stock Returns during Pandemics, in Real Time." *NBER Working Paper*, No. 26950.

Baldwin, R., and B. Weber Di Mauro. 2020. "Introduction." In *Mitigating the COVID Economic Crisis: Act Fast and Do Whatever it Takes*, edited by R. Baldwin and B. Welder Di Mauro, 1–24. London: CEPR Press.

Barro, R., J. F. Ursua, and J. Weng. 2020. "Lessons from the 'Spanish Flu' for the Coronavirus's Potential Effects on Mortality and Economic Activity." online mimeo.

Chen, C. D., C. C. Chen, W. W. Tang, and B. Y. Huang. 2009. "The Positive and Negative Impacts of the SARS Outbreak: A Case of the Taiwan Industries." *The Journal of Developing Areas* 43 (1): 281–293. doi:10.1353/jda.0.0041.

Chen, M. H., S. S. Jang, and W. G. Kim. 2007. "The Impact of the SARS Outbreak on Taiwanese Hotel Stock Performance: An Event-study Approach." *International Journal of Hospitality Management* 26 (1): pp. 200–212. doi:10.1016/j.ijhm.2005.11.004.

Djalante, R., J. Lassa, D. Setiamarga, B. Haryanto, A. Sudjatma, M. Indrawan, B. Haryanto, et al. 2020. "Review and Analysis of Current Responses to COVID-19 in Indonesia: Period of January to March 2020." *Progress in Disaster Science* 6: 100091. doi:10.1016/j.pdisas.2020.100091.

Dolado, J. J., and H. Lütkepohl. 1996. "Making Wald Tests Work for Cointegrated VAR Systems." *Econometric Reviews* 15 (4): pp.369–386. doi:10.1080/07474939608800362.

Elliot, L. 2020. "Prepare for the Coronavirus Global Recession." *The Guardian*, Media report. https://www.theguardian.com/business/2020/mar/15/prepare-for-the-coronavirus-global-recession

Fahlenbrach, R., K. Rageth, and R. M. Stulz. 2020. "How Valuable Is Financial Flexibility When Revenue Stops? Evidence from the COVID-19 Crisis." *Fisher College of Business Working Paper*, WP 2020-07.

Forbes, K., and R. Rigobon. 2001. "Measuring Contagion: Conceptual and Empirical Issues." In *International Financial Contagion*, edited by S. Claessens and K. J. Forbes, pp. 43–66. Springer, Boston, MA. doi:10.1007/978-1-4757-3314-3_3.

Gerding, F., T. Martin, and F. Nagler. 2020. "The Value of Fiscal Capacity in the Face of a Rare Disaster." *SSRN Electronic Journal*. doi:10.2139/ssrn.3572839.

Goldstein, M. 1998. "The Asian Financial Crises: Causes, Cures and Systemic Implications." Policy Analysis in International Economics No.55. Washington, DC: Institute for International Economics, 77.

Gourinchas, P.-O. 2020. "Flattering the Pandemic and Recession Curves." In *Mitigating the COVID Economic Crisis*, edited by R. Baldwin and B. Welder Di Mauro, 31–40. London: CEPR Press.

Hannan, E. J., and B. G. Quinn. 1979. "The Determination of the Order of an Autoregression." *Journal of the Royal Statistical Society: Series B (Methodological)* 41 (2): 190–195.

Ichev, R., and M. Marinč. 2018. "Stock Prices and Geographic Proximity of Information: Evidence from the Ebola Outbreak." *International Review of Financial Analysis* 56: 153–166. doi:10.1016/j.irfa.2017.12.004.

Kwiatkowski, D., P. C. B. Phillips, P. Schmidt, and Y. Shin. 1992. "Testing the Null Hypothesis of Stationarity against the Alternative of a Unit Root." *Journal of Econometrics* 54 (1–3): 159–178. doi:10.1016/0304-4076(92)90104-Y.

Li, L., Z. Yang, Z. Dang, C. Meng, J. Huang, H. Meng, D. Wang, et al. 2020a. "Propagation Analysis and Prediction of the COVID-19." *Infectious Disease Modelling* 5: 282–292. doi:10.1016/j.idm.2020.03.002.

Li, R., S. Pei, B. Chen, Y. Song, T. Zhang, W. Yang, and J. Sharman. 2020b. "Substantial Undocumented Infection Facilitates the Rapid Dissemination of Novel Coronavirus (Sars-cov2)." *Science*. doi:10.1126/science.abb3221.

Lima, L., C. F. Vasconcelos, J. Simao, and H. Ferreira de Mendonça. 2016. "The Quantitative Easing Effect on the Stock Market of the USA, the UK and Japan: An ARDL Approach for the Crisis Period." *Journal of Economic Studies* 43 (6): 1006–1021. doi:10.1108/JES-05-2015-0081.

Marais, E., and S. Bates. 2006. "An Empirical Study to Identify Shift Contagion during the Asian Crisis." *Journal of International Financial Markets, Institutions and Money* 16 (5): 468–479. doi:10.1016/j.intfin.2005.08.001.

Nicolaides, P. 2020. "Application of Article 107(2)(b) TFEU to Covid-19 Measures: State Aid to Make Good the Damage Caused by an Exceptional Occurrence." *Journal of European Competition Law & Practice* lpaa026. doi:10.1093/jeclap/lpaa026.

Ozili, P. K., and T. Arun. 2020. "Spillover of COVID-19: Impact on the Global Economy." *SSRN Electronic Journal.* doi:10.2139/ssrn.3562570.

Phillips, P. C. B. 1995. "Fully Modified Least Squares and Vector Autoregression." *Econometrica* 63 (5): 1023–1078. doi:10.2307/2171721.

Phillips, P. C. B., and P. Perron. 1988. "Testing for a Unit Root in Time Series Regression." *Biometrika* 75 (2): 335–346. doi:10.1093/biomet/75.2.335.

Ramelli, S., and A. Wagner. 2020b. "What the Stock Markets Tells Us about the Consequences of COVID-19." In *Mitigating the COVID Economic Crisis,* edited by R. Baldwin and B. Welder Di Mauro, 63–7. London: CEPR Press.

Ramelli, S., and A. Wagner. 2020a. "Feverish Stock Price Reactions to the Novel Coronavirus." *SSRN Electronic Journal.* doi:10.2139/ssrn.3550274.

Saikkonen, P., and H. Lutkepohl. 1996. "Infinite-Order Cointegrated Vector Autoregressive Processes." *Econometric Theory* 12 (5): 814–844. doi:10.1017/S0266466600007179.

Schwarz, G. E. 1978. "Estimating the Dimension of a Model." *Annals of Statistics* 6 (2): 461–464. doi:10.1214/aos/1176344136.

Summers, L. H. 2000. "International Financial Crises: Causes, Prevention, and Cures." *American Economic Review* 90 (2): 1–16. doi:10.1257/aer.90.2.1.

Toda, H. Y., and T. Yamamoto. 1995. "Statistical Inference in Vector Autoregressions with Possibly Integrated processes." *Journal of Econometrics* 66 (1–2): 225–250. doi:10.1016/0304-4076(94)01616-8.

World Economic Forum. 2020. *The Global Risks Report 2020.* Geneva: World Economic Forum.

Appendices

Appendix A

Table A1. Descriptive statistics.

a. Tranquil period

Variable	Mean	St. dev.	Skewness	Kurtosis	Min	Max	IO
SGL	7.779827	0.043883	−0.264111	3.426663	7.634506	7.877591	1
SPA50	8.435829	0.042645	−0.075176	2.757101	8.322431	8.538831	0
SPEURO	7.350181	0.035908	−0.18528	3.171133	7.235187	7.437483	1
SPX	7.975533	0.052154	−0.400026	3.306886	7.802982	8.083335	1
SPC500	8.013961	0.054398	−0.432114	3.546217	7.831006	8.12378	0
SPJ500	7.45831	0.037849	0.812729	2.762838	7.377328	7.545728	1
S5UTIL	5.713308	0.056288	−0.523413	2.516177	5.575419	5.797334	1
SPN	6.123346	0.051496	0.009745	2.082188	6.01606	6.229024	1
S5CONS	6.390875	0.055592	−0.650592	2.473844	6.245913	6.476926	1
S5INDU	6.463237	0.048214	−0.919056	4.653318	6.270043	6.54204	1
S5TELS	5.102332	0.056035	−0.408285	2.869132	4.930726	5.211779	1
S5COND	6.826569	0.04963	−1.000171	3.296925	6.648389	6.899663	1
SPF	6.120265	0.054606	0.258372	2.903057	5.96548	6.239476	1
S5HLTH	6.967744	0.040139	1.136799	4.267188	6.872905	7.085341	1
S5INFT	7.21219	0.090675	−0.493321	2.991402	6.941045	7.386904	1
SPSIPH	8.412655	0.060078	0.266197	3.091495	8.292356	8.586591	1
S5RE	5.430389	0.057081	−1.014941	3.88225	5.236282	5.516489	1

b. COVID-19 crisis period – Quarter 1, 2020

Variable	Mean	St. dev.	Skewness	Kurtosis	Min	Max	IO
SGL	7.803889	0.124376	−1.170681	2.869989	7.489731	7.903537	1
SPA50	8.482986	0.087235	−1.209563	3.35393	8.239556	8.573961	1
SPEURO	7.332204	0.144818	−1.186429	2.845893	6.993584	7.441631	1
SPX	8.022815	0.119531	−1.15776	2.902893	7.71307	8.127449	1
SPC500	8.075688	0.057509	−1.113435	3.224113	7.923696	8.14787	1
SPJ500	7.454462	0.100438	−1.037084	2.696535	7.229353	7.541508	1
S5UTIL	5.77771	0.107441	−1.463796	4.327183	5.428249	5.883684	1
SPN	5.856963	0.298355	−0.986647	2.429102	5.192623	6.136301	1
S5CONS	6.435482	0.075281	−1.367806	3.636496	6.216506	6.500313	1
S5INDU	6.447701	0.160176	−1.19023	2.964014	6.021169	6.576762	1
S5TELS	5.164337	0.10556	−1.049685	2.574725	4.925513	5.262535	1
S5COND	6.839461	0.117665	−1.167483	2.983564	6.561215	6.954906	1
SPF	6.116916	0.173403	−1.102204	2.648291	5.682048	6.246514	1
S5HLTH	7.030728	0.087122	−1.265765	3.461304	6.76963	7.106311	1
S5INFT	7.376749	0.101928	−1.018177	2.940396	7.122375	7.496436	1
SPSIPH	8.495017	0.130542	−1.092636	2.700247	8.197368	8.615481	1
S5RE	5.441869	0.123468	−1.478024	4.015351	5.066511	5.559566	1

c. COVID-19 crisis period – Quarter 2, 2020

Variable	Mean	St. dev.	Skewness	Kurtosis	Min	Max	IO
SGL	7.739272	0.05761	−0.322936	2.803972	7.594486	7.841024	1
SPA50	8.438827	0.045686	0.330945	2.188294	8.34608	8.524291	1
SPEURO	7.216119	0.060667	0.283788	1.945311	7.098609	7.328855	1
SPX	7.980141	0.058527	−0.699221	3.60039	7.812176	8.080977	1
SPC500	8.063437	0.038389	0.175884	2.253413	7.980786	8.13569	1
SPJ500	7.406253	0.055498	−0.070765	1.945837	7.286199	7.496219	1
S5UTIL	5.677635	0.039516	−0.253045	2.864989	5.57204	5.759942	0
SPN	5.635597	0.094544	−0.396608	3.470272	5.36148	5.860957	1
S5CONS	6.392484	0.022306	−0.796868	4.895759	6.310064	6.434803	0
S5INDU	6.301119	0.069257	0.311026	2.457267	6.164787	6.465491	1

(Continued)

Table A1. (Continued).

c. COVID-19 crisis period – Quarter 2, 2020							
Variable	Mean	St. dev.	Skewness	Kurtosis	Min	Max	IO
S5TELS	5.145981	0.066774	−0.767876	2.899023	4.968702	5.234365	1
S5COND	6.859505	0.085178	−0.870638	3.426767	6.624185	6.971537	1
SPF	5.928949	0.064715	0.243078	3.044666	5.784963	6.091921	0
S5HLTH	7.045179	0.038751	−1.958608	7.155167	6.900751	7.097185	1
S5INFT	7.404745	0.077326	−0.571589	2.72072	7.20614	7.518135	1
SPSIPH	8.463757	0.060978	−1.337241	3.9804	8.286939	8.533895	1
S5RE	5.342802	0.056358	−0.435568	3.097414	5.197779	5.456816	0

Note: Table A1.a, A1.b and A1.c report descriptive statistics of daily log-data. First column displays mean. second column displays standard errors. Third and fourth columns display raw skewness and kurtosis coefficients, respectively. Fifth and sixth show the smallest and largest observations, respectively. Seventh column displays the order of integration. As in Marais and Bates (2006) we use Phillips-Perron and KPSS tests to determine the integration order.

Appendix B

Table B1. TYDL causality test results and causal intensities during tranquil period.

H1 hypothesis [X→Z]	Imax	k	p = k + Imax	Marginal significance levels of the TYDL	Decision	Causal intensities$_{ZX}$
SPC500 → SGL	1	2	3	0.4143	Accept H0	SPC500 ↛ SGL
SPC500 → SPX	1	2	3	0.2028	Accept H0	SPC500 ↛ SPX
SPC500 → SPJ500	1	1	2	0.0104	Accept H1	0.9243
SPC500 → SPA50	0	1	1	0.1536	Accept H0	SPC500 ↛ SPA50
SPC500 → SPEUR	1	1	2	0.1386	Accept H0	SPC500 ↛ SPEUR
SPC500 → S5UTIL	1	1	2	0.4403	Accept H0	SPC500 ↛ S5UTIL
SPC500 → SPN	1	1	2	0.1332	Accept H0	SPC500 ↛ SPN
SPC500 → S5CONS	1	1	2	0.8652	Accept H0	SPC500 ↛ S5CONS
SPC500 → S5INDU	1	1	2	0.1858	Accept H0	SPC500 ↛ S5INDU
SPC500 → S5TELS	1	1	2	0.3236	Accept H0	SPC500 ↛ S5TELS
SPC500 → S5COND	1	2	3	0.2655	Accept H0	SPC500 ↛ S5COND
SPC500 → SPF	1	1	2	0.1908	Accept H0	SPC500 ↛ SPF
SPC500 → S5HLTH	1	1	2	0.7030	Accept H0	SPC500 ↛ S5HLTH
SPC500 → S5INFT	1	2	3	0.1461	Accept H0	SPC500 ↛ S5INFT
SPC500 → SPSIPH	1	1	2	0.0837	Accept H1	1.6703
SPC500 → S5RE	1	1	2	0.4697	Accept H0	SPC500 ↛ S5RE
SPX → SGL	1	2	3	0.1217	Accept H0	SPX ↛ SGL
SPX → SPC500	1	2	3	0.0001	Accept H1	1.0082
SPX → SPJ500	1	2	3	0.0000	Accept H1	0.9379
SPX → SPA50	1	2	3	0.0000	Accept H1	1.0595
SPX → SPEUR	1	2	3	0.0077	Accept H1	0.9318
SPJ500 → SGL	1	2	3	0.1559	Accept H0	SPJ500 ↛ SGL
SPJ500 → SPX	1	2	3	0.1815	Accept H0	SPJ500 ↛ SPX
SPJ500 → SPC500	1	1	2	0.6488	Accept H0	SPJ500 ↛ SPC500
SPJ500 → SPA50	1	1	2	0.8146	Accept H0	SPJ500 ↛ SPA50
SPJ500 → SPEUR	1	2	3	0.2080	Accept H0	SPJ500 ↛ SPEUR
SPJ500 → S5UTIL	1	1	2	0.4186	Accept H0	SPJ500 ↛ S5UTIL
SPJ500 → SPN	1	2	3	0.2123	Accept H0	SPJ500 ↛ SPN
SPJ500 → S5CONS	1	2	3	0.7662	Accept H0	SPJ500 ↛ S5CONS
SPJ500 → S5INDU	1	2	3	0.1712	Accept H0	SPJ500 ↛ S5INDU
SPJ500 → S5TELS	1	2	3	0.1686	Accept H0	SPJ500 ↛ S5TELS
SPJ500 → S5COND	1	2	3	0.1954	Accept H0	SPJ500 ↛ S5COND
SPJ500 → SPF	1	2	3	0.7158	Accept H0	SPJ500 ↛ SPF
SPJ500 → S5HLTH	1	2	3	0.1958	Accept H0	SPJ500 ↛ S5HLTH
SPJ500 → S5INFT	1	2	3	0.1631	Accept H0	SPJ500 ↛ S5INFT
SPJ500 → SPSIPH	1	2	3	0.8702	Accept H0	SPJ500 ↛ SPSIPH
SPJ500 → S5RE	1	1	2	0.9421	Accept H0	SPJ500 ↛ S5RE

(*Continued*)

Table B1. (Continued).

H1 hypothesis [X→Z]	lmax	k	p = k + lmax	Marginal significance levels of the TYDL	Decision	Causal intensitiese$_{ZX}$
SGL → SPX	1	2	3	0.0021	Accept H1	1.0266
SGL → SPC500	1	2	3	0.0000	Accept H1	1.0325
SGL → SPJ500	1	2	3	0.0000	Accept H1	0.9608
SGL → SPA50	1	2	3	0.0000	Accept H1	1.0856
SGL → SPEUR	1	2	3	0.0007	Accept H1	0.9474
SGL → S5UTIL	1	1	2	0.2912	Accept H0	SGL ↛ S5UTIL
SGL → SPN	1	1	2	0.9450	Accept H0	SGL ↛ SPN
SGL → S5CONS	1	1	2	0.8256	Accept H0	SGL ↛ S5CONS
SGL → S5INDU	1	1	2	0.5462	Accept H0	SGL ↛ S5INDU
SGL → S5TELS	1	1	2	0.6271	Accept H0	SGL ↛ S5TELS
SGL → S5COND	1	1	2	0.2278	Accept H0	SGL ↛ S5COND
SGL → SPF	1	1	2	0.1423	Accept H0	SGL ↛ SPF
SGL → S5HLTH	1	1	2	0.7860	Accept H0	SGL ↛ S5HLTH
SGL → S5INFT	1	1	2	0.0080	Accept H1	0.9353
SGL → SPSIPH	1	1	2	0.4747	Accept H0	SGL ↛ SPSIPH
SGL → S5RE	1	1	2	0.2740	Accept H0	SGL ↛ S5RE
SPA50 → SGL	1	2	3	0.0169	Accept H1	0.9362
SPA50 → SPX	1	2	3	0.0098	Accept H1	0.9554
SPA50 → SPC500	0	1	1	0.0035	Accept H1	0.9517
SPA50 → SPJ500	1	1	2	0.0244	Accept H1	0.8774
SPA50 → SPEUR	1	2	3	0.0062	Accept H1	0.8778
SPA50 → S5UTIL	1	1	2	0.5088	Accept H0	SPA50 ↛ S5UTIL
SPA50 → SPN	1	2	3	0.0198	Accept H1	0.7254
SPA50 → S5CONS	1	1	2	0.7680	Accept H0	SPA50 ↛ S5CONS
SPA50 → S5INDU	1	2	3	0.0045	Accept H1	0.7684
SPA50 → S5TELS	1	1	2	0.3791	Accept H0	SPA50 ↛ S5TELS
SPA50 → S5COND	1	2	3	0.0209	Accept H1	0.8136
SPA50 → SPF	1	2	3	0.0740	Accept H1	0.7310
SPA50 → S5HLTH	1	1	2	0.5469	Accept H0	SPA50 ↛ S5HLTH
SPA50 → S5INFT	1	2	3	0.0050	Accept H1	0.8713
SPA50 → SPSIPH	1	1	2	0.0400	Accept H1	1.0003
SPA50 → S5RE	1	1	2	0.3867	Accept H0	SPA50 ↛ S5RE
SPEUR → SGL	1	2	3	0.8401	Accept H0	SPEUR ↛ SGL
SPEUR → SPX	1	2	3	0.1660	Accept H0	SPEUR ↛ SPX
SPEUR → SPC500	1	1	2	0.0002	Accept H1	1.0923
SPEUR → SPJ500	1	2	3	0.0000	Accept H1	1.0483
SPEUR → SPA50	1	2	3	0.0000	Accept H1	1.1492
SPEUR → S5UTIL	1	1	2	0.2026	Accept H0	SPEUR ↛ S5UTIL
SPEUR → SPN	1	1	2	0.2030	Accept H0	SPEUR ↛ SPN
SPEUR → S5CONS	1	1	2	0.9250	Accept H0	SPEUR ↛ S5CONS
SPEUR → S5INDU	1	1	2	0.1863	Accept H0	SPEUR ↛ S5INDU
SPEUR → S5TELS	1	1	2	0.3779	Accept H0	SPEUR ↛ S5TELS
SPEUR → S5COND	1	1	2	0.0576	Accept H1	0.9311
SPEUR → SPF	1	2	3	0.0149	Accept H1	0.8363
SPEUR → S5HLTH	1	1	2	0.6773	Accept H0	SPEUR ↛ S5HLTH
SPEUR → S5INFT	1	1	2	0.0264	Accept H1	0.9918
SPEUR → SPSIPH	1	1	2	0.4286	Accept H0	SPEUR ↛ SPSIPH
SPEUR → S5RE	1	1	2	0.0311	Accept H1	0.7438

Note: To take into account the highest number of potential causal links while minimizing the risk of imprecision, a 10% significance level was used for all causality tests.

Table B2. TYDL causality test results and causal intensities during the COVID-19 crisis period (Quarter 1, 2020).

H1 hypothesis [X→Z]	lmax	k	p = k + lmax	Marginal significance levels of the TYDL	Decision	Causal intensities e_{ZX}
SPC500 → SGL	1	2	3	0.7560	Accept H0	SPC500 ↛ SGL
SPC500 → SPX	1	2	3	0.7249	Accept H0	SPC500 ↛ SPX
SPC500 → SPJ500	1	1	2	0.8070	Accept H0	SPC500 ↛ SPJ500
SPC500 → SPA50	1	1	2	0.6753	Accept H0	SPC500 ↛ SPA50
SPC500 → SPEUR	1	1	2	0.6436	Accept H0	SPC500 ↛ SPEUR
SPC500 → S5UTIL	1	1	2	0.6788	Accept H0	SPC500 ↛ S5UTIL
SPC500 → SPN	1	2	3	0.8840	Accept H0	SPC500 ↛ SPN
SPC500 → S5CONS	1	1	2	0.7251	Accept H0	SPC500 ↛ S5CONS
SPC500 → S5INDU	1	2	3	0.6814	Accept H0	SPC500 ↛ S5INDU
SPC500 → S5TELS	1	2	3	0.4686	Accept H0	SPC500 ↛ S5TELS
SPC500 → S5COND	1	2	3	0.4418	Accept H0	SPC500 ↛ S5COND
SPC500 → SPF	1	2	3	0.8761	Accept H0	SPC500 ↛ SPF
SPC500 → S5HLTH	1	2	3	0.4660	Accept H0	SPC500 ↛ S5HLTH
SPC500 → S5INFT	1	2	3	0.6678	Accept H0	SPC500 ↛ S5INFT
SPC500 → SPSIPH	1	2	3	0.5807	Accept H0	SPC500 ↛ SPSIPH
SPC500 → S5RE	1	1	2	0.6404	Accept H0	SPC500 ↛ S5RE
SPX → SGL	1	2	3	0.0605	Accept H1	0.9751
SPX → SPC500	1	2	3	0.2791	Accept H0	SPX ↛ SPC500
SPX → SPJ500	1	2	3	0.0131	Accept H1	0.9312
SPX → SPA50	1	2	3	0.0000	Accept H1	1.0493
SPX → SPEUR	1	3	4	0.5124	Accept H0	SPX ↛ SPEUR
SPJ500 → SGL	1	2	3	0.1030	Accept H0	SPJ500 ↛ SGL
SPJ500 → SPX	1	2	3	0.0097	Accept H1	1.0750
SPJ500 → SPC500	1	1	2	0.0598	Accept H1	1.0793
SPJ500 → SPA50	1	1	2	0.0669	Accept H1	1.1358
SPJ500 → SPEUR	1	2	3	0.6102	Accept H0	SPJ500 ↛ SPEUR
SPJ500 → S5UTIL	1	2	3	0.2395	Accept H0	SPJ500 ↛ S5UTIL
SPJ500 → SPN	1	2	3	0.2810	Accept H0	SPJ500 ↛ SPN
SPJ500 → S5CONS	1	1	2	0.0431	Accept H1	0.8623
SPJ500 → S5INDU	1	2	3	0.1467	Accept H0	SPJ500 ↛ S5INDU
SPJ500 → S5TELS	1	2	3	0.0103	Accept H1	0.6801
SPJ500 → S5COND	1	2	3	0.0732	Accept H1	0.9152
SPJ500 → SPF	1	2	3	0.1228	Accept H0	SPJ500 ↛ SPF
SPJ500 → S5HLTH	1	2	3	0.0025	Accept H1	0.9426
SPJ500 → S5INFT	1	2	3	0.0050	Accept H1	0.9889
SPJ500 → SPSIPH	1	2	3	0.0108	Accept H1	1.1380
SPJ500 → S5RE	1	2	3	0.0277	Accept H1	0.7279
SGL → SPX	1	2	3	0.0058	Accept H1	1.0267
SGL → SPC500	1	2	3	0.1479	Accept H0	SGL ↛ SPC500
SGL → SPJ500	1	2	3	0.0014	Accept H1	0.9564
SGL → SPA50	1	2	3	0.0394	Accept H1	1.0778
SGL → SPEUR	1	3	4	0.4940	Accept H0	SGL ↛ SPEUR
SGL → S5UTIL	1	4	5	0.0000	Accept H1	0.7416
SGL → SPN	1	4	5	0.0007	Accept H1	0.6664
SGL → S5CONS	1	2	3	0.0012	Accept H1	0.8228
SGL → S5INDU	1	1	2	0.2270	Accept H0	SGL ↛ S5INDU
SGL → S5TELS	1	2	3	0.0547	Accept H1	0.7298
SGL → S5COND	1	3	4	0.0148	Accept H1	0.8751
SGL → SPF	1	2	3	0.1148	Accept H0	SGL ↛ SPF
SGL → S5HLTH	1	1	2	0.6241	Accept H0	SGL ↛ S5HLTH
SGL → S5INFT	1	2	3	0.0594	Accept H1	0.9423
SGL → SPSIPH	1	3	4	0.1519	Accept H0	SGL ↛ SPSIPH
SGL → S5RE	1	3	4	0.0009	Accept H1	0.6979
SPA50 → SGL	1	2	3	0.4137	Accept H0	SPA50 ↛ SGL
SPA50 → SPX	1	2	3	0.0857	Accept H1	0.9376
SPA50 → SPC500	1	1	2	0.6788	Accept H0	SPA50 ↛ SPC500
SPA50 → SPJ500	1	1	2	0.5748	Accept H0	SPA50 ↛ SPJ500
SPA50 → SPEUR	1	2	3	0.8286	Accept H0	SPA50 ↛ SPEUR
SPA50 → S5UTIL	1	1	2	0.4503	Accept H0	SPA50 ↛ S5UTIL

(*Continued*)

Table B2. (Continued).

H1 hypothesis [X→Z]	lmax	k	p = k + lmax	Marginal significance levels of the TYDL	Decision	Causal intensitiese$_{ZX}$
SPA50 → SPN	1	2	3	0.6166	Accept H0	SPA50 ↛ SPN
SPA50 → S5CONS	1	1	2	0.1994	Accept H0	SPA50 ↛ S5CONS
SPA50 → S5INDU	1	2	3	0.1149	Accept H0	SPA50 ↛ S5INDU
SPA50 → S5TELS	1	2	3	0.0615	Accept H1	0.5172
SPA50 → S5COND	1	2	3	0.6017	Accept H0	SPA50 ↛ S5COND
SPA50 → SPF	1	2	3	0.2715	Accept H0	SPA50 ↛ SPF
SPA50 → S5HLTH	1	1	2	0.0569	Accept H1	0.8279
SPA50 → S5INFT	1	2	3	0.0621	Accept H1	0.8676
SPA50 → SPSIPH	1	2	3	0.3982	Accept H0	SPA50 ↛ SPSIPH
SPA50 → S5RE	1	2	3	0.0308	Accept H1	0.6394
SPEUR → SGL	1	3	4	0.0502	Accept H1	0.7451
SPEUR → SPX	1	3	4	0.0084	Accept H1	1.0817
SPEUR → SPC500	1	1	2	0.0243	Accept H1	1.0928
SPEUR → SPJ500	1	2	3	0.0000	Accept H1	1.0178
SPEUR → SPA50	1	2	3	0.0049	Accept H1	1.1465
SPEUR → S5UTIL	1	1	2	0.5367	Accept H0	SPEUR ↛ S5UTIL
SPEUR → SPN	1	2	3	0.0404	Accept H1	0.6690
SPEUR → S5CONS	1	6	7	0.0000	Accept H1	0.8729
SPEUR → S5INDU	1	7	8	0.0022	Accept H1	0.8611
SPEUR → S5TELS	1	3	4	0.0056	Accept H1	0.7019
SPEUR → S5COND	1	3	4	0.0045	Accept H1	0.9282
SPEUR → SPF	1	8	9	0.3346	Accept H0	SPEUR ↛ SPF
SPEUR → S5HLTH	1	7	8	0.0111	Accept H1	0.9483
SPEUR → S5INFT	1	3	4	0.0058	Accept H1	0.9989
SPEUR → SPSIPH	1	3	4	0.0222	Accept H1	1.1626
SPEUR → S5RE	1	3	4	0.0003	Accept H1	0.7415

Note: To take into account the highest number of potential causal links while minimizing the risk of imprecision, a 10% significance level was used for all causality tests.

Table B3. TYDL causality test results and causal intensities during the COVID-19 crisis period (Quarter 2, 2020).

H1 hypothesis [X→Z]	lmax	k	p = k + lmax	Marginal significance levels of the TYDL	Decision	Causal intensitiese$_{ZX}$
SPC500 → SGL	1	1	2	0.3515	Accept H0	SPC500 ↛ SGL
SPC500 → SPX	1	1	2	0.5671	Accept H0	SPC500 ↛ SPX
SPC500 → SPJ500	1	1	2	0.3261	Accept H0	SPC500 ↛ SPJ500
SPC500 → SPA50	1	1	2	0.0084	Accept H1	1.0473
SPC500 → SPEUR	1	1	2	0.2238	Accept H0	SPC500 ↛ SPEUR
SPC500 → S5UTIL	1	1	2	0.2497	Accept H0	SPC500 ↛ S5UTIL
SPC500 → SPN	1	1	2	0.8325	Accept H0	SPC500 ↛ SPN
SPC500 → S5CONS	1	1	2	0.1997	Accept H0	SPC500 ↛ S5CONS
SPC500 → S5INDU	1	1	2	0.5645	Accept H0	SPC500 ↛ S5INDU
SPC500 → S5TELS	1	1	2	0.5621	Accept H0	SPC500 ↛ S5TELS
SPC500 → S5COND	1	1	2	0.3744	Accept H0	SPC500 ↛ S5COND
SPC500 → SPF	1	1	2	0.5348	Accept H0	SPC500 ↛ SPF
SPC500 → S5HLTH	1	1	2	0.2347	Accept H0	SPC500 ↛ S5HLTH
SPC500 → S5INFT	1	1	2	0.5257	Accept H0	SPC500 ↛ S5INFT
SPC500 → SPSIPH	1	1	2	0.3662	Accept H0	SPC500 ↛ SPSIPH
SPC500 → S5RE	1	1	2	0.3259	Accept H0	SPC500 ↛ S5RE
SPX → SGL	1	1	2	0.5708	Accept H0	SPX ↛ SGL
SPX → SPC500	1	1	2	0.0213	Accept H1	1.0150
SPX → SPJ500	1	1	2	0.0000	Accept H1	0.9292
SPX → SPA50	1	1	2	0.0003	Accept H1	1.0597
SPX → SPEUR	1	1	2	0.0178	Accept H1	0.9059
SPJ500 → SGL	1	1	2	0.6544	Accept H0	SPJ500 ↛ SGL
SPJ500 → SPX	1	1	2	0.8395	Accept H0	SPJ500 ↛ SPX

(Continued)

Table B3. (Continued).

H1 hypothesis [X→Z]	lmax	k	p = k + lmax	Marginal significance levels of the TYDL	Decision	Causal intensitiese$_{ZX}$
SPJ500 → SPC500	1	1	2	0.4248	Accept H0	SPJ500 ↛ SPC500
SPJ500 → SPA50	1	1	2	0.2256	Accept H0	SPJ500 ↛ SPA50
SPJ500 → SPEUR	1	1	2	0.1724	Accept H0	SPJ500 ↛ SPEUR
SPJ500 → S5UTIL	1	1	2	0.8723	Accept H0	SPJ500 ↛ S5UTIL
SPJ500 → SPN	1	1	2	0.2199	Accept H0	SPJ500 ↛ SPN
SPJ500 → S5CONS	1	2	3	0.3847	Accept H0	SPJ500 ↛ S5CONS
SPJ500 → S5INDU	1	1	2	0.9131	Accept H0	SPJ500 ↛ S5INDU
SPJ500 → S5TELS	1	2	3	0.8940	Accept H0	SPJ500 ↛ S5TELS
SPJ500 → S5COND	1	2	3	0.7880	Accept H0	SPJ500 ↛ S5COND
SPJ500 → SPF	1	1	2	0.8218	Accept H0	SPJ500 ↛ SPF
SPJ500 → S5HLTH	1	1	2	0.6934	Accept H0	SPJ500 ↛ S5HLTH
SPJ500 → S5INFT	1	2	3	0.9045	Accept H0	SPJ500 ↛ S5INFT
SPJ500 → SPSIPH	1	1	2	0.2990	Accept H0	SPJ500 ↛ SPSIPH
SPJ500 → S5RE	1	1	2	0.5523	Accept H0	SPJ500 ↛ S5RE
SGL → SPX	1	1	2	0.7273	Accept H0	SGL ↛ SPX
SGL → SPC500	1	1	2	0.0313	Accept H1	1.0473
SGL → SPJ500	1	1	2	0.0000	Accept H1	0.9580
SGL → SPA50	1	1	2	0.0003	Accept H1	1.0927
SGL → SPEUR	1	1	2	0.0167	Accept H1	0.9335
SGL → S5UTIL	1	1	2	0.9442	Accept H0	SGL ↛ S5UTIL
SGL → SPN	1	1	2	0.6406	Accept H0	SGL ↛ SPN
SGL → S5CONS	1	1	2	0.1612	Accept H0	SGL ↛ S5CONS
SGL → S5INDU	1	1	2	0.0796	Accept H1	0.8171
SGL → S5TELS	1	1	2	0.6495	Accept H0	SGL ↛ S5TELS
SGL → S5COND	1	1	2	0.4027	Accept H1	SGL ↛ S5COND
SGL → SPF	1	1	2	0.1135	Accept H0	SGL ↛ SPF
SGL → S5HLTH	1	1	2	0.5833	Accept H0	SGL ↛ S5HLTH
SGL → S5INFT	1	1	2	0.7186	Accept H0	SGL ↛ S5INFT
SGL → SPSIPH	1	1	2	0.9340	Accept H0	SGL ↛ SPSIPH
SGL → S5RE	1	1	2	0.0785	Accept H1	0.6929
SPA50 → SGL	1	1	2	0.3949	Accept H0	SPA50 ↛ SGL
SPA50 → SPX	1	1	2	0.6168	Accept H0	SPA50 ↛ SPX
SPA50 → SPC500	1	1	2	0.0602	Accept H1	0.9535
SPA50 → SPJ500	1	1	2	0.9678	Accept H0	SPA50 ↛ SPJ500
SPA50 → SPEUR	1	1	2	0.3954	Accept H0	SPA50 ↛ SPEUR
SPA50 → S5UTIL	1	1	2	0.1779	Accept H0	SPA50 ↛ S5UTIL
SPA50 → SPN	1	1	2	0.8460	Accept H0	SPA50 ↛ SPN
SPA50 → S5CONS	1	1	2	0.1034	Accept H0	SPA50 ↛ S5CONS
SPA50 → S5INDU	1	1	2	0.6477	Accept H0	SPA50 ↛ S5INDU
SPA50 → S5TELS	1	1	2	0.7693	Accept H0	SPA50 ↛ S5TELS
SPA50 → S5COND	1	2	3	0.9397	Accept H0	SPA50 ↛ S5COND
SPA50 → SPF	1	1	2	0.9675	Accept H0	SPA50 ↛ SPF
SPA50 → S5HLTH	1	1	2	0.1197	Accept H0	SPA50 ↛ S5HLTH
SPA50 → S5INFT	1	2	3	0.9191	Accept H0	SPA50 ↛ S5INFT
SPA50 → SPSIPH	1	1	2	0.2510	Accept H0	SPA50 ↛ SPSIPH
SPA50 → S5RE	1	1	2	0.2605	Accept H0	SPA50 ↛ S5RE
SPEUR → SGL	1	1	2	0.5113	Accept H0	SPEUR ↛ SGL
SPEUR → SPX	1	1	2	0.6138	Accept H0	SPEUR ↛ SPX
SPEUR → SPC500	1	1	2	0.2086	Accept H0	SPEUR ↛ SPC500
SPEUR → SPJ500	1	1	2	0.0003	Accept H1	1.0463
SPEUR → SPA50	1	1	2	0.0111	Accept H1	1.1744
SPEUR → S5UTIL	1	1	2	0.7982	Accept H0	SPEUR ↛ S5UTIL
SPEUR → SPN	1	1	2	0.4765	Accept H0	SPEUR ↛ SPN
SPEUR → S5CONS	1	1	2	0.1263	Accept H0	SPEUR ↛ S5CONS
SPEUR → S5INDU	1	1	2	0.7803	Accept H0	SPEUR ↛ S5INDU
SPEUR → S5TELS	1	1	2	0.9447	Accept H0	SPEUR ↛ S5TELS
SPEUR → S5COND	1	1	2	0.9509	Accept H0	SPEUR ↛ S5COND
SPEUR → SPF	1	1	2	0.8751	Accept H0	SPEUR ↛ SPF
SPEUR → S5HLTH	1	1	2	0.1553	Accept H0	SPEUR ↛ S5HLTH
SPEUR → S5INFT	1	1	2	0.9737	Accept H0	SPEUR ↛ S5INFT
SPEUR → SPSIPH	1	1	2	0.3610	Accept H0	SPEUR ↛ SPSIPH
SPEUR → S5RE	1	1	2	0.4863	Accept H0	SPEUR ↛ S5RE

Note: To take into account the highest number of potential causal links while minimizing the risk of imprecision, a 10% significance level was used for all causality tests.

Table B4. Summary of the TYDL causality test results during the tranquil and the COVID-19 crisis periods.

H1 hypothesis [X→Z]	Decision		
	Tranquil period	Quarter 1, 2020	Quarter 2, 2020
SPC500 → SGL	Accept H0	Accept H0	Accept H0
SPC500 → SPX	Accept H0	Accept H0	Accept H0
SPC500 → SPJ500	Accept H1	Accept H0	Accept H0
SPC500 → SPA50	Accept H0	Accept H0	Accept H1
SPC500 → SPEUR	Accept H0	Accept H0	Accept H0
SPC500 → S5UTIL	Accept H0	Accept H0	Accept H0
SPC500 → SPN	Accept H0	Accept H0	Accept H0
SPC500 → S5CONS	Accept H0	Accept H0	Accept H0
SPC500 → S5INDU	Accept H0	Accept H0	Accept H0
SPC500 → S5TELS	Accept H0	Accept H0	Accept H0
SPC500 → S5COND	Accept H0	Accept H0	Accept H0
SPC500 → SPF	Accept H0	Accept H0	Accept H0
SPC500 → S5HLTH	Accept H0	Accept H0	Accept H0
SPC500 → S5INFT	Accept H0	Accept H0	Accept H0
SPC500 → SPSIPH	Accept H1	Accept H0	Accept H0
SPC500 → S5RE	Accept H0	Accept H0	Accept H0
SPX → SGL	Accept H0	Accept H1	Accept H0
SPX → SPC500	Accept H1	Accept H0	Accept H1
SPX → SPJ500	Accept H1	Accept H1	Accept H1
SPX → SPA50	Accept H1	Accept H1	Accept H1
SPX → SPEUR	Accept H1	Accept H0	Accept H1
SPJ500 → SGL	Accept H0	Accept H0	Accept H0
SPJ500 → SPX	Accept H0	Accept H1	Accept H0
SPJ500 → SPC500	Accept H0	Accept H1	Accept H0
SPJ500 → SPA50	Accept H0	Accept H1	Accept H0
SPJ500 → SPEUR	Accept H0	Accept H0	Accept H0
SPJ500 → S5UTIL	Accept H0	Accept H0	Accept H0
SPJ500 → SPN	Accept H0	Accept H0	Accept H0
SPJ500 → S5CONS	Accept H0	Accept H1	Accept H0
SPJ500 → S5INDU	Accept H0	Accept H0	Accept H0
SPJ500 → S5TELS	Accept H0	Accept H1	Accept H0
SPJ500 → S5COND	Accept H0	Accept H1	Accept H0
SPJ500 → SPF	Accept H0	Accept H0	Accept H0
SPJ500 → S5HLTH	Accept H0	Accept H1	Accept H0
SPJ500 → S5INFT	Accept H0	Accept H1	Accept H0
SPJ500 → SPSIPH	Accept H0	Accept H1	Accept H0
SPJ500 → S5RE	Accept H0	Accept H1	Accept H0
SGL → SPX	Accept H1	Accept H1	Accept H0
SGL → SPC500	Accept H1	Accept H0	Accept H1
SGL → SPJ500	Accept H1	Accept H1	Accept H1
SGL → SPA50	Accept H1	Accept H1	Accept H1
SGL → SPEUR	Accept H1	Accept H0	Accept H1
SGL → S5UTIL	Accept H0	Accept H1	Accept H0
SGL → SPN	Accept H0	Accept H1	Accept H0
SGL → S5CONS	Accept H0	Accept H1	Accept H0
SGL → S5INDU	Accept H0	Accept H0	Accept H1
SGL → S5TELS	Accept H0	Accept H1	Accept H0
SGL → S5COND	Accept H0	Accept H1	Accept H1
SGL → SPF	Accept H0	Accept H0	Accept H0
SGL → S5HLTH	Accept H0	Accept H0	Accept H0
SGL → S5INFT	Accept H1	Accept H1	Accept H0
SGL → SPSIPH	Accept H0	Accept H0	Accept H0
SGL → S5RE	Accept H0	Accept H1	Accept H1
SPA50 → SGL	Accept H1	Accept H0	Accept H0
SPA50 → SPX	Accept H1	Accept H1	Accept H0
SPA50 → SPC500	Accept H1	Accept H0	Accept H1
SPA50 → SPJ500	Accept H1	Accept H0	Accept H0
SPA50 → SPEUR	Accept H1	Accept H0	Accept H0
SPA50 → S5UTIL	Accept H0	Accept H0	Accept H0

(*Continued*)

Table B4. (Continued).

H1 hypothesis [X→Z]	Decision		
	Tranquil period	Quarter 1, 2020	Quarter 2, 2020
SPA50 → SPN	Accept H1	Accept H0	Accept H0
SPA50 → S5CONS	Accept H0	Accept H0	Accept H0
SPA50 → S5INDU	Accept H1	Accept H0	Accept H0
SPA50 → S5TELS	Accept H0	Accept H1	Accept H0
SPA50 → S5COND	Accept H1	Accept H0	Accept H0
SPA50 → SPF	Accept H1	Accept H0	Accept H0
SPA50 → S5HLTH	Accept H0	Accept H1	Accept H0
SPA50 → S5INFT	Accept H1	Accept H1	Accept H0
SPA50 → SPSIPH	Accept H1	Accept H0	Accept H0
SPA50 → S5RE	Accept H0	Accept H1	Accept H0
SPEUR → SGL	Accept H0	Accept H1	Accept H0
SPEUR → SPX	Accept H0	Accept H1	Accept H0
SPEUR → SPC500	Accept H1	Accept H1	Accept H0
SPEUR → SPJ500	Accept H1	Accept H1	Accept H1
SPEUR → SPA50	Accept H1	Accept H1	Accept H1
SPEUR → S5UTIL	Accept H0	Accept H0	Accept H0
SPEUR → SPN	Accept H0	Accept H1	Accept H0
SPEUR → S5CONS	Accept H0	Accept H1	Accept H0
SPEUR → S5INDU	Accept H0	Accept H1	Accept H0
SPEUR → S5TELS	Accept H0	Accept H1	Accept H0
SPEUR → S5COND	Accept H1	Accept H1	Accept H0
SPEUR → SPF	Accept H1	Accept H0	Accept H0
SPEUR → S5HLTH	Accept H0	Accept H1	Accept H0
SPEUR → S5INFT	Accept H1	Accept H1	Accept H0
SPEUR → SPSIPH	Accept H0	Accept H1	Accept H0
SPEUR → S5RE	Accept H1	Accept H1	Accept H0

Appendix C. China's key policy responses to COVID-19

China has been severely affected by the COVID-19 with more than 83,449 confirmed cases and 4,634 confirmed deaths as of 25 June 2020. To contain the epidemic, the Chinese government implemented stringent containment measures, including the prolongation of the National Lunar New Year holiday, the lockdown of Hubei Province, large-scale nationwide mobility and activity restrictions, social distancing, the uses of QR codes to track the path of the virus and thereby contain outbreaks, foreign entry restrictions and a 14-day quarantine period for returning migrant workers to contain imported cases. As a result, the Chinese economy contracted by 6.8% in Q1-2020 compared to Q1-2019.

To overcome the human and economic effects of this medical shock, RMB 4.2 trillion, which represents more than 4% of the Chinese GDP, of discretionary fiscal stimulus has been announced by the government. Key steps include: (i) public investment, (ii) higher expenditure to prevent and control epidemics, (iii) the development and production of medical equipment, (iv) faster payment of unemployment insurance, (v) tax relief and exemption from social security contributions. Many measures have also been taken by the Government to limit the tightening in financial conditions.

For its part, the People's Bank of China has eased its monetary policy and acted to preserve financial market soundness by (i) injecting RMB 5.7 trillion into the banking system via open market operations, (ii) supporting medical and basic necessity manufacturers, micro, small and medium enterprises as well, as the agricultural sector by expanding relending and rediscounting facilities at low interest rates, (iii) reducing the interest rate on excess reserves from 72 to 35 basis points, (iv) reducing the reverse repo rates, as well as the medium-run lending facility rates, (v) supporting lending to SME through an RMB 400 billion zero-interest 'funding-for-lending' program to finance 40% of new unsecured loans from local banks and (vi) easing restrictions on the investment quota for foreign institutional investors.

Health risk and the efficient market hypothesis in the time of COVID-19

Evangelos Vasileiou, Aristeidis Samitas, Maria Karagiannaki and Jagadish Dandu

ABSTRACT

In this note, we show that the stock markets do not always incorporate all the available information because in many cases they slowly evaluate the news. Using simple statistical analysis, we show that the response of the markets to the available information in certain time periods is irrational and inefficient. The COVID-19 outbreak gives financial economists an example of health risk underestimation, and of an unexpectedly slow response during a stress period; issues that should be examined in the future under a behavioral view.

1. Introduction

2019 ended with some worrying news regarding a cluster of cases of pneumonia in Wuhan, China. Many people underestimated this information, and some serious omissions by the authorities led to one of the deadliest pandemics of the last decades. The new virus was named Severe Acute Respiratory Syndrome CoronaVirus 2 (SARS-CoV-2) and causes the disease COVID-19.

The new virus spread worldwide and was a challenge for epidemiologists and other scientists, and also for financial economists. In what ways does a pandemic affect an economy and the financial system? Studies show ramifications such as inflation, reduced consumption, slowdown of the economic activity, and decrease in investments amongst others (see, for example, Smith et al. 2005; Keogh-Brown and Smith 2008; Keogh-Brown et al. 2010). In this note, we focus on the response of the stock markets to the COVID-19 outbreak. According to the Efficient Markets Hypothesis (EMH), stock prices at any point in time 'fully reflect' available information (Fama 1970). Was there any point in time when the stock markets did not reflect rationally all the available information during the COVID-19 outbreak?

We seek to present in a simple and clear way the news and the response of the world's developed stock markets (Australia, Austria, Belgium, Canada, Denmark, Finland, France, Germany, United Kingdom, Spain, Ireland, Israel, Italy, United Kingdom, Netherlands, New Zealand, Norway, Portugal, Singapore, Sweden, Switzerland, Japan, and United States)[1] during the COVID-19 outbreak. We choose to test our assumption using the specific sample because the developed stock markets should be precisely the ones where it would be expected for the EMH to hold true (Borges 2010). The results show that the markets are not always efficient and rational, and in some cases, they present the opposite of expected outcomes.

Section 2 presents a timeline of the COVID-19 outbreak and the theoretical framework, Section 3 presents the empirical findings, and Section 4 concludes the note.

2. COVID-19: timeline and theoretical framework

It was 31.12.2019 when the World Health Organization (WHO) China Country Office was informed of cases of an unknown etiology pneumonia detected in Wuhan City, China. On 14.01.2020 WHO reports[2]:

- According to the Chinese Government '... there is no clear evidence that the virus passes easily from person to person.'
- 'To date, investigations are still under way to assess the full extent of the outbreak. Wuhan city is a major domestic and international transport hub. More comprehensive information and ongoing investigations are also required to better understand the epidemiology, clinical picture, source, modes of transmission, and extent of infection; as well as the countermeasures implemented.' and
- 'Based on information provided by national authorities, WHO's recommendations on public health measures and surveillance for novel coronaviruses apply. WHO does not recommend any specific health measures for travelers.'

On 23 January, transport in Wuhan, Huanggang and Ezhou was severely restricted. On 30 January, WHO declared a Public Health Emergency of International Concern (PHEIC).[3] On 11.02.2020 the novel coronavirus was given a name: Severe Acute Respiratory Syndrome Coronavirus 2 (SARS-CoV-2), and its disease is called COVID-19.[4] On 22 February, the Italian authorities reported clusters of cases in Lombardy,[5] and taking into consideration the connection between the member countries of the European Union, the virus could be anywhere in Europe. In the USA, on 25.02.2020 the Center for Disease Control and Prevention (CDC) warned of coronavirus outbreaks.[6] On 11 March, WHO Director General Dr Tedros Adhanom Ghebreyesus characterized COVID-19 as a - pandemic.[7] After the pandemic declaration, most countries of the world implemented lockdowns in order to contain the spread of the virus.[8]

The extended lockdowns worsened the economic impact of the pandemic and governments throughout the world announced stimulus packages. The European Central Bank (ECB) announced a €750 billion Pandemic Emergency Purchase Programme (PEPP) on 18.03.2020 and the USA announced a 2 USD trillion stimulus pack on 24.03.2020.[9] Leaders of the European Union (EU) agreed to a comprehensive package of €1,824.3bn[10] during the Special European Council, 17–21 July 2020. Figure 1, presents the timeline of these events.

In the contemporary globalized environment, a highly contagious virus may spread fast and lead to a pandemic. Data say that in December 2019 and up to the Wuhan travel restrictions there were on average more than 160 thousand flights per day in the world.[11] Therefore, the virus could be anywhere because Wuhan is a domestic and international transport hub and most of the countries implemented lockdown measures after the

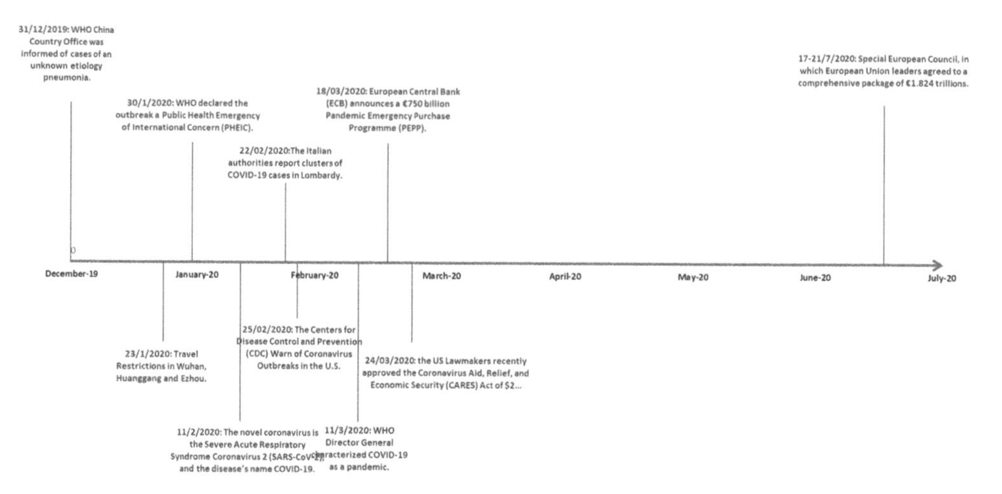

Figure 1. Timeline of the COVID-19 outbreak. Dates format Month-Year.

pandemic declaration. Before travel restrictions were put in place, most of the flights in the world either arrived in or departed from destinations in developed countries; therefore, in these countries, the virus was much more likely to travel sooner and in high quantity.

Moreover, developed countries have at least two additional reasons to worry about the virus impact. Firstly, their urban population as percentage of their total population (Table 1, column 2) is significantly high, and as WHO mentions[12]:

> The disease can spread from person to person through small droplets from the nose or mouth which are spread when a person with COVID-19 coughs or exhales. .... This is why it is important to stay more than 1 meter (3 feet) away from a person who is sick.

Do people normally keep more than 1 meter away from other people on trains, buses, etc., in urban areas? In normal conditions, the reply is negative. Therefore, if a virus with the characteristics of SARS-CoV-2 is not contained soon, its spread in urbanized communities could be significantly high. The percentage of urbanized population in the countries included in our sample is 82.11% on average.

Secondly, older people are more at risk of developing severe illness from COVID-19[13], and in many of the developed economies of our sample, the elderly are a significant part of the total population. Table 1 shows the population ages 65 and above as a percentage of the total population (column 3), according to the World Bank data.[14] The average value of the specific sample is 18.52% and, in some countries, older people constitute 27.58% of the total population. This means that if the virus spreads in an urbanized community where many older people live it has significantly more possibilities to lead to a heavier death toll.

The news regarding the virus spread increases the uncertainty about the health risk and the economy. Many governments try to find the optimal plan against COVID-19 in order to protect the lives of their citizens, while at the same time trying to lessen the impact of strict lockdowns on the economy. The theory suggests that fear for the consequences of COVID-19 and increased policy uncertainty[15] should lead to increased volatility in the financial markets (Antonakakis, Chatziantoniou, and Filis 2013; Baker,

Table 1. Urban population and population ages 65 and above (% of total population) of the countries of our sample.

Country	Urban population (% of total population)	Population ages 65 and above (% of total population)
Australia	86.01	15.66
Austria	58.30	19.00
Belgium	98.00	18.79
Canada	81.41	17.23
Denmark	87.87	19.81
Finland	85.38	21.72
France	80.44	20.03
Germany	77.31	21.46
United Kingdom	83.40	18.40
Spain	80.32	19.38
Ireland	63.17	13.87
Israel	92.42	11.98
Italy	70.44	22.75
United Kingdom	83.40	18.40
Netherlands	91.49	19.20
New Zealand	86.54	15.65
Norway	82.25	17.05
Portugal	65.21	21.95
Singapore	100.00	11.46
Sweden	87.43	20.10
Switzerland	73.80	18.62
Japan	91.62	27.58
United States	82.26	15.81

Source: World Bank data for 2018 (https://data.worldbank.org).

Bloom, and Davis 2016). The increased health risk due to a pandemic increases the investors' risk aversion (Decker and Schmitz 2016) and reduces consumption (Haacker 2004) and together these factors lead financial markets to a decline.[16]

Finally, we should highlight a specific characteristic of the recent pandemic that plays a significant role in our analysis: COVID-19 is a unique case because the consequences are not local, and globalization has changed the factors that may influence the performance of the stock markets (Goodell 2020). Recent studies that use data from the COVID-19 period show that the deaths in one country influence not only the performance of the local stock markets (Al-Awadhi et al. 2020) but also the stock markets of other countries and commodities (Ali, Alam, and Rizvi 2020). Therefore, when the virus has not been defeated globally and still threatens human lives, the stock markets of the interconnected economies should theoretically be under pressure.

3. COVID-19: what the data say

Figure 2 presents the performance of the world's developed stock markets. It is easily observed that most stock markets did not appear to worry about the COVID-19 outbreak and presented positive returns from the beginning of 2020 up to some days after the PHEIC declaration. Only after 21.02.2020, did the stock markets start to suffer losses because, as we presented above, the first reports that COVID-19 had spread to Europe and the USA surfaced on 22.02 and 25.02, respectively. The sharp decline period continues up to 18.03.2020 for most of the stock markets of our sample. After 18.03.2020, the stock markets present growth possibly because the governments announce relief programs and stimulus packs.

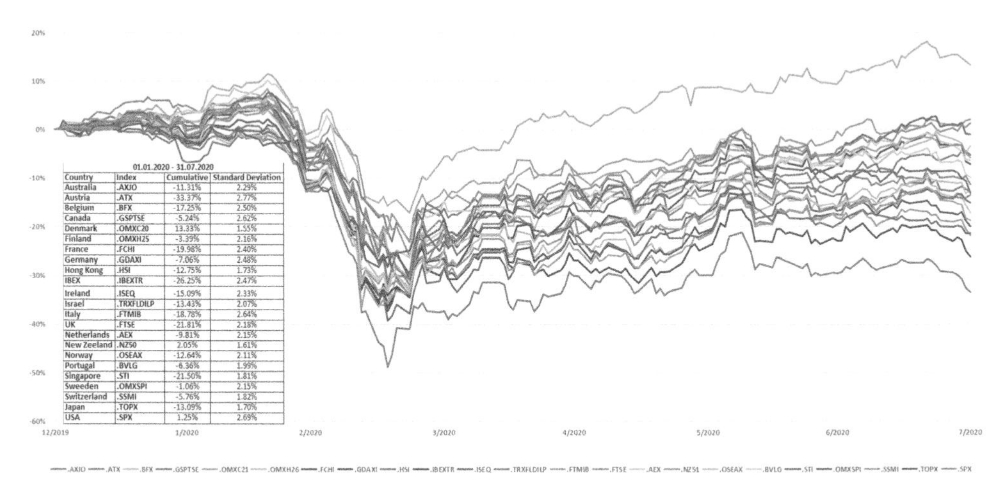

01.01.2020 - 31.07.2020			
Country	Index	Cumulative	Standard Deviation
Australia	.AXJO	-11.31%	2.29%
Austria	.ATX	-33.37%	2.77%
Belgium	.BFX	-17.25%	2.50%
Canada	.GSPTSE	-5.24%	2.62%
Denmark	.OMXC20	13.33%	1.55%
Finland	.OMXH25	-3.39%	2.16%
France	.FCHI	-19.98%	2.40%
Germany	.GDAXI	-7.06%	2.48%
Hong Kong	.HSI	-12.75%	1.73%
IBEX	.IBEXTR	-26.25%	2.47%
Ireland	.ISEQ	-15.09%	2.33%
Israel	.TRXFLDILP	-13.43%	2.07%
Italy	.FTMIB	-18.78%	2.64%
UK	.FTSE	-21.81%	2.18%
Netherlands	.AEX	-9.81%	2.15%
New Zeeland	.NZ50	2.05%	1.61%
Norway	.OSEAX	-12.64%	2.11%
Portugal	.BVLG	-6.36%	1.99%
Singapore	.STI	-21.50%	1.81%
Sweeden	.OMXSPI	-1.06%	2.15%
Switzerland	.SSMI	-5.76%	1.82%
Japan	.TOPX	-13.09%	1.70%
USA	.SPX	1.25%	2.69%

Figure 2. The performance of the developed stock markets during the COVID-19 outbreak.

Therefore, we divide the first 7 months of the COVID-19 outbreak into the following periods:

(i) *Period 1 (01.01.2020–29.01.2020)*: the day after the first notice regarding COVID-19 by the WHO up to the day before the PHEIC declaration,
(ii) *Period 2 (30.01.2020–21.02.2020)*: after the PHEIC declaration and up to the day before the report by Italian authorities,
(iii) *Period 3 (22.02.2020–10.03.2020)*: the day on which the stock markets started to fall sharply and up to the day before the pandemic declaration,
(iv) *Period 4 (11.03.2020–18.03.2020)*: the day of the pandemic declaration up to the day when the ECB announced the PEPP which is also the day that most stock indices reached their minimum values since the beginning of the COVID-19 outbreak, and
(v) *Period 5 (19.03.2020–31.07.2020)*: the days after the first announcement of the relief programs up to the end of the examined period.

Table 2 presents the cumulative returns and the standard deviation of the sample's stock indices during the respective periods in local currencies using data from the Eikon database, and adopting the following formulas

- The daily returns, which are estimated by the formula

$$\textbf{Daily Returns Per Index}_t = \frac{\textbf{Index Price}_t}{\textbf{Index Price}_{t-1}} - 1 \quad (1)$$

where t is the Index Price on day t and t-1 is the index Price in the previous date,

- The cumulative returns, which are estimated by the formulae

Table 2. Performance of the world's developed stock markets during selective subperiods of the COVID-19 outbreak.

Country	Index	Period 1	Period 2	Period 3	Period 4	Period 5	Whole Period
(a) Cumulative returns							
Australia	S&P/ASX 200 (.AXJO)	5.20%	1.53%	−16.80%	−16.61%	19.68%	−11.31%
Canada	Toronto Stock Exchange (.GSPTSE)	2.63%	1.89%	−16.17%	−21.64%	37.95%	−5.24%
Hong Kong	Hang Seng Index (.HSI)	−3.65%	0.55%	−7.02%	−12.21%	10.33%	−12.75%
Israel	THOMSON REUTERS ISRAEL Index (.TRXFLDILP)	1.36%	0.78%	−19.68%	−16.88%	26.93%	−13.43%
UK	FTSE 100 Index (.FTSE)	−0.78%	−1.06%	−19.50%	−14.76%	16.08%	−21.81%
New Zeeland	S&P/NZX 50 INDEX (.NZ50)	1.61%	3.40%	−9.74%	−13.24%	24.04%	2.05%
Norway	OSLO SE ALL-SHARE INDEX (.OSEAX)	−0.57%	−0.02%	−21.68%	−14.52%	31.25%	−12.64%
Singapore	FTSE STRAITS TIMES INDEX (.STI)	−1.25%	−0.05%	−10.96%	−14.37%	4.30%	−21.50%
Switzerland	SWISS MARKET INDEX (.SSMI)	2.29%	2.31%	−17.23%	−9.32%	19.99%	−5.76%
Japan	TOPIX STOCK PRICE INDEX (.TOPX)	−1.24%	−1.53%	−15.97%	−9.66%	17.72%	−13.09%
USA	S&P 500 (.SPX)	1.32%	1.97%	−13.65%	−16.80%	36.40%	1.25%
Austria	AUSTRIAN TRADED INDEX (.ATX)	−1.68%	0.51%	−25.02%	−30.94%	30.21%	−33.37%
Belgium	BEL 20 INDEX (.BFX)	0.23%	2.86%	−22.63%	−18.36%	27.06%	−17.25%
Denmark	OMX COPENHAGEN 20 INDEX (.OMXC20)	4.60%	5.38%	−14.55%	−10.55%	34.52%	13.33%
Finland	OMX HELSINKI 25 INDEX (.OMXH25)	2.21%	3.58%	−20.89%	−17.83%	40.37%	−3.39%
France	CAC 40 Index (.FCHI)	−0.39%	1.26%	−23.10%	−19.02%	27.40%	−19.98%
Germany	DAX Index (.GDAXI)	0.72%	1.76%	−22.86%	−19.41%	45.86%	−7.06%
IBEX	IBEX TOTAL RETURN (.IBEXTR)	0.27%	3.58%	−24.53%	−15.90%	11.88%	−26.25%
Ireland	ISEQ OVERALL PRICE INDEX (.ISEQ)	−0.20%	0.99%	−19.52%	−25.06%	39.69%	−15.09%
Italy	FTSE MIB Index (.FTMIB)	2.80%	2.52%	−27.86%	−15.39%	26.27%	−18.78%
Netherlands	AMSTERDAM EXCHANGES INDEX (.AEX)	0.11%	2.00%	−21.48%	−16.63%	34.94%	−9.81%
Portugal	PSI ALL SHARE GROSS RETURN Index (.BVLG)	3.48%	5.74%	−19.94%	−13.73%	23.90%	−6.36%
Sweeden	OMX STOCKHOLM_PI (.OMXSPI)	1.87%	4.62%	−18.73%	−17.06%	37.72%	−1.06%
Median Values		0.72%	1.89%	−19.52%	−16.61%	27.06%	−12.64%
EU		1.17%	2.90%	−21.76%	−18.32%	31.65%	−12.09%
Non-EU		0.63%	0.89%	−15.31%	−14.54%	22.24%	−10.38%
Average Correlation		0.294	0.546	0.791	0.748	0.642	0.711
(b) Standard Deviation							
Australia	S&P/ASX 200 (.AXJO)	0.77%	0.53%	2.59%	6.46%	2.08%	2.29%
Canada	Toronto Stock Exchange (.GSPTSE)	0.29%	0.49%	3.39%	8.34%	2.13%	2.62%
Hong Kong	Hang Seng Index (.HSI)	1.25%	1.19%	1.80%	2.11%	1.79%	1.73%
Israel	THOMSON REUTERS ISRAEL Index (.TRXFLDILP)	0.62%	1.42%	2.52%	3.67%	1.99%	2.07%
UK	FTSE 100 Index (.FTSE)	0.75%	0.83%	2.69%	5.07%	2.08%	2.18%
New Zeeland	S&P/NZX 50 INDEX (.NZ50)	0.53%	0.69%	1.59%	2.43%	1.69%	1.61%
Norway	OSLO SE ALL-SHARE INDEX (.OSEAX)	0.74%	0.91%	3.30%	4.59%	1.83%	2.11%

(Continued)

Table 2. (Continued).

Country	Index	Period 1	Period 2	Period 3	Period 4	Period 5	Whole Period
Singapore	FTSE STRAITS TIMES INDEX (.STI)	0.64%	0.89%	2.06%	1.61%	1.96%	1.81%
Switzerland	SWISS MARKET INDEX (.SSMI)	0.65%	0.79%	2.44%	4.40%	1.67%	1.82%
Japan	TOPIX STOCK PRICE INDEX (.TOPX)	0.94%	0.91%	2.22%	2.79%	1.65%	1.70%
USA	S&P 500 (.SPX)	0.65%	0.82%	3.91%	8.52%	2.18%	2.69%
Austria	AUSTRIAN TRADED INDEX (.ATX)	0.68%	0.91%	2.64%	5.64%	2.54%	2.77%
Belgium	BEL 20 INDEX (.BFX)	0.84%	1.05%	2.76%	6.32%	2.31%	2.50%
Denmark	OMX COPENHAGEN 20 INDEX (.OMXC20)	0.98%	1.01%	2.30%	3.19%	1.29%	1.55%
Finland	OMX HELSINKI 25 INDEX (.OMXH25)	0.90%	0.91%	2.41%	4.07%	2.05%	2.16%
France	CAC 40 Index (.FCHI)	0.81%	0.84%	2.76%	5.75%	2.23%	2.40%
Germany	DAX Index (.GDAXI)	0.97%	0.94%	2.57%	5.39%	2.36%	2.48%
IBEX	IBEX TOTAL RETURN (.IBEXTR)	0.78%	0.88%	2.63%	7.57%	2.13%	2.47%
Ireland	ISEQ OVERALL PRICE INDEX (.ISEQ)	0.83%	0.87%	2.33%	4.46%	2.19%	2.33%
Italy	FTSE MIB Index (.FTMIB)	1.03%	1.17%	3.37%	8.31%	2.06%	2.64%
Netherlands	AMSTERDAM EXCHANGES INDEX (.AEX)	0.82%	0.98%	2.69%	4.58%	1.98%	2.15%
Portugal	PSI ALL SHARE GROSS RETURN Index (.BVLG)	0.63%	0.60%	3.06%	5.54%	1.62%	1.99%
Sweeden	OMX STOCKHOLM_PI (.OMXSPI)	0.92%	0.81%	2.26%	4.77%	2.02%	2.15%
Median Values		0.78%	0.89%	2.59%	4.77%	2.05%	2.16%
EU		0.85%	0.92%	2.65%	5.47%	2.07%	2.30%
Non-EU		0.71%	0.86%	2.59%	4.54%	1.91%	2.06%

$$Cumulative\ Returns\ per\ period = \left[\prod_{i=1}^{N}(1+r_i)\right] - 1 \tag{2}$$

where r_i = the daily return of the stock index in day i, and i=1,2, . . ., N the first day of the period up to the last one, and

$$Standard\ Deviation\ per\ period = \sqrt{\frac{\sum_{i=1}^{N}\left(r_i - r_{average}\right)^2}{N-1}} \tag{3}$$

where $r_{average}$ = the mean return during the examined period.

Table 2 shows the cumulative returns per period, and the shaded cells the negative returns periods, while Table 2 shows the standard deviations per examined sub-period. Let us look at these periods more closely:

(i) Period 1. As we have already presented, in the globalized world, with thousands of flights per day, the virus can travel far and fast; yet, the statistics show a normal January for the stock markets (most countries present positive returns, and not high standard deviations). Was this rational? EMH supporters may argue that during this period there is no official warning about widespread of COVID-19 outside China; therefore, the performance of the stock markets could be characterized rational.

(ii) Period 2. After the PHEIC announcement, the stock markets have now information through official channels that the health risk has significantly increased, and according to the respective financial literature sooner or later it will turn to economic/financial risk. Surprisingly, most indices present positive returns, and slightly increased standard deviation relative to period 1. Was it rational to underestimate the health risk when up to 21.02.2020 most of the countries had not taken strict measures in order to reduce the virus spread?

(iii) Period 3. COVID-19 has spread to many countries, and after a delay, the stock indices present a sharp decline and increased standard deviations (Table 2) for the respective period, which is an indication that the stock markets have incorporated the health risk in their prices.

(iv) Period 4. The financial markets continue the sharp decline for some days, which is logical: COVID-19 cases and the death toll rise rapidly and many countries have adopted social distancing and lockdown measures that significantly reduce the economic activity. The health risk turns to economic and financial risk.

(v) Period 5. After the sharp decline comes a period of significant growth. However, the reason for this growth period is not that the COVID-19 issue has been resolved. Thousands of new COVID-19 cases and deaths are documented worldwide per day during this period. The financial relief programs could be an explanation for a growth period, but the COVID-19 risk still threatens peoples' lives and the economies. A growth period amid a raging pandemic and a devastating mounting death toll is not in line with the studies that present a negative relationship between stock market performance and the number of COVID-19 deaths and cases (Al-Awadhi et al. 2020; Ali, Alam, and Rizvi 2020). Therefore, is the growth that some stock markets presented during the outbreak rational?[17] Even if the growth period is rational, is the rapid growth period rational also?

In the last lines of Table 2, we divide the sample into two sub-groups; EU and non-EU countries, and we present the average returns and standard deviations per group and per examined period. During the decline periods (periods 3 and 4) EU stock markets suffered more losses than the non-EU countries, but during the growth periods, 1, 2, and 5, EU countries presented greater returns. Could this be linked to the impact of COVID-19 on specific areas? For example, the non-EU group includes Asian countries in which COVID-19 appeared first, and this could be an explanation for the differences during periods 1 and 2. Similarly, during periods 3 and 4, COVID-19 spreads to the rest of the world and the delay of the EU countries to incorporate the health risk leads to the sharper decline of the EU indices relative to the non-EU indices.

Is it the spread of the pandemic the only factor that could explain the almost 2%, on average, greater losses that the EU indices suffered relative to the non-EU countries during the entire examined period? Could the timely/delayed responses of the authorities of each country, e.g. lockdown measures,[18] stimulus packages, etc., influence not only the impact of the pandemic but also the performance of the stock markets? How did the currencies of these developed countries perform during the COVID-19 outbreak? These issues could be the main objective of future research.

Moreover, another issue for the further study could be the correlation of the indices performance during the COVID-19 outbreak. The last line of Table 2 shows the average value of the correlations of the examined indices.[19] The results show that during crises periods, periods 3 and 4, the correlation is increased. This is an indication that health risk is a systemic risk and shows that when the health crisis spread all the stock markets fell.

Finally, as we show in this study, there are some periods, e.g. period 2, during which the empirical evidence deviates from the theory, i.e. that the increased health risk increases risk aversion and leads to market decline, but eventually, the financial theory is confirmed, e.g. in period 3. These contrarian evidence shows that the early COVID-19 studies may be subject to some limitations because the pandemic is still here. For example, 7 months after the first announcement regarding COVID-19 we can say that there was a delay in incorporating the health risk. Can we say that the theory is questioned during period 5 (rapid growth) or is there another factor, such as the stimulus packages, that drives the markets? We can reach definitive and more detailed conclusions when the pandemic period ends and when more data will be available. However, some early findings such as the irrationality of market performance during some periods of the COVID-19 outbreak can be used to draw initial conclusions.

4. Discussion and conclusions

This note shows how the stock markets responded to the news regarding the COVID-19 outbreak. The results show that stock markets initially performed as in a normal period (period 1), which means that nothing worrying was expected from the COVID-19 news. Such a response may be characterized as rational by an EMH supporter who may suggest that there was no official report for significant spread worldwide, which is a logical explanation.

Can we say that the performance of the stock markets was rational during Period 2? The PHEIC has already been announced, yet stock markets present a performance which is similar to the one in Period 1. Even after the PHEIC, most countries did not take any restriction measures, e.g. social distance measures, lockdowns, travel restrictions, to contain the spread of the highly contagious virus and millions of passengers per day were allowed to travel worldwide. Is it rational that most indices present positive returns for the period 30.01.2020–21.02.2020? An explanation for this unexpected behavior could be that it can be difficult for rational traders to undo the dislocations caused by less rational traders (Barberis and Thaler 2003).

Therefore, these results do not confirm that prices 'fully reflect' all the available information at any point in time: the data up to 21.02.2020 show a normal period and that nothing worrying is coming (positive returns, and no significantly high standard deviations). Thus, either the health risk, due to the PHEIC, and the possibility of a pandemic do not influence the markets' performance or the markets are inefficient and failed to incorporate the available information.

Period 3 indicates that although there is a delay in the response of the markets, the health risk does eventually influence the performance of the stock market: when the news shows that COVID-19 has spread to many countries, including some countries where there are already too many cases (e.g. the Italian report on 22.02.2020), the stock markets start a sharp decline (period 3, the PHEIC has been announced); an additional sharp decline period is documented when COVID-19 was declared a pandemic (period 4). Therefore, periods 3 and 4 confirm the assumption that '... stock prices overreact to firm-specific information, but react with a delay to common factors' (Jegadeesh and Titman 1995).

The rapid growth during period 5, which as explained seems to incorporate the benefits of the relief programs, but underestimate the fact that COVID-19 still threatens humanity, may be linked to the overreaction hypothesis because investors '... tend to overweight recent information and underweight prior (or base rate) data' (De Bondt and Thaler 1985). COVID-19 has not disappeared, so is this rapid growth period rational? It is worth mentioning that volatility is unexpectedly high for a rapid growth period. Particularly, periods 3 and 5 have on average similar standard deviations (2.67% in period 3 and 2.20% in period 5), but opposite performance (average returns −18.77% and +27% for period 3 and 5, respectively). These results are in contrast to the leverage effect, which is the tendency of the stock prices to present higher volatility during large price falls than the respective volatility during growth periods. Should we reexamine the risk–return relationship and consider alternative viewpoints? Could volatility during Period 5 be attributed to controversial perceptions regarding the influence of relief programs versus the COVID-19 threat? The pandemic gives us the opportunity to examine how the market reacts when the money supply significantly increases.[20]

The aforementioned is not the only lesson we can study from COVID-19. Some ideas for future research are the following:

- Important studies regarding information asymmetry and capital markets (Healy and Palepu 2001) have already been published. Reduced information asymmetry leads to lower risk periods and price dispersion (Grover, Lim, and Ayyagari 2006), increases the market efficiency (Wittenberg-Moerman 2008) and this way contributes to a more stable financial environment. The recent health crisis may give us additional insight regarding inside information that involves broad social system topics, such as public health, i.e. authorities and government officials have prior knowledge regarding the public health issues and may take advantage of non-public information. Scholars and regulators may find it useful to examine whether or not

information regarding public health issues should be announced publicly in an effort to avoid information asymmetries.
- The relief programs may be considered as a positive measure for the reduction of the economic impact of the pandemic, but the increased money supply may lead to an increase in inflation. According to financial theory, inflation influences the stock market prices either negatively (Fama and Schwert 1977) or positively at long periods (Boudoukh and Richardson 1993). The COVID-19 pandemic together with the increased money supply gives financial economists the opportunity to examine the specific inflation-market performance relationship using real data.
- Health policy issues regarding how we could avoid or reduce the impact of a next pandemic, e.g. in the recent health crisis, significant shortages of personal protective equipment (PPE) were observed even among healthcare workers (Ranney, Griffeth, and Jha 2020).[21] Authorities and scholars should examine ways to ensure adequate PPE and other equipment in the future and agree on health policies which will protect citizens and limit the spread when a new pandemic breaks out.
- The recent pandemic gives us the opportunity, using real data, to examine the behavior of the investors under a stress health period (Decker and Schmitz 2016), and/or the macroeconomic impact of a pandemic (Keogh-Brown et al. 2010).
- Most studies test market efficiency under the assumption of the random walk hypothesis, and/or using runs tests, variance ratio tests (Worthington and Higgs 2004; Borges 2010). Even if the performance of the stock market is random, e.g. in the second period, does it mean that it is rational and efficient? The financial markets sooner or later may incorporate the news; however, as we present, during the COVID-19 outbreak the stock markets did not always incorporate the available information at any point in time, e.g. period 2. Therefore, the 'at any point in time' that is mentioned in Fama (1970) may not always be true. How can we test efficiency in short-term periods? Do we need a new approach?[22]

The COVID-19 outbreak gives us the opportunity to test what is missing from the asset pricing models in order to understand how the world of financial markets work, how the investors respond to significant crisis periods, and how we might build more accurate models.

Notes

1. As they are classified by the MSCI https://www.msci.com/market-classification.
2. https://www.who.int/csr/don/12-january-2020-novel-coronavirus-china/en/.
3. The term Public Health Emergency of International Concern is defined in the International Health Regulations as 'an extraordinary event which is determined, as provided in these Regulations: (i) to constitute a public health risk to other States through the international spread of disease; and (ii) to potentially require a coordinated international response'. This definition implies a situation that: is serious, unusual or unexpected; carries implications for public health beyond the affected State's national border; and may require immediate international action.(source: https://www.who.int/ihr/procedures/pheic/en/).
4. https://www.who.int/emergencies/diseases/novel-coronavirus-2019/technical-guidance/naming-the-coronavirus-disease-(covid-2019)-and-the-virus-that-causes-it.

5. https://www.ecdc.europa.eu/en/publications-data/outbreak-novel-coronavirus-disease-2019-covid-19-situation-italy.
6. https://www.nytimes.com/2020/02/25/health/coronavirus-us.html.
7. https://www.who.int/news-room/detail/29-06-2020-covidtimeline.
8. https://en.wikipedia.org/wiki/Template:COVID-19_pandemic_lockdowns.
9. https://abcnews.go.com/Business/futures-us-financial-markets-spike-overnight-hit-limit/story?id=69765921.
10. https://www.consilium.europa.eu/en/meetings/european-council/2020/07/17-21/.
11. https://www.flightradar24.com/data/statistics.
12. https://www.who.int/news-room/q-a-detail/q-a-coronaviruses.
13. https://www.who.int/news-room/feature-stories/detail/who-delivers-advice-and-support-for-older-people-during-covid-19#:~:text=The%20COVID%2D19%20pandemic,potential%20underlying%20health%20conditions.
14. https://data.worldbank.org/indicator/SP.POP.65UP.TO.ZS.
15. https://regulatorystudies.columbian.gwu.edu/regulatory-policy-uncertainty-under-covid-19.
16. A rational evaluation could be the following: when the health risk increases, the chances of adopting lockdown and social distancing measures also increase; and if such a scenario is confirmed, economic activity and corporate profits fall, while the growth expectations are revised downward. All these lead to increased risk and reduced stock prices.
17. e.g. the DAX index presents more than 45% growth, and many other indices, such as the S&P500, CAC40, Toronto, ISEQ etc., present more than a 30% increase.
18. A very good source for the specific issue regarding the lockdown measures worldwide is https://www.bbc.co.uk/news/world-52103747.
19. Correlation (ρ) between two indices, A and B, is estimated by the formula

$$\rho_{A,B} = \frac{\sum_{i=1}^{n}\left(r_{Ai}-\overline{r_A}\right)\times\left(r_{Bi}-\overline{r_B}\right)}{\sqrt{\sum_{i=1}^{n}\left(r_{Ai}-\overline{r_A}\right)^2\times\left(r_{Bi}-\overline{r_B}\right)^2}}$$

where r_{Ai} and r_{Bi} is the daily return of the index A and B, respectively, on day i = 1,2, . . ., n, and $\overline{r_A} and \overline{r_B}$ is the average return of the index A and B during the examined period.The average correlation ($\bar{\rho}$) during each examined period is the average value of all the pairs of the correlations of our sample.
20. Vasileiou (2020a) examines the case of the US stock market and shows that during the COVID-19 period the stock market is not efficient.
21. Additional news https://healthmanagement.org/c/hospital/news/medical-equipment-deficit-and-provision-during-pandemic, https://www.who.int/news-room/detail/03-03-2020-shortage-of-personal-protective-equipment-endangering-health-workers-worldwide, https://www.washingtonpost.com/health/2020/07/08/ppe-shortage-masks-gloves-gowns/.
22. e.g. Vasileiou (2020b) presents a quantum mechanics view of EMH.

Acknowledgments

We would like to thank the anonymous reviewer(s) for the excellent comments that significantly improved our paper.

Disclosure statement

No potential conflict of interest was reported by the author(s).

References

Al-Awadhi, A. M., K. Al-Saifi, A. Al-Awadhi, and S. Alhamadi. 2020. "Death and Contagious Infectious Diseases: Impact of the COVID-19 Virus on Stock Market Returns." *Journal of Behavioral and Experimental Finance*: 100326. doi:10.1016/j.jbef.2020.100326.

Ali, M., N. Alam, and S. A. R. Rizvi. 2020. "Coronavirus (COVID-19)–An Epidemic or Pandemic for Financial Markets." *Journal of Behavioral and Experimental Finance*: 100341. doi:10.1016/j.jbef.2020.100341.

Antonakakis, N., I. Chatziantoniou, and G. Filis. 2013. "Dynamic Co-movements of Stock Market Returns, Implied Volatility and Policy Uncertainty." *Economics Letters* 120 (1): 87–92. doi:10.1016/j.econlet.2013.04.004.

Baker, S. R., N. Bloom, and S. J. Davis. 2016. "Measuring Economic Policy Uncertainty." *The Quarterly Journal of Economics* 131 (4): 1593–1636. doi:10.1093/qje/qjw024.

Barberis, N., and R. Thaler. 2003. "A Survey of Behavioral Finance." Chap. 18 In *Handbook of the Economics of Finance*. 1 Part B vols. edited by G. M. Constantinides, M. Harris, and R. M. Stulz, Vol 1, Part B, 1053–1128. North Holland, Amsterdam: Elsevier. doi:10.1016/S1574-0102(03)01027-6.

Borges, M. R. 2010. "Efficient Market Hypothesis in European Stock Markets." *The European Journal of Finance* 16 (7): 711–726. doi:10.1080/1351847X.2010.495477.

Boudoukh, J., and M. Richardson. 1993. "Stock Returns and Inflation: A Long-horizon Perspective." *The American Economic Review* 83 (5): 1346–1355. https://www.jstor.org/stable/2117566

De Bondt, W. F., and R. Thaler. 1985. "Does the Stock Market Overreact?" *The Journal of Finance* 40 (3): 793–805. doi:10.1111/j.1540-6261.1985.tb05004.x.

Decker, S., and H. Schmitz. 2016. "Health Shocks and Risk Aversion." *Journal of Health Economics* 50: 156–170. doi:10.1016/j.jhealeco.2016.09.006.

Fama, E. F. 1970. "Efficient Capital Markets: A Review of Theory and Empirical Work." *The Journal of Finance* 25 (2): 383–417. https://www.jstor.org/stable/2325486

Fama, E. F., and G. W. Schwert. 1977. "Asset Returns and Inflation." *Journal of Financial Economics* 5 (2): 115–146. doi:10.1016/0304-405X(77)90014-9.

Goodell, J. W. 2020. "COVID-19 and Finance: Agendas for Future Research." *Finance Research Letters*: 101512. doi:10.1016/j.frl.2020.101512.

Grover, V., J. Lim, and R. Ayyagari. 2006. "The Dark Side of Information and Market Efficiency in E-markets." *Decision Sciences* 37 (3): 297–324. doi:10.1111/j.1540-5414.2006.00129.x.

Haacker, M. 2004. "The Impact of HIV/AIDS on Government Finance and Public Services." Chap. 7 In *The Macroeconomics of HIV/AIDS*. USA: International Monetary Fund. doi:10.5089/9781589063600.071.

Healy, P. M., and K. G. Palepu. 2001. "Information Asymmetry, Corporate Disclosure, and the Capital Markets: A Review of the Empirical Disclosure Literature." *Journal of Accounting and Economics* 31 (1–3): 405–440. doi:10.1016/S0165-4101(01)00018-0.

Jegadeesh, N., and S. Titman. 1995. "Overreaction, Delayed Reaction, and Contrarian Profits." *The Review of Financial Studies* 8 (4): 973–993. doi:10.1093/rfs/8.4.973.

Keogh-Brown, M. R., and R. D. Smith. 2008. "The Economic Impact of SARS: How Does the Reality Match the Predictions?" *Health Policy* 88 (1): 110–120. doi:10.1016/j.healthpol.2008.03.003.

Keogh-Brown, M. R., S. Wren-Lewis, W. J. Edmunds, P. Beutels, and R. D. Smith. 2010. "The Possible Macroeconomic Impact on the UK of an Influenza Pandemic." *Health Economics* 19 (11): 1345–1360. doi:10.1002/hec.1554.

Ranney, M. L., V. Griffeth, and A. K. Jha. 2020. "Critical Supply Shortages—The Need for Ventilators and Personal Protective Equipment during the COVID-19 Pandemic." *New England Journal of Medicine* 382 (18): e41. https://www.nejm.org/doi/full/10.1056/NEJMp2006141

Smith, R. D., M. Yago, M. Millar, and J. Coast. 2005. "Assessing the Macroeconomic Impact of a Healthcare Problem: The Application of Computable General Equilibrium Analysis to Antimicrobial Resistance." *Journal of Health Economics* 24 (6): 1055–1075. doi:10.1016/j.jhealeco.2005.02.003.

Vasileiou, E. 2020a. "Efficient Markets Hypothesis in the Time of COVID-19." *Forthcoming in Review of Economic Analysis.* https://openjournals.uwaterloo.ca/index.php/rofea/article/view/1799/2125

Vasileiou, E. 2020b. "Are Markets Efficient? A Quantum Mechanics View." *Journal of Behavioral Finance*: 1–7. doi:10.1080/15427560.2020.1772260.

Wittenberg-Moerman, R. 2008. "The Role of Information Asymmetry and Financial Reporting Quality in Debt Trading: Evidence from the Secondary Loan Market." *Journal of Accounting and Economics* 46 (2–3): 240–260. doi:10.1016/j.jacceco.2008.08.001.

Worthington, A., and H. Higgs. 2004. "Random Walks and Market Efficiency in European Equity Markets." *The Global Journal of Finance and Economics* 1 (1): 59–78. https://eprints.qut.edu.au/2319/1/2319.pdf

Behavioral finance and market efficiency in the time of the COVID-19 pandemic: does fear drive the market?

Evangelos Vasileiou

ABSTRACT

In this study, we examine the efficiency of the US stock markets during the COVID-19 outbreak using a fundamental financial analysis approach, the constant growth model and a behavioral model including a Google-based Index. We juxtapose the released news and the performance of the US stock market during the COVID-19 outbreak and we show that during some periods the health risk was significantly underestimated and/or ignored. The Efficient Market Hypothesis (EMH) suggests that prices incorporate all the available information at any point in time, yet as we show a systemic factor, the health risk, was not always rationally incorporated in stock prices. The Runs-tests confirm our assumption that the market was not efficient during the examined period. The reason for this inefficiency could be that something is missing from traditional finance models, such as the impact of fear of COVID-19. For this reason we employ a Coronavirus Fear Index (CFI) based on Google searches and using Granger causality we provide empirical evidence that the fear drives the S&P500 performance, and using a GARCH model we show that the fear negatively influences the performance of the US stock market.

1. Introduction

There are many studies in the financial literature regarding how – and how fast – the markets react to: a stock split (Fama et al. 1969), inflation (Schwert 1981), accounting information (Brennan 1991) etc. Moreover, there is a significant body of literature regarding market overreaction (De Bondt and Thaler 1985; Baytas and Cakici 1999) and financial contagion (Allen and Gale 2000; Claessens and Forbes 2013). However, there are not many empirical studies that examine the reactions of the stock markets when pandemics break out.[1]

This study endeavors to contribute to existing financial literature by examining the behavior of the financial markets during global health stress periods such as the current period we live in. A brief timeline of the pandemic follows. In late December 2019, a new virus, Novel Coronavirus (2019-nCoV), emerged. The virus causes a deadly disease, the Coronavirus Disease (COVID-19), and quickly spread worldwide. On 11 March 2020, this new disease was declared a pandemic threatening millions of lives worldwide. The world did not have recent experience in the last decades of a pandemic that influences the economic and social life to the extent that COVID-19 has. Therefore, it is not only the coronavirus that is novel, but this level of economic disruption is also unprecedented.[2] In this study, we examine the response of the world's highest capitalized stock market when new stress conditions emerge.

Before we present our assumptions regarding efficiency, we should mention some characteristics regarding the new virus and its impact on the economy. According to World Health Organization (WHO)[3]: '*The disease can spread from person to person through small droplets from the nose or mouth which are spread when a person with COVID-19 coughs or exhales. . . . . This is why it is important to stay more than 1 meter (3 feet) away from a person who is sick.*' Why would a pandemic, such as the COVID-19, be a huge risk for the global economy[4]?

If such a disease is not contained before it spreads, it will cause many people to get ill because people do not always keep 1 meter apart from each other in their workplaces and in their social life. This, in turn, will stress the healthcare system, and lead to a large number of deaths. A way to reduce the impact of COVID-19 is to adopt social distancing measures,[5] together with area lockdowns. Under these circumstances, economic activity will significantly decline, and the expected returns and growth expectations of the companies will be revised downward. As a result, stock prices should fall.

This study juxtaposes the released information regarding the COVID-19 outbreak and market performance. The main objective is to examine if we should focus on the efficiency of the financial markets, or if we should include in academic discussions the rationality and/or predictability of the behavior of the stock prices. R. Thaler in a very interesting discussion with E. Fama regarding the Efficient Markets Hypothesis (EMH) and behavioral finance says: 'The distinction I make is whether the behavior is predictable for a rational model[6,7]'. This is a point on which both prominent scholars agreed, and a point on which this study is focused.

According to the EMH, all the available information is incorporated in the stock prices at any point in time (Fama 1970); therefore, at any point in time the performance of the stock markets should follow the financial theory. If it does not, either the markets are not efficient, or the theory should be revised because something is missing. In order to provide empirical evidence to answer our questions, we test our assumptions using data from the U.S. stock market and particularly the S&P 500 stock index during the period 31.12.2019–31.10.2020 for at least two reasons: (i) it is the largest stock market of the world and it belongs to the developed stock markets, thus it would be expected to be efficient (Borges 2010), and (ii) the US is the country that experience the highest death tolls from COVID-19 worldwide.

We use a simple financial analysis theoretical framework in order to show the evaluation process of the stock market prices and the performance of the stock markets in specific periods during the COVID-19 outbreak. We test whether the market's response to the news always follows the rules of financial theory. Moreover, we applied econometric tests, runs-tests, to quantitatively show whether or not the US stock market is efficient. Finally, we provide empirical evidence that in the 2020 pandemic period some data that were initially considered as the most appropriate variables to explain the market's performance (COVID-19 cases) should be revised, and that a Google-based fear index we suggest in this study better explains the U.S. stock market's behavior during the examined period. The empirical evidence shows that this index incorporates a significant behavioral variable, i.e. the health fear, that is generally missing from EMH model. This means that a Google-Based Fear Index may contribute to building more accurate models and to understanding how the financial world works in periods of extreme health stress.

The rest of this paper goes as following: Section 2 presents the COVID-19 outbreak news and analyzes the theoretical framework, Section 3 shows what the data say, Section 4 econometrically tests the EMH. Section 5 shows that a fear index based on Google Searches could be a significant quantitative tool which shows that health risk drives the US stock market and that has negative impact on market's performance during the examined period. Finally, Section 6 concludes the study.

2. COVID-19 outbreak, health risk and price evaluation: a theoretical framework

COVID-19 started in December 2019 in the city of Wuhan in the Hubei providence in China and was officially reported as 'Pneumonia of unknown cause – China' by the WHO, on 31 December 2019.[8] The WHO reported on 9 January 2020 (amongst others)[9]: *'WHO does not recommend any specific measures for travelers. WHO advises against the application of any travel or trade restrictions on China based on the information currently available'*. On 23 January 2020, the Chinese authorities decided to lock down Wuhan, but at that time there were already confirmed cases not only in other Chinese provinces, but also in other countries.[10] On 30 January, the WHO declared the outbreak a Public Health Emergency of International Concern (PHEIC).[11] On 11 February 2020, WHO named the disease caused by the new virus COVID-19. On 24 February the White House requests 2.5 USD billion to deal with the coronavirus emergency (hereafter '2.5 b. request'),[12] and on 25 February the U.S. Centers for Disease Control and Prevention (CDC) warns of Coronavirus Outbreaks in the U.S.[13] On 11 March, WHO Director General Tedros Adhanom Ghebreyesus characterized COVID-19 as a pandemic.[14]

In a recent study, Vasileiou (2020) argues that the travel restrictions that were adopted for Wuhan on 23 January gave sufficient time for the virus to travel worldwide, given that there were more than 160 thousand flights per day around the world (and the US is one of the most popular destinations).[15] This means that travelers who were potentially carrying the virus – not only from China, but from other countries as well – could fly to the U.S.[16,17]. Moreover, if an easily transmitted virus, such as COVID-19, travels to an urbanized country, it can spread too fast within the community because people do not usually keep 1 or 2-m distance in buses, trains, malls etc. (Vasileiou et al. 2020). The U.S. urban population as percentage of the total population is 82.459%,[18] thus when the virus traveled to the US there were increased possibilities that it would spread within the community.

In the following paragraphs, we briefly show how investors evaluate asset prices. Figure 1 enables us to graphically present the evaluation process traditional finance. A rational investor prefers as high as possible returns at the lowest possible risk (which is measured by standard deviation). An investor examines several n-scenarios regarding each financial decision: from the best case (e.g. economic growth, technological innovations, and advances) to the worst-case scenario (e.g. a war), and several probabilities for

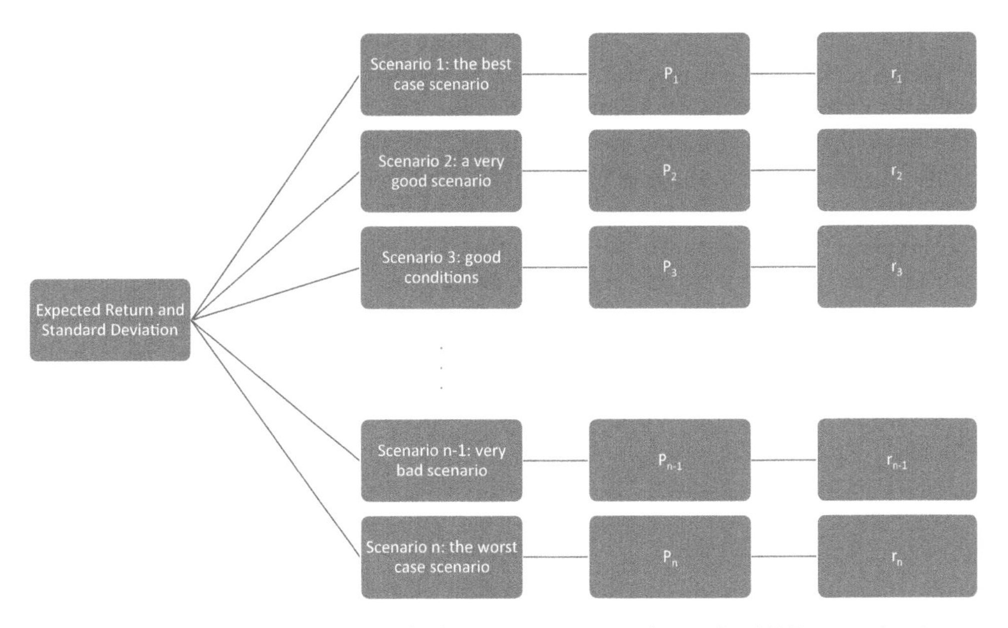

Figure 1. The expected return and standard deviation scenarios during the COVID-19 outbreak.

each scenario to be confirmed. The expected rates of return and the standard deviations for the scenario-based approach are estimated using the following formulas:

$$Expected\ Rate\ of\ Return = \hat{r} = \sum_{i=1}^{n} P_i \times r_i \tag{1}$$

where P_i = the probability of occurrence of some financial conditions that lead to a respective return r_i, i = the event/scenario 1, 2, . . ., n, and

$$StandardDeviation = \sigma = \sqrt{(r_i - \hat{r})^2 \times P_i} \tag{2}$$

Each investor has several scenarios and considers different possibilities for each scenario to play out in the real world. All the perceptions of the investors shape the behavior of the markets. When new information is released, the scenarios and their respective probabilities are revised and influence the market's performance $(\hat{r}, \sigma)$. If the investors (and by extension the stock market) did not consider the possibility of a negative scenario such as a pandemic, according to Equations (1) and (2), the expected returns are overestimated and the risk is underestimated.

When the news leads to conclusions which suggest that the possibility of COVID-19 becoming a pandemic is very likely, then the possibilities for a negative scenario are significantly increased, the expected returns are low, and the risk high. Such a scenario leads to lower stock investments turnover, probably because investors may choose other asset classes to invest in, such as bonds and time deposits, and stock prices decline. Depending on the released news, the probabilities of the examined scenarios to happen change and/or new scenarios may be included in the evaluation process.

In traditional finance, there is an additional, corporate finance approach that enables us to explain how a pandemic affects the market. During a pandemic, many people get sick, many people die, and the healthcare system struggles to cope with a surge in hospitalizations. A usual practice in order to contain the spread of the virus is to implement social distancing measures and lockdowns, which causes the economic activity to slow down (Almond and Mazumder 2005; Garrett 2008; Keogh-Brown et al. 2010). The slowdown of the economic activity leads a lot of businesses to reduce their production, which in turn leads to employee dismissals, income shrinkage and reduced consumption, and so forth. In this environment, companies have reduced profits, the growth expectations are revised negatively, and asset prices are reduced, because investors will require increased returns in order to participate in the stock market during a negative period. Moreover, the health risk increases the investors' risk aversion (Decker and Schmitz 2016), which is a behavioral influence on the market decline.

According to the popular Constant Growth Model (CGM, also known as Gordon Model),[19] the stock prices are estimated by the formula:

$$P = \frac{D_1}{r_{req} - g} \tag{3}$$

where P = is the value of the stock/index in our case,

D_1 = the value of the first dividend expected which has a positive influence on the stock/index price,

r_{req} = the required rate of return or the minimum acceptable compensation for the investors in order to bear the investment's real risk, which negatively influences the stock prices, and

g = the expected growth rate, which has a positive influence on the stock prices.

Therefore, stock prices will fall when a pandemic breaks out because

- The upcoming economic slowdown may reduce the dividends (D_1),
- The expected growth rate will be revised downward, and
- The required rate of return will increase because investors will demand higher compensation in order to invest in this risky environment (Guiso, Sapienza, and Zingales 2018), and because the health risk makes investors more risk averse (Decker and Schmitz 2016).

When COVID-19 is successfully contained and/or the virus is finally defeated, the financial risk associated with the disease will be reduced, and all these aforementioned factors will again influence the market but this time positively.

Either we adopt the scenario-based approach, or the corporate finance-based approach, when new information emerges, the basic measures that lead to the financial decisions, Equations (1)–(3), change, and these changes influence the asset prices. If we assume that investors are always rational and the asset pricing models are accurate, the stock markets will always incorporate all the available information in their prices. In such a case, the stock markets will be efficient. However, in a stress period like the COVID-19 pandemic, are all investors rational? And how is rationality defined?

The new information was available to all investors; however, the evaluation of this information may be different. For example, some investors may think that if the virus threatened countries around the world, US included, the authorities would have warned them. For this group of investors, a warning from the authorities is the significant information that should be incorporated into the evaluation process, e.g. PHEIC. However, there could be another group of investors who assume that in the contemporary environment with many flights per day globally, an easily transmitted virus could be anywhere, and who withdraw their investments, under the fear of a pandemic outbreak.[20] For the latter group of investors, the characteristics of the virus and the delayed measures by the authorities to contain the virus in Wuhan before it traveled to other places is the information. Which of these groups is the rational/irrational one? How does traditional financial theory incorporate fear and rationality?

Thus, certain behavioral factors should be taken into consideration because the rationality issue in this case may be too complex to analyze and measure using only traditional financial theory. What do behavioral studies suggest for market behavior during health stress periods? When the investors feel that their health is in danger, they have higher risk aversion, and this leads markets to decline (Decker and Schmitz 2016). Testing risk aversion during the pandemic period, Yue, Gizem Korkmaz, and Zhou (2020) reached similar conclusions providing empirical evidence that households who know someone infected with COVID-19 lose confidence in the economy and become risk-averse. These findings are consistent with the early studies that show a negative relationship between the number of COVID-19 cases and the performance of the financial markets (Al-Awadhi et al. 2020; Ali, Alam, and Rizvi 2020; Ashraf 2020). Subsequent studies provide useful information that Google searches and news coverage using terms related to the COVID-19 pandemic may incorporate significant fear sentiments (Chen, Liu, and Zhao 2020; Haroon and Rizvi 2020). In our study, we test if the number of cases or a Google-related index is a more appropriate indicator for the market's performance.

3. COVID-19 outbreak and S&P500 performance: what the data say

Taking into consideration the abovementioned, in order to evaluate the rationality and the efficiency of the US stock market we examine its performance during the following sub-periods:

- *1st sub-period: 02.01.2020–29.01.2020*: the day after the first notice by the Chinese authorities up to the day before the PHEIC declaration
- *2nd sub-period: 30.01.2020–21.02.2020*: after the PHEIC declaration and up to the day before the warning of the CDC for COVID-19 Outbreaks in the U.S.
- *3rd sub-period: 25.02.2020–10.03.2020*: from the CDC warning day and up to the day before the pandemic declaration
- *4th sub-period: 11.03.2020–30.10.2020*: the post-pandemic declaration.

Figure 2 graphically presents the performance of S&P500 during the examined period and its sub-periods using the following formulas:

$$Returns_t = \frac{S\&P500_i}{S\&P500_{i-t}} - 1 \tag{4}$$

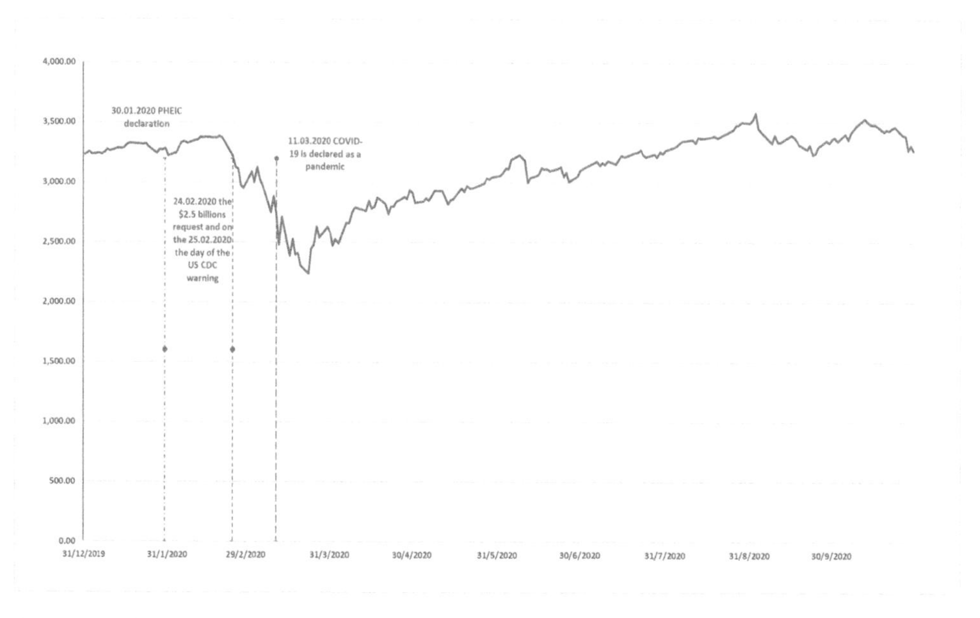

Figure 2. Performance of S&P 500 during 31.12.2019–30.10.2020.

where *i* is the Price of the Index in the current day, and t is the price of the index t days before, e.g. for the daily returns t = 1. The standard deviations for the respective sub-periods are given by the formula:

$$Standard\ Deviation\ per\ period = \sqrt{\frac{\sum_{i=1}^{N}\left(r_i - r_{average}\right)^2}{N-1}} \tag{5}$$

where $r_{average}$ = the mean return of the daily returns during the examined period.

Table 1 presents the returns and standard deviations during the examined sub-periods.

What the data say for each sub-period, and some comments

3.1. *1st sub-period*

From the end of 2019 up to the PHEIC declaration, the US stock market presents a growth of 1.32%, and 0.64% daily standard deviation. If anyone looks at Figure 2 and Table 1 for the 1st sub-period without having any information about a new easily transmitted virus, (s)he could assume that they refer to a normal period and that there is nothing to worry about.

Table 1. Risk returns during the COVID-19 outbreak.

Examined Period	1st sub-period 31/12/2019–29/1/2020	2nd sub-period 29/1/2020–21/2/2020	3rd sub-period 21/2/2020–10/3/2020	4th sub-period 10/3/2020–30/10/2020	Whole examined period 31/12/2019–30/10/2020
Returns	1.32%	1.97%	−13.65%	13.45%	1.21%
Daily Standard Deviation	0.64%	0.79%	3.75%	2.41%	2.35%

Therefore, during the first period the stock market either underestimates the news regarding the novel coronavirus, or they only accept news regarding the threat of virus when it is announced by public authorities. The EMH supporters may suggest that in the 1st sub-period the reaction is normal because there is no official report that something worrying is happening outside Asia.

3.2. 2nd sub-period

After the PHEIC announcement and up to the request for the 2.5 billion supplementary funds and the warnings by the CDC, the stock market presents a further growth of 1.97% and the daily standard deviation increases to 0.79%. Is there any explanation for the positive returns after a PHEIC declaration? The PHEIC is a clear message from officials that the health risk can no longer be ignored and following this declaration nobody can argue that the news regarding the disease is reassuring. Again, the stock market may have either not incorporated the PHEIC report in their evaluation or they may have underestimated it. Is this behavior rational and efficient?

In our opinion, the rationality and the efficiency of the markets during this period is at the very least debatable. For example, if the returns during the second sub-period were negative and the standard deviations significantly higher than the previous period, would such a performance be characterized as inefficient and irrational?

The same news, different possible outcomes: theoretically the news of increased health risk (PHEIC) should lead to negative returns, but reality shows positive returns. When the news is similar, the performance of the stock markets should not have significant deviations if we consider the market as efficient. Returns that are different than expected may mean that either the stock market significantly underestimated the health risk, or that the theory which assumes a positive relationship between health risk and risk aversion should be revised. If the stock market underestimated the health risk, was this behavior rational and expectable? Could something else, e.g. a health risk measurement, be missing from this framework? How could we measure the health risk?

3.3. 3rd sub-period

When the negative news of 24–25/2 was released, the stock market presented a sharp decline and a significantly increased standard deviation because confirmed cases and deaths due to COVID-19 started to emerge: period's return −13.65% and daily standard deviation 3.75%. These results demonstrate support for the theory: when the health risk increases, risk aversion increases, and the stock prices should fall. Therefore, since at least the PHEIC and up to this point, stock markets irrationally underestimated the health risk, until the 2.5 b. request and the CDC warnings precipitated the sharp decline. Could a rational model forecast when the markets will stop underestimating a crucial factor, such as the health risk?

3.4. 4th sub-period

The COVID-19 pandemic declaration on 11/3 led to further decline for a few days; however, the announcement of the stimulus pack on 24/3 contributed to the stabilization of the stock markets. The stock market during this sub-period presented 13.45% growth and 2.41% standard deviation. Is the rapid growth of the stock market rational during this period? The pandemic still threatens people's lives, and during this period the number of cases and deaths increase not only in the US, but worldwide also.

Therefore, during some periods, e.g. the 2nd and the 4th period, the stock markets present performance measures that are not consistent with a rational evaluation. Moreover, if we examine the first 10 months of the pandemic, the stock market present 1.21% growth, which is a performance that is usually associated with a normal period. Is this rational? Only the increased standard deviation, 2.35%, may lead us to the conclusion that the period was not normal. Does this mean that the markets are not efficient? Before we discuss in most detail the results, we need quantitative proof of market efficiency; thus, in the next section, we econometrically test the efficiency of the stock markets.

4. Statistical tests for the efficiency of the S&P 500 Index

In this section, we present the descriptive and econometric results of the S&P 500 daily returns during the period of the pandemic outbreak. Table 2 presents the descriptive statistics of our sample. The Jarque-Bera test shows that the returns are not normally distributed. This means that parametric tests are not appropriate for our sample.

According to the EMH, there are several tests that are presented in the financial literature and are used in order to examine the EMH[21]: serial correlation test (ACF test), runs test, unit root test (Kwiatkowski et al. 1992), multiple variance ratio test (Chow and Denning 1993), and the non-parametric variance ratio test using ranks and signs (Wright 2000). In our study, the sample is small and not normally distributed, therefore the runs-test is considered the most appropriate amongst the abovementioned (Islam, Watanapalachaikul, and Clark 2007).

In theory, when the markets are efficient, the positive and negative daily returns do not follow a specific pattern. The Runs test analyzes if a repeated consequence of positive (or negative) returns,[22] which is a run, is randomly generated. If the series is random, which is a basic assumption of the EMH, there is a specific number of runs that should be counted; otherwise, the time series is impacted by an underlying variable.[23] For a random time series, the expected number of runs should be on average (μ):

$$\mu = \frac{2 \times N_p \times N_n}{N} + 1 \tag{3}$$

and the expected deviation of the number of runs (σ) is

Table 2. Descriptive statistics of S&P500 daily returns.

	S&P 500 daily returns
Mean	0.033%
Median	0.274%
Maximum	9.383%
Minimum	−11.984%
Std. Dev.	2.346%
Skewness	−0.470
Kurtosis	9.475
Jarque-Bera	376.3473

*Indicates statistical significance at 1% confidence level.

$$\sigma = \sqrt{\frac{2 \times N_p \times N_n \times (2 \times N_p \times N_n - N)}{N^2 \times (N - 1)}} = \sqrt{\frac{(\mu - 1) \times (\mu - 2)}{\mathrm{N} - 1}} \quad (4)$$

where N_p = number of positive observations, N_n = number of negative observations, and $N = N_p + N_n$ the total number of observations. Therefore, the Z-statistic is

$$z = \frac{U - \mu}{\sigma} \quad (5)$$

where U = the number of runs.

What do all these equations mean? Table 3 presents the findings of the runs test. For the tested period, we have 211 observations with 90 negative and 121 positive observations. If this time series is randomly distributed, we expect that it will have on average 104.223 runs, with a standard deviation ±7.088. The sample shows that we have 124 runs, which does not fall within the expected number of runs confidence interval (104.223 ± 7.088), and this means that we cannot accept the randomness hypothesis (p-value 0.005 < 0.05).

The main conclusion we draw from this section is that the stock market was not efficient for a long period of the COVID-19 outbreak. Initially, the stock markets underestimated the health risk, sub-periods 1 and 2, but eventually incorporated it in period 3. The delay of the stock market reaction due to the COVID-19 health risk could be associated with the tendency of the stock markets to react with a delay to common factors (Jegadeesh and Titman 1995). Can we predict the exact time when the stock market stops under-evaluating a systemic factor, such as the health risk in our case, or is this difficult for a rational asset pricing model? When the stock markets do not incorporate rationally the available information, e.g. period 2, are they considered efficient or should Fama's (1970) 'at any point in time' be revised/reworded? As Fama mentions in the interview for the EMH[24] '... is a model, it is not completely true', so we can assume that for a period of time the markets may not be efficient. The next question regarding period 2 is after how many days of delay should the stock markets not be considered efficient? Theoretically, a 3-week delay is not a short period.

The EMH is widely critiqued, and there are behavioral and neuro finance approaches which show that the human brain can lead investors to non-rational decisions (Peterson 2007; Thaler and Sunstein 2009; Kahneman 2011; Sahi 2012). For example, in some cases humans may be over-optimistic about their abilities. In our case, U.S. authorities may have believed that the impact of COVID-19 on the US would not be severe, and/or that the strong US health system could respond to the COVID-19 outbreak, and for this reason

Table 3. The runs-test of S&P 500 daily returns during the examined period.

	Runs Test
Number of Runs	124
Expected Mean Number of Runs	104.223
Expected Standard Deviation Number of Runs	7.088
Number of Positive Observations	121
Number of Negative Observations	90
Runs Test Value (Z)	2.790
p-value	0.005

early protective measures were not taken. Investors and market analysts may have the same perceptions and as a result up to 24.02.2020 the health risk was underestimated.[25]

The rapid growth of the 4th sub-period could be explained by the conclusions of De Bondt and Thaler (1985) that investors tend to overweight recent information (stimulus pack) and underweight the previous (COVID-19 pandemic). Is the rapid growth period rational when the major issue of the sharp decline, COVID-19, still threatens peoples' health? Does this growth period mean that stock markets believe the stimulus package is enough for economic recovery because COVID-19 will be defeated soon by therapeutics and/or a vaccine? If there is a new wave of COVID-19 before health scientists find a solution, will this stimulus pack be enough, or will supplementary funds be needed? If new funds are needed, but not given, a new financial crisis period will come.

In our opinion, something is missing from traditional financial economics models because the traditional estimation process only includes economic variables. If we quantitatively capture the health risk/fear, we may be able to explain the seemingly irrational behavior of the aforementioned periods. Moreover, the fact that the runs test shows that the returns of the stock market were not randomly distributed implies that there may exist a crucial variable that is omitted from a rational evaluation.

5. Number of COVID-19 cases vs Google Based Fear Index: which is a better explanatory variable for market performance?

What is the crucial variable that may be missing? Certainly a variable that is linked to the health risk. However, if what is missing is obvious, could the real issue be a reliable measure of the health risk? The first studies that tried to explain what drives the financial markets during the COVID-19 period show that the number of COVID-19 deaths and cases have a negative influence on market performance (Al-Awadhi et al. 2020; Ali, Alam, and Rizvi 2020; Ashraf 2020). Ashraf (2020) provides empirical evidence that stock markets react more proactively to the growth in number of confirmed cases than to the growth in number of deaths. The number of cases could incorporate the expected losses in the economy, because the higher the COVID-19 cases, the lower the productivity and the fear of the investors, which leads to greater risk aversion. What do the data say for the examined period?

Figure 3 graphically shows the S&P500 performance and the number of new COVID-19 cases per day.[26] The graphical representation shows that after late-March the number of new COVID-19 cases significantly increase, and the stock market presents a growth period. The correlation of the S&P500 and the New COVD-19 Cases is 0.245 during our sample period; therefore, this measure could be useful in order to explain the performance of the stock markets during the early stages of the pandemic, but not in the longer term.

The stimulus packages may be a significant boost for economic recovery (Vasileiou 2020), but when the number of cases increases, the health risk and risk aversion also increase.[27] Therefore, the stimulus packages should have a positive influence on market prices and the increased number of COVID-19 cases should have a negative influence. Can the rapid growth of the 4th sub-period be explained? Could the assumption that risk aversion is linked to the number of cases not hold when a long health stress period is examined? This means that the number of cases may not be the appropriate measure to incorporate/represent the health risk.

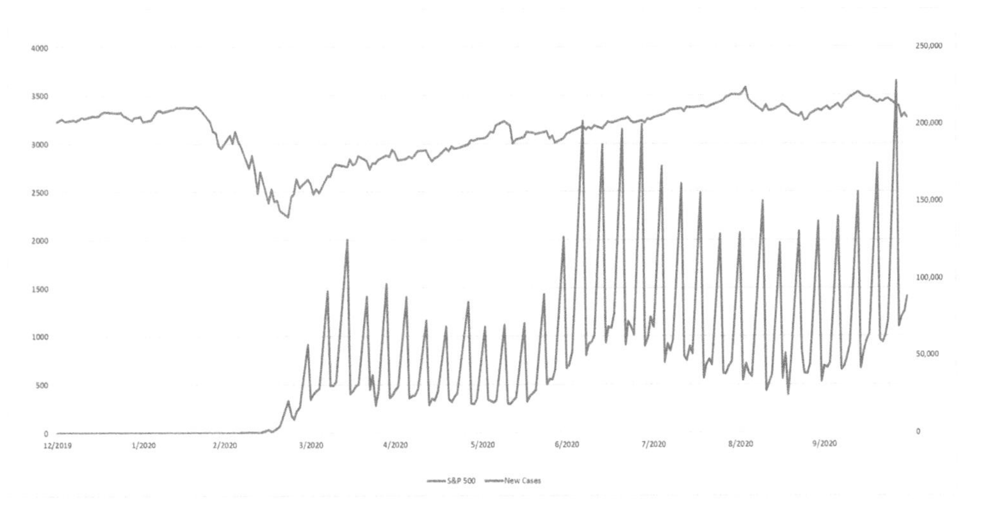

Figure 3. S&P 500 performance and number of new COVID-19 cases during the period 31.12.2019–30.10.2020.

In order to measure the health fear, we try to employ a Coronavirus Fear Index (CFI) based on the Google searches of the term 'Coronavirus.' The index has a 0–100 range. The higher the number of Google searches for the term 'Coronavirus,' the higher the fear of the US citizens regarding the pandemic, and the higher the value of the Index. The S&P500 performance and the CFI Index during the examined period are graphically presented in Figure 4 and the strong negative correlation, which is equal to –0.873, can be easily observed.

Therefore, comparing Figures 3 and Figures 4 and the respective correlations, we can assume that the CFI could better explain the S&P500 performance during the examined

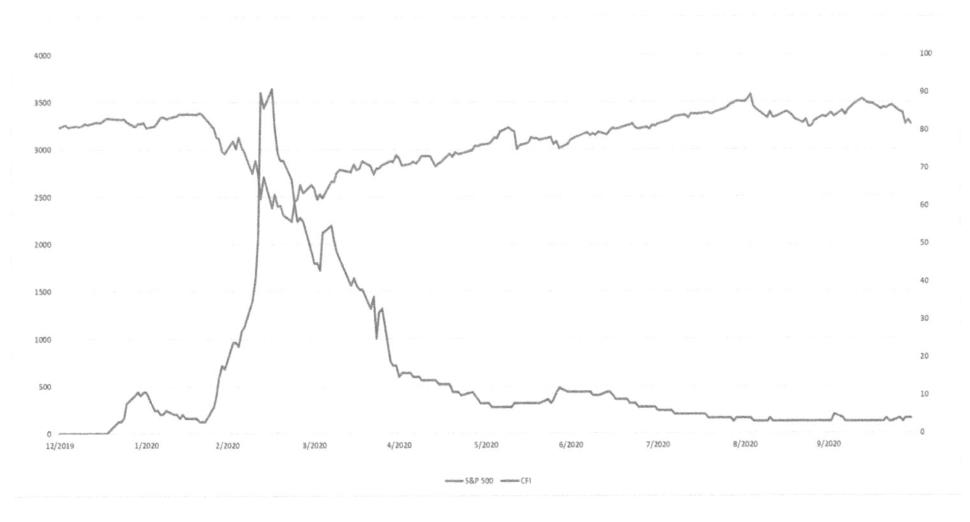

Figure 4. S&P 500 performance and Coronavirus Fear Index (CFI) during the period 31.12.2019–30.10.2020.

Table 4. Linear Granger causality.

Causality	F-Statistic	Prob.
CFI does not Granger Cause S&P500	5.1847	0.0064*
S&P500 does not Granger Cause CFI	0.05967	0.9421

Schwarz Information Criterion indicates that the optimal lag period is 2.

period. We further investigate this relationship, and we try to draw statistical conclusions for the causality of these variables, using the Granger causality test (Granger 1969)

$$S\&P500_t = c_0 + \sum_{i=1}^{n} c_{1i} S\&P500_{t-i} + \sum_{i=1}^{m} c_{2i} CFI_{t-i} + \varepsilon_{1t} \tag{4}$$

$$CFI_t = d_0 + \sum_{i=1}^{n} d_{1i} CFI_{t-i} + \sum_{i=1}^{m} d_{2i} S\&P500_{t-i} + \varepsilon_{2t}$$

where S&P500 is the S&P500 index price, and CFI is the Coronavirus Fear Index. In our case, the optimal lag length is 2 and is determined by the Schwarz Information Criterion (Shen, Urquhart, and Wang 2019). The Granger Causality test shows that there is unidirectional causality from CFI to S&P500, which indicates that the CFI is a significant driver of the S&P500 index price (Table 4).

Finally, in order to econometrically present our suggestion, we employ a GARCH (1,1) model which is usually applied in similar studies (Corbet, Larkin, and Lucey 2020). The model has the following mean equation

$$R_t = a_0 + b_1 \times dNC\_m_{t-1} + b_2 \times dCFI_{t-1} + \varepsilon_t \tag{5}$$

where dNC_m_{t-1} and $dCFI_{t-1}$is the growth of the number of New Cases (NC) and the Coronavirus Fear Index (CFI), because if the NC and the CFI grow this means that the pandemic is spreading within the community and that fear is increasing (and vice versa), and ε_t is the error term $\varepsilon_t \tilde{N}(0, \sigma_t)$.

For the variance equation of our model we use the following formula

$$\sigma_t^2 = \omega + \beta_1 \times \varepsilon_{t-1}^2 + \beta_2 \times \sigma_{t-1}^2 \tag{6}$$

where $\beta 1$ and $\beta 2$ are the coefficients of the ARCH (ε_{t-1}^2)and GARCH (σ_{t-1}^2) terms, respectively, and ω represents the long-term average value of volatility. The variance equation cannot be negative; therefore, the ω, β_1, and β_2 terms should be positive and the sum of the coefficients $\beta 1$, $\beta 2$ should be less than one to secure the covariance stationarity. Table 5 reports the results of the model and the ARCH-LM and the Q-statistics for the econometric validation of the model. The results show that the CFI has a strong, significant negative impact on the performance of the S&P500 stock market during the examined period, and that the variable of the NC does not have a significant impact. The model does not suffer from autocorrelation and ARCH-LM issues, and for the variance equation the coefficients are positive, and their sum is less than 1, which secures the covariance stationarity.

Table 5. Econometric analysis of S&P500.

Mean Equation	
	Coefficient
α_0	0.001443
α_1	1.29E-08
α_2	−0.002344*
Conditional Variance Equation	
ω	1.02E-05*
β_1	0.243212*
β_2	0.730640*
Q-statistics and ARCH LM Tests for the econometric validation	
Q1	2.5385
Q2	4.1842
LM_1	0.002261
(Prob. Chi-Square)	(0.9621)
LM_2	0.004718
(Prob. Chi-Square)	(0.9976)

*Denotes the statistical significance at the 1% confidence level.

6. Conclusions

This paper shows that the US stock market did not always react as the financial theory suggests during the period 31.12.2019–30.10.2020. For a long period of time, it seems to significantly underestimate (and/or ignore) the health risk associated with the COVID-19 outbreak. This means that the prices of the stock market do not always incorporate all the available information, which is in contrast to the EMH. In some periods, e.g. the 1st sub-period before the PHEIC announcement, EMH supporters may assume that the positive returns and the low standard deviation is rational behavior because no worrying news was confirmed by officials. However, can we say the same for the positive returns during the second sub-period when the PHEIC was announced but no stimulus packages were announced? We recall that during the second sub-period the stock market presents another 1.97% growth. Afterward, even with a delay the stock markets finally incorporated the health risk, and the stock prices fell. This is consistent with the stock markets' delayed reactions when systemic issues emerge (Jegadeesh and Titman 1995).

During the 3rd sub-period, up to the pandemic declaration, the stock market presents a sharp decline, which is rational behavior. However, when the stimulus package was announced, (24.03.2020) a rapid growth period followed that day, and the post-pandemic declaration period presents a 13.45% growth. Is this behavior rational? The number of COVID-19 cases and deaths increases, but the market seems to react as if COVID-19 has been defeated by a medicine and/or a vaccine. This behavior partly confirms the conclusions by De Bondt and Thaler (1985) that investors overweight the information that a stimulus pack will boost the economy, but they seem to underweight the previous information, that the COVID-19 pandemic which led to the financial crisis still exists.

Thus, the performance of the US stock market seems to ignore during some sub-periods the health risk. This means that it should not be efficient because stock prices do not always incorporate all the available information. Runs tests econometrically confirmed our assumption that the US stock market was not efficient during the examined period, which is an interesting and not expected outcome when we examine the world's largest stock market. We tried to find a measure that could enable us to examine this behavior.

The early studies show that the number of new COVID-19 cases is an appropriate measure to explain the market decline during the initial pandemic outbreak; however, the negative relationship was not confirmed when a longer period of time was tested. Therefore, this measure does not incorporate the fear index, so we employed a Coronavirus Fear Index (CFI) based on Google searches enables us to incorporate the health risk into financial markets analysis. The higher the number of Google searches using the term 'Coronavirus,' the higher the fear of the pandemic. Using a Granger causality procedure, we show that the CFI drives the stock market prices, and applying a GARCH (1,1) model, we provide empirical evidence that the CFI has a statistically significant negative impact on the stock market performance, while the new COVID-19 cases do not.

Concluding this study, we show that when extreme conditions emerge, economic variables alone may not be sufficient to explain the markets' behavior. Financial decisions do not always wait for the next official financial statements or the economic indicators to be announced. Behavioral factors, such as fear may be better indicators to explain investor decisions, and Google Searches may be a useful tool to quantitatively incorporate the behavioral influence on financial models and bridge the gap between behavioralists and EMH supporters. The findings show that fear of COVID-19 was at its highest level up to mid-March, and afterward it started to decline. The increase of fear explains the market decline, and the reduction of the fear index in combination with the stimulus package explains the rapid growth period. Possibly, a prolonged pandemic and a protracted period of health risk lead to a situation where citizens and investors are getting used to the idea of COVID-19. Further studies based on internet-based behavioral indicators, e.g. based on Google Searches, on Twitter, etc., may enable us to bridge the gap between behavioralists and the EMH supporters, and built more accurate models.

Notes

1. There are some studies which examine the economic and health impact of pandemics, Almond and Mazumder (2005), Garrett (2008) and Keogh-Brown et al. (2010) etc., but not the response of the stock markets during pandemic periods.
2. https://qz.com/1818061/robert-shiller-says-the-coronavirus-disruption-is-different-from-other-economic-crises/.
3. https://www.who.int/news-room/q-a-detail/q-a-coronaviruses.
4. Bill Gates has given a speech in which he describes a situation similar to the current https://www.youtube.com/watch?v=6Af6b_wyiwI.
5. The social distancing measures were also recommended by the WHO for SARS https://www.who.int/csr/resources/publications/CDS_CSR_ARO_2004_2.pdf.
6. The interview is available on https://www.youtube.com/watch?v=bM9bYOBuKF4&t=1879s, and the part we mentioned at 28:39–28:53.
7. Eugene Fama and Richard Thaler are distinguished professors and Nobel laureates. Fama E. is the father of the Efficient Market Hypothesis, and he was awarded the Nobel Prize in 2013 for his empirical analysis of asset prices. The impact of Eugene Fama's work has extended beyond the field of research, e.g. his results influenced the development of index funds. Thaler R. was awarded the Nobel Prize in 2017 for his contribution in behavioral economics. He has analyzed economic decision-making with the aid of insights from psychology. He has paid special attention to three psychological factors: the tendency not to behave completely rationally, notions of fairness and reasonableness, and lack of self-control. For a brief introduction into the work of these two distinguished professors, visit

https://www.nobelprize.org/prizes/economic-sciences/2013/fama/facts/, https://www.nobelprize.org/prizes/economic-sciences/2017/thaler/facts/. A conclusion regarding their approach: Thaler does not accept that markets are always efficient.
8. https://www.who.int/csr/don/05-january-2020-pneumonia-of-unkown-cause-china/en/.
9. https://www.who.int/china/news/detail/09-01-2020-who-statement-regarding-cluster-of-pneumonia-cases-in-wuhan-china.
10. https://www.bbc.com/news/world-asia-china-51217455.
11. https://www.who.int/westernpacific/emergencies/covid-19.
12. https://edition.cnn.com/interactive/2020/03/politics/coronavirus-trump-cdc-timeline/.
13. https://www.nytimes.com/2020/02/25/health/coronavirus-us.html.
14. *** .
15. See the data before the COVID-19 outbreak https://www.flightradar24.com/data/statistics.
16. https://www.nytimes.com/2020/04/04/us/coronavirus-china-travel-restrictions.html.
17. On 2 February there was a travel ban for travelers from China. https://apnews.com/article/5ca1c6f1bff5cf4d24392d10a27de7ca.
18. https://data.worldbank.org/indicator/SP.URB.TOTL.IN.ZS?locations=US.
19. See Gordon and Shapiro (1956) and Gordon (1959).
20. A rational financial decision in early January could be the following: we have the information for a new highly transmissible virus which may have a significant impact on the health of the population, and consequently on economies worldwide. An individual investor may withdraw his/hers investments from the stock markets and turn to other financial assets, because the growth would not be significant if the virus was contained, but the losses could be severe if the virus caused a pandemic.
21. See Khan and Vieito (2012).
22. In our study, we use as criterion whether an observation is positive or negative. Other criteria could also be used, e.g. whether the observation is above/below the median or the mean returns of the examined period. We have run the runs-tests adopting all these criteria and the results are similar to those presented in this section.
23. Vasileiou (2020) shows that for the US case the stimulus pack and the COVID-19 outbreak news significantly impacted the S&P500 performance.
24. https://www.youtube.com/watch?v=bM9bYOBuKF4 on 2:30–2:30.
25. In many cases, the general perception may influence other investors who may initially have different views regarding the economic conditions and eventually make them adopt the general view (Akerlof and Shiller 2010; Kim and Willett 2014).
26. Data for the COVID-19 cases were derived from the European Centre for Disease Prevention and Control https://www.ecdc.europa.eu/en/geographical-distribution-2019-ncov-cases.
27. An Increased number of cases leads to increased possibilities that investors might have a confirmed COVID-19 case in their social circle, and this increases risk aversion (Yue, Gizem Korkmaz, and Zhou 2020).

Disclosure statement

No potential conflict of interest was reported by the author(s).

References

Akerlof, G. A., and R. J. Shiller. 2010. *Animal Spirits: How Human Psychology Drives the Economy, and Why It Matters for Global Capitalism*. New Jersey, USA: Princeton University Press.

Al-Awadhi, A. M., K. Al-Saifi, A. Al-Awadhi, and S. Alhamadi. 2020. "Death and Contagious Infectious Diseases: Impact of the COVID-19 Virus on Stock Market Returns." *Journal of Behavioral and Experimental Finance* 27: 100326. doi:10.1016/j.jbef.2020.100326.

Ali, M., N. Alam, and S. A. R. Rizvi. 2020. "Coronavirus (Covid-19)–an Epidemic or Pandemic for Financial Markets." *Journal of Behavioral and Experimental Finance* 27: 100341. doi:10.1016/j.jbef.2020.100341.

Allen, F., and D. Gale. 2000. "Financial Contagion." *Journal of Political Economy* 108 (1): 1–33. doi:10.1086/262109.

Almond, D., and B. Mazumder. 2005. "The 1918 Influenza Pandemic and Subsequent Health Outcomes: An Analysis of SIPP Data." *American Economic Review* 95 (2): 258–262. doi:10.1257/000282805774669943.

Ashraf, B. N. 2020. "Stock Markets' Reaction to COVID-19: Cases or Fatalities?" *Research in International Business and Finance* 54: 101249. doi:10.1016/j.ribaf.2020.101249.

Baytas, A., and N. Cakici. 1999. "Do Markets Overreact: International Evidence." *Journal of Banking & Finance* 23 (7): 1121–1144. doi:10.1016/S0378-4266(98)00133-2.

Borges, M. R. 2010. "Efficient Market Hypothesis in European Stock Markets." *The European Journal of Finance* 16 (7): 711–726. doi:10.1080/1351847X.2010.495477.

Brennan, M. J. 1991. "A Perspective on Accounting and Stock Prices." *The Accounting Review* 66 (1): 67–79.

Chen, C., L. Liu, and N. Zhao. 2020. "Fear Sentiment, Uncertainty, and Bitcoin Price Dynamics: The Case of COVID-19." *Emerging Markets Finance and Trade* 56 (10): 2298–2309. doi:10.1080/1540496X.2020.1787150.

Chow, K., and K. Denning. 1993. "A Simple Multiple Variance Ratio Test." *Journal of Econometrics* 58: 385–401. doi:10.1016/0304-4076(93)90051-6.

Claessens, S., and K. Forbes, eds. 2013. *International Financial Contagion*. New York: Springer Science & Business Media.

Corbet, S., C. Larkin, and B. Lucey. 2020. "The Contagion Effects of the Covid-19 Pandemic: Evidence from Gold and Cryptocurrencies." *Finance Research Letters* 35: 101554. doi:10.1016/j.frl.2020.101554.

De Bondt, W. F., and R. Thaler. 1985. "Does the Stock Market Overreact?" *The Journal of Finance* 40 (3): 7. doi:10.1111/j.1540-6261.1985.tb05004.x.

Decker, S., and H. Schmitz. 2016. "Health Shocks and Risk Aversion." *Journal of Health Economics* 50: 156–170.93-805. doi:10.1016/j.jhealeco.2016.09.006.

Fama, E. F., L. Fisher, M. C. Jensen, and R. Roll. 1969. "The Adjustment of Stock Prices to New Information." *International Economic Review* 10 (1): 1–21. doi:10.2307/2525569.

Fama, E. F. 1970. Efficient Capital Markets: A Review of Theory and Empirical Work." *The Journal of Finance* 25 (2): 383–417. doi:10.2307/2325486.

Garrett, T. A. 2008. "Pandemic Economics: The 1918 Influenza and Its Modern-day Implications." *Federal Reserve Bank of St. Louis Review* 90: 75–93. March/April.

Gordon, M. J. 1959. "Dividends, Earnings, and Stock Prices." *The Review of Economics and Statistics* 41 (2): 99–105. doi:10.2307/1927792.

Gordon, M. J., and E. Shapiro. 1956. "Capital Equipment Analysis: The Required Rate of Profit." *Management Science* 3 (1): 102–110. doi:10.1287/mnsc.3.1.102.

Granger, C. W. 1969. "Investigating Causal Relations by Econometric Models and Cross-spectral Methods." *Econometrica: Journal of the Econometric Society* 37 (3): 424–438. doi:10.2307/1912791.

Guiso, L., P. Sapienza, and L. Zingales. 2018. "Time Varying Risk Aversion." *Journal of Financial Economics* 128 (3): 403–421. doi:10.1016/j.jfineco.2018.02.007.

Haroon, O., and S. A. R. Rizvi. 2020. "COVID-19: Media Coverage and Financial Markets Behavior – A Sectoral Inquiry." *Journal of Behavioral and Experimental Finance* 27: 100343. doi:10.1016/j.jbef.2020.100343.

Islam, S. M., S. Watanapalachaikul, and C. Clark. 2007. "Some Tests of the Efficiency of the Emerging Financial Markets: An Analysis of the Thai Stock Market." *Journal of Emerging Market Finance* 6 (3): 291–302. doi:10.1177/097265270700600304.

Jegadeesh, N., and S. Titman. 1995. "Overreaction, Delayed Reaction, and Contrarian Profits." *The Review of Financial Studies* 8 (4): 973–993.

Kahneman, D. 2011. *Thinking, Fast and Slow*. New York: Farrar, Straus and Giroux.

Keogh-Brown, M. R., S. Wren-Lewis, W. J. Edmunds, P. Beutels, and R. D. Smith. 2010. "The Possible Macroeconomic Impact on the UK of an Influenza Pandemic." *Health Economics* 19 (11): 1345–1360. doi:10.1002/hec.1554.

Khan, W., and J. P. Vieito. 2012. "Stock Exchange Mergers and Weak Form of Market Efficiency: The Case of Euronext Lisbon." *International Review of Economics & Finance* 22 (1): 173–189. doi:10.1016/j.iref.2011.09.005.

Kim, Y., and T. D. Willett. 2014. "News and the Behavior of the Korean Stock Market during the Global Financial Crisis." *Korea and the World Economy* 15 (3): 395–419.

Kwiatkowski, D., P. C. Phillips, P. Schmidt, and Y. Shin. 1992. "Testing the Null Hypothesis of Stationarity against the Alternative of a Unit Root." *Journal of Econometrics* 54 (1–3): 159–178. doi:10.1016/0304-4076(92)90104-Y.

Peterson, R. L. 2007. "Affect and Financial Decision-making: How Neuroscience Can Inform Market Participants." *The Journal of Behavioral Finance* 8 (2): 70–78. doi:10.1080/15427560701377448.

Sahi, S. K. 2012. "Neurofinance and Investment Behaviour." *Studies in Economics and Finance* 29 (4): 246–267. doi:10.1108/10867371211266900.

Schwert, G. W. 1981. "The Adjustment of Stock Prices to Information about Inflation." *The Journal of Finance* 36 (1): 15–29. doi:10.1111/j.1540-6261.1981.tb03531.x.

Shen, D., A. Urquhart, and P. Wang. 2019. "Does Twitter Predict Bitcoin?" *Economics Letters* 174: 118–122. doi:10.1016/j.econlet.2018.11.007.

Thaler, R. H., and C. R. Sunstein. 2009. *Nudge: Improving Decisions about Health, Wealth, and Happiness.* New York: Penguin.

Vasileiou, E. 2020. "Efficient Markets Hypothesis in the Time of COVID-19." *Review of Economic Analysis* 12: 2.

Vasileiou, E., A. Samitas, M. Karagiannaki, and D. Jagadish. 2020. "Health Risk and the Efficient Market Hypothesis in the Time of COVID-19." *International Review of Applied Economics.* forthcoming.

Wright, J. 2000. "Alternative Variance-ratio Tests Using Ranks and Signs." *Journal of Business and Economic Statistics* 18 (1): 1–9.

Xu, S., and Y. Li. 2020. "Beware of the Second Wave of COVID-19." *The Lancet* 395 (10233): 1321–1322. doi:10.1016/S0140-6736(20)30845-X.

Yue, P., A. Gizem Korkmaz, and H. Zhou. 2020. "Household Financial Decision Making Amidst the COVID-19 Pandemic." *Emerging Markets Finance and Trade* 56 (10): 2363–2377. doi:10.1080/1540496X.2020.1784717.

Analysis of containment measures and economic policies arising from COVID-19 in the European Union

Javier Cifuentes-Faura

ABSTRACT
The crisis caused by COVID-19 differs from previously crises due to its particularities. Many countries have been affected by the pandemic, although not all have acted in the same way or imposed the same level of restrictions. This paper analyses the virus containment measures carried out by some of the European countries most affected by the pandemic. It concludes that those that acted early have been less affected. In addition, it examines possible policies to be developed at the European Union level to combat the crisis.

1. Introduction

The coronavirus known as COVID-19 emerged in China in late 2019 and spread rapidly worldwide, causing millions of infections and over a million deaths, affecting virtually every country. The World Health Organization declared this situation as a health emergency and catalogued it as a pandemic at the international level (Sohrabi et al. 2020). The Coronavirus crisis is predicted to be the biggest economic crisis since the Great Depression of the 1930s. Due to the health crisis, the economy was drastically affected (McKibbin and Fernando 2020; Mann 2020; Carlsson-Szlezak, Reeves, and Swartz 2020), with a decrease in total consumer spending (Baker et al. 2020). Global financial markets recorded sharp declines, and volatility was at similar or even higher levels than in the financial crisis that began in 2008. In addition to the threat to people's health posed by COVID-19, there are also concerns about its economic effects (Fetzer et al. 2020).

It is an unprecedented crisis because of its peculiarities, characterized by a supply shock and a demand shock at the same time (Barua 2020). Restrictions on the movement of people aggravated these supply and demand effects.

This paper examines the virus containment measures implemented by the European countries most affected by the pandemic, with the aim of detecting whether those countries that anticipated taking restrictive measures managed to minimize the impact of the pandemic. Likewise, some of the economic policies to be developed at EU level to combat the crisis derived from COVID-19 are also analysed (expenditure measures, policies aimed at the labour market, businesses, those relating to mortgages, consumer loans and specific subsidies or aids granted), with these being selected as the most influential and prominent during the pandemic. As this is a dynamic situation, measures are examined from the beginning of the pandemic to mid-July 2020, where the cut-off point for data collection for this paper was set.

2. Measures taken in selected EU countries

Most countries in Europe – and indeed the rest of the world – took drastic measures including confinement or quarantine of the population. And while all European countries were affected by the coronavirus, Italy, Spain, France, the United Kingdom and Germany had the highest number of cases according to data constantly updated by John Hopkins University. A study of these countries was carried out together with another sample of countries that at the time of this work was considered representative in order to understand the effectiveness of the measures applied (cancellation of public events and meetings of several people, closure of borders and non-core shops, and suspension of movements considered as non-core).

The outbreak is considered to have started (BO = Beginning of Outbreak) when there were more than 100 positive cases of COVID-19 in the country.[1] The peak of the pandemic was reached months after the outbreak began in each country. After the first coronavirus death in each country, France, the United Kingdom, Italy and Spain were the European countries that took the longest to close schools or close borders (Table 1). Interestingly, these are also the countries most affected.

Table 2 shows as of 1 July 2020 the number of completed tests, the number of citizens testing positive, and the number of confirmed deaths.

The evolution of the pandemic in each country was different, as were the actions taken. Countries such as Portugal with fewer cases per 1,000 inhabitants compared to other countries such as Spain or Belgium carried out a higher number of tests per 1,000 inhabitants (Figure 1).

Table 1. Days taken by countries to enact measures after outbreak and first death.

	School closures		Border closure		Canceled events		Non-essential shops closed		Suspended non-essential movements		Non-essential production shutdown[3]	
Country	BO[1]	FD[2]	BO	FD	BO	FD	BO	FD	BO	FD	BO	FD
Austria	7	3	-	-	2	0	8	4	8	4	-	-
Belgium	9	4	14	9	8	3	11	6	11	6	-	-
Czech Republic	0	0	4	0	0	0	2	0	4	0	-	-
France	16	30	-	-	0	14	14	28	17	31	-	-
Germany	14	6	15	7	19	11	-	-	21	13	-	-
Greece	0	0	3	4	0	0	4	5	11	12	-	-
Hungary	0	1	0	2	0	0	0	2	-	-	-	-
Italy	11	13	16	18	11	13	16	18	16	18	32	34
Poland	2	4	1	3	0	0	1	3	11	13	-	-
Portugal	3	0	3	0	0	0	3	0	3	0	-	-
Spain	13	12	14	13	8	7	13	12	14	13	27	26
United Kingdom	18	18	-	-	12	12	16	16	19	19	-	-
Median Values	7,75	7,58	7,78	6,22	5	5	8	8,55	12,27	11,72	-	-

[1]BO: Beginning of the outbreak
[2]FD: First deceased
[3]The activities involved in the market supply chain and in the operation of the services of centres producing essential goods and services, as well as certain health centres, services and establishments, are considered essential.
0: means that the country took action before counting more than 100 cases in the country
(-) means that the country has not taken that action
Source: Prepared by the author on the basis of information provided by John Hopkins University

Table 2. Data on various European countries as of 1 July 2020.

Country	Tests	Cases	Deaths
Austria	620,866	17,777	705
Belgium	989,052	61,509	9,754
Czech Republic	560,682	11,954	349
France	1,454,588	164,801	29,843
Germany	6,376,054 (1)	194,725	8985
Greece	315,982	3,409	192
Hungary	277,750	4,155	585
Italy	5,445,476	240,578	34,767
Poland	1,546,510	34,393	1,,463
Portugal	1,222,190	42,141	1,576
Spain	3,644,458 (2)	249,659	28,363
United Kingdom	6,035,588	312,654	43,730
Median Values	2,021,215	111,479	11,512

(1) Until 5/7/2020
(2) Until 2/7/2020
Source: Our World on the data

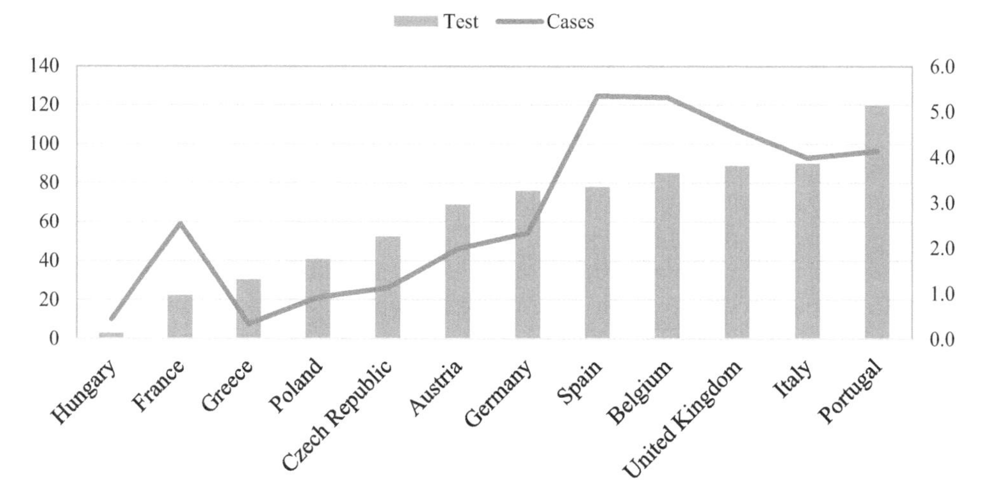

Figure 1. Test and confirmed cases per 1,000 inhabitants at the beginning of July 2020. Source: own elaboration

Austria, Greece, the Czech Republic or Poland, despite the low number of infections compared to others, reacted more quickly and restrictively than other countries, with the aim of getting out of the crisis more quickly. Table 3 presents different averages used by different European countries to reduce the impact of COVID-19.

Germany managed to have one of the lowest death rates in Europe, yet had not declared home confinement of the population (except in specific areas). It had only imposed some restrictions, recommending that people stay at home and follow certain directions when going out on the streets. This low mortality is mainly due to the fact that Germany is one of the countries where the most rapid tests for the disease were carried out, allowing the authorities to reduce the spread of the pandemic by isolating those diagnosed. In addition, it employed an effective containment strategy among the elderly, with an efficient use of its hospital capacity (Bennhold 2020).

Table 3. Measures imposed by governments to mitigate the effects of COVID-19 during containment.

Country	State of emergency (start day)	Home confinement (start day)	Outdoor activities	Non-essential services closing days
Austria	No	Yes (16 March)	Yes, but not in groups.	36
Belgium	No	Yes (18 March)	Yes, physical activities are allowed, but sitting in parks is prohibited.	30
Czech Republic	Yes (12 March)	Yes (16 March)	Yes, at first it was mandatory to wear masks.	46
France	Yes (21 March)	Yes (17 March)	Yes, allowed, but less than a kilometer from home	50
Germany	No	No, except for some areas	Yes, but alone or with a person from the same household.	53
Greece	No	Yes (23 March)	Yes, allowed alone or in pairs.	41
Hungary	Yes (11 March)	Yes (28 March)	Yes, with a distance of one and a half meters.	36
Italy	Yes (31 Enero)	Yes (9 March)	No, outdoor exercise is prohibited.	54
Poland	Yes (20 March)	Yes (25 March)	Yes, allowed alone or in pairs.	39
Portugal	Yes (19 March)	Yes (16 March)	Yes, but individually.	48
Spain	Yes (14 March)	Yes (14 March)	No, outdoor exercise is prohibited.	67
United Kingdom	Yes (23 March)	Yes (23 March)	Yes, but only once a day, alone or with people from the same household.	23

Source: own elaboration

Spain and Italy were the only countries that prohibited the cessation of all productive activity for two weeks, except for those supplying essential services (Fernández Riquelme 2020). This situation, while helping to reduce the pandemic, generated a fall in the country's GDP.

To ensure compliance with the confinement, Italy approved a decree establishing fines of up to 3,000 euros and penalties of up to five years in prison for those who violate it. In the case of the Lombardy region – the main focus of contagion in Italy – the Italian authorities established penalties of 400 euros for those going out without wearing masks. In the case of Spain, depending on the seriousness of the offence committed, citizens were exposed to fines (ranging from EUR 601 to EUR 10,400), up to prison sentences, which could vary depending on the seriousness of the offence. In France, anyone who broke confinement was punished by a fine of 135 euros, although it could be increased to 1,500 euros in the event of a repeat offence within 15 days. If the rules were violated more than three times in 30 days, the penalty could be up to six months in prison and a fine of 3,750 euros. In the United Kingdom, failure to comply with the measures was punishable by a fine of £1,000, and failure to pay could lead to imprisonment. In Germany, depending on the area, the situation varied; in Berlin, people not complying could be fined between 10 and 100 euros; in the Land of North Rhine-Westphalia, it was 200 euros; in Bavaria, fines were up to 25,000 euros.

3. Economic policies in selected EU countries

The health emergency caused by COVID-19 led to economic and social crisis, and it will be necessary for the leaders of the various political forces to work together to enact new measures. In contrast to the last economic crisis, the banking sector was better capitalized and more liquid (Bisseker 2020; Remolina 2020).

The pandemic affected all countries, but both the drop in output in 2020 and the strength of the rebound in 2021 differ significantly: 'The EU economy is forecast to contract by 8.3% in 2020 and grow by 5.8% in 2021. The contraction in 2020 is, therefore, projected to be significantly greater than the 7.7% projected for the euro area and 7.4% for the EU as a whole in the Spring Forecast' (European Comission 2020). The economic impact is uneven (Table 4). Germany will suffer the least from the recession (an estimated 7.8% drop in GDP), compared to Italy and Spain, where a 12.8% drop in GDP is expected, according to the International Monetary Fund. Public debt is soaring in all countries, especially in Italy, where post-COVID public debt is estimated at 155.7% of GDP.

3.1. *France*

Among the main expenditure measures, France established a Solidarity Fund with a tax exemption corresponding to the loss of turnover in one year for companies with a turnover of less than 1 m euros and an annual taxable profit of less than 60 k euros and for self-employed workers, micro-entrepreneurs and the liberal professions who experience a sharp fall in turnover (loss of 50% of turnover in one year in March 2020) or who were subject to administrative closure. It also offered 5 k euros for businesses with at least 1 employee threatened with bankruptcy. In addition, it opened a credit line (20bn) for strategic industrial enterprises in need of state support with an increase in the capacity of the Economic and Social Development Fund aimed at medium-sized enterprises.

3.2. *Germany*

In Germany, additional expenditure in the health sector totals EUR 18.9bn. The federal guarantees for loans granted by the KfW promotion bank to the business sector were extended. The federal government guaranteed up to EUR 30bn in compensation payments from credit insurers. It established an Economic Stabilisation Fund administered by the German Finance Agency (Finanzagentur); and a programme of direct subsidies of about EUR 50bn to the approximately 3 million small business owners.

3.3. *Italy*

In Italy, 845 m of funding was earmarked for extra recruitment in the health system and acquisition of medical devices with an increase of 1.65bn euros for the National Emergency Fund and an increase in the overtime fund for health workers by 150 m

Table 4. Main economic indicators 2019–2020.

Country	Public debt 2019	Debt Per Capita 2019	Estimated public debt 2020 (post-COVID)	GDP 2019 (pre-COVID)	Estimated GDP 2020	Estimated GDP 2021
France	2,380,106	35,517	115%	2,425,313 M	−12.5%	+7.3%
Germany	2,053,033	24,730	75%	3,435,210 M.	−7.8%	+5.4%
Italy	2,409,841	39,925	155.7%	1,787,664 M.	−12.8%	+6.3%
Spain	1,188,867	25,241	109.3%	1,244,757 M.	−12.8%	+6.3%
United Kingdom	2,223,544	33,363	100.9%	2,523,313 M	−10.2%	+6.3%

Source: Prepared by the author on the basis of IMF data

euros along with 340 m euros to increase hospital beds and intensive care and 8.1bn for the strengthening and reorganisation of health care. The total financial aid package for the support of households, workers and enterprises in 2020 is equivalent to 4.5% of GDP.

3.4. Spain

In Spain, the Contingency Fund for the Ministry of Health was increased by 1bn euros to cover expenses related to increased health care needs. 2.8bn was established for the regions through the early transfer of funds under the 2020 regional funding framework. 25 m was made available to ensure that vulnerable children affected by the suspension of educational activity in schools had basic access to food. An extraordinary subsidy for self-employed workers affected by the suspension of economic activity and additional budgetary funds of 110 m was allocated to finance R&D&I for the development of drugs and vaccines for COVID-19. On 16 June 2020, the Government approved the creation of the COVID-19 Fund, amounting to 16bn, with funds transferred to the regions to finance the pandemic and compensate for their loss of income.

3.5. United Kingdom

In the United Kingdom, spending on measures to support public services, businesses and individuals increased by nearly 190 USDbn and the direct cost of fiscal policy measures since March is estimated at £184 billion, just over 8% of GDP in 2019 (FischRating 2020).

Furthermore, the **European Green Deal** is expected to be the great lever for Europe's reconstruction and economic recovery from the COVID-19 crisis (Colli 2020). The European Council simultaneously approved the Multiannual Financial Framework and the Next Generation EU[2] programme to address the needs created by the pandemic. This programme will involve an investment of EUR 750bn, of which EUR 672.5bn will go into the Recovery and Resilience Facility (EUR 360bn will be loans and 312.5bn transfers). These funds are distributed as follows: 37% for ecological transition, 20% for digitisation of the economy and 43% for boosting economic and social cohesion, in line with the objective of achieving the European Union's green and ecological transition.

Based on the information published on the websites of the ministry of economy of each country, Table 5 presents the main policies aimed at the labour market, companies and those relating to consumer mortgages/loans and specific subsidies or aid granted. Some of the industry-specific measures are described, as governments have focused on assisting and refloating the most affected sectors, such as airlines and tourism. In addition, the main aid and policies of these countries are included in order to contribute to the reconstruction of the economy in a sustainable way.

4. Economic policies at EU level

To mitigate the impact of the coronavirus crisis on the economy, the EU has relaxed European budgetary rules.

Table 5. Review of government support for businesses and individuals.

Measures	Labour market	Business and SMEs	Mortgages/Loans	Grants	Industry-specific measures	Green recovery
Spain	• People on a Redundancy Scheme receive an unemployment allowance. • Part-time workers, cooperative members and permanent workers who are dismissed eligible for unemployment benefits. • Workers with temporary contracts that expire after the declaration of the state of alert and are not entitled to unemployment benefits may receive an extraordinary allowance.	• Deferment and fractioning of tax payments for companies and self-employed persons. • Flexibility in tax deferrals for a period of six months, on request, with interest rate reductions. • A line of financing is approved to meet liquidity needs.	• Moratorium if there is a reduction in income.	• Minimum Living Income for people in situations of unemployment and extreme poverty. • The social benefit for energy supply ('social bonus') automatically extended until 15 September.	• Iberia and Vueling signed a - 1.01bn euro syndicated loan guaranteed by the Instituto de Crédito Oficial (ICO). In Spain, companies in the tourism sector have been financed through an ICO financing line with an amount in excess of 10.5bn euros.	• The Plan for the Recovery, Transformation and Resilience of the Spanish Economy is inspired by Agenda 2030 and the United Nations' Sustainable Development Goals. Around 72bn euros will be allocated between 2021 and 2023:
Italy	• No worker may be dismissed for two months. • Subsidies for workers who lose their jobs and for the self-employed	• Deferral of tax payments until September 2020; possibility for companies to convert deferred tax assets into tax credits • SMEs benefit from a 3-month cut in bill payments and the abolition of the regional tax on productive activities in June. Able to recover up to 60% of rent paid for premises in the last 3 months. • Cancellation of the June liability for IRAP, the regional tax on turnover, for all companies with a turnover of up to EUR 250 m and self-employed persons. • Government-guaranteed loans at advantageous rates for companies in need of liquidity.	• Moratorium on mortgage payments if job lost. • Payment of taxes and bills suspended until May, and payment of mortgages suspended until September in the case of employees who lost their jobs.	• Social bond to finance unemployment benefits.	• Government to keep Alitalia afloat with an injection of 600 m euros, as part of its nationalization project. • Workers in tourism sector will receive subsidies. • 55bn euro plan to recover tourism, with measures such as the granting of a bonus of up to 500 euros to families with measures to spend on tourism structures in the country itself.	• 209bn euros (81.4 in grants and 127.4 in loans) for Recovery and Resilience Plan that meets the objectives of the European Green Deal. They will focus on building rehabilitation, electric vehicle recharging points and a hydrogen strategy to improve the climate.

(*Continued*)

Table 5. (Continued).

Measures	Labour market	Business and SMEs	Mortgages/Loans	Grants	Industry-specific measures	Green recovery
France	• A mechanism was set up for partial unemployment and compensation for workers who are forced to stay at home.	• Deferral of contributions and direct taxes; loans to companies. • Solidarity fund for small businesses with less than one million euros of annual turnover that have lost income or had it reduced by at least 70% and deferment of electricity and gas payments, as well as rent.	• Deferment of first home mortgage payment.	• Creation of a 'baby-sitter bonus' so that those who have to continue working can leave their children.	• Air France agreed with government, which owns 14% of the airline, a loan of 7bn euros, of which 4bn to be state-guaranteed loans, but contributed by a consortium of French and international banks, and remaining 3bn a direct state loan. 18bn euro Tourism Rescue Plan, of which 1.3bn is direct public investment and the rest includes exemptions and unemployment benefits.	• 30bn will be used to strengthen the transition to a green economy, of which 11bn will be used to strengthen rail freight and to implement cycling as a means of transport. • 7bn to renovate buildings in terms of energy and 9bn to support research and innovation companies, in order to develop hydrogen as an energy source.
United Kingdom	• Government to cover social security and pension payments with a monthly salary limit of £2,500. • Sick pay from day one (rather than day four) • Increased benefits for those out of work or on low incomes • Increased support available to self-employed people. • Income support for self-employed (80% of earnings for first phase and 70% in second phase)	• Financial support for larger companies through the purchase of short-term debt that reduces the financing and deferral of outstanding tax debts for companies and self-employed persons in difficulty. • Funding for innovative companies through Innovate UK. • Coronavirus Business Interruption Loan Schemes (CBILS) offering Government-guaranteed loans. • Allow SMEs and employers to reclaim Statutory Sick Pay (SSP) paid for sickness absence due to COVID-19. • The Bounce Back Loan for SMEs affected by the pandemic to receive loans of up to 25% of annual turnover (with a cap of £50 k) from accredited lenders.	• Delay of up to three months in mortgage payments for citizens experiencing difficulties as a result of the pandemic.	• Extra food packages for vulnerable people	• British Airways has increased the liquidity thanks to several loans guaranteed by the government. • British Airways has received aid amounting to 300 million pounds. This guaranteed loan is in addition to the 1.38 billion dollar credit line of the British airline.	• The government will invest £160 million in wind energy will be used to create new jobs and lead a green revolution. • Ports and factories building turbines will be modernised, creating 2,000 jobs and another 60,000 jobs in the supply chain. • The United Kingdom currently has a wind power capacity of 10 gigawatts, so the Government intends to build turbines to generate power.

(Continued)

Table 5. (Continued).

Measures	Labour market	Business and SMEs	Mortgages/Loans	Grants	Industry-specific measures	Green recovery
Germany	• Kurzarbeitergeld (Money for Reduction of Work): aimed at employees who had to reduce working hours and reduce their payroll (until 31.12.2020). • The employment agency will pay the employees between 60% and 67% of the net salary.	• Subsidies for companies suspending activities and suffering loss of sales of at least 60% in April and May 2020 compared to same period in 2019. • A rescue fund of up to EUR 50bn for the self-employed and small businesses. • 25bn euros for SMEs, up to 150bn euros for fixed costs for 3 months, to prevent company bankruptcies. • Reduction of VAT from 1 July to 31 December from 19% to 16% and reduced VAT from 7% to 5%.	• Students receive interest-free loans of up to 650 euros per month through the state development bank Kreditanstalt für Wiederaufbau and for those students in 'particularly serious emergencies' non-refundable grants.	• Family bonus: 300 euros per child for eligible families	• Lufthansa to receive 9bn euro aid from government, giving in return a 20% stake in the company to the government through the subscription of shares in a capital increase. • State guarantee scheme of EUR 840 m to cover vouchers issued by tour operators for cancelled travel packages.	• 50bn to sectors related to green growth, such as renewable energy or sustainable transport. • 40bn of the total will be allocated to technological developments to combat climate change and to promote digitalisation. • 10bn will be allocated to modernising mobility and advancing its sustainability, with aid for buying electric vehicles.

Source: own elaboration

4.1. Tax policies

Before the coronavirus, there was a debate about how much national income should be allocated to the EU budget. The European Commission's proposal was for 1.11% of national income. The situation caused by COVID has a significant impact on the financial situation of public administrations. National governments will have to borrow several percentage points of total GDP. Among the main fiscal policies developed by the EU are those that seek to provide an immediate fiscal boost, such as additional government spending on medical resources, subsidies to SMEs and public investment, as well as revenue forgone such as the cancellation of certain taxes and social security contributions. These types of measures lead immediately to the deterioration of the budget balance without any direct compensation afterwards.

It is likely that some firms will experience not only liquidity but also solvency problems, which cannot be addressed by monetary policy and even less so by (micro- and macro-) prudential policies, so that fiscal intervention will be necessary. There have also been payment deferrals, which include taxes and social security contributions, and which, in principle, must be paid back later. These measures improve the liquidity positions of individuals and companies, but do not cancel out their obligations. These measures therefore cause a deterioration in the budget balance in 2020, but improve it later. Measures that include liquidity guarantees or credit lines have been put in place, and may not weaken the budget balance in 2020, but would create contingent liabilities that could become actual expenditure in 2020 or later.

4.2. European Union solidarity fund and European globalization adjustment fund

The European Union Solidarity Fund was created to intervene in the event of major natural disasters and to provide European solidarity to the affected areas in Europe. It was established in response to the major floods in the summer of 2002 in Central Europe. Since then, 24 European countries have been helped with more than EUR 500 m and it has been used for 80 disasters of various kinds. In the wake of the COVID-19 pandemic, the Solidarity Fund has been extended. The estimated expenditure on emergency response measures to support the population and limit the spread of the disease within four months from the date the country took its first public action to combat the crisis should exceed EUR 1.5bn, at 2011 prices, or 0.3 of gross national income.

In addition, the European Globalization Adjustment Fund supports workers who lose their jobs as a result of major structural changes in world trade patterns caused by globalization or the global economic and financial crisis. This Fund should be an instrument of European solidarity to help workers who are affected by company restructuring as a result of this pandemic. This fund has a maximum budget of EUR 150 m per year for the period 2014–20 and can finance up to 60% of the cost of projects designed to help redundant workers find a new job or set up their own business.

There could be a problem of interest rates rising suddenly in some Member States, making their debts unsustainable, and the ECB's open market operations plan would probably have to be activated.

4.3. Coronabonds

In addition, the possibility of issuing so-called coronabonds (Bénassy-Quéré et al. 2020) is being considered. These community bonds imply a joint and several responsibility on the part of all the states. The credit line granted would reduce the risks to the economic stability of all countries, while allowing Member States to maintain their efforts by making the cost of borrowing less dependent on the individual fiscal situations of each country. Access to capital markets would be easier because the risk of the whole would be lower and more liquidity could be raised than separately. However, not all countries agree with these measures, as it would mean a mutualisation of debt, and some would have to cover the obligations of others.

4.4. Policy recommendation

The European Central Bank (ECB) can help counter an attack on a member state by buying unlimited amounts of sovereign bonds, through a conditional adjustment programme. The ECB has a negative deposit rate which combined with low interest rates has led to indebtedness and rising asset prices in the Eurozone, weakening the banking, pension fund and life insurance sectors. In addition, the European Stability Mechanism (ESM) can support banking institutions, providing assistance and support to those countries in greatest economic difficulty, so as to ensure financial stability in the euro area. The ESM provides assistance to countries in the euro area that are experiencing or are at risk of experiencing economic difficulties. It is authorised to grant loans for the purpose of macroeconomic adjustment, to purchase debt on primary and secondary debt markets, to provide precautionary financial assistance in the form of credit lines and to finance recapitalisations of financial institutions by lending to the governments of its member countries.

Simply renaming existing budget appropriations or announcing large headlines based on virtual multipliers will not be sufficient. Support must be allocated in the EU to deal with the consequences of COVID-19 such as the European Solidarity Fund and the European Globalization Adjustment Fund.

The EU should also make reallocations. The budgetary appropriations for the structural funds in the 2020 budget should be mobilized and used to combat this crisis. Assistance should be provided to all Member States, regardless of their participation in the structural funds or the distribution of unspent money by country. Specific budget items could be reallocated to the European disaster relief plan, within the EU budget, at the same time as negotiations are underway to reach a political agreement that would compensate the potential beneficiaries of the reallocated funds through an exceptional allocation in the 2021 budget. Cooperation between Member States outside the framework of the EU budget will also be very important.

4.5. Limitations and future research

Among the limitations of this work is that economic policies across the EU and globally are volatile, as governments publish new policies on a weekly basis, so data are accurate up to the selected deadline for data collection (mid-July). An opportunity for future research is to compare data at a later period when the pandemic has stabilized and to test the effectiveness of measures that were finally put in place. The selection of specific countries (those most affected by the pandemic rather than all of them) is also a limitation and an area for future research.

5. Conclusions

The coronavirus epidemic caught many political and economic institutions off guard. COVID-19 is expected to produce the biggest economic crisis in years, and the world is expected to enter a major economic recession. After the last global financial crisis and the euro crisis, measures were designed and proposed to combat a possible crisis originating, once again, in the financial sector. However, this crisis is totally different.

The measures taken by European countries to contain the virus have varied. Data were collected up to mid-July 2020. Spain and Italy, the countries most affected by the pandemic, had been the only ones to ban the cessation of all productive activity. Germany had managed to have one of the lowest death rates in Europe and to impose fewer restrictions than other countries. Its success was due to its decentralised testing system and laboratory infrastructure, as well as being the European country where most rapid tests for the disease were carried out.

Some countries acted early, so that fewer people were affected and they could get out of the crisis earlier. Others, however, took longer to take action, and may therefore have had more people infected.

Once virus containment measures had been imposed, economic policies needed to be formulated to alleviate the situation and minimize the damage. Many of these measures were aimed at supporting companies in the short term, allowing tax breaks and credit lines with favourable conditions, or providing subsidies to avoid bankruptcies. Those countries that took longer to take action would have to pursue more restrictive policies and allocate more spending to bring about economic recovery.

The European Union must coordinate a common European response to the pandemic. It will be necessary to start from European solidarity, avoiding confrontations between countries, where aid is offered to the most affected sectors and individuals. In this way, all governments should participate in a European economic reconstruction that will lead to complete digitalisation, promote sustainable industry and put in place prevention and public health measures. Measures taken at European level and agreed upon by all countries are likely to be more effective than those taken individually. The European Union Solidarity Fund and European Globalization Adjustment Fund may be some of the most effective for economic recovery.

We must move towards an expansive fiscal policy scenario, in line with a Keynesian vision. Keynes' redistributive theories must be accompanied by a comprehensive investment plan. Stimulus policies must be created from the demand side, injecting liquidity to reverse any depressive cycle, through fiscal policy, or by issuing public debt. In this way, it will be possible to contribute to a fall in unemployment and to economic recovery.

Notes

1. 100 days are considered as the beginning of the outbreak as in works like https://ourworldindata.org/coronavirus/country/spain?country=~ESP
2. More information on Next Generation EU is available at https://ec.europa.eu/info/live-work-travel-eu/health/coronavirus-response/recovery-plan-europe/pillars-next-generation-eu_es

Disclosure statement

No potential conflict of interest was reported by the author(s).

References

Baker, S. R., R. A. Farrokhnia, S. Meyer, M. Pagel, and C. Yannelis. 2020. "How Does Household Spending Respond to an Epidemic? Consumption during the 2020 COVID-19 Pandemic" University of Chicago, Working Paper.

Baldwin, R. Y., and B. Di Mauro 2020. "Economics in the Time of COVID-19." CEPR Press.

Barua, S. 2020. "Understanding Coronanomics: The Economic Implications of the Coronavirus (COVID-19) Pandemic." *Paper No. 99693*. Online at https://mpra.ub.uni-muenchen.de/99693/ MPRA

Bénassy-Quéré, A., G. Corsetti, A. Fatás, G. Felbermayr, M. Fratzscher, C. Fuest, F. Giavazzi, et al. 2020. "COVID-19 Economic Crisis: Europe Needs More than One Instrument", *VoxEU.org*, 05 April, Accessed 20 April 2020. https://voxeu.org/article/long-run-view-coronabonds-debate

Bennhold, K. 2020. "A German Exception? Why the Country´s Coronavirus Death Rate Is Low." *The New York Times*. Available at: https://www.nytimes.com/2020/04/04/world/europe/germany-coronavirus-death-rate.html

Bisseker, J. 2020. "¿Cuál es el impacto del COVID-19 en los bancos europeos?" Available at: https://www.estrategiasdeinversion.com/analisis/bolsa-y-mercados/el-experto-opina/cual-es-el-impacto-del-COVID-19-en-los-bancos-n-445183

Carlsson-Szlezak, P., M. Reeves, and P. Swartz 2020. "Understanding the Economic Shock of Coronavirus. Harvard Business Review." Accessed 20 April 2020 https://hbr.org/2020/03/understanding-the-economic-shock-of-coronavirus

Colli, F. 2020. "The End of 'Business as Usual'?" *COVID-19 and the European Green Deal*. Available at http://www.egmontinstitute.be/content/uploads/2020/05/EPB60.pdf?type=pdf

European Comission. 2020. "Summer 2020 Economic Forecast: An Even Deeper Recession with Wider Divergences." Accessed 16 July 2020 https://ec.europa.eu/commission/presscorner/detail/en/ip_20_1269

Fernández Riquelme, S. 2020. "Primera Historia De La Crisis Del Coronavirus En España." *La Razón histórica. Revista hispanoamericana de Historia de las Ideas* 46: 12–22.

Fetzer, T., L. Hensel, J. Hermle, and C. Roth (2020). "Coronavirus Perceptions and Economic Anxiety." arXiv preprint arXiv:2003.03848.

FischRating. 2020. "UK Coronavirus Measures Add to Fiscal Cost, Consolidation Plan to Come." Accessed 15 July 2020. https://www.fitchratings.com/research/sovereigns/uk-coronavirus-measures-add-to-fiscal-cost-consolidation-plan-to-come-10-07-2020

Letzing, J. 2020. "How Many Policy Tools are Left to Soften the Impact of COVID-19?" *World Economic Forum*. Accessed 27 March 2020. https://www.weforum.org/agenda/2020/03/COVID-19-coronavirus-policy-toolseconomic-impact/

Mann, C. L. 2020. "Real and Financial Lenses to Assess the Economic Consequences of COVID-19." In *Economics in the Time of COVID-19*, edited by R. Baldwin and B. W. Di Mauro, London: A VoxEU.org Book, Centre for Economic Policy Research. Accessed 26 March 2020. https://voxeu.org/system/files/epublication/COVID19.pdf

McKibbin, W., and R. Fernando. 2020. "The Economic Impact of COVID-19." In *Economics in the Time of COVID-19*, edited by R. Baldwin and B. W. Di Mauro, London: A VoxEU.org Book, Centre for Economic Policy Research. Accessed 26 March 2020. https://voxeu.org/system/files/epublication/COVID-19.pdf

OECD. 2020. "Coronavirus: The World Economy at Risk. OECD Interim Economic Assessment." 2 March. Organization for Economic Cooperation and Development. Available at: https://www.oecd.org/berlin/publikationen/Interim-Economic-Assessment-2-March-2020.pdf

Remolina, N. 2020. "Respuestas De Supervisores Y Reguladores Financieros Al COVID-19 (Financial Regulators' Responses to COVID/19)." Instituto Iberoamericano de Derecho y Finanzas (IIDF).

Sohrabi, C., Z. Alsafi, N. O'Neill, M. Khan, A. Kerwan, A. Al-Jabir, C. Iosifidis, and R. Agha. 2020. "World Health Organization Declares Global Emergency: A Review of the 2019 Novel Coronavirus (COVID-19)." *International Journal of Surgery* 76: 71–76. doi:10.1016/j.ijsu.2020.02.034.

Covid 19: Ramifications for progress towards the sustainable development goals (SDGs) in Nigeria

O'Raye Dicta Ogisi and Toritseju Begho

ABSTRACT

This paper examines whether the impact of COVID-19 at the household level is an obstacle to achieving the sustainable development goals of no poverty (SDG1), zero hunger (SDG2), good health and wellbeing (SDG3) and decent work and economic growth (SDG8). We limit our investigation to farm households given their precarious situation. We analyse data from the World Bank National Longitudinal Phone Survey (COVID-19 NLPS) and the 2018/2019 General Household Survey (GHS). An exact McNemar's test determined that there was a statistically significant difference in the proportion of households that skipped a meal (p =.002), ran out of food (p =.036) or went a whole day without food (p <.001) pre- and during- COVID-19. Approximately 81% perceived COVID-19 as a substantial threat to their income. This was buttressed by the finding that 75% reported a decrease in their total income since the outbreak of COVID-19. Overall, the findings in this paper suggest that COVID-19 posed a substantial threat to the attainment of SDGs 1, 2, 3 and 8. In the long term, government would need to mitigate the impact of COVID-19 through targeted social protection programs and policies to ensure that the country is on track to achieve the SDGs.

1. Introduction

Sub-Saharan Africa has one of the highest proportion of households living on less than 1.25 USD a day (United Nations, 2015). The UN Millennium Development Goals Report (2015) estimated the percentage of Sub-Saharan Africans that lives in extreme poverty at 41% of the population in 2015. Despite recent efforts to reverse the trend, the region continues to lag behind other regions of the world. Nigeria is the second of five countries that constitute 60% of the world's 1 billion extremely poor people (World Bank 2015). In Nigeria, small farmers make up 88% of the farming population, with over 72% of these smallholders living below the poverty line (FAO 2018). This implies that despite the crucial role small farmers play in feeding the country, many are still unable to break out of poverty or to attain food security. In addition to hunger and poverty, Nigerian farmers face a myriad of challenges ranging from climate change to post-harvest losses, land ownership to limited access to technology (Apata et al. 2018; Mgbenka, Mbah, and Ezeano 2016). There is evidence that the outbreak of COVID-19 is adding to these challenges.

From previous experience – for example, with 2014–16 Ebola outbreak in Africa – the regions that experience the most adverse effects are those where a substantial number are living close to the poverty line (Fallah et al. 2015; Kapiriri and Ross 2020).

Driven by the sustainable development goals (SDGs), the pathway taken by the Nigerian government to achieve the goals of ending hunger, poverty and unemployment had been on course before the outbreak of COVID-19. Thus, in this paper, we examine the effect of COVID-19 on households, and the obstacle COVID-19 poses to achieving the SDGs. We focus on SDG1 (no poverty), SDG2 (zero hunger), SDG3 (good health and wellbeing) and SDG8 (decent work and economic growth). Actions to attain these goals have taken centre stage in the government's current and future development plans.[1]

The paper is organized as follows. Section 2 discusses COVID-19 as a threat at the household level, and obstacles to progress towards the SDGs. Data and estimation methods are described in Section 3. The results and discussion are presented in Section 4. Section 5 concludes.

2. COVID-19 as a threat to progress towards the *SDGs in Nigeria*

On 30 January 2020, the Director–General of the World Health Organisation (WHO) declared the novel coronavirus outbreak (2019-nCoV) a Public Health Emergency of International Concern (PHEIC). The Nigerian government on 31 January, through the Nigeria Centre for Disease Control, established a Coronavirus Preparedness Group tasked with monitoring and reviewing the outbreak globally, evaluating the risk of spread, and improving the country's position ahead of an outbreak. These steps coincided with the categorisation of Nigeria among the high-risk countries in Africa by the WHO (Ezigbo and Ifijeh 2020). Nigeria confirmed the first case of the coronavirus in sub-Saharan Africa on 27 February. In March 2020 the Nigerian government declared a lockdown in the Federal Capital Territory, Lagos and Ogun states. All states eventually imposed lockdown. The lockdowns restricted group gatherings, travelling and all activities categorised as nonessential. These restrictions negatively impacted the economy, including agricultural production – processing as well as the supply chain (Penrhys-Evans 2020). There were large income losses across agricultural-related jobs (Abdul 2020).

Following the conclusion of the Millennium Development Goals (MDGs), the Sustainable Development Goals were a global call to action for people, planet and prosperity, aiming to enhance economic, social and environmental dimensions of social development. The 2030 Agenda for Sustainable Development consists of 17 sustainable goals.

Nigeria was committed to the SDGs since its adoption. Credible progress was made in the domestication process of the SDGs, integrating them into the country's Economic Recovery and Growth Plan, with the development of the home-grown 'Integrated Sustainable Development Goals' to make policy more responsive to the SDGs (Nigeria's Voluntary National Review, 2020). However, Nigeria is ranked 160 out of the 166 countries on the 2020 SDG Index scores (Sachs et al. 2020) implying that much more action still needs to be taken by the Nigerian government as shown in Table 1.

Table 1. Progress of Nigeria on SDGs 1, 2, 3 and 8.

SDG goal	Indicators	2016	2018
1 End poverty in all its forms everywhere	Proportion (overall) of people living on less than $1.25 a day	62.2	**
	Proportion of population covered by social protection floors/systems, by sex, distinguishing children, unemployed persons, older persons, persons with disabilities, pregnant women, newborns, work-injury victims and the poor and the vulnerable	8.29	↑ 2.37
	People residing in households that have access to basic services (%)		
	• improved sanitation.	35.9	↑ 6.1
	• improved water source.	64.1	↑ 2.9
2 Zero hunger	Children under the ages of five are suffering from acute malnutrition	10.6	↑ 0.8[T]
3 Ensuring healthy lives and promoting well-being at all ages	Maternal mortality ratio (per 100,000 live births)	576	↓ 64
	Births attended by skilled health personnel (%)	43	*
	Mortality rate for children below 5 years (per 1000 live births)	128	↑ 4
	Women of reproductive age (aged 15–49 years) who have their need for family planning satisfied with modern methods (%)	13.4	**
8 Inclusive and sustainable economic growth, employment and decent work for all	Annual growth rate of real GDP (%)	−1.58	↑ 3.48
	Annual growth rate of real GDP per capita (%)	−28.24	↑ 26.9
	Unemployment rate	14.4	↓ 8.9
	Youth (aged 15–24 years) not in education, employment or training (%)	20.9	**
	Number of children aged 5–17 years engaged in child labour (%)	188	↓ 77

*No significant change, **No record, ↑ increase, ↓ decrease in comparison to baseline (2016), [T] data for 2017
Source: NIGERIA Integration of the SDGs into National Development Planning: A Second Voluntary National Review; Tull (2019).

2.1. COVID-19 as a potential driver of household hunger, poverty, and food insecurity

COVID-19 affected various constituents of household food security in Nigeria. Prior to lockdown, households that could afford to stock up food staples purchased more than usual. This stockpiling in addition to disruptions in food supply chain drove prices up in regions where supply was limited. For instance, the price of a 50 kg bag of rice rose to NGN21000[2] from NGN18000, and the price of yam rose from NGN500 to NGN1200 (Akinfenwa 2020). Such increases in the price of staple food pushed them beyond the reach of many farm households, increasing food insecurity, particularly for the 26 million undernourished Nigerians.

Income losses associated with COVID-19 also drove poor farmers to seek alternative income-earning activities – involving migration which increased the risk of spreading the virus. For many farmers, there was the conundrum of whether to follow lockdown rules at the risk of losing their livelihoods or continue farming and risk exposure to COVID-19.[3]

2.2. Impact of COVID-19 on farm households' lives and well-being

Healthy life expectancy in Nigeria is 49 years, thus earning Nigeria a place in the bottom six countries in the world (Soto, Moszoro, and Pico 2020). About one-third of Nigerian smallholder farmers are above 50 years[4] (Anderson et al. 2017). There are links in the severity of COVID-19 and age (Zheng et al. 2020; Liu et al. 2020). Thus, a considerable proportion of farmers in Nigeria is at higher risk. More so, the effect of the virus is acute for individuals with underlying health conditions (Chen et al. 2020; Clark et al. 2020).

Figure 1 reflects Nigerians low confidence in the publicly provided primary healthcare Tilley-Gyado et al. 2016). Many small farmers have to travel 5–9 km to access decent healthcare (Anyiro 2010; Titus, Adebisola, and Adeniji 2015). The lack of basic amenities such as access to clean water for regular hand washing put many rural dwelling farmers at risk. For the millions of farm household that live in rural communities, it is may be unfeasible to social distance, and in the outbreak of the virus to self-isolate.

In addition to COVID –19 posing new-unanticipated health risks, lockdowns have ramifications for SGD3 (especially 3.3)[5] as an effort towards ending the epidemics such as AIDS, tuberculosis, malaria is either delayed or suspended as the focus shifts to COVID-19. Benjaminsen (2020) reported that activities targeted at malaria prevention have largely been deferred. For instance, there has been delays or complete halt in the distribution of mosquito nets and access to other preventive medicines. In addition, the pandemic could lead farmers with pre-existing illnesses to either stay away from hospitals or become neglected due to the shift in health focus.

There are emerging findings globally on the impact of COVID-19 on mental health. Individuals have reported effects on wellbeing ranging from being worried about the future to feeling stressed and anxious (Smith et al. 2020; Lim et al. 2020; Bhuiyan et al. 2020). To address these health-care concerns, the government budgetary allocation to health in 2020 reached a five-year-high. However, with less than 5% of the total annual budget allocated to expenditure on health, it remains well short of the 15% target set by the African Union governments since 2001 (BudgIT 2020).

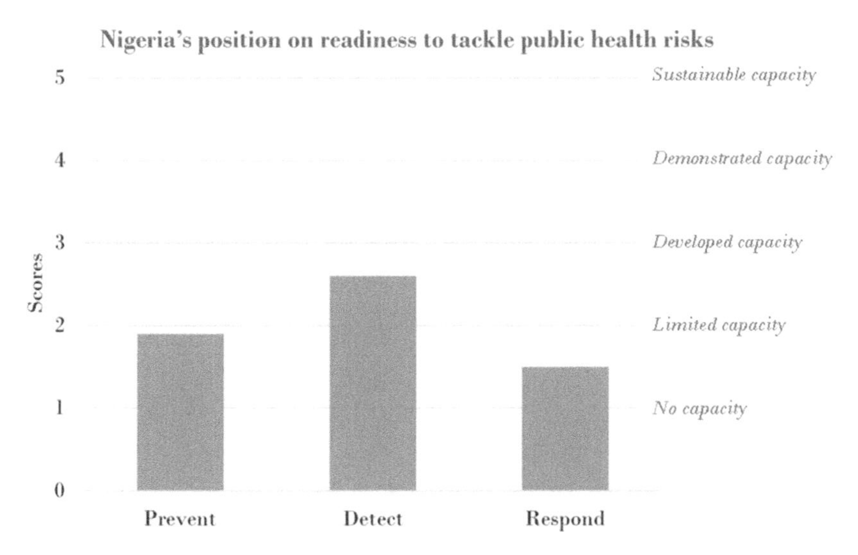

Figure 1. Nigeria's position on readiness to tackle public health risks in 2017 (Adapted from Dixit, Ogundeji, and Onwujekwe 2020 using data from World Health Organisation 2017).

2.3. COVID-19 effect on employment and economic growth

By the end of 2020, approximately 39.4 million people will be unemployed in Nigeria (BusinessDay 2020a). For many households that supplement farm income with wages, regular cash flows depend on household members working. However, this additional source of income may be threatened by COVID-19 posing a risk to full and productive employment. Also, agricultural labourers are likely to be directly affected when farmers are unable to work at full capacity.

Nigeria depends on oil revenues that had already fallen with lower prices triggered by a collapse in demand (Olarewaju 2020). There is evidence of inflation (see Colato 2020; NBS 2020) attributed partly to the pandemic, with food inflation increasing from 14.98% in March to a two-year high of 15.03% in April (Reuters 2020). The increase in consumer prices rose from 0.84% in March to 1.02% in May 2020 (FocusEconomics 2020). It is anticipated that Nigeria's economy would contract by 3.2%, with a recession that had not been witnessed in the past four decades (Nigeria Development Update (NDU) World Bank, 2020). In an economic downturn, the effects are particularly pronounced among lower-income groups and in rural areas (Tisdell and Sen 2004). The projection is that COVID-19 will drive 5 million more Nigerians into poverty in 2020 (NDU, 2020).

2.4. Government action to off-set the economic effects of COVID-19

The Nigerian government have taken steps to cushion the effect of COVID-19 through a stimulus package of 50 billion nairas (EUR 121 million) targeted to support households and micro and small enterprises (Ozili and Arun 2020). The government also announced three-month interest holidays for beneficiaries of microloans of the Government Enterprise and Development Programme (GEEP). Part of the government (at federal and state levels) effort to cushion the effects of the COVID-19 pandemic was through the distribution of food to support vulnerable households. Approximately 77,000 metric tonnes of food consisting mainly of grains were drawn from the National Food and Strategic Reserve – a source which could be depleted if the effect of the pandemic persists. The government announced a cash transfer of 52 USD (representing 4 months advance payment of the monthly stipend of 13 USD) to poor and vulnerable household National Social Register (NSR). However, those on the register constitute around 12% of the people that live below the poverty line (Dixit, Ogundeji, and Onwujekwe 2020). However, there are concerns (see Ajibo, Chukwu, and Okoye 2020; Eranga 2020; BusinessDay 2020b) that these measures are inadequate, and partially excludes the informal sector in which many vulnerable and poor households fall.

3. Methods

We analyse data from the World Bank National Longitudinal Phone Survey (COVID-19 NLPS) consisting of a sample of 1,950 households covering all regions of the country from which we extracted 954 farm households. These households participated in 2018/19 General Household Survey (GHS) approximately a year prior to the outbreak of COVID-19. The GHS data which provided a reliable baseline for comparison are the fourth round of a nationally representative survey made up of a sample of 5,000 households. The COVID-19 NLPS data is collected with the aim of providing close to real-time update on the socio-economic effects of the pandemic. The data covered aspects of food security, employment, access to basic services, income and coping strategies. We compare aspects of food security before and during the outbreak of COVID-19 and changes in household income and employment. We employ descriptive comparison to the same sample of farm household pre-COVID-19 (in 2019) and during COVID-19 (from March 2020).

4. Results and discussion

4.1. Results

To examine the effect of COVID-19 on food security, we investigate the situation in 2019 prior to the global outbreak of the pandemic. The results show that 31% of the farm household were food secure as they did not have to worry about not having enough food to eat either because of lack of money or other resources. On the other hand, 69% were faced with at least one of the following food insecurity issues arising from the household not having enough money or other resources for food. Affected households were either unable to eat healthy and nutritious/ preferred foods, ate only a few kinds of foods, skipped a meal, ate less than they thought they should, household ran out of food, were hungry but did not eat, went without eating for a whole day, restricted consumption in order for children to eat, borrowed food, or relied on help from others outside the household. This highlights the precarious position of farm household even before the outbreak of COVID-19.

Comparing these findings with the period following COVID-19 restrictions in Nigeria, the results show significant effects of COVID-19 on farm household food security. Households where members skipped a meal ran out of food or went a whole day without food increased from 38%, 34% and 12% in the previous year to 74%, 58% and 36% respectively after the outbreak of COVID-19 as presented in Figure 2. An exact McNemar's test determined that there was a statistically significant difference in the proportion of households that skipped a meal ($p = .002$), ran out of food ($p = .036$) or went a whole day without food ($p < .001$) pre – and during – COVID-19.

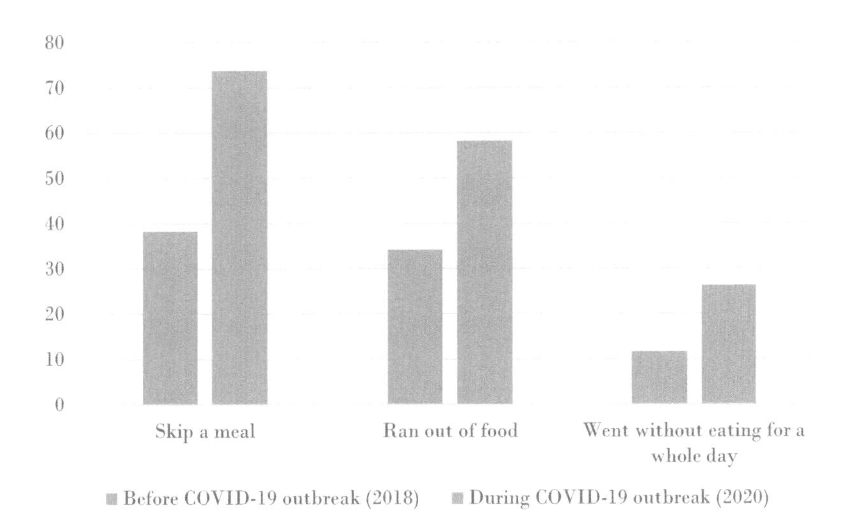

Figure 2. Food insecurity before and during COVID-19.

This finding is in line with the projection of the World Food Program (2020) that COVID-19 will double the number of people facing food crises – with Nigeria contributing significantly to that number, being one of the 10 countries that constituted the worst food crises in 2019. Access to basic food is also affected by COVID-19 restrictions. Due to the pandemic, an average of 21% of the farm households were unable to buy food staples such as rice, beans and processed cassava as shown in Figure 3. At current trends, the household will continue to be at high risk of losing access to food because of shocks associated with COVID-19. With the access to basic food being difficult, the risk of hunger and food insecurity is exacerbated among the half (approximately 51%) of the farm household that are unable to stock up on more food than normal.

The results show that the main reasons reported by farm households for being unable to buy food were lack of money and high food prices – as reported in Figure 4. This is in line with Adeshokan (2020) reporting prices of basic food commodities increasing by up to 50%. This is a major cause for concern as prior to COVID-19 in 2019, at the national level about 56% of The Nigerian households total expenditure was spent on food (according to the consumption expenditure pattern report of the National Bureau of Statistics 2019). This high proportion of total expenditure on food is likely to increase significantly thus resulting in households struggling to meet other basic needs such as housing and children's education. Further, the closure of markets or other travel restrictions being at the bottom of the factors hindering access to food (as presented in Figure 4) is evidence of how COVID-19 intensified financial vulnerabilities of the many households living on less than 1.25 USD a day without savings, credit or insurance.

Since the outbreak of COVID-19, 34% have been unable to perform their normal activities on the farm. This will have a trickle-down effect in terms of unemployment for informal workers that supply farm labour. Crucially, when COVID-19 restrictions coincide with farming activities that require high labour demand – such as planting or harvesting – it would have severe consequence for food supplies at its source.

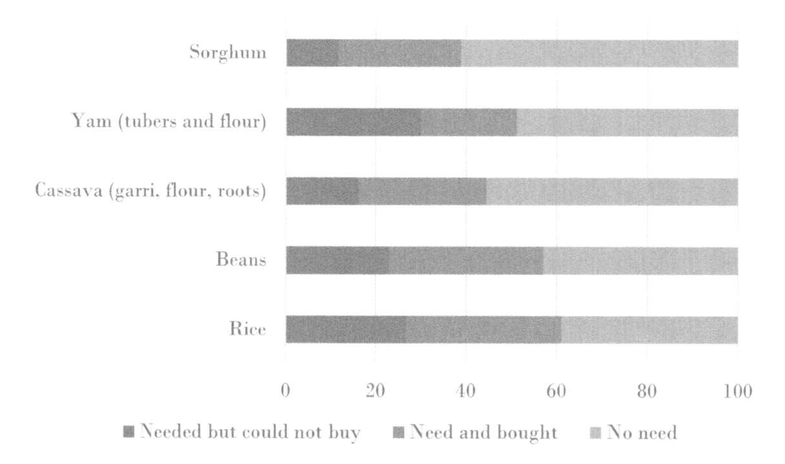

Figure 3. Access to basic food during COVID-19.

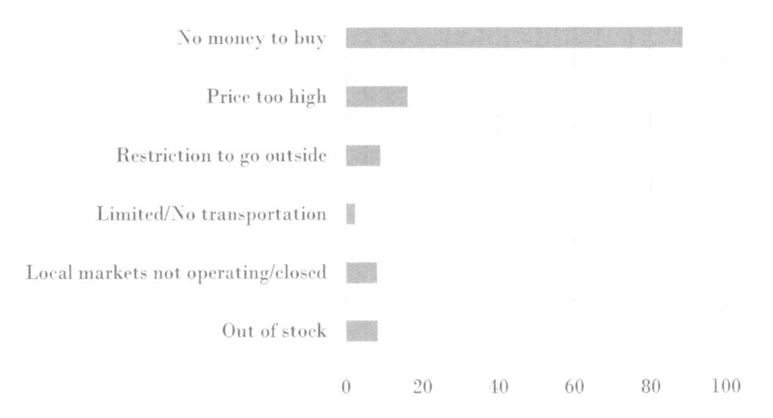

Figure 4. Reasons households are unable to purchase food during COVID-19.

COVID-19 was perceived by 81% of the farm household as a substantial threat to their income; 80% reported a decrease in their total income since the outbreak. Remittances from home and abroad and assistance from outside the household – two important sources of income for many poor farm households – had decreased, as presented in Table 2. This widespread loss in income emanating from both within the country and abroad could be attributed to the simultaneous effect of the pandemic across the country and around the world.

We compared the proportion of farm households that reported a decrease in total income during the pandemic with those whose income stayed the same pre and during the pandemic. We calculated a z-statistic of 49.9 which is greater than the critical value, 1.96 associated with a significance level $\alpha = 0.05$. Thus, we conclude that there was a statistically significant difference between the proportions ($p < .000$).

This decrease in income for many farmers coincided with the planting season. As a result of the inability to afford farm inputs, farmers resorted to either reducing the area planted, planting more variety of crops as some sort of insurance or delaying planting altogether.

Households in food crises are likely to have a weakened immune system, thus increasing the risk of developing severe COVID-19 symptoms. Approximately, 75% of the households feel very worried about the possibility of either them or someone in their household

Table 2. Changes in household income by source due to COVID-19.

Income source	N	Increased	Stayed the same	Decreased
Household farming, livestock or fishing	935	8.8	19.5	71.8
Nonfarm family business	633	7.6	9.3	83.1
Wage employment of household members	308	2.9	43.2	53.9
Remittances from abroad	30	0.0	33.3	66.7
Remittances from family within the country	187	2.7	21.9	75.4
Assistance from other nonfamily individuals	211	7.6	12.8	79.6
Income from properties, investments or savings	144	11.1	26.4	62.5
Pension	50	2.0	82.0	16.0
Assistance from the Government	33	18.2	27.3	54.5
Assistance from NGOs/charitable organization	33	18.2	3.0	78.8
Other	8	12.5	25.0	62.5
Total household income	895	4.9	14.5	80.6

Source: Authors compilation with data from 2020 COVID-19 National Longitudinal Phone Survey (COVID-19 NLPS) baseline.

becoming seriously ill from COVID-19. This anxiety could impact on mental wellbeing. The findings in this paper are similar to global findings, e.g. Roy et al. (2020) in India where over two-thirds of respondents reported being worried for themselves and their close ones. In addition, the findings support the postulation by Frissa and Dessalegn (2020) that the poor health-care systems could result in the immense impact of COVID-19 on mental health and wellbeing, especially if mental health services in Sub-Saharan Africa are not improved.

4.2. Discussion

Following the spread of the virus, the primary risks to food security arose from food supply chain disruption and loss of incomes and remittances. There is thus a need for government action regarding the provision of financial and food assistance. In addition, by the government declaring as 'essential' all services responsible for food production and supply, the food supply chain could be kept running. However, it is crucial to ensure those involved in the chain comply with necessary safety rules and guidelines. Another way in which COVID-19 affected food security decreases in purchasing power. The sharp and unanticipated rise in food prices increased the cost of households' typical consumption basket.

The pandemic in the face of corruption also triggered social vices. There were accusations that authorities hoarded food and nonfood items handed to the government by a private-sector coalition against the coronavirus (CA-COVID). This resulted in COVID-19 relief materials in warehouses across one-third of the 36 states being ransacked. Legacies of corruption compromised the pandemic relief measures, denying poor households much-needed support – jeopardizing efforts targeted at the attainment of the SDGs.

5. Conclusion

COVID-19 restrictions disrupted economic activities for farm households, sparking food security concerns. The COVID-19 pandemic laid bare once again the hungry farmer paradox. With few buffers for situations of diminished purchasing power, many farm households are vulnerable to shocks. COVID-19 thus created a substantial threat at the household level and was an obstacle to the attainment of SDGs 1, 2, 3 and 8 in Nigeria.

While COVID-19 will be defeated in due course, recovery plans and actions will determine the impact it will leave behind. Conducting a post-COVID-19 need assessment is an important early step to recovery. Social protection targeting poor households is urgently needed. It is crucial that farm households have access to appropriate support and resources – not only to recover but to build resilience and reduce vulnerability to future shocks.

Notes

1. The government's Economic Recovery and Growth Plan (2017–20) was designed to sustain economic growth while promoting social inclusion and investing in people. The Nigeria Agenda 2050 plan and the Medium-Term National Development Plan (MTNDP) aims to move 100 million Nigerians out of poverty over the next 10 years.
2. US$1 is equivalent to NGN 361 (Central Bank of Nigeria rate, June 2020).

3. Nigeria ranks fourth globally in a number of undernourished people, with 13.07% of the population in 2018 undernourished (Worldometers 2020).
4. This age differs from most developing countries and particularly several in Africa where (according to the FAO 2014) the estimated average age of farmers is about 60. However, as 61% of the Nigerian population is under 25 (Central Intelligence Agency 2020), farming can be seen to be unattractive to the young.
5. SDG3 (3.3): By 2030, end the epidemics of AIDS, tuberculosis, malaria and neglected tropical diseases and combat hepatitis, water-borne diseases, and other communicable diseases.

Disclosure statement

The authors declare that they have no competing interests.

Funding

The authors received no specific funding for this work.

ORCID

Toritseju Begho http://orcid.org/0000-0003-2137-2826

Availability of data and material

The data that support the findings of this study are the Nigeria National Bureau of Statistics-General Household Survey, Panel (GHS-Panel) 2018-19 and Nigeria National Bureau of Statistic COVID-19 National Longitudinal Phone Survey (COVID-19 NLPS) 2020, baseline available in [www.microdata.worldbank.org] at [https://microdata.worldbank.org/index.php/catalog/3712] and [https://microdata.worldbank.org/index.php/catalog/3557].

References

Abdul, I. M. 2020. Covid-19, Lockdown and Transitory Food Insecurity in Nigeria. *Food & Agribusiness Management* 1 (1): 26–30.

Adeshokan, O. 2020. “Coronavirus: Food Insecurity Fallout from Nigeria’s Lockdown.” Accessed 06 July 2020. https://www.theafricareport.com/27676/coronavirus-food-insecurity-fallout-from-nigerias-lockdown/

Ajibo, H. T., N. E. Chukwu, and U. U. Okoye. 2020. “COVID-19, Lockdown Experiences and the Role of Social Workers in Cushioning the Effect in Nigeria.” *Journal of Social Work in Developing Societies* 2: 2.

Akinfenwa, G. 2020. “COVID-19: Food Prices Hit 15.03% High in 2 Years.” Accessed 06 July 2020. https://guardian.ng/features/covid-19-food-prices-hit-15-03-high-in-2-years/

Anderson, J. B., C. Marita, D. Musiime, and M. Thiam 2017. “National Survey and Segmentation of Smallholder Households in Nigeria: Understanding Their Demand for Financial, Agricultural, and Digital Solutions.” No. 122092, 1–93. World Bank.

Anyiro, C. O. 2010. “The Impact of Inaccessible Health Care Services on Agricultural Production by Rural Farmers in Umuahia North Local Government Area, Abia State, Nigeria.” *Advances in Agriculture & Botanics* 23: 265–271.

Apata, T. G., Y. G. N’Guessan, K. Ayantoye, A. Badmus, O. Adewoyin, S. Anugwo, and A. Ajakpovi. 2018. “Tenacity of Small Farms and Poverty Levels: Evidence of Relationship among Farming Households in Nigeria.” *Research on Crops* 194: 775–786.

Benjaminsen. 2020. "World Malaria Day: Covid-19's Wrecking Ball on SDG 3?" Accessed 2 July 2020. https://lidc.ac.uk/world-malaria-day-covid-19s-wreaking-ball-on-sdg3/

Bhuiyan, A. I., N. Sakib, A. H. Pakpour, M. D. Griffiths, and M. A. Mamun. 2020. "COVID-19-related Suicides in Bangladesh Due to Lockdown and Economic Factors: Case Study Evidence from Media Reports." *International Journal of Mental Health and Addiction.* doi:10.1007/s11469-020-00307-y.

BudgIT. 2020. "2020 Budget Analysis and Opportunities." Accessed 5 July 2020. https://yourbudgit.com/wp-content/uploads/2020/03/2020-Budget-Analysis.pdf

BusinessDay. 2020a. "NBS to Release Newest Unemployment Report by End of July." Says Finance Minister. Accessed 17 July 2020. https://businessday.ng/lead-story/article/nbs-to-release-newest-unemployment-report-by-end-of-july-says-finance-minister/

BusinessDay. 2020b. "Lamentation Still Trails Lagos, FG's Palliative Package as Middlemen Hijack Programme." Accessed 18 May 2020. http//:lamentation-still-trails-lagos-fgs-palliative-packages-as-middlemen-hijack-programme/amp/

CBN. 2020. Accessed 5 July 2020. https://www.cbn.gov.ng/rates/ExchRateByCurrency.asp

Chen, N., M. Zhou, X. Dong, J. Qu, F. Gong, Y. Han and T. Yu. 2020. "Epidemiological and Clinical Characteristics of 99 Cases of 2019 Novel Coronavirus Pneumonia in Wuhan, China: A Descriptive Study." *The Lancet* 39510223: 507–513. doi:10.1016/S0140-6736(20)30211-7.

Clark, A., M. Jit, C. Warren-Gash, B. Guthrie, H. H. Wang, S. W. Mercer and F. Checchi. 2020. "Global, Regional, and National Estimates of the Population at Increased Risk of Severe COVID-19 Due to Underlying Health Conditions in 2020: A Modelling Study." *The Lancet Global Health* 8 (8): e1003-e1017. doi:10.1016/S2214-109X(20)30264-3.

Colato. 2020. "Focuseconomics. Nigeria: Inflation Hits over Two-year High in May." Accessed 28 June 2020. https://www.focus-economics.com/countries/nigeria/news/inflation/inflation-hits-over-two-year-high-in-may-0

Dixit, S., Y. K. Ogundeji, and O. Onwujekwe 2020. "How Well Has Nigeria Responded to COVID-19?" Accessed 05 July 2020. https://www.brookings.edu/blog/future-development/2020/07/02/how-well-has-nigeria-responded-to-covid-19/

Eranga, I. O. E. 2020. "COVID-19 Pandemic in Nigeria: Palliative Measures and the Politics of Vulnerability." *International Journal of Maternal and Child Health and AIDS* 9 (2): 220.

Ezigbo, O., and M. Ifijeh 2020. "Coronavirus Spread: WHO Lists Nigeria Among High Risk Countries." This Day Newspaper, Accessed 15 June 2020.

Fallah, M. P., L. A. Skrip, S. Gertler, D. Yamin, and A. P. Galvani. 2015. "Quantifying Poverty as a Driver of Ebola Transmission." *PLoS Neglected Tropical Diseases* 912: e0004260. doi:10.1371/journal.pntd.0004260.

FAO. 2014. Food security for sustainable development and urbanization: Inputsfor FAO´s contribution to the 2014 ECOSOC Integration Segment. 27-29 May.

FAO. 2018. "Small Family Farms Country Factsheet." Accessed 6 July 2020. http://www.fao.org/3/I9930EN/i9930en.pdf

Frissa, S., and B. W. S. Dessalegn 2020. The mental health impact of the COVID-19 pandemic: Implications for sub-Saharan Africa.

Iloani, F. A., S. E. Sunday, Z. Adaramola, C. Agabi, V. O. C. C. Okeke, U. S. Usman, L. Opoola, E. Agha, C. T. Alabi, and S. M. Ogwu 2020. "Nigeria: Job Cuts Displace Workers As COVID-19 Hits Employers." Accessed 13 June 2020. https://www.dailytrust.com.ng/job-cuts-displace-workers-as-covid-19-hits-employers.html

Kapiriri, L., and A. Ross. 2020. "The Politics of Disease Epidemics: A Comparative Analysis of the SARS, Zika, and Ebola Outbreaks." *Global Social Welfare* 71: 33–45. doi:10.1007/s40609-018-0123-y.

Lim, W. S., C. K. Liang, P. Assantachai, T. W. Auyeung, L. Kang, W. J. Lee, … M. Y. Chou. 2020. "COVID-19 and Older People in Asia: AWGS Calls to Actions." *Geriatrics & Gerontology International* 20 (6): 547–558.

Liu, K., Y. Chen, R. Lin, and K. Han. 2020. "Clinical Features of COVID-19 in Elderly Patients: A Comparison with Young and Middle-aged Patients." *Journal of Infection* 80 (6): e14–e18.

Mgbenka, R. N., E. N. Mbah, and C. I. Ezeano. 2016. "A Review of Small Holder Farming in Nigeria: Need for Transformation." *International Journal of Agricultural Extension and Rural Development Studies* 32: 43–54.

National Bureau of Statistics NBS. 2019. "Consumption Expenditure Pattern in Nigeria." Accessed 8 July 2020. https://nigerianstat.gov.ng/elibrary

National Bureau of Statistics NBS. 2020. Accessed 13 July 2020. https://nigerianstat.gov.ng/elibrary

Nigeria Development Update NDU World Bank. 2020. "Nigeria in Times of COVID-19: Laying Foundations for a Strong Recovery. Nigeria Development Update." Accessed 7 July 2020. https://reliefweb.int/sites/reliefweb.int/files/resources/Nigeria-in-Times-of-COVID-19-Laying-Foundations-for-a-Strong-Recovery.pdf

Nigeria's 2020 Voluntary National Review (VNR). 2020. "NIGERIA Integration of the SDGs into National Development Planning A Second Voluntary National Review. The Office of the Senior Special Assistant to the President on SDGs OSSAP-SDGs." The Federal Secretariat, Phase II. Abuja, Nigeria. https://sustainabledevelopment.un.org/content/documents/26308VNR_2020_Nigeria_Report.pdf

Olarewaju. 2020. "Nigeria's post-COVID-19 Recovery Plan Has Some Merit. But It Misses the Mark." Accessed 06 July 2020. https://theconversation.com/nigerias-post-covid-19-recovery-plan-has-some-merit-but-it-misses-the-mark-140974

Ozili, P. K., and T. Arun 2020. Spillover of COVID-19: Impact on the Global Economy. Available at SSRN 3562570.

Penrhys-Evan. 2020. "COVID-19 in West Africa: The Impacts for Agricultural Enterprises - FAC Blog." Accessed 9 July 2020. https://www.future-agricultures.org/blog/covid-19-in-west-africa-the-impacts-for-agricultural-enterprises/

Reuters. 2020. "UPDATE 1-Nigeria Inflation Rose for Eighth Month in April on Higher Food Prices." Accessed 2 July 2020. https://uk.reuters.com/article/nigeria-inflation/update-1-nigeria-inflation-rose-for-eighth-month-in-april-on-higher-food-prices-idUKL8N2D340B

Roy, D., S. Tripathy, S. K. Kar, N. Sharma, S. K. Verma, and V. Kaushal. 2020. "Study of Knowledge, Attitude, Anxiety & Perceived Mental Healthcare Need in Indian Population during COVID-19 Pandemic." *Asian Journal of Psychiatry* 51: 102083. doi:10.1016/j.ajp.2020.102083.

Sachs, J., G. Schmidt-Traub, C. Kroll, G. Lafortune, G. Fuller, and F. Woelm 2020. "The Sustainable Development Goals and COVID-19." Sustainable Development Report 2020. Cambridge: Cambridge University Press

Smith, L., L. Jacob, A. Yakkundi, D. McDermott, N. C. Armstrong, Y. Barnett, G. F. López-Sánchez, S. Martin, L. Butler, and M. A. Tully. 2020. "Correlates of Symptoms of Anxiety and Depression and Mental Wellbeing Associated with COVID-19: A Cross-sectional Study of UK-based Respondents." *Psychiatry Research* 291: 113138. doi:10.1016/j.psychres.2020.113138.

Soto, M., M. W. Moszoro, and J. Pico 2020. Nigeria—Additional Spending Toward Sustainable Development Goals.

The Millennium Development Goals Report. 2015. United Nations, New York.

Tilley-Gyado, R., O. Filani, I. Morhason-Bello, and I. F. Adewole. 2016. "Strengthening the Primary Care Delivery System: A Catalytic Investment toward Achieving Universal Health Coverage in Nigeria." *Health Systems & Reform* 24: 277–284. doi:10.1080/23288604.2016.1234427.

Tisdell, C. A., and R. K. Sen, Eds. 2004. *Economic Globalisation: Social Conflicts, Labour and Environmental Issues*. UK: Edward Elgar Publishing.

Titus, O. B., O. A. Adebisola, and A. O. Adeniji. 2015. "Health-care Access and Utilization among Rural Households in Nigeria." *Journal of Development and Agricultural Economics* 75: 195–203.

Tull, K. 2019. "Stunting, Wasting and Education in Nigeria." K4D Helpdesk Report 540. Brighton, UK: Institute of Development Studies.

UN. 2015. "Sustainable Development Goals: 17 Goals to Transform Our World." Accessed 6 July 2020. http://www.un.org/sustainabledevelopment/

UNDP. 2020. "Putting the UN Framework for Socio-Economic Response to Covid-19 into Action: Insights. Brief Prepared by the United Nations Development Programme June 2020." [Accessed 15 July 2020. file://san/Homes/tbegho/My%20Documents/Downloads/Brief2-COVID-19-final-June2020.pdf

World Bank. 2015. "Half of the World's Poor Live in Just 5 Countries." Accessed 7 July 2020. https://www.worldbank.org/en/topic/poverty#:~:text=Half%20of%20the%20world's%20poor%

20live%20in%20just%205%20countries,-Share%20of%20poor&text=Of%20the%20world's%20736%20million,Congo%2C%20Ethiopia%2C%20and%20Bangladesh

World Food Program. 2020. "2020 Global Report on Food Crises." Accessed 15 July 2020. https://docs.wfp.org/api/documents/WFP-0000114546/download/?_ga=2.206711258.896920919.1595968379-1042484375.1595968379

World Health Organisation. 2017. *Joint External Evaluation of IHR Core Capacities of the Federal Republic of Nigeria*. Geneva: World Health Organization. Accessed 13 June 2020. https://apps.who.int/iris/bitstream/handle/10665/259382/WHO-WHE-CPI-REP-2017.46-eng.pdf?sequence=1

Worldometers. 2020. "Undernourished People in the World Nigeria." Accessed 15 July 2020. https://www.worldometers.info/undernourishment/

Zheng, Z., F. Peng, B. Xu, J. Zhao, H. Liu, J. Peng, … C. Ye. 2020. "Risk Factors of Critical & Mortal COVID-19 Cases: A Systematic Literature Review and Meta-analysis." *Journal of Infection* 81 (2): e16-e25. doi:10.1016/j.jinf.2020.04.021.

The political risk factors of COVID-19

J. Eduardo Vera-Valdés

ABSTRACT

This paper analyses a broad range of macro variables to assess the effects they have on the number of cases and deaths due to COVID-19. We consider 23 explanatory variables on health, political, and economic factors for 94 countries. Given the vast number of explanatory variables analysed, the paper employs advanced statistical tools for the analysis. We use regularised regression and dimension reduction methods to increase estimation efficiency. We find that alcohol drinking is associated with an increase in the number of cases and deaths due to COVID-19. In this regard, our results support the World Health Organization's recommendation of reducing alcohol drinking during the pandemic. Furthermore, our results show that the level of trust inside the society is associated with both the number of cases and deaths. A higher level of trust in medical personnel is associated with fewer cases, while a higher level of trust in the government is associated with fewer deaths due to COVID-19. Finally, hospital beds per thousand inhabitants are a statistically significant factor in reducing the number of deaths. Our results are robust to the estimation method, and they are of interest to governments and authorities responsible for the control of the pandemic.

1. Introduction

The COVID-19 pandemic has resulted in a major health crisis costing hundreds of thousands of lives around the World. Furthermore, as a way to mitigate the spread of the virus and reduce the number of cases and deaths, governments had to impose several restrictions on movement and commerce. These restrictions resulted in significant economic downturns whose total effects will not be known for several years; see (Rodríguez-Caballero and Vera-Valdés 2020). Even though the pandemic is still ongoing, much knowledge has been gained in the past months.

We are starting to isolate some of the potential risk factors on an individual level. In particular, several articles have found evidence for some of the comorbidities of COVID-19. The most prevalent comorbidities seem to be hypertension, diabetes, cardiovascular disease, and respiratory system disease; see (Atkins et al., 2020; Chudasama et al. 2020; Yang et al. 2020). Moreover, some evidence has been obtained regarding the effect that pollution and human habits like smoking and alcohol drinking have on morbidity; see (Alqahtani et al. 2020; Gupta et al. 2020; Hendryx and Luo 2020; Zoran et al. 2020).

This paper adds to the literature on risk factors of COVID-19 on a macro-level. The data shows notable differences in the number of deaths per million inhabitants between countries. Nonetheless, the difference does not seem to be explained due to development, as the cases of Belgium, the United Kingdom, and the United States show. There may be other political or economic variables that may explain the difference in the number of deaths between countries. The goal of this paper is to identify factors that can be of use to design policies aimed at mitigating the number of cases and deaths due to COVID-19.

To achieve this goal, this paper analyses data on health-related variables, political conditions, pollution levels, economic variables, and trust-related variables. We consider 23 variables for 94 countries. The high number of regressors for a macro analysis may result in a lack of degrees of freedom and possible multicollinearity in the estimation and less efficient estimates. Thus, we use advanced statistical tools to alleviate these concerns.

The surge of machine learning has resurfaced several statistical tools to deal with the problem of not enough degrees of freedom. We use two of the most popular statistical tools to deal with this problem: i) regularised regression via the lasso estimator, see (Hastie, Tibshirani, and Wainwright 2015; Tibshirani 1996), and ii) dimension reduction via principal component regression, see (Jolliffe 1982; Park 1981).

We find that a higher level of alcohol consumption in a country is associated with a higher number of cases and deaths due to COVID-19. Moreover, our results show the importance that trust has on controlling the effects of the pandemic. In particular, we find that trust in medical personnel is negatively associated with the number of cases, while trust in government is negatively related to the number of deaths. In this regard, our results show that collective, coordinated actions are needed to slow the spread of the virus.

This article proceeds as follows. The next section presents the data used in this study. Section 3 presents the results from the analysis, while Section 4 concludes.

2. Data

All data used in this paper were obtained from Our World in Data. The website is a collaborative effort between the researchers of the Oxford Martin Programme on Global Development at the University of Oxford, and the non-profit organisation Global Change Data Lab. We use data on a broad range of health, political, economic, pollution and trust variables.

Besides the health-related measurements, the selected variables capture the distinct political and economic circumstances at each country before the start of the pandemic. We are interested in assessing if a more open and trusting society can cope better with the pandemic. Moreover, following recent results at the micro-level (Gupta et al. 2020; Hendryx and Luo 2020; Zoran et al. 2020), the dataset also allows us to test the comorbidity of pollution at the macro-level.

We first clean the data by removing countries with missing values in any of the variables in Table 1. Then, we consider the last available observation for each country. Even though there is an ongoing debate regarding a probable under-counting of COVID-19 cases and deaths, the statistical tools used for the analysis will not produce biased results as long as the under-counting is proportionally similar for all countries, allowing for some random variation between them. Notwithstanding that the pandemic is not

Table 1. Presents an overview of the data considered in this study.

	Name of variable	Description
Pollution	*Pollution*	Population-weighted average level of exposure to concentrations of suspended particles measuring less than 2.5 microns in diameter. (μg/m^3).
	DeathsPollution	Number of deaths per 100,000 population from both outdoor and indoor air pollution. Age-standardized.
Health	*SmokeDaily*	Estimates of the prevalence of daily smoking, defined as the percentage of men and women, of all ages, who smoke daily.
	Drinking	Share of adults aged 15 and older who drank any form of alcohol within the previous 12 months.
	UnsafeWater	Share of deaths from unsafe water sources.
	Sanitation	Death rates from unsafe sanitation measured as the number of deaths per 100,000 individuals.
	Overweight	Share of adults that are overweight or obese.
	Cardiovascular	Annual number of deaths per 100,000 people from cardiovascular disease.
	Diabetes	Diabetes prevalence (% of population aged 20 to 79).
	Aged65	Share of the population that is 65 years and older.
	HospBeds	Hospital beds per 1,000 people (OECD, Eurostat, World Bank, national government records and other sources).
Trust Variables	*Corruption*	Transparency International's Corruption Perception Index. Scores are on a scale of 0–100, where 0 means that a country is perceived as highly corrupt.
	TrustShare	Share of respondents who answered 'a lot' or 'some' to the question: 'How much do you trust your national government?'
	TrustMedics	Share of people who trust doctors and nurses in their country.
Political Variables	*Literacy*	Estimates of the share of the population older than 14 years that is able to read and write.
	HumanRights	Degree to which governments protect and respect human rights. The values range from −3.8 to around 5.4 (the higher the better).
	PoliticalRegime	The scale goes from −10 (full autocracy) to 10 (full democracy).
Economic Variables	*GiniIndex*	Gini Index. World Bank inequality data. A higher Gini index indicates higher inequality.
	EconomicFreedom	Calculated by the Fraser Institute. Measures the degree to which individuals are free to choose, trade, and cooperate with others. Scores are on a scale of 0–10, where 10 represents maximum economic freedom.
	HealthShare	Public health expenditure (%GDP).
	PopDensity	Number of people divided by land area, measured in square kilometers.
	GDPpcp	Gross domestic product at purchasing power parity (constant 2011 international dollars).
	Poverty	Share of the population living in extreme poverty, most recent year available since 2010.
Dep. Var.	*TotCases*	Total confirmed cases of COVID-19 per 1,000,000 people as of 7 August 2020.
	TotDeaths	Total deaths attributed to COVID-19 per 1,000,000 people as of 7 August 2020.

Data considered. Source: Our World in Data.

over, we believe that the results presented in this paper can be of use in the design and implementation of policies aimed at mitigating the effects of the current wave of the pandemic and help societies to be better prepared for the next one.

The dataset contains 94 countries once we remove missing observations. As such, the analysis covers a broad range of countries with heterogeneous characteristics. Furthermore, countries included in the analysis cover 62% of the global population.[1]

2.1. Standardised data

It is a well-known result that using raw data in a regularised regression can negatively affect the results. Given that regularised regressions penalise the size of the estimates, they are no longer free to take large values that may be associated to variables measured in a reduced scale in comparison to the independent variable, see (Hastie, Tibshirani, and

Friedman 2009). To alleviate these concerns, we standardise the data for all variables. Nonetheless, normalising the data does not qualitatively change the parametric estimation by ordinary least squares. The estimated coefficients adjust to the standardisation, given that they are free to increase with the scaling. In this regard, standardising the data makes it easier to compare estimators.

Moreover, standardised data are easier to analyse and present graphically. Figure 1 presents boxplots for the standardised data. The boxplots are a nonparametric graphical representation of the distribution of the data. They provide a clear representation of the data dispersion, which is preserved after standardisation. Also shown are the 10 countries with the most total of deaths due to COVID-19 (black diamonds), and the 10 countries with the least total of deaths (grey diamonds).

As the figure shows, there is considerable heterogeneity between countries. In particular, the boxplots show that the data covers a broad range of values. Furthermore, there seem to be some extreme values for some of the variables, particularly in exposure to pollution and population density. This further shows the broad range of countries considered in the analysis. That is, the countries considered in this analysis seem to cover a wide subset of the world.

Looking at the characteristics of the countries with the most and least amount of deaths (black and grey diamonds, respectively), we notice that the countries with the most and

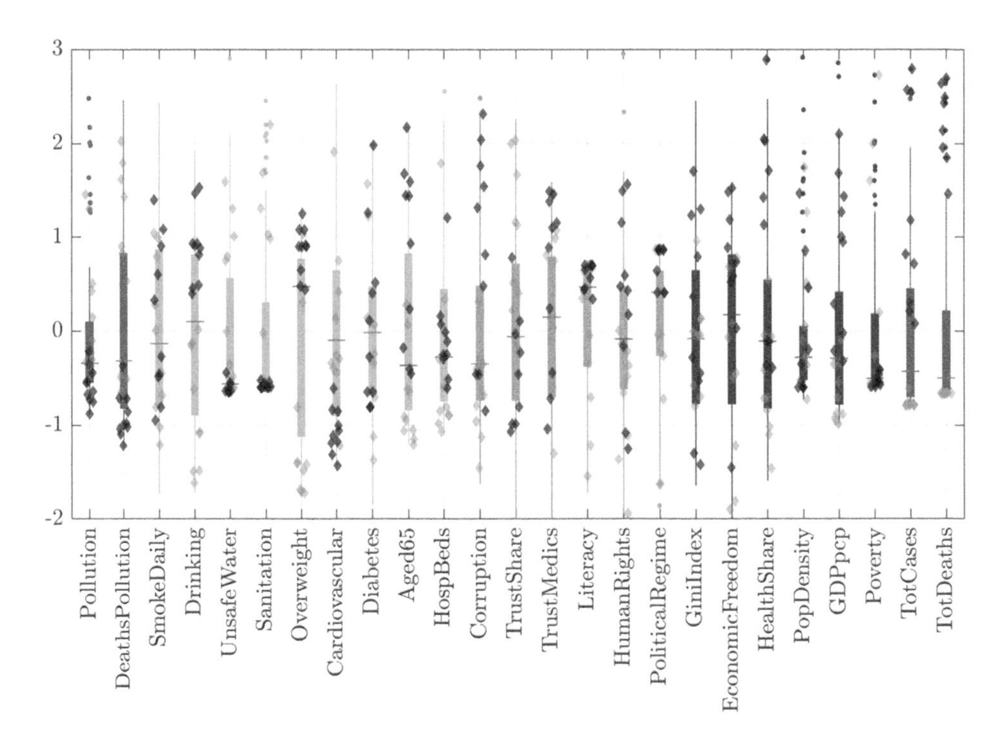

Figure 1. Boxplot of standardised data in Table 1. On each box, the central mark indicates the median, and the bottom and top edges of the box indicate the 25th and 75th percentiles, respectively. The whiskers extend to the most extreme data points not considered outliers, and the outliers are plotted individually. Also shown are the 10 countries with the most total of deaths due to COVID-19 (black diamonds), and the 10 countries with the least total of deaths (grey diamonds).

least amount of deaths due to COVID-19 are quite disperse for most of the variables. That is, there does not seem to be a clear separation from the median for the characteristics of the countries with the most and least amount of deaths; that is, there are black and grey diamonds above and below the median. The exception being *Drinking, Overweight*, and *PoliticalRegime*. Thus, we may expect these variables to have some statistical explanatory power. Nonetheless, the graphical analysis only considers the isolated nonparametric distribution from each variable since we do not control for correlations between the variables. A variable could become significant once we control for other characteristics. Furthermore, a sample size of 20 countries is too small to obtain some statistical significance. Thus, this paper uses a broad range of statistical tools capable of controlling for correlations and using the whole sample size to explain the data.

2.2. Principal component analysis

As Table 1 and Figure 1 show, we have a large number of regressors for a macro-level analysis. A regression considering all of the regressors could potentially suffer from multicollinearity and having too few degrees of freedom which result in a lack of efficiency in the estimates.

Principal component regression is an alternative to regularised regression for dealing with multicollinearity and too few degrees of freedom. The idea behind principal component regression is to reduce the dimension of the space spanned by the regressors. The method first obtains the principal components for the regressors and uses only the ones that capture most of the variance. Typically, only a few principal components are needed to explain most of the variation in the data. This reduces the dimensionality of the regression, which alleviates the possible multicollinearity problem and increases the degrees of freedom.

To estimate principal components regression, we first divide the regressors in five categories.

- PollutionVars: *Pollution, DeathsPollution.*
- HealthVars: *SmokeDaily, Drinking, UnsafeWater, Sanitation, Overweight, Cardiovascular, Diabetes, Aged65, HospBeds.*
- TrustVars: *Corruption, TrustShare, TrustMedics.*
- PoliticalVars: *Literacy, HumanRights, PoliticalRegime.*
- EconomicVars: *GiniIndex, EconomicFreedom, HealthShare, PopDensity, GDPpcp, Poverty.*

Figure 2 presents the biplots, a graphical representation of the magnitude and sign of each variable's contribution to the first two principal components, for the five categories. Each observation in terms of those components is shown inside each biplot, while the arrows show the direction into which each variable moves the most.

As can be seen from the biplots, the first principal component (the x-axis) captures almost all of the variance for each of the categories. That is, the data is quite dispersed in the direction of the first principal component and not as disperse in the direction of the second principal component. Indeed, the first principal component captures more than 80% of the variance for the *PollutionVars* (84%),

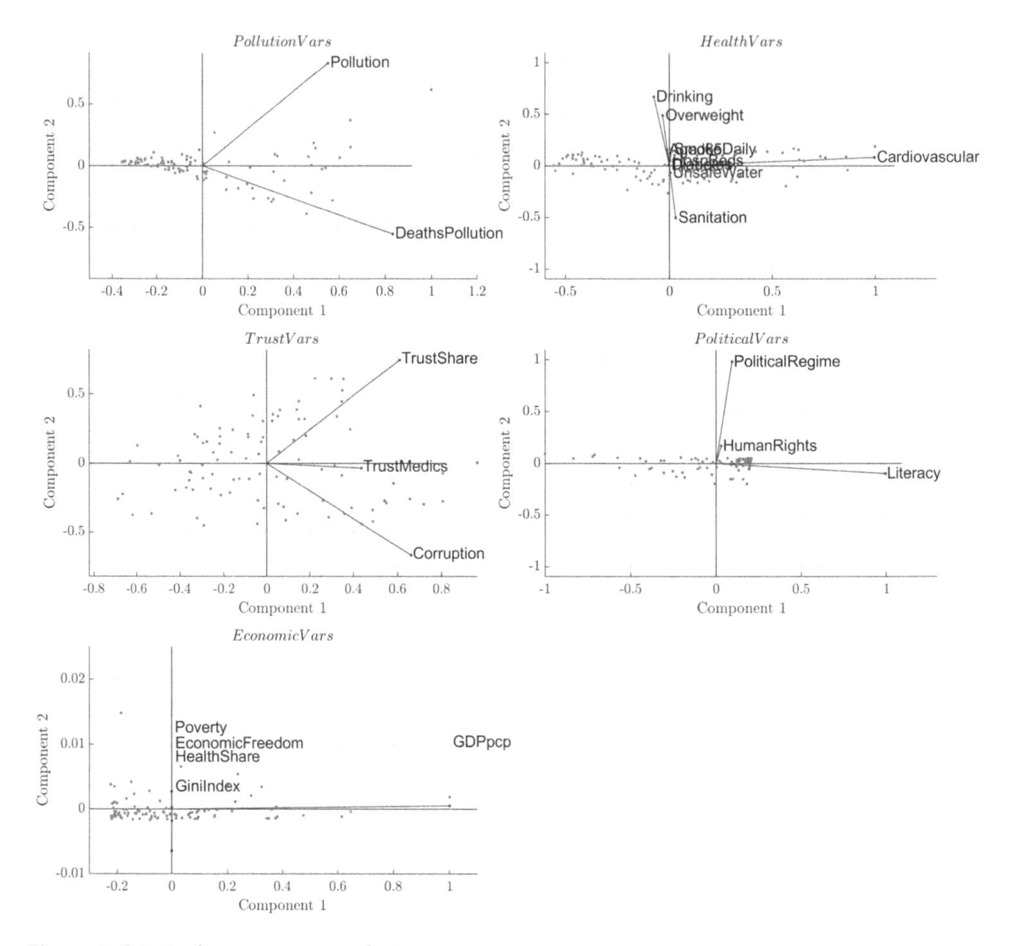

Figure 2. Principal components analysis.

HealthVars (90%), *PoliticalVars* (95%), and *EconomicVars* (99%) categories. The only exception is the variance explained by the first component of the *TrustVars* category that captures (58%) of the variance. These results suggest using only one principal component for the first four categories, while the first and second principal component for the *TrustVars* category may be needed in the analysis.

Furthermore, note that principal component analysis explicitly controls for collinearity in the data. Principal components are selected as the directions into which the regressors move together the most; that is, in the directions of higher collinearity. Principal component regression then uses these directions instead of the whole set of regressors to control for multicollinearity. As shown above, at most two principal components are needed to explain most of the variance of the data, greatly reducing the size of the model.

This section described the data considered in this analysis. A total of 23 explanatory variables are considered. They cover a broad range of characteristics on a large sample of countries. In particular, we argue that individual characteristics by themselves may not be enough to explain the difference in the number of cases or deaths. Thus, this paper uses advanced statistical tools to assess the joint effect that they have on the number of cases and deaths due to COVID-19. Furthermore, we discuss principal component analysis as an alternative method to increase the degrees of freedom and alleviate multicollinearity concerns. We show that for most variables considered, only the first principal component is needed to explain most of the variance of the data.

3. Results

This section presents the results from the statistical analysis of the data presented in Section 2. We use modern statistical tools to get a better understanding of the effects of the political and economic variables on the impact of the pandemic at the macro-level. To ease the exposition, we present the results separately from the confirmed number of cases and the total number of deaths, both measured per million of inhabitants.

3.1. Confirmed cases of COVID-19 per million inhabitants

We consider a linear specification for the total number of cases of COVID-19 per million of inhabitants explained by the health, political, and economic-related macro variables to get a sense of their effects. The model is thus given by

$$TotCases = \alpha + X\beta + \in, \tag{1}$$

where X is a matrix containing the 23 regressors presented in Table 1.

Table 2. Results from parametric estimators for number of cases of COVID-19 - per million inhabitants. Dep. Var., Est., pVal, *RMSE, DoF, Adj.* R^2, *Num. Obs* stand for dependent variable, estimates, p-values, root-mean squared error, degrees of freedom, adjusted R-squared, and number of observations, respectively.

Ordinary least squares estimation is considered by using all of the regressors in the specification. The estimation is thus simple to implement, and standard errors and p-values are easily obtained. Nonetheless, as previously discussed, including such a large set of regressors may significantly reduce the degrees of freedom and could potentially result in estimation problems due to multicollinearity. In turn, few degrees of freedom and multicollinearity problems reduce the efficiency of the estimates.

The results from the ordinary least squares estimation show that Drinking seems to be positively associated with an increase in the number of cases of COVID-19. This result may point to the fact that gatherings of people increase the spread of the virus, particularly in closed environments like nightclubs, pubs, and bars. Thus, policies aimed at controlling the opening and functioning of indoor alcohol drinking places may play a major role in controlling the pandemic. For example, South Africa recently banned the sale of alcohol to mitigate the effects of the pandemic.[2] Moreover, some countries in our sample have active bans on alcohol sale. Results from the analysis excluding these countries (there are five countries with total bans and seven with total or partial bans) are qualitatively the same, and they are available upon request. Thus, our results are robust when controlling for countries with bans on alcohol sale.

Furthermore, the table shows that *TrustMedics* is negatively related to the number of cases of COVID-19 per million inhabitants. This may point out that societies that trust the recommendations from the health authorities are better equipped to slow the spread

Table 2. Presents the results from estimating Equation (1) using three distinct statistical tools.

Dep. Var: *TotCases*	Ordinary least squares			Forward stepwise selection			Lasso
Variable	Est.	SE	pVal.	Est.	SE	pVal.	Est.
(Intercept)	0.000	0.088	1.000	0.000	0.083	1.000	–
Pollution	−0.051	0.156	0.744	–	–	–	–
DeathsPollution	−0.125	0.341	0.715	–	–	–	–
SmokeDaily	0.140	0.165	0.400	–	–	–	–
Drinking	0.400	0.202	0.051*	0.393	0.157	0.014**	0.165
UnsafeWater	−0.228	0.561	0.686	–	–	–	–
Sanitation	0.476	0.794	0.551	–	–	–	–
Overweight	0.245	0.274	0.374	0.272	0.180	0.135	0.226
Cardiovascular	−0.003	0.193	0.989	–	–	–	−0.085
Diabetes	−0.109	0.124	0.381	–	–	–	–
Aged65	−0.359	0.253	0.160	−0.224	0.192	0.246	−0.058
HospBeds	−0.222	0.169	0.194	−0.145	0.121	0.234	−0.006
Corruption	0.025	0.247	0.919	–	–	–	–
TrustShare	0.115	0.170	0.501	0.162	0.146	0.270	–
TrustMedics	−0.306	0.167	0.071*	−0.266	0.141	0.063*	−0.089
Literacy	0.033	0.240	0.891	–	–	–	–
HumanRights	−0.297	0.180	0.102	−0.267	0.137	0.055*	−0.023
PoliticalRegime	0.143	0.128	0.269	0.165	0.110	0.140	0.022
GiniIndex	0.199	0.136	0.146	0.206	0.108	0.060*	0.200
EconomicFreedom	0.003	0.142	0.981	–	–	–	–
HealthShare	0.064	0.177	0.719	–	–	–	–
PopDensity	0.099	0.117	0.402	–	–	–	–
GDPpcp	0.332	0.206	0.111	0.365	0.159	0.024**	0.139
Poverty	−0.440	0.320	0.173	−0.221	0.142	0.123	−0.109
RMSE		0.854			0.854		0.796
DoF		70			82		83
Adj. R^2		0.270			0.354		–
Num. Obs.		94			94		94

of the virus. In this regard, constant honest communication from the health authorities may help in controlling the pandemic.

As previously argued, the large set of regressors considered in Equation (1) could potentially produce too few degrees of freedom and multicollinearity problems. One common measurement used to assess multicollinearity problems is to compute the variance inflation factor (VIF) for each regressor. The VIF for the j-th regressor is computed by:

$$VIF\left(\beta_j\right) = \frac{1}{1 - R^2_{X_j|X_{-j}}},$$

where $R^2_{X_j|X_{-j}}$ is the R-squared from a regression of the j-th variable onto all of the other variables. The idea is that if $R^2_{X_j|X_{-j}}$ is close to one, then multicollinearity is suspected and the *VIF* will be large; see (James et al. 2013). The *VIF* is not a statistical test in the sense that there does not exist a distribution associated to it, and thus no critical values can be obtained. As a rule of thumb, a *VIF* value that exceeds 10 indicates a problematic amount of multicollinearity. In our complete specification in Equation (1), four variables are found to be probable candidates for multicollinearity problems according to their *VIF*.[3] Thus, the significance of our estimates could be affected making the estimation find less variables to be significant that if no multicollinearity problems were detected. A related problem to multicollinearity is how to deal with the variables that are under suspicion of multicollinearity. One way to get rid of multicollinearity could be to remove some of the variables that are highly correlated. Nonetheless, we may wrongly remove one of the variables with the most explanatory power. Thus, in the following we use systematic procedures to deal with multicollinearity.

To alleviate the concerns on the degrees of freedom and multicollinearity problems, the table also presents results from estimating Equation (1) using forward stepwise selection. The idea behind forward stepwise selection is to start with the simplest model containing only the constant term and add variables one at a time following some fitness criteria. A typical rule is to add a regressor only if it increases the adjusted *R*-squared of the regression, and we stop adding regressors when we can no longer increase the adjusted *R*-squared. Recall that, unlike the standard *R*-squared that always increases as we add more regressors, the adjusted *R*-squared computes a trade-off between explanatory power and number of regressors included. Thus, we add an extra regressor to the specification only if the added explanatory power more than compensates the loss of the degree of freedom by the extra regressor, see (James et al. 2013). The estimation is thus simple but computationally burdensome. The advantage of forward stepwise selection is that the selected model is usually much smaller than the complete model, which results in more degrees of freedom and less multicollinearity problems. In our estimation by forward stepwise selection, no regressor is found to be concern for multicollinearity problems according to their *VIF*. Thus, forward stepwise selection helps in increasing estimation efficiency.

The increase in efficiency gained from forward stepwise selection allows us to isolate some other factors that may explain the different number of cases of COVID-19 - per million inhabitants between countries.

First, in agreement with ordinary least squares, forward stepwise selection identifies *Drinking* and *TrustMedics* as significant variables capable of explaining the number of cases.

Furthermore, forward stepwise selection finds that *HumanRights* is negatively associated with the number of cases. This may suggest that protecting and respecting human rights may allow the population of a country to decide the best way to avoid contagious on a macro-level. As argued by the (World Health Organization 2020a), 'human rights frameworks provide a crucial structure that can strengthen the effectiveness of global efforts to address the pandemic. Protecting human rights can help address public health concerns, by requiring, for example, that proactive measures such as ensuring accurate information are made available and that stigmatising and discriminatory behaviour and practices are identified and stopped'.

Then, both *GiniIndex* and *GDPpcp* are positively associated with the number of cases. In conjunction, these factors suggest that more developed countries with high levels of economic inequality are associated with a higher number of cases. This may point to the fact that the population in this type of countries are typically more individualistic, and thus less prone to act in a way that benefits society in general at a small personal cost. The current debate around the wearing of masks in the United States, Mexico, and Brazil is an example of an egoistic behaviour that makes it harder to stop the spread of the virus. As pointed by (Cheng, Lam, and Leung 2020), 'mass masking is a useful and low-cost adjunct to social distancing and hand hygiene during the COVID-19 pandemic. This measure shifts the focus from self-protection to altruism, actively involves every citizen, and is a symbol of social solidarity in the global response to the pandemic'. Thus, the results suggest that societies that show more solidarity are better equipped to control the spread of the virus.

Moreover, focusing on the significant variables from forward stepwise selection, we can expand the list of countries considered in the analysis. An additional 35 countries, bringing the total to 129 countries covering 94% of the population, are included in the reduced specification once we list all countries without missing observations in these variables only. The results from the reduced specification, reported in Table A2 in Appendix A.3, are qualitatively the same as the ones in Table 2, showing the robustness of the results.

A further alternative to reduce the dimensionality of the estimation is regularised regression. In this paper, we focus on the lasso estimator. Lasso adds a penalty term as a function of the size of the estimates to the residual sum of squares defined by ordinary least squares. That is, lasso solves the problem given by

$$min_{\beta} = (TotCases - \alpha - x\beta)^{'}(TotCases - \alpha - x\beta) + \lambda|\beta|_{\ell_1},$$

where λ is the weight associated to the penalty term, and $|\beta|_{\ell_1}$ is the ℓ_1-norm given by $|\beta|_{\ell_1} = \sum_{i=1}^{n} |\beta_i|$ where $\beta' = (\beta_1, \ldots, \beta_n)$. The use of ℓ_1-norm allows the lasso estimator to make variable selection. That is, the lasso is capable of selecting the variables that increase the fit of the model and removing the rest. As such, lasso estimation increases the degrees of freedom and controls for multicollinearity by constructing a smaller model. The weight λ is typically selected by cross-validation so that the model is fit in a subset of the data and evaluated in the remaining observations. We select the λ with the best fit to the data.

One drawback of lasso estimation is that standard errors and p-values for inference are no longer a byproduct of the estimation.[4] Nevertheless, lasso estimates can give us an indication regarding which variables better seem to explain the number of cases of COVID-19 per million inhabitants.

Results from the lasso estimation in Table 2 are much in line with forward stepwise selection except for the replacement of *Cardiovascular* for *TrustShare*. As such, the main outcomes are maintained.

A final alternative to deal with the high dimensionality of the specification is presented in Table 3. The table shows the results from principal component regression for *TotCases*. Principal component regression is a dimensionality reduction method to estimate a linear model with a large number of regressors; see (Jolliffe 1982; Park 1981). The idea is to project the regressors into a lower-dimensional space spanned by the principal components, and estimate the specification in this lower-dimensional space. The method thus alleviates multicollinearity concerns and increases degrees of freedom which result in more efficient estimates.

Principal component regression uses ordinary least squares in the equation given by

$$\begin{aligned} TotCases = {} & \alpha + \beta_1 PollutionVars + \beta_2 HealthVars + \beta_3 PoliticalVars + \beta_4 EconomicVars \\ & + \beta_5 TrustVars + \in, \end{aligned} \tag{2}$$

Table 3. Results estimation by principal components regression for number of cases of COVID-19 per million inhabitants. Dep. Var., Est., pVal, *RMSE, DoF, Adj.* R^2, *Num. Obs.* stand for dependent variable, estimates, *p*-values, root-mean squared error, degrees of freedom, adjusted *R*-squared, and number of observations, respectively.

Dep. Var: *TotCases*	Principal component regression			Principal component regression		
Variable	Est.	SE	pVal.	Est.	SE	pVal.
(Intercept)	0.000	0.091	1.000	0.000	0.091	1.000
PollutionVars	−0.091	0.213	0.669	−0.137	0.224	0.543
HealthVars	−0.235	0.114	0.043**	−0.233	0.115	0.045**
PoliticalVars	0.172	0.182	0.347	0.158	0.184	0.393
EconomicVars	0.289	0.160	0.075*	0.346	0.182	0.061*
TrustVars	−0.317	0.128	0.015**	−0.365	0.147	0.015**
TrustVars 2PC	–	–	–	0.091	0.136	0.504
RMSE		0.881			0.883	
DoF		88			87	
Adj. R^2		0.224			0.220	
Num. Obs.		94			94	

where the variables are obtained by principal component analysis as described in Section 2.2. Furthermore, as previously discussed, the first principal component already explains more than 80% of the variation for all variables besides *TrustVars* where two first principal components may be needed in the analysis.

Notice that by construction, Equation (2) has fewer regressors than Equation (1), and thus more degrees of freedom. Moreover, no variable is found to be of concern for multicollinearity problems according to their *VIF*.

Moreover, from Table 3 notice the decrease in the adjusted *R*-squared an increase in root-mean-squared error from the specification with only the first principal component against the one including two first principal components for *TrustVars*. These statistics suggest that including two first principal components result in worse explanatory power. Thus, we continue the analysis considering only the specification with just one first principal component for all variables.

The results from principal component regression in Table 3 show that *HealthVars*, *EconomicVars*, and *TrusVars* are significantly related to the number of cases per million inhabitants. Recalling that *Drinking* is contained in the *HealthVars* category (with negative loading as shown in Figure 2 and Appendix A.4), *TrustMedics* is contained in the *TrustVars* category (with positive loading), and that *GiniIndex* and *GDPpcp* are contained in the *EconomicVars* category (both with positive loadings), the results from principal component regression are much in line with the results from the forward stepwise selection and lasso estimation. As such, the results are quite robust to the estimation method.

3.2. Deaths by COVID-19 per million inhabitants

In this section, we model the total number of deaths by COVID-19 per million of inhabitants using a linear specification on the health, political, and economic-related variables. The model is thus given by

$$TotDeaths = \alpha + X\beta + \in, \tag{3}$$

where X is a matrix containing the 23 regressors presented in Table 1.

Analogously to the analysis for the number of cases, we estimate Equation (3) using several statistical methods. The results from the estimations using ordinary least squares, forward stepwise selection, and lasso are presented in Table 4.

The results from ordinary least squares estimation using all of the variables show that only *HospBeds* and *HumanRights* seem to be significantly associated with the number of deaths, both with negative signs. These results suggest that hospital capacity measured in the number of beds available per thousand inhabitants helps in controlling the number of deaths due to COVID-19. This result supports the high priority that several countries set around hospital capacity to deal with the effects of COVID-19, particularly after noticing the impact of the pandemic in Italy and Spain; see (Moghadas et al. 2020; Remuzzi and Remuzzi 2020). In particular, having more available hospital beds to treat patients worst hit by COVID-19 is shown to reduce the number of deaths.

Moreover, countries that better respect human rights are associated with a fewer number of deaths due to COVID-19. As previously argued, this result may relate to a population that is freer to decide how to avoid getting infected or once infected how to look for proper care. In particular, governments should pay explicit attention to the needs and vulnerabilities faced by the most vulnerable that subjects them to a higher risk of infection and undermines the broader COVID-19 response. Human rights guarantees

Table 4. Results from parametric estimators for number of deaths by COVID-19 per million inhabitants. Dep. Var., Est., pVal, *RMSE, DoF, Adj.* R^2, *Num. Obs* stand for dependent variable, estimates, *p*-values, root-mean squared error, degrees of freedom, adjusted *R*-squared, and number of observations, respectively.

Dep. Var: *TotDeaths*	Ordinary least squares			Forward stepwise selection			Lasso
Variable	Est.	SE	pVal.	Est.	SE	pVal.	Est.
(Intercept)	0.000	0.089	1.000	0.000	0.084	1.000	–
Pollution	−0.063	0.158	0.694	–	–	–	–
DeathsPollution	0.088	0.346	0.800	0.028	0.217	0.897	–
SmokeDaily	0.061	0.168	0.717	–	–	–	–
Drinking	0.251	0.205	0.224	0.361	0.147	0.016**	0.109
UnsafeWater	−0.08	0.569	0.889	–	–	–	–
Sanitation	0.189	0.805	0.815	–	–	–	–
Overweight	0.123	0.278	0.660	–	–	–	0.217
Cardiovascular	−0.212	0.196	0.283	−0.137	0.131	0.298	−0.221
Diabetes	−0.182	0.126	0.152	–	–	–	–
Aged65	0.002	0.257	0.993	–	–	–	–
HospBeds	−0.352	0.172	0.044**	−0.286	0.123	0.022**	−0.005
Corruption	−0.054	0.251	0.831	–	–	–	–
TrustShare	−0.174	0.172	0.315	−0.18	0.104	0.087*	−0.026
TrustMedics	−0.100	0.169	0.557	–	–	–	–
Literacy	0.094	0.244	0.701	–	–	–	–
HumanRights	−0.348	0.182	0.060*	−0.306	0.136	0.026**	–
PoliticalRegime	0.048	0.130	0.711	–	–	–	–
GiniIndex	−0.049	0.138	0.724	–	–	–	–
EconomicFreedom	0.097	0.144	0.502	–	–	–	–
HealthShare	0.23	0.18	0.206	0.253	0.142	0.080*	0.070
PopDensity	0.122	0.119	0.308	–	–	–	–
GDPpcp	0.216	0.209	0.305	0.209	0.164	0.207	–
Poverty	−0.271	0.324	0.406	−0.188	0.149	0.210	–
RMSE		0.867			0.813		0.816
DoF		70			84		88
Adj. R^2		0.249			0.339		–
Num. Obs.		94			94		94

and protections require special measures be put in place to ensure protection from discrimination and to ensure access to information, social services, health care, social inclusion, and education for vulnerable groups in national COVID-19 responses; see (World Health Organization 2020a).

The high number of regressors, and thus the lower degrees of freedom and possible multicollinearity problems, could be one of the reasons behind the few significant estimates computed by ordinary least squares. As previously discussed, one way to alleviate these concerns is to estimate the model using forward stepwise selection to systematically obtain a smaller model. Results from Table 4 using forward stepwise selection show that besides *HospBeds* and *HumanRights* already found to be significant by ordinary least squares, *Drinking*, *TrustShare*, and *HealtShare* are also found to be significantly associated to the number of deaths due to COVID-19 per million inhabitants.

The results from *Drinking* are qualitatively similar to the analysis for the number of cases. Societies with a higher share of the population that drinks alcohol are associated with a higher number of deaths due to COVID-19. This result may be related to the argument for the number of cases. Societies with a higher proclivity to alcohol drinking may be more prone to infection. Furthermore, once infected, alcohol-related health conditions may perversely affect recovery. As argued in (World Health Organization 2020b), 'Alcohol use, especially heavy use, weakens the immune system and thus reduces the ability to cope with infectious diseases'. In this regard, our results support the World Health Organization's recommendation of reducing alcohol drinking during the pandemic.

Furthermore, the positive coefficient for *TrustShare* advocates that societies that trust their governments are better equipped to control the number of deaths due to COVID-19. This may relate to more people believing, and thus following, the government's guidelines regarding COVID-19 mitigation policies. Thus, our results indicate that governments should gain the trust of their citizens as a way to reduce the number of deaths during the pandemic. In this regard, a clear and honest set of guidelines should be implemented.

The result regarding *HealthShare* seems counterintuitive at first. The sign of the coefficient appears to suggest that higher public spending on health care is associated with a more significant number of deaths. Nonetheless, note that spending on health care services includes treatments for cancer, diabetes, and a broad range of cardiovascular diseases. As found by (Dieleman et al. 2017), 'Increases in the US health care spending from 1996 through 2013 were largely related to increases in health care service price and intensity but were also positively associated with population growth and ageing and negatively associated with disease prevalence or incidence'. Thus, it may be the case that countries that spend more in health care are those with a higher proportion of older individuals, with more comorbidities to COVID-19. In this regard, the result from *HospBeds* is particularly revealing. Our results suggest that countries should consciously assign a proportion of their health care spending on policies directly aimed to care for COVID-19 patients to reduce the number of deaths. Nonetheless, note that our explanatory variable only considers available hospital beds. A further determinant for a successful recovery is access to a respirator if needed. In this regard, the effect that respirator availability has on the number of deaths is left open for future research.

Focusing on the significant variables from the forward stepwise selection exercise, we can expand the list of countries considered in the analysis. An additional 26 countries, bringing the total to 120 countries covering 70% of the population, are included in the reduced specification once we list all countries without missing observations in these variables. The results from the reduced specification, reported in Table A3 in Appendix A.3, are qualitatively the same as the ones in Table 4, showing the robustness of the results.

The results from lasso estimation broadly agree with the ones from forward stepwise selection except for *HumanRights*. In this regard, the main outcomes are maintained.

Finally, Table 5 presents the results from principal components regression for *TotDeaths*.

To model *TotDeaths*, principal component regression uses ordinary least squares in the equation given by

$$TotDeaths = \alpha + \beta_1 PollutionVars + \beta_2 HealthVars + \beta_3 PoliticalVars + \beta_4 EconomicVars + \beta_5 TrustVars + \in, \quad (4)$$

where the regressors are defined as in Equation (2). Following the discussion in the section for the number of cases, we consider only one first principal component for all variables.

Notice that the results from principal component regression are much in line with the results on the high-dimensional specification in Equation (3). In particular, *HealthVars*, *EconomicVars*, and *TrustVars* seem to be significantly associated with the number of deaths due to COVID-19 per million inhabitants.

Recalling that *Drinking* and *HospBeds* are contained in the *HealthVars* category (with negative and positive loading, respectively), *HealthShare* is contained in the *EconomicVars* (with positive loading), and *TrustShare* is contained in the *TrustVars* category (with positive loading), the results from principal component regression are much in line with the results from the forward stepwise selection and lasso estimation. As such, the results from the analysis of the number of deaths due to COVID-19 are robust to the estimation method.

Table 5. Results estimation by principal components regression for number of deaths by COVID-19 per million inhabitants. Dep. Var., Est., pVal, *RMSE, DoF, Adj.* R^2, *Num. Obs.* stand for dependent variable, estimates, *p*-values, root-mean squared error, degrees of freedom, adjusted *R*-squared, and number of observations, respectively.

Dep. Var: *TotDeaths*	Principal component regression		
Variable	Est.	SE	pVal.
(Intercept)	0.000	0.089	1.000
PollutionVars	−0.132	0.209	0.530
HealthVars	−0.320	0.112	0.005**
PoliticalVars	0.089	0.178	0.619
EconomicVars	0.263	0.167	0.098*
TrustVars	−0.243	0.125	0.055*
RMSE		0.862	
DoF		88	
Adj. R^2		0.257	
Num. Obs.		94	

4. Conclusions

We have analysed a broad range of health, political, and economic variables at a macro-level to assess the effects that they may have on the number of cases and deaths due to COVID-19. The data contains information on 23 variables for 94 countries. Given the vast amount of regressors, we use a broad range of advanced statistical tools for the analysis. We use regularised regression, forward stepwise selection, and principal component regression to increase the degrees of freedom and control for possible multicollinearity problems which results in increased estimation efficiency. The increase in efficiency allows us to isolate some of the macro-level factors that may explain the difference in the number of cases and deaths due to COVID-19 across countries.

Our results suggest that alcohol drinking has perverse consequences on the effects of the pandemic. We find that at a macro-level, alcohol drinking is positively associated with both the number of cases and deaths due to COVID-19. In this regard, our results support the World Health Organization's advice that people should minimise their alcohol consumption during the pandemic.

Furthermore, we find that higher GDP per capita and income inequality are associated with an increase in the number of cases. The combination of these two factors may point to the fact that an individualistic society is less prone to adopt the necessary altruistic behaviour that may be needed to control the pandemic. As previously argued, this result may relate to the neglect of the use of masks in some of the countries worst hit by COVID-19.

Moreover, our analysis does not support the notion that pollution levels increase the morbidity of COVID-19, at least at a macro-level. Pollution was not found to be a significant factor for either the number of cases or deaths. In this regard, it may be the case that the effect of pollution is a much more local affair that is not maintained in the aggregate at the country level.

Finally, our results highlight the importance that trust has on controlling the pandemic. We find that higher levels of trust in medical personnel are associated with a lower number of COVID-19 cases per million inhabitants. This, of course, reflects the fact that the more people trust the medical staff, the easier it will be for people to follow their recommendations to control the spread of the virus. Moreover, trust in government is found to be significantly associated with the number of deaths due to the pandemic. A higher level of trust in government translates into a lower level of deaths due to COVID-19. Thus, our results highlight that governments with clear and honest communication are better at controlling the perverse effects of the pandemic.

Overall, our results show that collective action is needed to control the pandemic. Countries that are better prepared to cope with COVID-19 are those that can react to the pandemic in a timely, coordinated fashion. Furthermore, the results are robust to the estimation method.

There are several limitations to the present study. As previously noted, under-counting of cases and deaths could bias our results. This is particularly relevant if only a subset of the countries systematically under-report the number of cases and deaths to obscure the true effects of the pandemic. Thus, a proper assessment of the validity of the reporting is called upon. Moreover, this paper considers several statistical tools, all based on a linear specification. Non-linear effects are omitted from the analysis. Finally, our analysis relies on cross-sectional data. Time-variant effects are not captured by the analysis. In this regard, the experience gained by governments from the previous wave of the pandemic cannot be inferred for the second and successive waves. A formal analysis of the changes in the governments' response after the first wave of the pandemic is left for future research.

Notes

1. The list of countries included in the dataset is presented in Appendix A.1, while summary statistics are presented in Appendix A.2. The cleaned data is available with DOI: 10.6084/m9.figshare.12786302.v1.
2. Thanks to the anonymous referee for bringing this to our attention.
3. The variables with *VIF* values greater than 10 are *DeathsPollution, UnsafeWater, Sanitation*, and *Poverty*.
4. Given that we use cross-validation for estimation, and thus use the data to select the weights, standard errors are not valid for the lasso. Statistically speaking, standard errors are not valid given that we use the data twice, for selecting and for estimating the final model, see (Kyung et al. 2010).

Acknowledgements

The author would like to thank the anonymous referee for the valuable comments which helped to improve the manuscript significantly.

Data availability statement

The data that support the findings of this study are available with DOI: 10.6084/m9.figshare.12786302.v1. These data were derived from resources freely available in the public domain in 'Our World in Data'. https://doi.org/10.6084/m9.figshare.12786302.v1

Disclosure statement

The author declares no conflict of interest.

ORCID

J. Eduardo Vera-Valdés http://orcid.org/0000-0002-0337-8055

References

Alqahtani, J. S., T. Oyelade, A. M. Aldhahir, S. M. Alghamdi, M. Almehmadi, A. S. Alqahtani, S. Quaderi, S. Mandal, J. R. Hurst, and G. C. Bhatt. 2020. "Prevalence, Severity and Mortality Associated with COPD and Smoking in Patients with COVID-19: A Rapid Systematic Review and Meta-Analysis." *PloS One* 15 (5): e0233147. doi:10.1371/journal.pone.0233147.

Atkins, J. L., J. A. H. Masoli, J. Delgado, L. C. Pilling, C.-L. Kuo, G. A. Kuchel, D. Melzer, and A. B. Newman. 2020. "Preexisting Comorbidities Predicting COVID-19 and Mortality in the UK Biobank Community Cohort." *The Journals of Gerontology: Series A* 75 (11): 2224–2230. doi:10.1093/gerona/glaa183.

Cheng, K. K., T. H. Lam, and C. C. Leung. 2020. "Wearing Face Masks in the Community during the COVID-19 Pandemic: Altruism and Solidarity." *The Lancet* 2019 (20): 2019–2020. doi:10.1016/S0140-6736(20)30918-1.

Chudasama, Y. V., C. L. Gillies, K. Appiah, F. Zaccardi, C. Razieh, M. J. Davies, T. Yates, and K. Khunti. 2020. "Multimorbidity and SARS-CoV-2 Infection in UK Biobank." *Diabetes & Metabolic Syndrome* 14 (5): 775–776. doi:10.1016/j.dsx.2020.06.003.

Dieleman, J. L., E. Squires, A. L. Bui, M. Campbell, A. Chapin, H. Hamavid, C. Horst, et al. 2017. "Factors Associated with Increases in US Health Care Spending, 1996-2013." *JAMA* 318 (17): 1668–1678. doi:10.1001/jama.2017.15927.

Gupta, A., H. Bherwani, S. Gautam, S. Anjum, K. Musugu, N. Kumar, A. Anshul, and R. Kumar. 2020. "Air Pollution Aggravating COVID-19 Lethality? Exploration in Asian Cities Using Statistical Models." *Environment, Development and Sustainability*. doi:10.1007/s10668-020-00878-9.

Hastie, T., R. Tibshirani, and J. Friedman. 2009. *The Elements of Statistical Learning*.New York, NY: Springer. doi:10.1007/978-0-387-84858-7.

Hastie, T., R. Tibshirani, and M. Wainwright. 2015. *Statistical Learning with Sparsity: The Lasso and Generalizations*. New York, NY: Chapman & Hall. doi:10.1201/b18401.

Hendryx, M., and J. Luo. 2020. "COVID-19 Prevalence and Fatality Rates in Association with Air Pollution Emission Concentrations and Emission Sources." *Environmental Pollution* 265: 115126. doi:10.1016/j.envpol.2020.115126.

James, G., D. Witten, T. Hastie, and R. Tibshirani. 2013. *An Introduction to Statistical Learning*. New York, NY: Springer. http://link.springer.com/10.1007/978–1–4614–7138–7.

Jolliffe, I. T. 1982. "A Note on the Use of Principal Components in Regression." *Journal of the Royal Statistical Society. Series C (Applied Statistics)* 31 (3): 300–303. doi:10.2307/2348005.

Kyung, M., J. Gill, M. Ghosh, and G. Casella. 2010. "Penalized Regression, Standard Errors, and Bayesian Lassos." *Bayesian Anal* 5 (2): 369–411. doi:10.1214/10-BA607.

Moghadas, S. M., A. Shoukat, M. C. Fitzpatrick, C. R. Wells, P. Sah, A. Pandey, J. D. Sachs, et al. 2020. "Projecting Hospital Utilization during the COVID-19 Outbreaks in the United States." *Proceedings of the National Academy of Sciences* 117 (16): 9122 LP– 9126. doi:10.1073/pnas.2004064117.

Park, S. H. 1981. "Collinearity and Optimal Restrictions on Regression Parameters for Estimating Responses." *Technometrics* 23 (3): 289–295. doi:10.2307/1267793.

Remuzzi, A., and G. Remuzzi. 2020. "COVID-19 and Italy: What Next?" *The Lancet* 395 (10231): 1225–1228. doi:10.1016/S0140-6736(20)30627-9.

Rodríguez-Caballero, C. V., and J. E. Vera-Valdés. 2020. "Long-lasting Economic Effects of Pandemics: Evidence on Growth and Unemployment." *Econometrics* 8 (37): 1–16. doi:10.3390/econometrics8030037.

Tibshirani, R. 1996. "Regression Selection and Shrinkage via the Lasso." *Journal of the Royal Statistical Society B* 58 (1): 267–288. doi:10.2307/2346178.

World Health Organization. 2020a. "Addressing Human Rights as Key to the COVID-19 Response". *World Health Organization Publication*, April, 1–4. http://familyplanning2020.org/sites/default/files/COVID/WHO-2019-nCoV-SRH-Rights-2020.1-eng.pdf

World Health Organization. 2020b. "Alcohol and COVID-19: What You Need to Know". *World Health Organization*. https://www.euro.who.int/__data/assets/pdf_file/0010/437608/Alcohol-and-COVID-19-what-you-need-to-know.pdf

Yang, J., Y. Zheng, X. Gou, K. Pu, Z. Chen, Q. Guo, R. Ji, H. Wang, Y. Wang, and Y. Zhou. 2020. "Prevalence of Comorbidities and Its Effects in Patients Infected with SARS-CoV-2: A Systematic Review and Meta-analysis." *International Journal of Infectious Diseases* 94: 91–95. doi:10.1016/j.ijid.2020.03.017.

Zoran, M. A., R. S. Savastru, D. M. Savastru, and M. N. Tautan. 2020. "Assessing the Relationship between Surface Levels of PM2.5 And PM10 Particulate Matter Impact on COVID-19 in Milan, Italy." *Science of the Total Environment* 738: 139825. doi:10.1016/j.scitotenv.2020.139825.

Appendix

A.1. List of countries

List of countries included in the analysis: Albania, Algeria, Argentina, Armenia, Australia, Austria, Bangladesh, Belgium, Benin, Bolivia, Brazil, Bulgaria, Burkina Faso, Burundi, Cameroon, Canada, Chile, Colombia, Costa Rica, Croatia, Denmark, Dominican Republic, Ecuador, El Salvador, Estonia, Ethiopia, Gabon, Gambia, Georgia, Ghana, Greece, Guatemala, Guinea, Haiti, Honduras, Hungary, Iceland, India, Indonesia, Iran, Iraq, Ireland, Israel, Italy, Jordan, Kazakhstan, Kenya, Kyrgyzstan, Latvia, Liberia, Lithuania, Luxembourg, Macedonia, Madagascar, Malawi, Malaysia, Mauritius, Mexico, Moldova, Mongolia, Montenegro, Morocco, Mozambique, Myanmar, Nepal, Nicaragua, Niger, Norway, Pakistan, Panama, Paraguay, Peru, Portugal, Romania, Russia, Slovakia, South Africa, South Korea, Spain, Sri Lanka, Sweden, Tanzania, Thailand, Togo, Tunisia, Turkey, Uganda, Ukraine, United Kingdom, United States, Uruguay, Yemen, Zambia, Zimbabwe.

A.2. Summary statistics

Table A1. Summary statistics.

Variable	Min	Median	Mean	Max
Pollution	5.20	22.00	32.79	203.74
DeathsPollution	9.40	46.46	59.53	160.50
SmokeDaily	3.70	16.40	17.47	36.90
Drinking	1.90	47.85	45.36	93.90
UnsafeWater	0.00	0.21	1.62	10.73
Sanitation	0.00	0.27	11.66	76.93
Overweight	18.10	56.85	48.65	70.20
Cardiovascular	85.76	235.17	246.21	539.85
Diabetes	0.99	6.77	6.83	22.02
Aged65	2.17	7.40	9.65	23.02
HospBeds	0.20	2.16	2.80	12.27
Corruption	14.00	37.00	43.30	88.00
TrustShare	10.95	50.45	51.55	92.34
TrustMedics	49.77	82.23	80.60	98.20
Literacy	19.10	94.84	86.45	100.00
HumanRights	−2.47	0.34	0.47	5.13
*PoliticalRegimea**	−7.00	8.00	6.18	10.00
GiniIndex	25.50	37.55	38.17	63.40
EconomicFreedom	4.84	7.00	6.87	8.07
HealthShare	0.79	3.84	4.07	10.02
PopDensity	1.98	78.74	126.41	1265.04
GDPpcp	702.23	12,703.05	17,788.49	94,277.97
Poverty	0.10	1.75	11.31	77.60
TotCases	6.60	1492.39	3265.22	19,181.16
TotDeaths	0.00	29.94	122.65	850.85

*We have updated Iceland's *PoliticalRegime* from a 1816 designation as a colony to a current democracy.

A.3. Reduced specification

Table A2. Results from parametric estimators for number of cases of COVID-19 - per million inhabitants. Dep. Var., Est., pVal, *RMSE, DoF, Adj. R^2, Num. Obs* stand for dependent variable, estimates, *p*-values, root-mean squared error, degrees of freedom, adjusted *R*-squared, and number of observations, respectively. The data covers 94% of the global population.

Dep. Var: *TotCases*	OLS Number of Cases		
Variable	Est.	SE	pVal.
(Intercept)	−0.058	0.062	0.354
Drinking	0.235	0.085	0.007***
TrustMedics	−0.115	0.071	0.106
HumanRights	−0.191	0.094	0.044**
GiniIndex	0.167	0.067	0.014**
GDPpcp	0.406	0.121	0.001***
RMSE	0.670		
DoF	123		
Adj. R^2	0.222		
Num. Obs.	129		

Table A3. Results from parametric estimators for number of deaths by COVID-19 - per million inhabitants. Dep. Var., Est., pVal, *RMSE, DoF, Adj. R^2, Num. Obs* stand for dependent variable, estimates, *p*-values, root-mean squared error, degrees of freedom, adjusted *R*-squared, and number of observations, respectively. The data covers 94% of the global population.

Dep. Var: *TotCases*	OLS Number of Deaths		
Variable	Est.	SE	pVal.
(Intercept)	−0.003	0.082	0.972
Drinking	0.445	0.121	0.000***
HospBeds	−0.257	0.090	0.005***
TrustShare	−0.142	0.081	0.082*
HumanRights	−0.297	0.125	0.019**
HealthShare	0.423	0.115	0.000***
RMSE		0.316	
DoF		114	
Adj. R^2		0.286	
Num. Obs.		120	

A.4. Principal components loadings

Table A4. Loadings from principal components analysis.

HealthVars		*EconomicVars*		*PoliticalVars*	
SmokeDaily	0.011	*GiniIndex*	−0.000	*Literacy*	0.995
Drinking	−0.074	*PopDensity*	−0.001	*HumanRights*	0.030
Overweight	−0.032	*GDPpcp*	0.999	*PoliticalRegime*	0.094
Aged65	−0.013	*Poverty*	−0.001	*TrustVars*	
Diabetes	−0.002	*EconomicFreedom*	0.000	*Corruption*	0.661
UnsafeWater	0.004	*HealthShare*	0.001	*TrustShare*	0.610
Sanitation	0.301	*PollutionVars*		*TrustMedics*	0.438
Cardiovascular	0.996	*Pollution*	0.553		
HospBeds	0.003	*DeathsPollution*	0.833		

A green new deal and debt sustainability for the post COVID-19 world

Juan Rafael Ruiz and Patricia Stupariu

ABSTRACT
This paper explores the design and impact on public finances of a global investment plan directed at supporting post-COVID19 reconstruction efforts by investing in climate change mitigation. We analyse current macroeconomic conditions in both developed and emerging economies and, subsequently, simulate various growth scenarios and observe the impact on public debt sustainability of implementing an economic stimulus oriented towards climate change mitigation.

1. Introduction

The COVID-19 crisis has led to the deepest global recession since the Second World War, hitting every region in the world and creating a context of radical uncertainty. More than half the global population has suffered lockdowns and strict containment measures, and the pandemic has triggered the most serious economic crisis in a century. Comparisons with other crises, like the 2008–09 global financial crisis, have significant limitations. COVID-19 has caused a global shock both in terms of supply and in terms of demand, impacting all sectors and all regions across the planet. Compared to the global financial crisis, unemployment has risen much more quickly in the COVID-19 crisis, while production and consumption have fallen much more significantly (OECD 2020). What's more, many of the efforts to limit the effects of the pandemic entail a sharp fall in economic activity, and the impact is asymmetric between countries, as well as within each country.

Most countries were not properly prepared for the pandemic for several reasons: i) austerity was the ordered response to manage the past financial crisis. This has also had an impact on healthcare systems[1]; ii) the risks were underestimated when the first outbreaks happened; iii) most countries did not have crisis management plans for pandemics[2]; and iv) there was a shortage of basic and essential equipment, such as face masks and respirators, leading countries to compete with one another in a race to acquire health supplies.

While it is true that the COVID-19 crisis could not be foreseen, the same cannot be said for climate change. For decades, there have been warnings about the dangers associated with climate change, which not only include temperature rises across the surface of the earth, rising sea levels, the decrease in snow cover and arctic ice, the displacement of species and the appearance and intensification of extreme atmospheric phenomena, but also greater risk of infectious disease propagation. As the UN's Intergovernmental Science-Policy Platform on Biodiversity and Ecosystem Services (IPBES) explains in a recently published report: 'human and animal movements in response to climate change are likely to allow microbes to make contact with new hosts, to potentially invade new niches and to infect even relatively unrelated hosts' (IPBES 2020, 25). At the same time, land-use changes that have a high impact in terms of CO2 emissions and loss of biodiversity are also the drivers behind the emergence of new zoonoses globally[3] (IPBES 2020; Mills, Gage, and Khan 2010; Jones et al. 2013). Thus, while it cannot be said that climate change directly leads to a rise in pandemics, there is evidence showing that dynamics behind climate change also influence the spreading of novel or known viruses and that people's and animals' adaptation responses can also play an important part in this process. Therefore, in the current coronavirus pandemic context, the benefits of fighting climate change are made even more evident.

Although the data show that the COVID-19 pandemic has caused the biggest drop in CO2 in history, this is as a result of the reclusion measures and the drop in commercial activity. The UN warns that the positive impact of improved air quality is only temporary, and that the social and economic devastation caused by climate change will, in the long term, be much greater than the impact of the current pandemic if measures are not taken to address it. UN Secretary General António Guterres argued during the 2020 forum of Small Island Developing States that 'currently, all eyes are on the COVID-19 pandemic, the biggest test the world has faced since the Second World War. We must work together to save lives, ease suffering, lessen the shattering economic and social consequences, and bring the disease under control, but, at the same time, let us not lose focus on climate change. [...] we can use the recovery from the effects of COVID-19 to secure a more sustainable and resilient future. [...] For that, we need ambitious climate action on mitigation, adaptation and finance.' The improvement in air quality is a very short-term effect that does not mean that climate change has been curbed, given that large amounts of carbon dioxide and other greenhouse gases, emitted due to human activity since the Industrial Revolution, have already accumulated in the atmosphere (Muhammad, Long, and Salman 2020). There is also the additional danger that efforts to mitigate the effects of climate change will be relaxed. The low cost of gasoline and global uncertainty over the state of the economy could hinder the sale of electric vehicles or complicate funding for projects related to renewable energy, as well as the development of new research. The IPCC (2019) highlights that limiting global warming to 1.5°C will require fast and far-reaching changes of an unprecedented scale in all aspects of society. The European Commission (2019) has taken a stand on this issue and aims for the EU to be carbon-neutral by 2050, but without global coordination it runs the risk of repeating the failure of the Millennium Development Goals.

To tackle the current crisis, an arsenal of health, economic and social measures have been introduced across the world in a bid to slow the negative effects of the pandemic in all its dimensions. This includes direct aid to households and businesses, guaranteed credit, asset purchase programs, unemployment protection, tax deferrals and the purchase of medical supplies. This has revealed the power of governments and its tools to influence the economy. However, the problems that existed before the pandemic have not gone away and it would be a mistake to plan a solution to the COVID-19 crisis that did not take into account that the reconstruction must jointly fight against the recession caused by current crisis as well as the inherited risks that predate the international health emergency. The COVID-19 pandemic was unexpected, but the same is not true of the climate crisis, which has been warned of for decades. Any exit strategy to the COVD-19 crisis that does not take into account climate change warnings will inevitably lead to an even greater crisis, of a scale impossible to accurately calculate, given the uncertainty and asymmetry of its impacts. What is known is that the consequences will be irreversible. For this reason, we are aiming to contribute to the debate through an analysis of the impact on public finances of a plan to address this challenge, given the existing debates over the role of public spending and public debt sustainability.

In the context immediately prior to the COVID-19 crisis, there was discussion about whether the economies of developing countries had reached a point of secular stagnation, in which most would continue to consistently record low growth rates (Teulings and Baldwin 2014). This debate coincided with the debate on the need to consider the investment required to deal with the challenge of global warming. For Barbier (2010) it is very unlikely that an increase in the green fiscal stimulus of G20 economies will significantly increase fiscal deficit and levels of public debt. He shows that a combination of the Green New Deal and regulatory reform could improve energy security and correct the trade imbalances in the economies most dependent on reducing their current-account deficits. In the same line, Sachs (2014) proposes financing green investment by issuing bonds, showing that this type of financing is Pareto improving for all generations relative to a business-as-usual scenario of no climate change mitigation. On this basis, he justifies the use of public debt as an instrument, given that all generations would benefit from the mitigation of global warming. Monasterolo and Raberto (2018) reach a similar conclusion, but from a different perspective. By simulating the introduction of green fiscal stimuluses, they conclude that these policies could promote growth and positively influence the prospects of businesses and the credit market. Climate bonds represent a solution that is beneficial on all levels, while green taxation would have immediate distributional effects. Fenton et al. (2014) warn that the inability to mobilise adequate and dependable funding to support measures against climate change in developing countries has turned into a source of international political tension and suggest the use of debt to share the burden. This would reduce the pressure of the national budgets of developing countries and facilitate funding in green investment, instead of austerity policies, whose design ignores the global dimension of climate change and the seriousness of the problem. Nersisyan and Wray (2019, 2020) consider up to what point it is possible to quantify the benefits of preventing an apocalyptic scenario and compare the current challenge of global warming with the measures proposed by Keynes to address the costs of the Second World War. In their analysis, they combine Keynesian elements with Modern Monetary Theory, concluding that the social costs of not taking action are so high that they justify the required investment. They add that, if the funding requirements are greater than estimated, other methods to fund investment used in extreme cases could be explored. For Blanchard (2019), the role of fiscal policy is key to achieving balanced growth that allows new debt to be issued so that the necessary investment can be made and sustainable development achieved. In his approach, debt is justified when private demand is weak, production is below its potential and monetary policy has reached its limit. He also believes the use of debt is justified when it finances infrastructure, whose risk-adjusted social gains are higher than the interest rates on debt. These arguments will be explored in more detail later.

This document develops a proposal of possible global implementation and examines what impact its application would have on the public accounts of the world's major economies. The research is divided into six sections. The first section focuses on how the COVID-19 crisis has impacted public finances and the historical relationship between several macroeconomic variables that are relevant to our analysis. This relationship is of great importance, as it indicates how frequent debt rollover processes have been in the historical development of these countries. The third section analyses the criteria conventionally used to justify large processes of fiscal expansion; and the fourth outlines the investment needed to reach a stage of sustainable development, as defined by the International Energy Agency (IEA), and proposes a distribution method for the total public investment needed among world's countries. The fifth section shows the macro effect on public debt of an investment plan in several growth scenarios and results are presented at an aggregate level for advanced and emerging and developed economies according to IMF classifications[4]. Due to China's relevance in this process, we present the results for this country separately. Lastly, the sixth section outlines the main conclusions of the study.

2. Long-term growth and debt sustainability

Growth forecasts for all regions have been drastically downgraded after the onset of the pandemic. The associated measures to mitigate its impact have slowed consumption and investment, and restricted labour supply and production. The effects of cross-border contagion have disturbed financial markets, global trade, supply chains, travel and tourism. The World Bank (2020) forecasts the biggest fall in production since the creation of comparable records. Table 1 presents the evolution of the main macroeconomic variables over the last year and the IMF forecasts up until 2022. A sharp fall in global GDP (−4.4%) can be seen in 2020, with a recovery (5.2%) forecast from 2021. The joint GDP of advanced economies will shrink (−5.3%) in 2020, with the fall especially pronounced in the European Union (−8.3%), although the region is expected to recover (5.2%) from 2021. In Emerging Market and Developing Economies (EMDEs), a smaller fall is forecast in 2020 (−3.3%) and a larger recovery (6%) in 2021. With respect to the evolution of the deficit, this is forecast to be around 18% in advanced economies in 2020 and fall gradually in 2021 (−5.7%) and 2022 (−3.5%). In EMDEs, a lower deficit is expected in 2020 (−8.5%) that will fall at a slower rate (−6.9% in 2021 and −5.8% in 2022). In advanced economies, public debt is forecast to rise 20 points in 2020, stabilizing at around 124% of GDP. In EDMEs, it is expected to rise 10 points in 2020 and stabilize at around 65% of GDP. Inflation during the entire period is forecast to remain below 2% in advanced economies, and at around 5% in EMDEs. Finally, unemployment in advanced economies is expected to rise from 4.8% in 2019 to 7.3% in 2020, and slowly fall in the following years. There is no unemployment forecast for EMDEs, but countries like China and Russia are not expected to be especially affected. However, one should keep in mind there is a non-negligible degree of uncertainty in the current context and it is possible that these forecasts become outdated in the near future.

Table 1. IMF forecasts of main macroeconomic variables.

Variable	Country Group Name	2019	2020	2021	2022
GDP	World	2.8	−4.4	5.2	4.2
GDP	Advanced economies	1.7	−5.8	3.9	2.9
	United States	2.2	−4.3	3.1	2.9
	Japan	0.7	−5.3	2.3	1.7
	Euro area	1.3	−8.3	5.2	3.1
	Emerging market and developing economies	3.7	−3.3	6	5.1
	China	6.1	1.9	8.2	5.8
	Russia	1.3	−4.1	2.8	2.3
Public debt/GDP	Advanced economies	104.2	124.1	124.2	124.3
	United States	108.7	131.2	133.6	134.5
	Japan	238	266.2	264	263
	Euro area	84	101.1	100	98.4
	Emerging market and developing economies	52.1	61.4	64	66.2
	China	52.6	61.7	66.5	71.2
	Russia	13.9	18.9	19	18.5
Primary deficit	Advanced economies	−1.9	−13	−5.7	−3.5
	United States	−4.1	−16.7	−6.9	−4.9
	Japan	−3.1	−13.9	−6.2	−3.1
	Euro area	0.8	−8.7	−3.6	−1.3
	Emerging market and developing economies	−3	−8.5	−6.9	−5.8
	China	−5.5	−10.9	−10.9	−9.9
	Russia	2.2	−4.9	−2.1	−0.5
Inflation	Advanced economies	1.4	0.8	1.6	1.6
	United States	1.8	1.5	2.8	2.1
	Japan	0.5	−0.1	0.3	0.7
	Euro area	1.2	0.4	0.9	1.2
	Emerging market and developing economies	5.1	5	4.7	4.3
	China	2.9	2.9	2.7	2.6
	Russia	4.5	3.2	3.2	3.2
Unemployment	Advanced economies	4.8	7.3	6.9	6
	United States	3.7	8.9	7.3	5.7
	Japan	2.4	3.3	2.8	2.4
	Euro area	7.6	8.9	9.1	8.4
	China	3.6	3.8	3.6	3.6
	Russia	4.6	5.6	5.2	4.7

Source: IMF

Almost every country across the globe has introduced sweeping social and economic measures in a bid to address the pandemic and its many consequences. These range from economic stimuluses to health and social measures. EU leaders have agreed to a recovery fund worth €672.5 billion for the entire EU, which includes €312 billion in grants and €360 billion in loans for the economies worst affected by the pandemic. EU leaders also agreed for the first time to issue joint debt in financial markets. This is an addition to the national efforts of each EU state to mitigate the COVID-19 crisis, which include diverse stimuluses, employment protection and loans to the business sector. The European Central Bank (ECB), for its part, has maintained interest rates at zero, relaxed collateral requirements for liquidity injections and launched the Pandemic Emergency Programme, with an overall envelope for asset purchases of €1.35 trillion, in an effort to reduce the funding costs of states and increase the concession of credit in the eurozone. The immediate effect of this program has been a decrease of the 10-year sovereign bond yields by almost 45 basis points (ECB 2020). In the United States, the Federal Reserve has cut rates to nearly zero and announced sweeping measures to stabilize the financial system. These measures include unlimited purchases of US government debt and mortgage-backed obligations, as well as large-scale purchases of corporate bonds and of securities issued by lower levels of government. The US government has also provided nearly 3 USD trillion in fiscal support, including over 1 USD trillion in loans to companies and to state and local governments. Additional measures, including another round of direct aid to households, are under consideration. In Japan, the Central Bank has increased its equity and corporate bonds purchasing program, increasing the size of its balance sheet by more than 10% of GDP since January and announcing an unlimited purchase of public debt. In China, there have also been significant injections of liquidity, valued at around 2.8% of GDP. Additional emissions of special bonds from the central and local government equivalent to around 2.6% of GDP have also been authorized. Across the globe, measures are being taken to mitigate the COVID-19 crisis and support the economy. But although the COVID-19 crisis is a global problem, these measures have been introduced without a common plan, indicating that there is room for improvement when it comes to political coordination.

In the worst years of the European debt crisis that hit the eurozone following the global financial crisis, the inaction of the ECB and the lack of a common plan placed the public debt of several countries under great strain. One decade on, debt-to-GDP ratios are much higher than, with interest rates close to 0%, compared to the 7% recorded in the worst moments of the sovereign debt crisis. Indeed, negative interest rates have even been recorded thanks to the monetary policy applied by the ECB, which demonstrates that, beyond conventional strategies, there are tools to keep interest rates on public debt under control, even though the level of debt may rise. In the case of US and Japanese public debt, interest rates are around 0%, despite the rise in the funding needs of their governments. As it is known, the historical relationship between the GDP growth rate (g) and the interest rate on public debt (r) has profound implications for debt sustainability, given that if the rate growth exceeds the interest rate, there is the possibility of reducing the debt/GDP ratio even in the absence of continuous budget surpluses. Globally, there is

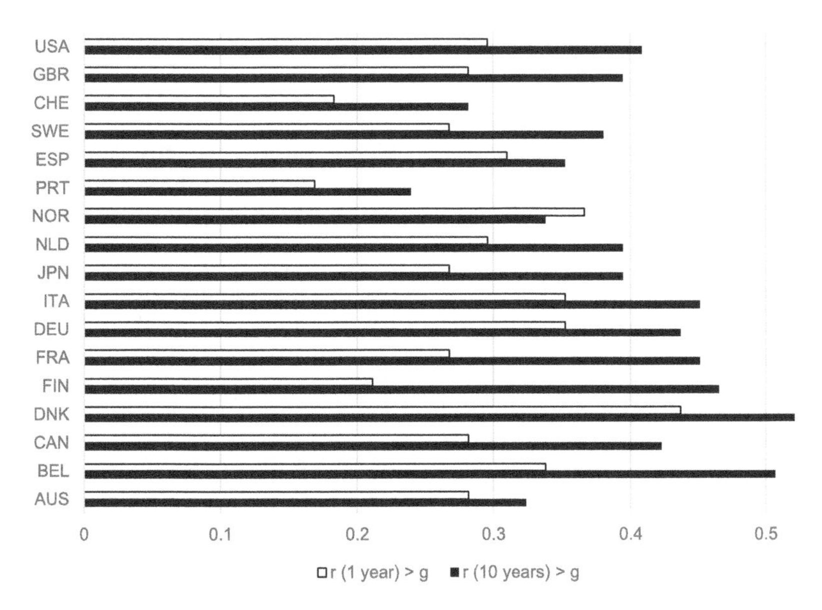

Figure 1. Frequency of r > g (1950–2020).

historical evidence that indicates that the r < g equation is the norm. Both in the most recent years and over a larger time period, the real interest rates of sovereign bonds have been fairly reduced (Ball, Elmendorf, and Mankiw 1998; Jordà et al. 2019; Blanchard 2019; Mehrotra y Sergeyev 2020) and in many cases persistently negative.

Based on the data from Jordà et al. (2019), it is possible to build a series of interest (r) and growth (g) rates for the main OECD countries. Figure 1 shows the frequency of r > g between 1950 and 2020, highlighting that growth has been greater than the interest rates on public debt for long periods of time. According to the data analysed, this relationship has been stable in the long term in all but two cases – Belgium and Denmark.[5] However, if we consider the last two decades, 38% for Denmark and 41% for Belgium of the observations show that r > g. In the short term, the relationship remains stable for the entire sample. As stated earlier, this evolution of rates in a context of an appropriate monetary policy is compatible with the rolling over of public debt and if this trend leads to a scenario of large fiscal multipliers there is great possibility that an expansive fiscal strategy will be successful. And there is such evidence suggesting that, when compared with traditional fiscal stimulus, investment geared towards green projects (e.g. renewable energy, green construction projects such as insulation retrofits or clean energy infrastructure) can create more jobs, yield higher short-term returns per dollar spent and lead to cost savings in the long term (Hepburn et al. 2020)

The next section will cover the criteria that are associated with the adequacy of carrying out fiscal expansion, which are related to monetary policy, private demand, the relation between actual and potential growth and the social return of public investments.

3. Conditions that support the role of an expansive fiscal policy

In the current context, where there is high indebtedness and great need for investment, the role of fiscal policy is key to achieving balanced growth that allows further indebtedness, while ensuring the debt-to-GDP ratio does not rise. Blanchard (2019) proposes that there are two scenarios that justify the role of fiscal policy in this context. The first is when private demand is weak, growth is below its potential and we are in a context where interest rates are close to or equal to zero, which confirms that monetary policy has reached its lower bound. In this scenario, the negative impact of the deficit is mitigated thanks to the role of fiscal multipliers and the low tax burden resulting from the interest rates on debt compared to the growth achieved due to public investment. The second condition that justifies this policy is the funding of infrastructure whose risk-adjusted social profitability exceeds the rate at which a government can emit debt. Spending on measures to fight global climate change meets this condition, as its social return is higher than the risk-free rate, which justifies the use of debt as a financing mechanism. In the following subsections, we show the current situation the monetary policy of the world's main economies is in, as well as the growth forecasts in the period immediately before they were hit by the COVID-19 crisis. The goal is to present the variables that describe the first of the above-mentioned conditions.

Table 2. Forecasts for Euribor, Federal funds rate and EA 10y goverment bond yields.

	March/June 2020				March/June 2019		
Year	2019	2020	2021	2022	2019	2020	2021
Three-month EURIBOR (percentage per annum, March)	−0.4	−0.4	−0.4	−0.4	−0.3	−0.2	0
Federal funds rate (Monthly, June)	2.4	0.1	0.1	0.1	2.4	2.1	2.4
EA Ten-year government bond yields (percentage per annum, March)	0.4	0.1	0.2	0.3	1	1.3	1.5

Source: ECB and FED

3.1. Monetary policy in a fragile economic context

The combination of the impact of the health crisis, instability and low growth suggests that the policy of low interest rates will continue for a long period of time. In Europe, the Euribor has recorded negative values uninterruptedly since February 2016. What's more, in addition to there being low growth rates in a context of low interest rates, the dire situation of the banks appears to have become chronic. Table 2 presents the change in interest rate forecasts from the ECB and FED between March/June of 2019 and March/June of 2020. In both cases, a sharp drop is seen in the expected rates, which are situated at around 0%. The ECB also offers forecasts of the average yields of government bonds issued in the eurozone. Monetary policy is expected to support further rate drops, going from values of around 1.5% to around 0%.

With regard to monetary policy, there is a scenario in which the first of the three conditions is undoubtedly met, given that once negative rates are reached there is no room to pursue this route further and forecasts suggest that this will continue for a long period of time, as it has been happening since 2012 up until today.

3.2. The role of waning demand

The second of the conditions traditionally proposed for the use of large fiscal multipliers is a context in which private demand is weak. Table 3 presents the projections made immediately before the pandemic hit for the world's main economies. In all cases, there is stagnant demand. In the eurozone, the forecasts made before the pandemic were for 1.1% growth in 2020 and 1.2% in 2021. In the US, the forecast growth was slightly higher, with

Table 3. ECB Macroeconomic projections (autumn 2019).

Variable	Year	Real GDP	Private consumption	Government consumption	Gross fixed capital formation	Exports	Imports
Euro	2019	1.1	1.1	1.6	4.3	2.4	3.2
Area	2020	1.2	1.2	1.5	2	2.1	2.6
	2021	1.2	1.2	1.3	1.9	2.3	2.7
USA	2019	2.3	2.6	2.3	2.2	0.3	2.2
	2020	1.8	2.2	1.7	1.1	1.5	2
	2021	1.6	2.1	0.6	1.1	1.6	1.8
China	2019	6.1	-	-	-	1.1	−1.7
	2020	5.8	-	-	-	1.4	1.1
	2021	5.6	-	-	-	2.5	2.2
Russia	2019	1.0	1.4	0.3	1.0	0.2	−0.1
	2020	1.4	1.5	0.8	2.0	1.3	1.4
	2021	1.4	1.6	1.0	2.2	1.4	1.7
Japan	2019	0.9	0.6	2.0	1.4	−1.5	−0.8
	2020	0.4	−0.2	1.2	0.9	0.6	0.3
	2021	0.6	0.5	0.6	0.7	0.8	0.5

Source: ECB

Table 4. Output gap estimates (November 2019).

Year	2018	2019	2020	2021
United States	−1.04	−0.77	−0.77	−0.76
Japan	2.21	2.55	2.47	2.69
Euro area	−0.41	−0.42	−0.55	−0.54
OECD – Total	−0.5	−0.64	−0.8	−0.86

Source: OECD

rates between 2.3% and 1.6%. And in Japan, the figure is between 0.9% and 0.4%. For China the range is 6.1% to 5.6%, while for Russia it was comprised between 1% and 1.4%. The figures for China may seem high, but they are the lowest in three decades. Even before the health crisis, there was very weak growth, in line with the thesis of secular stagnation.

3.3. The evolution of the output gap

Table 4 presents OECD forecasts in the evolution of the output gap at the end of 2019, the moment immediately before the COVID-19 crisis. It can be seen that most OECD economies were slightly below potential GDP.

Note to Table 4: International organisms do not provide output gap estimates for Russia and China.

Of the three variables conventionally used to describe a context favorable for large fiscal multiples, this one is the most controversial. Orphanides and van Norden (2002, 2005) highlight the inconsistency of this measure on the grounds that ex-post reviews of the estimated output gap are the same size as the very initial estimation. What's more, such revisions are constant. In the same vein, Brooks and Basile (2019) conclude that it is not compatible for countries with relatively strong economic growth over the last decade to have the same gaps as countries with negative economic growth, as is the case with Spain and Germany. Heimberger and Kapeller (2017) and Heimberger, Kapeller, and Schütz (2017) propose that the risk of using a faulty measure could lead to misguided policies. Output gap estimates also differ substantially depending on the methodology used such that figures published by different national and international organisms can yield contradictory results in terms of countries being below or above potential output at the same time.

Based on what has been seen till now, it is possible to conclude that the world's main economies meet the three indicators that would give rise to large fiscal multipliers before the beginning of the COVID-19 crisis. The next section outlines the investment needed to reach a stage of sustainable development, as defined by the International Energy Agency (IEA), and proposes a distribution method for the total cost of the public investments.

4. Return to growth based on a plan that addresses the climate emergency

Faced with the current health, social and economic impact of the pandemic, it is highly likely most countries fulfil the conditions commonly used to justify the use of fiscal policy: monetary policy has reached its limit once negative interest rates are reached; anemic demand, even before the negative effects of the pandemic; and below potential GDP. What's more, tackling the climate emergency meets the conditions of the second route in which Blanchard (2019) justifies an increase in public investment. In other words, a growth plan based on addressing the climate emergency is not only justified by conventional indications, but also by its social returns, given that inaction will have an enormous cost to the economy, society, as well as the environment. While the quantifications on the negative effects of climate change are imperfect, we cannot ignore them – the latest findings warn that there is no time for gradual measures, nor for more delays in active policies (IPCC 2018, 2019). The choices made in the next two decades will determine the living conditions of future generations and, if we are to avoid the worst consequences, we must respond today with a fast and far-reaching plan.

The problems of the climate emergency may be felt on a local level but the challenge is global, and so must too be the response, as well as the investment needed to address it. An economy compatible with a scenario of less than 2°C temperature rise needs quick reorientation and massive capital flows. The IEA (2018) estimates in its World Energy Outlook that it is possible to achieve a similar GDP level as that of 2014 under three different growth scenarios. These scenarios are outlined in Figure 2. Each bubble represents the same amount of GDP achieved with different levels of CO2 emissions, as a consequence of less emissions and energy demand due to carrying out investment needed to achieve a more efficient productive system. Scenario A, or the sustainable development policy scenario, represents the production, energy demand and CO2 emissions, if there is an investment plan as described below. Scenario B represents the expected evolution under the current policies.

Table 5 lists the amount of investment needed and in what areas if a scenario of global sustainable development is to be achieved, and compares this to scenario B. In a scenario of global sustainable development, total investment rises to more than 65,461 USD billion within 20 years. This scenario requires 26% more investment than the one based on currently stated policies. With respect to the areas of investment, there are two main groups. The first is divided into investment in fuel and power, where there is a significant reallocation. This change means there is a drop in investment in fossil fuels: investment in oil and natural gas falls 24% in the first decade and 43% in the second, while investment in

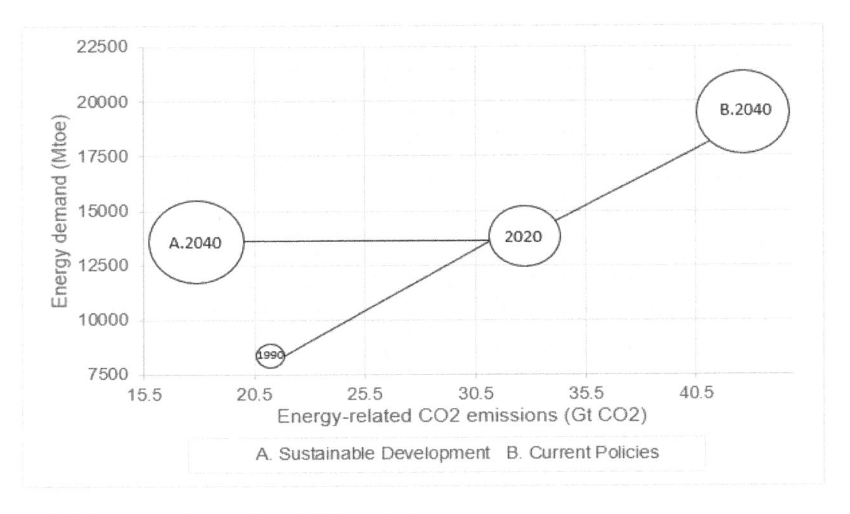

Figure 2. Global energy demand and CO2 emissions.

Table 5. Investments in the energy sector – Average annual values.

	A. Sustainable Development		B. Stated Policies		Increase of A over B	
Investment	2021–30	2031–40	2021–30	2031–40	2021–30	2031–40
Fuels and power:	1,844	2,230	1,753	1,954	5%	14%
Fuels:	676.5	561	869	881	−22%	−36%
¯ Oil and natural gas	610.8	464	800	809	−24%	−43%
¯ Coal	20.4	18	49	37	−58%	−51%
¯ Biofuels and biogases	45.3	80	20	36	127%	122%
Power:	1,168	1,669	884	1,073	32%	56%
¯ Generation:	704.6	783	478	522	47%	50%
Fossil fuels	59.6	58	86	78	−31%	−26%
Nuclear	53.1	59	52	47	2%	26%
Renewables	591.9	666	340	396	74%	68%
¯ Electricity networks	441.4	829	393	517	12%	60%
¯ Battery storage	21.8	57	13	35	68%	63%
End-use:	857.8	1,614	574	922	49%	75%
¯ Energy efficiency	536.7	809	364	537	47%	51%
¯ Renewables and other	321	805	211	385	52%	109%
Total	2,702	3,844	2,327	2,877	16%	34%

	Cumulative investment (2021–2040)
A scenario	65,461
B scenario	52,040
Increase of A over B	26%

Source: IEA

coal drops 58% and 51%, respectively. Meanwhile, there is strong investment in biofuels and biogasses (127%, 122% of increase with respect to current levels). Investment in power generation increases 47% in the first decade and 50% in the second. Within this category, there is a sharp fall in investment in fossil fuel power (−31%, −26%) and an increase in renewable energy (74%, 68%). With respect to the rest of investment related to power generation, there is a significant increase in electricity networks (12%, 60%) and battery storage (68%, 63%). The second group of investment concerns end-use areas related to the energy efficiency of industry, building and renewables. New spending is focused on this group. It can be seen that investment to improve energy efficiency increases 47% in the first decade of the plan and 51% in the second, with respect to the scenario based on current policies. Meanwhile, the implementation of renewable energy sees the biggest growth of this area, with rises of 52% and 109% in the respective decades.

The IEA (2019) estimates that 70% of the investment needed to reach a scenario of sustainable development will be made directly, both by private and public entities, with the state financing the largest part of the investment. Governments will play the most important role as it is up to them to influence the institutional, regulatory and market context, which in turn will influence the will and capacity of the financial and industrial community to mobilise large-scale investment in green energy. Policies and government regulation will define the scenario that we are heading towards. The amount of investment needed for sustainable development can only be achieved by fairly distributing the costs of global energy transition. Below, we propose a method to divide the costs based on statistics from the Carbon Dioxide Information Analysis Centre (CDIAC) and Global Carbon Project (GCO) of the cumulative CO_2 emissions of each country and the World Bank's country classification by income groups. We have created the following distribution index based on the following formula:

$$I = \alpha IDH \cdot \varphi CO2 \quad (1)$$

In this formula, I represents the investment corresponding to each country, α is the vector that complies transformed values of the World Bank's Human Development Index for each country, and ᴪ is a parameter of the proportion of CO2 emitted. In this equation, we assign α values between 0 and 1 in 33 BPS intervals of the development index, with countries with the lowest income levels assigned 0. Countries with medium-low income levels are assigned a value of 0.33, those with medium-high levels 0.66 and those with the highest income 1. These values are then weighted by ᴪ which represents the percentage of total annual CO2 emissions that correspond to each country. For any country, this is calculated as the country's emissions divided by the sum of total global emissions (including international aviation and shipping and 'statistical differences' in carbon accounts). For our calculations we use 2017 data, the latest available in a dataset compiled by Our World in Data based on CDIAC and GCO sources.[6] In this way, we calculate the percentage of investment that corresponds to each country based on their contribution to said index until a scenario of sustainable growth is reached. Once we have selected the variables that make up the index, we weight the proportion that corresponds to each country by dividing its index value by the total sum of the index. In this way, we distribute the investments for the 2020–2030 period and the 2030–2040 period among the weighting that each country has received. The proposed method serves to illustrate a distribution system based on criteria guided by clarity, pragmatism, universality and social justice. Evidently, it is not the only possible method and its extrapolation to reality will depend on political negotiation with all countries. That said, the proposed method meets the positive criteria mentioned above: a) clarity: it is a direct method that does not depend on the calculation of non-observable variables that could fluctuate depending on the model used for their analysis; 2) simplicity: its calculation does not involve great cost or complexity; 3) social justice: it is fair that at the beginning the countries which pollute the most, should invest the most, while less developed countries are not penalized; 4)

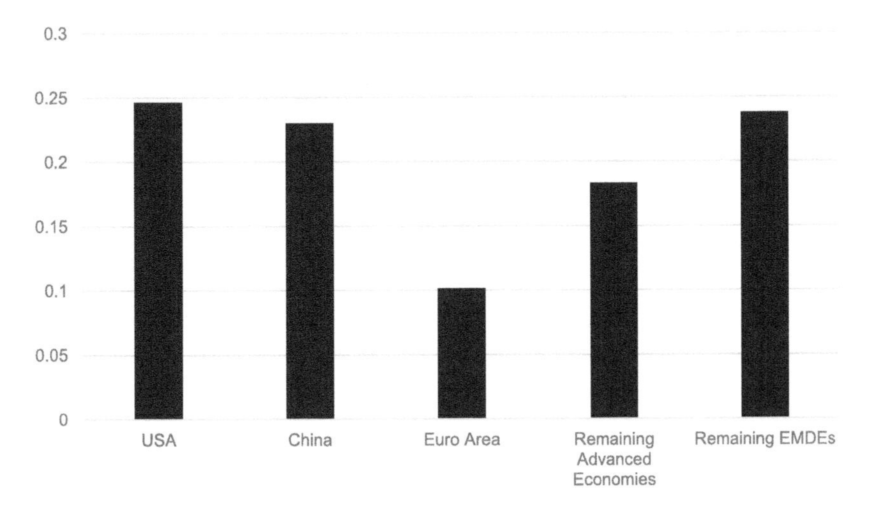

Figure 3. Investment breakdown by region.

universality: the climate change challenge transcends borders, so it is imperative that a criteria to approach the problem comes from a global perspective.

In Figure 3, we show the percentage of investment that corresponds to each country. The US and China have the largest percentage, with 25% and 23% respectively. Ten percent of investment would correspond to the eurozone, 18% to the remaining advanced economies and 24% to the rest of the EMDEs.

5. Results

Using the calculations from the previous section, we propose several scenarios based on different growth paths of GDP, deficit, inflation and interest rates on debt. For future values, we use forecasts from the ECB and FMI, but these are only for the next two to three years. For this reason we propose a what-if analysis, as is common in situations where there is a high grade of uncertainty about the future evolution of variables due to the extended time horizon relevant to the analysis. We present three scenarios to orientate the discussion and examine the potential effects in the evolution of debt. These scenarios do not pretend to predict the future, but rather open a window to assess the viability of this distribution policy under different conditions. The range covered is wide enough to see that, despite the great effort required, positive effects can be achieved, even in a scenario of ongoing global stagnation as has never been seen before in the world. In each scenario, we propose two alternatives. In the first, we apply the 'golden rule' so that the deficit generated as a result of the investment to confront global warming is separated from the conventional deficit. In the second scenario, without additional policies, we calculate the total deficit without distinguishing between the deficit produced by green investment.

In the high-growth scenario, we use values that are two percentage points above the historic growth, and in the stagnation scenario we use values that are two percentage points lower than the cumulative historic growth. This is done for both advanced economies and EDMEs. In the case of China, we opted to reduce the cumulative growth rate both in the high-growth and stagnation scenario due to the large size of its historic growth. In the case of deficit, we maintain the average historical values for the three regions in the high-growth scenario, and lower this value in the stagnation scenario. In all scenarios, we propose uninterrupted deficits. The same is proposed for interest rates. The values are presented in Appendix I. For the simulation, the following debt equation is used:

$$D_t = \frac{1 + r_t}{(1 + \pi_t) \times (1 + g_t)} \times D_{t-1} - PDR_t + e_t \tag{2}$$

In this equation, D represents the value of the debt in each period, r is the interest rate, π represents inflation, g is real GDP growth, PDR is the primary surplus or deficit and e the disruption or deficit-debt adjustment. The results of each country are shown below.

5.1. Results of a high-growth context

Figure 4 presents the evolution of the debt in the high-growth scenario. Advanced economies are in black, EDMEs in grey and China in light grey. A dotted line is used

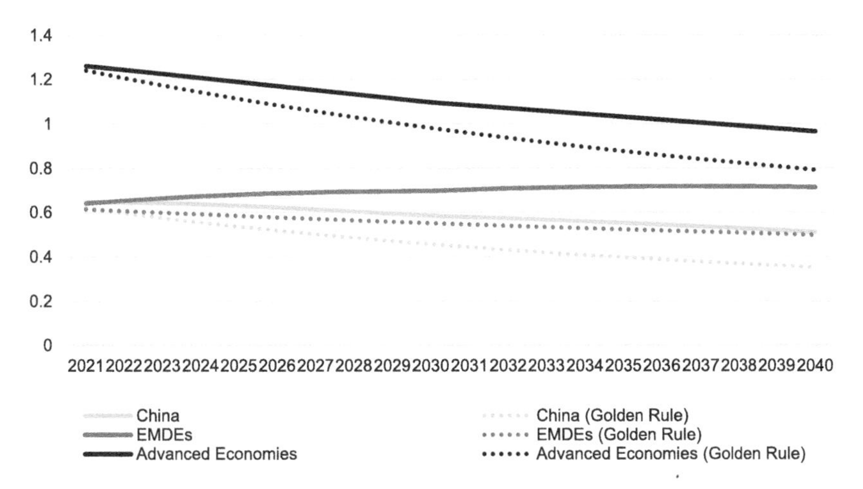

Figure 4. High-growth scenario.

to represent each group of countries in the golden rule scenario, while a continuous line represents a scenario without additional policies. A sharp negative slope can be seen in advanced economies under both the golden rule scenario and the scenario without additional policies. In the case of China, the scenario under the golden rule is notably better than the scenario without additional policies, although in both situations there is a deleveraging trend that oscillates between 13 and 26 percentage points over GDP. Only the EMDEs would register a slight uptick in debt, which would increase to 71% of GDP in a situation without additional policies – a rise of seven points. Meanwhile, in the golden rule scenario, debt in EMDEs would fall 12 points to 50% of GDP.

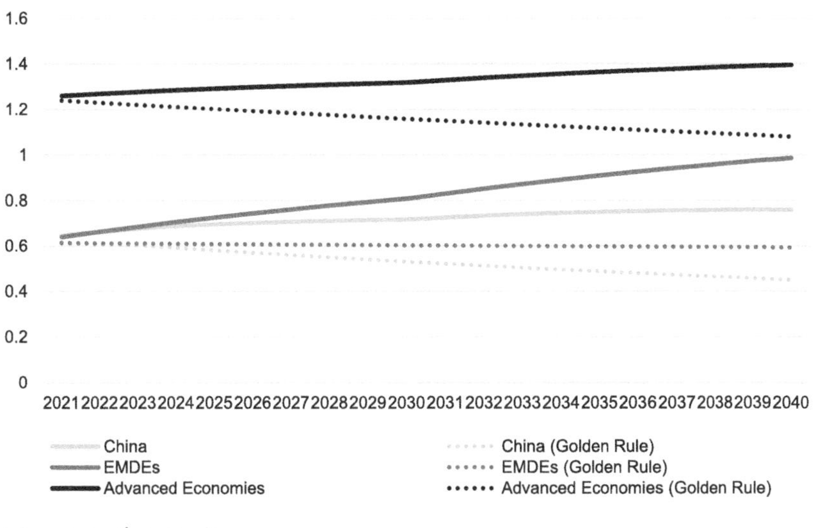

Figure 5. Low-growth scenario.

5.2. *Results of a low growth context*

The scenario of low growth (Figure 5) is the only one where there is tension in the dynamic relation between debt and GDP. Nevertheless, we observe that, despite the proposed anemic growth, the scenario under the golden rule invites some optimism, with the debt-to-GDP ratio remaining below initial levels. This would lead to a stage in which debt is maintained at current levels, at the same time as the productive model has been successfully changed to tackle the challenge of climate change. Under this scenario, debt is seen to rise 12 points at the end of the investment period for China, 13 points for the group of advanced economies and 35 points for EMDEs, which are situated slightly below the 100% threshold of debt-to-GDP at the end of the investment period. EMDEs experience a significant rise in their debt levels, but are far from the levels recorded by the most advanced economies. If the golden rule option is applied, this is the scenario in which there would be greatest relief on debt levels. By the end of the investment period, global indebtedness would fall to 108% of GDP for advanced economies, 59% of GDP for EMDEs and 45% of GDP for China.

5.3. *Results based on historic values*

With respect to the evolution of debt in the scenario based on historical values (Figure 6), China would experience a significant fall, with its debt-to-GDP ratio falling 30 points. Advanced economies would also manage to reduce their debt levels: under the golden rule scenario it would fall by 16 points and in the scenario without additional policies, its leverage would be situated at similar levels to today's. Finally, EMDEs would experience a slight uptick in its debt ratio in the golden rule scenario, reaching 68% of GDP at the end of the investment period, while in the scenario without additional policies, it would rise slightly to more than 90% of GDP.

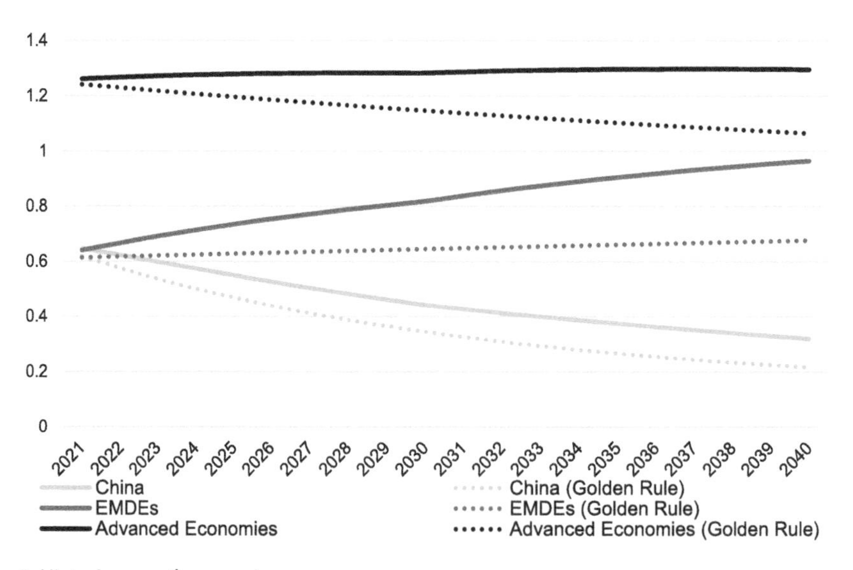

Figure 6. Historic-growth scenario.

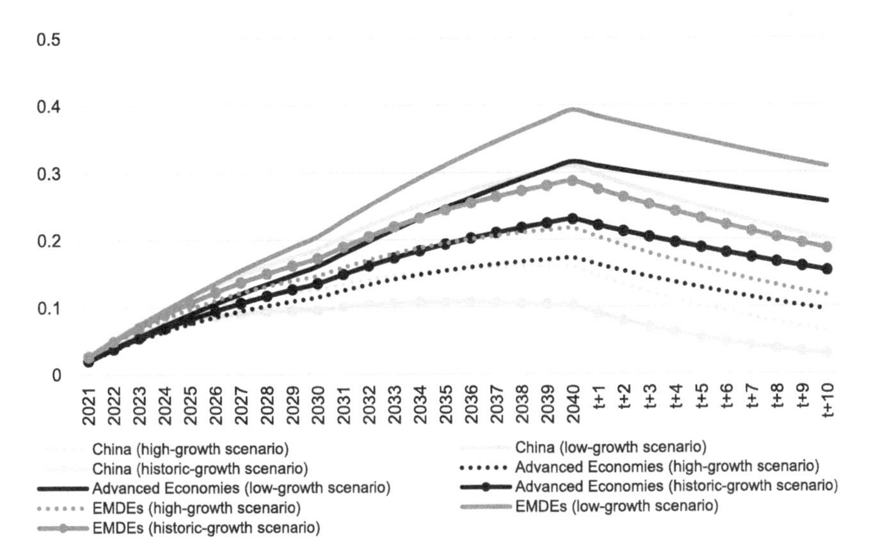

Figure 7. Evolution of debt to tackle climate change.

5.4. Evolution of debt

To conclude, Figure 7 represents the evolution of the debt accumulated from climate change in a scenario without additional policies. This scenario has the worst results of the three projections. We observe that during the two decades corresponding to the investment period, the cumulative debt for EMDEs would be 39% of GDP in the low growth scenario, leading to a rollover process where in the 10 years until the end of the investment period, debt would fall by eight points. In the low-growth scenario, China and advanced economies behave in a similar way. In China, the debt accumulated from climate change would reach 20% of GDP in the 10 years after the investment period, while in advanced economies, the downward trend is more pronounced, reaching a maximum of 32% of GDP. In the high-growth scenario, the accumulated debt at the end of the investment period would be 22% of GDP for EMDEs and 16% for China. In the following 10 years after the end of the investment period, the debt-to -GDP ratio would be 6% of GDP in China, 10% of GDP in advanced economies and 12% of GDP in EMDEs. Lastly, in the scenario based on historic values, only China would see better results than in the high-growth scenario, with its debt-to-GDP ratio at 3% in the 10 years after the end of the investment period. In this scenario, the distance between the advanced economies and the EDMEs is small. Ten years after the end of the investment period, advanced economies starting at debt levels of 23% would have lowered their green debt to 15% of GDP, while in EDMEs, debt would go from a maximum of 28% of GDP to 18% at the end of the period.

6. Conclusions

The compatibility of a post-COVID-19 development model that addresses the investment needed to tackle climate change is not only desirable from an ecological, political and social point of view, but is also possible from the point of view of debt sustainability.

But, as we have warned, it is necessary to consider the results of this study with caution, given that the projections are based on the implementation of one political proposal, among all those possible, and on the design of scenarios. Nevertheless, it offers a sweeping image of the possible impact, where in a climate of international cooperation, it is possible to reach satisfactory results, both for advanced economies that start with high levels of debt, as for EMDEs which, although would see their level of debt rise compared to today's levels in some scenarios, would still be far from the current levels of advanced economies in all scenarios.

The fact that taking action to mitigate the effects of global change has a greater impact on social wellbeing than the impact of not taking action justifies an ambitious investment plan. Any exit strategy to the COVD-19 crisis that does not take into account the climate change emergency will very likely lead to an even greater crisis, of a scale impossible to accurately calculate, given the uncertainty and asymmetry of its impacts. What is known is that the consequences will be very severe. The plan described in this document is ambitious as it considers all the investment needed to achieve the IEA's scenario of sustainable development. Furthermore, the plan has been designed without taking into account possible direct transfers nor other monetary policy options, such as the monetization of part of the public debt.

With respect to the projection, we see that a debt refinancing process is possible and that a plan based on the green golden rule and one without additional policies are compatible with a deleveraging process, especially in a growth scenario. The evolution of the debt within a growth scenario would remain within thresholds that are acceptable under current standards. Tensions are only registered in the case of a stagnation scenario, however, an important deleveraging trend is seen in the decade after the end of the investment period. Both in the growth scenario and the scenario based on historical values, the deleveraging process is faster than the other scenarios. The green debt would oscillate between a maximum of 19% of GDP and a minimum of 3%.

Some policy recommendations can be distilled from our analysis. The fight against COVID-19 has reminded us that there are great challenges ahead that require coordinated policies on a planetary scale. Making the necessary investments to mitigate future climate change is the biggest global challenge we face in the immediate future. Numerous reports by international groups of experts leave no doubt that the time horizon for action is short (IPCC 2018). Such policies should focus on decarbonizing the energy system and increasing its efficiency, both of which are fundamental pillars of the transition to an economy that generates close to zero greenhouse gas emissions. These investments have to be necessarily carried out globally since carbon emissions have a global effect regardless of their origin. The countries that have achieved a higher degree of development and accumulated emissions are the ones who should lead this process of global change by decarbonizing more rapidly so that developing and emerging countries can use up a larger share of the remaining carbon budget to increase social welfare levels. Meeting the challenge in a common way might also serve to open a new chapter of cooperation in the international community and reduce current tensions and armed conflict.

The compatibility of a post-COVID-19 development model that meets the investment needs to face climate change is not only desirable from an ecological, political and social point of view, but it is also possible from the point of view of financial sustainability. Additionally, one interesting proposal based on our proposed index would be an annual recalibration of the parameter corresponding to CO2 emissions, encouraging a virtuous race to the bottom by establishing a mechanism that discourages all countries from increasing emissions.

The main limitations of these proposals are political and stem from short termism and international tensions among countries pursuing individual economic growth and disregarding global impacts of their actions. A change of focus of global powers is necessary in order for them to interiorize that leading this transformation process is the way toward ensuring sustainable growth for the future. It is not at all clear that this change of focus will be achieved. The method of investment distributions that we propose responds to the principles of clarity, universality, pragmatism and social justice, but it is not the only possibility.

We aim at further contributing to this debate by carrying out future research regarding alternative distributional methods and institutional frameworks. Among the latter, one option would be the setting up of international institutions that could work as automatic stabilizers for the different participants so that green investments can continue to be carried out in case of possible tensions in sovereign interest rates. We consider a main line of research to be the design of mechanisms involving the participation of all countries and covering both investments and the response to tensions in a coordinated way.

Notes

1. The number of hospital beds per capita in OECD countries decreased at around 0.7% annually between 2008 and 2018.
2. Except for Asian countries that were hit by the SARS pandemic and north-European countries, where crisis management plans are mandatory.
3. The list of epidemic outbreaks of new and potentially dangerous virus for humans is long, with six relevant threats over the last 20 years: SARS, MERS, Ebola, the H5N1 ('avian') and H1N1 ('swine') influenzas.
4. The classification is available at: https://www.imf.org/external/pubs/ft/weo/2020/01/weodata/groups.htm
5. For these two countries, most observations of $r > g$ correspond to the 1977–1999 period (23 out of 37 for Denmark and 22 out of 36 for Belgium). In general, all countries concentrated the bulk of $r > g$ during the 1980s and early 1990s with the onset of the second oil crisis and the implementation of policies focused on ending the monetization of debt. In Denmark there are additional factors that contributed to this situation: the aftermath of the 1987–1993 banking crisis, that involved austerity policies, devaluations, high inflations and high interest rates. While in the case of Belgium, the peg of the Belgian franc to the German mark led to a notable increase in interest rates, in addition to suffering the effects of the biggest recession since the Second World War in the years 1992–1993.
6. Data has been converted by Our World in Data from tons of carbon to tons of carbon dioxide (CO_2) using a conversion factor of 3.664 and they are available at https://ourworldindata.org

Disclosure statement

No potential conflict of interest was reported by the author(s).

ORCID

Juan Rafael Ruiz http://orcid.org/0000-0002-4447-1483

References

Ball, L., D. W. Elmendorf, and N. G. Mankiw. 1998. "The Deficit Gamble." *Journal of Money, Credit and Banking* 30 (4): 699–720. doi:10.2307/2601125.
Barbier, E. B. 2010. *A Global Green New Deal: Rethinking the Economic Recovery.* New York: Cambridge University Press.
Blanchard, O. 2019. "Public Debt and Low Interest Rates." *American Economic Review* 109 (4): 1197–1229. doi:10.1257/aer.109.4.1197.
Brooks, R., and G. Basile 2019. "Campaign against Nonsense Output Gaps." *Global Macro Views, Institute of International Finance*, 23 May.
ECB. 2020. *Economic Bulletin.* no. 5/2020.
European Commission. 2019. *The European Green Deal.* Brussels: European Commission.
Fenton, A., H. Wright, S. Afionis, J. Paavola, and S. Huq. 2014. "Debt Relief and Financing Climate Change Action." *Nature Climate Change* 4: 650–653. doi:10.1038/nclimate2303.
Heimberger, P., and J. Kapeller. 2017. "The Performativity of Potential Output: Pro-cyclicality and Path Dependency in Coordinating European Fiscal Policies." *Review of International Political Economy* 24 (5): 904–928. doi:10.1080/09692290.2017.1363797.
Heimberger, P., J. Kapeller, and B. Schütz. 2017. "The NAIRU Determinants: What's Structural about Unemployment in Europe?" *Journal of Policy Modeling* 39 (5): 883–908. doi:10.1016/j.jpolmod.2017.04.003.
Hepburn, C., B. O'Callaghan, N. Stern, J. Stiglitz, and D. Zenghelis 2020. "Will COVID-19 Fiscal Recovery Packages Accelerate or Retard Progress on Climate Change?" Smith School Working Paper 20-02.
IEA. 2018. *World Energy Outlook.* Paris: IEA.
IEA. 2019. *World Energy Outlook.* Paris: IEA.
IPBES. 2020. *Workshop Report on Biodiversity and Pandemics of the Intergovernmental Platform on Biodiversity and Ecosystem Services.*
IPCC. 2018. *Global warming of 1.5°C. An IPCC Special Report on the impacts of global warming of 1.5°C above pre-industrial levels and related global greenhouse gas emission pathways, in the context of strengthening the global response to the threat of climate change, sustainable development, and efforts to eradicate poverty.* [V. Masson-Delmotte, P. Zhai, H. O. Pörtner, D. Roberts, J. Skea, P.R.Shukla,A. Pirani, W. Moufouma-Okia, C.Péan, R. Pidcock, S. Connors, J. B. R. Matthews, Y. Chen, X. Zhou, M. I. Gomis, E. Lonnoy, T. Maycock, M. Tignor, T. Waterfield(eds.)].In Press.
IPCC. 2019. *Climate change and land: An IPCC special report on climate change, desertification, land degradation, sustainable land management, food security, and greenhouse gas fluxes in terrestrial ecosystems.* [P.R. Shukla, J. Skea, E. Calvo Buendia, V. Masson-Delmotte, H.-O. Pörtner, D. C. Roberts, P. Zhai, R. Slade, S. Connors, R. van Diemen, M. Ferrat, E. Haughey, S. Luz, S. Neogi, M. Pathak, J. Petzold, J. Portugal Pereira, P. Vyas, E. Huntley, K. Kissick, M. Belkacemi, J. Malley, (eds.)]. In press.
Jones, B. A., D. Grace, R. Kock, S. Alonso, J. Rushton, M. Y. Said, D. McKeever, et al. 2013. "Zoonosis Emergence Linked to Agricultural Intensification and Environmental Change." *Proceedings of the National Academy of Sciences of the United States of America* 110 (21): 8399–8404. doi:10.1073/pnas.1208059110.
Jordà, Ò., K. Knoll, D. Kuvshinov, M. Schularick, and A. M. Taylor. 2019. "The Rate of Return on Everything, 1870–2015." *The Quarterly Journal of Economics* 134 (3): 1225–1298. doi:10.1093/qje/qjz012.
Mehrotra, N., and D. Sergeyev 2020. "Debt Sustainability in a Low Interest Rate World." *CEPR Discussion Paper*, No. DP15282.

Mills, J. N., K. L. Gage, and A. S. Khan. 2010. "Potential Influence of Climate Change on Vector-borne and Zoonotic Diseases: A Review and Proposed Research Plan." *Environmental Health Perspectives* 118 (11): 1507–1514. doi:10.1289/ehp.0901389.
Monasterolo, I., and M. Raberto. 2018. "The EIRIN Flow-of-funds Behavioural Model of Green Fiscal Policies and Green Sovereign Bonds." *Ecological Economics* 144 (C): 228–243. doi:10.1016/j.ecolecon.2017.07.029.
Muhammad, S., X. Long, and M. Salman. 2020. "COVID-19 Pandemic and Environmental Pollution: A Blessing in Disguise?" *Science of the Total Environment* 728: 138820. doi:10.1016/j.scitotenv.2020.138820.
Nersisyan, Y., and L. R. Wray 2019. "How to Pay for the Green New Deal." *Working Papers Series*, 931, Levy Economics Institute.
Nersisyan, Y., and L. R. Wray 2020. "Can We Afford the Green New Deal?" *Public Policy Brief*, 148, Levy Economics Institute.
OECD. 2020. *OECD Employment Outlook 2020: Worker Security and the COVID-19 Crisis*. Paris: OECD Publishing.
Orphanides, A., and S. Van Norden. 2002. "The Unreliability of Output-Gap Estimates in Real Time." *The Review of Economics and Statistics* 84 (4): 569–583. doi:10.1162/003465302760556422.
Orphanides, A., and S. Van Norden 2005. "The Reliability of Inflation Forecasts Based on Output Gap Estimates in Real Time." *CEPR Discussion Paper*, 4830.
Sachs, J. D. 2014. "Climate Change and Intergenerational Well-being." In *The Oxford Handbook of the Macroeconomics of Global Warming*, edited by L. Bernard and W. Semmler, 248–259. Oxford: Oxford University Press.
Teulings, C., and R. Baldwin. 2014. *Secular Stagnation: Facts, Causes, and Cures*. London: CEPR.
World Bank. 2020. *Global Economic Prospects, June 2020*. Washington, DC: World Bank.

Appendix

Appendix I

Scenario	Variable	Advanced Economies	EMDEs	China
High-growth	g	3.6%	5.0%	6.0%
	π	3.0%	3.0%	3.0%
	r	2.0%	4.0%	4.0%
	deficit	2.0%	0.9%	1.2%
Low-growth	g	1.6%	1.0%	3.0%
	π	1.0%	2.0%	2.0%
	r	1.0%	2.0%	2.0%
	Deficit	1.0%	0.5%	0.6%

COVID-19 and the Chinese economy: impacts, policy responses and implications

Kerry Liu

ABSTRACT

COVID-19, the disease caused by novel coronavirus SARS-CoV-2, has greatly affected financial markets, economies and societies worldwide. This study focuses on China and examines a series of issues including: the impact of COVID-19 on the Chinese economy, China's policy responses to this shock such as fiscal, monetary and institutional measures, and implications such as the nature, gains and costs of China's policy responses. This study also explores problems that need to be answered in the future. In view of the importance of China in the world regarding the size of its economy, its contribution to world growth, and its increasing influence, this study makes timely and important contributions to policy makers and investors around the world.

1. Introduction

The 2019–20 coronavirus pandemic is an ongoing pandemic of coronavirus disease 2019 (COVID-19). As a response, many countries have implemented quarantine policies to curb the spread of this disease. These have led to the disruption of business activities in many economic sectors such as retail, transportation and tourism, and schools among others. Governments and central banks from the world have launched a series of stimulus programs. The impacts from COVID-19 on global economies and the implications are significant.

This study especially focuses on the Chinese economy. While the outbreak of COVID-19 was first identified in China in December 2019, the situation in China has gradually become stabilized after mid-March. Chinese businesses began an orderly resumption of work and production since March 2020. At the same time, other economies such as the US are lagging behind China in terms of containing the further spread of COVID-19 and reopening. While daily confirmed cases may be able to show this difference[1], Google Trends search[2] results (Figure 1) also confirm this finding. Thus, China provides a good full-cycle case study on how the COVID-19 has impacted the economy, how the government has responded to this shock, and their implications.

There are already a few COVID-19-related economic studies. First, regarding the impacts on macroeconomy, current studies (Fernandes 2020; Atkeson, 2020; McKibbin, 2020) are mainly based on hypothetical scenario analyses. A scenario analysis, which is a method of evaluating potential future events by considering

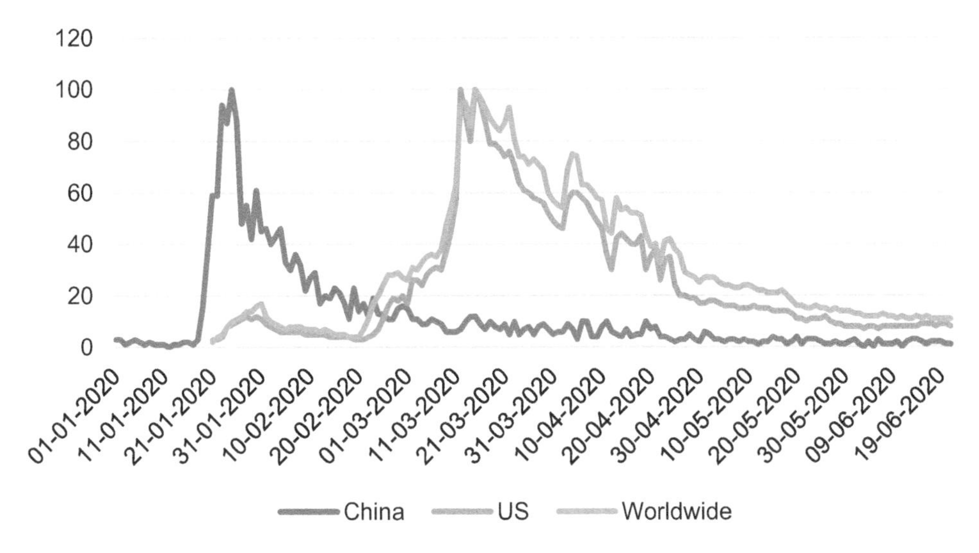

Figure 1. COVID-19 index: China, US and the world: 1 January 2020–21 June 2020. Source: Google Trends *Note: there are too few search results during 1–20 January 2020 for the regions of the US and the world, thus they are not reported in the Google Trends result.*

possible alternate outcomes, does not give an exact picture of future. The research based on historical data becomes more significant, meaningful and precise as the future events slowly become the past. This is exactly what is happening to the Chinese economy. Second, regarding economic policy responses, Elgin, Basbug, and Yalaman (2020) conducted a review of different economic policy measures adopted by 166 countries as a response to the COVID-19 pandemic. At the same time, Elgin, Basbug, and Yalaman (2020) also admitted that this index, which is as of 31 March 2020, needs update regularly. Multilateral organizations such as the World Bank and IMF (International Monetary Fund) have also conducted some research on policy responses from governments around the world (Loayza and Pennings 2020; IMF, 2020) but on a very general basis. This study focuses on the policy responses from the Chinese authorities with more details and deeper analysis. Third, the most important of all is the implications of the impacts and policy responses to the Chinese economy. As China accounted for the largest share of world growth during 2013–18 (twice the share of the US), and will account for a similar share of growth during 2019–24 (Reuters 2019), the performance of the Chinese economy matters not only to China but also to the world. From this point of view, policy makers and investors from the world will be keen to know how the COVID-19 has affected or will affect China's reform process. For example, in 2015, China started to implement supply-side structural reform including cutting industrial overcapacity and corporate deleveraging. In 2016, the Chinese central government's stated position on real estate was changed to 'houses are for living in, not for speculation'. In 2018, the prevention of financial systemic risks by deleveraging became one of China's key tasks during 2018–20. So, will COVID-19 affect or has COVID-19 affected these reforms? This study will also focus on this perspective.

The structure of this paper is as follows. Section 2 looks at the impacts of COVID-19 on the Chinese economy including GDP (overall output and sector performance) and job market. Section 3 conducts a review on China's policy responses including fiscal policy, monetary policy and institutional reform. Section 4 analyses the implications of China's policy response such as supply-side reform and financial system. Section 5 concludes this paper.

2. The impact of COVID-19 on the Chinese economy

Responding to the outbreak of COVID-19, the Chinese authorities have launched a series of measures to contain the pandemic. For example, the Spring Festival was extended. Schools' open date was significantly delayed. There was a large-scale lockdown across China including the whole Hubei Province and other regions. While social distancing rule[3] has not been popular, the 14-day quarantine period measure has been widely adopted across China.[4] As the result, the Chinese economy was significantly affected. In this section, the impact of COVID-19 on the Chinese economy is analysed. As China does not publish its income approach-based quarterly national account, the production approach and expenditure approach are used. This section also discusses the impact on China's job market.

Table 1 shows that China's (production approach-based) national economic output contracted 6.8% on a year-on-year basis in Q1, 2020. This is the worst performance of the Chinese economy since it started its national economic accounting system in 1992. The most severely impacted is the accommodation and catering sector, which contracted 35.3%, followed by wholesale and retail sector. It does make sense as during the lockdown period, people would significantly reduce their business or personal travels. There had been widespread reports that the shock to the hospitality industry was devastating. The most recent data of the Dragon Boat Festival during 25–27 June 2020 show that China's national tourism revenue has dropped 68.8% on a year-on-year basis (People.com.cn 2020a). Also, as people had to stay at home, the wholesale and retail sector[5] was also significantly affected. However, Table 2 shows that the IT sector (information transmission, software and information technology) and financial service sector are the only two that experienced a growth. T-tests also show that they are not significantly different from the mean level. The main reason is the rising online services during the lockdown period. For example, entertainment, shopping, education, work and medical consultation have increasingly become digitalized. Employing an EGARCH model to analyse the effects of COVID-19 on Chinese stock markets, Liu (2020a) found that the IT sector is the only one that responded significantly positively. While at present, financial service sector experienced a growth such as through the expanding of bank loans and hiking securities trading activities,[6] Liu (2020a) found that in the future the financial service sector may also be negatively affected. Further discussion is conducted in Section 3.

Table 2 shows the performance of the Chinese economy based on the expenditure approach. Regarding fixed asset investment, Table 2 shows that its growth experienced the largest drop in history too. The subsectors including manufacturing sector, infrastructure sector and real estate sector all experienced the largest contraction of investment. However, fixed-asset investment from real estate sector has

Table 1. The performance of the Chinese economy during COVID-19 period 1.1. Production approach (Year-on-year growth, %).

	National GDP	Accommodation and Catering	Wholesale and Retail	Constructi-on	Transport, Warehousi-ng and Postal Services	Manufacturing	Leasing and Business Services	Industrial	Real Estate	Agriculture	Other Industries	Financial Services	IT
2019	6.1	6.3	5.7	5.6	7.1	5.7	8.7	5.7	3	3.1	5.9	7.2	18.7
Q1, 2020	−6.8***	−35.3***	−17.8***	−17.5***	−14***	−10.2***	−9.4***	−8.5***	−6.1***	−2.8***	−1.8***	6	13.2
Q2, 2020	3.2**	−18.0***	1.2**	7.8	1.7**	4.4**	−8***	4.1	4.1	3.4	−0.9***	7.2	15.7

Table 2. Expenditure approach A. Fixed asset investment (FAI; accumulated year-on-year growth, %).

	Total FAI	Manufacturing	Infrastructure	Infrastructure (excluding electricity)	Real Estate
2019	5.4	3.10	3.33	3.80	9.90
Jan-2020	NA[1]	NA[1]	NA[1]	NA[1]	NA[1]
Feb-2020	−24.5***	−31.5***	−26.86***	−30.3***	−16.3**
Mar-2020	−16.1***	−25.2***	−16.36***	−19.7***	−7.7*
Apr-2020	−10.3***	−18.8***	−8.78**	−11.8***	−3.3
May-2020	−6.3**	−14.8**	−3.31*	−6.3**	−0.3
June-2020	−3.1*	−11.7**	−0.07	−2.7*	1.9

Table 3. Retail sales (year-on-year growth, %).

2019	8.0
Jan-2020	NA[1]
Feb-2020	−20.51***
Mar-2020	−15.8***
Apr-2020	−7.5***
May-2020	−2.8**
June-2020	−1.8**

gradually recovered, which is also confirmed by the t-test (further analysis is conducted in Part 3.2D), while the manufacturing sector is still struggling although has improved. This sluggish rebound of manufacturing investment shows weak expectation for the future. Table 3 shows that China's retail sales were also hit the most significantly during Jan – Feb 2020, but has gradually recovered from March although still weak.

Table 4 shows the performance of China's foreign trade. Regarding goods trade, it shows that initially the major shock is on supply side, i.e., China's factories were shut down in January and February. After China's factories are gradually resuming their operation from March, this shock has become mitigated. In fact, the April and May data show that China's goods export almost matches its 2019 trend data. At the same time, although goods import data show that the demand shock is big, t-tests show that this impact is insignificant. Service trade data show that the significant shock is on China's service import, i.e., mainly overseas tourism, as the result of constraints on cross-border flow of people or even total shutdown of borders. China's service trade has experienced an increasing deficit during the past decade. For example, in 2008, China's service trade surplus was US$ 4.4 billion. In 2018, this has changed to a trade deficit of US$ 258.2 billion.[7] The shock of COVID-19 on China's service trade will help improve China's balance of international payments.

As a result of the shock from COVID-19, China's job market was also significantly affected. From April 2018, China's National Bureau of Statistics started to publish the survey-based unemployment rate. Its definition of (un)employment is consistent with those from the International Labour Organization. Thus, these two labour market indicators, i.e., urban unemployment rate: 31 major cities, and urban employment rate, are the most reliable official ones. They have increased to 5.9% in May 2020 for urban employment rate: 31 major cities, and 6.2% in February 2020 for urban employment rate. They are both the highest since the availability of data. However, they may be significantly underestimated. The major factor is China's huge amount of peasant workers, who can be workers in cities, and peasants when not working in cities. A market economist estimated that the real unemployment rate could be around 20% (Bloomberg News 2020a).

Table 4. Foreign trade (3-month moving average for monthly data; year-on-year growth, %).

	Goods Trade		Service Trade	
	Export	Import	Export	Import
2018 (trend[2])	2	2	5	7
2019 (trend[2])	0	2	NA[3]	NA[3]
Jan-2020	−7.4	3.2	0.1	−9.9
Feb-2020	−13.3	−2.8	−7.9	−17.4*
Mar-2020[4]			−1.3	−26.0***
Apr-2020	−2.2	−10.8	−6.5	−29.0***
May-2020	−0.1	−9.7		

Source: Wind, National Bureau of Statistics, General Administration of Customs Note:

0. Table 1 also shows the performance of the Chinese economy in Q2/June 2020. This will be discussed at Subsection 3.2
1. Due to the Spring Festival effect (in either January or February), China's statistics bureau does not respectively publish the January data but rather the combined one of January and February
2. As China's foreign trade data are volatile, the Hodrick-Prescott filter method is used, which is a mathematical tool to remove the cyclical component of a time series from raw data. The raw data are from annual growth date during 1984–2019.
3. As of 29 June 2020, China's annual service trade data have not been published yet
4. While China's General Administration of Customs usually publishes the January data, it combined the goods trade data of January and February in 2020. Thus, the 3-month moving average data in March becomes unavailable. As a result, while the significant change may happen in March, this information has become unavailable.
5. *** means $p < 0.001$, ** means $p < 0.01$, * means $p < 0.05$. Series A includes either a sample of quarterly GDP data of past ten years (2010–2019) except for manufacturing, IT and Leasing and Business Services sectors which started from Q1, 2015, a sample of monthly FAI, retail sales and goods trade data of past ten years except for infrastructure FAI excluding electricity which started from April 2014, or a sample of monthly service trade data since January 2015. Series B includes the quarterly or monthly data in 2020. The methodology is to perform t-tests for equality of means between series A and B

3. China's policy responses to the shock of COVID-19 on the Chinese economy

As Liu (2020b) argued, the policy body that was responsible for analysing the current economic situation and guiding the implementation of relevant policies is the CPC (Communist Party of China) Politburo during the 2018–19 US – China trade war. The implementing bodies include the Chinese governments, agencies and the People's Bank of China (PBC, China's central bank). However, during the COVID-19 period, the decision-making body has been changed to the Standing Committee of the CPC Politburo (Xinhua News 2020a, b), a much smaller body than the CPC Politburo. It may reflect the urgency and significance of policy responses to the shock from COVID-19 or is the result of other factors. According to the CPC Politburo meetings held in 27 March and 17 April 2020, China's fiscal policies were required to be more proactive, and monetary policy should be more flexible. At the same time, China should further implement supply-side reforms. In this section, the fiscal policy measures, monetary policy measures and supply-side reform measures from the Chinese authorities are reviewed.

3.1. Fiscal policy

Regarding fiscal policy, IMF (IMF (International Monetary Fund) 2020a) summarized the major measures including increased spending on epidemic prevention and control, production of medical equipment, accelerated disbursement of unemployment insurance and extension to migrant workers, tax relief and waived social security contributions, and public investment. Furthermore, the tax relief and waived social security contributions policy especially targets micro- and small-sized enterprises. At the same time, for the first time since the Global Financial Crisis (January 2009), China's public revenue experienced a negative growth during 2020 (as of June). Thus, the Chinese governments have increased their issuance of government bonds including central government bond and local government bond. As of May 2020, China's central government bond issuance has increased 51.7% on a year-on-year basis. Local government issuance has increased 65.13%.[8] As the result, China's target fiscal deficit as a percentage of GDP has been increased to 3.6% in 2020, the highest since 2010.

As China's deficit ratio only includes the budgets for general public finance, but exclude the budgets for government-managed funds, the real deficit figure may be higher. For example, the Chinese central government also issued RMB 1 trillion (equivalent to US$ 143 billion) special government bonds. A total of 30% of them are (to be) used in epidemic-related expenditure, and the rest is (to be) used in investment in infrastructure projects. As of May 2020, the Chinese local governments also issued RMB 2.3 trillion (equivalent to US$ 329 billion) special local government bonds, which are mainly used in investments in infrastructure projects, and replenishing capital for small- and medium-sized banks as well. Both of these two special bonds are excluded from the budgets for general public finance.

Furthermore, China's fiscal stimulus mainly focuses on corporate[9] supporting programs, and less on households. For example, China's support to households includes unemployment-related assistance, relief funds for people in need, and shopping coupons.[10] They are together around RMB 33.2 billion (equivalent to US$ 4.7 billion),[11] representing 0.03% of GDP. The real amount of fiscal funds provided to corporates should be much larger than those provided to households.[12] This reflects the corporate-centric nature of the Chinese economy although consumption is playing an increasingly important role.

Most importantly of all, one of China's less known fiscal policy is its investment in new-type infrastructure projects including 5 G, big data centre, artificial intelligence, and Industrial Internet of Things. They are broadly related to internet, information and technology sectors. They may be more appropriate to be classified into supply-side reform. Further discussions are conducted in Subsection 2.3.

3.2. Monetary and credit policy

In this subsection, China's monetary policy measures are reviewed. Furthermore, Liu (2020b) found that while China adopted a de facto expansionary monetary policy responding to the US-China trade war during 2018–19, the credit expansion was marginal.[13] Thus, the credit conditions, which are also important, are reviewed in this subsection.

China's monetary policy framework is in the transition from quantity-based policy tools such as reserve requirement ratio (RRR) adjustments to the interest rate channel[14] (Liu 2019a). Accordingly, the PBC has adopted both of these two types of tools.

Specifically, the PBC has cut its RRR three times during January–July 2020. The first was conducted on 6 January 2020 by cutting 0.5% for all financial institutions. The second was conducted on 16 March 2020 by cutting 0.5–1% for all financial institutions which have met the financial inclusion criteria, and additional 1% for joint-stock commercial banks. The third time was conducted on 15 April 2020 and 15 May 2020 by cutting 0.5% each time for small financial institutions which mainly serve micro- and small-sized enterprises. Besides RRR cuts, the PBC has also expanded its re-lending and re-discounting facilities for the purposes such as medical facilities supply, business reopening and supporting small- and medium-sized banks.

The characteristics of the PBC's quantity-based policy tools is that most of them are targeted policies, i.e., supporting financial institutions that have met or will meet financial inclusion loans criteria. The financial inclusion loans include lending to households and micro- and small-sized enterprises, entrepreneurial guarantee loans, and sole trader loans and so on. They are generally at a disadvantageous status in accessing credit. Targeted policy will help alleviate their financial constraint. For example, using a sample of listed small businesses between 2003 and 2018, Lin, Lerong, and Yang (2020) found that the implementation of targeted easing policies in China has significantly reduced the financing constraints of small businesses as measured by the cash flow sensitivity.

Besides these targeted easing policies, the PBC has also launched a series of policies that directly help ease the credit conditions. For example, the target growth rate of Chinese large banks'[15] lending to micro- and small-sized enterprises has increased from 30% in 2019 to 40% in 2020. Deferred principal and interest payment policy for loans to micro- and small-sized enterprises has been extended to end of March 2021 while the PBC will compensate medium- and small-sized banks 1% of principal. Commercial banks are encouraged to expand their uncollateralized micro- and small-sized enterprises loans while 40% of the loans during 31 March–31 December 2020 will be guaranteed by the PBC.

As the result, China's total social financing[16] year-on-year growth (stock) has reached 12.8% as of June 2020, the highest since February 2018. China's M2 growth has reached 11% as of June 2020, the highest since January 2017[17]. Specifically, as of May 2020, China's financial inclusive loans to micro- and small-sized enterprises have increased 25.4%,[18] far higher than the growth rates of general loans, M2, total social financing and nominal GDP.

One key feature of China's expansionary monetary and credit policies (with fiscal policies as well) is the targeted supports to micro- and small-sized enterprises. The major consideration is that China's micro- and small-sized enterprises play a dominant role in providing job opportunities. For example, according to China's Fourth National Economic Census, as of 2018, micro- and small-sized enterprises contribute to 79.4% of total employments.[19]

Besides quantity-based policy tools, the PBC has also cut the key policy rates. For example, the key reference rates of China's interbank market FR007 (fixed 7-day repurchase rate by both deposit-taking institutions and non-deposit-taking institutions) and FDR007 (fixed 7-day repurchase rate pledged by interest rate bonds by deposit-taking institutions) have dropped from around 3% at the end of 2019 to below 1.5% in May 2020. However, China's interest rate pass-through is less efficient than advanced economies. Especially, the performance of the real economy has a significant effect on interest rate pass-through (Liu 2019a). In August 2019, the PBC announced that Loan Prime Rate (LPR), which is the interest rate that banks charge their most creditworthy customers, would become another (dominant) reference rate (besides FR007 and FDR007) for lending. Accordingly, the

1-year and 5-year LPRs have decreased from 4.15% and 4.80% on 20 January 2020 to 3.85% and 4.65% on 20 April 2020, respectively, and remain unchanged as of 20 July 2020[20]. As the result, the lending rates for general loans and commercial papers have both dropped while housing mortgage rates almost remain unchanged.[21]

3.3. Institutional reforms

Responding to the shock from the COVID-19 on the Chinese economy, the Chinese authorities have also implemented institutional reforms. The most important is 'new-type' infrastructure investment, which, however, attracts less attention from the media and China watchers. China also stated that it would further implement factor market reform[22] and other institutional reforms.

First, in March 2020, the Chinese authorities announced its plan of investing in 'new-type' infrastructure projects including 5 G, big data centre, artificial intelligence, and Industrial Internet of Things. The specific details have not been disclosed yet. Based on some estimates from market economists, the size of investment will be hundreds of billions dollar or even more. Based on a panel data set for 30 Chinese regions during 2010–15, Liu (2021c) found that unlike 'old-type' infrastructure such as road, port and airport, there is a time lag but greater effect from 'new-type' infrastructure investment on growth. Also, the human capital factor plays an enhancing role. China's 'new-type' infrastructure investment broadly echoes its plan of supply-side reform. For example, the time lag effect means that the Chinese government pursues a long-term strategy more than a short-term stimulus. Moreover, China's 'new-type' infrastructure investment is also closely related to its controversial 'Made in China 2025′ plan. The 10 key sectors listed in China's Made in China 2025 include new information technology (Liu 2018). China's Internet Plus Advanced Manufacturing Plan, which is also part of the Made in China 2025, intends to create new information technology solutions such as cloud computing, big data, the internet of things, e-commerce and artificial intelligence. China's overall goal is to enable China to become the world's manufacturing powerhouse (Liu 2018). However, as it became the focus of the US-China trade war, China has begun to downplay this plan since mid-2018 (SCMP (South China Morning Post) 2018; Reuters 2018). Furthermore, the 'new-type' infrastructure investment is also closely associated with China's digital silk road program (part of Belt and Road Initiative, further discussion in Section 4). These projects will greatly help China's agenda of building a China-led digital and telecommunication infrastructure network regionally and globally. The COVID-19 and the 'success' of China's health surveillance technologies including smartphone apps, coloured health code and facial recognition have made this agenda more feasible.

Second, in April 2020, the Chinese authorities issued a guideline document on establishing a more market-oriented factor allocation system (Xinhua News 2020c). The background is China's factor market is still under strict regulation and control. Huang and Wang (2010) argued that the fundamental cause of China's structural imbalance problems such as overinvestment, low consumption share of GDP and income inequality is the repressed factor cost, which is associated with heavily distorted markets for labour, capital, land, resources and the environment. This document tries to show the

Chinese authority's intention of further implementing supply-side-oriented reform but does not provide a detailed plan or timetable. For example, this document emphasized the important of reforming China's Hukou system.[23] However, the phrases are almost the same as those announced in March 2019 (see Liu 2020b). This document also mentioned the importance of interest rate liberalization. However, further interest rate liberalization is less likely at least in the short term considering that the lending rates will certainly rise if the deposit interest rates are to be further liberalized.[24] This will impede rather than facilitate the recovery of the Chinese economy.

The similar scenario happened back to 2013, when Chinese leaders constructed a master plan for putting the economy on a sustainable growth path. This plan provided a road map for change that would span 15 broad areas and 60 specific tasks including economic, financial, social and environmental policies. While abolishing the one-child-per-couple policy to increase labour supply and further opening up China's domestic market are positive initiatives, overall progress is very small. Generally speaking, it probably means that there are no agreements on these kind of policy initiatives among various stakeholders. As a result, the policy document may just state some general (and sometimes conflicting) goals. The final result will be simply left to the time.

Third, in May 2020, the Chinese authorities released a master document on improving China's socialist market economy (Xinhua News 2020d). As it is a top-down guideline document, it may not to be expected to provide a detailed roadmap. While it is supply-side oriented, the overall direction is mixed. It emphasized the importance of state ownership, and the comprehensively leading role of the Chinese Communist Party in implementing reforms. It also reiterated China's determination of further opening up its domestic market, and the role of further open-up in reform,[25] which is consistent with China's policy roadmap during the 2018–19 US-China trade war (Liu 2020b). For example, the Belt-and-Road-Initiative-centred foreign economic relations will be further enhanced. There will be more free trade zones and free trade ports such as the release of master plan of building Hainan Free Trade Port[26] on 1 June 2020. The personal bankruptcy legislation will also be enhanced including the release of China's first personal bankruptcy law draft in Shenzhen on 4 June 2020 (Reuters 2020).

On one hand, responding to the shock from the COVID-19, the Chinese authorities have launched a series of provocative fiscal policies and expansionary monetary and credit policies. China's responses may not be exceptional among major economies in the world. For example, Loayza and Pennings (2020) suggested that the first step is the crisis management, and the main objective is to avoid collapse of the real economy (and financial markets) through relief measures. On the other hand, the Chinese authorities have also launched some institutional reforms including specific policies and reform statements. The most prominent is China's plan of 'new-type' infrastructure investment. Besides, some other essential policy initiatives have also been announced. However, some of them may be symbolic, demonstrating to domestic and foreign investors that the Chinese authorities are still determined to further its market-oriented reforms. As COVID-19 has disrupted global supply chains, there is discussion that companies should exit China (Govindarajan and Bagla 2020) or have moved out of China (Gartner Survey 2020).[27] Thus, expectation on China's further reform is very important.

Regarding policy responses, there are also some problems that need further research in the future. For example, first, as mentioned at the beginning of this section, China's decision-making body has been changed to the Standing Committee of the CPC Politburo. Is this temporal or permanent? How does this relate to the Party's status and Xi's role? Second, future studies can conduct comparative analysis on policy responses around the world. The differences of policy responses in terms of size, structure and nature may be explained by factors such as severity of COVID-19 shock, political system, economic structure and so on.

4. Discussion

The impacts of COVID-19 on the Chinese economy, and correspondingly, the policy responses from the Chinese authorities, have profound implications. In this section, a series of issues are discussed including the nature of China's policy responses and its effects on China's reform agenda (gains and costs).

4.1. Nature of China's policy responses

During the Politburo Standing Committee meeting held on 15 April 2020, Chinese decision-makers clearly stated that the first important goal of China's policy responses is employment (Xinhua News 2020b). Unlike other developed economies, the Chinese system of basic income or massive unemployment insurance is underdeveloped. As discussed previously, China's micro- and small-sized enterprises contribute to around 80% of job opportunities. Accordingly, China's fiscal policies, monetary and credit policies primarily focus on supporting micro- and small-sized enterprises.

At the same time, the Chinese authorities have also adopted a series of measures to promote employment. For example, on 15 July 2020, China's 13 ministries including the National Development and Reform Commission issued a document to support diversified employment such as online services including webcasting, sole trader,[28] and shared economy and so on (People.com.cn 2020b). It is expected that job creation will be a key task of the Chinese authorities in the foreseeable future.

Furthermore, China's quick policy reverse in order to get the economy grow again has its deep cause. The idea that a government aims for a particular economic growth rate and steer the economy to achieve it is unusual (The Economist 2016). China is arguably the only large industrial country that sets economic growth target. As the Chinese economy is widely interconnected through ownership and control among various players such as state-owned enterprises, non-state-owned enterprises, banking and financial system and real estate sector with the Party (government) as the core, if the whole Chinese economy is regarded as one single firm: China Inc., this will easily make sense. Maximizing output growth is alike maximizing shareholder' wealth. This concept may also be related to China's communist ideology.

4.2. Gains and costs of china's policy responses

Table 1 shows that the Chinese economy grew 3.2% on a year-on-year basis in Q2, 2020, indicating a significant rebound. On one hand, this rebound is impressive as

China may be the only country that will experience a positive growth in 2020 among major economies (IMF (International Monetary Fund) 2020b). China's job market is still challenging but so far (as of June 2020) has improved. – On the other hand, Table 1 shows that while financial service and IT sectors have consistently performed well, there is a huge reversal of construction sector. It demonstrates the significant role of construction such as real estate and infrastructure investment in the rebound (see Table 2). Table 2 A also shows that there was a weak recovery of manufacturing investment. Simultaneously, the rebound of retail sales (Table 3) is also weak. The struggling recovery in import (Table 4) means that China's contribution to world growth may not be as large as before. They all show that the rebound of the Chinese economy in Q2, 2020 is still fragile.

At the same time, the Chinese economy's quick recovery is also at some costs. In this subsection, a series of issues are discussed including overcapacity, debt, financial system and assets markets.

4.3. Overcapacity

Overcapacity has been a problem for the Chinese economy for a long time. Liu (2019b) performed a review of past six overcapacity problems since the 1990s with a focus on the most recent one in 2015.

During the COVID-19 period, the overcapacity issue re-emerged. For example, the capacity utilization ratio for China's industrial sector (the largest sector of the Chinese economy) dropped to just 67.3% in Q1, 2020 and recovered to 74.4% in Q2, 2020, which is still the lowest since Q1, 2017[29].

While China's overcapacity issue in 2015 is mainly about supply side, thus cutting overcapacity was the key task (Liu 2019b), this round of overcapacity issue is mainly about demand side. Subdued domestic and overseas demands are the main causes. China's fiscal and monetary stimulus, which primarily aims to support the corporate sector, may only contribute marginally to this round of overcapacity issue. However, if overseas markets continue to be weak no matter because of weak demand or economic decoupling from China (Johnson and Gramer 2020; Tan 2020), this overcapacity issue will become a supply-side issue again.

4.4. Debt and deleveraging

Another great cost of the Chinese economy's quick recovery is the rapid accumulation of debt again. The below Figure 2 shows the debt level of the Chinese economy by sector: non-financial corporate, financial corporate, household, and public sector (central government and local government). All items are calculated as the fraction of debt over quarterly nominal GDP.

Figure 2 shows that all sectors' leverage ratios have increased in Q1, 2020. Especially, the non-financial corporate sector's leverage ratio has reversed its declining trend during Q2, 2017 – Q4, 2019, and reached its peak in history in Q1, 2020. Financial corporate sector's leverage ratio has also reversed its declining trend since Q2, 2017. Household sector's leverage ratio has been continuously rising. After being stable since 2014, China's public sector's leverage ratio has also increased and reached its peak in Q1, 2020.

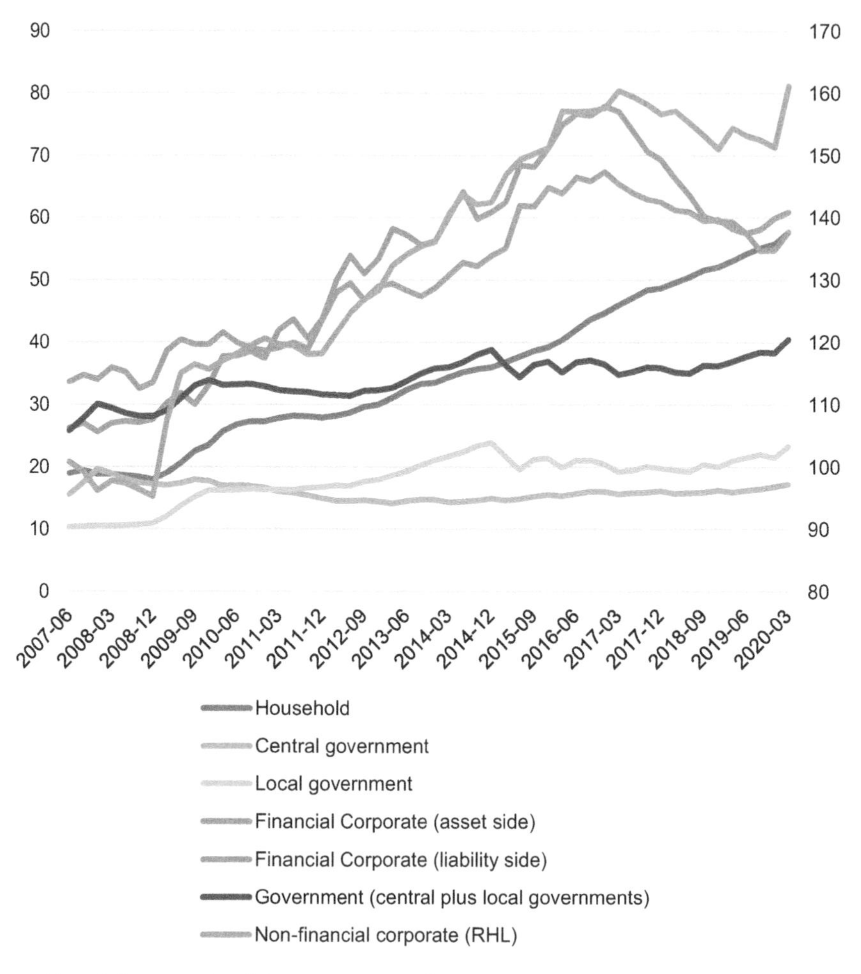

Figure 2. China's leverage level (unit: per cent of GDP). Source: Wind, Chinese Academy of Social Science

Liu (2021b) conducted a review on China's debt by sector and China's deleveraging strategies adopted since 2016, and concluded that some positive progress had been achieved as shown in Figure 2. Regarding non-financial corporate sector, Liu (2021b) argued that the fundamental causes of the rapid accumulation of Chinese non-financial corporate debts are China's financial repression, i.e., very low (controlled) interest rates, and its banking-centric (credit-driven) financing model. China's policy responses to COVID-19 including lowering lending rates and massive lending are exactly the drivers of debt accumulation. Regarding financial corporate sector, Liu (2021b) found that a rate cut together with a lower reserve requirement ratio can accelerate the growth of China's intra-financial system debts. Also, a decline of real economy performance is significantly associated with the acceleration of intra-financial system debts growth. These are exactly what have happened during the COVID-19 period. Regarding household sector, Liu (2021b) found that when the monetary policy is expansionary in the form of an RRR cut, a lending rate cut or expansionary broad credit (M2), the mortgage loans growth will accelerate. These are also what have happened during the COVID-19 period. Also, an accelerating growth of real estate price is positively associated with an accelerating mortgage loans growth. This is also happening in China (more detailed discussions in Part 3.2D). While Liu (2021b) concluded that China's government debt is generally not a big concern for investors and policy makers, the rising public sector debt also contributes to the rising debt level of the overall Chinese economy.

It seems that the COVID-19 and China's economic policy responses have eroded some if not all of the achievements of the Chinese authorities' deleveraging reform adopted from 2016. Especially for the non-financial corporate sector, which accounts for the majority of Chinese debt, it has returned back where it was. These have important implications. First, the Chinese economy has become weaker as the result of rapid debt accumulation. Liu (2021a) conducted a literature review and found that the average impact of debt becomes negative when the debt reaches a certain level, and the high debt appears to reduce growth mainly by lowering the efficiency of investment. Empirical evidences (Maliszewski et al. 2016) show that the Chinese economy may experience severe disruptions in the future in the form of either financial crises or growth slowdowns or both. Second, how to further deleverage the post-COVID-19 China will be more challenging. Liu (2021b) argued that monetary policy does play a significant role in credit booms in various sectors. As the result, the Chinese authorities decided to align the growth of M2 and total social financing with the nominal GDP growth. The COVID-19 has broken the Chinese authorities' reform plan. Liu (2021b) also questioned the sustainability of China's present deleveraging strategy such as the debt for equity swap program for non-financial corporate sector. COVID-19 has made this issue more challenging.

4.5. *Financial system*

China's policy responses have also significantly affected the Chinese financial system. Specifically, Chinese banking sector's performance has become worse, and the systemic risk of the Chinese financial system has also increased.

First, Chinese banking sector will face more challenges in the future. In order to support Chinese corporate sector especially the micro- and small-sized enterprises, Chinese regulators have asked Chinese banking sector to give up RMB 1.5 trillion (equivalent to US$ 212 billion) in profits (Bloomberg News 2020b). These profits cuts are mainly in three ways including: reduction of net interest income through lending rate cut; reduction of penalty interest payments and high-interest bridge loans and guarantee fees; and reduction of non-interest income including net fee and commission income. Chinese banking sector's non-performing loan ratio has increased, and may rise further in the future.

Second, the systemic risk of the Chinese financial system has also increased. One of the three key tasks in 2018 (until 2020) is the prevention of Chinese financial systemic risks by deleveraging. This task had been reiterated during the 5 CPC Politburo meetings during 2018–19 (Liu 2020b). Based on this strategy, the shadow banking activities have been generally under strict regulations. As a result of this, Chinese financial sector leverage has also been continuously declining since Q2, 2017 (see Figure 2). However, as Figure 2 shows, China's policy responses have reversed this trend too. This rising financial sector leverage demonstrates potentially regulatory arbitrage. This may help increase the volatility of asset prices (Liu 2019c), distort the mechanisms of asset pricing, decrease the efficiency of resource allocation, and enhance the systemic risk of the whole financial system in China (People's Bank of China (PBC) 2017). The comprehensive implementation of the *Guiding Opinions on Regulating the Asset Management Business of Financial Institutions*, which was issued in April 2018 intending to fundamentally regulate Chinese asset management industry, has been further delayed in order to support the real economy (Caixin Global 2020).

4.6. Assets markets

China's asset markets are closely associated with monetary policy. For example, using a series of univariate regressions, rolling correlations and error correction models, Liu (2019d) found an increasing effectiveness of reserve requirements ratio cuts on assets markets. Specifically, the effects of RRR adjustment on real estate price growth rate for the first-tier cities have become very strong since late 2016. Also, the effects of RRR adjustments on Chinese stock markets have become stronger after 2015. This round of expansionary monetary and credit policy has profound effects on Chinese assets markets.

First, China's real estate market has become further inflated. While it may be controversial to claim that Chinese real estate markets are bubble-driven, it is undeniable that a consistently rising market has caused serious risks to Chinese financial system and the economy (Liu 2019b). Shortly after the recovery from the COVID-19, the real estate price of Chinese first-tier cities including Beijing, Shanghai, Shenzhen and Guangzhou began to pick up from March 2020. According to Liu (2019d), second-tier and third-tier cities will respond a little late. While the official data of household mid- and long-term loans (mainly mortgage loans) have significantly increased, a large fraction of funds is also from COVID-19 supporting loans.[30] This makes the Chinese authorities' official policy that houses are for living in, not for speculation under challenge. As part of this new position, the Chinese government announced restrictions on real estate sales. Once a buyer purchases a property, it cannot be traded for a certain period thereafter – in most cases, 2 years. This policy worked in curbing the real estate boom in 2015–16. As a response, Chinese local governments have to strengthen this policy of restrictions on real estate sales again. While it is part of China's macroprudential policy, China's visible hand has become stronger and the market force has been further weakened.

Second, Chinese stock markets are booming again. During 1 January–21 July 2020, China's Shenzhen stock exchange index grew 29.8%, outperforming all major markets. Shanghai stock exchange composite index grew 8.9%, third to Nasdaq composite index and Shenzhen index. A booming equity market will help China's Made-in-China 2025 program by making high-tech start-ups easier to access equity investments when the Chinese governments are suffering fiscal blow from COVID-19. As the US-China trade war is still on going and the technology war is intensifying, it becomes very important to have a healthy domestic financing system for these high-tech firms. As the result, China's Sci-Tech innovation board was launched in July 2019. Furthermore, a booming equity market will help deleverage the Chinese economy. However, while the Chinese authorities successfully changed the investment style of Chinese stock markets during 2016–17 (Liu 2019b), it will be more challenging to manage a consistent bull market that can help realize China's agenda.

5. Concluding remarks

The COVID-19 has caused severe shocks to the world including societies, economies and financial markets. This study focuses on China, and addresses a series of issues including the impact of COVID-19 on the Chinese economy, China's policy responses to this shock and the implications such as the nature, gains and costs of China's policy responses. In view of the importance of China in the world regarding the size of its economy, its contribution to world growth, and China's increasing influence around the world, this study makes timely and important contributions to policy makers and investors as well around the world.

China's official data show that that China's national economic output contracted 6.8% on a year-on-year basis in Q1, 2020, which is its worst performance since 1992. China's job market was also significantly affected. As a response, the Chinese authorities have implemented a series of policy responses. One notable difference is that China's fiscal stimulus mainly focuses on corporate supporting programs, and less on households. Also, China's expansionary monetary policy is mainly in the form of targeting micro- and small-sized enterprises. Future studies can conduct a comparative analysis on policy responses around the world. As the result, the Chinese economy has rebounded in Q2, 2020 although some indicators show that this recovery is still fragile.

At the same time, there are also costs with China's policy responses. While they may marginally contribute to the worsening overcapacity issue, the direct and most severe consequence is the rising (again) leverage across all sectors especially the non-financial corporate sector. Chinese banking and financial system have become weaker. While booming equity markets will be helpful, real estate markets have been further inflated again, thus posing additional risk to the economy and financial system. It seems that China's supply-side structural reform has been disrupted by this COVID-19. In view of the unprecedented nature of this pandemic, China's policy responses may be not that unusual. At the same time, the Chinese authorities are still determined to further upgrade its industrial structure by promoting investment in 'new-type' infrastructures.

There are still unanswered questions. For example, first, how will China's status of global supply chain evolve in the future? Foreign direct investment (FDI) in China generally considers two factors: return and risk. Regarding return side, China's quick economic recovery will increase investment return in China. When other economies such as Vietnam, Mexico and the US and so on have also recovered, the attractiveness of China as an FDI destination will relative decrease. Regarding the risk side, there is discussion on economic decoupling of China. The geopolitical risk resulted from the China-US confrontation may continue to the upcoming US' Presidential election and beyond. So, this issue may be better for further examination based on a medium- to long-term horizon.

Second, how will China's Belt and Road Initiative (BRI) be impacted? As the overcapacity issue re-emerged, Chinese firms may pay more attention to BRI to boost sales. At the same time, some developing countries have been severely hit by COVID-19, thus causing suspension of some BRI infrastructure projects. It is also reported that some countries asked for debt relief or renegotiation (The Economist

2020). It may not be surprising if another (or more) case like Hambantota Ports[31] or China-Iran deal[32] will emerge in the future. As the BRI is the China's version globalization, the BRI will continue to serve China's global geopolitical and economic agenda but probably with some adjustments such as focusing more on high-quality projects and field projects such as health and digital silk road. Many countries have become poorer than before COVID-19. At the same time, China's foreign reserves[33] are almost stable. From the realism perspective, the BRI may become more attractive. However, this is a so important and ongoing issue, it needs constant monitoring and more research in the future.

Third, how will China's foreign policy evolve? The Chinese economy has become weaker than before this pandemic, but relatively stronger than the rest of the world such as the US which is lagging behind China in terms of containing COVID-19 and re-opening. This change of power balance may impact China's foreign policy. For example, based on a time series model, Liu (2021d) found that the relative size of GDP between Mainland China and Taiwan is significantly associated with the reduced number of Taiwan's formal diplomatic recognition.[34] Another example is the China-India border conflict in June 2020[35]. This topic is marginally related to the theme of this paper, but worth serious research in the future.

Notes

1. For data information, see Coronavirus COVID-19 Global Cases by the Centre for Systems Science and Engineering at Johns Hopkins University. https://gisanddata.maps.arcgis.com/apps/opsdashboard/index.html#/bda7594740fd40299423467b48e9ecf6.
2. Google Trends (https://trends.google.com/trends/) is a website by Google that analyses the popularity of top search queries in Google Search across various regions and languages. Numbers represent search interest relative to the highest point on the chart for the given region and time. A value of 100 is the peak popularity for the term. A value of 50 means that the term is half as popular. A score of 0 means there was not enough data for this term. For China, the key word is 肺炎 (in Pinyin: Fei Yan; In English: coronavirus/pneumonia). For US and the world, the key word is coronavirus.
3. Lai et al. (2020) identified three major groups of non- pharmaceutical interventions to contain COVID-19 in China including intercity travel restrictions, early identification and isolation of cases, and contact restrictions and social distancing measures together with personal preventive actions. At the same time, one important factor may be missing, i.e., wearing face masks. As Feng et al. (2020) claimed, the use of face masks has become ubiquitous in China or even compulsory. In reality, wearing face mask is of higher priority than social distancing. At the same time, Liu and Zhang (2020) stated that there is a lack of research on face masks.
4. For an international comparison of the strictness of lockdown, please see Hale et al. (2020).
5. While retail sales were significantly hit, the online sales performed relatively better. For example, during January – June 2020, China's online retails sales (goods) have increased 14.3% on a year-on-year basis. As online sales (goods) only account for 25.2% of total retail sales, its outperformance only partially contributes to the rebound of retail sector (data source: Wind, National Bureau of Statistics).
6. For example, China's stamp duty revenue from stock trading is Renminbi (Chinese currency, RMB. Approximately RMB 7 = US$ 1 during 2020 as of 23 July) 19.6 billion and 19.1 billion in February and March 2020, the highest since China's 2015–16 stock market crash (see https://en.wikipedia.org/wiki/2015%E2%80%932016_Chinese_stock_market_tur

bulence for more detailed information). Source: Wind, China Securities Regulatory Commission. Wind (https://www.wind.com.cn/en/) is the mostly widely used Chinese economic and financial data and information provider. It serves more than 90% of the financial firms in the Chinese market, and 75% of the qualified foreign institutional investors in China.

7. Source: Wind, General Administration of Customs.
8. Source: https://www.chinabond.com.cn/Channel/19012917# (in Chinese). They include both general (central and local) government bonds and special (central and local) government bonds.
9. Corporate means businesses including both state-owned and non-state-owned enterprises.
10. The issuance of shopping coupons is mainly at local level. Various Chinese provincial and city governments have issued different types of shopping coupons targeting sectors such as accommodation and catering (the most severely hit, see Table 1.1), retail (the second most severely hit, see Table 1.1), sports, fitness and recreation, culture and tourism and so on. The funds are either fully from local governments, or shared between local governments and businesses.
11. For unemployment-related assistance data, see http://www.xinhuanet.com/politics/2020-04/11/c_1125840488.htm (in Chinese). For relief funds for people in need data, see http://www.xinhuanet.com/fortune/2020-04/11/c_1125840378.htm (in Chinese). For shopping coupons data, see http://www.xinhuanet.com/fortune/2020-05/13/c_1125977369.htm (in Chinese). China's GDP in 2019 (current price) is RMB 99,086.5 billion (Source: Wind).
12. IMF (International Monetary Fund) (2020a) estimated that the around RMB 4.2 trillion (or 4.1% of GDP) of discretionary fiscal measures have been announced by the Chinese authorities as of 25 June 2020. While there may be a gap between the announced amount and real amount, it is of no question that corporate sector receives a majority of these funds.
13. In China, credit includes Renminbi (Chinese currency) and foreign currency loans, entrusted loans, trust loans, undiscounted bank acceptance draft, and bonds. According to Liu (2020b), there are three reasons why credit expansion was low during 2018–19: the Chinese authorities' consistent deleveraging strategy; China's macro prudential assessment regulations, meaning that Chinese financial institutions are under strict regulations regarding on-balance sheet and off-balance sheet activities; the underperformance of the real economy.
14. According to Ma and Ji (2016), there are two drivers of this change: first, the relations between quantity-based policy tools and economic growth and inflation have become weaker, thus making it difficult to stabilize the economy through quantity-based policy tools; second, as the result of financial innovation, it has become more difficult to predict the amount of money needed, thus leading to the higher volatility of interest rates.
15. The Chinese banking system includes 6 largest banks – the Industrial and Commercial Bank of China, China Construction Bank, Bank of China, Agricultural Bank of China, the Bank of Communications, and Postal Saving Bank of China. The Chinese government owns the majority of these banks' shares; private shareholders own a small fraction. There are also 12 mid-sized joint-stock commercial banks, 133 small city commercial banks, and over 2,000 rural commercial banks/credit unions. Finally, there are 3 policy banks – the Agricultural Development Bank of China, China Development Bank, and the Export–Import Bank of China.
16. The total social financing measures the total funds the real economy has obtained from the financial system over a certain period of time.
17. Source: Wind, People's Bank of China. M2 includes currency in circulation, corporate demand and term deposits, household demand and term deposits, and other deposits from such as non-deposit-taking financial institutions and Housing Provident Fund.
18. Source: https://finance.sina.com.cn/roll/2020-07-11/doc-iirczymm1708236.shtml (in Chinese). While China's such data are usually published on a quarterly basis, this information is from the PBC's news conference.
19. Source: http://www.stats.gov.cn/tjsj/zxfb/201912/t20191218_1718313.html (in Chinese).

20. Source: Wind, People's Bank of China.
21. The main purpose of keeping mortgage rates unchanged is to try to not further inflate the real estate bubble although real estate buyers (for both first home buyer or investors) are less concerned about interest rate as the price hike will generally compensate the interest loss if any. At the same time, while most other countries have allowed mortgage holders to defer making payments, this policy in China is generally bank-specific and of small scale.
22. Specifically, China would further reform the markets of labour, land, capital, technology and data. At the same time, while energy sector is under the heavy regulation, it is not the focus of future reform.
23. A hukou is a record in a government system of household registration required by law in mainland China, and determines where citizens are allowed to live. It is a tool for social and geographic control.
24. Although China's deposit rates have been officially liberalised, they are still under a self-regulation mechanism in order to prevent their quick rise. The main purpose is to repress the interest rates in order to support economic growth.
25. China's reform can be generally classified into two categories: domestic reform and open-up of domestic markets to foreign investors. After over thirty years of reform since 1978, the easiest part of domestic reform has been almost finished, and the remaining such as factors of production markets reform are more challenging. During the past couple of years, China has shifted its focus from domestic reform to opening up domestic markets to foreign investors such as shortening the negative list of foreign investments, open-up of domestic bond and equity markets and so on.
26. Hainan (in Chinese: 海南) is China's smallest and southernmost province. Its GDP in 2019 is RMB 530.9 billion (equivalent to US$ 76.9 billion), ranking 28th among China's 31 provincial level regions. Its foreign trade in 2019 is US$ 18.1 billion, ranking 26th (source: wind, National Bureau of Statistics).
27. A Gartner survey of 260 global supply chain leaders in February and March 2020 found that 33% had moved sourcing and manufacturing activities out of China or plan to do so in the next two to three years (Gartner Survey 2020). This result is consistent with another survey conducted by the American Chamber of Commerce in China in March 2020 (AmChamChina (American Chamber of Commerce in China) 2020). These companies may have relocated to Vietnam and/or Mexico (New York Times 2020a; Kearney 2020).
28. A sole trader means a person runs its own business as an individual and is self-employed. It legally exits in the Chinese economy for a long time. But many of these online-related job categories were not included in the employment statistics. In July 2020, the Chinese authorities have revised the statistics document accordingly. Together with preferential policies, the employment statistics may improve.
29. Source: Wind, National Bureau of Statistics.
30. Chinese regulator CBIRC also acknowledged this. See http://finance.caixin.com/2020-07-11/101578721.html?originReferrer=weibo_caixinwang (in Chinese).
31. The Hambantota Port is a Sri Lanka maritime port with a majority of its construction funding from the Export–Import Bank of China. As the port incurred heavy losses, making debt repayment difficult, its majority shares were then sold to state-owned China Merchants Port Holdings following a debt-for-equity swap program in 2017.
32. It is reported in July 2020 that China may invest in Iran for US$ 400 billion within next 25 years in various sectors including banking, telecommunications, ports, railways etc, and enhance deep military cooperation as well (New York Times 2020b).
33. China's foreign reserves inflow includes four parts: goods trade surplus, service trade surplus, foreign portfolio investment and foreign direct investment (FDI). While China's FDI suffered a negative growth as of June 2020, the rest have experienced a moderate growth. As a result, China's foreign reserves are almost stable. The Chinese authorities can also exert (or have exerted) strict capital control measures mainly targeting private firms and

personal use to control capital outflow. Thus, from the perspective of funds availability, the BRI may not suffer a significant effect.

34. The rationale is that a (relative) bigger GDP means more economic resources such as (goods and service) trade, loan and investment and so on, thus gaining an advantage in a check book diplomacy. At the same time, Taiwan's international status has improved during the (post) COVID-19 period such as the enactment of the Taiwan Allies International Protection and Enhancement Initiative Act in March 2020, and the following historical Taiwan visit from a US health minister in August 2020. These two factors, i.e., economic and non-economic ones, may not be conflicting with each other but rather complementary.
35. For more information, see https://www.bbc.com/news/topics/c1newxlp4qwt/china-india-border-dispute.

Acknowledgements

The author would like to thank two anonymous referees for very timely and valuable comments on an earlier version of this article. All errors are the author's sole responsibility.

Disclosure statement

No potential conflict of interest was reported by the author(s).

ORCID

Kerry Liu http://orcid.org/0000-0003-0581-4049

References

AmChamChina (American Chamber of Commerce in China). 2020. "Supply China strategies under the Impact of COVID-19 of large American companies operating in China". April. Retrieved from https://www.amchamchina.org/about/press-center/amcham-statement/supply-chain-challenges-for-us-companies-in-china

Atkeson, A. 2020. "What will be the economic impact of Covid-19 in the Us? Rough estimates of disease scenarios". No. w26867. National Bureau of Economic Research,

Bloomberg News. 2020a. "China brokerage retracts estimate that real jobless level is 20%". 27 April. Retrieved from https://www.bloomberg.com/news/articles/2020-04-27/china-brokerage-retracts-estimate-that-real-jobless-level-is-20

Bloomberg News. 2020b. "Killing bank profits is a pretty desperate move". 19 June. Retrieved from https://www.bloomberg.com/opinion/articles/2020-06-18/china-asking-banks-to-route-profit-to-smes-shows-lending-failed

Elgin, C., G. Basbug, and A. Yalaman. 2020. "Economic policy responses to a pandemic: Developing the COVID-19 economic stimulus index." *Covid Economics* 1 (3): 40–53. http://www.amcham-egypt.org/bic/pdf/corona1/Covid%20Economics%20by%20CEPR.pdf#page=44

Feng, S., et al. 2020. "Rational use of face masks in the COVID-19 pandemic." *The Lancet Respiratory Medicine* 8.5 (5): 434–436. doi:10.1016/S2213-2600(20)30134-X.

Fernandes, N., 2020. "Economic effects of coronavirus outbreak (COVID-19) on the world economy" (March 22). Available at SSRN: https://ssrn.com/abstract=3557504 or 10.2139/ssrn.3557504.

Gartner Survey. 2020. "Gartner survey reveals 33% of supply chain leaders moved business out of china or plan to by 2023". 24 June. Retrieved from https://www.gartner.com/en/newsroom/press-releases/2020-06-24-gartner-survey-reveals-33-percent-of-supply-chain-leaders-moved-business-out-of-china-or-plan-to-by-2023

Global, C. 2020. "Extensions possible for new asset management rule compliance: Regulator". 3 February. Retrieved from https://www.caixinglobal.com/2020-02-03/extensions-possible-for-new-asset-management-rule-compliance-regulator-101511116.html

Govindarajan, V., and G. Bagla. 2020. "As covid-19 disrupts global supply chains, will companies turn to india? " *Harvard Business Review*. 25 May. retrieved from https://hbr.org/2020/05/as-covid-19-disrupts-global-supply-chains-will-companies-turn-to-india

Hale, T., S. Webster, A. Petherick, T. Phillips, and B. Kira. 2020. *Oxford COVID-19 Government Response Tracker*. Oxford: Blavatnik School of Government.

Huang, Y., and B. Wang. 2010. "Cost distortions and structural imbalances in China." *China & World Economy* 18 (4): 1–17. doi:10.1111/j.1749-124X.2010.01201.x.

IMF (International Monetary Fund). 2020a. "Policy responses to Covid-19". Retrieved From https://www.imf.org/en/Topics/imf-and-covid19/Policy-Responses-to-COVID-19

IMF (International Monetary Fund). 2020b. "World economic outlook update". 20 June. Retrieved from https://www.imf.org/en/Publications/WEO/Issues/2020/06/24/WEOUpdateJune2020

Johnson, K., and R. Gramer. 2020. "The great decoupling." *Foreign Policy*. 14 May. Retrieved from https://foreignpolicy.com/2020/05/14/china-us-pandemic-economy-tensions-trump-corona virus-covid-new-cold-war-economics-the-great-decoupling/

Kearney. 2020. "Trade war spurs sharp reversal in 2019 reshoring index, foreshadowing COVID-19 test of supply chain resilience". Retrieved from https://www.kearney.com/docu ments/20152/5708085/2020+Reshoring+Index.pdf/ba38cd1e-c2a8-08ed-5095-2e3e8c93e142?t=1586876044101

Lai, S., et al. 2020. "Effect of non-pharmaceutical interventions to contain COVID-19 in China." *Nature* 1–7. doi:10.1038/s41586-020-2293-x.

Lin, C., H. Lerong, and G. Yang. 2020. "Targeted monetary policy and financing constraints of chinese small businesses." *Small Business Economics* 1–18. doi:10.1007/s11187-020-00365-5.

Liu, K. 2018. "Chinese manufacturing in the shadow of the china–us trade war." *Economic Affairs* 38 (3): 307–324. doi:10.1111/ecaf.12308.

Liu, K. 2019a. "The determinants of china's lending rates and interest rates pass-through: A cointegration analysis." *Research in Economics* 73 (1): 66–71. doi:10.1016/j.rie.2019.02.002.

Liu, K. 2019b. "China's visible hand: An analysis of the chinese government's intervention in its economy during 2015–17." *Journal of Business and Economic Studies* 23 (1): 36–54.

Liu, K. 2019c. "Chinese shadow banking: The case of trust funds." *Journal of Economic Issues* 53 (4): 1070–1087. doi:10.1080/00213624.2019.1668338.

Liu, K. 2019d. "China's reserve requirements and their effects on economic output and assets markets during 2008-2018." *International Journal of Monetary Economics and Finance* 12 (3): 212–232.

Liu, K., 2020a. "The effects of COVID-19 on chinese stock markets: An EGARCH approach" (April 26). *Economic and Political Studies*. Forthcoming. Available at SSRN: https://ssrn.com/abstract=3612461

Liu, K. 2020b. "China's policy response to the China US trade war: An initial assessment." *The Chinese Economy* 53 (2): 158–176. doi:10.1080/10971475.2019.1688003.

Liu, K. 2021a. "Chinese local government debt: Institutional change, roles in economic growth and pricing." *International Journal of Economic Policy in Emerging Economies*. Forthcoming.

Liu, K. 2021b. "Deleveraging China." *International Review of Applied Economics*. 35 (1): 91–109. doi:10.1080/02692171.2020.1836136.

Liu, K. 2021c. "How Does China's Information and Communications Technology Infrastructure Investment Promote Economic Growth? ". Unpublished working paper

Liu, K. 2021d. "Cross-Strait relations between taiwan and China: The economic imbalance and its implications". China Report. Forthcoming.

Liu, X., and S. Zhang. 2020. "COVID-19: Face masks and human-to-human transmission." *Influenza and Other Respiratory Viruses* 14 (4): 472–473. doi:10.1111/irv.12740.

Loayza, N. V., and S. Pennings. 2020. "Macroeconomic policy in the time of COVID-19: A primer for developing countries." March. 10.1596/33540

Ma, J., and M. Ji. 2016. "新货币政策框架下的利率传导机制. "Interest rate passthrough under the new framework of monetary policy". The People's Bank of China, China Financial Forum Working Paper. No. 2016. 54.

Maliszewski, W., S. Arslanalp, J. G. Caparusso, S. Guo, J. S. W. Kang, R. Lam, and L. Zhang, 2016, "Resolving China's corporate debt problem". IMF Working Paper 16/203.

New York Times. 2020a. "Companies may move supply chains out of China, but not necessarily to the U.S.". 22 July. Retrieved from https://www.nytimes.com/2020/07/22/business/companies-may-move-supply-chains-out-of-china-but-not-necessarily-to-the-us.html

New York Times. 2020b. "Defying U.S., China and Iran near trade and military partnership". 22 July. Retrieved from https://www.nytimes.com/2020/07/11/world/asia/china-iran-trade-military-deal.html

News, X. 2020a. "中共中央政治局召开会议 中共中央总书记习近平主持会议 The politburo of the central committee of the communist party of China held a meeting, and the general secretary of the CPC central committee Xi Jinping presided over the meeting". 27 March. Retrieved from http://www.xinhuanet.com/politics/leaders/2020-03/27/c_1125778940.htm (in Chinese)

News, X. 2020b. "中共中央政治局召开会议 习近平主持. The politburo of the cpc central committee held a meeting chaired by Xi Jinping". 17 April. Retrieved from http://www.xinhuanet.com/politics/leaders/2020-04/17/c_1125871992.htm (in Chinese)

News, X. 2020c. "中共中央 国务院关于构建更加完善的要素市场化配置体制机制的意见 Opinions of the central committee of the communist party of china and the state council on building a more perfect market-oriented allocation system for factors". 9 April. Retrieved from http://www.gov.cn/zhengce/2020-04/09/content_5500622.htm (in Chinese)

News, X. 2020d. "中共中央 国务院关于新时代加快完善社会主义市场经济体制的意见 Opinions of the central committee of the communist party of china and the state council on accelerating the improvement of the socialist market economic system in the new era". 18 May. retrieved from http://www.gov.cn/zhengce/2020-05/18/content_5512696.htm (in Chinese)

People.com.cn. 2020a. "端午假期旅游收入同比恢复31.2% 节日效应明显 Dragon boat holiday travel income recovered 31.2% YoY". 29 June. Retrieved from http://finance.people.com.cn/n1/2020/0629/c1004-31762353.html (in Chinese)

People.com.cn. 2020b. "发改委等13部门发文支持网络直播等多样化自主就业13 ministries including the national development and reform commission issued a document to support diversified independent employment such as webcasting". 15 July. Retrieved from http://finance.people.com.cn/n1/2020/0715/c1004-31784572.html (in Chinese)

People's Bank of China (PBC). 2017. "*China Financial Stability Report 2017*". China Financial Publishing House

Reuters. 2018. "Exclusive: Facing U.S. Blowback, Beijing softens 'made in China 2025' message". Retrieved from https://www.reuters.com/article/us-usa-trade-china-madeinchina2025-exclu/exclusive-facing-u-s-blowback-beijing-softens-made-in-china-2025-message-idUSKBN1JL12U

Reuters. 2019. "China has replaced U.S. as locomotive of global economy: Kemp". 6 November. Retrieved from https://www.reuters.com/article/us-economy-global-kemp-column/china-has-replaced-u-s-as-locomotive-of-global-economy-kemp-idUSKBN1XF211

Reuters. 2020. "Shenzhen drafts china's first personal bankruptcy laws as virus pressures economy". 4 June. Retrieved from https://www.reuters.com/article/us-china-economy-bankruptcy/shenzhen-drafts-chinas-first-personal-bankruptcy-laws-as-virus-pressures-economy-idUSKBN23B1EG

SCMP (South China Morning Post). 2018. "Beijing tries to play down 'made in China 2025' as donald trump escalates trade hostilities". Retrieved from https://www.scmp.com/news/china/policies-politics/article/2152422/beijing-tries-play-down-made-china-2025-donald-trump

Tan, S.-L. 2020. "Australia Sees 'Partial Economic Decoupling' from China as Canberra Weighs Risks of over Reliance after Coronavirus Disruptions". *South China Morning Post*. 4 July. Retrieved from https://www.scmp.com/economy/china-economy/article/3091769/australia-sees-partial-economic-decoupling-china-canberra

The Economist. 2016. "Grossly deceptive plans: China's obsession with GDP targets threatens its economy". 28 January. Retrieved from https://www.economist.com/news/china/21689628-chinas-obsession-gdp-targets-threatens-its-economy-grossly-deceptive-plans

The Economist. 2020. "The belt and road initiative: Break time". 6 June. Retrieved from https://www.economist.com/china/2020/06/04/the-pandemic-is-hurting-chinas-belt-and-road-initiative

Part II

Covid-19, Inequality, and Government Responses

The 'Great Reset' to tackle Covid-19 and other crises

Jonathan Michie and Maura Sheehan

The 2021 World Economic Forum pledged a 'Great Reset', recognising that the Covid-19 crisis would be compounded by several other crises, actual and threatened, including the climate crisis, financial crises, social and economic inequality, and the threat of further pandemics.[1]

This is the second Special Issue of the *International Review of Applied Economics* focussing on the Covid-19 pandemic. The first, on 'The Political Economy of Covid-19' (Volume 35, Number 2, March 2021) included an article by John Child, which argued that while the pandemic intensified many of the economic and social problems that societies were already facing, the public response to the crisis points to a constructive way forward, widening participation in organisational decision-making as an approach to addressing the problems, which will continue to be with us – in effect, to enable a 'Great Reset' to be actually put into practice on the ground, and realised.[2]

The articles in this follow-up Special Issue also relate to the connections made by the World Economic Forum to the other serious challenges facing humanity, and in particular inequality – which in turn can exacerbate the risk of financial crises, and the threat of climate crisis.

1. The Covid-19 pandemic and inequality

In terms of social and economic inequality, the worse off tended to be hit harder by the effects of the Covid-19 pandemic, both globally and within individual countries. In the UK, death rates tended to be higher in poorer communities, where housing is more crowded, making 'social distancing' difficult, and employment more likely to be in 'front line' jobs, such as health or transport, which cannot be performed from home. In 'The Impact of Covid-19 on the Indian Economy', Deepak Kumar Behera, Maryam Sabreen and Deepika Sharma estimate the loss of output over the financial year 2020–21 in India at between 1.7% and 7.6%, with the loss of jobs amounting to anything from 1.56 million to 35.4 million. Such losses in output and employment are caused most immediately by lockdowns and other restrictions. But Christa D. Court, João-Pedro Ferreira, Geoffrey J. D. Hewings and Michael L. Lahr point out that such measures dampen economic activity of 'non-essential' sectors in particular, and that this affects other industries and countries that supply parts, machinery and services *via* global value chains. 'Accounting for global value chains: Rising global inequality in the wake of COVID-19?' uses the World Input-Output Database to show how a hypothetical decline in the worldwide consumption of a set of non-essential sectors affects the global distribution of GDP and employment. While richer countries consume relatively more non-essential goods and services, by considering the interdependencies among developed and developing economies they find that low-income countries are likely to suffer steeper declines in their GDP and employment. Specifically, for each 1% decline in the demand for non-essential products, the Gini index across nations is expected to rise by 0.3%. That is, global inequality is likely to rise, and economies with less-diverse sets of industries are more vulnerable to such global shocks.

In 'Impact of Pandemics on Income Inequality: Lessons from the past', Pinaki Das, Santanu Bisai and Sudeshna Ghosh examine how past pandemics impacted upon income inequality. They find that pandemics have had a statistically significant positive impact upon income inequality, particularly for the high-income group but also for their entire set of 70 countries, but that the impact of the pandemics was negative upon the upper-middle-income group of countries. Their study demonstrates how past pandemics generated policy responses that influenced the distribution of income, and that a weakened role of the state was responsible for worsening inequality.

2. Government responses to the Covid-19 pandemic

In 'The Covid-19 pandemic and economic stimulus in India: Has it been a hostage of macroeconomic complications?', Himadri Shekhar Chakrabarty, Partha Ray and Parthapratim Pal analyse the efficacy of the economic stimulus package in response to the Covid-19 pandemic, arguing that India was cautious in formulating policy measures, especially when the authorities deferred spending measures, while the need of the hour was direct fiscal spending, and that the reason may be linked to India's twin fiscal and current account deficits, along with the fear of a possible adverse response by foreign investors and capital flight.

In 'An Empirical Analysis of COVID-19 Responses: Comparison of US with the G7', Mahua Barari, Srikanta Kundu and Saibal Mitra compare the US policy response to the Covid-19 pandemic with its G7 counterparts. The G7 countries, while economically and ideologically aligned, instituted very different policies to mitigate the spread of the disease, with varying degrees of compliance. They found that countries that eased their lockdown measures moderately while enforcing nationwide mask mandates and comprehensive contact tracing generally performed better in mitigating the spread of new infections, and that countries with higher degree of compliance did better. The US was ranked mostly in the bottom half of the G7 group but was not always the worst.

In 'The Korean government's public health responses to the Covid-19 epidemic through the lens of industrial policy', Hee-Young Shin explores the idea that the success of the Korean government's non-pharmaceutical interventions can be best understood through the lens of an industrial policy framework, rather than merely administrative efficiency. The paper emphasizes that the Korean government has over many years maintained sustained R&D support, tax subsidies, and various forms of public–private partnerships to help nurture and grow domestic infant industry in such strategic industrial areas as information-communication technology, biotechnology and health care, and pharmaceutical industry; and argues that it was this industrial policy that enabled the public health authority to implement successfully a series of non-pharmaceutical public health measures to suppress and mitigate the spread of the coronavirus.

3. Conclusion: the impact of government policy

The papers in this Special Issue analyse the impact that the Covid-19 crisis had on economic outcomes, including output, employment, and inequality. These impacts came both from direct government restrictions designed to reduce the spread of Covid-19, and from the knock-on effects via global supply chains. How effective the Government measures were both in stopping the spread of the disease, and in limiting the detrimental economic impacts varied, depending in part on the extent to which Governments took countervailing fiscal measures. The previous Special Issue reported research finding that the degree of trust amongst the population in Government and the health authorities was a significant factor (Eduardo Vera-Valdés 2021), and likewise the papers in this Special Issue point to the importance not just of the measures introduced but also of the degree of *compliance* with such measures, and to the importance of an industrial policy framework having created capabilities for the successful introduction and implementation of public health measures.

Notes

1. For a brief report and discussion, see https://theconversation.com/davos-2021-to-achieve-a-great-reset-we-cant-count-on-the-same-old-globalists-to-lead-the-way-153508
2. For further elaboration and discussion, see Michie and Sheehan (2021) and Child (2021).

Disclosure statement

No potential conflict of interest was reported by the author(s).

References

Child, John. 2021. "Organizational Participation in Post-covid Society – Its Contributions and Enabling Conditions." *International Review of Applied Economics* 35 (2, March): 117–146. doi:10.1080/02692171.2020.1774976.

Eduardo Vera-Valdés, J. 2021. "The Political Risk Factors of Covid-19." *International Review of Applied Economics* 35 (2, March): 269–287. doi:10.1080/02692171.2020.1866973.

Michie, Jonathan, and Maura Sheehan. 2021. "Building Back Better?" *International Review of Applied Economics* 35 (2, March): 111–116. doi:10.1080/02692171.2021.1882035.

The Covid-19 pandemic and economic stimulus in India: has it been a hostage of macroeconomic complications?

Himadri Shekhar Chakrabarty, Partha Ray and Parthapratim Pal

ABSTRACT

This paper analyzes the efficacy and skepticism surrounding the economic stimulus package announced by the Indian authorities in response to the Covid-19 pandemic in 2020. While the end of the pandemic is yet to be on the horizon, countries across the world have been undertaking economic stimulus packages of varied nature, depth, and quantum. A scrutiny of these packages show that India has been cautious in formulating policy measures and balancing inter-temporal objectives. The disaggregated economic stimulus package in India belies the justification of it being an adequate stimulus in managing the mammoth crisis, especially when the authorities had resorted to more deferred spending measures while the need of the hour was direct fiscal spending. Specifically, this study argues that the causes behind the fiscal conservativeness might be linked to India's twin deficits in the fiscal and current account fronts, along with the fear of a potential capital flight and a possible adverse response by the foreign investors.

1. Introduction

Over the last two decades, India has emerged as a major economy in the world. The Gross Domestic Product (GDP) of the Indian economy has grown at an annual average rate of nearly 7% since the new millennium and reached around USD 3 trillion (at the market exchange rate) by 2019. Notwithstanding such an impressive GDP growth rate, India has not done well in terms of income distribution, health and education indicators, hunger, nutrition, and gender-equality indices. The Human Development Index of 2020 ranked India 131st among the 189 countries ranked.[1]

With its multiple handicaps of a large population, widespread poverty, densely populated habitats, poor social indicators, and dismal medical facilities, India was not well prepared to face a pandemic like Covid-19. Not surprisingly, India experienced large number of Covid-19 infections, and it is likely that the economic and human impact of the pandemic prove far higher than anything the country had experienced since its independence. In terms of number of cases, India was second to the U.S.; in terms of number of deaths, India's position was third, after Brazil.

Provision and quality of health-care services have never attracted adequate political attention in India. Historically, total health expenditure in India has hovered between

3.3% and 3.8% of Gross Domestic Product (GDP), with the proportion of *public* health expenditure being less than 1% of GDP.[2] Thus, in the context of the pandemic crisis in India, increased public investment in health, infrastructure, and social sectors is expected to improve its ability to cope with the Covid-19 crisis and help it rebound. Studies in the past have pointed out that the complementarity of private and public investment is generally high in developing countries. Especially in an economy like India, where lack of infrastructure and low 'ease of doing business' hinder private investment, there is a possibility that the right kind of public investment may crowd-in private investment (Belloc and Vertova 2006; Bahal, Raissi, and Tulin 2018). Specifically, in an economy that was slowing down even before the pandemic, and faced unprecedented contraction due to a prolonged lockdown of markets, it was expected that the government would introduce a substantial stimulus to mitigate the economic and humanitarian fallout of the Covid-19 pandemic.

However, so far, India's fiscal stimulus has been modest. Why has India responded so meekly to the gravest human challenge it has faced since its independence? This paper looks at various dimensions of this issue. It puts forward hypotheses that India's twin deficit (viz., fiscal deficit as well as current account deficit) problem, along with a dependence on foreign portfolio investors could have constrained India's actions to deal with the pandemic.

The rest of the paper is organized as follows: Section 2 puts forward the details of the Indian economic stimulus package. Section 3 provides a detailed account of the reasons behind India's fiscal rectitude and the resulting low stimulus package. Section 4 concludes.

2. India's economic stimulus package

Given the compelling reasons discussed above, one would have expected that India's economic stimulus package would be substantial. We will argue in this section that this is far from the case.

The Government of India's first significant response to the pandemic came in the form of a nation-wide lockdown on 22 March 2020, which was aimed to limit the spread of the virus. This came at a time when the economy's structural parameters were already looking grim. India's quarterly growth rates had decelerated since the first quarter of 2015 (Figure 1).[3] The Covid-19 shock on top of the ongoing slowdown resulted in an astounding decline in quarterly GDP by 23.9%, which happens to be the sharpest contraction in quarterly GDP among the G20 countries.

India's initial response came in the form of a combined fiscal and monetary stimulus. The Indian Prime Minister's announcement of INR 20 trillion stimulus package on 20 May 2020 was later followed by three rounds of additional stimulus.[4] While the first addition to the package on 8 July 2020 was an extension of the previously announced economic stimulus package, the next two complete packages were announced on 12 October 2020 and 12 November 2020. One feature of the stimulus package was that the emphasis was on keeping the immediate fiscal outlays low, with much stronger dependence on monetary policy. It is possible that the government adopted a cautious stance on the fiscal front due to an already tight budgetary constraint (Pal and Ray 2020a, 2020b; Chakrabarty, Ray, and Pal 2020). As we discussed later, the government was

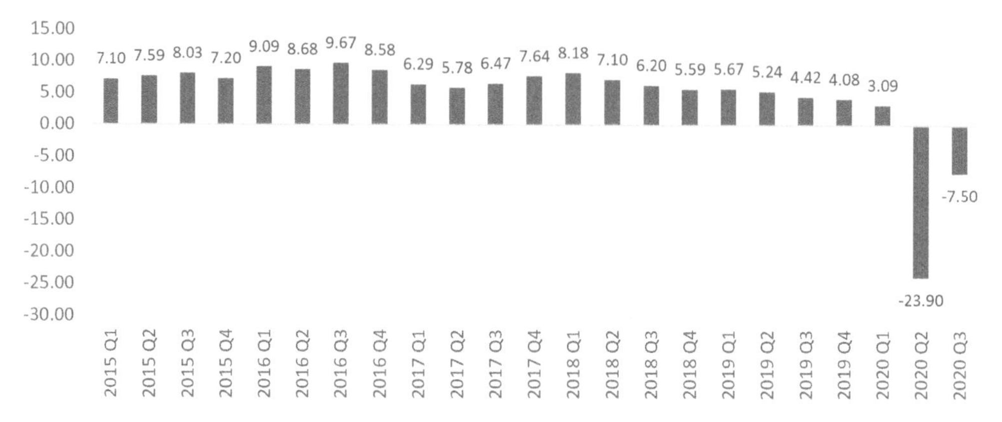

Figure 1. India's real GDP growth (in per cent). As per Indian convention, quarterly growth rates are calculated on an annualized basis, i.e., over the corresponding quarter of the previous quarter. Source: Ministry of Statistics and Programme Implementation, Government of India

possibly under the impression that a bigger fiscal deficit would have led to a sovereign rating downgrade,[5] which, among other things, would have pushed up the cost of financing the deficit.

India's economic stimulus package had very distinct modules, and just adding them up could suffer from the fallacy of composition. The package includes the previously announced monetary stimulus in the form of liquidity infusion by the Reserve Bank of India (RBI), amounting to around INR 12.71 trillion. The remaining amount of the package, worth INR 17.16 trillion was distributed across several tranches, catering to various sectors of the economy. The details of the package are given in Table 1.[6] We have segregated various tranches of the economic stimulus package into three components: a) monetary stimulus from the Reserve Bank of India; b) fiscal stimulus; and c) others, including guaranteed and non-guaranteed liquidity schemes.

The size of the announced economic stimulus package, as claimed by the government, has been arrived by summing up direct fiscal measures, liquidity support, guaranteed schemes, and interventions by the Reserve Bank of India. The tepid direct fiscal support even after three rounds of additional allocation amounting to 33% of total stimulus further suggests that the government was under certain compulsions of fiscal rectitude (Table 1). According to our estimate, net of the monetary policy measures, long-term policy prescriptions, and guarantee schemes for liquidity, the effective fiscal stimulus would be around 4.9%. Moreover, many direct fiscal measures include extensions of previous budgetary announcements and long-term proposals for structural changes in the economy.[7]

Out of the total economic stimulus, the segregation across various components are as follows (Table 2).

2.1. Fiscal and monetary policy nexus

As far as the components related to non-income support are concerned, the first point of contention is whether the monetary policy announcements by the RBI (close to 6.2% of GDP till 31 October 2020) can be attributed to government

Table 1. Summary of India's economic stimulus package for Covid-19 (Till 31 October 2020).

No	Type of Support	Amount (in Billion)	% of Nominal GDP (of 2019–20)
I	Monetary Stimulus: Reserve Bank of India Measures	12,712	6.22
II	Fiscal Stimulus	5,805	4.90
	1. *Pradhan Mantri Garib Kalyan* (PMGK) *Yogana*	1,700	0.83
	2. Health Sector Package	150	0.07
	3. Revenue loss due to tax concessions	78	0.04
	4. Income transfer/support	3,877	1.90
	a) Fund of Funds for Micro Small and Medium Enterprises (MSME)	500	0.24
	b) EPF Support for Business and Workers	28	0.01
	c) Reduction in Employees' Provident Fund rates	68	0.03
	d) Reduction in Tax Deducted at Source rates	500	0.24
	e) Free Food grain for Migrant Workers	35	0.02
	f) Interest Subvention for Micro Units Development and Refinance Agency Loans	15	0.01
	g) Credit facility for street vendors	50	0.02
	h) Food Micro Enterprises	100	0.05
	i) Housing Credit Linked Subsidy Scheme Middle Income Group	700	0.34
	j) Pradhan Mantri Matsya Sampada Yojana	200	0.10
	k) Agriculture and Animal Husbandry related	1,200	0.59
	l) Viability Gap funding	81	0.04
	m) Additional Mahatma Gandhi National Rural Employment Guarantee Act allocation	400	0.20
	5. Additional allocation under PMGK Yojana	829	0.41
	6. Additional allocation under *Atmanirbhar Bharat Abhiyaan* 2.0	730	0.36
	7. Additional allocation under *Atmanirbhar Bharat Abhiyaan* 3.0	2651	1.30
	a) Housing for all	180	0.09
	b) Rural Employment	160	0.08
	c) Industrial Infrastructure and Equity infusion	162	0.08
	d) Research and Development grant for vaccine development	9	0.00
	e) Boost for project exports	30	0.01
	f) Manufacturing sector incentives	1459	0.71
	g) Agriculture subsidy	650	0.32
III	Others	7,150	3.50
	8. Non-guarantee liquidity schemes	2,300	1.13
	a) Emergency Working Capital through National Bank for Agriculture and Rural Development	300	0.15
	b) Additional credit through Kisan Credit Card	2,000	0.98
	9. Fully/Partially Guaranteed Liquidity Schemes	4,850	2.37
	a) Working Capital facility for MSME	3,000	1.47
	b) Subordinate debt for MSME	200	0.10
	c) Special Liquidity Scheme for Non-Banking Finance companies/Housing Finance/Micro-Finance Institutes	300	0.15
	d) Partial credit guarantee for Non-Banking Finance companies	450	0.22
	e) Liquidity Injection for Power Distribution Companies	900	0.44
IV	Total	29,876	14.62

(1) As per Advanced Estimate of 2019–20 (Economic Survey 2019–20, Statistical Appendix, Table A14) the nominal GDP of 2019–20 is taken to be Rs 2,04,422.33 billion.
(2) Loose Translations of the vernacular components of the Economic Stimulus Package: (i) *Pradhan Mantri Garib Kalyan Yojana*: Prime Minister's Poor Welfare Scheme; (ii) *Pradhan Mantri Matsya Sampada Yojana*: Prime Minister's Scheme for Agro-Marine Processing; (iii) *Atmanirbhar Bharat Abhiyaan*: Self-reliant India campaign; (iv) *Kisan Credit Card*: Farmer's Credit Card.
Sources: (1) Presentations on Atma Nirbhar Bharat of the Finance Minister (June 13–16, 2020 and 12 November 2020).
(2) Economic Survey 2019–20, Government of India (GOI, 2020).

support measures and should be included as part of the economic stimulus package. Specifically, the package seems to have also included several non-guaranteed and guaranteed liquidity measures, which are fundamentally monetary in nature and are in the RBI's domain. Here the authorities focused heavily on boosting liquidity, but

Table 2. Composition of economic stimulus of India (measures announced in 2020).

No.	Type of Measure	Percentage Share
1	Pure Monetary Stimulus by RBI	42.55
2	Guarantees	16.23
3	Non-guarantee Liquidity Scheme	7.70
4	Initial Income Support	19.43
5	Additional Income Support	14.09
6	Total	100.0

Source: Authors' Calculations

its actions were inadequate for treating insolvency, especially when both have affected the economy.

The liquidity and solvency crisis of the entire business sector can be traced back to the twin shocks of demonetization and hastily implemented new indirect tax regime namely the Goods and Services Tax (GST) in 2016 and 2017. The Micro, Small and Medium Enterprises (MSME) sector, which relies heavily on the easy availability of credit, experienced the maximum deceleration in credit growth during this phase due to a sharp decline in economic activity (Behera and Wahi 2018; RBI 2017). The demonetization of higher value currency notes in November 2016 caused a reduction in the ready supply of cash and, therefore, the MSME sector faced obstacles in meeting their working capital requirements and in paying their suppliers (Lahiri 2020).[8] A year later, the GST, a form of value-added tax, was introduced to eradicate the cascading effect of a multiplicity of indirect taxes that existed in India. However, the teething challenges in the implementation of GST and the costs of compliance with the new regime led to increased costs and reduced profits within the MSME sector.

Further, the liquidity of the MSME sector got tightened with the need to pay taxes every month as opposed to the previous regime where taxes were paid at quarterly intervals and the delay in getting input tax credit from their suppliers. In addition, financial fragility was observed in the scheduled commercial banks and non-banking financial companies (NBFCs) during 2011–2019 due to a sharp rise in the share of non-performing assets in gross advances. Since 2018, a large number of NBFCs, which manage their liabilities through debt instruments and not through regular commercial deposits, were labeled with the 'default' status by credit rating agencies, leading to conservative lending and contagion effect on industrial sectors due to the credit squeeze (Dasgupta 2020).

Taking the financial sector's lending fatigue in perspective, the government's reluctance to spend extensively during the pandemic did force the banks to lend, even though it may have increased the risk for the banks. A 100% credit guarantee might distort the credit allocation of banks with a limited amount of incentive to scrutinize loan applications leading to moral hazard problems and even a rise in non-guaranteed lending (Acharya and Kulkarni 2019; Wilcox and Yasuda 2019; Cowan, Drexler, and Yañez 2015). Further, owing to the risk-averse nature of public sector banks' lending activities in periods before the pandemic and ongoing process of` mergers, the credit guarantee mechanism, especially to the MSME sector, hit a roadblock (Nair and Das 2019). This is also reflected in the Reserve Bank of India's Financial Stability Report (RBI 2020), which states that credit growth of Scheduled Commercial Banks across all groups, which had considerably weakened during the first half of 2019–20, slid further to 5.9% by March 2020 and remained muted, post the initial months of the pandemic.

2.2. *Inter-temporal imbalance*

Some of the proposals especially related to infrastructure development, were an extension of previous annual budgetary proposals, which either remained incomplete earlier or there were some added budgetary allocations. By introducing long-term initiatives like *Pradhan Mantri Matsya Sampada Yojana*, Promotion of Herbal Cultivation, Agri-Infrastructure Fund, among others, the economic stimulus package has been made analogous to budgetary announcements. This is where the inter-temporal perspective of fiscal multipliers comes into the picture wherein a distinction is made between impact multiplier and cumulative multiplier (Ilzetzki, Mendoza, and Végh 2013; Batini, Eyraud, and Weber 2014). While the former measures the ratio of the change in output to a change in government expenditure at the time in which the impulse to government expenditure occurs, the latter measures the cumulative change in output per unit of additional government expenditure over a longer horizon. The Government of India had perhaps focused more on the cumulative multiplier effects when the need of the hour required direct income support. The long-run effects, captured by the cumulative multiplier are more for capital expenditure as it involves the creation of assets while revenue expenditures are in the form of subsidies, tax cut, or direct fiscal transfers, and tend to have short-run effects (Jain and Kumar 2013; Bose and Bhanumurthy 2015; RBI 2019). Similarly, transfers by the government, much like the income support as part of the economic stimulus package, result in higher disposable income for households, leading to higher private consumption expenditure. India's economic stimulus package required a concerted effort to boost the short-term demand in the economy, especially after the prolonged lockdown. However, the government's priorities were possibly fixated on the long-term outcomes and hence resorted to capital expenditure.

Historically, India's revenue expenditure has dominated the total government expenditure and increased steadily compared to capital expenditure (Figure 2). This is primarily because of the existence of a large public sector and salaries and pension expenses thereof along with significant subsidies and interest payments on debt, due to the presence of a large amount of rural and urban poor. Over the years, owing to strict fiscal rules, whenever the ruling government had to stick to its fiscal deficit targets, capital expenditure has generally been compromised and often remained largely procyclical. During the 2008–09 Global Financial crisis, revenue expenditure constituted around 84%, and the remainder accounted for the capital component (RBI, Annual Report, 2008–09) with major emphasis on tax cuts and increased expenditure on both investment and consumption. Though it resulted in the rise in fiscal deficit from 2.7% of GDP in 2007–08 to 6.0% of GDP in 2008–09, India was able to overcome the crisis quickly. Among recent studies Goyal and Sharma (2018) show that the short-run impact multiplier is the highest for revenue expenditure while the cumulative multiplier is highest for capital expenditure. These results are consistent even after considering the monetary policy response and supply shocks.

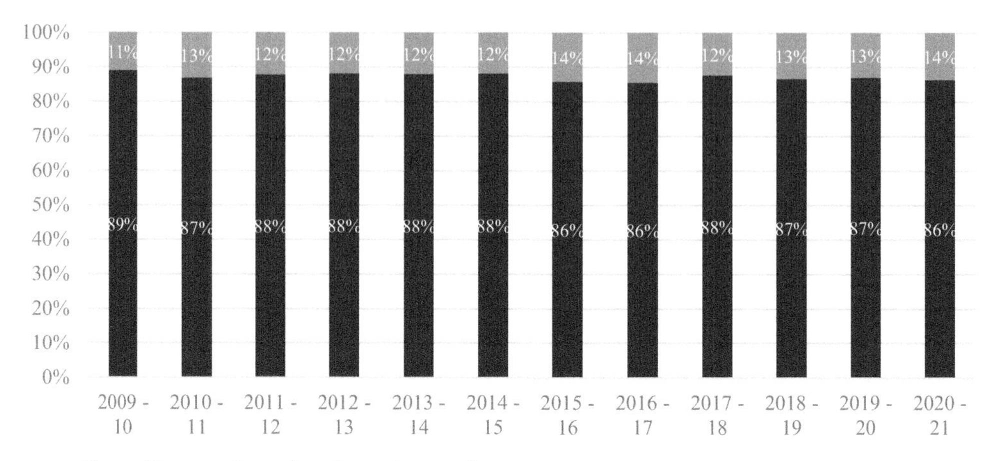

Figure 2. Distribution of revenue and capital expenditure in total government expenditure in India. (Percentage of total expenditure). Source: Handbook on Indian Economy, RBI

Thus, in the context of the pandemic, the government might have prioritized more short-term spending measures. This is for three reasons. First, with many of the migrant labourers moving to their respective homes, there could be short-term labor supply shortages leading to delay in effect of capital investment. In such a scenario, direct income support, in the form of revenue expenditure, was expected to yield higher multiplier effects than long-term measures. Secondly, the pandemic reignited the debate between lives and livelihood, which could be supported substantially through impact multiplier reforms. The migrant crisis led to a humanitarian crisis.[9] Amidst the stringent imposition of lockdowns, the plight of migrant unskilled and semi-skilled labourers, who got stuck in different parts of the country without jobs, access to shelter and food, and other basic needs was deplorable (Dandekar and Ghai 2020). Thus, a substantive relief package through a direct cash transfer and based on the minimum floor wage level for the reverse-migrants was deemed necessary as part of the stimulus (Lele, Bansal, and Meenakshi 2020). And finally, in a period of excess capacity and unprecedented low interest rates, crowding-out is unlikely.

2.3. Overemphasis on guarantees

The first and most expensive tranche of the economic stimulus package was entirely on sovereign guarantees for the MSME sector. The apparent advantage of such guarantees for the government is to prevent an immediate outflow of funds in the present and defer all future liabilities. At a time when revenue collections are abysmal, this was the chosen solution to infuse liquidity in the economy by nudging the banks and NBFCs to spend. Illustratively, credit growth was low, hovering between 6% and 7%. This low credit offtake is attributed to weak business investment because of excess capacity in the Indian economy.[10] Post lockdown, there was further reduction in demand. Given the deficient and declining demand, it is likely that credit guarantees may be unable to compensate for an inadequate fiscal stimulus. Furthermore, for a crisis of this magnitude, while monetary policy can make credit cheaper, it cannot bring money into the hands of workers, and hence fiscal spending needed to be adequate (Pal and Ray 2020a).

However, India was not the only country to frontload its economic stimulus package through credit guarantees. India allocated around 3.5% of its GDP to credit guarantees. Among a list of 43 countries whose data on guarantees could be extracted from the IMF Policy response tracker, India stood close to being in the middle holding the 21st position in terms of guarantees as a percent of GDP (Figure 3).

The proportion of India's guarantees (3.5% of GDP) is more than the average of most emerging market economies (0.4% of GDP) (Alberola et al. 2020), but less than the average of advanced and high-income countries (6.6% of GDP). Guarantees in low-income countries are not necessarily sustainable due to incomplete information about the operational efficiency and fund management in the various enterprises. There may be additional transactional costs imposed on the lending and borrowing parties due to the involvement of a third party like the government (Meyer and Nagarajan 1996). As far as the fiscal cost is concerned, its magnitude will depend on the scope of the scheme, the extent of deliberate underpricing and unexpected excess underwriting losses, and administrative efficiency (Honohan 2010). While one of the primary motivations behind the move of sovereign guarantees by the government in a crisis could be linked to a very limited need for an upfront cash commitment, such guarantees can spur the growth of contingent liabilities for the government. These contingent liabilities are a potential obligation for the government, which depends on possible future adverse events. They are a cause of fiscal risk if they materialize into an actual liability, which could trigger large increases in public debt.

As far as the top 10 countries resorting to sovereign guarantees are concerned, it is important to understand their fiscal space in financing them. The share of guarantees in tax revenues for Italy and Germany is well beyond 100%, and the share of guarantees to debt is among the highest. However, India's guarantees to tax revenue ratio lies in the moderate regime of around 22% and guarantees to the gross debt being around 4.9%, calculated at 2019 rates. Therefore, it may appear that compared to other countries, India had fiscal space to increase guarantees to the vulnerable sectors but it must be kept in

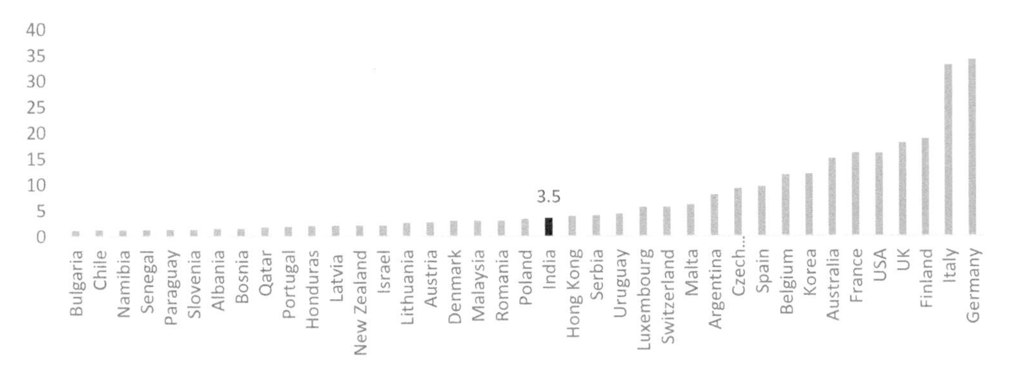

Figure 3. Size of guarantees announced by countries in response to Covid-19 (as a percentage of GDP). Source:1)IMF Policy Tracker https://www.imf.org/en/Topics/imf-and-Covid19/Policy-Responses-to-Covid-19 2)Covid-19 Financial Response Tracker Visualization (CFRTV) https://som.yale.edu/faculty-research-centers/centers-initiatives/program-on-financial-stability/Covid-19-tracker

mind that India has been issuing several guarantees from before, especially to the MSME sector, which add to its off-budget liabilities. There are also reports that the government has resorted to off-budget methods of financing to meet its capital expenditure requirements, affecting transparency norms and artificially reducing the fiscal deficit. Debt sustainability assessment should consider these contingent liabilities (CAG, 2017 2019, Misra, Gupta, and Trivedi 2020).

The government's decision to use sovereign guarantees for MSMEs as part of the economic stimulus package is based on the assumption that the MSMEs would recover, once the pandemic loses its sting and there are fewer supply chain disruptions. But the same assumption could boomerang and hit the fiscal coffers hard if the performance of MSMEs falls short of expectation. In this regard, it has been argued that contingent liabilities in the form of government guarantees are appropriate when the government is best placed to anticipate risk, control risk exposure, and minimize the cost of risk (Cangiano et al. 2006). According to them, guarantees have two sources of uncertainties – whether the government has to pay in the future, and if yes, what is the timing and amount for it. Further, guarantees create a bias of being used as a fiscal stimulus measure as it does not create an immediate impact on the budget. It is therefore important to be transparent about the fiscal risks created by guarantees.

3. Reasons for fiscal rectitude: some conjectures

The limited fiscal stimulus in India defies logic for two reasons. First, the impact of the Covid-19 pandemic in India was substantial in terms of the extent of the infection, lives lost, jobs lost, and output foregone. Second, compared with the economic stimulus of around 3.5% of GDP during the global financial crisis of 2008–2009, this time the economic stimulus was only slightly more, amounting to 4.9% of GDP, net of the monetary policy measures, and guaranteed and non-guaranteed schemes for liquidity, despite GDP growth being negative for two consecutive quarters. To explain this phenomenon, we put forward the following hypothesis.[11]

3.1. Budgetary underestimations and the twin deficit

We conjecture that a major reason behind India's fiscal conservatism is its twin deficit problem, viz., the coexistence of a fiscal deficit and a current account deficit (Figure 4).

On the fiscal deficit, while there was some improvement in and around 2010, in recent times the budget outcomes have deviated significantly from the expected course. Moreover, given the discipline imposed by the Fiscal Responsibility and Budget Management Act there may not be much room for fiscal maneuverings. In particular, the Union Budget 2020–21 was overly optimistic and did not include any significant stimulus to boost domestic demand, and revenue projections in the 2020 budget were based on unrealistic expectations (Pal and Ray 2020a). The Covid-19 pandemic put a further strain on the budgetary resources. After the pandemic, tax and non-tax revenue collections will take time to return to normalcy, especially after being through one of the most stringent lockdowns among countries.

On the other hand, there is an urgent need for increased government expenditure. Given the growing imbalance between expected receipts and spending, the government may be

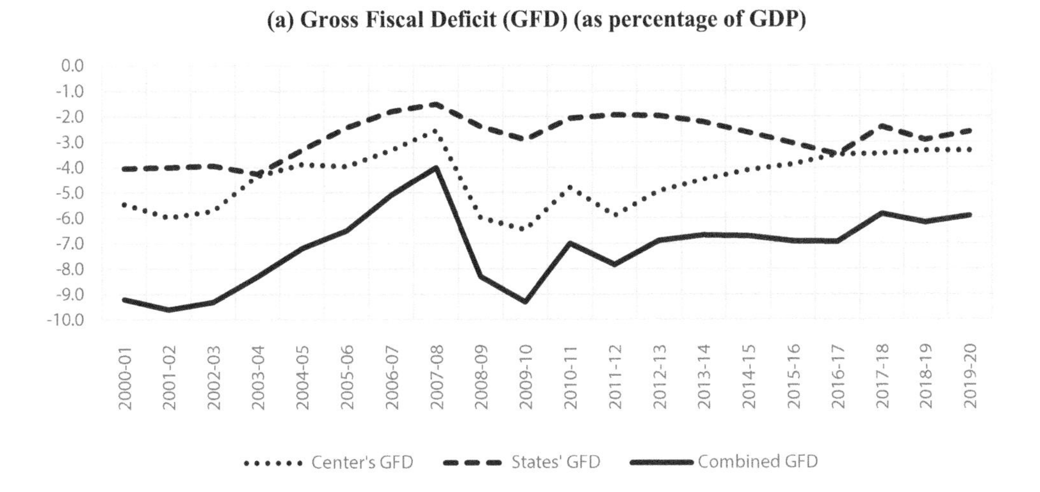

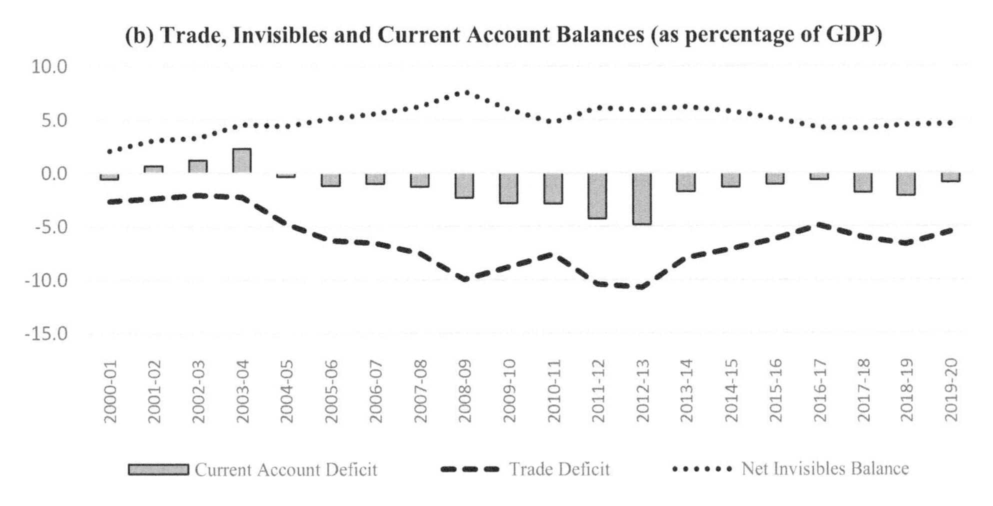

Figure 4. India's twin deficit. (a) Gross Fiscal Deficit (GFD) (as percentage of GDP) Source: Database on Indian Economy, Reserve Bank of India.

acting cautiously to keep the fiscal deficit under control. But then the question arises: what is the sanctity of the provisions of the Fiscal Responsibility and Budget Management Act in the face of an unprecedented economic shock like the pandemic? It is here that the current account deficit imposes another constraint on the government's budgetary envelope.

Without an active export basket and with inelastic import demand dominated by items like oil, gold and electronics, India tends to have a trade deficit perennially. Since 2000–01, other than during a brief three-year period from 2001–02 to 2003–04, the Indian current account has been in deficit (Ray and Pal 2019). Thanks to the net inflows on account of invisibles (comprising primarily remittances and services exports, driven by information technology-related services), the current account deficit has been manageable (Figure 4(b)).[12]

However, the manageability of the current account comes out of some peculiarities in India's capital inflows, which are dominated by foreign institutional investors (FIIs). Compared with foreign direct investment (FDI), FIIs flows are traditionally much more volatile. In fact, whenever there are issues with FII flows, the Indian rupee (INR) has been under a severe attack, as happened during June–August 2013 and August–October 2018 (Ray 2014; Pal and Ray 2018). In the current context, the initial trends of capital outflows on account of withdrawal by FII turned into a problem of abundance in the more recent time period with an attendant appreciation of INR and a booming stock market. While the initial outflows could perhaps be in line with the pursuit of 'flight to safety' by the FIIs, later inflows could have been on account of massive liquidity infusion under the garb of quantitative easing by the major central banks like the Federal Reserve in USA or the European Control Bank (Figure 5).[13]

This apart, there are apprehensions about elements of underestimation in the official fiscal deficit number. A rough and ready idea of the extent of misestimation can be arrived at by comparing the 'General Government net borrowing' as per IMF and 'Gross Fiscal Deficit' as per RBI. While both these include fiscal deficit of the central as well as state governments, IMF does not take disinvestment proceeds arising out of the sale of shares of public sector undertakings (Figure 6).[14] Considering the fact that for the financial year April 2020 – March 2021 disinvestment proceeds have been ambitiously budgeted at INR 1.2 trillion (or approximately USD 16.2 billion), there is a likelihood this target may not be achieved. Thus, the final GFD number could turn out to be much more. This might have prompted the government to be conservative in adopting the fiscal stimulus.

3.2. *Fear of rating downgrade*

While there are push and pull factors behind the foreign portfolio investment in times of crisis, international rating agencies tend to play a significant role. Interestingly, India's outlook has undergone changes to 'Negative' from November 2019, by Moody's, and from June 2020 by Fitch (Table 3). Ratings provide an estimate of the probability that borrowers will not fulfill the obligations in their debt issues and hence carries significant value to investors.

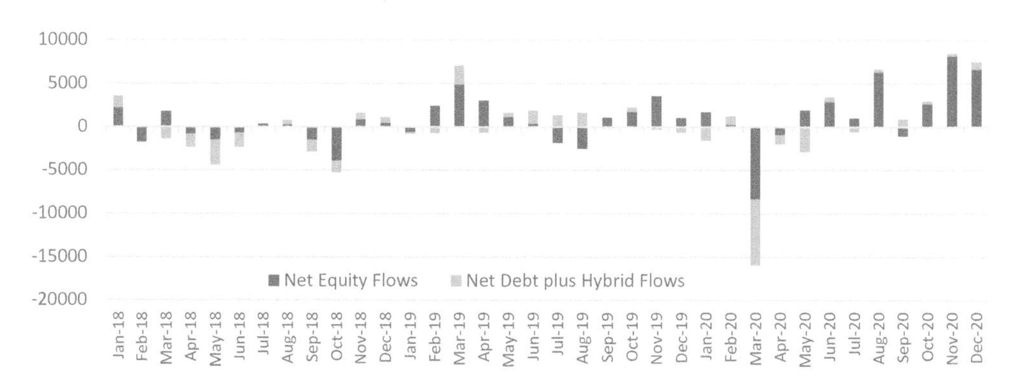

Figure 5. Foreign portfolio flows to India (USD Million). Source: https://www.fpi.nsdl.co.in/web/Reports/Yearwise.aspx?RptType=6

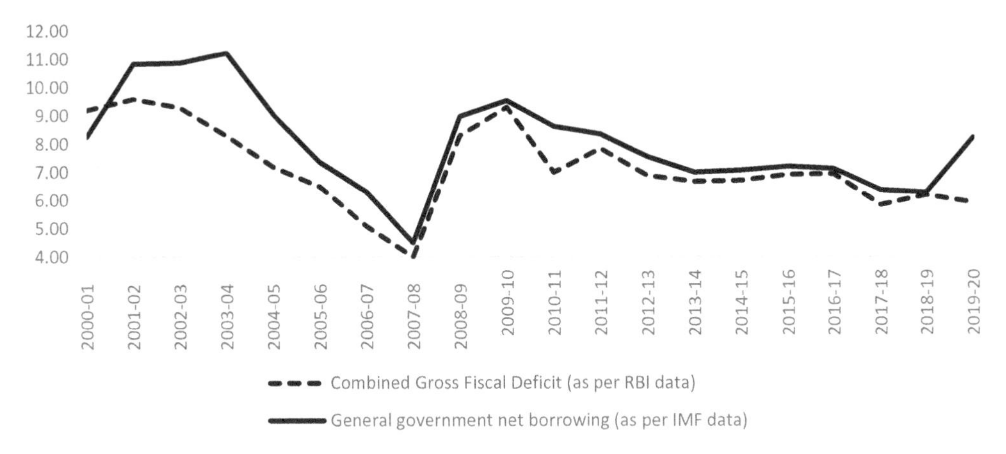

Figure 6. Fiscal deficit as per government of India and IMF. Source: (1) Database on Indian Economy, RBI; (2) World Economic Outlook Database, October 2020

Table 3. India's credit rating by two leading rating agencies.

Moody's			Fitch		
Date	Rating	Outlook	Date	Rating	Outlook
Dec-11	Baa3	Stable	Dec-11	BBB-	Stable
Apr-15	Baa3	Positive	Dec-15	BBB-	Stable
Nov-16	Baa3	Positive	Jul-16	BBB-	Stable
Nov-17	Baa2	Stable	May-17	BBB-	Stable
Nov-19	Baa2	Negative	Dec-19	BBB-	Stable
Jun-20	Baa3	Negative	Jun-20	BBB-	Negative

Standard and Poor's has been maintaining India's outlook as stable since September 2014.
Source: https://www.moodys.com/ and https://www.fitchratings.com/

Press reports suggest that while speaking in a virtual meeting under the Saudi Arabia presidency, on 18 July 2020, attended by the G20 group of finance ministers and central bank governors, the Indian Finance minister Nirmala Sitharaman criticized the credit rating agencies and indicated that any credit downgrade could limit policy options for emerging market economies in their fight against coronavirus pandemic. Specifically, she also spoke about the procyclicality of credit rating downgrades by the rating agencies and its deterrent impact on policy options, particularly for EMEs.[15] As far as econometric evidence is concerned, Balajee, Tomar, and Udupa (2020) show that countries with lower ratings and stringent lockdowns announced a lower proportion of economic stimulus and delayed their announcement. Out of a sample of 116 countries, only 67 had declared their economic stimulus in response to the pandemic as early as mid-April. India was found to be one of the vulnerable countries based on the mean stringency and mean credit ratings of the country. These vulnerable countries would need external support in terms of long-term loans from multilateral organizations. The fear of sovereign rating downgrade makes it difficult for the countries to raise resources to combat the pandemic and disincentive to invest among the institutional investors. Even in previous crisis episodes, it has been observed that the contagion effect of sovereign credit ratings spills over to private sector credit markets, and investors are not insulated from differences in country risks arising out of higher dispersion of emerging market spreads across countries (Dell'Ariccia, Schnabel, and Zettelmeyer 2006). In essence, the fear of a possible capital flight has constrained Indian authorities' flexibility to provide a substantial economic stimulus even with adverse medical and health indicators.[16] Given the heterogeneity in pandemic impact across countries, a flight of capital could soon be followed by a flight to quality or the more stable countries and ensuing devaluation of the domestic currency. The sovereign credit ratings affect the country's exchange rate with stronger market reactions to negative in contrast to positive credit signals, and to large rating adjustments (Baum, Schäfer, and Stephan 2016; Alsakka and Gwilym 2012). With one of the rating agencies, Moody's expecting India's public debt to GDP ratio to rise from 72% of GDP to 84% of GDP in 2020–21 along with a rising proportion of non-performing assets in banks, this might have led to a tepid fiscal response.

3.3. *Compulsions of political business cycle*

The political business cycle theories originating from Nordhaus (1975), which have gradually transitioned into political budget cycles since Rogoff (1990), explain how policy instruments are manipulated before elections. Procyclical fiscal policy is often driven by myopic motivations by the government and with electoral incentives among politicians to signal their ability to manage the economy better. Electoral competition and special interest pressures may also induce similar behavior (Alesina, Campante, and Tabellini 2008; Abbott and Jones 2013; Lim 2020). The literature for India shows that electoral budget cycles seem to be operative (Rajaraman 2008), although Khemani (2004) suggests a somewhat contrarian view. Unlike in the 2008–09 Global Financial Crisis, the pandemic did not hit India just preceding elections.[17] Elections in Kerala, West Bengal, Tamil Nadu & Puducherry, and Assam are due in mid-2021, which may have implications for allocation and disbursal of funds.

Interestingly enough the last few tranches of fiscal stimulus, which were announced in October and November, coincided with elections in the state of Bihar and had several benefits for propelling demand. However, fears of a further rise in retail inflation (7.6% in October) could lead to re-prioritization of the fiscal stimulus. Erratic rainfall did substantial damage to crops and pushed up food prices as well. Moreover, the gradual relaxation of lockdown stringency, which significantly contributed to the suspension of output in business, transport, and different companies, might inflict further upward pressures on retail prices. In such a situation, the government might again tread cautiously.

4. Concluding observations

Despite an impressive growth performance since the 1990s, India lacked progress in terms of health and social-sector indicators. With adverse initial condition, in terms of its preparedness for a pandemic, one would have expected a pro-active and substantial economic stimulus so that social-sector expenditure in general and health expenditure in particular could have been geared up to minimize the adverse impact of the pandemic. However, we have argued in this paper that the twin deficit problem of India, along with a dependence on foreign portfolio investors, made India's active economic stimulus rather modest.[18] In essence, India is an economy where despite having a booming services sector and an impressive growth performance, dependence on foreign capital has made the country vulnerable, leading to social welfare being sacrificed due to this environment of macroeconomic constraints.

Notes

1. http://hdr.undp.org/en/content/latest-human-development-index-ranking.
2. Of 182 countries for which health expenditure as a proportion of GDP was available for the period 2017 from the World Bank's World Development Indicators, India ranked 160th, despite being the second-largest country in the world by population and the seventh largest country by size. As far as health infrastructure is concerned, countries with a high human development index have, on average, 55 hospital beds, over 30 physicians and 81 nurses per 10,000 people and an average least developed country has 7 hospital beds, 2.5 physicians and 6 nurses for the same number of people, according to the United Nations Development Programme (UNDP). Shockingly, for India, there are 7 hospital beds, 7.8 physicians and 21 nurses and midwives available per 10,000 population.
3. Responding to the decelerating growth rates, the Reserve Bank of India had already initiated an expansionary monetary policy, reducing interest rates from January 2019.
4. Based on the exchange rates of Indian Rupee on 12 November 2020, India's economic stimulus package is equivalent to around US$410 billion, British Pounds 300 billion, Euro 340 billion and Chinese Yuan 2650 billion.
5. Sovereign rating downgrade would imply that bonds issued by the Indian governments would be 'riskier' than before, due to weaker economic growth and worsening fiscal health.
6. As on 31 October 2020 based on information sought by a private petitioner, only 1.2 trillion was sanctioned as credit guarantees from the first tranche of the package by the Government, which amounts to around 10% of the initial tranche. The low disbursal of funds notwithstanding the large-scale losses to individuals, families and businesses even after 7 months of the first case of the pandemic, does not augur well for the economy to kickstart. See https://timesofindia.indiatimes.com/india/rs-20l-cr-pandemic-package-barely-10-disbursed-says-rti/articleshow/79677830.cms.
7. Figures published by the International Monetary Fund are closer to our estimates. According to the calculations of IMF, the direct spending plus and foregone or deferred revenue part of the stimulus is around 1.9% of GDP. There is an additional announcement of Rs 150 billion for health infrastructure, which is approximately 0.1% of GDP by their calculation. 'Below the line measures', that is measures without an immediate bearing on government's deficit is another 4.9% of the GDP. See https://www.imf.org/en/Topics/imf-and-Covid19/Policy-Responses-to-Covid-19#Ifordetails.
8. On 8 November 2016, the Government announced the demonetization of all INR 500 and INR 1,000 banknotes to reduce the size of the shadow economy, and the use of illicit and counterfeit cash to fund illegal activity and terrorism.
9. 238 migrant workers died while migrating homes, from physical sickness or accidents during transit: https://www.indiatoday.in/news-analysis/story/migrant-workers-deaths-govt-says-it-has-no-data-but-didn-t-people-die-here-is-a-list-1722087-2020-09-16). However, the Government failed to collect data on migrant deaths. According to the United Nation's World Food Programme (WFP), an estimated 265 million people could be pushed to the brink of starvation by the end of 2020. As far as jobs are concerned, the Centre for Monitoring India Economy Private Limited suggested that the labour force participation rate had dropped from 42.6% at the beginning of the lockdown on March 22 to 38.2% in May, 2020 and currently hovers around 40% with unemployment close to 10% on 13 December 2020.
10. The Indian economic recovery seems led by profits, not wages (livemint.com).
11. India experienced deceleration of growth over the last three years; the IMF in its June 2020 World Economic Outlook projected the Indian economy contracting by 4.5% in 2020.

12. In fact, the recent improvement in current account balance (as well as trade balance) of India has been primarily due to the subdued imports on account of an economic contraction and not necessarily due to any exuberance in exports.
13. Technically, FPI = FII + Capital raised under American Depository Receipts and Global Depository Receipts.
14. IMF's 2018 Article IV Consultation Report for India noted, 'The difference between the authorities' and IMF presentations primarily reflects higher-than-budgeted privatization proceeds, which are recorded below the line in the IMF presentation'; see IMF (2018).
15. https://pib.gov.in/newsite/PrintRelease.aspx?relid=210160.
16. This happened despite the fact that India's foreign exchange reserves is growing and reached a record US$ 538.19 billion as of 14 August 2020 (https://timesofindia.indiatimes.com/business/india-business/forex-reserves-climb-3-623-billion-to-record-538-191-billion/articleshow/77548073.cms).
17. Even during 2008, coinciding with the election year, some of the fiscal stimulus was prior to the fall of Lehman Brothers and was in the nature of election year sops.
18. The US Treasury Department's report on 'Macroeconomic and Foreign Exchange Policies of Major Trading Partners of the United States' of December 2020, noted, 'The (Indian) authorities responded with modest direct fiscal support of around 2% of GDP and substantial monetary easing' (p. 11).

Acknowledgments

The authors extend sincere thanks to the anonymous referees of this journal for their insightful and detailed comments and suggestions.

Disclosure statement

No potential conflict of interest was reported by the author(s).

ORCID

Partha Ray http://orcid.org/0000-0002-9600-5484

References

Abbott, A., and P. Jones. 2013. "Procyclical Government Spending: A Public Choice Analysis." *Public Choice* 154 (3–4): 243–258. doi:10.1007/s11127-011-9816-9.

Acharya, V. V., and N. Kulkarni 2019. "Government Guarantees and Bank Vulnerability during a Crisis: Evidence from an Emerging Market." NBER Working Paper No. w26564.

Alberola, E., Y. Arslan, G. Cheng, and R. Moessner. 2020. "The Fiscal Response to the Covid-19 Crisis in Advanced and Emerging Market Economies." BIS Bulletin, No. 23. https://www.bis.org/publ/bisbull23.pdf

Alesina, A., F. R. Campante, and G. Tabellini. 2008. "Why Is Fiscal Policy Often Procyclical?" *Journal of the European Economic Association* 6 (5): 1006–1036. doi:10.1162/JEEA.2008.6.5.1006.

Alsakka, R., and O. Gwilym. 2012. "Foreign Exchange Market Reactions to Sovereign Credit News." *Journal of International Money and Finance* 31 (4): 845–864. doi:10.1016/j.jimonfin.2012.01.007.

Bahal, G., M. Raissi, and V. Tulin. 2018. "Crowding-out or Crowding-in? Public and Private Investment in India." *World Development* 109: 323–333. doi:10.1016/j.worlddev.2018.05.004.

Balajee, A., S. Tomar, and G. Udupa 2020. "COVID-19, Fiscal Stimulus, and Credit Ratings." Fiscal Stimulus, and Credit Ratings, April 15.

Batini, N., L. Eyraud, and A. Weber 2014. "A Simple Method to Compute Fiscal Multipliers (No. 14-93)." International Monetary Fund Working Paper.

Baum, C. F., D. Schäfer, and A. Stephan. 2016. "Credit Rating Agency Downgrades and the Eurozone Sovereign Debt Crises." *Journal of Financial Stability* 24: 117–131. doi:10.1016/j.jfs.2016.05.001.

Behera, H., and G. Wahi 2018. "How Have MSME Sector Credit and Exports Fared? (No. 13)." Mint Street Memo

Belloc, M., and P. Vertova. 2006. "Public Investment and Economic Performance in Highly Indebted Poor Countries: An Empirical Assessment." *International Review of Applied Economics* 20 (2): 151–170. doi:10.1080/02692170600581086.

Bose, S., and N. R. Bhanumurthy. 2015. "Fiscal Multipliers for India." *Margin: The Journal of Applied Economic Research* 9 (4): 379–401. doi:10.1177/0973801015598585.

Cangiano, M. M., B. Anderson, M. M. Alier, M. Petrie, and M. R. Hemming. 2006. "Public-Private Partnerships, Government Guarantees, and Fiscal Risk." International Monetary Fund.

Chakrabarty, H. S., P. Ray, and P. Pal. 2020. "Deciphering India's Stimulus Package: Adding Apples with Oranges? Indian Institute of Management, Calcutta." Working Paper Series WPS, (846).

Comptroller and Auditor General (CAG). 2017. "Report of the Comptroller and Auditor General of India on Compliance of the Fiscal Responsibility and Budget Management Act, 2003 for the Year 2016–17." Report No. 20 of 2018, January, Union Government (Civil), Department of Economic Affairs (Ministry of Finance). https://www.cag.gov.in/uploads/download_audit_report/2018/Report_No_20_of_2018_Compliance_of_the_Fiscal_Responsibility_and_Budget_Management_Act_2003_Department_of_Economic_Affairs_Minis.pdf

Cowan, K., A. Drexler, and Á. Yañez. 2015. "The Effect of Credit Guarantees on Credit Availability and Delinquency Rates." *Journal of Banking and Finance* 59: 98–110. doi:10.1016/j.jbankfin.2015.04.024.

Dandekar, A., and R. Ghai. 2020. "Migration and Reverse Migration in the Age of COVID-19." *Economic and Political Weekly* 55 (19): 28–31.

Dasgupta, Z. 2020. "Economic Slowdown and Financial Fragility: The Structural Malaise of India's Growth Process." *Economic and Political Weekly* 55 (13): 46–53.

Dell'Ariccia, G., I. Schnabel, and J. Zettelmeyer. 2006. "How Do Official Bailouts Affect the Risk of Investing in Emerging Markets?" *Journal of Money, Credit and Banking* 38 (7): 1689–1714. doi:10.1353/mcb.2006.0091.

Government of India. 2020. "Economic Survey". https://www.indiabudget.gov.in/economicsurvey/

Goyal, A., and B. Sharma. 2018. "Government Expenditure in India: Composition and Multipliers." *Journal of Quantitative Economics* 16 (1): 47–85. doi:10.1007/s40953-018-0122-y.

Honohan, P. 2010. "Partial Credit Guarantees: Principles and Practice." *Journal of Financial Stability* 6 (1): 1–9. doi:10.1016/j.jfs.2009.05.008.

Ilzetzki, E., E. G. Mendoza, and C. A. Végh. 2013. "How Big (Small?) are Fiscal Multipliers?" *Journal of Monetary Economics* 60 (2): 239–254. doi:10.1016/j.jmoneco.2012.10.011.

IMF. 2018. "India: 2018 Article IV Consultation Report." https://www.imf.org/~/media/Files/Publications/CR/2018/cr18254.ashx

Jain, R., and P. Kumar 2013. "Size of Government Expenditure Multipliers in India: A Structural VAR Analysis." Reserve Bank of India Working Paper Series, 7.

Khemani, S. 2004. "Political Cycles in a Developing Economy: Effect of Elections in the Indian States." *Journal of Development Economics* 73 (1): 125–154. doi:10.1016/j.jdeveco.2003.01.002.

Lahiri, A. 2020. "The Great Indian Demonetization." *Journal of Economic Perspectives* 34 (1): 55–74. doi:10.1257/jep.34.1.55.

Lele, U., S. Bansal, and J. V. Meenakshi. 2020. "Health and Nutrition of India's Labour Force and COVID-19 Challenges." *Economic & Political Weekly* 55 (21): 13.

Lim, J. J. 2020. "The Political Economy of Fiscal Procyclicality." *European Journal of Political Economy* 65: 101930. doi:10.1016/j.ejpoleco.2020.101930.

Meyer, R. L., and G. Nagarajan. 1996. "Credit Guarantee Schemes for Developing Countries: Theory, Design and Evaluation." Prepared for Africa Bureau of USAID. Barents Group, Washington, DC.

Misra, S., K. Gupta, and P. Trivedi 2020. "RBI Working Paper Series No. 08 Subnational Government Debt Sustainability in India: An Empirical Analysis."

Nair, T., and K. Das. 2019. "Financing the Micro and Small Enterprises in India." *Economic & Political Weekly* 54 (3): 37.

Nordhaus, W. D. 1975. "The Political Business Cycle." *The Review of Economic Studies* 42 (2): 169–190. doi:10.2307/2296528.

Pal, P., and P. Ray. 2018. "Recent Downfall of the Indian Rupee." *Economic and Political Weekly* 53 (41): 12–16.

Pal, P., and P. Ray 2020a. "It Takes Two to Tango: Can Monetary Stimulus Compensate for an Inadequate Fiscal Stimulus in India?." Working Paper of International Development Economics Associates (IDEAs). https://www.networkideas.org/wpcontent/uploads/2020/05/Two_to_Tango.pdf

Pal, P., and P. Ray 2020b. "To Spend or Not to Spend? the Austerity Debate in Retrospect." IIM Calcutta Working Paper No. WPS-849. https://www.iimcal.ac.in/sites/all/files/pdfs/wps_849.pdf

Rajaraman, I. 2008. "The Political Economy of the Indian Fiscal Federation." India Policy Forum, 2007-08, New Delhi: NCAER. http://testnew.ncaer.org/image/userfiles/file/Indira%20Rajaraman.pdf

Ray, P. 2014. "The Rupee in Distress: June–August 2013." ICRA Bulletin on Money and Finance, July, 51–62.

Ray, P., and P. Pal 2019. "Who Is Afraid of the Exchange Rate." The India Forum, July 5. https://www.theindiaforum.in/sites/default/files/pdf/2019/07/05/who-is-afraid-of-the-exchange-rate.pdf

RBI. 2017. "Macroeconomic Impact of Demonetisation – A Preliminary Assessment." March. https://rbidocs.rbi.org.in/rdocs/Publications/PDFs/MID10031760E85BDAFEFD497193995BB1B6DBE602.PDF

RBI. 2019. "Expert Committee on Micro, Small and Medium Enterprises (MSMEs) (Chairman: U K Sinha)." Mumbai: RBI.

RBI. 2020. "Financial Stability Report Issue No.21." https://rbidocs.rbi.org.in/rdocs//PublicationReport/Pdfs/0FSRJULY2020C084CED43CD1447D80B4789F7E49E499.PDF

Rogoff, K. 1990. "Equilibrium Political Budget Cycles." *American Economic Review* 80: 21–36.

Wilcox, J. A., and Y. Yasuda. 2019. "Government Guarantees of Loans to Small Businesses: Effects on Banks' Risk-taking and Non-guaranteed Lending." *Journal of Financial Intermediation* 37: 45–57. doi:10.1016/j.jfi.2018.05.003.

Accounting for global value chains: rising global inequality in the wake of COVID-19?

Christa D. Court, João-Pedro Ferreira, Geoffrey J.D. Hewings
and Michael L. Lahr

ABSTRACT
Production processes depend on fragmented and interdependent value chains; nowadays, a single product often includes components produced in dozens of countries. Many public health measures being implemented to prevent the spread of COVID-19 have dampened economic activity of 'non-essential' sectors. The decreased production affects other industries and countries that supply parts, machinery, and services via global value chains. Using the World Input-Output Database, we show how a hypothetical decline in the worldwide consumption of a set of non-essential sectors affects the global distribution of GDP and employment. While richer countries consume relatively more non-essential goods and services, we find, by considering the interdependencies among developed and developing economies, that low-income countries are likely to suffer steeper declines in their GDP and employment. Specifically, for each 1% decline in the demand for non-essential products, the GINI index across nations is expected to rise by 0.3%. That is, global inequality is likely to rise, contradicting some earlier findings. Finally, we show that economies with less-diverse sets of industries are more vulnerable to such global shocks. This study highlights the role of value chains in analyzing the spatial spread of the impacts and their contribution to amplifying world imbalances.

1. Introduction

Major economic shocks whether caused by economic recessions or natural events (such as floods, hurricanes, earthquakes) generate differing macroeconomic impacts upon economies. Sectors affected vary with the nature and duration of the shock, as well as the focus of any government interventions (such as economic stimuli or quantitative easing). The novel coronavirus disease (COVID-19) event was unprecedented in terms of the speed and intensity of the negative economic impacts incurred; for example, in the United States (US), close to 40 million people filed unemployment claims within just 10 weeks of when major lockdowns were implemented. Further, while only a small set of sectors were directly affected by lockdown measures, many of them employed large shares of lower-income individuals from vulnerable populations. Due to differences in health-care provision by income alone, the poor were more vulnerable to the virus; this enhanced risk forced many to fall into poverty conditions. Ultimately, however, all sectors of the economy were significantly affected.

The nature and strength of value chains determines the nature of indirectly affected sectors. Value chains are increasingly fragmented and, hence, involve activities in multiple countries (Montresor and Vittucci Marzetti 2010). A shock in one country affects other economies and, thereby, ultimately amplifies or reduces world inequalities. This distributional effect of international trade has been discussed by Fajgelbaum and Khandelwal (2016) who showed that, because they are heterogeneous in income, households have different consumption propensities. These different product preferences are manifest as differential demand elasticities with respect to income, particularly when the goods are imported. Hence, an analysis of the COVID-19 event needs to address this heterogeneity in combination with the value-chain effects to ascertain the full asymmetry of the total impacts.

This paper begins by providing some context on the possible economic impacts of the pandemic. Section 3 is a description of the model and data that we use to calculate how the impacts spread worldwide and how they affect countries differently due to dissimilarities in their income levels and economic structures. In Section 4, we probe the nature of the COVID-19 shock by focusing on declines in consumption of non-essential products. We discuss the findings in Section 5, in which we also present a more realistic shock based on a stringency/lockdown index. The final section offers some conclusions and directions for future research.

2. The context

The emergence, spread, and severity of COVID-19 triggered public health measures that abruptly disrupted daily lives and livelihoods around the world. As incidence of the disease peaks and wanes across the globe with staggered timing, some economies remain relatively open, while others remain under more restrictive public health measures, and still others reopen to a 'new normal' as the number of new hospitalized cases slows.

During 2020, particularly after the winter surge in COVID-19 cases, the range and severity of the measures applied has varied according to distinct national or regional policies. Uncertainty abounds, it is clear that a more equal, sustainable, and peaceful world depends on the policy choices made during and after this pandemic, policy choices that can and should be informed by analyses of the underlying mechanisms that determine global economic activity.

The general loss of economic activity is critical to individuals and countries that have a significant share of their population living in poverty. Husain et al. (2020) of the World Food Programme conclude that the depth and breadth of hunger will increase. Barnett-Howell and Mobarak (2020) argue that, independently of where the gross domestic product (GDP) falls, workers and communities in less-developed countries are less willing to accept lockdown measures if they struggle to obtain basic goods, especially as the duration of lockdown periods extends. Krishnakumar and Rana (2020) highlight, via insight from India, the impossibility of social distancing among people who do not have formal employment contracts. Similar conclusions have emerged from studies in developed countries. Adams-Prassl et al. (2020) underline how the current pandemic disproportionately affects low-skilled individuals, while Reeves and Rothwell (2020) demonstrate how a more fragile economic and social status increases one's chance of losing a job. Barro and Ursúa (2008) report similar issues that existed during the so-called Spanish Flu pandemic at the end of World War I. Economists participating in the IGM Forum (Initiative on Global Markets 2020) almost unanimously expect that this shock will result in both income and wealth distribution effects at both national and global scales.

Noticeable shifts in economic activity appear to have resulted from implemented public health measures as well as from changes in consumer behavior; additional impacts should be expected, however. Trade patterns are changing and exchange rates are also being affected (McKibbin and Fernando 2020), and this also affects interest rates (Jordà, Singh, and Taylor 2020). Some poorer countries encumbered by large public debt are having difficulties mobilizing resources to stimulate the economy in the post-pandemic period (Pierros 2020; Bolton et al. 2020). New debt created by national social supports will cause inflation to rise differentially in the near- to medium-term. In past financial crises, households adjusted in the short run by cutting expenditures on durables, cutting health-care visits, and cutting school attendance, which might enlarge the effects in the long term (Harrison and McMillan 2007). The wealthy, who typically spend on luxury goods and international travel, find themselves unable to do so; they enhance their savings instead. Indeed, as a result, tourism-dependent cities and regions have lost substantial portions of their economic base (Gössling et al., 2020). Availability, costs, and storage requirements of currently approved vaccines might inhibit efficient and widespread vaccination in certain developing countries, leading to more extended periods of income loss associated with tourism declines.

The prices of oil and other raw materials largely produced in developing countries have already declined by 20% during the first half of 2020 (Bloomberg 2020). The prices of basic needs are likely to rise (Watanabe 2020), and private debt will likely increase everywhere; this will put upward pressure on interest rates, which in turn might limit future investment (Coibion, Gorodnichenko, and Weber 2020). As jobs and labor income fall at the bottom end of the pay scale, migrant remittances from developed countries to developing countries are also likely to shrink (Hevia and Neumeyer 2020; World Bank 2020b). Indeed, significant heterogeneity has been observed across receiving countries; Central and South American countries experienced a 17% year-over-year decline in April 2020 but have noted substantial recovery in the rest of the year (Pew Research Center 2020). Finally, as governments focus on fixing domestic ills, the pandemic will undoubtedly induce major downward adjustments to official development assistance packages (Ataguba 2020). Laborde, Martin, and Vos (2020) and Milanovic (2020) suggest that this shock is likely to have larger effects in the more-developed countries and, thereby, possibly reducing international inequalities, as developed nations are likely to experience larger direct impacts from the lockdowns.

The asymmetric nature of the pandemic's spread and intensity, the variety of government responses planned to date, as well as the inherent uncertainty associated with it all, makes forecasting its general equilibrium economic impacts a substantial challenge. In the face of the rise of economic uncertainty and turbulence, insight is needed into the dynamic economic spillovers and feedback at play across nations with the hope of identifying key strengths and weaknesses in interregional and international supply chains. Thus, our contribution to the literature is insight into global economic impacts of the pandemic from the perspective of global value chains. Drawing on multiregional input-output (MRIO) models and global value chain (GVC) analysis, we demonstrate how changes in the economic impacts of demand spread between regions.

We follow Krugman (2020) and Ramos et al. (2020) by likening the COVID-19 pandemic to a disaster event that largely affects the demand for the so-called 'non-essential' goods and services. Krugman (2020) suggests the pandemic lockdowns are not simply shocks to aggregate demand, but rather each is more akin to a medically induced coma that shuts down specific functions to avoid system-wide damage. He identifies the shutdown functions as 'non-essential' goods and services.

There is no straightforward, widely accepted definition for 'essential' and 'non-essential' in this context. Woo (2019) suggests that the aggregate demand for 'non-essential' goods becomes zero when their prices are sufficiently high; thus, luxury goods are a good example of a set of non-essential goods since their demands are quite price and income elastic. In the context of the COVID-19 pandemic, Leibovici and Santacreu (2020) conservatively identify food, defense, and medical goods as essential and anything else as non-essential. Snyder (2009) notes that some essential goods require non-essential goods in the course of their production. Thus, from the perspective of households, Leibovici and Santacreu's definition of 'essential' goods must be broadened to include motor vehicles, motor fuels, major kitchen appliances, and other goods and services 'vital' to the purchase, maintenance, and preparation of food goods.[1] We adopt a more practical definition of 'non-essential' products – one grounded in the government classifications used for lockdown measures. We examine sectors that have been most exposed to specific regulations imposed in the US (Identifying Critical Infrastructure during COVID-19, CISA 2020), UK (Critical Workers information, GOVUK 2020), and the European Union (Policy measures taken against the spread and impact of the coronavirus – 7 May 2020, EC 2020). The set of industries closed via regulation has been fairly uniform across these countries. Authorities have closed dentists, barbershops, entertainment, cultural and religious facilities, bars, restaurants, indoor recreation and fitness facilities, and clothing stores. They have been deemed 'non-essential' partly because, in the past, some households have proved that they could live without the goods and services provided by these industries and partly because these industries typically cannot accommodate social-distancing recommendations between employees and/or customers.[2]

We assess how a shock in demand for such products influences gross value-added (GVA), employment, labor compensation, and capital compensation across different industries and different countries. By combining data on production processes and international trade available within an MRIO database, we go beyond an analysis of the direct effects – the simple demand decline in selected sectors of some countries – to also measure the indirect effects embodied in global supply chains.

3. World input-output database and value-chain analysis

By combining data on production processes and international trade available within the World Input-Output Database (WIOD), we go beyond the simple decline in demand in some sectors of some countries (direct effects) to also capture how the indirect effects spread throughout global supply chains. We assess how this decline in demand for non-essential goods and services might affect inequality and delineate the sectors that are critical in determining these impacts for many less developed economies. Finally, we also simulate a shock based on the level of stringency of measures adopted by each country.

We use the latest WIOD data (Dietzenbacher et al. 2013; Timmer et al. 2015). This database combines information on interactions among industries and regions by detailing intra and interindustry transactions. It also details the heterogeneity in labor income in different industries among distinct countries (Parteka and Wolszczak-Derlacz 2015).

As with most of any other economic framework, the use of WIOD restricts the scope of our economic scenario modelling. First, input-output (IO) analysis, as we implement it, is a static model so technology is fixed over time. It is difficult to simulate changes in preferences, or how countries might alter the origins of goods they use (spatial substitution). Prices are also fixed; so, we cannot discern how product prices might change in light of altered international demands and supplies. Further, we cannot predict how changes in the prices of intermediate goods might affect the relative costs of other factors, like labor or capital.

With these limitations in mind, it is important to highlight that WIOD is our exclusive source of three aspects for understanding international trade flows: (i) the international distribution of trade; (ii) the interindustry economic structure of the countries involved in trade; and (iii) the share of intra-industry trade. The structure of the WIOD is presented in Figure 1.

WIOD data are in basic prices (US$ millions) and cover 44 regions (43 countries plus the 'Rest of the World' [ROW] region) for 2014. Wholesale, Retail, and Transportation margins are included as production inputs of the respective industries. $\mathbf{Z}$ is the intermediate consumption matrix and represents the links between industries in each country and between countries associated with the production process. z^{nn} represents the domestic trade in each country. Instead, z^{1n} represents the products produced in region 1 and sold to industries located in region n. Alternatively, z^{n1} represents the production of industries located in region n that were used in the production activity of region 1. $\mathbf{Y}$ represents the final demand matrix, and total final demand $\mathbf{y} = \mathbf{Yi}$, where $\mathbf{i}$ is a vector of ones that sums $\mathbf{Y}$ row-wise across final demand types. $\mathbf{v}^1$ is the vector of value-added for industries in country 1 while $\mathbf{x}^1$ is the vector of total output of that same country.[3] Finally, WIOD also includes socio-economic accounts that contain national industry-level data on employment, labor compensation, and the compensation of capital, among others.

$$\begin{bmatrix} \mathbf{z}^{11} & \cdots & \mathbf{z}^{1n} \\ \vdots & \ddots & \vdots \\ \mathbf{z}^{n1} & \cdots & \mathbf{z}^{nn} \end{bmatrix} \begin{bmatrix} \mathbf{y}^{11} & \cdots & \mathbf{y}^{1n} \\ \vdots & \ddots & \vdots \\ \mathbf{y}^{n1} & \cdots & \mathbf{y}^{nn} \end{bmatrix} = \begin{bmatrix} \mathbf{x}^{1} \\ \vdots \\ \mathbf{x}^{n} \end{bmatrix}$$

$$\begin{bmatrix} \mathbf{v}^{1} & \ldots & \mathbf{v}^{n} \end{bmatrix}$$

$$\begin{bmatrix} \mathbf{x}^{1} & \ldots & \mathbf{x}^{n} \end{bmatrix}$$

Figure 1. WIOD matrix structure.

This information is transformed to yield **A**, the spatial requirements matrix. For this, the elements in **Z** are column-wise normalized by the total output of each industry, **x**. The Leontief matrix (**L**) is obtained by:

$$\mathbf{L} = (\mathbf{I} - \mathbf{A})^{-1} \qquad (1)$$

where **I** is an identity matrix of the same dimension as matrix **A**.

The multipliers represented in this matrix include the direct and indirect effects and are used to estimate the impacts of real or hypothetical changes in the final demand ($\Delta\mathbf{y}$). Indeed, equation 4 measures the effects of such impacts while accounting for the direct and indirect effects:

$$\mathbf{x}^* = \mathbf{L}\mathbf{y}^* \qquad (4)$$

The total final demand less our rough estimate of the marginal decline in non-essential goods is denoted by $\mathbf{y}^*$. Thus, $\mathbf{x}^*$ denotes the expected output to be converted to other economic indicators via appropriate transformation coefficients (Miller and Blair 2009). This setup allows us to identify those industries that are most affected by the final demand change and how the impacts on them unfurl throughout the global value chain. WIOD has been used in numerous investigations. Timmer et al. (2014), for example, show how the international fragmentation of labor embodied in the manufacture of German automobiles has changed over time. Ye, Meng, and Wei (2015) investigate the production of electrical and optical equipment from China and Mexico and of automobiles in Japan and Germany. Xiao et al. (2020) examine how value chains have recently become more regionalized internationally and less global in nature. Chen et al. (2018) evaluate the EU-wide country and regional impacts of BREXIT using an MRIO approach that is very similar to the one employed in this paper. This very brief survey highlights several studies that have investigated the roles played by different countries and industries in global value chains using WIOD.

4. COVID-19 shock in non-essential products and services

Public health measures enacted around the world have been designed to reduce non-essential interaction (and as a result, the economic activity associated with these interactions). Greater insight into the uncertainty and risk associated with potential severing of existing global value chains can surely help some countries' planning and trade policy efforts. Undoubtedly, current economic interdependencies could exacerbate global imbalances in the event of such a crisis.

This is not a simple issue. Not only does the definition of what constitutes an 'essential' industry vary by country, but it is best if the nature and magnitude of the event – in this case, the COVID-19 pandemic – are fully understood.[4] In Section 2, we discussed our definition of 'essential' industries and how it was reflected in the policy measures to 'flatten the curve' by some of the most important economies in the world (see Appendix 1 for the list of industries that we included).

In essence, we start by assessing how a homogeneous 1% across-the-board decline in the demand of non-essential goods and services across all world regions distributes geographically and asymmetrically affects national economies. This scenario displays the role of international trade in changing imbalances. We then depart from a homogeneous shock to observe what we contend is a more realistic heterogeneous impact. This second scenario addresses the international economic spillover and feedback effects associated with the stringency of lockdown measures that countries applied to minimize the public health and economic effects of the COVID-19 pandemic. We aggregate our results into three country types based on relative national wealth (levels of GDP per capita) plus the rest of the world (ROW). We analyze ROW separately since it is composed of a diverse set of economies with very different income-levels.

Table 1 shows that high-income economies, which produce about 40% of world GDP and are responsible for nearly 46% of GVA, are home to less than 10% of the world's population. This contrasts with the low-income countries that constitute more than 47% of the world's population and just 28% of GDP and 23% of the GVA.

4.1. Scenario 1: A 1% marginal decline in the demand for non-essential goods

Two aspects distinguish how a relatively equal shock in non-essential sectors affects economies asymmetrically. First, if an economy has greater exposure to the consumption of non-essential goods and services, then a 1% decrease in their consumption represents a larger share of the nation's total demand and, as a consequence, of its economy. For example, entertainment and cultural events have affected some economies rather heavily since they are structured to cater to international visitors. Table 2 shows how essential vs. non-essential demand varies across economies.

Low-income countries tend to consume low shares of production from non-essential sectors (37.3%) as people spend a larger portion of their income on essential goods and services. For ROW, the share is slightly higher (40.6%). Middle- and high-income countries lean slightly more heavily upon non-essential sectors. It is (perhaps overly) simple to observe that COVID-19 will have the largest immediate impact on richer countries, as mentioned earlier. We suggest that this is an incomplete and, hence, naïve perspective. International interdependencies are omitted and are well known to have the potential to change the story substantially. Indeed, the entries in Table 2 do not consider the origin of the production of goods and services consumed. For example, just

Table 1. Description of the countries represented in each income group.

	GDP per capita (US$)	Countries	Share of World Population	Share of World Output	Share of World GVA
Low-income	< 10 K	Bulgaria, Brazil, China, Indonesia, India, Mexico, Turkey	47.4%	28.1%	23.3%
Middle-Income	10k – 40k	Croatia, Cyprus, Czech Rep., Estonia, Greece, Hungary, Italy, Japan, Korea, Latvia, Lithuania, Malta, Poland, Portugal, Romania, Russia, Slovakia, Slovenia, Spain	7.6%	16.1%	16.6%
High-Income	> 40k	Australia, Austria, Belgium, Canada, Finland, France, Germany, Denmark, Ireland, Netherlands, Norway, Luxembourg, Sweden, Switzerland, Taiwan, USA, UK	9.7%	39.9%	45.7%
ROW			35.3%	15.9%	14.5%

Source: WIOD (2020) and World Bank (2020)

16.7% of clothing consumed by US households is produced domestically, while the rest is imported from abroad. Similarly, some countries produce more for their own markets while other economies are more export-based. Limited intermediate self-supply of demand provides the basis for a first round of 'spillovers' to other countries. Figure 2 shows how a 1% decline in non-essential goods affects each group's production; the colors represent the part that corresponds to the origin of the consumption.

Figure 2 shows that a 1% decrease in the consumption of non-essential sectors worldwide could end up affecting low-income countries and ROW more because they produce goods consumed elsewhere in the world. In contrast, high-income countries account for just 8% of the production of non-essential sectors used by low-income countries. Consumption within low-income countries accounts for less than 1% of production in high-income countries. Indeed, 92% of production by high-income countries depends on their own consumption of output from non-essential sectors; for middle-income countries the figure is 86%, and for the ROW it is 83%.

This analysis provides greater insight into how countries could be affected by a specific economic shock. Including global value chains and information on intranational dependence realigns initial thoughts derived from numbers similar to those presented in Table 2. Thus, the use of IO techniques contemplates the role of the 'locally' produced inputs that are embodied throughout the production phase. Using this approach, we can see how the economies of richer and poorer countries are inextricably intertwined through international trade and determine which are likely to be more affected by a decline in consumption.[5] Such analysis has been applied to study the economic impacts of the

Table 2. Share of essential vs. non-essential goods in total household consumption.

	Low-income	Middle-Income	High-income	ROW
Non-essential	37.3%	45.4%	41.2%	40.6%
Essential	62.7%	54.6%	58.8%	59.4%

Source: WIOD (2020)

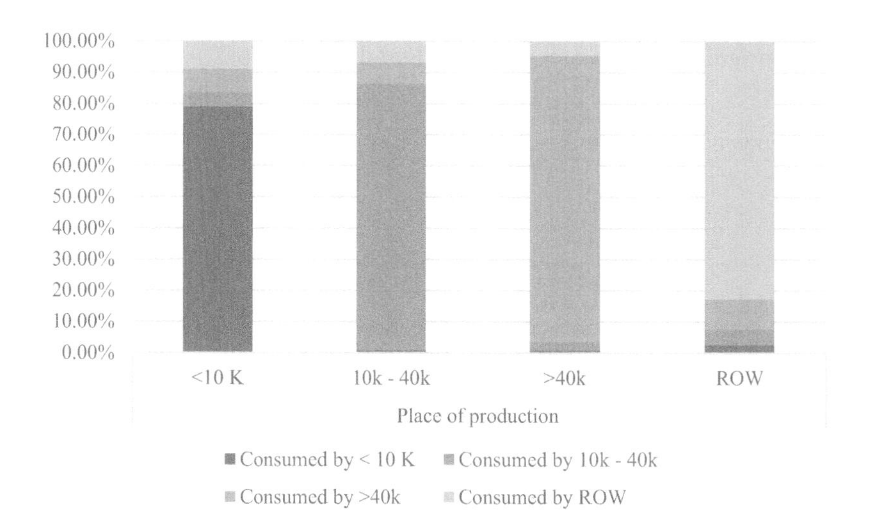

Figure 2. Destination of non-essential product production by place of consumption.

Japanese earthquake of 2011 in the automobile industry (Arto *et al.*, 2015) or the case of floods in Rio de Janeiro (Haddad and Teixeira, 2015).

4.2. Discussion of scenario 1 results

We now present a picture of how the economic shock of the COVID-19 pandemic will disperse across the globe. Table 3 shows outcomes for each group of economies of a global marginal decline of just 1% in households' demands for non-essential goods.

The result of the 1% decline in demand presented in Table 3 is a shock of 3.4 USD trillion to global final demand. Multiplier (general equilibrium) effects yield a reduction in total output of 8.2 USD trillion. This accounts for impacts across the entire value chain. In terms of GVA, Table 3 shows that low-income countries are most affected, followed by the ROW. According to all indicators, high-income countries are the least exposed to the hypothetical shock. It is in middle-income countries, however, where employment is affected the most severely; these are countries concentrated in southern and Western Europe, where tourism and labor-intensive manufacturing dominate their economies.

An important conclusion from this scenario is that inequality levels should be expected to rise in the wake of a pandemic shock. This is due to international trade links and spillover effects, which disperse economic impacts globally. To develop deeper insights into how economies might respond, we decompose GVA changes into labor and capital compensation by country to understand the relative importance of each factor.[6] Figure 3a-c display Lorenz curves to demonstrate the likely changes in the distribution of GVA, labor, and capital compensation per capita and the respective GINI index before and after the shock on non-essential products.

The GINI index is expected to increase across all three dimensions, meaning international inequalities will grow due to disparities in the distribution of capital and labor compensation. Next, all three panels of Figure 3 show that a 1% decline in the consumption of non-essential goods raises the GINI index of GVA per capita distribution to 0.4041. This value results from greater inequality inherent in the distribution of capital compensation per capita and labor compensation, which rises at a lower rate.

In the context of growing disparities, different sectors play distinct roles. Table 4 offers the list of the country sectors most affected by indirect impacts in low-income countries and ROW; it also shows their share of the total indirect impacts by the country.

Note that each region's economic structure is critical to its integration into global value chains; this is revealed by the asymmetry of transmission chains. While the output of some countries decreases because their industries are associated with natural

Table 3. Decrease in GVA and employment embodied in a 1% decline in non-essential goods.

		Total Economic Impacts	
	Shock as a Share of GVA	Change in the GVA	Change in Employment
Low-Income	0.55%	−0.52%	−0.47%
Middle-Income	0.47%	−0.46%	−0.49%
High-Income	0.41%	−0.41%	−0.46%
ROW	0.48%	−0.46%	*

*WIOD socio-economic data do not have numbers for employment in this region

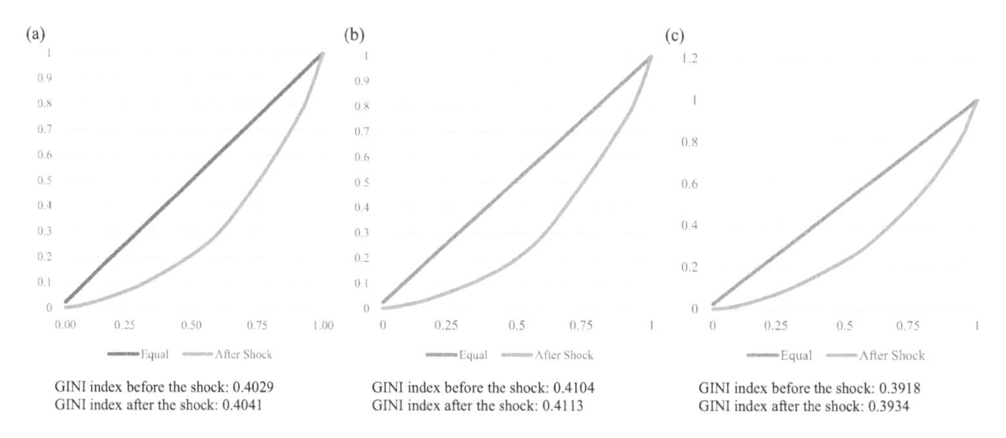

Figure 3. (a) Lorenz curve and GINI index for world GVA per capita distribution. (b) Lorenz curve and GINI index for labor compensation per capita distribution. (c) Lorenz curve and GINI index for capital compensation per capita distribution.

Table 4. Top industries with higher share in total national indirect impacts.

Country	Top 1	Top 2	Top 3	Top 4	Top 5	Top 6	TOTAL
Brazil	B (6.4%)	G47 (6.4%)	C24 (5.8%)	K64 (4.7%)	H49 (4.5%)	C19 (4.5%)	32.2%
Bulgaria	C24 (10.3%)	G46 (8.0%)	F (6.8%)	H49 (5.6%)	D35 (5.1%)	K64 (4.7%)	40.4%
China	C24 (10.9%)	C20 (6.4%)	B (6.3%)	C23 (5.6%)	D35 (4.8%)	C13-C15 (4.7%)	38.7%
Indonesia	B (15.5%)	G46 (7.4%)	C19 (6.0%)	C10-C12 (5.6%)	G47 (4.3%)	A01 (4.1%)	42.9%
India	C24 (10.6%)	H49 (7.7%)	G47 (7.4%)	C20 (6.0%)	F (5.7%)	G46 (4.5%)	41.9%
Mexico	N (10.6%)	B (9.7%)	C29 (9.3%)	C24 (7.3%)	G46 (6.2%)	C20 (5.4%)	48.6%
Turkey	C13-C15 (13.9%)	H49 (8.9%)	C24 (6.0%)	G46 (5.8%)	G47 (4.7%)	M74-M75 (4.6%)	43.9%
ROW	B (17.1%)	D35 (10.8%)	C24 (6.8%)	G46 (4.4%)	F (4.2%)	C20 (3.9%)	47.1%

resources, others are mainly tied to international trade through manufacturing. The top 6 industries of the 56 in WIOD account for an important share of the decline in total indirect output (ranging from 32.2% to 48.6%). For low-income countries, the industries that are most intensely involved in the relevant transmission chains from the hypothetical shock are 'Mining', 'Manufacturing of Basic Metals' and 'Manufacture of chemicals and chemical products'. These industries, together with other tradable manufacturing and service activities are the main drivers of global decline in lower-income economies, not because they are non-essential but because they are *embodied* in production that is deemed non-essential consumption.

A final aspect is that ROW obscures important heterogeneity; it includes countries with a variety of income levels; Figure 4 shows the sectoral effects on ROW aggregated into ten sectors. Using the data in Figure 4 and information available for 48 African economies in the *African Economic Outlook* published by OECD (2020a), we can hypothesize how these economies are likely to fair, due to their economic structure. For this, we weight their economic structure via corresponding changes in industry GVA shares in ROW. Table 5 shows the list of the eight most exposed economies to this hypothetical shock and the primary industry exposing that economy.

Table 5 suggests these countries might suffer larger declines and those most affected are the ones specializing in activities related to mining, trade and tourism or manufacturing.

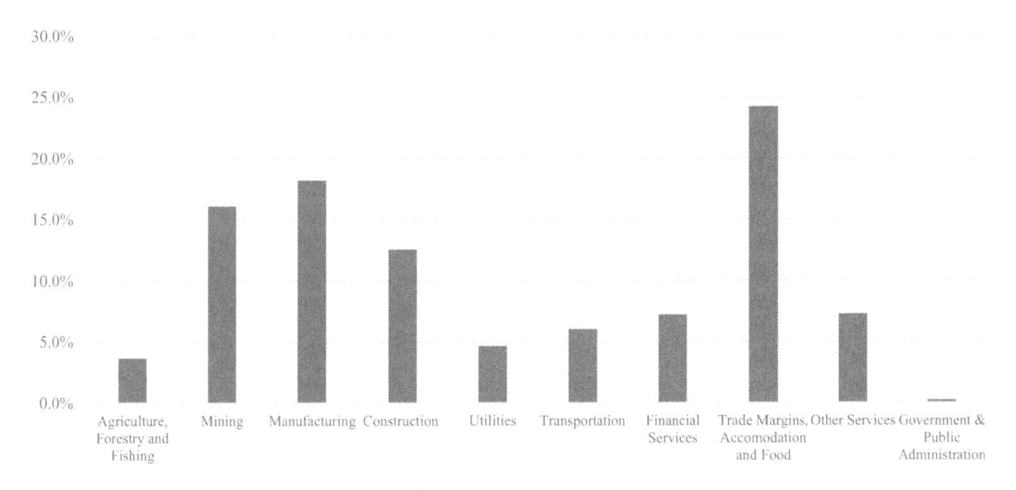

Figure 4. Decomposition of total sectoral impacts in the ROW region.

Table 5. Top countries exposed to a negative 1% shock in non-essential goods.

Country	Expected decline in GVA	Most important sector
Equatorial Guinea	0.71%	Mining (89%)
Angola	0.67%	Mining (47%)
Congo	0.66%	Mining 65%
Seychelles	0.60%	Trade and Tourism (31%)
Gabon	0.58%	Mining (57%)
Nigeria	0.57%	Mining (41%)
Eswatini	0.55%	Manufacturing (44%)
Mauritius	0.55%	Trade and Tourism (19%)

This reinforces the Husain et al. (2020) conclusion about the major threat to fragile and less diverse African economies. Thus, countries whose GDP depends on other sectors seem more likely to weather such a disruption. It remains unclear how the response to COVID-19 will play out, it seems clear that we must look at the critical role of global value chains.

4.3. Scenario 2: A non-homogeneous shock based on lockdown data

The multifarious nature of measures adopted to counteract the dangers associated with COVID-19's spread do not lend themselves to ready adaptation in traditional economic models; this is particularly the case for models that rely on historical trends. For example, as China restricted activity in Wuhan in reaction to cases of the new virus, forecasts in early 2020 continued to predict a strong year for most of the world's economies. By May, with European and American economic data from March now available, times series models reflected a decrease albeit with some questions remaining on the extent and duration of the crisis. Generally, rapid recovery was expected after a poor second quarter in 2020. By June, with a full month of historic data (April 2020) the IMF (2020a) predicted that US GDP would shrink by 8.0%, the Eurozone's by 10.2% and worldwide GDP would reduce on average by 4.9%. By mid-August 2020, forecasters seemed to have matters in hand as some lockdown measures were finally lifted. The updated IMF forecast (2020b) was more sanguine with world GDP dipping on average by 4.4%, with the US and the Eurozone now declining 4.3% and 8.3%, respectively. OECD (2020b) initial predictions were more severe – a reduction of world GDP by 6% – but its September revisions were similar – 4.5% by September (OECD 2020c). By the end of the year, the IMF (2020c) reported, in a press release, that there was 'slowing momentum in economies where the pandemic is resurging'.

During 2020, the Oxford COVID-19 Government Response Tracker (Hale et al. 2020) developed a stringency/lockdown index – OxCGRT – as a way to compare the policies followed by different countries in distinct periods. OxCGRT is a composite-index based on nine indicators including variables such as school workplace closures or travel bans. The values are then rescaled to a value that ranges from 0 to 100 (100 = strictest). While admittedly imperfect, OxCGRT provides some insight into how mitigation measures might impact life and, consequently, economic activity. We incorporate this stringency/lockdown index to produce a scenario in WIOD that yields additional insights into repercussions on world economies, given variations in COVID-19 restrictions. In this scenario, we allow demand for non-essential goods to drop between 1.5% and 0.5% according to the annual average value of this index by country. The values shown in Table 6 are based on an annual average estimated using the daily values from January 1 to 22 November 2020. Table 6 shows the depth of the effect on final demand across countries was highly associated with this stringency index.

Table 6. Stringency/Lockdown index by country (annual average).

	Top Group	Medium Group	Low group
Stringency/ Lockdown index value	> 50	<50 and >40	< 40
Countries	Australia, Brazil, Canada, China, Cyprus, France, India, Indonesia, Italy, Ireland, Mexico, Portugal, Russia, Spain, Turkey, United Kingdom, US	Austria, Belgium, Czech Rep., Denmark, Greece, Germany, Hungary, Latvia, Lithuania, Netherlands, Malta*, Poland, Romania, Slovakia, Slovenia, South Korea, Sweden, Switzerland, ROW*	Bulgaria, Croatia, Estonia, Finland, Japan, Luxembourg, Norway, Taiwan
Shock in the final demand of non-essential products	– 1.50%	– 1.00%	– 0.5%

Source: Our estimations based on Oxford COVID–19 Government Response Tracker.
* The values for Malta and the ROW were estimated using other indicators available in this source.

Table 7. Decrease in GVA and employment embodied in the OxCGRT lockdown scenario.

		Total Economic Impacts	
	Shock as a Share of GVA	Change in the GVA	Change in Employment
Low-Income	– 0.81%	– 0.69%	– 0.60%
Middle-Income	– 0.49%	– 0.44%	– 0.48%
High-Income	– 0.50%	– 0.47%	– 0.49%
ROW	– 0.52%	– 0.46%	*

Table 7 summarizes the results obtained for Scenario 2. It generally yields conclusions that are similar in nature to those gained in Scenario 1, albeit somewhat exaggerated. That is, a non-homogeneous shock grounded in the OxCGRT stringency/lockdown ratio generates larger deleterious economic effects in the low-income countries, many of which implemented stricter mitigation measures (e.g., Mexico and BRIC nations [Brazil, Russia, India, and China]). High-income countries (e.g. France, Ireland, Italy, United Kingdom, and US) also deployed strict mitigation measures in the name of public health to protect against severe economic and health effects of COVID-19. Nevertheless, as in our homogeneous scenario, this differential shock represents a smaller part of the GVA and employment in high-income countries when compared to low-income countries and the ROW.

5. Conclusions

The world's present understanding of the economic repercussions of the COVID-19 pandemic remains at best naïve. Changes in the mitigation measures implemented during 2020 and continuing into 2021 show that countries are still moving through different stages of the pandemic and nobody knows for certain what sectoral and technological changes will persist once things 'return to normal'. This is particularly the case of the international nature of supply chains. Our presentation of the economic repercussions of the COVID-19 pandemic is a first attempt at assessing the nature and extent of the global impacts. As information becomes available, our knowledge of the nature and spread of the global value-chain impacts will evolve and deepen. As with all analyses of unexpected events, a prime concern centers on the asymmetry of the direct and indirect impacts across geographies. We have perhaps provided the first insights into this area for the COVID-19 pandemic but subsequent research should focus on the degree to which the 'new normal' will mirror the pre-COVID economy. It seems natural that economies (particularly more affluent ones) will rethink their exposure to dependence on external value chains, particularly those with strong links to China.

Future distribution of income and changes in economic activity across countries also depends on some variables that we opted not to examine: price changes, possible sovereign debt crises, implementation of additional barriers to trade, migration shocks, and impacts on international aid and remittance flows, among others. Nonetheless, our approach using world MRIO tables provides substantial insight into how international trade induces global economic changes. As we learn more about how economies have been affected by COVID-19 and about the relevant success or failure of government responses, more realistic scenarios can be evaluated. One could even attempt a cost/benefit analysis of alternative government responses, if deployed worldwide. Either of these alternatives can include hypothetical scenarios as suggested by Porsse et al. (2020) involving an increase in government expenditure as a counterpart of the initial shock or a better informed scenario of heterogeneity impacts on labor demand and supply at the sector level (Brinca, Duarte, and Faria E Castro 2020). Also, new data and updated multi-country databases like WIOD will help to improve further analyses of the impacts of COVID-19, including impacts on trade patterns. Nevertheless, our work makes it clear that national economies are not isolated, and that global value chains must be considered to yield a comprehensive depiction of economic outcomes.

This initial work underlines that the world is likely to become a somewhat more unequal place after this pandemic with low-income countries, particularly some fragile African economies, raw material producers, and tourism-dependent countries suffering the most. Accordingly, policy decisions will gain coherence if they consider the complexities of production and the sectoral dependencies established. Major disruptions of supply chains might be prevented, contributing to a quicker and smoother recovery from this 'ongoing' crisis that, as the World Bank recognizes (2020a), has the potential to thrust an additional 150 million people into extreme poverty around the world by 2021.

Notes

1. Our definition of non-essential goods and services, presented in Appendix 1, only pertains to final demand. By definition, any intermediate production that supports the production of 'essential' final goods is itself essential.
2. Recall at the start of the pandemic that our understanding of the means and mode of transmission of SARS-CoV2 and the use and efficiency of mitigation measures such as masks was incomplete.
3. For each industry, WIOD presents other components that are not considered for value-added or intermediate-consumption estimations, specifically, 'taxes less subsidies on products' and 'international transport margins'. With respect to final demand, WIOD also offers a view on the aggregate 'Direct purchases abroad by residents' and 'Purchases on the domestic territory by non-residents', which allows characterization of exports and imports associated with tourism.
4. This is not yet the case as we revisit this paper in January 2021. Although it may be that many aspects what has been truly 'essential' will never be fully comprehended.
5. A great example of this with fascinating detail has been developed for case of the iPad in the article 'iPadded: The trade gap between America and China is much exaggerated' (*The Economist*, 21 January 2012).
6. The labor and capital compensation analysis excludes the ROW economy as this is not represented in the WIOD socio-economic accounts.

Disclosure statement

No potential conflict of interest was reported by the author(s).

ORCID

Christa D. Court http://orcid.org/0000-0002-2690-9015
João-Pedro Ferreira http://orcid.org/0000-0002-6726-7856
Geoffrey J.D. Hewings http://orcid.org/0000-0003-2560-3273
Michael L. Lahr http://orcid.org/0000-0002-2602-2465

References

Adams-Prassl, A., T. Boneva, M. Golin, and C. Rauh. (2020). "Inequality in the Impact of the Coronavirus Shock: Evidence from Real Time Surveys." *IZA Discussion Papers, No. 13183*, Institute of Labor Economics (IZA): Bonn

Arto, I., V. Andreoni, and J. Rueda Cantuche. (2015). "Global Impacts of the Automotive Supply Chain Disruption following the Japanese Earthquake of 2011." *Economic Systems Research* 27 (3): 306–323. doi:10.1080/09535314.2015.1034657.

Ataguba, J. (2020). "COVID-19 Pandemic, a War to Be Won: Understanding Its Economic Implications for Africa." *Applied Health Economics and Health Policy* 18 (3): 325–328. doi:10.1007/s40258-020-00580-x.

Barnett-Howell, Z., and A. Mobarak. (2020). "The Benefits and Costs of Social Distancing in Rich and Poor Countries." arXiv preprint arXiv:2004.04867, April 13. Available online in May 2020 at: https://arxiv.org/pdf/2004.04867.pdf

Barro, R., and J. Ursúa. (2008). "Macroeconomic Crises since 1870." *(No. w13940).* National Bureau of Economic Research.

Bloomberg. (2020). "Bloomberg Commodity Index." Available online in May 2020: https://www.bloomberg.com/quote/BCOM:IND

Bolton, P., L. Buchheit, P. Gourinchas, G. Gulati, C. Hsieh, U. Panizza, and B. Weder Di Mauro. (2020). "Born Out of Necessity: A Debt Standstill for COVID-19." *Center for Economic Policy Research; Policy Insight No. 103*; Duke Law School Public Law & Legal Theory Series No. 2020-23.

Brinca, P., J. Duarte, and M. Faria E Castro. (2020). Measuring labor supply and demand shocks during COVID-19. *Federal Reserve Bank of St. Louis Working Paper* 2020-011E. St. Louis, USA.

Chen, W., B. Los, P. McCann, R. Ortega-Argilés, M. Thissen, and F. Van Oort. (2018). "The Continental Divide? Economic Exposure to Brexit in Regions and Countries on Both Sides of the Channel." *Papers in Regional Science* 97: 25–54. doi:10.1111/pirs.12334.

CISA. (2020). "Identifying Critical Infrastructure during Covid-19." Available online in May 2020: https://www.cisa.gov/identifying-critical-infrastructure-during-covid-19

Coibion, O., Y. Gorodnichenko, and M. Weber. (2020). "The Cost of the COVID-19 Crisis: Lockdowns, Macroeconomic Expectations, and Consumer Spending." *(No. w27141). National Bureau of Economic Research.*

Dietzenbacher, E., B. Los, R. Stehrer, M. Timmer, and G. De Vries. (2013). "The Construction of World Input-Output Tables in the WIOD Project." *Economic Systems Research* 25: 71–98. doi:10.1080/09535314.2012.761180.

EC. (2020). "Policy Measures Taken against the Spread and Impact of the Coronavirus." 7 May 2020. Available online in May 2020 at: https://ec.europa.eu/info/sites/info/files/coronovirus_policy_measures_7_may.pdf

Fajgelbaum, P., and A. Khandelwal. (2016). "Measuring the Unequal Gains from Trade." *The Quarterly Journal of Economics* 131 (3): 1113–1180. doi:10.1093/qje/qjw013.

Gössling, S., D. Scott, and C. Hall. (2020). "Pandemics, Tourism and Global Change: A Rapid Assessment of COVID-19." *Journal of Sustainable Tourism* 29 (1): 1–20. doi:10.1080/09669582.2020.1758708.

GOVUK. (2020). "Critical Workers." Available Online in May 2020: https://www.gov.uk/government/publications/coronavirus-covid-19-maintaining-educational-provision/guidance-for-schools-colleges-and-local-authorities-on-maintaining-educational-provision

Haddad, E. A. and E. Teixeira. (2015). "Economic impacts of natural disasters in megacities: The case of floods in São Paulo, Brazil.„ *Habitat International*, 45 (2): 106–113. doi:10.1016/j.habitatint.2014.06.023

Hale, T., N. Angrist, N. Cameron-Blake, L. Hallas, B. Kira, S. Majumdar, A. Petherick, T. Phillips, H. Tatlow, and S. Webster. (2020). "Variation in Government Responses to COVID-19 Version 8.0." *Blavatnik School of Government Working Paper.* 22 October 2020. Available online in November 2020 at: www.bsg.ox.ac.uk/covidtracker

Harrison, A., and M. McMillan. (2007). "On the Links between Globalization and Poverty." *The Journal of Economic Inequality* 5 (1): 123–134. doi:10.1007/s10888-006-9041-9.

Hevia, C., and P. Neumeyer. (2020). "A Perfect Storm: COVID-19 in Emerging Economies. VoxEU CEPR Policy Portal." Available online in May 2020 at: https://voxeu.org/article/perfect-storm-covid-19-emerging-economies

Husain, A., S. Sandström, F. Greb, J. Groder, and C. Pallanch. (2020). *COVID-19 - Potential Impact on the World's Poorest People.* Rome: World Food Programme.

IMF. (2020a). *World Economic Outlook Update, June 2020*. Washington D.C., USA: IMF.

IMF. (2020b). *World Economic Outlook Update, September 2020*. Washington D.C., USA: IMF.

IMF. (2020c). "Continued Strong Policy Action to Combat Uncertainty." Visited In: https://blogs.imf.org/2020/11/19/continued-strong-policy-action-to-combat-uncertainty/

Initiative on Global Markets. (2020). "Inequality and the COVID-19 Crisis." Available online in May 2020: http://www.igmchicago.org/surveys/inequality-and-the-covid-19-crisis/

Jordà, Ò., S. Singh, and A. Taylor. (2020). "Longer-run Economic Consequences of Pandemics (No. W26934)." *National Bureau of Economic Research*.

Krishnakumar, B., and S. Rana. 2020. "COVID 19 in India: Strategies to Combat from Combination Threat of Life and Livelihood." *Journal of Microbiology, Immunology and Infection* 53 (3): 389–391. doi:10.1016/j.jmii.2020.03.024.

Krugman, P. (2020). "Notes on the Coronacoma (Wonkish): This Is Not a Conventional Recession, and G.D.P. Is Not the Target". *The New York Times*, April 1. Available online in May 2020: https://www.nytimes.com/2020/04/01/opinion/notes-on-the-coronacoma-wonkish.html

Laborde, D., W. Martin, and R. Vos. (2020). "Poverty and Food Insecurity Could Grow Dramatically as COVID-19 Spreads." *IFPRI Blog, Research Post*, International Food Policy Research Institute, Washington, D.C., April 16. Available online in May 2020 at: https://www.ifpri.org/blog/poverty-and-food-insecurity-could-grow-dramatically-covid-19-spreads

Leibovici, F., and A. M. Santacreu. (2020). "International Trade of Essential Goods during a Pandemic (No. 2020-010)."

McKibbin, W., and R. Fernando. (2020). *The global macroeconomic impacts of COVID-19: Seven scenarios*. A report by The Brookings Institution, Washington, D.C., March 2. Available online in May 2020 at: https://www.brookings.edu/wp-content/uploads/2020/03/20200302_COVID19.pdf

Milanovic, B. (2020). "The World after COVID-19: Inequality within Rich Countries Will Increase, Globalization Will Reverse, Politics Will Remain Turbulent." *Promarket*, Stigler Center, University of Chicago, April 8. Available online in May 2020: https://promarket.org/2020/04/08/the-world-after-covid-19-inequality-within-rich-countries-will-increase-globalization-will-reverse-politics-will-remain-turbulent/

Miller, R., and P. Blair. (2009). *Input-Output Analysis: Foundations and Extensions*. 2nd ed. Cambridge, UK: Cambridge University Press.

Montresor, S., and G. Vittucci Marzetti. (2010). "Outsourcing and Structural Change. Application to a Set of OECD Countries." *International Review of Applied Economics* 24 (6): 731–752. doi:10.1080/02692171.2010.512147.

OECD. (2020a). *African Economic Outlook*. OECD, Paris, France.

OECD. (2020b). *OECD Economic Outlook, Interim Report June 2020*. OECD, Paris, France.

OECD. (2020c). *OECD Economic Outlook, Interim Report September 2020*. OECD, Paris, France.

Parteka, A., and J. Wolszczak-Derlacz. (2015). "Integrated Sectors – Diversified Earnings: The (Missing) Impact of Offshoring on Wages and Wage Convergence in the EU27." *Journal of Economic Inequality* 13: 325–350. doi:10.1007/s10888-014-9290-y.

Pew Research Center. (2020). "Amid COVID-19, Remittances to Some Latin American Nations Fell Sharply in April, Then Rebounded," https://www.pewresearch.org/fact-tank/2020/08/31/amid-covid-19-remittances-to-some-latin-american-nations-fell-sharply-in-april-then-rebounded/

Pierros, C. (2020). "Income Distribution, Structural Competitiveness and Financial Fragility of the Greek Economy." *International Review of Applied Economics* 34 (1): 50–74. doi:10.1080/02692171.2019.1620704.

Porsse, A., K. De Souza, T. Carvalho, and V. Vale. (2020). "The Economic Impacts of COVID-19 in Brazil Based on an Interregional CGE Approach." Regional Science Policy & Practice.

Ramos, P., J.-P. Ferreira, L. Cruz, and E. Barata. (2020). "Os Modelos Input-Output, a Estrutura Setorial Das Economias E O Impacto Da Crise Da COVID 19." *Gabinete de Estratégia e Estudos do Ministério da Economia, no 150*. Lisbon, Portugal

Reeves, R., and J. Rothwell. (2020). "Class and COVID: How the Less Affluent Face Double Risks." *Upfront*. Brookings Institution, Washington, D.C., March 27. Available online in May 2020 at:

https://www.brookings.edu/blog/up-front/2020/03/27/class-and-covid-how-the-less-affluent-face-double-risks/

Snyder, J. (2009). "What's the Matter with Price Gouging?." *Business Ethics Quarterly* 19 (2): 275–293. doi:10.5840/beq200919214.

Timmer, M., A. Erumban, B. Los, R. Stehrer, and G. De Vries. (2014). "Slicing Up Global Value Chains." *Journal of Economic Perspectives* 28 (2): 99–118. doi:10.1257/jep.28.2.99.

Timmer, M., E. Dietzenbacher, B. Los, R. Stehrer, and G. De Vries. (2015). "An Illustrated User Guide to the World Input–Output Database: The Case of Global Automotive Production." *Review of International Economics* 23: 575–605. doi:10.1111/roie.12178.

Watanabe, T. (2020). "The Responses of Consumption and Prices in Japan to the COVID-19 Crisis and the Tohoku Earthquake." *Center on Japanese Economy and Business Working Papers, 373*, Columbia University. Available online in May 2020 at: https://academiccommons.columbia.edu/doi/10.7916/d8-qs4v-q792

Woo, W. C. (2019). "Structural Change with Non-essential and Elastic Goods." *Structural Change and Economic Dynamics* 49: 62–73. doi:10.1016/j.strueco.2019.04.001.

World Bank. (2020a). "*COVID-19 to Add as many as 150 Million Extreme Poor by 2021.*" PRESS RELEASE NO: 2021/024/DEC-GPV. World Bank press, Washington D.C., USA.

World Bank. (2020b) "COVID-19: Remittance Flows to Shrink 14% by 2021," https://www.worldbank.org/en/news/press-release/2020/10/29/covid-19-remittance-flows-to-shrink-14-by-2021

Xiao, H., B. Meng, J. Ye, and S. Li. (2020). "Are Global Value Chains Truly Global?." *Economic Systems Research* 32: 540–564. doi:10.1080/09535314.2020.1783643.

Ye, M., B. Meng, and S. Wei. (2015). "Measuring Smile Curves in Global Value Chains." *IDE Discussion Papers 530, Institute of Developing Economies*. Japan External Trade Organization (JETRO).

Appendix 1

		Non-Essential Product	WORLD Final Demand	% Share Output
A01	Crop and animal production, hunting and related service activities		1,720,495	35%
A02	Forestry and logging		60,962	16%
A03	Fishing and aquaculture		203,143	48%
B	Mining and quarrying	X	385,224	6%
C10-C12	Manufacture of food products, beverages and tobacco products		3,732,428	54%
C13-C15	Manufacture of textiles, wearing apparel and leather products	X	1,220,319	44%
C16	Manufacture of wood and of products of wood and cork, except furniture; manufacture of articles of straw and plaiting materials	X	75,884	8%
C17	Manufacture of paper and paper products	X	110,494	11%
C18	Printing and reproduction of recorded media	X	53,963	11%
C19	Manufacture of coke and refined petroleum products		915,714	24%
C20	Manufacture of chemicals and chemical products	X	585,270	14%
C21	Manufacture of basic pharmaceutical products and pharmaceutical preparations		407,111	33%
C22	Manufacture of rubber and plastic products	X	204,216	12%
C23	Manufacture of other non-metallic mineral products	X	106,747	5%
C24	Manufacture of basic metals	X	163,820	4%
C25	Manufacture of fabricated metal products, except machinery and equipment	X	389,481	16%
C26	Manufacture of computer, electronic and optical products		1,242,024	31%
C27	Manufacture of electrical equipment	X	707,336	30%
C28	Manufacture of machinery and equipment n.e.c.	X	1,574,112	44%
C29	Manufacture of motor vehicles, trailers and semi-trailers	X	2,299,236	51%
C30	Manufacture of other transport equipment	X	783,274	54%
C31_C32	Manufacture of furniture; other manufacturing	X	646,322	53%
C33	Repair and installation of machinery and equipment		114,640	36%
D35	Electricity, gas, steam and air conditioning supply		1,065,574	20%
E36	Water collection, treatment and supply		164,245	44%
E37-E39	Sewerage; waste collection, treatment and disposal activities; materials recovery; remediation activities and other waste management services		107,529	19%
F	Construction	X	9,638,708	80%
G45	Wholesale and retail trade and repair of motor vehicles and motorcycles	X	802,516	58%
G46	Wholesale trade, except of motor vehicles and motorcycles	X	3,239,469	41%
G47	Retail trade, except of motor vehicles and motorcycles	X	3,529,145	70%
H49	Land transport and transport via pipelines		1,590,384	39%
H50	Water transport	X	201,960	30%
H51	Air transport	X	324,782	42%
H52	Warehousing and support activities for transportation	X	269,441	17%
H53	Postal and courier activities		41,843	11%
I	Accommodation and food service activities	X	2,661,914	70%
J58	Publishing activities	X	296,221	45%
J59_J60	Motion picture, video and television programme production, sound recording and music publishing activities; programming and broadcasting activities	X	330,663	46%
J61	Telecommunications		1,120,769	46%

(*Continued*)

(Continued).

		Non-Essential Product	WORLD Final Demand	% Share Output
J62_J63	Computer programming, consultancy and related activities; information service activities		1,006,729	48%
K64	Financial service activities, except insurance and pension funding		1,350,191	29%
K65	Insurance, reinsurance and pension funding, except compulsory social security		1,131,146	53%
K66	Activities auxiliary to financial services and insurance activities		207,572	25%
L68	Real estate activities		6,456,706	75%
M69_M70	Legal and accounting activities; activities of head offices; management consultancy activities	X	428,326	12%
M71	Architectural and engineering activities; technical testing and analysis	X	335,591	29%
M72	Scientific research and development		411,096	51%
M73	Advertising and market research	X	79,168	14%
M74_M75	Other professional, scientific and technical activities; veterinary activities	X	228,782	20%
N	Administrative and support service activities		774,580	21%
O84	Public administration and defense; compulsory social security		7,997,598	91%
P85	Education		3,383,033	91%
Q	Human health and social work activities		6,135,295	94%
R_S	Other service activities	X	2,286,816	68%
T	Activities of households as employers; undifferentiated goods- and services-producing activities of households for own use	X	147,138	74%
U	Activities of extraterritorial organizations and bodies		81	100%

Impact of pandemics on income inequality: lessons from the past

Pinaki Das, Santanu Bisai and Sudeshna Ghosh

ABSTRACT

This paper examines how past pandemics impacted income inequality measured through the Gini measure of inequality net of taxes. It explores how five major pandemics, namely, SARS in 2003, H1N1 in 2009, MERS in 2012, Ebola in 2014, and Zika in 2016 impacted the distribution of income across high income, upper-middle-income and lower-middle-income countries. How the inequality across quintiles share in income is impacted was explored. We used comprehensive panel data sets covering annual observations from 1995 to 2017 for 70 countries. The generalized least square estimation shows that the pandemics have a statistically significant positive impact upon income inequality particularly for the high-income group and also for the entire set of 70 countries. However, the impact of the pandemics is negative upon the upper-middle-income group of countries. The estimation is robust controlling for additional macroeconomic variables. The study demonstrates that past pandemics may generate a policy response that impacts the distribution of income. A weakened role of the state has been responsible for worsening inequality.

1. Introduction

Historical lessons teach us that pandemics do not affect all in a uniform way. The Black Death (1347–1351) reduced the world's population from an estimated 450 million to between 350 and 375 million in 1400; the highest number of deaths was found among the poorer households. The explicit impact of the pandemic on the distribution of income emerges from the fact that the spread of a deadly virus leads to fatality specifically among the most helpless sections of the population (Furceri et al. 2020). Following the paper of Ma, Rogers, and Zhou (2020), we discuss how the five major pandemics of the past, namely, SARS in 2003, H1N1 in 2009, MERS in 2012, Ebola in 2014, and Zika in 2016, impacted the distribution of income. The most widespread was the spreading of the H1N1 virus which spread across 148 countries with fatalities reaching 19,000. In terms of mortality rates, the Ebola and MERS were most disastrous followed by SARS, Zika and HINI. Table A1 provides a list of countries which were affected by the past pandemics.

It is important to understand how pandemics may trigger income inequality across different countries. Such analysis shows how policy interventions can be made for distributive purposes to avoid a rise in already high levels of income inequality. To date, there is little discussion in the literature regarding in what magnitude pandemics may affect income inequality. Furceri et al. (2020) using data from the World Bank and the International Labour Organization explored the impact of past pandemics like H1N1 on income inequality. Furthermore, the study examined the potential impact of COVID-19 upon income inequality. Based on impulse response function they conclude that the effect of COVID-19 on future inequality in the distribution of income would be worse than the earlier pandemics. The results show that real GDP will be 2.6% lower than average in around 210 countries from the period the pandemic was officially declared and these adverse implications continue for another 5 years. The study concludes that the impact of pandemics will vary considerably depending upon the country-specific characteristics, cultural context, and initial levels of income distribution. However, the study concludes that further research needs to be done to study the extent of variation of impact of pandemics across different countries and what would be the potential impact on the vulnerable sections of the population.

The main objective of the current paper is to address this lacuna in the literature. Our analysis utilizes econometric techniques and dense distinctive data sets to examine the impact of pandemics on income inequality, particularly in the long-run. The study is the first of its kind to explore the impact of pandemics on income inequality measured by Gini inequality measure across countries classified by high-income groups, upper-middle-income groups, lower-middle-income groups and low-income groups based on World Bank Atlas method of classification. Further, it utilizes income inequality across quintile share of income to examine how pandemics impact inequality across different income shares. Such an exploration will add new insights on how pandemics impact inequality at a disaggregate level. Apart from utilizing major economic factors as control variables like economic growth, terms of trade to avoid misspecification bias the study has incorporated institutional factors to examine the role of institutions in impacting inequality. Section 2 reports the literature. Section 3 discusses the methodology and data sets. The major results are discussed in Section 4. Section 5 provides a brief discussion. Section 6 concludes.

2. Review of the literature

2.1. Inequality in income: major drivers

A large body of literature discusses how inequality is impacted by economic growth, macroeconomic variables, demographic variables and institutional variables, but both the theoretical and empirical discussion is ambiguous on the way the major determinants impact inequality owing to methodological concerns, choice of data sets and periods. Based on the findings of the literature we have identified the following economic, demographic, political and institutional variables and further government size as major drivers of inequality for major panel-based country studies. However, there may be country-specific discussion about other transmission channels which is beyond the scope of the current study.

2.1.1. GDP per capita (economic variable)

Following the hypothesis of Kuznets (1955) we find the inverted 'U'-shaped behaviour across national income and income inequality. However, the study by Deininger and

Squire (1996) contradicts the Kuznets hypothesis. The studies by Barro (2000) discuss how economic growth can be inequality reducing or augmenting depending upon the initial levels of development. Lee and Son (2016) examined the impact of income inequality on economic growth based on panel data for a wide set of developed and developing countries using the methodology of the generalized method of moments. The study explains that there can be negative effects on growth when the sample of less developed countries with relatively new data sets is examined. The study explains that differences in results as to the impact of inequality on growth can be explained by problems associated with the omitted control variables and how the differences in inequality in the distribution of income have evolved over time, particularly in the transitional economies of Eastern Europe and the Sub-Saharan region.

2.1.2. Trade openness and global integration (economic variable)

Trade has been the major explanatory factor for competition and efficiency in many countries. In mature economies trade openness has resulted in offshoring and a rise in skill premiums, which has reduced inequality (Feenstra and Hanson 2003). However, trade openness could also lower inequality by increasing demand for low-skilled workers in emerging economies (Munch and Skaksen 2008). Foellmi and Oechslin (2010) argue that with increasing globalization the less developed economies are exposed to free trade but the benefits of trade are unequally distributed. This leads to rising inequality. The imperfections in the credit market are responsible for the imperfections in the distribution from gains from trade which exacerbates inequality in the distribution of income.

2.1.3. Availability of credit and market conditions (economic variable)

Availability and access to credit markets with financial development may improve resource allocation and thus can lower-income inequality Dabla-Norris et al. (2015). The study by Greenwood and Jovanovic (1990) discusses that financial development and credit market imperfections in the early stages of development may lead to a rise in income inequality but the benefits of financial development get redistributed with the process of economic development. The earlier discussion of the 1990s states that inequality is negatively affected by growth through two conduits. The first is through tendencies of rent-seeking behaviour owing to weak institutional setup and abuse of political power. The second is through higher taxation and regulation owing to the demands of voters. According to Banerjee and Newman (1991) and Galor and Zeira (1993) imperfections in credit markets may deter borrowing for investment in physical and human capital formation; in such instance inequality may rise. The study further discusses that there exists an optimal level of inequality that leads to minimal level of market imperfections. Gutiérrez-Romero (2021) using data over 1991 to 2015 across 138 countries, discussed the causes of imperfections in the credit market and the dualistic economy which has implications for inequalities in the nations.

2.1.4. Infrastructure development and physical capital formation (economic variable)

According to Calderón and Chong (2004) and Chatterjee and Turnovsky (2012) empirical verification of the relationship between physical capital formation and inequality in income distribution is rather scarce. However, it can be understood that technological innovation and physical capital formation enhance productive opportunities and this may raise the levels of asset of the poor which may help to reduce inequality.

2.1.5. Inflation (economic variable)

Inflation does not affect all income earners in the same way so it can potentially decrease or increase income inequality depending on how it impacts wage income, capital income and government redistribution. The study by Dolmas, Huffman, and Wynne (2000) discusses that democratic countries may tend to reduce inflation through central bank policy prescriptions and in many instances central bank has financed growth through inflation which increased income inequality.

2.1.6. Human capital formation (demographic variable)

Investment in education and human capital formation can play a crucial role in reducing income inequality as it enhances productivity and access to job market opportunities (Becker and Chiswick 1966). The endogenous growth theories postulated in the studies of Mankiw, Romer, and Weil (1992) and Lucas (1988) suggest that investment in human capital formation helps countries to augment their skill-base, participate in labour markets, and fight poverty which promotes growth and socio-economic development. However Knight and Sabot (1983) discuss that there are two effects of human capital formation on income distribution, namely, the 'composition effect' and 'compression effect'. The 'composition effect' raises the size of the educated population and first raises inequality but subsequently lowers it. The 'compression effect' is that returns on education decline as more and more people get education and this eventually lowers income inequality. So, the net effect of investment in education depends upon the net of these two effects (Dincer and Gunalp 2012).

Recent literature discusses that human capital formation is a major factor in impacting inequality in the distribution of income. According to Lee and Lee (2018) human capital calculated by the educational levels attained by a worker is a crucial determining component of the earnings of the concerned worker over a lifetime. The governments of many developing countries have invested in the nation's educational development to reduce educational inequality which would help in reducing income inequality. Such a process through skill formation leads to a decline in the inequality of distribution of income.

2.1.7. Taxes and social sector spending by government (government size)

Many studies (e.g. Anyanwu 2016; Dabla-Norris et al. 2015) discuss that size of government can be proxied for impact of social spending and redistribution. The studies show that large governments are able to run social transfer programmes and thereby negatively impact income distribution. Richardson and Immervoll (2011) explain that redistribution is often used in the literature identically with the process of reduction in the inequality of distribution of income. Tax and benefit transfers which reduce inequality are regarded as progressive redistribution. Duncan and Peter (2016) based on measures of tax progressivity (e.g. top statutory personal income tax rate) over 1981–2005 for a panel set of countries discuss how tax progressivity reduces income Gini. The paper discusses that tax progressivity is an equalizing instrument and helps in pro-poor distribution provided the country's legal institutions are strengthened. Following the pioneering study of Reynolds and Smolensky (2013) a fiscal redistribution is progressive if post-fiscal redistribution of inequality measure by Gini is less than the pre-fiscal redistribution and the redistribution is regressive in the opposite. A sizeable existing empirical literature finds that fiscal policy is a primary instrument for governments to impact income distribution (International Monetary Fund 2015, 2017; Doumbia and Kinda 2019).

2.1.8. Democracy, culture and institutional context

Gradstein and Milanovic (2004) note that the literature has discussed widely institutions, political structures, and economic growth, and their impact on inequality. Democratic institutions lead to expansion of adult suffrage and give decision-making power to the poor which has high redistributive implications, lowering inequality (Alesina and Rodrik 1994; Persson and Tabellini 1994).

2.2. Pandemics and inequality

The effect of the COVID-19 pandemic on the world's economies is estimated to exacerbate income inequality. The earlier discussion notes that inequalities may arise from many factors. The current pandemic through social restrictions and mandated closures expands the nature of such factors causing inequality. The pandemic's socio-economic implications include limited work opportunities, which requires an increased responsibility of the state for social sector spending.

Ma, Rogers, and Zhou (2020) draw lessons from past epidemics, namely, Flu (1968), SARS (2003), H1N1 (2009), MERS (2012), Ebola (2014), and Zika (2016), finding that epidemics cause GDP growth to decline by three percentage points in countries worst hit by epidemics in comparison to the relatively less afflicted countries. Jordà, Singh, and Taylor (2020) finds that pandemics cause considerable after-impact shocks on the macroeconomy which may continue for decades contrary to devastations made by wars. Alfani (2021) discusses that the current crisis emanating from COVID–19 could become worse for countries which not only lack good quality affordable health-care system but also do not have social security networks. The pandemics will worsen inequalities owing to loss of jobs particularly for the economically vulnerable groups. The current paper modifies and extends the studies by Ma, Rogers, and Zhou (2020) to include a larger group of countries and using updated data that captures increasing global integration to describe how past pandemics impact inequality in the distribution of income measured by Gini inequality across different income groups.

The literature studying the pandemics impact on the macroeconomy, growth and inequality have documented the global impact of pandemics across various dimensions of inequality like consumption-based inequality, income-based inequality, population-weighted consumption and Gini measure. The essential conclusion from the literature is that COVID-19 has endangered life and livelihood particularly for the less-educated who cannot stay at home and work safely. As Case and Deaton (2021) discuss, that social distancing and economic shut down has helped to meet the public health needs during pandemic but there is a trade-off with the economy. This will exacerbate inequality. To what extent inequality will rise both within and between countries depends upon governmental efforts. Based on this literature the subsequent discussion formulated the hypothesis for the present study.

Against the backdrop of health disasters and pandemics, governments try to combat the effects through policy measures. In the current situation fiscal packages and healthcare packages are announced to combat the pandemic. However, the extent to which fiscal policy stimulus will impact the targeted population is uncertain. Progressive fiscal transfer by governments and social investment impact on inequality tend to vary. If regional differences are considered then the long-standing socio-economic features of different regions explained through cultural context, global integration, democracy, market imperfections and infrastructural development along with many other factors are slow changing.

Hypothesis I: *The impact of the pandemics is not uniform across all regions classified by income groups across the globe. It depends on global integration, infrastructure development, institutional context and levels of development.*

The discussion in the existing literature explains that pandemics can cause an increase in the inequality of income distribution. This is because policymakers and authorities have mandated stay-at-home orders, lockdowns and social distancing. These policies will create job losses particularly for the low skilled, across lower quintiles in the income distribution, where the jobs cannot be done remotely. Accordingly, loss of jobs would increase inequality across income groups.

Hypothesis II: *The pandemic will lead to rise in inter-group income inequality within a country across various income quintile groups.*

3. Model, methods and data sets

3.1. Model specification

This section explains the panel data regression models that we utilize to explore empirically the relation between pandemics and inequality of income over time. According to Hsiao (2007), the application of panel data regression models generates a greater number of degrees of freedom than available in the cross-section or time-series model specification. Furthermore, it improves the precision of the parameter estimation.

3.1.1. Model I

Equation (1) explains the impact of pandemics on the inequality of income distribution along with other macroeconomic variables.

$$InGini_{it} = \alpha + \beta\, Dummy_t + \beta_{1i} InX_{it} + t_t + \delta_i + \varepsilon_{it} \quad (1)$$

where Gini denotes the Gini coefficient of inequality (net of taxes), X are the vectors of control variables. The subscripts $i = 1, \ldots, N$, indicate the country and $t = 1, \ldots, T$ denote the time. The vector X consists of the macroeconomic variables including gross domestic product per capita, inflation, physical capital formation, trade openness and democracy index. The inclusion of the explanatory variables enables us to control for economic growth, global integration, the impact of price changes, socio-political contexts and demography.[1] The preceding section has explained the importance of these control variables in the inequality literature.

Dummy is the dummy variable to include the impact of the pandemics. The dummy variable takes the value one during the years of pandemic outbreak and zero otherwise. It takes the value one during SARS (2003), HINI (2009), MERS (2012), Ebola (2014) and Zika (2016) and the value zero otherwise. It is expected that the inclusion of dummy to indicate the outbreak of pandemics will have an adverse impact on the inequality of the distribution of income. δ denotes the unobserved country-level fixed effect, t denotes the time fixed effect and ε is the usual error term. *In* indicates the logarithmic transformation of the concerned variables. All variables except the dummy are converted into the logarithmic counterpart. The conversion of the observations into the natural logarithmic form decreases the problems related to the distributional properties (Alam and Paramati 2016). Furthermore, in the log transformation, the estimated coefficients will be the elasticities.

3.1.2. Model II

Pandemics generate global shock which affects income inequality not only between countries but within a country. A growing concern has emerged in the literature about what may be the probable distributive implications of the current pandemic (COVID-19) across different income groups within a country. To add to the existing seam of the literature this research explores how the past pandemics have impacted income shares of the top and the bottom income quintiles. Equation (2) explains how the outbreak of past pandemics impact income share across each income quintile, controlling for major macroeconomic variables, as outlined in Model I.

$$InQ_{kit} = \alpha + \beta\, Dummy_t + \beta_{1_i} InX_{it} + t_t + \delta_i + \varepsilon_{it} \qquad (2)$$

Here Q_k denotes the kth quintile share of the income group; X are the vectors of control variables as described in Equation (1). Dummy is the dummy variable to include the impact of the pandemics. δ denotes the unobserved country-level fixed effect, t denotes the time fixed effect and ε is the usual error term.

3.2. Econometric specification

The static panel data regression model as outlined in Equations (1) and (2), respectively, will be estimated through fixed and random effects. The parameters of the fixed and random effect models are estimated through the ordinary least squares (OLS) estimation, generalized least squares (GLS) estimation and least squares dummy variables (LSDV) estimation, respectively. To check with the importance of the decomposition of the constant and error term the Wald and the Breush and Pagan Lagrange Multiplier test and Restricted F-test are applied. The Hausman specification test enables us to choose the best fit model.

3.3. Data sets

3.3.1. Dependent variable

This paper uses inequality data set from Solt (2020) using version 9 of the Standardized World Income Inequality Database (SWIID). To the best of our knowledge, the data set covers the largest set of countries and spans over the largest period. To discuss inequality, we utilize the Gini coefficients (for Model I) based on net inequality which is calculated by considering tax and transfers.

The data on income quintile share (Model II) is obtained from the World Income Inequality Database (WIID4) which has dense time-series data on income inequality for both the developing and the developed countries. The income quintile share measures inequality in the distribution of income. It is calculated as the ratio of total income enjoyed by the top 20% of the population (the top quintile) to that enjoyed by the bottom 20% of the population (bottom quintile) which has the lowest quintile.

3.3.2. Explanatory variables

The data sets for the explanatory variables are largely based on the World Development Indicators, World Bank except for the democracy index which is drawn from Polity IV Project Online (2013) following Marshall (2017). Table 1 provides a detailed description of the data and their sources. All observations are based on an annual frequency ranging from 1995 to 2017. A set of 70 countries constrained by the availability of data is utilized in this study. The countries are further divided into sub-panels based on the World Bank Atlas Method of classification into high, upper-middle, lower-middle- and low-income

Table 1. Description of the variables and data source.

Description of variables	Unit	Symbol	Source
Gini index of inequality net of taxes and transfer payments.	Index ranging from 0 to 100, higher the value higher is the inequality.	Gini	Standardized World Income Inequality Database, URL: https://fsolt.org/swiid
The quintile method of classification expresses the share of income going to each fifth of population, the fifth quintile is the richest 20%.	It is expressed in terms of percentage of total income.	Q	World Income Inequality Database (WIID) URL: https://www.wider.unu.edu/database
Measure of economic growth is GDP per capita -gross domestic product divided by population	GDP per capita expressed in constant 2010 US$	GDP	World Development Indicators, World Bank, URL: https://databank.worldbank.org
Measure of trade openness.	It is the sum of exports and imports of goods and services expressed as a share of GDP.	TR	
Measure of inflation	Consumer price index, base year 2010, proxy inflation.	CPI	
Measure of physical capital formation	Gross capital formation as a percentage share of GDP expressed the outlays on additions to fixed assets, inventories and plant and machinery. Data sets are expressed in constant 2010 U.S.$	K	
Measure of democracy	An index measure on scale of −10 to +10.	DEM	Polity 2 index of Polity IV Project, URL:https://www.systemicpeace.org/polityproject

Source: Compilation Author.

groups. Such a method of classification will improve our understanding of the differential impact of pandemics on income inequality across different income groups. Table A1 provides the list of selected countries.

4. Results

4.1. Preliminary exploratory analysis

Figure 1 plots the inequality situation across countries at a disaggregate level across the low, lower middle-income, upper middle-income and high-income countries. Based on Figure 1 we find that two major types of classification on the inequality is evident (i) for the high-income countries there is evidence of declining inequality and (ii) there is a strong indication of increasing inequality for the lower-middle-income group of countries and low-income group of countries. Furthermore, Figure 2 plots the scatter diagram of the association of inequality explained through the Gini measure along with the major explanatory variables.

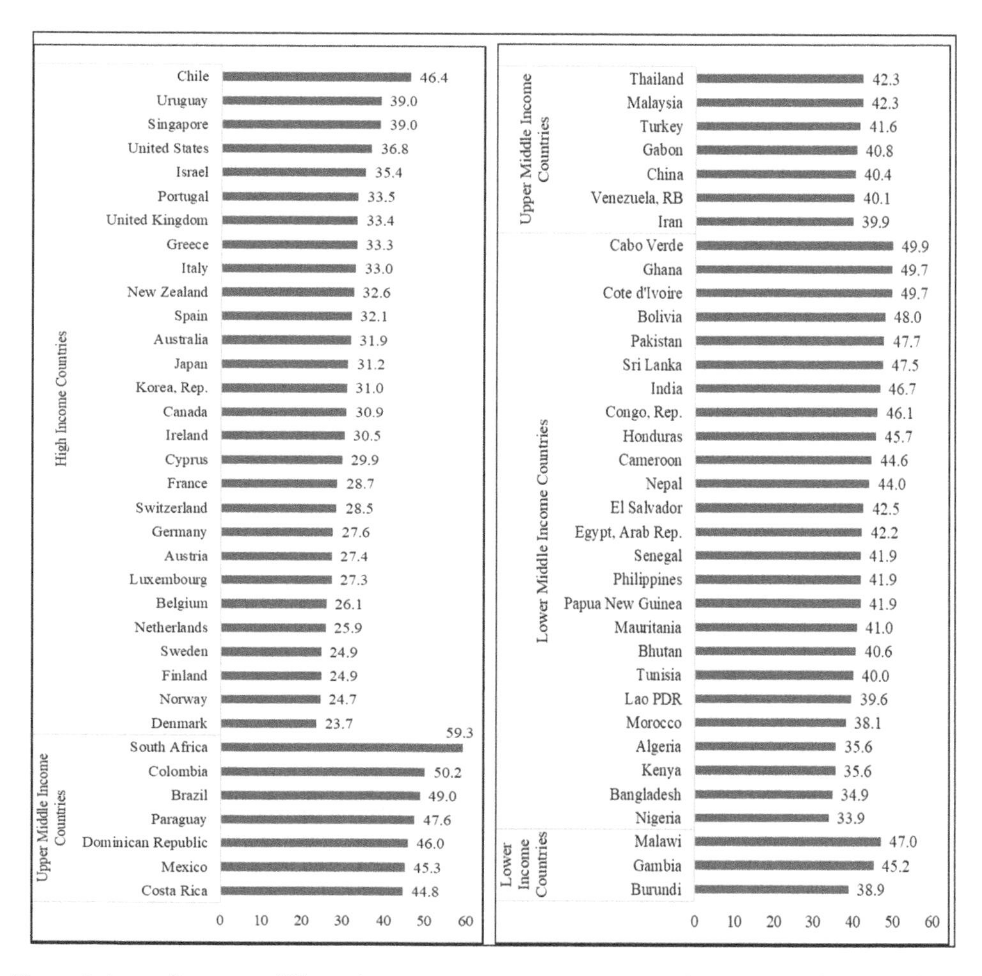

Figure 1. Inequality across different income groups among countries. Source: Compilation Authors.

4.2. Results of econometrics estimation

Table 2 presents the findings of the GLS estimation across the whole panel consisting of a group of 70 countries and further disaggregated by income groups. The impact of the past pandemic as demonstrated through dummy1 (SARS in 2003), dummy2 (H1N1 in

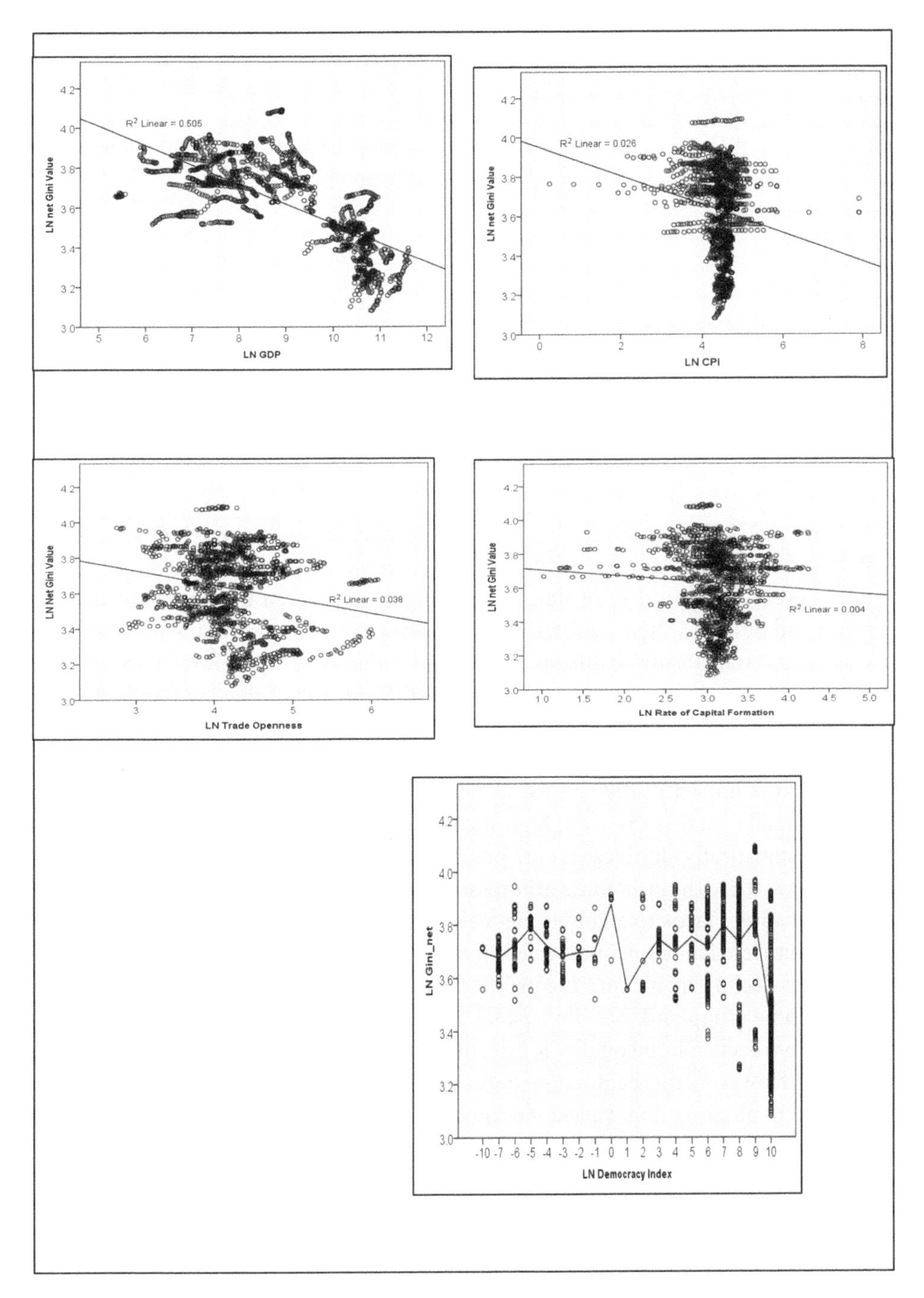

Figure 2. Scatter plot: inequality in income and major drivers. Source: Compilation Authors.

Table 2. Random-effects GLS estimation across country groups.

Dependent variable	High-income group		Upper middle-income group		Lower-middle group		All Countries	
ln Gini	Coefficient	Prob	Coefficient	Prob	Coefficient	Prob	Coefficient	Prob
dummy1	0.0294	0.00	−0.022	0.00	−0.0032	0.54	0.0126	0.00
dummy2	0.0134	0.01	−0.036	0.00	−0.0089	0.12	0.0011	0.75
dummy3	0.0122	0.05	−0.022	0.03	−0.0068	0.33	0.0044	0.33
dummy4	0.0057	0.39	0.003	0.76	−0.0125	0.10	0.0026	0.59
dummy5	0.0063	0.34	−0.012	0.28	−0.0031	0.68	0.0004	0.94
ln GDP	−0.0686	0.00	0.089	0.00	0.0032	0.82	−0.0292	0.00
ln CPI	−0.0599	0.00	−0.013	0.00	0.0182	0.01	−0.0209	0.00
ln TR	0.0477	0.00	−0.003	0.83	−0.0563	0.00	−0.0018	0.79
ln K	0.0121	0.33	0.024	0.15	0.0004	0.95	−0.0045	0.35
ln DEM	−0.0109	0.00	0.003	0.00	0.0003	0.57	0.0006	0.19
Constant	4.2434	0.00	3.027	0.00	3.8864	0.00	3.9894	0.00
Number of observations	644		322		575		1610	
R-sq: overall	0.27		0.05		0.02		0.49	
R-sq: within	0.22		0.42		0.11		0.03	
R-sq: between	0.28		0.02		0.05		0.52	
Wald chi2(10)	174.42*		197.35*		60.22*		81.90*	
Breusch and Pagan LM test, chibar2(01)	5007.60*		1272.61*		4474.00*		15009.19*	
F test that all u_i = 0: F(27, 606)	203.40*		110.30*		195.90*		316.13*	
Hausman chi2(0)	0.00		0.00		0.00		0.00	

*Denotes the level of significance at 1% level.
Source: Compilation Author.

2009), dummy3 (MERS in 2012), dummy4 (Ebola in 2014) and dummy5 (Zika in 2016) is positive upon the Gini measure of inequality for the whole panel and the higher income group. However, the results are statistically insignificant when the impact of dummy3, dummy4 and dummy5 dummy variables is concerned. The impact of the past pandemics is negative and statistically significant for dummy1, dummy2 and dummy3 for the upper middle-income group, furthermore, the results of the impact of the past pandemics upon the lower middle-income group are negative though the results are statistically insignificant. These results support Hypothesis I.

As far as the impact of the control variables is concerned GDP per capita negatively impacts inequality across the set of high-income countries, and the panel as a whole. The results are statistically significant. One per cent rise in GDP per capita leads to a fall in inequality by 0.06% (high-income group) and 0.02% (panel as a whole). However, a rise in GDP per capita leads to a rise in inequality for the upper-middle and lower-middle-income countries. Trade openness in conformity with the earlier studies in the literature has led to a decline in income inequality for the upper-middle-income group, lower-middle-income group and the whole panel. As per expectations improvement of democracy leads to a decline in inequality for the high-income group, the results are statistically significant. However, the democracy index is inequality augmenting for other income groups. Such puzzling but varied findings on the relation between democracy and inequality across income groups can be rationalized by following the arguments of (Gradstein, Milanovic, and Ying 2001). In sum the results based on Table 2 support Hypothesis I.

Table 3 reports the results of the impact of the past pandemics upon inequality across different income quintiles, of the set of 70 countries under observation, the impact of the past pandemics, particularly the SARS in 2003, H1N1 in 2009 and MERS in 2012, are

Table 3. Random-effects GLS regression estimates across income quintiles.

Dependent variable	lnq1		lnq2		lnq3		lnq4		lnq5	
ln(quintiles)	Coefficient	Prob	Coefficient	Prob	Coefficient	Prob	Coefficient	Prob	Coefficient	Prob
dummy1	−0.015	0.45	−0.015	0.188	−0.015	0.054	−0.009	0.068	0.009	0.218
dummy2	−0.020	0.40	−0.015	0.244	−0.014	0.142	−0.001	0.888	0.013	0.156
dummy3	−0.050	0.10	−0.015	0.378	−0.004	0.713	−0.007	0.347	0.007	0.536
dummy4	0.034	0.31	0.002	0.911	−0.006	0.639	−0.004	0.645	0.002	0.859
dummy5	0.004	0.90	0.013	0.494	0.005	0.714	0.004	0.591	−0.003	0.787
ln GDP	0.176	0.00	0.130	0.00	0.095	0	0.043	0.000	−0.088	0.00
ln CPI	−0.036	0.12	−0.018	0.155	−0.010	0.278	−0.002	0.658	0.005	0.567
ln TR	−0.001	0.97	−0.011	0.64	−0.011	0.51	−0.017	0.067	0.003	0.841
ln K	−0.177	0.00	−0.088	0.001	−0.075	0	−0.031	0.006	0.054	0.003
ln DEM	−0.004	0.32	−0.004	0.094	−0.004	0.003	−0.002	0.010	0.003	0.036
Constant	0.847	0.01	1.563	0	2.175	0	2.849	0.000	4.410	0
Number of observations	1081		1081		1081		1081		1081	
Observations per group	23		23		23		23		23	
R-sq: overall	0.03		0.03		0.04		0.02		0.02	
R-sq: within	0.31		0.4		0.46		0.4		0.47	
R-sq: between	0.24		0.33		0.37		0.28		0.39	
Wald chi2(10)	45.8*		57.34*		74.4*		54.59*		61.6*	
Breusch and Pagan LM test, chibar2(01)	5098.1*		5713.1*		5047.9*		3461.3*		5099*	
F test that all u_i = 0: F(27, 606)	46.21*		55.4*		45.64*		29.1*		46.1*	
Hausman chi2(0)	0		0		0		0		0	

*Denotes the level of significance at 1% level.
Source: Compilation Author.

negative upon the inequality of incomes shares across quintiles q1, q2, q3 and q4. However, the impact of the past pandemics upon inequality upon q5 is positive.

As far as the impact of the control variables is concerned it conforms with the earlier findings in the literature. The results based on Table 3, which is based on Equation (2), support Hypothesis II.

5. Discussion

To throw light on the possible impact of the COVID-19 pandemic upon income inequality across countries the current paper explores how past pandemics impacted Gini income inequality across high-income groups, upper-middle-income groups and lower-middle-income groups. Furthermore, the study also explores the impact of past pandemics upon income inequality across income shares across different income quintiles. Past pandemics have raised income shares of the top income quintiles and raised income inequality in the high-income countries. These results confirm the earlier literature findings of Alfani (2021) and Ma, Rogers, and Zhou (2020). Such findings imply that the pandemics have increased opportunities for capital income earners in the high-income countries and lowered prospects for employment for those with basic education and semi-skills. These observations are consistent with Case and Deaton (2021) because the richer sections of the population in the wealthier nations have opportunities to earn during crisis owing to the pandemic situation.

The findings suggest that the tax-transfer policy has become decreasingly regressive (e.g. see Reynolds and Smolensky 2013) as far as redistributive instruments in the high-income countries are concerned. So, the impact of the pandemic in these countries augments inequality. As far as the emerging economies in the upper middle-income and the lower-income group of countries are concerned redistributive mechanisms through transfers in the health and education sectors may have helped in reducing inequality in income, confirming the findings of the International Monetary Fund (2015, 2017; Doumbia and Kinda 2019). For these groups of countries, the redistributive gains from education and health transfers dominate over the inefficiency costs associated with the pandemics. The findings of the current study in conformity with the studies of Lee and Lee (2018) and Lee and Vu (2020) explain that the government's efforts to raise investment in human capital formation through redistribution helps in the reduction of inequality. In light of these findings, the study calls for strategic interventions which should be aimed towards lessening the inequality of income and wealth. The study by Duncan and Peter (2016) in line with the current study explains that government's redistributive mechanisms help in reducing the inequality in income. The stark differences in results across the high-income countries and upper-middle and lower-middle-income countries could be attributed to the dichotomy owing to the demographic differences in the two sets of countries (Dabla-Norris et al. 2015).[2] The findings of this study are difficult to generalize because they are based on specific past pandemics which have hit the different parts of the globe differently. Nevertheless, they are in line with existing evidence particularly from the recent studies of Furceri et al. (2020) and Ma, Rogers, and Zhou (2020).

As far as the impact of the control variables on Gini inequality is concerned (Model I) we find that the impact of GDP per capita confirms the hypothesis of Kuznets (1955). Furthermore for Model II the study confirms the results based on the work by Barro (2000) and Lee and Son (2016). Trade openness favours redistribution for the upper-middle and lower-middle-income groups which rely on labour-intensive methods of export promotion confirming the earlier literature (e.g. see Munch and Skaksen 2008). Regarding the effect of the democracy index the study confirm the earlier works of Alesina and Rodrik (1994), Persson and Tabellini (1994), Gradstein (2001) and Gradstein and Milanovic (2004). According to Gradstein, Milanovic, and Ying (2001) the impact of democracy works indirectly upon inequality. Democracy works through culture and ideology to reduce inequality in the distribution of income. Cultural values play important roles in determining policies to reduce inequality in the distribution of income.

6. Conclusion and policy suggestions

This study has examined how past pandemics impact income inequality measured through the Gini measure of inequality net of taxes in a panel model. The paper discusses that past pandemics have a significant impact upon inequality of income. The study has utilized OLS, GLS, and LSDV estimation. We use comprehensive and dense time-series data covering annual observations from 1995 to 2017 for 70 countries. These countries are classified across income groups based on the World Bank Atlas Method of classification to examine whether there is variation as far as the impact of the pandemics upon different income groups is concerned. Furthermore, the impact of the pandemics upon inequality across different quintile income share is also explored. During the period chosen in our analysis, there were outbreaks of several pandemics including SARS, H1N1, MERS, Ebola, and Zika. We use a dummy variable for the occurrence of the pandemic in the particular year for the concerned country. Pandemics may have a direct impact upon the inequality of income distribution and augment inequality owing to heterogeneity in economic opportunities. The spread of diseases restricts job opportunities for low skill workers and may increase opportunities for capital earners. Furthermore, pandemics may indirectly reduce inequality in the distribution of income owing to the direct intervention of the government in the health and education sector. Such findings have important policy implications because our policymakers are trying to address the health and economic consequences of the COVID-19 pandemic. The Generalized Least Square Estimation show that the pandemics have a statistically significant positive impact upon income inequality particularly for the high-income groups and when considering the entire set of 70 countries. However, the impact of the pandemics is negative upon the upper-middle-income group of countries. The results are statistically significant. The estimation is robust controlling for additional macroeconomic variables and institutional quality indicators that are identified in the literature as drivers of inequality for example economic development, trade openness, capital formation and inflation. The institutional quality is measured through the democratic system of governance. The results confirming the hypothesis of the study show that the impact of pandemics upon income inequality is not identical across regions and income groups. The study essentially demonstrates that the occurrence of past pandemics generated policy responses that may in turn have impacted the distribution of income.

6.1. Limitations and directions of future research

Our findings open the scope for research in the following directions: (i) since the study shows that the past pandemics have a varying impact depending upon income group, future studies can explore how the recent pandemic may impact countries with different initial income distribution; with different country-based characteristics and as well as differences in stringency measures adopted by the respective governments and (ii) further studies can examine the impact of COVID-19 across inequality in terms of race, age and gender. The pandemic has had a particular impact upon the vulnerable excluded population because of limited access to health-care and employment opportunities.

6.2. Policy suggestions

Income inequality has risen in all major countries and the inequality is sharp at the top income shares. Learning from the lessons of the past pandemics it is likely that the COVID-19 pandemic would be inequality reinforcing for these countries. The COVID-19 pandemic has caused a division across those who can work remotely and those who cannot. A waning role of the state as far as redistributive policies are concerned has been exacerbating the inequality. The task ahead is the need to orient towards more responsive and inclusive policies to reduce the negative economic outcomes of the pandemic. Most countries of the world are responding to the immediate impact of the pandemic by adopting stringency measures to contain the contagious effect. Policies have been adopted to give economic stimulus to the vulnerable groups. Beyond the immediate course of actions, a lot of attention needs to be put on the long-term impact of COVID-19 and how it will impact inequality of income across the globe. New policies need to be formulated which are inclusive and robust in the post-pandemic situation and this can be successfully achieved through responsible collaboration and dialogue across nations.

Notes

1. The choice of the variables to explore the transmission channel upon inequality is constrained by (i) availability of data across large country sets and across time; (ii) WDI data sets have large missing values; (iii) multicollinearity issues and thereby determining the best set of variables and last (iv) trying to obtain data sets which encompass all countries and across the time. As the study by Dabla-Norris et al. (2015) discuss that there is no 'one-size-fits-all approach to tackling inequality'. So, lot depends on the decision of the choice of drivers, country context, policies and institutions. Thus, it is difficult to ascertain the set of determinants of inequality particularly across diverse nations. Given the constraints the present study has identified the variables from the literature which are encompassing through cross-section and time.
2. We could not explore the impact of the past pandemics on the inequality conditions of the low-income group owing to a large set of missing observations.

Disclosure statement

No potential conflict of interest was reported by the author(s).

Data availability statement

Data used for this study is available at figshare: http://doi.org/10.6084/m9.figshare.13896074.

Code availability

The STATA Software was used.

Funding

No funding is involved with this research.

ORCID

Sudeshna Ghosh http://orcid.org/0000-0002-2026-1676

References

Alam, M. S., and S. R. Paramati. 2016. "The Impact of Tourism on Income Inequality in Developing Economies: Does Kuznets Curve Hypothesis Exist?" *Annals of Tourism Research* 61: :111–126. doi:10.1016/j.annals.2016.09.008.

Alesina, A., and D. Rodrik. 1994. "Distributive Politics and Economic Growth." *The Quarterly Journal of Economics* 109 (2): 465–490. doi:10.2307/2118470.

Alfani, G. 2021. "Economic Inequality in Preindustrial Times: Europe and Beyond." *Journal of Economic Literature* 59 (1): 3–44. doi:10.1257/jel.20191449.

Anyanwu, J. C. 2016. "Empirical Analysis of the Main Drivers of Income Inequality in Southern Africa." *Annals of Economics & Finance* 17 (2): 337–364.

Banerjee, A. V., and A. F. Newman. 1991. "Risk-bearing and the Theory of Income Distribution." *The Review of Economic Studies* 58 (2): 211–235. doi:10.2307/2297965.

Barro, R. J. 2000. "Inequality and Growth in a Panel of Countries." *Journal of Economic Growth* 5 (1): 5–32.

Becker, G. S., and B. R. Chiswick. 1966. "Education and the Distribution of Earnings." *The American Economic Review* 56 (1/2): 358–369.

Calderón, C., and A. Chong. 2004. "Volume and Quality of Infrastructure and the Distribution of Income: An Empirical Investigation." *Review of Income and Wealth* 50 (1): 87–106. doi:10.1111/j.0034-6586.2004.00113.x.

Case, A., and A. Deaton. 2021. *Deaths of Despair and the Future of Capitalism*. Princeton, USA: Princeton University Press.

Chatterjee, S., and S. J. Turnovsky. 2012. "Infrastructure and Inequality." *European Economic Review* 56 (8): 1730–1745. doi:10.1016/j.euroecorev.2012.08.003.

Dabla-Norris, E., K. Kochhar, N. Suphaphiphat, F. Ricka, and E. Tsounta. 2015. "Causes and Consequences of Income Inequality: A Global Perspective." *IMF Staff Discussion Paper SDN/15/13*. Washington: International Monetary Fund. Accessed 22 March 2021. https://www.imf.org/external/pubs/ft/sdn/2015/sdn1513.pdf

Deininger, K., and L. Squire. 1996. "A New Data Set Measuring Income Inequality." *The World Bank Economic Review* 10 (3): 565–591. doi:10.1093/wber/10.3.565.

Dincer, O. C., and B. Gunalp. 2012. "Corruption and Income Inequality in the United States." *Contemporary Economic Policy* 30 (2): 283–292. doi:10.1111/j.1465-7287.2011.00262.x.

Dolmas, J., G. W. Huffman, and M. A. Wynne. 2000. "Inequality, Inflation, and Central Bank Independence." *Canadian Journal of Economics/Revue Canadienne d'économique* 33 (1): 271–287. doi:10.1111/0008-4085.00015.

Doumbia, D., and M. T. Kinda. 2019. *Reallocating Public Spending to Reduce Income Inequality: Can It Work?* Washington: International Monetary Fund. Accessed 22 March 2021. wpiea2019188-print-pdf.pdf

Duncan, D., and K. S. Peter. 2016. "Unequal Inequalities: Do Progressive Taxes Reduce Income Inequality?" *International Tax and Public Finance* 23 (4): 762–783. doi:10.1007/s10797-016-9412-5.

Feenstra, R., and G. H. Hanson. 2003. "Global Production Sharing and Rising Inequality: A Survey of Trade and Wage." In *Handbook of International Trade*, edited by E. K. Choi and J. C. Harrigan (pp. 146–85). Malden, MA: Blackwell.

Foellmi, R., and M. Oechslin. 2010. "Market Imperfections, Wealth Inequality, and the Distribution of Trade Gains." *Journal of International Economics* 81 (1): 15–25. doi:10.1016/j.jinteco.2010.03.001.

Furceri, D., P. Loungani, J. D. Ostry, and P. Pizzuto. 2020. "Will COVID-19 Affect Inequality? Evidence from past Pandemics." *Covid Economics* 12 (1): 138–157.

Galor, O., and J. Zeira. 1993. "Income Distribution and Macroeconomics." *The Review of Economic Studies* 60 (1): 35–52. doi:10.2307/2297811.

Gradstein, M., and B. Milanovic. 2004. "Does Liberté = Égalité? A Survey of the Empirical Links between Democracy and Inequality with Some Evidence on the Transition Economies." *Journal of Economic Surveys* 18 (4): 515–537. doi:10.1111/j.0950-0804.2004.00229.x.

Gradstein, M., B. Milanovic, and Y. Ying. 2001. "Democracy and Income Inequality: An Empirical Analysis." *Policy Research Working Paper; No. 2561*. Washington, DC: World Bank.

Greenwood, J., and B. Jovanovic. 1990. "Financial Development, Growth, and the Income Distribution." *Journal of Political Economy* 98: 1076–1107. doi:10.1086/261720.

Gutiérrez-Romero, R. 2021. "Inequality, Persistence of the Informal Economy, and Club Convergence." *World Development* 139: 105211. doi:10.1016/j.worlddev.2020.105211.

Hsiao, C. 2007. “Panel Data Analysis—Advantages and Challenges.” *Test* 16 (1): 1–22. doi:10.1007/s11749-007-0046-x.

International Monetary Fund. 2015. “Making Public Investment More Efficient.” *IMF Policy Paper*. Accessed 22 March 2021. http://www.imf.org/external/np/pp/eng/2015/061115.pdf

International Monetary Fund. 2017. “Tackling Inequalities.” *Fiscal Monitor*, 48. Washington: International Monetary Fund. Fall. Accessed 22 March 2021. https://www.imf.org/en/Publications/FM/Issues/2017/10/05/fiscal-monitor-october-2017

Jordà, Ò., S. R. Singh, and A. M. Taylor. 2020. “Longer-run Economic Consequences of Pandemics.” *No. w26934*. National Bureau of Economic Research.

Knight, J. B., and R. H. Sabot. 1983. “Educational Expansion and the Kuznets Effect.” *The American Economic Review* 73 (5): 1132–1136.

Kuznets, S. 1955. “Economic Growth and Income Inequality.” *The American Economic Review* 45 (1): 1–28.

Lee, D. J., and J. C. Son. 2016. “Economic Growth and Income Inequality: Evidence from Dynamic Panel Investigation.” *Global Economic Review* 45 (4): 331–358. doi:10.1080/1226508X.2016.1181980.

Lee, J. W., and H. Lee. 2018. “Human Capital and Income Inequality.” *Journal of the Asia Pacific Economy* 23 (4): 554–583. doi:10.1080/13547860.2018.1515002.

Lucas, J. R. 1988. “On the Mechanics of Economic Development.” *Journal of Monetary Economics* 22: 3–42. doi:10.1016/0304-3932(88)90168-7.

Ma, C., J. Rogers, and S. Zhou. 2020. “Modern Pandemics: Recession and Recovery”. *BOFIT Discussion Paper No. 16-2020*. Accessed 16 October 2020. https://papers.ssrn.com/sol3/papers.cfm?abstract_id=3668472

Mankiw, N. G., D. Romer, and N. D. Weil. 1992. “A Contribution to the Empirics of Economic Growth.” *The Quarterly Journal of Economics* 107 (2): 407–437. doi:10.2307/2118477.

Marshall, M. G. 2017. “Major Episodes of Political Violence (MEPV) and Conflict Regions, 1946–2016.” *Center for Systemic Peace* 17. Accessed 9 December 2020. http://www.systemicpeace.org/warlist/warlist.htm

Munch, J. R., and J. R. Skaksen. 2008. “Human Capital and Wages in Exporting Firms.” *Journal of International Economics* 75 (2): 363–372. doi:10.1016/j.jinteco.2008.02.006.

Persson, T., and G. Tabellini. 1994. “Is Inequality Harmful for Growth?” *The American Economic Review* 84 (3): 600–621.

Reynolds, M., and E. Smolensky. 2013. *Public Expenditures, Taxes, and the Distribution of Income: The United States, 1950, 1961, 1970*. New York: Academic Press.

Richardson, L., and H. Immervoll. 2011. “Redistribution Policy and Inequality Reduction in OECD Countries: What Has Changed in Two Decades?” *LIS Working Papers 571*. Luxembourg: LIS Cross-National Data Center. Accessed 22 March 2021. https://ideas.repec.org/p/lis/liswps/571.html

Solt, F. 2020. “Measuring Income Inequality across Countries and over Time: The Standardized World Income Inequality Database.” *Social Science Quarterly* 101 (3): 1183–1199. doi:10.1111/ssqu.12795.

Appendix A.

Table A1. Country classification: the selected countries and the past pandemics.

Serial no.	Low-income countries	Lower-middle-income countries	Upper-middle-income countries	High-income countries
1	Burundi (HINI-2009)	Algeria (HINI-2009)	Brazil (HINI-2009) (Zika-2016)	Australia (SARS-2003) (HINI-2009)
2	Gambia (HINI-2009)	Bangladesh (HINI-2009)	China (SARS-2003) (HINI-2009) (MERS-2012)	Austria (HINI-2009) (MERS-2012)
3	Malawi (HINI-2009)	Bhutan (HINI-2009)	Colombia (HINI-2009) (Zika-2016)	Bahamas (HINI-2009)
4		Bolivia (HINI-2009) (Zika-2016)	Costa Rica (HINI-2009) (Zika-2016)	Belgium (HINI-2009)
5		Cabo Verde (HINI-2009)	Dominican Republic (HINI-2009) (Zika-2016)	Canada (SARS-2003) (HINI-2009) (Zika-2016)
6		Cameroon (HINI-2009)	Gabon (HINI-2009)	Chile (HINI-2009) (Zika-2016)
7		Congo, Rep. (HINI-2009)	Iran (HINI-2009) (MERS-2012)	Cyprus (HINI-2009)
8		Cote d'Ivoire (HINI-2009)	Malaysia (SARS-2003) (HINI-2009) (MERS-2012)	Denmark (HINI-2009)
9		Egypt, Arab Rep. (HINI-2009) (MERS-2012)	Mexico (HINI-2009)	Finland (HINI-2009)
10		El Salvador (HINI-2009) (Zika-2016)	Paraguay (HINI-2009) (Zika-2016)	France (SARS-2003) (HINI-2009) (MERS-2012)
11		Eswatini (HINI-2009)	South Africa (SARS-2003) (HINI-2009)	Germany (HINI-2009) (SARS-2003) (MERS-2012)
12		Ghana (HINI-2009)	Thailand (SARS-2003) (MERS-2012)	Greece (HINI-2009) (MERS-2012)
13		Honduras (HINI-2009) (Zika-2016)	Turkey (HINI-2009) (MERS-2012)	Iceland (HINI-2009)
14		India (SARS-2003) (HINI-2009)	Venezuela (HINI-2009)	Ireland (HINI-2009) (SARS-2003)
15		Kenya (HINI-2009)		Israel (HINI-2009)
16		Lao PDR (HINI-2009)		Italy (SARS-2003) (HINI-2009) (MERS-2012) (Ebola-2014)
17		Mauritania		Japan (HINI-2009)

(Continued)

Table A1. (Continued).

Serial no.	Low-income countries	Lower-middle-income countries	Upper-middle-income countries	High-income countries
18		Morocco (HINI-2009)		Korea, Rep. (SARS-2003) (MERS-2012)
19		Nepal (HINI-2009)		Luxembourg (HINI-2009)
20		Nigeria (HINI-2009)		Malta (HINI-2009)
21		Pakistan (HINI-2009)		Netherlands (HINI-2009) (MERS-2012)
22		Papua New Guinea (HINI-2009)		New Zealand (SARS-2003) (HINI-2009)
23		Philippines (SARS-2003) (HINI-2009) (MERS-2012)		Norway (HINI-2009)
24		Senegal		Portugal (HINI-2009)
25		Sri Lanka (HINI-2009)		Singapore (SARS-2003) (HINI-2009)
26		Tunisia (HINI-2009) (MERS-2012)		Spain (SARS-2003) (HINI-2009) (Ebola- 2014)
27				Sweden (SARS-2003) (HINI-2009)
28				Switzerland (SARS-2003) (HINI-2009)
29				United Kingdom (SARS-2003) (HINI-2009) (MERS-2012) (Ebola-2014)
30				United States (SARS-2003) (HINI-2009) (MERS-2012) (Ebola-2014)
31				Uruguay (HINI-2009) (Zika-2016)

Source: Compilation Authors.

The Korean government's public health responses to the COVID-19 epidemic through the lens of industrial policy

Hee-Young Shin

ABSTRACT

The paper explores the idea that the success of the Korean government's non-pharmaceutical interventions in response to the COVID-19 epidemic can be better understood through the lens of industrial policy framework than many descriptive public policy literatures that have merely focused on administrative efficiency. It is emphasized in this paper that the Korean government has maintained sustained R&D support, tax subsidy, and various forms of public–private partnerships to help nurture and grow domestic infant industry in such strategic industrial areas as information-communication technology, biotechnology and health care, and pharmaceutical industry for a long time, and this soft industrial policy has enabled the public health authority to implement a series of successful non-pharmaceutical public health measures to suppress and mitigate the spread of the novel coronavirus.

1. Introduction

The Korean government's non-pharmaceutical public health responses to the COVID-19 epidemic have been widely praised by many public health experts and researchers around the world. In the absence of vaccines and effective medical treatment, the government's public health measures such as mask wearing, social distancing, and extensive contact tracing are crucial non-pharmaceutical interventions to suppress and mitigate the spread of the novel coronavirus. On this ground, the Korean health authority's systematic responses to the COVID-19 have proven to be highly effective and successful: Its rapid support for the development and nationwide deployment of the novel coronavirus test kit and its timely establishment of expedite contact tracing mechanism to detect and suppress the spread of the novel coronavirus have so far successfully managed to lower the total number of infected patients and the fatality rate measured in both absolute and per capita term, compared to many other OECD member countries in Europe (notably, the UK, France, Germany, and Italy) and North America (such as the US and Canada).

This paper examines the government's COVID-19 related public health measures through the lens of industrial policy framework, and it explores the possibility that the relatively successful performance of non-pharmaceutical interventions in response to the COVID-19 epidemic is made possible, in large part, thanks to the Korean government's decade-long industrial policy programs to nurture and develop domestic strategic industry in information technology, healthcare, and pharmaceutical sector.

The industrial policy involves the public sector's artificial allocation of resource to private enterprises to help and encourage them to develop and provide public goods that are deemed too risky to produce in the absence of the government's nonmarket coordination mechanism. This industrial policy can take the form of the R&D investment, tax subsidy, and public–private partnerships granted to incentivize private enterprises to develop, produce, and deliver the necessary public goods. The paper argues that the rapid development and deployment of the novel coronavirus test kits, the flexible expansion of the diagnostic testing capacity, the information-communication technology (ICT) based contact tracing capacity to identify and detect epidemiological links of patients and clusters, and the rapid development and delivery of protective medical equipment and treatment of the patients in such a short time are largely indebted to the sustained financial support and effective public-private partnerships in high tech industry.

To demonstrate this point, the paper proceeds as follows: In the next section the paper reviews the recent studies on the effectiveness of the Korean government's public health responses to the COVID-19 epidemic and discusses the need of introducing a new perspective. The paper then overviews the evolution of the COVID-19 epidemic and reconstructs the timeline of the major public health measures adopted by the Korean government. The third section attempts to analyze the performance of these policies through the lens of the industrial policy framework. It is in this section where we highlight and discuss how the Korean government's long-lasting strategic investment and public–private partnerships in major domestic industry such as information technology, biotechnology and health care, and pharmaceutical industry shape the form and effectiveness of the public health authority's non-pharmaceutical interventions. The fourth section identifies some of issues and challenges surrounding the government's active industrial policy and discuss how to address these problems. These issues include the institutional requirement for conducting effective industrial policy and the relationship between the government's industrial policy and other monetary and macroeconomic policies. The last section concludes the previous discussion by restating and summarizing the core argument in this paper.

2. Recent studies on the effectiveness of public health responses to COVID-19 epidemic in Korea

Early studies on the Korean government's responses to the COVID-19 epidemic have legitimately focused on the government's remarkable and successful administrative strategies for '3 T' (testing, tracing, and treatment). One of the earliest academic paper on the Korean government's public health response is Oh et al. (2020). Oh et al. (2020) tabulated the timeline of the Korean government's public health response strategies and identified (1) the early activation of national response protocols, (2) rapid development and deployment of diagnostic testing capacity, (3) scaling up the measures to prevent community spread (including extensive contact tracing and quarantine), and (4) redesigning and mobilizing medical and clinical resources to treat severely symptomatic COVID-19 patients as the most crucial factors behind its early success.

In a similar vein, both You (2020) and Kang et al. (2020) emphasize the epidemic preparedness and early warning system that was established from very early stage of the COVID-19 epidemic and discuss the effectiveness of (1) the activation of the Emergency National Infectious Disease Management Plan that the Korean government has developed and upgraded over many years, which guides the central government and local health agencies in responding to the health emergency situation, (2) the public-private partnership in developing and deploying diagnostic testing kits and other medical equipment, and (3) technology-based contact tracing measures designed and implemented to mitigate the community spread of the virus, among other.

If these studies are focusing on the public health authority's administrative capacity to deal with the epidemic, other strand of research highlights the effectiveness of the government's non-pharmaceutical interventions from a statistical point of view. For example, Kim and Castro (2020) offers an early assessment of the effectiveness of the government's public health measures in mitigating the virus transmission dynamics (Kim and Castro 2020). Cooper, Mondal, and Antonopoulos (2020) conducts the SIR model-based parameter estimation for China, Korea, India, Australia, and selected states in US using country-specific data (from December 2019 to July 2020), and concludes that the wide range of differences in infection and recovery rate among the country lies in the timing and effectiveness of non-pharmaceutical interventions taken by each government.

The statistical and empirical analysis of this kind is also consistent with many international journalists' reports as well as the Korean government's own accounts for the matter. BBC, Reuters, and New York Times, for example, published a series of special reports on the Korean government's public health policies from early March 2020 (Terhune et al. 2020; Parodi et al. 2020; Fisher and Choe 2020, to name a few). In response to repeated multi-governmental requests from other countries and international institutions, even the Ministry of Economy and Finance of Korea published a booklet titled 'Tackling COVID-19: Health, Quarantine, and Economic Measures of South Korea' in late March (Ministry of Economy and Finance 2020). Other government agencies also published their own informational booklets (Government of the Republic of Korea 2020a, 2020b, 2020c; KCDC 2020), which confirmed the similar assessment of the government's overall strategies.

Even though all these studies are useful and informative, there remain several questions that have not been fully addressed in these previous studies. For example, one may want to ask how it was possible for the Korean public health authority to develop and deploy massive diagnostic testing kits in such a short time. How was it possible for the health authority to conduct such an extensive ICT-based contact tracing operation? How could the government manage to produce and distribute specialty face masks and other personal protective equipment in the face of surging demand? And finally, but not less importantly, how could a local pharmaceutical company develop and produce a COVID-19 treatment candidate in such a short time that has significantly contributed to lowering the mortality rate during the latest phase of the epidemic?

This paper attempts to address these questions by relying on the hypothesis that the Korean government's long-lasting industrial policy framework that is designed and implemented to nurture and develop domestic infant industry in such strategic areas as information technology, bio-health, and pharmaceutical industry has laid the ground for the effective implementation of these public health measures and has significantly contributed to the relatively successful outcome amid the COVID-19 epidemic.

The industrial policy is the government's particular policy framework that is designed to achieve a targeted economic performance. We can define the industrial policy as part of a broad economic development strategy that encompasses the government's efforts to enhance industrial diversification and upgrading and to promote the use of advanced technology and innovations in production and products (Cf. Chang 1993). According to Rodrik, it is a policy to 'stimulate specific economic activities and promote structural change.'(Rodrik 2009, 3) By nature, industrial policy is closely connected with other economic policies such as trade policy, interest rate and exchange rate management policy and many other broad macroeconomic stabilization programs. It can often involve an authoritative and selective allocation of resources (both financial support and raw materials) for development, production, and comprehensive delivery (including the public sector's procurement) of the goods and services produced by private companies.

Historically, the industrial policy and the overall development strategy took various forms. During the 19th century many western European countries heavily relied on tariff, outright ban and prohibition of export and import, export subsidy and tariff rebates on input used for exports granted to domestic firms, [1] all of which were designed to protect domestic infant industry and to promote their export performance. Nowadays, these 'hard' and visible industrial policies have been replaced by many 'soft' and less visible forms. Examples of these soft industrial policies include the government's broad industrial and investment planning (or guideline), selective approval and the promotion of the public-private partnership in startup business in some strategic industrial sectors, the public sector's R&D support, tax credit, and tax rebate for R&D investment and innovation in production line, the governmental support for expedite patent protection and monitoring of the intellectual property right, the government's inducement for (competing) private companies to form a cooperative business network to develop and expand the production of new products across the industry, and the establishment of institutions and incentive scheme that promote public-private cooperation and partnership.

In the neoclassical economics literature, this industrial policy, or any other forms of the government's artificial intervention in the private business operation has long been demonized as the bastion of cronyism, corruption and rent-seeking, and inefficiency. Contrast to this prevailing notion, however, there have been many influential works done by heterodox economists and sociologists who have investigated the crucial role played by the government's effective industrial policy during the industrialization process of East Asian economies (Amsden 1992, 2003a, 2003b; Chang 1993, 2006; Wade 1990) and more generally during the early stage of capitalist economic development in the West (Chang 2003. See also List [1837] 1983, [1841] 1885).[2] In addition, industrial policy is not at all a bygone feature. Mainstream economists' theoretical demonization notwithstanding, many advanced capitalist economies in OECD are still relying on various forms of industrial policies in practice to enhance their domestic firms' international competitiveness and to promote economic diversification (Wade 2012, 2015).

This paper relies on this 'industrial policy-led-developmentalist argument' in its core and attempts to highlight some industrial policy aspects of the Korean government's non-pharmaceutical interventions in response to the COVID-19 epidemic. The paper argues that the Korean experience has shown that well-designed public–private partnership in developing and delivering public goods enabled by the long-lasting industrial policy framework is one of the most important contributing factors to the successful epidemic mitigation strategies.

3. The evolution of the COVID-19 epidemics and the performance of non-pharmaceutical interventions in Korea

Before moving on to the main discussion point, however, let us briefly overview how the COVID-19 epidemic has played out so far and how the Korean government and public health authority have adopted a series of non-pharmaceutical interventions to suppress and mitigate the epidemic.

Since the first imported case was detected in late January 2020, there have been three distinctive phases of the COVID-19 epidemic in Korea. The first full-blown spread of the novel coronavirus began from mid-to-late February, as the number of confirmed cases and those who were suspected to have close contacts with locally transmitted patients grew exponentially. This explosive growth in the number of confirmed cases was mainly associated with a massive religious assembly of a particular Christian group, known as Shinchonji Church of Jesus. The coronavirus easily spread among those who attended this group's religious gathering held in a tightly packed mega church building. This spike in the number of confirmed cases that marked the first wave of the COVID19 epidemic in Korea lasted until early-May (May 10).

The second wave of the COVID-19 epidemic began from around early August. The number of confirmed cases rose sharply again from weekly average of less than 50 to a peak of 441 cases on 28 August 2020. This second-round spike was directly linked to another super spreader event, a massive political demonstration held at the center of the capital city, Seoul. A conservative opposition political party and groups of Christian fundamentalists joined their forces to organize and hold this political rally against the law. Unlike the first wave of the COVID-19 epidemic, however, the public health authority was not able to implement its preventative measures because of fierce oppositions and resistance by highly politicized Christian group members. They resisted providing the list of participants in the rally and even instructed their members not to cooperate with health-care officials. Due to these non-cooperative behaviors, the health authority failed to conduct proper contact tracing measure that was designed to prevent further community transmission. Even though the Korean government ultimately managed to contain the arduous situation, it took more than 30 days to bring down the number of confirmed cases below 100 (by September 20).

The third and concurrent phase of the COVID19 epidemic began from mid-October. Daily confirmed cases rose from the low of 60s in mid-October to 110s on November 4 and these numbers continued to rise. Compared to first two waves, the concurrent phase of the virus infection is not triggered by any single super spreader event. Instead, small scale, multi-sited, persistent infection cases in child and elderly care facilities, churches and other religious buildings, and private educational facilities have occurred all around the country infrequently. The median age of new confirmed cases has become lower than the second phase, as more and more younger and asymptomatic patients are suspected to spread the virus.

The following figure shows these distinct phases of the COVID-19 epidemic from 18 February 2020 (Day 1) to 20 February 2021 (Day 398) (Figure 1) and the number of cumulative deaths associated with the COVID-19 as of 20 February 2021 (Figure 2):

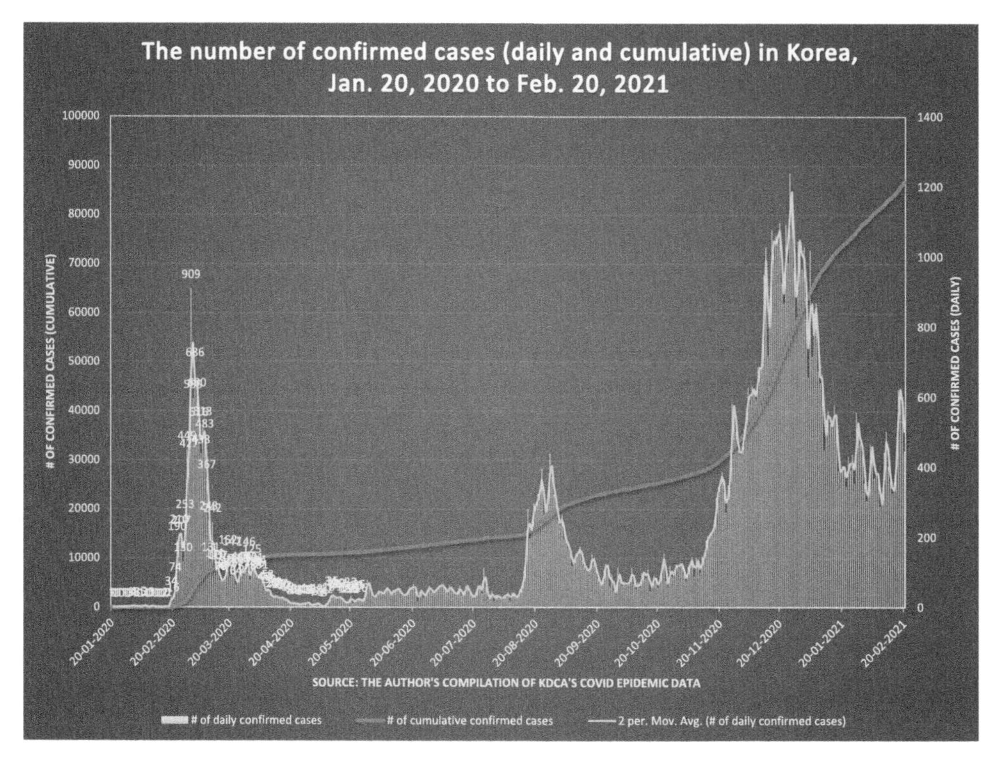

Figure 1. The number of confirmed cases (daily and cumulative) in Korea, 20 January 2020 to 20 February 2021.

From very early stage of the epidemic, the public health authority led by the Central Disease Control Headquarter established an emergency warning system and began to formulate the pandemic response protocols that have been maintained throughout the entire period of the epidemic with some flexible adjustments.

For example, in response to the surge in the confirmed case during the first wave, the public health authority temporarily expanded its public health measures (1) to obtain the membership list of the religious group to conduct preemptive diagnostic testing for those who had contacts with infected patients and to quarantine those who were suspected and confirmed. The government also (2) established a series of medical criteria that enabled local health authorities and medical professionals to discern and treat those who were asymptomatic or 'mildly' symptomatic patients differently from those who were showing severe symptoms. The government also (3) developed a system to convert public buildings and vocational training centers as designated quarantine sites to accommodate the growing need of this separate treatment. If the infected patients are mildly symptomatic but unable to stay at home for their own self-quarantine for various reason, and if the incoming travelers are confirmed to be infected at the point of entry, they are all escorted to stay at least 14 days in these designated quarantine sites.[3] It is in this period when the government (4) recommended the public mask wearing and physical distancing measure after successfully managing the steady supply of specialty face masks and personal protective equipment. Ultimately, these efforts brought down the number of newly confirmed cases by early May in the first wave.

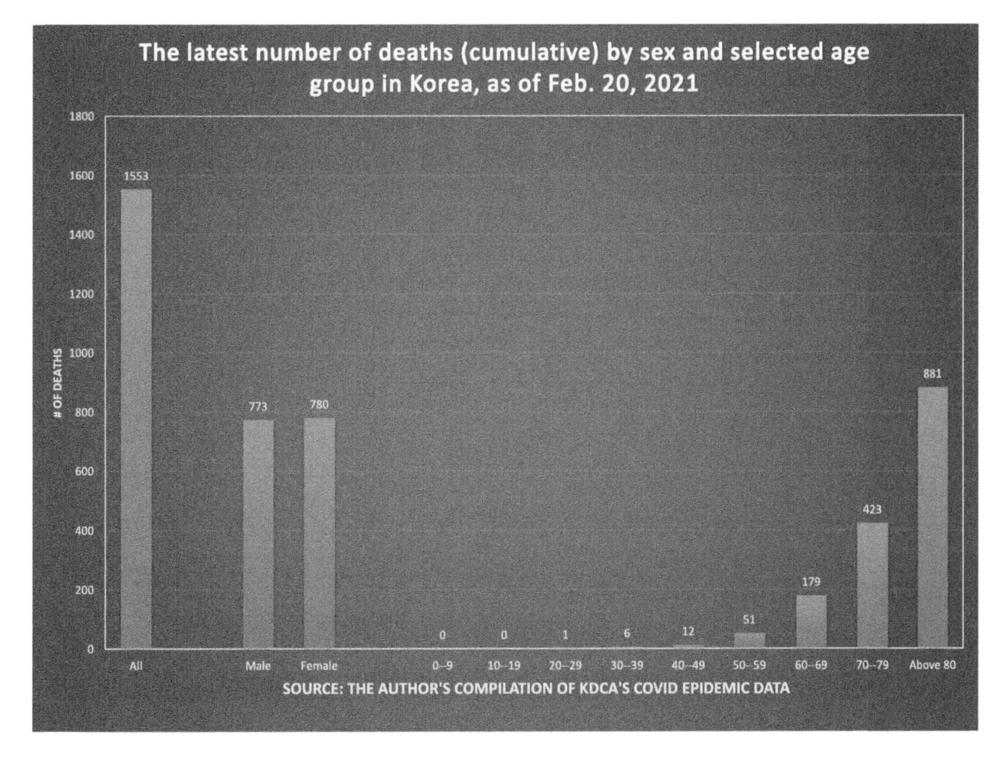

Figure 2. The latest number of deaths (cumulative) by sex and selected age group in Korea, 20 January 2020 to 20 February 2021.

The following figure shows the timeline of major public policy responses adopted during the first wave of the epidemic (see Figure 3).

4. The Korean government's public policy responses to COVID-19 epidemic through the lens of industrial policy

Most of these public health measures may not seem directly related with industrial policy per se. However, the nature of some of these non-pharmaceutical interventions are often determined by the administrative and technological capacity of the public health authority, which is, in turn, shaped by the Korean government's sustained public investment in some priority industrial sectors. In addition, the success of some of these policies is also made possible, primarily by the outcome that the government's industrial policy has laid out for decades. Let us illustrate this point by focusing on the following four aspects.

4.1. The government's sustained soft industrial policy under changing environments and the legal framework for public health measures

The Korean government has sustained its public investment on many strategic industries for a long time. This strategic industry includes biotechnology and health care industry, information-communication technology sector, and pharmaceutical industry, in addition to the traditional support for heavy-chemical, automobile, semiconductor, and

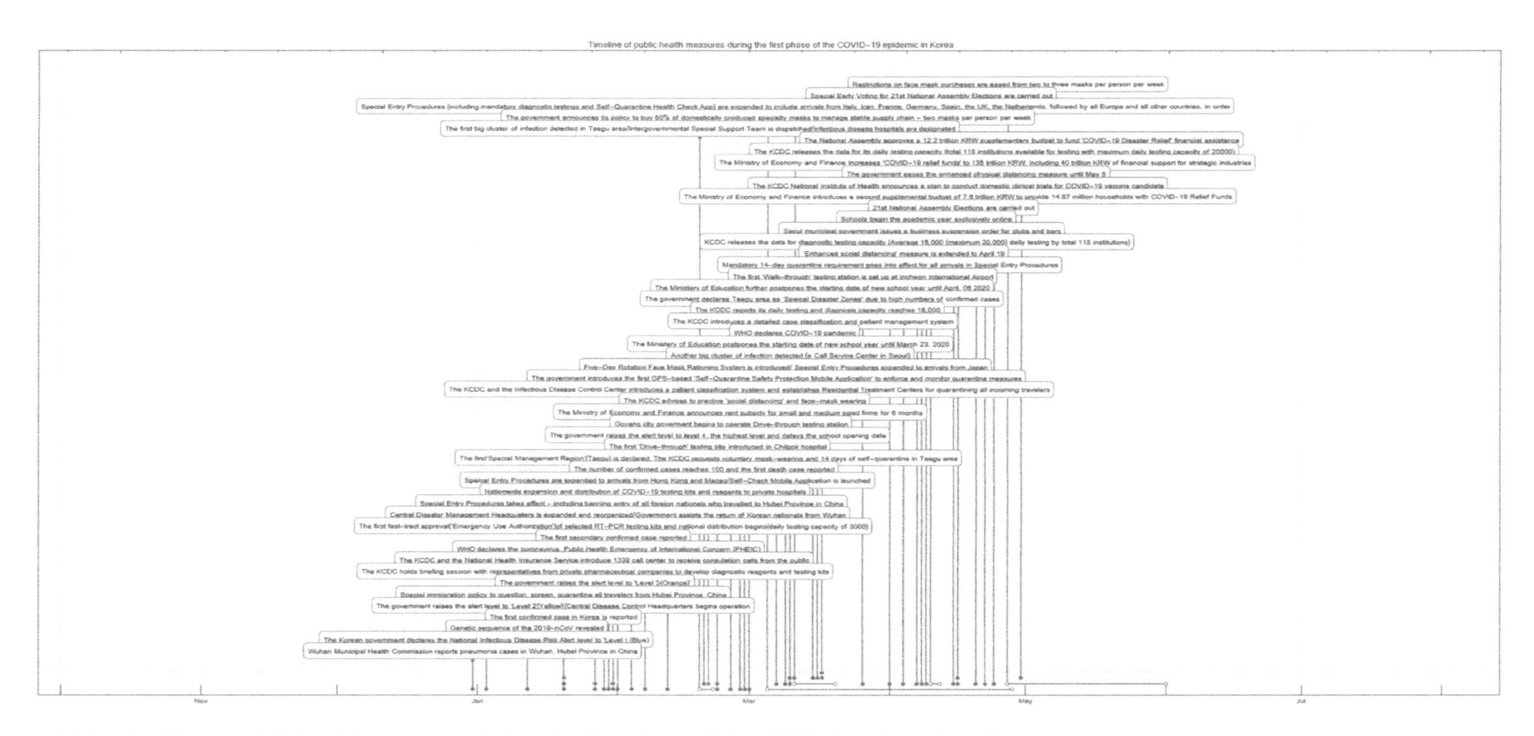

Figure 3. The timeline of public health measures during the first phase of the COVID-19 epidemic in Korea.

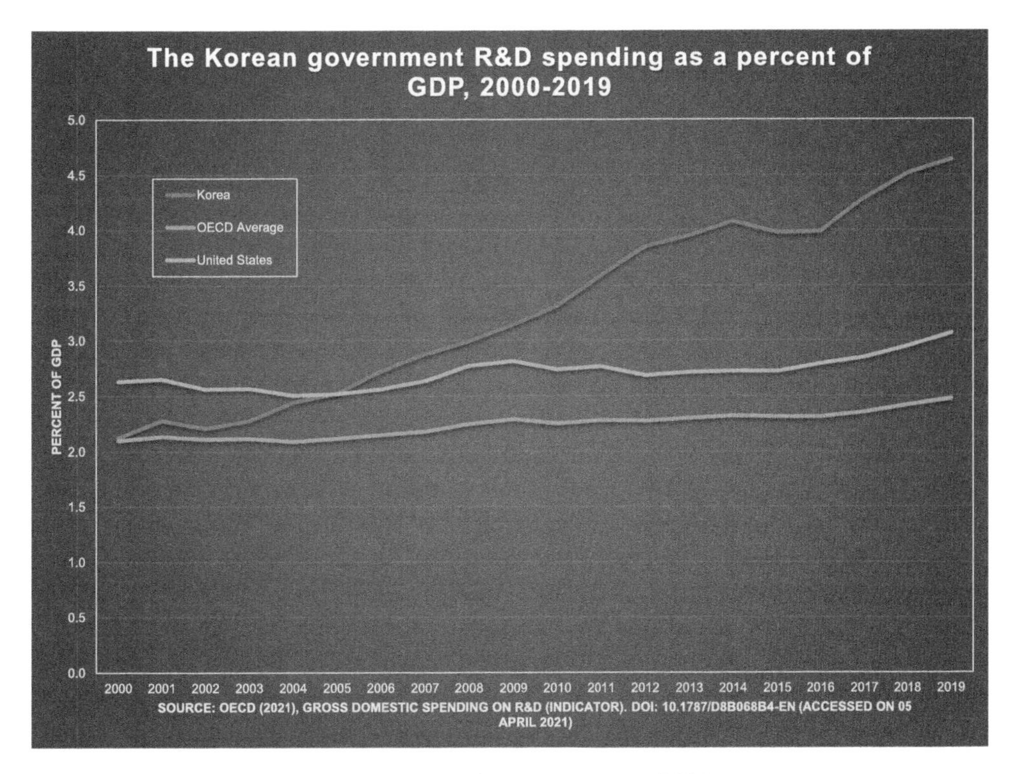

Figure 4. The Korean government's R&D spending as a percent of GDP, 2000–2019.

shipbuilding industry that the country has been renowned for. The exact institutional relationship between the government and private companies in different industrial sectors has evolved over time, and, in some cases, was radically restructured by both intentional policy choice and external pressures. For example, financial market liberalization policy and deregulation adopted during the early 1990s was an intentional policy choice made by the government policymaker, while further trade and capital account liberalization imposed during and after the Asian Financial Crisis in 1998–99 was part of the IMF-US Treasury's bailout conditionality (Wade and Veneroso 1998). Since then, the relationship between the government and private business sector has substantially altered (Cf. Chang 2006; Lee et al. 2019). It is also important to note that the Korean government's aggressive pursuit of signing in bilateral and regional trade agreements with the US, the EU, and many other countries including China in 2010s has also shaped the way how the government's industrial policy is formed and implemented in Korea (See Note [6] below).

Throughout these tumultuous changes, however, the government has sustained many 'soft' industrial policies, including the government's R&D support, industrial lending to individual companies in strategic industrial sectors, and various tax credit and subsidy for product innovation and patent. For example, the Korean government's support for R&D was just 2% of GDP in 2000, but it grew to more than 4.5% of GDP in 2019, which is the second next to the State of Israel in percentage term (see Figure 4). In this year, Korea's total R&D spending (including R&D spending by corporate business firms) is the fifth highest in absolute term among the entire OECD countries, totalling 89.06 trillion won. It is under this policy framework that small and medium-sized enterprises (SMEs) in biotechnology, health care, and pharmaceuticals, artificial intelligence and cybersecurity, and broadband-based technology firms began to emerge in the 2010s, some of which have played a critical role amid the current COVID-19 epidemic.

The successively upgraded legal framework for public health matter also plays an important role. During this epidemic, the Korean government activated the national infectious disease alert system from very early on (3 January 2020), just three days after Wuhan Municipal Health Commission reported pneumonia cases in Wuhan, Hubei Province in China (31 December 2019). According to the National Infectious Disease Management Plan that has been updated and upgraded multiple times in the past (Lee et al. 2013; Ministry of Health and Welfare of Korea and WHO 2015),[4] the Center for Public Health Emergency Preparedness and Response under Korea Centers for Disease Control and Prevention (KCDC) reported this case to the intergovernmental emergency meeting and urged to establish the Central Disaster Management Headquarters (Head: Minister of Health and Welfare) that comprises of the Central Disease Control Headquarters (Head: Director of KCDC), provincial and municipal health agencies (Head: Provincial Governor or Mayor) (Government of the Republic of Korea 2020a, 33).

Among many objectives of the KCDC specified by this legal framework, establishing private-public cooperation system in coping with the infectious disease, developing emergency response guidelines for all medical institutions and public health centers, and planning and organizing epidemiological investigation teams are the key factors that set the trajectory of the path of COVID-19 infection and of later public policy responses. It is under this legal framework that the head of the KCDC and the government officials convened an emergency meeting joined by representatives from private bio-health and pharmaceutical companies, in which they shared the crucial information about the emerging infectious disease and the need of urgent development of diagnostic testing kits. Under the same legal framework, the Central Disease Control Headquarters directed the governmental resource to help private companies to expand their production capacity for manufacturing personal protective equipment and facemask in anticipation of acute surges in the number of infected patients.

4.2. Public-private partnerships in developing and deploying diagnostic test kits, personal protective equipment, and specialty facemask

The first remarkable outcome of this public-private cooperation system was a rapid development and deployment of the coronavirus test kits and the expansion of the diagnostic testing and assessment capacity. The KCDC developed and evaluated the real-time reverse transcription polymerase chain reaction (rRT-PCR) diagnostic method for coronavirus in late January 2020, partnering with the Korean Society for Laboratory Medicine (KSLM) and the Korean Association of External Quality Assessment Service (KAEQAS). KCDC then shared this formula with private biotech companies, encouraging them to develop their own PCR-based test kits in the hurriedly convened meeting.

Within a week, four private bio-tech companies (Kogene Biotech, Seegene, SolGent, and SD Biosensor) developed their own sample test kits and successively passed the KCDC's quality assessment. The Korean Ministry of Food and Drug Safety (KMFDS), in turn, activated 'fast-tract authorization' for these newly developed PCR-based test kits in early February 2020. Of course, most of these companies have been the biggest beneficiaries of the government's R&D support for bio-health and technology industry for a long time.

In addition to this development, the Central Disease Control Headquarters rapidly expanded the operation of screening centers (including 71 drive-through testing centers initiated by private hospitals and medical doctors) and walkthrough screening stations (which is also developed by non-governmental sector) that collect specimens, as well as more than 90 medical institutions (including 18 public health and environment institutes) that were capable of processing and assessing specimens with an rRT-PCR testing technique (You 2020, 803).

Amid the first wave, the government also mobilized and redirected financial resource and raw materials to expand the production of personal protective equipment (PPE) and specialty facemask. At first, the government expended its emergency financial support (corporate loans and subsidy) to domestic manufacturing companies so that they could easily scale up the production line for manufacturing PPE and facemask, and even adopted a policy of exclusive public procurement during the acute surge in the number of confirmed cases. The government maintained a policy of buying up to 80% of domestically produced specialty masks to manage the stable supply chain, from March 05 to April 27. With this sufficient inventory, the government delivered them to frontline workers in medical facilities and then domestic citizens through local pharmacies and many public offices. This public procurement policy and rationing system – 'two to three masks per person per week' policy (effective on 5 March 2020), which was later replaced by five-day face mask rationing system (effective on 9 March 2020), and by free purchase of face mask without waiting time interval (effective on 27 April 2020) – proved to be highly effective in preventing private sector's wasteful competition in obtaining raw materials for production and potential price gauging that otherwise could have posed a serious difficulty in persuading the public to wear mask voluntarily. Even though there were some public frustration and acrimonious blames waged by conservative politicians and mass media (calling the measure 'mask socialism'), the government has managed to deliver the basic medical equipment and face mask efficiently and equitably throughout the entire period of the epidemic.[5]

We can discuss various aspects of these developments from a variety of perspectives. But one thing seems obvious. The long-lasting R&D support and subsidy granted to nurture and grow domestic high-tech industry has made it possible for these companies to build and develop their core skills and technologies. In the absence of the government's timely information sharing with private sector, of its clear signal for the need of producing mass testing kits, and the government's financial support for ramping up the domestic manufacturing capacity combined with the public procurement policy, it would have been very difficult (if not impossible) for private biotech companies to produce high-quality test kits on time and for private manufacturing companies to supply the specialty mask and other personal protective equipment during the acute surge in the number of patients.

4.3. The technological infrastructure behind the ICT-based contact tracing

The contact tracing is a monitoring process of the movement of a confirmed patient, with which public health agencies identify and inform persons who might have been in contact with the patient. Korean health agencies have conducted extensive contact tracing, utilizing various information and communication technology (ICT) and the intergovernmental cooperation that is enabled by the updated Infectious Disease Control and Prevention Act in 2016.

A special contact tracing team under the KCDC is dedicated to identifying the location and movement of the confirmed patient by (1) conducting a thorough interview with the patient, by (2) collecting data from credit card transaction records as well as GPS data from mobile phone, and CCTV, etc. This somewhat intrusive data collection is then used to alert (using smartphone) the public who might have been in close contact with the patient, so that they can get COVID-19 test as earliest as possible. The same data has also been used to identify the epidemiological link among the patients and potential clusters of infections (The government of Republic of Korea 2020c).

This contact tracing mechanism was established in the aftermath of the failed response to 2015 MERS outbreak in Korea. The KCDC proposed the need of amending the existing Infectious Disease Control and Prevention Act (Article 76–2), which ultimately enabled the public health agencies to collect these personal data (KCDC 2020). Under this new legal framework, the public health authority was able to conduct its technology-based extensive contact tracing efforts that ultimately helped its overall mitigation strategies.

One may argue that this personal data collection may infringe privacy, even if this practice is perfectly legal. But the main point of the discussion here is not about privacy concern, but about how this way of data collection and ICT-based contact tracing is made possible. This extensive collection and the use of person's location data requires in the first place a widespread development of information technology infrastructure such as high-speed internet that is free and publicly available and telecommunication network that enables the widespread usage of mobile phone across the region.

This advanced ICT infrastructure in Korea has been also developed by the government's decade-long public investment geared toward nurturing and developing high-tech information technology industry. Just as the government's sustained R&D support granted to bio-health and pharmaceutical industry, information communication technology industry has been an important strategic industry pursued by the public sector in Korea. Only based on this advanced technological infrastructure was the public health authority able to establish and operate its highly effective contact tracing as a part of its broad epidemic mitigation strategy.

4.4. Public–private partnerships in developing and delivering vaccines, medical treatments, and low dead space syringe

The Korean government has also collaborated with the private sector in making coronavirus treatments and vaccines, as well. The Korea National Institute of Health (KNIH) developed a monoclonal antibody treatment with Celltrion and embarked a trial of antigen-containing part of the virus vaccine with SK Bioscience (KCDC 2020;

You 2020, 803). For this cooperation, the government granted additional 100 billion won (about 89 USD million) R&D fund (on 3 June 2020) and made it possible for Celltrion to manufacture the first successful antibody treatment. The Ministry of Food and Drug Safety approved clinical trials for this drug candidate as early as 7 August 2020, and authorized emergency use on 15 December 2020.

When it comes to developing an independent COVID-19 vaccine, Korean firms (consortium comprising five private companies) have not yet shown any successful outcome. Nonetheless, the Korean government helped strike a favorable deal for SK Bioscience, for example, to secure manufacturing contract with the AstraZeneca and many other vaccines developed by leading pharmaceutical companies and institutes. This manufacturing contract with these companies includes a provision for technology transfer and long-term co-development and cooperation for other vaccine development projects, which will surely help SK Bioscience acquire an advanced technology and expertise in the area of vaccine development in the future. The government's sustained R&D support for bio and health care sector and its effective public-private partnerships in dealing with infectious disease is in this way providing an important momentum for further development of this industry.

The Korean government's effort to establish various forms of public–private partnerships has not been limited to the development of vaccine and medical treatments. It has also helped bridging the partnership within private corporate sector. For example, PoongLim Pharmatech has developed and retained a core skill to design low dead space syringe (LDSS), while Samsung Biologics has maintained a massive productive capacity in potential use. The Ministry of SMEs and Startups proposed a cooperative business deal between the two companies, spelling out how to scale up production level, how to fairly reward and compensate their respective contribution to the production, and how the government will help support their private business partnership for both domestic use of the product and export.

5. Discussion: issues, challenges, and reforms

5.1. Democratic accountability, bureaucratic efficiency, and public support

Throughout this paper, we have argued that the Korean government's non-pharmaceutical interventions have achieved a remarkable success in suppressing and mitigating the COVID-19 epidemic and some of these policies are made possible by the government's soft industrial policy implemented in the form of long-lasting R&D support for information technology, biotechnology and health care, and pharmaceutical industry. But this core argument should not mask the importance of the basic institutional requirement for the effective implementation of industrial and public health policy. This requirement includes the government's democratic accountability, bureaucratic competence and efficiency, and broad-based public support.

First, the Korean government has maintained a policy of transparent and timely communication to build consensus and to maintain broad-based public support throughout the entire period of the epidemic, and the public's expectation about the performance has been very high. When it comes to implementing the proposed rules, the governance within the bureaucracy and administrative capacity in Korea have shown high degree of competence in delivering the outcome. In the absence of high degree of democratic accountability, bureaucratic efficiency in administering the public policy, and the broad-based public support, the proposed public–private partnership must have been mistrusted and most of the COVID-19 mitigation measures could not have been implemented effectively in the first place.

In addition, the Korean government's soft industrial policy such as the sustained R&D spending and the public-private partnership in many industrial sectors has never been seriously questioned by the public in Korea for a long time, even though there have been always some debates over the priority and the ownership of policy making (who set the priority, how the priority is being set and why). This broad-based public support for the active role of the government in industrial management is perhaps the historical by-product of successful industrialization experience in the past and the government's efforts for making transparent information sharing and communication about the goal, performance, and the limitation of a particular industrial policy program.

5.2. Intergovernmental coordination and monitoring of performance

In the past, both the Ministry of Finance (1948–1994, later renamed as the Ministry of Economy and Finance in 1994) and the Presidential Economic Planning Board (1961–1994) played a crucial role in designing and implementing 'hard' and 'visible' industrial policies in Korea, especially during the mid-1960s and 1970s. Since the early 2000s, however, the implementation of the government's industrial policies has been reformulated as part of an ongoing process of intergovernmental deliberation, competition, and cooperation among various ministerial agencies. And any actual implementation of the soft industrial policy has been done by these different ministerial agencies.[6]

Of course, the Ministry of Economy and Finance still plays a very important role because the proposal for the central government's overall budgetary planning is still under its discretion. Compared to previous decades, however, other departments and the central government agencies have gained their policy autonomy and administrative capacity to implement and monitor their own departmental expenditure since the immediate aftermath of the Asian financial crisis in the late 1990s. It is under this ministerial cooperative environment that the Ministry of Science and ICT, for example, has developed their own independent R&D support and grant system in the core science and engineering, just as the Ministry of Health and Welfare and the Ministry of Food and Drug Safety has developed their own public health research and administrative capacity, supporting the KCDC and KNIH's R&D activities. The Ministry of SMEs and Startups has also played a particularly important role during this epidemic in coordinating many SMEs to produce personal protective equipment and high-quality face mask as well as bridging one SME's skill for designing LDSS with mass production capacity of a big corporation. Heightened congressional oversights and the public monitoring have been accompanied by in all these interdepartmental implementations of soft industrial policies over many years.

5.3. Coordination with other economic (fiscal and monetary) policies

Industrial policy aims to develop a particular industrial sector for economic development and diversification. Therefore, it often requires a certain coordination with other economic policies. During the whole period of the epidemic, the central bank in Korea (Bank of Korea) has adopted a series of expansionary monetary policies including the operation of emergency credit facilities for banks and nonbank financial companies. The Bank of Korea has also engaged in unlimited purchase of bonds and commercial papers issued by nonfinancial corporate business firms, the measure that has not been seen before in the entire history of the Korean central banking.

Compared to the central bank's nonconventional monetary policy stance, the Ministry of Economy and Finance has maintained an extremely frugal policy stance. Even though it has adopted a series of expansionary fiscal policies in the form of provisioning emergency disaster relief funds and supplemental budgetary programs, the total amount of the fiscal expenditure has not been enough to support struggling households who bear the brunt of the economic consequences of the epidemic. The Korean government has maintained a broadly sound balance sheet for decades and it has a great room for adopting more aggressive expansionary fiscal policies that can directly subsidize the income and employment for the public. But for various ideological and political reason, the Ministry has maintained an extremely frugal policy stance, which has often created fierce debates among policymakers and the public alike.

5.4. Policy design for democratic control and socialization of economic gains

Finally, there is another important question that is often missing in the industrial policy literature. It is about how to democratize the governance and corporate management in the publicly subsidized private firms through industrial policy and how to socialize the economic gains from the successful outcome of the same industrial policy framework. As a result of the government's sustained financial support and the effective operation of the public–private partnership amid the epidemic, some private companies have been able to produce diagnostic test kits, high-quality protective equipment, and face mask that they have been exporting all around the world. The companies that produce and export these products have expanded their business operations, and the market value of their capital assets have grown exponentially consequently. How can we then socialize profits currently appropriated by the CEOs and shareholders of these companies, which are heavily indebted to the government's sustained support? How can we design a policy framework that help enhance democratic governance of these companies so that they can show better and socially responsible corporate management practice?

One can think of the government's majority shareholding of these companies so that they can continuously operate under the public control, prioritizing public interest over short-term gains from quasi-monopoly profit. One can also think of the government's indirect control in the form of strict governance and financial policy requirement imposed on these companies in such a way that they are required to reinvest retained earnings to nurture and develop related high-tech venture, rather than merely increasing the dividend pay-outs to shareholders. On the issue of democratic governance and control, however, we have not seen yet any alternative outcome in Korea.

6. Conclusion

This paper seeks to analyze the performance of the Korean government's public health measures in response to the COVID-19 epidemic through the lens of industrial policy framework. One cannot fully explain the relatively successful performance of non-pharmaceutical interventions adopted in response to the COVID-19 epidemic without understanding the Korean government's soft industrial policy programs to nurture and develop domestic strategic industry around information technology, bio and healthcare technology, and pharmaceutical industry, and its institutionalized public-private cooperation framework. For this hypothesis, this paper specifically examines the case of effective operation of the public–private partnership in developing and deploying diagnostic test kits, medical protective equipment, and antibody treatment, as well as ICT-based contact tracing and epidemiological investigation. Though some of these public health measures may not be necessarily reducible to the government's industrial policy category, the advanced technological nature of these policies is largely associated with and even indebted to the Korean government's sustained industrial policy and public investment for a long time. After demonstrating this point, the paper also discussed the way in which the Korean government's soft industrial policy is interrelated with other macroeconomic and monetary policies and suggested some ideas for bringing democratic control and governance issue to the fore in the industrial policy framework and how to socialize profit gains from successful business operations that are heavily indebted to public supports.

Notes

1. The tariff rebate on inputs used for exports, also known as 'duty drawback scheme' is the government's monetary compensation and incentive program given to private enterprises that manufacture internationally tradable outputs relying on inputs imported from abroad. Under this scheme, the government provides rebate for tariff cost added to the price of imported inputs to partially relieve the immediate financial burden associated with tariff-adjusted input price. This micro incentive policy can be made to help increase domestic firms' export target and international competitiveness. One useful study of this 'duty drawback scheme' used in South Korea and Taiwan, see Wade (1991).
2. This paper does not aim to revisit existing theoretical debates over market failure and the case for industrial policy. Interested readers on this issue can find useful references from Rodrik (2009), Wade (2012, 2015), Chang (1993, 2006), and Chang and Andreoni (2020). The paper focuses on how the existing industrial policy framework in Korea has helped formulate and implement highly successful mitigation strategies adopted by public health authority in this country.
3. The purpose and actual usage of publicly designated quarantine sites have changed as time goes by. At the beginning, the public health authority used these converted public buildings to help accommodate the urgent need of quarantining returning Korean nationals who either traveled or resided in Wuhan area in China, the epicenter of the novel coronavirus outbreak. However, beginning from late January of 2020, the Korean government gradually expanded its 'special entry screening' programs applied to all incoming travelers to mandatorily get the COVID-19 testing and quarantine for about 14 days in these designated sites. The selected quarantine sites were designated and directly managed by the Central Disease Control Headquarter at first, but later local government health agencies took the charge of flexible operation of these sites. For more detailed information about this special entry screening and quarantine measures, see KDCA (2020).

4. The immediate impetus for upgrading the existing National Infectious Disease Control and Prevention Act was the recognition of multi-governmental coordination failures in coping with the prior outbreaks of infectious diseases such as 2014's Ebola and the Middle East Respiratory Syndrome (MERS) in 2015. The Korea Centers for Disease Control and Prevention under the Ministry of Health and Welfare proposed the need of amending the existing law in 2016, and the amended act was passed in National Assembly in the same year. The amended law streamlined the intergovernmental coordination process and empowered the public health authority's access to personal data for identifying epidemiological links of the virus.
5. This is stark contrast to what happened in the US under the Trump Administration. Even after the administration grudgingly declared national emergency (in March 2020) after repeated underestimation and denials of the potential danger of the COVID-19 epidemic, US CDC and NIH (under severe budget constraint) and many private labs were not able to produce properly functioning COVID-19 test kits and frontline workers – medical doctors and nurses and many other 'essential workers' were not able to obtain basic personal protective equipment and specialty face mask for a long time. It was hardly believable and tragic to see so many dedicated doctors and nurses were forced to wear patchworked plastic trash bags before approaching COVID-19 patients in many American hospitals for so long. The National Defence Act that temporarily allows extraordinary presidential power to mobilize private sector resources in the face of emergency did not help turn the corner around because of long-lasting deindustrialization of domestic manufacturing base and difficulties in obtaining basic raw materials critical for producing these products.
6. We cannot fully trace the history and implications of the change in planning and implementation of industrial policy framework in Korea. But from a broad historical point of view, we can identify the following distinct periods, in which the existing industrial policy framework underwent substantial changes and modifications. An early attempt to restructure the key governmental agencies that played a dominant role in industrial planning and to abolish the government's practice for industrial policy was made in the early 1980s. This 'neoliberal rationalization and restructuring of industry' was largely driven by the negative consequences of excessive external debt accumulated in the aftermath of global oil shocks in the late 1970s. The persistent democratic social movements and the transition toward the civilian government in political sphere materialized in the late 1980s and early 1990s also involved a radical shift away from the existing hard industrial policy framework as well. The Kim Young-Sam Administration attempted to abolish the presidential Economic Planning Board and reshuffled the Ministry of Finance in 1994, while pursuing domestic financial market deregulation and external capital account liberalization policies in the name of coping with 'SEGEWHA' (meaning 'globalization' in Korean). It is well known that this pro-globalization policy stance ended up with the Asian financial crisis in 1997-98, which transformed the Korean industrial policy framework further. Even in these tumultuous changes in the relationship between the government and private business sector, the government's pursuit of soft industrial policies and budgetary practice has remained as one dominant feature of the contemporary Korean political economy. Interested readers can find more detailed references for this aspect from Chang (2006) and Lee and Rhyu (2019) among other.

Acknowledgements

The author is grateful to anonymous reviewers' and editors' comments and suggestions that helped substantially improve the manuscript. It is the author's sole responsibility, however, for the errors and/or mistakes remained in the article.

Disclosure statement

No potential conflict of interest was reported by the author(s).

ORCID

Hee-Young Shin http://orcid.org/0000-0002-3124-1195

References

Amsden, Alice H. 1992. *Asia's Next Giant: South Korea and Late Industrialization*. London and New York: Oxford University Press.

Amsden, Alice H. 2003a. *The Rise of "The Rest": Challenges to the West from Late-Industrializing Economies*. London and New York: Oxford University Press.

Amsden, Alice H. 2003b. *Beyond Late Development: Taiwan's Upgrading Policies*. Boston: MIT Press.

Chang, Ha-Joon. 1993. "The Political Economy of Industrial Policy in Korea." *Cambridge Journal of Economics* 17 (2): 131–157. doi:10.1093/oxfordjournals.cje.a035227.

Chang, Ha-Joon. 2003. "Kicking Away the Ladder: Infant Industry Promotion in Historical Perspective." *Oxford Development Studies* 31 (1): 21–32. doi:10.1080/1360081032000047168.

Chang, Ha-Joon. 2006. *The East Asian Development Experience: The Miracle, the Crisis, and the Future*. London: Zed Books.

Chang, Ha-Joon, and Antonio Andreoni. 2020. "Industrial Policy in the 21st Century." *Development and Change* 51 (2): 324–351. doi:10.1111/dech.12570.

Cooper, Ian, Argha Mondal, and Chris G. Antonopoulos. 2020. "A SIR Model Assumption for the Spread of COVID-19 in Different Communities." *Chaos, Solitons and Fractals*, no. Vol: 139. doi:10.1016/j.chaos.2020.110057.

Fisher, Max, and Sang-Hun Choe. 2020. "How South Korea Flattened the Curve." *The New York Times*, March 23.

Government of the Republic of Korea. 2020a. *Flattening the curve on COVID-19 - How Korea responded to a pandemic using ICT*, May 11.

Government of the Republic of Korea 2020b. *COVID-19, Testing Time for Resilience*, May 11.

Government of the Republic of Korea 2020c. *All About Korea's Response to COVID-19*, October 7.

Kang, JaHyun, YunYoung Jang, JinHwa Kim, S-H. Han, K R. Lee, M. Kim, J S. Eom et al. 2020. "South Korea's Responses to Stop the COVID-19 Pandemic." *American Journal of Infection Control* 48 (9): 1080–1086. DOI:10.1016/j.ajic.2020.06.003.

Kim, Sun, and Marcia C. Castro. 2020. "Spatiotemporal Pattern of COVID-19 and Government Response in South Korea (As of May 31, 2020)." *International Journal of Infectious Diseases* 98: 328–333. doi:10.1016/j.ijid.2020.07.004.

Korea Centers for Disease Control and Prevention. 2020. "Frequently Asked Questions." *KCDC Press Release*, April 24.

Korea Disease Control and Prevention Agency. 2020. "All about Korea's Response to COVID-19." *KDCA Press Release*, October.

Lee, Hye-Young, Min-Na. Oh, Yong-Shik Park, C. Chu, T-J. Son. 2013. "Public Health Crisis Preparedness and Response in Korea." *Osong Public Health and Research Perspectives* 4 (5): 278–284. doi:10.1016/j.phrp.2013.09.008.

Lee, Seungjoo, and Sany-young Rhyu, eds. 2019. *The Political Economy of Change and Continuity in Korea – Twenty Years after the Crisis*. Springer.

List, Friedrich. [1837] 1983. *The Natural System of Political Economy*. Translated and edited by Henderson, W.O. London: Frank Cass and Company.

List, Friedrich. [1841] 1885. *The National System of Political Economy*. Translated by Lloyd, Sampson S. London: Longmans, Green and Co.

Ministry of Economy and Finance. 2020. *Tackling COVID-19: Health, Quarantine and Economic Measures of South Korea*, March 23.

Ministry of Health and Welfare of Korea and World Health Organization. 2015. *Middle East Respiratory Syndrome*, Republic of Korea-World Health Organization Joint Mission Report. October 1.

Oh, Juhwan, Jong-Koo Lee, Dan Schwarz, H L. Ratcliffe, J F. Markuns, L R. Hirschhorn. 2020. "National Response to COVID-19 in the Republic of Korea and Lessons Learned for Other Countries." *Health Systems and Reform* 6 (1): e1753464. doi:10.1080/23288604.2020.1753464.

Parodi, Emilio, Stephen Jewkes, Sangmi Cha, and Ju-min Park. 2020. "Special Report: Italy and South Korea Virus Outbreaks Reveal Disparity in Deaths and Tactics." *Reuters*, March 12.

Rodrik, Dani. 2009. "Industrial Policy: Don't Ask Why, Ask How." *Middle East Development Journal* 1 (2009): 1–29.

Terhune, Chad, Dan Levine, Hyunjoo Jin, and Jane Lanhee Lee. 2020. "Special Report: How Korean Trounced U.S. In Race to Test People for Coronavirus." *Reuters*, March 18.

Wade, Robert H. 1990. *Governing the Market: Economic Theory and the Role of Government in East Asian Industrialization*. New Jersey: Princeton University Press.

Wade, Robert H. 1991. "How to Protect Exports from Protection: Taiwan's Duty Drawback Scheme." *The World Economy* 14 (3): 299–309. doi:10.1111/j.1467-9701.1991.tb00850.x.

Wade, Robert H. 2012. "Return of Industrial Policy?" *International Review of Applied Economics* 26 (2): 223–239. doi:10.1080/02692171.2011.640312.

Wade, Robert H. 2015. "The Role of Industrial Policy in Developing Countries." In Alfredo Calcagno, Sebastian Dullien, Alejandro Márquez-Velázquez, Nicolas Maystre, and Jan Priewe (Eds.), *Rethinking Development Strategies after the Financial Crisis - Vol. 1 Making the Case for Policy Space*:1–14. New York and Geneva: UNCTAD.

Wade, Robert H., and Frank Veneroso. 1998. "The Asian Crisis: The High-Debt Model versus the Wall Street-Treasury-IMF Complex." *New Left Review*. No. 228, Mar/Apr.

You, Jongeun. 2020. "Lessons from South Korea's Covid-19 Policy Response". *The American Review of Public Administration* 50 (6–7): 801–808. doi:10.1177/0275074020943708.

The impact of COVID-19 on the Indian economy

Deepak Kumar Behera, Maryam Sabreen and Deepika Sharma

ABSTRACT

This paper estimates the loss of output and employment for the Indian economy over the financial year 2020–21 as a result of the COVID-19 pandemic. Using a capacity utilization ratio method, we estimate that the countrywide lockdown disrupted both demand and supply, with a loss of GVA for 2020–21 of 1.7% under an optimistic approach, and a fall in employment of 0.34%, with a loss of 1.56 million jobs. The pessimistic approach suggests a fall in GVA of almost 10%, with employment falling by 7.6%, and around 35.4 million jobs lost in 2020–21. Future growth will depend on the duration of the containment measures, the exit strategy from the lockdown, and the success of the policy responses in restoring business and consumer confidence, by increasing aggregate demand through fiscal expansion to foster investment and employment.

1. Introduction

The outbreak of the coronavirus disease (COVID-19) first in China and its subsequent rapid spread to other countries led the World Health Organization (WHO) to declare it a public health emergency of international concern. To curb the spread of the virus, many countries imposed full or partial lockdowns, including the imposition of social distancing, self-isolation at home, closure of institutions and public facilities, restrictions on mobility, and so on. The lockdown measures adopted for its curtailment had serious economic implications, and the global economy will likely experience its worst recession since the Great Depression of the 1930s, with over 170 countries likely to experience negative per capita gross domestic product (GDP) growth.

India is currently the second worst-hit nation after the USA recorded the first case of the disease on 30 January 2020. Awareness of its detrimental consequences led the government to restrict the movement of the entire population of the country by declaring nationwide five consecutive lockdowns (starting from 24 March 2020), which resulted in a slump in overall economic activity. The unprecedented lockdown was expected to have a significant adverse effect on the economy due to the dual problem of a fall in demand and investment, cutting GDP growth (Dev and Sengupta 2020). With the Corona outbreak, supply chains were disrupted. Closing of units during lockdown and the inability of workers to reach work resulted in lost production and dissaving among businesses (Kumar 2020).

Prior to the occurrence of the COVID-19 pandemic, the Indian economy had experienced a significant slowdown over the previous few quarters (NSO, 2020a). This dampened employment growth, which is evident from the Annual Periodic Labour Force Survey (PLFS) Report published by the National Statistical Office (NSO).

To tackle COVID-19, Red, Orange, and Green zones were identified based on the severity of the outbreak in those areas. The Red and Orange zones were among the worst-hit areas, where economic activities came to a near standstill. In the Green Zone area, economic activities were allowed to remain functional with strict guidelines. Once the process of unlocking the economy began, many restrictions continued. The loss incurred by the lockdown was estimated at 26 billion U.S. dollars (Keeylery 2020); the top six industries that account for 60% of industrial output were largely in the red and orange zones. According to the Asian Development Bank (ADB), the Covid-19 outbreak could cost the Indian economy between 387 USD million and 29.9 USD billion in personal consumption losses. Different agencies provided different growth estimates for 2020–21. The International Monetary Fund (IMF) projected 1.9%. Fitch Solutions forecast real GDP to contract by 4.5%, while Moody's Investors Service forecast a 'zero' growth rate for India, whereas S&P Global Ratings forecast the Indian economy to shrink by 5%; CRICIL forecast economic growth of 1.8%; Goldman Sachs, Nomura, Fitch predict −5%, where CARE rating predicts −1.5 to −1.6%.

The Indian government introduced a special economic package under Atmanirbhar Bharat Abhiyan Scheme on 12 May 2020, consisting of a mix of reforms that include infrastructure building, support to stressed businesses, and a certain amount of direct cash support that accounts for the 10% of India's GDP to boost the economy.

The present paper estimates output at the aggregate as well as the sectoral level for the year 2020–21, as well as employment growth, using output data released by the NSO published on 29 May 2020. Section II explaining the theoretical framework. Section III deals with data sources and methodology. Section IV revisits the structural pattern of output and employment in the economy since 2011–12. Section V presents the estimation of output for 2020–21, with projections of employment discussed in Section VI. Section VII presents the major conclusions. Finally, limitations and areas for future research are discussed in Section VIII.

2. Theoretical perspective of output–employment relation

Keynes (1936) advocated fiscal stimulus in a recession to expand employment and output in the economy. The Harrod-Domar model implies that economic growth depends on policies to increase investment, by increasing savings and using that investment more efficiently through technological advances to achieve full employment. Development theories argued that employment determination implicitly or explicitly assumes a close positive relationship between output and employment that varies during the long-run and short-run (Wilson 1960). It is the structural aspects of the labour market (representing the supply side) which determine the rate of employment generation in the economy, rather than the demand-side factors. Even when growth performances have been satisfactory, an increase in capital-labour and capital-output ratios can accelerate income growth but not employment. With a constant capital–labour ratio, the growth in capital formation would augment employment growth at slower income-growth rates, but increasing capital-labour ratios would mean higher income growth at reduced employment growth. Given the conflict between income and employment growth, ironically, income growth is often favoured (Thirlwall 2005).

A Keynesian approach is more relevant when the economy is going through a recession. In a recession, people respond to the threat of unemployment by increasing savings and reducing their spending. This is a rational choice, but contributes to an even bigger decline in aggregate demand and output. Thus, government intervention may be needed. Keynes argued that in a recession, private sector savings rose sharply, leading to unused savings. Thus, government spending is merely making use of unemployed resources. Bond yields on government borrowing will not rise because the private sector wants to buy government bonds.

Wheelock (2020), in his US-based comparison of the current economic slowdown with the Great Depression of the 1930s, argues that the COVID-19 contraction was sharper but shorter. Quddus (2020) argues that the pandemic has defeated the best defences that science and public health could offer, and unlike during the 2008 Global financial crisis, monetary policy would not be effective in the current situation. Valla (2020) calls for a coordinated policy mix, stressing fiscal policy. For Woodford (2020) fiscal policy without monetary policy intervention can achieve the best results. Kaul (2020) too advocated the idea of Keynes according to which the government should become the spender of last resort to pull the economy out of the COVID-19 economic crisis. Azmi (2020) also calls for a Keynesian remedy to provide fiscal stimulus to neutralise the effects of the pandemic. Romana (2020) tried expanding Tobin's Keynesian models by analysing their local stability, and evolution in the present situation. By using Keynesian adjustments in the models, he concluded that the Covid-19 situation is a strong exogenous negative supply shock, reducing the potential production of goods and services leading to depression through the effect on aggregate demand in the medium/long term accompanied by rise in inflation, inflation expectations, and the real interest rate (Romana 2020). Thus, his policy prescriptions include expansionary fiscal and active monetary policies that would ease the economic impact of the pandemic (Romana 2020). Similarly, Guerrieri et al. (2020) proposed that the first best policy is to shut down contact-intensive sectors and provide insurance payments to affected workers followed by a policy measure where standard fiscal stimulus is less effective, while an expansionary monetary policy unimpeded by the zero-lower bound, is expected to have amplified effects. Gopinath (2020) study suggested that broader monetary stimuli such as policy rate cuts or asset purchases can lift confidence and support financial markets if there is a marked risk of a sizable tightening in financial conditions (with actions by large central banks also generating favourable spill-overs for vulnerable countries).

3. Data source and methodology

To estimate the above objectives, the present study uses data covering the period 2011–12 to 2019–20, from two data sources. First, annual and quarterly Gross Value Added (GVA) and its sectoral components at 2011–12 constant prices are from National Account Statistics (NAS) and employment data under the usual principal and subsidiary status approach emanating from the National Sample Survey Office (NSSO). The employment data i.e. Key indicators of Employment and Unemployment in India

2011–12 and Annual PLFS Report 2017–18 are considered for the analysis. Sectoral components under per National Industrial Classification (NIC) 2018 are categorised into nine broad industries: Agriculture and allied activities (A&A); Mining (MIN); Manufacturing (MNF); Electricity, Gas, and Water (EGW); Construction (CON); Trade, Hotel, and Restaurant (THR); Transport, Storage, and Communication (TSC); Finance, Insurance, Real Estate, and Business (FIRB); Community, Social, and Personal & other services (CSP).

The methodology entails the use of compound annual growth rate (CAGR) to show the temporal and spatial trends. To estimate output growth for 2020–21, two broad scenarios were considered (Table 1). Scenario-1 is an optimistic approach to estimate the output for 2020–21 by adopting the GDP capacity utilization ratio i.e. the ratio of the actual output to the potential output. It assumes that even if the COVID-19 pandemic disrupts the economy very badly, this is offset by the mix of reforms, infrastructure building, support to stressed businesses, and a certain amount of direct cash support that are initiated by the government to boost the economy positively. To calculate the capacity utilization ratio, output under advance estimates (potential output), and provisional estimates (actual output) data for 2019–20 are used. The ratios are then used to perform an interpolation to construct the output data for 2020–21.

Scenario-2 is the pessimistic approach. To estimate annual output data, quarterly data for 2018–19 (assuming no growth, the nation can produce at least the same level of output that was produced) and 2019–20 (as actual output produced) are used to calculate the capacity utilization ratio and adjusted accordingly. The adjustment is done based on the assumption that due to lockdown in the first quarter, the output of one and half quarters is wiped out baring a few sectors. In the second quarter, even though the lockdown would not be there, many sectors would be facing the demand constraints, supply chain disruption, and input supply problem (Das and Mishra 2020). There is an expectation that all sectors may achieve normally in the third and the fourth quarter. After computing each quarter for every sector, it adds across sectors to find the total estimated output.

For employment projection, employment elasticity for 2017–18 is multiplied with GDP growth for 2019–20 to construct the employment figure for 2019–20. Then, employment growth for 2020–21 is estimated separately for Scenario 1 & 2 by multiplying the GDP growth for 2020–21 with the elasticity capacity utilization ratio (actual elasticity over potential elasticity).

4. Structural pattern of output and employment in India since 2011-12

Achieving the twin targets of sustained and rapid economic growth with a high rate of employment has been the prime objective of the Indian development agenda since the beginning of the post-independence era. The last decade and a half showed that employment opportunities created were inadequate despite rapid growth. The general perception in the country is that although GDP growth has accelerated, it has not been accompanied by a commensurate increase in employment leading to a worsening in the employment situation in the post-reform periods (Rao 1979; Bhattacharya and Mitra 1997; Kaur and Dhindsa 2002; Gandhi and Ganesan 2002; Bhattacharya and Sakthivel 2004; Papola 2005; Unni and Raveendran 2007; Dev 2008;; Bhaduri 2008; Papola and

Table 1. Formula for estimating output and employment under scenario 1 & 2.

Estimation	Scenarior-1 (Optimistic Approach)	Scenarior-2 (Pessimistic Approach)
Output (Y_t)	$Yt = \sum^{(YxCUR)_{t-1,i}}$ $CUR_{t-1} = \left(\frac{ActualY}{PotentialY}\right)_{t-1}$ $Y_t{}^g = \left(\left\{Exp*\left[\frac{L_nY_{t-L_n}Y_{t-1}}{T}\right]\right\} - 1\right)x100$ where CUR: capacity utilization ratio, Y^g: Estimated output growth, Exp: exponential, t^{th} year, i^{th} sector, T: total time period	$Yi = \sum_{K=4}^{1} Q(YxCUR)_{t-1,i}$ $CUR_{t-1} = \left(\frac{Q^{ActualY_{t-1}}}{Q^{PotenialY_{t-2}}}\right)$ $Y_t{}^g = \left(\left\{Exp*\left[\frac{L_nY_{t-L_n}Y_{t-1}}{T}\right]\right\} - 1\right)x100$ Where CUR: capacity utilization ratio Q is quarterly, Y^g: Estimated output growth, Exp: exponential k = 1 to 4, t^{th} year, i^{th} sector, T: total time period
Employment (E_t)	$Et = Et - 1*[1 + \left(\frac{E_t{}^g}{100}\right)^T]$ $E_t{}^g = \sum^{(} Y_t{}^g xe^{CUR})ij$ $e^{CUR=\left(\frac{e^{Actual}}{e^{Potential}}\right)}$ $e^{Actual} = \left(\frac{E^g}{Y^g}\right)_{T-1}$ $e^{Potential} = \left(\frac{E^g}{Y^g}\right)_{T-2}$ Where E^g is estimated employment growth, e is employment elasticity, T: total time period	$Et = Et - 1*[1 + \left(\frac{E_t{}^g}{100}\right)^T]$ $E_t{}^g = \sum^{(} Y_t{}^g xe^{CUR})ij$ $e^{CUR} = \left(\frac{e^{Actual}}{e^{Potential}}\right)$ $e^{Actual} = \left(\frac{E^g}{Y^g}\right)_{T-1}$ $e^{Potential} = \left(\frac{E^g}{Y^g}\right)_{T-2}$ Where E^g is estimated employment growth, e is employment elasticity, T: total time period

Source: Author's interpretation

Sahu 2012; Mehrotra and Parida 2019). This jobless growth can be attributed to the fact that high growth rates have not been preceded by the remarkable growth of the manufacturing sector that depends on highly capital-intensive techniques in productions, which is one of the peculiar features of the transition in the Indian economy for which it can be considered as a perverse trend when no notable transformation in the occupational structure of the economy accompanies the relative growth of sub-sector (Behera 2015).

The structure of the economy can be better understood through the sectoral distribution of GDP and employment. Table 2 suggests that the share of agriculture in GDP in India has declined from around 19% in 2011–12% to 15% in 2017–18% and 14.6% in 2019–20, while that of the industry declined from 32.5% to 31.4% and 30.2% during the corresponding period, while that of services increased from around 49% to 53.4% and 55.2%. Among the sub-sectors in industry, manufacturing, the only sector in the industry, has registered an increase of 0.75% in 2017–18 as compared to 2011–12 but fell by 0.72% during 2019–20 due to a fall in output of six core industries. For services, all sub-sectors have shown an increasing share with finance, insurance, and the real estate business sector the highest.

Looking at the growth pattern in the economy, India registered an average of 6.86% output growth during 2011–12 to 2017–18 but 4.96% in 2019–20 over 2017–18. Though all the broad sectors registered declining growth, the highest growth was seen in the services sector. Sectoral growth indicated from here that the agriculture sector registered lesser growth i.e. 3.22% compared to services but performed better than industry. Among the sub-sectors of the industrial sector, except construction, all other sectors showed declining growth, with mining registering negative growth during 2019–20. The massive fall in growth for manufacturing caused the overall growth of the industrial sector to decline. The turnaround in the service sector, which has acted as an engine of growth in India's development process, has been reflected in many of its leading indicators, that is, finance, insurance, real estate, and business sector followed by trade and transport sectors

Table 2. Percentage share and growth rate of GDP and employment during 2011–12 to 2017–18.

	GDP					Employment		
	Percentage Share			Growth Rate		Percentage Share		
Sector	2011–12	2017–18	2019–20	2011–17	2017–19	2011–12	2017–18	Growth Rate
A&A	*18.53*	*15.14*	*14.65*	*3.33*	*3.22*	*47.51*	*44.14*	*−1.49*
Industry	*32.50*	*31.42*	*301.19*	*6.26*	*2.88*	*24.61*	*24.82*	*−0.14*
MIN	3.22	3.04	2.67	5.82	−1.49	0.55	0.41	−5.04
MNF	17.39	18.14	17.42	7.62	2.85	12.96	12.15	−1.34
EGW	2.30	2.27	2.32	6.61	6.15	0.54	0.59	1.21
CON	9.59	7.97	7.77	3.62	3.64	10.56	11.67	1.40
Services	*48.97*	*53.44*	*55.17*	*8.43*	*6.64*	*27.89*	*31.04*	*1.52*
THR+ TSC	17.43	19.13	19.38	8.53	5.64	16.36	17.88	1.21
FIRB	18.88	21.61	21.92	9.29	5.71	1.17	1.26	0.96
CSP	12.66	12.70	13.87	6.93	9.66	10.36	11.90	2.05
Total	*100.00*	*100.00*	*100.00*	*6.86*	*4.96*	*100.00*	*100.00*	−0.28

Note: A&A: Agriculture and allied activities; MIN: Mining; MNF: Manufacturing; EGW: Electricity, Gas and Water; CON: Construction; THR+TSC: Trade, Hotel and Restaurant, Transport storage and Communication; FIRB: Finance, Insurance, Real Estate and Business; CSP: Community, Social and Personal & other services.

Source: Author's estimation, NSSO (2013, 2019)

during 2011–17 but the trend changed during 2017–20 where community, social, personal, and other services showed increasing growth.

An analysis of the structure of employment by industrial activities shows that a majority of the workforce is engaged in the agricultural sector despite a continuously declining share. However, the ground lost by the agricultural share of employment has been largely gained by the services sector without much addition to the industrial sector, which is said to have missed the transformation trajectory. Data reveal that the share of agricultural employment has declined from 47.51% to 44.14%. The industrial and services sector has been showing an increasing share from 24.61% to 27.89% to 24.82% and 31.04%, respectively, over the period under study. Within the industrial sector, the manufacturing sector showed a declining rate in 2017–18, but the construction sector benefited from the Mahatma Gandhi National Rural Employment Guarantee Act (MGNREGA), which mainly involves construction work. Within the services sector, all the sub-sectors registered an increasing share of employment in 2017–18 as compared to 2011–12. The trade and transport sector absorbed a majority of the workforces followed by the community and social services. These trends indicate that though the industrial sector should be the engine of the modern developmental process, countries that have been late entrants into the development process like India seem to have missed this transformation trajectory because of the need to absorb highly capital-intensive technology. Therefore, industry, particularly the manufacturing sector, has shown a significant increase in terms of income but not in terms of employment. The services sector consequently became a default sector in absorbing surplus labour.

In terms of employment growth, the Indian economy registered a negative growth rate of employment of −0.28% per annum during the period 2011–12 to 2017–18 despite a higher output growth in the Indian economy during the same year. As a result, there occurred a massive fall in employment by an absolute number of around 7 million jobs over the period under study. Sectoral employment growth suggested that barring the service sector, the other two sectors have been recording negative growth trends, with employment growth becoming a natural casualty of this decline in growth. Regarding the industrial sector, the construction sector has shown higher employment growth followed by electricity, gas, and water, while the manufacturing sector registered negative rates of growth despite high employment share in the sector. Within the services sector, the highest employment growth has been recorded in community, social, personal, and other services, followed by trade and transport services. Finance, insurance, real estate, and business sectors show the highest output growth among services, but this is not commensurate with employment growth. It has also been observed that the small contributions made by the commodity-producing sectors to an increase in employment have been disappearing lately, making the system more dependent on construction and services. Service sector despite a high output growth has not had commensurate employment growth due to firstly, high productivity services contributing so little to employment that even significant low wage employment in traditional services that contribute little to GDP could not restore a semblance of proportionality between employment and output growth; secondly, sectors that have a large potential to generate employment are growing slowly. Thirdly, the fast-growing services sector also witnesses high productivity growth as a result, the employment potential is lower in these sectors. Fourth, a slower rise in employment in the sector has concentrated in those services where labour productivity has risen or is skilled labour-intensive. Technological improvements and efficiency gains have further reinforced this trend. If a high-growth sector does not contribute to absorbing a large number of workers, the welfare implication of the growth trajectory is bound to be adverse.

The above explanation brings to the forefront that employment growth has not matched the GDP growth rate in the case of India. Moreover, before moving to the next section, which analyses the future employment growth, it is important to analyze the elasticity of employment, which is a standard measure for undertaking economic analysis presenting the rate of employment creation from the growth of output. In other words, employment elasticities provide a numerical measure of how employment growth varies with output growth. Employment elasticity figures for the total economy and broad sectors are presented in Figure 1. Overall employment elasticity for the economy during 2011–12 to 2017–18 has been negative (−0.041). This implies that there is a clear trend towards the declining labour absorptive capacity of growth in the economy. At the sectoral level, the construction sector displays the highest employment elasticity followed by the community, social, personal, and other services. The employment elasticity of output in agriculture, wherein the largest share of workers are concentrated, has been showing a negative trend followed by the manufacturing and mining sector. The negative elasticity of agriculture suggests that this sector may fail to create enough jobs for the rapidly growing rural labour force. With a view to adopting structural adjustments proposed under the New Economic Policy (NEP), many firms in the public sector have recently tried to reduce their employment in the industry sector. Hence, this negative employment elasticity reflects the fact that there has been a considerable decline in overall elasticity during this period.

To achieve high employment growth, it is thus necessary that GDP must grow at a higher pace to take care of the current employment challenge of absorbing the backlog and to those who are new entrants in labour force. Since fast growth in GDP is desired, it is essential that aggregate employment intensity is increased by focusing on those sectors where long-term employment elasticity is high. Hence, the next section will estimate the

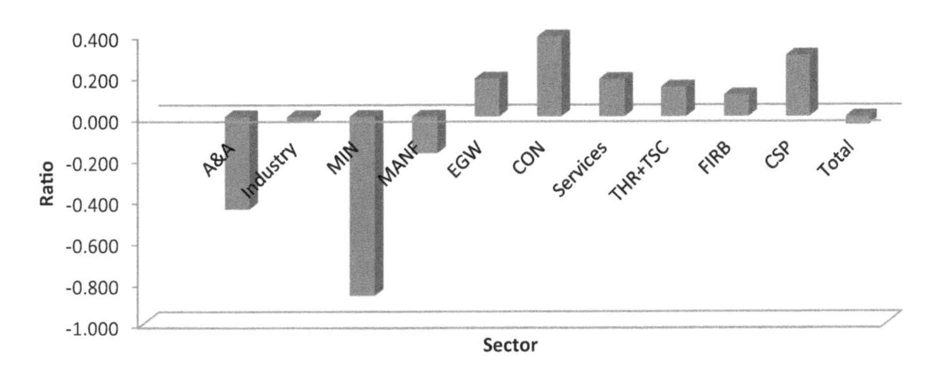

Figure 1. Sectoral employment elasticity. **Note**: Agriculture and allied activities (A&A); Mining (MIN); Manufacturing (MNF); Electricity, Gas and Water (EGW); Construction (CON); Trade, Hotel and Restaurant (THR); Transport, Storage and Communication (TSC); Finance, Insurance, Real Estate and Business (FIRB); Community, Social, and Personal & other services (CSP).

output growth for 2020–21, by keeping in mind the current pandemic situation in the country, to project the future employment growth in the economy.

5. Estimating output for 2020–21

The COVID-19 pandemic in India led to unprecedented closure of normal activities. It is expected the pandemic would have a severe adverse effect on the Indian economy in 2020–21. Keeping in mind the pre-pandemic economic status of the country and the impact of COVID-19 on the economy, output growth for 2020–21 has been estimated under two scenarios (Scenario1: Optimistic Approach; Scenario 2: Pessimistic Approach). This exercise has been undertaken both at aggregate as well as sectoral level. It is obvious that the following estimation is an approximate one but gives an idea considering the most recent structure of the economy.

Table 3 represents the estimation of output for 2020–21 under Scenario 1. According to the estimation, output will have a negative growth of 1.72% with the loss of Rs.228,399 in 2020–21 as compared to 2019–20. This estimation is made with the assumption that a major stimulated package declared by the government may control the growth. Except for agriculture and electricity, all other broad sectors are showing negative growth. The highest decline is estimated in the mining sector (−5.43%) followed by construction (−4.96%) and manufacturing (−2.40%).

Table 4 represents scenario 2 which shows the country's output will register growth of −9.65%. This estimation is made by keeping in mind that due to lockdown, many sectors during the first and second quarters would be facing demand constraints, supply chain disruption, and input supply problem which will negatively affect production in almost all industries. Sectors like the trade, transport and manufacturing sectors would register the highest negative growth as compared to other sectors that will lead to an aggregate loss of Rs. 1,283,503 in 2020–21 as compared to 2019–20. Community, social and personal services have shown to be the most promising sector during the pandemic.

6. Projection of employment for 2019–20 and 2020–21

Table 5 reveals that estimated employment decreased at a rate of −0.02% between 2017 and 18 to 2019–20 with a loss of two million jobs. The possible decrease in employment is due to low output growth. The year 2019–20 showed that most of the core industry

Table 3. Estimating GDP for 2020–21 under scenario-1.

	2019–20			Estimated GDP		
Sector	Potential	Actual	CUR	2020–21 (Rs. Crore	Gain/Loss (Rs. Crore)	Growth Rate
A&A	1,907,605	1,948,110	1.021	1989475	41365	2.12
MIN	376,119	355,680	0.946	336352	−19328	−5.43
MNF	2,374,176	2,317,280	0.976	2261747	−55533	−2.40
EGW	301,966	308,833	1.023	315856	7023	2.27
CON	1,087,210	1,033,277	0.950	982019	−51258	−4.96
THR+ TSC	2,616,095	2,577,944	0.985	2540349	−37595	−1.46
FIRB	3,027,407	2,915,680	0.963	2808076	−107604	−3.69
CSP	1,849,803	1,844,316	0.997	1838845	−5471	−0.30
Total	13,540,381	13,301,120		13072721	−228399	**−1.72**

Note: CUR: Capacity Utilization Ratio
Source: Author's estimation, NSO (2020a)

Table 4. Estimating GDP for 2020–21 under scenario-2.

	CUR				Adjusted CUR				Estimated GDP		
Sector	Q1	Q2	Q3	Q4	Q1*	Q2**	Q3	Q4	2020–21 (Rs. Crore)	Gain/Loss (Rs. Crore)	Growth Rate
A&A	1.030	1.035	1.036	1.059	1.034	1.035	1.036	1.059	2028959	80849	4.15
MIN	1.047	0.989	1.022	1.052	0.767	0.710	1.022	1.052	321545	−34135	−9.60
MNF	1.030	0.994	0.992	0.986	0.607	0.571	0.992	0.986	1829568	−487712	−21.05
EGW	1.088	1.039	0.993	1.045	0.930	0.880	0.993	1.045	296353	−12480	−4.04
CON	1.052	1.026	1.000	0.978	0.497	0.472	1.000	0.978	766265	−267012	−25.84
THR+ TSC	1.035	1.041	1.043	1.026	0.530	0.536	1.043	1.026	2043193	−534751	−20.74
FIRB	1.060	1.060	1.033	1.024	0.947	0.946	1.033	1.024	2862103	−53577	−1.84
CSP	1.077	1.109	1.109	1.101	0.897	0.930	1.109	1.101	1869630	25314	1.37
Total									**12017617**	**−1283503**	**−9.65**

Note: * is estimated by taking the latest data of Gross Domestic Product for the First Quarter (Q1) of 2020–21
** adjusted by considering the same ratio used in Q1
Source: Author's estimation, NSO (2020a, 2020b)

Table 5. Projecting employment for 2019–20.

Sector	Employment (in Million) 2017–18	Employment Elasticity	Estimated Employment (in Million) 2019–20	Gain/Loss	Growth Rate
A&A	205.30	−0.448	199.40	−5.89	−1.45
MIN	1.91	−0.866	1.95	0.04	1.13
MNF	56.51	−0.176	55.93	−0.58	−0.51
EGW	2.74	0.182	2.81	0.06	1.12
CON	54.28	0.387	55.82	1.54	1.41
THR+ TSC	83.16	0.142	84.50	1.34	0.80
FIRB	5.86	0.104	5.93	0.07	0.59
CSP	55.35	0.296	58.56	3.21	2.86
Total	465.10	−0.041	**464.90**	−0.20	**−0.02**

Source: Author's estimation

output fell resulting in high unemployment. Among the sectoral growth, except agriculture and manufacturing, others have registered a positive growth wherein the community, social, personal, and other services grew with the highest rate i.e. 2.86% in 2019–20. The construction sector recorded 1.41% growth adding 1.54 million jobs during 2017–20. The agriculture-sector employment continues to decline at the rate of 1.45% still employing 42.9% of the total workforce.

With the outbreak of COVID-19, millions of job losses are expected. This shows in our estimation presented in Table 6 projecting employment for 2020–21 under scenario 1. By considering output estimation for 2020–21 under an optimistic approach, it is found that with the negative output growth, employment will grow at a rate of −0.34% losing 1.56 million jobs during 2019–20 to 2020–21. With the reverse migration, the agricultural sector sees some hope for absorbing surplus labour in 2020–21, which is also reflected in terms of its output. The electricity, gas, and water sector has also seen a positive growth of employment, but the share is minimal to the total. However, construction saw a sharp decline in employment growth as most of the construction activities were halted during the first quarter and will remain affected throughout the year. Business activities too registered negative growth, losing 2.2 million jobs. Supply shocks and demand constraints adversely affected the manufacturing sectors. The silver lining is that the loss of

Table 6. Projecting employment for 2020–21 under scenario-1.

Sector	Elasticity CUR	GDP Growth 2020–21 2.12	Estimated Employment 2020–21 Growth Rate	Employment (in Million)	Gain/Loss (in Million) over 2019–20
A&A	1.002	−5.43	2.13	203.64	4.24
MIN	0.872	−2.40	−4.74	1.86	−0.09
MNF	1.025	2.27	−2.46	54.56	−1.37
EGW	1.065	−4.96	2.42	2.88	0.07
CON	1.003	−1.46	−4.98	53.04	−2.78
THR+ TSC	1.002	−3.69	−1.46	83.26	−1.24
FIRB	1.002	−0.30	−3.70	5.71	−0.22
CSP	1.000		−0.30	58.39	−0.17
Total			−0.34	**463.34**	**−1.56**

Source: Author's estimation

employment is expected to be low due to the major stimulus package to boost investment.

The worst employment loss due to COVID-19 is presented in Table 7 with the assumption that with demand reduction, there will also be widespread supply chain disruptions. There are many who stayed at home, some who cannot undertake work from home, and many have returned from their workplace due to no work. With almost no economic activity during the first quarter of 2020–21 and expected to further halt the production for a couple of months, it is estimated to have large-scale job losses. It is expected that with −9.65% growth of output, employment will register negative growth of 7.62% during 2019–20 to 2020–21 with a loss of 35.4 million jobs. The most affected sectors are to be trade and transport, construction, and manufacturing. It is the agricultural sector which is expected to absorb most of the migrant labour with 8.28 million workers with a growth rate of 4.16%. Community, social and personal services too expect to accommodate an additional eight million workers with a growth rate of 1.37%. It is assumed that mining and most of the sectors that were exempted from the lockdown, can at most work with 50% capacity under the imposition of the physical distancing guideline. However, these sectors do not see any growth of output, which would adversely affect the employment growth in the economy. Joblessness among the contractual and daily wageworkers would be the highest and this section of people would be the worst affected workforce group for 2020–21. Even though a strong association between GDP

Table 7. Projecting employment for 2020–21 under scenario-2.

Sector	Elasticity CUR	GDP Growth 2020–21	Estimated Employment 2020–21 Growth Rate	Employment (in Million)	Gain/Loss (in Million) over 2019–20
A&A	1.002	4.15	4.16	207.689	8.289
MIN	0.872	−9.60	−8.37	1.787	−0.163
MNF	1.025	−21.05	−21.56	43.869	−12.061
EGW	1.065	−4.04	−4.30	2.689	−0.121
CON	1.003	−25.84	−25.93	41.348	−14.472
THR+ TSC	1.002	−20.74	−20.79	66.932	−17.568
FIRB	1.002	−1.84	−1.84	5.821	−0.109
CSP	1.000	1.37	1.37	59.364	0.804
Total		−9.65	−7.62	**429.498**	**−35.402**

Note: CUR: Capacity Utilization Ratio
Source: Author's estimation

per capita and the percentage of jobs that can be performed at home has been advocated, the percentages of jobs that can be performed at home is low (Saltiel 2020; Dingel and Neiman 2020); the larger share of agriculture and self-employment in the economy, the lower the ability to work from home (Gottlieb, Grobovšek, and Poschke 2020). The trends in output amd employment growth under scenario 1 and 2 are presented in the figure 2 and 3 respectively.

7. Conclusion

The COVID-19 pandemic completely changed India's economic growth scenario for the year 2020–21. This pandemic induced crisis came at a time when India's GDP growth had been experiencing a significant slowdown, with unemployment rising. In this connection, it is expected that due to lockdown's nationwide closures of business activities and social distancing effects, the growth of GVA during 2020–21 is estimated to be −1.72% under scenario 1 and under scenario 2 – 9.65%. With the negative output growth, employment will register negative growth of 0.34% losing 1.56 million jobs during 2019–20 to 2020–21 under scenario 1 and −7.62% during 2019–20 to 2020–21 with 35.4 million jobs under scenario 2.

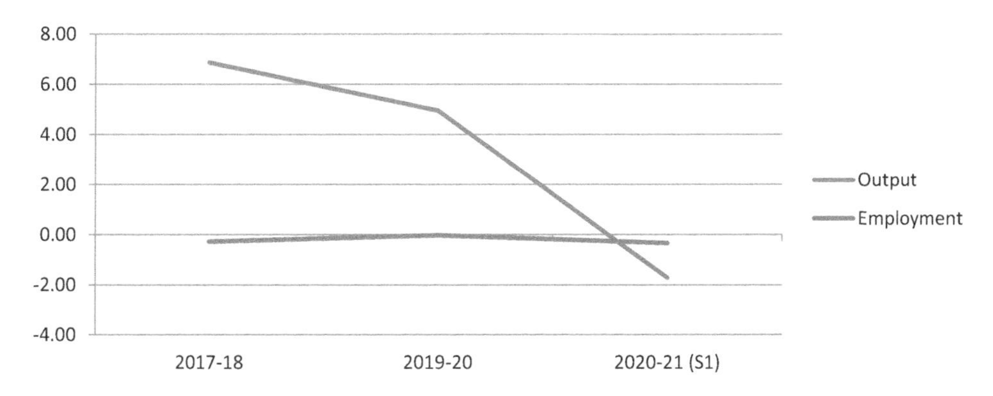

Figure 2. Output and employment growth from 2011–12 to 2020–21 under scenario 1.

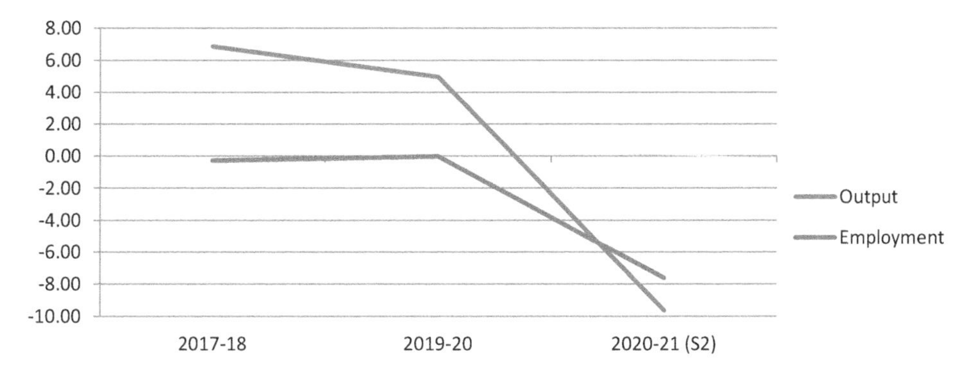

Figure 3. Output and employment growth from 2011–12 to 2020–21 under scenario 2.

Though various economic packages were introduced, these were limited to a particular level of public spending that did little to prevent economic decline. Excess stress on liquidity and supply-side distress management is ineffective without the revival of demand (Ghosh 2020). Substantial fiscal stimulus was needed (Subramanian 2020).

It is important to ponder on the possibility of whether India can afford the necessary stimulus package to overcome the adverse economic, social, and health impact of the pandemic. As far as food security measures are concerned, India has enough food grain stocks in the Food Corporation of India (FCI). Even if the Universal Public Distribution System (PDS) is adopted under which 80% of the population is covered, each person can get 10 kg of food grain for 6 months (Sinha, 2020). The only shortcoming is the inability on the part of the government to reach out to the needy due to bureaucratic and other challenges.

An alternative way of financing the fiscal stimulus is by letting the Reserve Bank of India directly buy government bonds offering money to the government account, and then write it off. Using foreign exchange reserve to finance the relief packages with the option of implementing a regime of Pigouvian taxes in the event of sudden and large capital flows (Singh 2020). Furthermore, wealth taxation or a uniform marginal tax rate of 4% on the wealth of the Rich List would earn a revenue equivalent to 1% of India's GDP. Similarly, another source of funding for government expenditure can be through donations based on philanthropic impulse for which. The Prime Minister's National Relief Fund (PMNRF) and newly established PM-CARES are two parallel funds. Thus, instead of focusing on whether India can afford a huge amount of fiscal expenditure as that is the only way to deal with the loss, the focus should be to find ways to finance the deficit that is expected to occur.

Apart from generating finance from within the economy, the government can resort to external borrowing to raise money externally, as the dollar is overvalued and expected to depreciate as the panic subsides and the earlier flight to safety is reversed. Tapping an IMF line of credit would both yield funds and reassure investors of bond issuance by India. In the budget of 2019–2020, the Finance Minister announced that a part of the gross borrowing program would be through external markets in foreign currencies by issuing overseas sovereign bonds. Interestingly, the share of external financing has jumped to 4.5% in Q1 of the financial year 2021 from 1.6% in the same quarter last year. The global market is likely to play an important source of demand for sovereign debt amid a supply glut as India plans to sell a record 12 trillion rupees of bonds this fiscal year.

The question is whether there exists the political will to implement the recovery measures. The COVID-19 pandemic is an unprecedented crisis that has exposed the lack of health infrastructure. The economic health too is affected, and we are in a situation of demand constraint and the global economic slowdown that resembles the great depression of 1929. This brings to the forefront the application of Keynesian policies in dealing with the current slump. Keynes advocated government intervention to regain prosperity and end economic depression, even at the cost of large fiscal deficits. India needs huge fiscal expenditure to help curb unemployment, which causes poverty. The need of the hour is to generate employment by investing in the creation of massive infrastructure projects that include schools, colleges, hospitals, highways, dams, steel plants, and so on. The Indian government's Atmanirbhar Bharat Yojna that offers financial stimulus packages to provide relief to the agricultural sector, MSME's, street vendors, non-bank financial companies, and real estate sector are very much in line with Keynesian economics, as the government has intended to spend more, create more agro-infrastructure, and put more money in the hands of the people, thus encouraging demand.

8. Limitations and areas for future research

Firstly, the current study is restricted to broad sectors and could be conducted at the disaggregated level. Micro-level analysis of sector-specific data could be used to estimate the output and employment loss due to the COVID-19 pandemic. Furthermore, the exact magnitude of the loss can be quantified after the post-COVID period. Secondly, it might be noted that economic growth is the outcome of a complex set of interactions of supply and demand factors. This exercise does not consider possible supply constraints in the post-pandemic scenario. Hence, future studies can carry out an in-depth analysis of labour supply shocks due to employment status, industry level, and occupation. Third, the results presented in this study are scenario analyses and based on the model that incorporates the decline in demand due to reduced production and income but does not fully capture the independent contraction in demand. It also does not include a decline in investor confidence and any financial repercussions. Finally, it is difficult to estimate the impact of social distancing and the overall decline of economic activity, but a detailed individual sectoral analysis might give a clearer picture.

Disclosure statement

No potential conflict of interest was reported by the author(s).

ORCID

Deepak Kumar Behera http://orcid.org/0000-0002-7972-9448
Maryam Sabreen http://orcid.org/0000-0002-3475-1692
Deepika Sharma http://orcid.org/0000-0001-8959-4340

References

Azmi, Feza T. 2020. "The Tumult of Recession: Of K-shaped Recover and Keynes". Forbes India. December 23. https://www.forbesindia.com/blog/economy-policy/the-turmult-of-recession-of-k-shaped-recovery-and-keynes/

Behera, D.K. 2015. "Occupational Transformation in India: Issues and Challenges." *Journal of Social, Political and Economic Studies* 40 (4): 413–445.

Bhaduri, Amit. January 2008. "Growth and Employment in the Era of Globalisation: Some Lessons from the Indian Experience." *ILO Asia-Pacific working Paper*, New Delhi.

Bhattacharya, B. B., and S. Sakthivel. 2004. "Economic Reforms and Jobless Growth in India in the 1990s." *Working Paper Series No.E/245/2004*, New Delhi: Institute of Economic Growth.

Bhattacharya, B.B, and Arup Mitra. 1997. "Changing Composition of Employment in Tertiary Sector: A Cross-Country Analysis." *Economic and Political Weekly* 32 (11): 529–534.

Das, Amarendra, and Subhankar Mishra. 2020. "India Growth Forecast for 2020–21." May 14. https://arxiv.org/pdf/2005.06461.pdf

Dev, S. Mahendra. 2008. "Employment: Trends, Issues and Policies." In *Inclusive Growth: Agriculture, Poverty and Human Development.* edited by. New Delhi: Oxford University Press.

Dev, S.M, and Rajeswari Sengupta. 2020. "Covid-19: Impact on Indian Economy." *Working Paper No.2020–013*, Mumbai: Indira Gandhi Institute of Development Research, April. http://www.igidr.ac.in/pdf/publication/WP-2020-013.pdf

Dingel, J. I, and B. Neiman. April 2020."How Many Jobs Can Be Done at Home?" *NBER Working Paper No. 26948*, Cambridge: Massachusetts. https://www.nber.org/papers/w26948

Gandhi, Jagadish, and P. Ganesan. 2002. "Service Sector and Employment Generation: Is It Real?" In *Economic Liberalisation and Its Implications for Employment*, edited by A Mathur and P S. Raikhy. 263–271. New Delhi: Deep and Deep Publication.

Ghosh, Jayati. 2020. "A Critique of the Indian Government's Response to the COVID-19 Pandemic." *Journal of Industrial and Business Economics* 47 (3): 519–530. doi:10.1007/s40812-020-00170-x.

Gopinath, Gita. 2020. "Limiting the Economic Fallout of the Coronavirus with Large Targeted Policies." *IMF blog*, March 9. https://blogs.imf.org/2020/03/09/limiting-the-economic-fallout-of-the-coronavirus-with-large-targeted-policies/

Gottlieb, C., J. Grobovšek, and M. Poschke. 2020. "Working from Home across Countries (No. 07-2020).Center for Interuniversity Research in Quantitative Economics." April 15 http://www.cireqmontreal.com/wp-content/uploads/cahiers/07-2020-cah.pdf

Guerrieri, Veronica, Guido Lorenzoni, Ludwig Straub, and Iván Werning. 2020. "Macroeconomic Implications Of Covid-19: Can Negative Supply Shocks Cause Demand Shortages?" *Working Paper 26918*, National Bureau Of Economic Research. http://www.nber.org/papers/w26918

Kaul, Vivek. 2020. "Keynes Can Rescue Modi Govt from COVID Economic Crisis but It First Needs Fund." The Print. June 15. https://theprint.in/opinion/keynes-can-rescue-modi-govt-from-covid-economic-crisis-but-it-first-needs-funds/441230/

Kaur, Kuldeep, and Paramjeet Dhindsa. 2002. "Growth of Tertiary Sector Employment in India." In *Economic Liberalization and Its Implications for Employment*, edited by A Mathur and P S. Raikhy. 272–284. New Delhi: Deep and Deep.

Keeylery, Sandhya. 2020. "Estimated Economic Impact from COVID-19 on India's GVA April-June 2020 by Sector." https://www.statista.com/statistics/1107798/india-estimated-economic-impact-of-coronavirus-by-sector/

Keynes, J.M. 1936. *The General Theory of Employment, Interest and Money*. London: Macmillan.

Kumar, Arun. 2020. "COVID-19 Crisis: Understanding the State of Economy during and after the Lockdown." *Economic and Political Weekly* 55 (19). May 9. https://www.epw.in/node/156901/pdf.

Mehrotra, Santosh, and J.K. Parida. 2019. "India's Employment Crisis: Rising Education Levels and Falling Non-agricultural Job Growth." *CSE Working Paper 2019-04*, AzimPremji University. https://cse.azimpremjiuniversity.edu.in/wpcontent/uploads/2019/10/Mehrotra_Parida_India_Employment_Crisis.pdf

National Sample Survey Office. 2013. *Key Indicators of Employment and Unemployment in India, July 2011-June 2012.* Ministry of Statistics and Programme Implementation, Government of India: New Delhi.http://mospi.nic.in/sites/default/files/publication_reports/KI-68th-E%26U-PDF.pdf

National Statistical Office. 2019. *Annual Report- Periodic Labour Force Survey, July 2017 – June 2018.* Ministry of Statistics and Programme Implementation, Government of India: New Delhi. May 29. http://www.mospi.gov.in/sites/default/files/publication_reports/Annual%20Report%2C%20PLFS%202017-18_31052019.pdf

National Statistical Office. 2020a. *Press Note on Provisional Estimates of Annual National Income 2019–2020 and Quarterly Estimates of Gross Domestic Product for the Fourth Quarter (Q4) of 2019–20.* Ministry of Statistics and Programme Implementation, Government of India:New

Delhi. http://www.mospi.gov.in/sites/default/files/press_release/PRESS%20NOTE%20PE%20and%20Q4%20estimates%20of%20GDP.pdf

National Statistical Office. 2020b. *Press Note on Estimates of Gross Domestic Product for the First Quarter (Q1) of 2020–21*. Ministry of Statistics and Programme Implementation, Government of India: New Delhi. http://www.mospi.gov.in/sites/default/files/press_release/PRESS_NOTE-Q1_2020-21.pdf

Papola, T.S. 2005. "Emerging Structure of Indian Economy: Implications of Growing Inter-sectoral Imbalances, Presented." In *88th Conference of The Indian Economic Association*, Andhra University, Visakhapatnam, December 27–29.

Papola, T.S., and P.P. Sahu. March 2012. *Growth and Structure of Employment in India: Long-Term and Post-Reform Performance and the Emerging Challenge*. New Delhi: Institute for Studies on Industrial Development.

Quddus, Munir. 2020. "The Legacy of Keynes in the Age of the Corona Virus Pandemic." April 6. https://www.pvamu.edu/blog/opinion-in-the-long-run-we-are-all-dead-the-legacy-of-keynes-in-the-age-of-the-coronavirus-pandemic/

Rao, V.K.R.V. 1979. "Changing Structure of Indian Economy: As Seen through National Accounts Data." *Economic and Political Weekly* 14 (50): 2049–2058.

Romana, I. E. 2020. "Keynesian Models of Depression. Supply Shocks and the COVID-19 Crisis." *IE Romana-arXiv Preprint* arXiv: 2007.07353.

Saltiel, F. 2020. "Who Can Work from Home in Developing Countries?" *Covid Economics* 7: 104–118.

Singh, Gurbachan. April 11, 2020. "Covid-19: Reserves to the Rescue." *Macroeconomics*. https://www.ideasforindia.in/topics/macroeconomics/covid-19-reserves-to-the-rescue.html

Sinha, D. 2020. "Food For All During Lockdown: State Governments Must Universalise PDS." TheWire. April 20. https://thewire.in/rights/covid-19-lockdown-food-supply-pds

Subramanian, S. 16 April 2020. "Doing the Maths: Why India Should Introduce a Covid Wealth Tax on the Ultra Rich." *Scroll*. https://scroll.in/article/959314/doingthe-maths-why-india-should-introduce-a-covid-wealth-tax-on-the-ultra-rich

Thirlwall, A.P. 2005. *Growth and Development with Special Reference to Developing Economies*. 8th ed. New York: Palgrave Macmillan.

Unni, J, and G. Raveendran. 2007. "Growth of Employment (1993–94 to 2004–05): Illusion of Inclusiveness?" *Economic and Political Weekly* 42 (3): 196–199.

Valla, Natacha. 2020. "Boosting the Economic Recovery or Closing a Green Deal in Europe? or Both?" *Intereconomics* 55 (6): 350–352. doi:10.1007/s10272-020-0930-0.

Wheelock, David C. 2020. "Comparing the COVID-19 Recession with the Great Depression." *Economic Synopses* 2020 (39). doi:10.20955/es.2020.39.

Wilson, G. 1960. "The Relationship Between Output And Employment." *The Review of Economics and Statistics* 42 (1, February 42): 37–43. doi:10.2307/1926093.

Woodford, M. 2020. "Effective Demand Failures and the Limits of Monetary Stabilization Policy." *NBER Working Paper Series* 27768. https://www.nber.org/system/files/working_papers/w27768/w27768.pdf

An empirical analysis of COVID-19 response: comparison of US with the G7

Mahua Barari, Srikanta Kundu and Saibal Mitra

ABSTRACT

We compare the US policy response to COVID-19 with its G7 counterparts between March and September 2020. The G7 countries, while economically and ideologically aligned, have instituted vastly different policies to mitigate the spread of the disease with varying degrees of compliance. To quantify the effect of policy responses on the spread of infections, we estimate beta for each country which is the slope coefficient of daily new cases in each country regressed against world new cases. First, we test for structural breaks in daily data for world new cases using the Bai Perron method which endogenously determines break points. We obtain five break dates that allow us to divide the time period into six windows and estimate betas separately for each window. Next, we rank the G7 countries based on their beta values for each window. Our empirical findings suggest that countries that eased their lockdown measures moderately while enforcing nationwide mask mandate and comprehensive contact tracing generally performed better in mitigating the spread of new infections. Furthermore, countries with higher degree of compliance saw improvement in their rankings. US was ranked mostly in the bottom half of the G7 group but not always the worst.

1. Introduction

2020 will go down in history as the year of the global pandemic stemming from COVID-19. By the end of March 2020, the disease has reached every corner of the world. Countries around the world have continued to struggle to strike a balance between mitigating the spread of the disease and avoiding an economic shutdown. However, the magnitude of the impact of the disease has varied widely across countries. The United States (US) is one of the world leaders in terms of total number of confirmed cases and deaths. Table 1 provides a snapshot in time of cumulative total of confirmed cases in the US between March and September compared to its G7 counterparts [Canada, France, Germany, Italy, Japan and the United Kingdom (UK)] comprising some of the largest and most advanced economies of the world.

Table 1. Share of world COVID cases and population for G7 countries.

	Share of world cases (%)			
	30-Mar	30-Jun	30-Sep	Share of world population (%)
Canada	0.84	1.01	0.47	0.48
France	5.41	1.60	1.63	0.84
Germany	7.71	1.90	0.86	1.08
Italy	13.15	2.35	0.93	0.78
Japan	0.25	0.18	0.25	1.62
UK	3.61	2.77	1.32	0.87
USA	19.25	25.29	21.32	4.25

As Table 1 indicates, there has been a staggering disparity of performance between the US and its G7 counterparts. The US, which is home to approximately 4.25% of the world's population, accounted for more than 25% of the world's total coronavirus cases back in June 302,020. Although the US share in world cases dropped down to 21.3% by September 302,020, it was still five times its share of world population. France had the second highest share of world cases in the G7 group on September 30 which was only twice its share in world population.

Clearly, there is ample empirical evidence to suggest that the US was one of the chronic underperformers in the world between March and September 2020 in containing the spread of the virus. However, in our view, comparing countries by tracking the trajectories of their new cases (or any other metric), while informative, presents an incomplete picture. For a deeper understanding and evaluation of COVID policy responses in mitigating the spread of the virus, we propose a new methodology in this paper. Borrowing the concept of beta from the financial literature, we suggest comparing the 'beta value' for new cases across countries over time. Ranking securities by their beta values is a common practice in the financial field. Beta measures whether a stock is outperforming or underperforming with respect to a market benchmark such as S&P 500. A beta value of greater than 1 indicates that the stock under consideration will outperform the market when the market index is rising but underperform when the market index is falling. The beta value of a stock can also be negative when its value moves against the market.

In a similar vein, we propose estimating beta value for daily new COVID cases in a country against a world benchmark and subsequently ranking countries based on their beta values. In our study, beta is the slope coefficient of daily new COVID cases in a country estimated against the world daily new cases. It measures whether new cases in a country are moving in the same or opposite direction of world benchmark and at a faster or slower pace. Therefore, it quantifies whether a country is outperforming or underperforming with respect to the rest of the world in containing the spread of the virus. The advantage of this approach is that we can rank countries in terms of their COVID response relative to the world using the calculated beta values. It is worth noting that one can apply our method to compare countries in terms of other metrics, such as the death rate.

While the concept of beta is straight forward, its calculation is complicated by the fact that beta is unlikely to stay constant for the whole period if structural breaks exist in time series data. Therefore, first we test for the presence of structural breaks in world daily new cases before estimating the beta values for each country. Structural changes have always been an important concern in econometric modelling of time series data. While setting break dates exogenously is fairly common, we add a new dimension to the growing body of COVID literature by endogenously determining structural break points occurring at multiple unknown dates. We accomplish this by applying the Bai-Perron (1998, 2003a, 2003b) methodology to world daily new cases spanning March through September 2020. The Bi-Perron algorithm gives rise to five different break points. We divide the entire period from March to September into six windows using the Bai-Perron break dates and subsequently estimate betas for each country separately for each of the six windows.

To compare US performance with respect to its peers in the G7 group, we rank the countries next based on their beta values for each window. Such rankings allow us to track, over time, the performance of each country separately relative to the world and assess the effectiveness of policies instituted by these countries in response to COVID 19. Our country rankings for the six windows indicate fluctuations in US rankings over time. There were periods of success followed by periods of struggle in coping with the virus. On a ranking scale of 1–7 where 1 is the best and 7 is the worst, the US performed the worst in the G7 group in June and July at the peak of summer. But it had a significant turnaround in August when its ranking jumped from 7 to 1. Unfortunately, the US could not keep its momentum going and its ranking dropped again to 5 in September. The performance of France was the worst in the G7 group in August and September.

To explain why some G7 countries were more successful in fighting the virus than others, we focus on government policy responses. We analyze country rankings using a government stringency index developed by the researchers at the University of Oxford. It is essentially a proxy for government-imposed lockdown measures based on nine factors. We combine the stringency index with other health policies such as nationwide mask mandate and contact tracing and also consider degree of compliance with such policies. Our empirical evidence suggests that countries that generally ranked higher in the G7 group moderately lowered their stringency index scores by summer but supplemented it with other policies such as a nationwide mask mandate and comprehensive contact tracing. Moreover, these countries also recorded a higher degree of compliance. It could be that the lack of a nationwide mask mandate combined with limited contact tracing and a lower degree of compliance explains why the US was ranked mostly in the bottom half of the G7 group in this study, albeit not always the worst.

Our paper is organized as follows. In section 2, we provide a brief literature review of a rapidly growing body of literature on COVID-19 to place our work in context. In section 3, we describe our empirical methodology by focusing on the theory underlying Bai-Perron structural break test. We present and analyze our results in section 4. We summarize our key findings as well as address limitations of our study in our concluding remarks in section 5.

2. Review of literature

Literature on the COVID pandemic is growing quickly to explain this ongoing phenomenon. Given that the disease is new and effective medical interventions are still in the nascent stage of development, governments have had to adopt non-medical measures, also referred to as Non- Pharmaceutical Interventions (NPI), aimed at containment and mitigation of the pandemic. These NPIs included stringent lockdown measures such as bans on public gatherings, stay at home orders, closures of public places, national and international mobility restrictions. They also included other public health measures such as requirements to wear face coverings and participate in contact tracing. In the review that follows, we will focus on studies that assess the impact of such measures on COVID cases and related deaths. Furthermore, we will summarize a growing body of literature in public health policy looking into why government COVID responses and their effectiveness varied across countries and the role the system of governance and compliance played in it.

Dergiades, Milas, and Panagiotidis (2020) assess the quantitative impact of such government interventions on COVID-19 related deaths using daily data covering January 1 to 30 April 2020 for 32 countries. Applying Perron and Yabu (2009) statistical methodology, they endogenously determine if a break exists in the linear trend of the logarithm of deaths per country and subsequently estimate the slope of the trend before and after the break. They hypothesize that if a country increases the strength of its policy response, a significant reduction in the trend slope should follow after a certain breakpoint. To quantify the stringency of policies conducted across countries, they use the Oxford COVID-19 Government Response Tracker (OxCGRT) index. Their overall findings suggest that the greater the strength of government interventions at an early stage, the more effective these are in slowing down or reversing the growth rate of deaths. In another similar study using the same Oxford COVID-19 Government Response Tracker, Carraro, Ferrone, and Squarcina (2020) analyze how different government policies affect the number of active COVID-19 cases in 166 countries, with a temporal lag of seven and fourteen days, using daily data ranging from Jan 1 to 15 May 2020. They find that confinement measures such as school closures and lockdowns are highly effective in reducing the diffusion of active cases, specifically more effective in high income countries. In a similar vein, Bonardi et al. (2020) study the overall effects of lockdown policies on the increase in new infections and deaths for 184 countries between 31 December 2019 to 4 May 2020. They find that partial lockdowns were as effective in reducing the number of infections and deaths as stricter measures, especially for developed countries. Their findings support their hypothesis that effectiveness of lockdown measures depend on individual opportunity costs of staying at home which are typically higher in developing countries where many people rely on informal economy to earn their living. They also find a speed premium in implementing lockdowns in that countries that acted fast fared better supporting Dergiades, Milas, and Panagiotidis (2020) findings in this respect. Focusing on a single country, Hartl, Wälde, and Weber (2020) investigate the impact of the German public shutdown as announced on 13 March 2020 on the spread of Covid-19. Using a simple linear trend model for log of cumulative confirmed cases, they search for a trend break using maximum likelihood method of estimation. They identify a trend break on March 20 when the growth rate of cases drops by half. They conclude that policy measures were effective in reducing the spread of the virus with a time lag of seven days as expected.

Another strand of literature focuses on the effect of wearing face masks in reducing the spread of the virus. Despite consensus in the scientific community regarding face covering in reducing the transmissibility of the virus, policies surrounding mask mandates have varied widely across countries and across regions within countries. For example, using country level data for the US between February 15 and August 30, Yilmazkuday

(2020) confirms that higher social interaction leads to higher COVID-19 cases and deaths across U.S. counties. Subsequently, he splits the counties into mask-wearing and non-mask-wearing counties and find that wearing a face mask helps in mitigating the spread of the virus only if more than 75% of people in a country 'always' wear a face mask. Furthermore, the negative effects of social interaction on COVID-19 are statistically eliminated when more than 85% of people in a country 'always' wear a face mask. Using the same panel dataset but a different methodology that exploits a large set of controls for correctly identifying the relationship, Welsh (2020) finds that a one percentage point increase in the number of individuals who say they often or frequently wear a mask when within six feet of people reduces COVID-19 deaths in a country by 10.5%, or six deaths in an average sized country.

Imposing a nationwide mask mandate or enforcing strict lockdown measures that, by design, curtail individual freedom has become a contentious political issue and highlights the role of the system of governance in place in a country. Peters (2012) argued that successful governance requires fulfilling at least four principle activities including goal selection, goal reconciliation and coordination, implementation and feedback/accountability. Kettl (2020) finds that the U.S. system of governance with its deep roots in traditions of federalism impeded a coordinated policy response to COVID-19. As he notes, in no other country was the level of friction between the national and subnational governments as high as it was in the US. Rothert, Brady, and Insler (2020) assess the impact of a scattered policy response in the US on the country-wide spread of the virus. Using both spatial econometric and time series methods, they study the impact of one state's containment measures on new infections in surrounding states and quantify the extent of inter-state spillovers. Their findings suggest presence of substantial spillovers and thus the need for a coordinated policy response. Desson et al. (2020) provide a comprehensive comparative analysis of the epidemiological situation and policy responses in France, Belgium and Canada representing a wide spectrum of governance structures under the umbrella of OECD nations. They conclude that actions taken by these three countries appear to have been largely dictated by existing health system capacity along with varying degrees of federalism and regional autonomy. They also note that increasing federalism has been associated with more fragmented strategies and less coordination across jurisdictions. Kavanagh and Singh (2020) explore the nature of relationship between public health and democratic form of government. They question the conventional wisdom that democracy is beneficial for public health and ask if there is an advantage to an authoritarian pandemic response.

To assess policy effectiveness, Pak, McBryde, and Adegboye (2021) investigate the role of compliance by the people in adhering to public health guidelines. Compliance with COVID policies entails significant costs in terms of both economic and social life disruptions. They focus on the level of public trust in government and its institutions and hypothesize that high public trust is positively related to compliance with stringent policy measures. Using survey data from 58 countries and the Oxford COVID-19 government response tracker, they offer empirical evidence in support of their hypothesis. In a similar vein, Bargain and Aminjonov (2020) also examine the role of trust and compliance in the face of a massive pandemic when compliance is required for collective survival. Using Google mobility index data along with European social survey data on trust and the Oxford government response tracker, they find that high trust regions in Europe decrease their mobility related to non-necessary activities significantly more than low-trust regions. Furthermore, the trust level increases with the degree of stringency. Greer et al. (2020) also agree that success of authoritarian public health measures depend on societal compliance. But in their view, compliance requires more than trust; it needs a political economy that allows people to stay at home without losing livelihood. Therefore, the extent of compliance is also shaped by pre-existing social policies in place in the country.

In an interesting Platteau and Verardi (2020a, 2020b) explore the role of a country's culture in spreading the virus. For example, the Japanese habit of maintaining a reasonable distance from people stands in stark contrast to the Western European habit. Moreover, due to air pollution in countries like South Korea, China and Japan, people are already accustomed to wearing face masks – a practice that is at odds with the culture in Western Europe. Their findings, based on an epidemiological model, suggest that in addition to public health policies and genetic make-up of population groups, cultural specificities matter in explaining international and inter-regional variations in the incidence of the virus and the impact of public interventions.

To summarize, our review suggests that more stringent lockdown policies, especially if adopted early on, are effective in reducing new cases and deaths. Furthermore, wearing masks help in reducing transmission of the virus and deaths. Studies also show that countries that have a system of governance rooted in federalism are more likely to have a scattered policy response due to lack of coordination between national and subnational governments thereby rendering these policies less effective. Studies further suggest that societal compliance is negatively impacted by policies that are deemed authoritarian. A country's culture may also play a role when it comes to spreading the virus or complying with public health policies.

Our goal in this paper is to study the policy effectiveness of NPIs of different countries in containing the spread of the Covid-19 virus. We add a new dimension to the growing literature by proposing a simple methodology that allows us to rank the countries by calculating their beta coefficients in different time windows identified by multiple structural breaks in the global daily new cases. We hypothesize that countries with more stringent NPIs (such as a higher stringency index and an enforceable mask mandate) and higher degree of compliance in a given time window will be ranked higher in the group in that window, all else being equal. Likewise, countries with less stringent NPIs combined with low level of compliance will be ranked lower. For countries with more stringent NPIs but low level of compliance or less-stringent NPIs with higher compliance, the ranking cannot be determined a priori and will lend itself to empirical investigation. Furthermore, we will explore how the system of governance and the level of compliance affect the ranking of a country in the group.

We apply our proposed methodology to rank US with respect to other members of the G7 group. We choose the G7 as our comparison group because these countries are economically as developed and ideologically aligned with the US to offer a useful comparison. At the same time, the G7 group consists of countries from three different continents that exhibit differing governance structure within the context of democracy. There also exists cultural differences across G7 nations resulting in varying degrees of compliance with policy measures. Therefore, the G7 group provides a useful case study to examine the role of governance and compliance in understanding the effectiveness of COVID policy in the developed world.

3. Estimation technique

In this study, we apply an advanced structural break test developed by Bai and Perron (1998, 2003a, 2003b) to endogenously determine break dates within the sample. As the COVID-19 virus travelled from one corner of the world to another, different countries faced the severity of contagion at different points in time. Naturally, policy responses undertaken by each country also varied over time in terms of strategy, severity and timing. Therefore, presence of structural breaks is expected in our time series data implying that the value of beta will not stay constant for the entire period. To estimate time varying beta, we need to determine the dates for structural breaks (if they are detected) so that we could divide the entire sample into separate windows.

There exists a substantial body of literature focusing on methods for detecting structural breaks in time series data. [For example, see Andrews (1993), Bai (1997), Liu, Wu, and Zidek (1997), Bai and Perron (1998, 2003a, 2003b)]. We use the Bai-Perron methodology in this study to determine the break dates. Their theoretical framework marks a significant improvement over previous studies since (i) it allows for multiple break points instead of single break point and (ii) break points are not handpicked a priori; instead they are determined endogenously within the model. Bai-Perron methodology is a two-step procedure. First, they test for the number of structural breaks in the data series if they exist and subsequently estimate the break dates. Bai and Perron 2003a) paper start by estimating the break dates treating the number of breaks to be known and discuss various tests for determining the number of breaks later in the paper. What follows is a brief intuitive discussion of the Bai and Perron 2003a) model.

3.1. Estimation of the break dates

Since our objective is to compare the G7 countries based on their beta values measured against the world benchmark, we apply the Bai-Perron break test to world data on new cases.[1] Bai and Perron (1998) start with a multiple linear regression model with m breaks and $m + 1$ windows. Based on the times series plot of world daily new COVID cases per million (as depicted by Figure 1 in section 4.2 below), we consider a quadratic trend function. The structure of the trend function can be written as a multiple linear regression model as follows

$$y_t = a_j + b_j t + c_j t^2 + u_t; t = T_{j-1} + 1, \ldots, T_j \quad (1)$$

For $j = 1, \ldots, m + 1$, $T_0 = 0$ and $T_{m+1} = T$. In equation (1), y_t represents the observed dependent variable which is a quadratic function of time t and a_j, b_j and c_j are regression coefficients corresponding to the jth window. The notation u_t denotes the error term for the tth time period. In our analysis we have considered a pure structural break test where all coefficients of the model are allowed to vary across windows.[2]

The purpose is to estimate the unknown regression coefficients together with the break points when T observations are available. The Bai-Perron estimation proceeds using the least square principle. For each m partition $(T_1, \ldots, T_m)$ denoted by T_j, the least square estimate of a_j, b_j and c_j are obtained by minimizing the residual sum of squares, S_T,

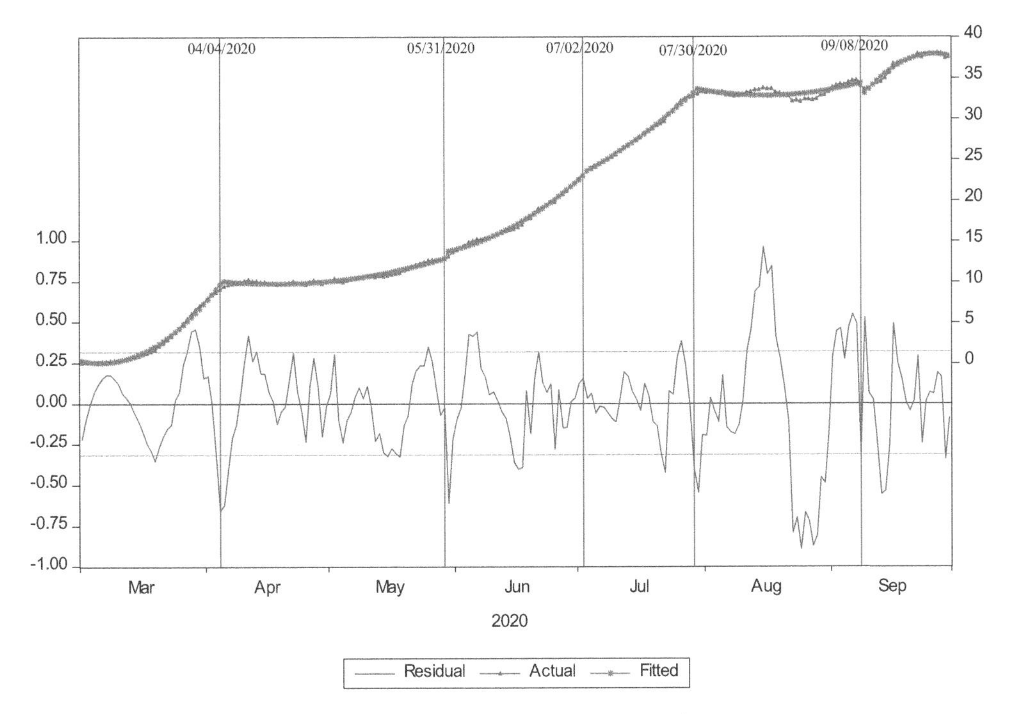

Figure 1. World daily new COVID-19 cases per million – actual and fitted.

$$S_T = \sum_{i=1}^{m+1} \sum_{t=T_{j-1}+1}^{T_j} \left[Yt - \left(a_j + b_j t + c_j t^2\right)\right]^2 \quad (2)$$

The estimated break points $\hat{T}_1, \hat{T}_2, \ldots, \hat{T}_m$ can be obtained by

$$\left(\hat{T}_1, \hat{T}_2, \ldots, \hat{T}_m\right) = \arg\min S_T(T_1, T_2, \ldots, T_m) \quad (3)$$

where the minimization of S_T is taken over all partitions $(T_1, \ldots, T_m)$.

3.2. *Testing multiple structural breaks*

To determine if structural breaks exist and how many, Bai and Perron (1998) propose a few different test statistics as summarized below.

(i) Thesup$F_T(k)$ test is a suprema F type test of no structural break (m = 0) against the alternative hypothesis of a fixed number of breaks $(m = k)$ where T represents the sample size. However, the usefulness of this test is somewhat limited as it requires specifying the number of breaks, m, under the alternative hypothesis.

(ii) Next, Bai and Perron (1998) consider tests of no structural break against an unknown number of breaks (with an upper bound) using a new class of tests called the double maximum (D_{max}) tests. They recommend using either unweighted D_{max} called the UD_{max} or the weighted D_{max} called the WD_{max} test where weights may reflect the imposition of some priors on the likelihood of various numbers of breaks. The weights depend on the number of regressors and the significance level of the tests.

(iii) Finally, Bai and Perron (1998) consider a sup F type test of the null hypothesis of l breaks against the alternative that an additional break exists denoted by $\sup F_T(l+1|l)$ test. This is a sequential test of the null hypothesis of l breaks against the alternative of $(l+1)$ breaks. The test is applied to each segment containing the observations $\hat{T}_{i-1}$ to $\hat{T}_i$ $(i = 1, \ldots, l+1)$. The null hypothesis is rejected if the overall minimal value of the sum of squared residuals (over all segments where an additional break is included) is sufficiently smaller than the sum of squared residuals from the ℓ breaks model.

Based on extensive simulation exercises, Bai and Perron (2003a) suggest the following useful strategy. A researcher may first look at the *UDmax* or *WDmax* tests to see if at least one break is present. If these tests indicate the presence of at least one break, then the number of breaks can be decided based upon a sequential examination of the $\sup F(l+1|l)$ statistics constructed using global minimizers for the break dates (i.e. ignore the test $F(1|0)$ and select m such that the tests $\sup F(l+1|l)$ are insignificant for $l \geq m$). This is the method Bai and Perron recommend for empirical application as it leads to the best results.

To ensure a minimum number of observations in each regime, a pre-specified trimming parameter (ε) is required. More specifically, the trimming parameter is defined as $\varepsilon = h/T$ where h is the minimum possible length of a segment and T is the total number of observations in the time series. Bai and Perron (2003b) provided the critical values for ε ranging from 0.05 to 0.25 with maximum number of regressors equal to 10. The value of ε, in our analysis, is set to 0.10 such that each regime contains a reasonable number of observations to estimate the parameters.

4. Data and empirical findings

4.1. Data

Our sample is based on daily data from March 1 until 30 September 2020. While the choice of a cut-off date is somewhat arbitrary in the middle of an ongoing pandemic, we choose September based on the advent of the B.1.1.7 variant (also known as the UK variant) in the UK in late September of 2020.[3] The data for this study comes from Our World in Data: https://ourworldindata.org/coronavirus. The measure we use for new cases is the daily new confirmed cases of COVID-19 (7-day smoothed) per million people and it is provided by the European Center for Disease Prevention and Control.[4] We retrieved this data for G7 countries and the world[5] directly from the website on October 11. To track the timing and stringency of government's policy response, we use a measure called the stringency index that is also available on this website. This index is sourced from the Oxford Coronavirus Government Response Tracker (OxCGRT). The OxCGRT calculates the stringency index as a composite measure of nine response metrics consisting of school closures; workplace closures; cancellation of public events; restrictions on public gatherings; closures of public transport; stay-at-home requirements; public information campaigns; restrictions on internal movements; and international travel controls. Hence, it is a measure of government-imposed lockdown restrictions and closures. On a scale of 1–100, a higher score indicates a stricter government response. If policy responses vary at the subnational level, the index captures the response level of the strictest sub-region. Despite this limitation, we believe the stringency index provides a reasonable approximation of the degree of lockdown imposed by a government.

4.2. Bai-Perron structural break test and dates

Since our objective is to compare G7 countries based on their beta values, we need common windows for all of them. To identify such dates, we apply the Bai-Perron test to the benchmark series, i.e. the world daily new cases. We start with the WD_{max} test to see if any break exists and subsequently determine the exact number of breaks using the sequential $\sup F_T(l+1|l)$ test. We use the least squares principle as suggested by Bai-Perron to determine the break dates. Based on the time series plot of world new cases, we fit a quadratic trend function to it. The actual and fitted graphs along with the break dates are given in Figure 1 below. From the bottom half of Figure 1 it is clear that after fitting a quadratic trend with structural breaks, the residuals revert to the mean implying the absence of any remaining trend.

We use the estimated break dates as shown in Figure 1 to identify 6 common windows as follows – Window 1 (March 1–April 4), Window 2 (April 5–May 31), Window 3 (June 1–July 2), Window 4 (July 3–July 30), Window 5 (July 31–September 8) and Window 6 (September 9–September 30). From the fitted model for each window, it is clear that the number of new cases rose in the first four windows though the rate of increase varied across windows. We observe the steepest rate of increase in the first window in the early stages of the pandemic as expected. This was followed by a period of significantly slower growth in the second window covering April and May, partly due to strict lockdown measures hurriedly put in place to stop the spread. Subsequently, there was a spike in rate of increase in new cases during the third and fourth window as countries worldwide started opening up their economies, with a sharper increase noted in July. Thereafter, in the fifth window spanning mostly August, the fitted line was relatively flat. In this window, we notice a slight upward movement in daily new cases that was also accompanied by higher fluctuations. Finally, in the last window covering most of September, the number of new cases started rising again but at a decreasing rate as depicted by the concave fitted curve.

4.3. Beta values and country rankings

For each window, we estimate the beta value for new cases for each country separately using equation (4) below.

$$N_{jkt} = \alpha_{jk} + \beta_{jk} N_{wkt} + \varepsilon_{jkt} \tag{4}$$

where N_{jkt} and N_{wkt} represent daily new confirmed COVID cases in the jth country and in the world respectively in period t of the kth window and ε represents the random error term. Thus, the slope coefficient β quantifies the changes in number of new cases in the jth country relative to unit change in new cases in the world.

Next, we rank the countries based on their beta values to assess their relative performance in tackling the pandemic. A country's rankings will depend on whether (i) the world benchmark is rising or falling and (ii) beta values are positive or negative and above or below one. For example, if new cases in the world are rising, a negative beta that exceeds one in absolute value will be the most desirable scenario. The next desirable scenario will entail a negative beta that lies below one. A positive beta that falls short of one will be the third preferred outcome followed by a positive beta that exceeds one. The ordering of outcomes will be reversed when the world new cases are falling with a positive beta exceeding one being the best-case scenario. All possible scenarios are outlined in Table 2.

In short, a negative (positive) beta value is preferred to a positive (negative) beta value when the world new cases are rising (falling). Moreover, a negative (positive) beta that exceeds 1 in absolute value is the most desirable outcome as it indicates that the daily new cases in a country are falling at a faster rate compared to the world benchmark.

In our study, we rank the countries based on a ranking scale of 1–7. We assign 1 to the best performing country in the G7 group and 7 to the worst. The estimated betas and associated country rankings are given in Table 3 below.

Based on our calculations reported in Table 3, although not always ranked the worst, the US was generally ranked in the bottom half of the group. Its standing in the G7 group fluctuated over time like any other member of the group. It comes as no surprise that Italy, France, and Germany performed the worst in March since the pandemic erupted in continental Europe early on before spreading to North America. Italy saw the biggest increase in infections with 994 new cases per million for every 100 new cases per million in the world. The situation improved for each country in April and May as their beta values moved from positive to negative territory from window 1 to window 2 suggesting that all members of G7 outperformed the world during this period in containing the spread of the virus. This was likely a direct outcome of the severe lockdown measures that were adopted by the G7 countries. Italy saw the biggest drop in beta value from window 1 to window 2 followed by France and Germany resulting in significant improvement in their country rankings. Specifically, Italy climbed from rank 7 to rank 1 by bringing the daily new cases down by 1668 per million for every 100 new cases per million in the world. This prompted many G7 governments to quickly reopen their struggling economies. The beta values moved up again in June and turned positive by July for all countries, although their values were close to 0 indicating that their new cases were mostly in line with the world new cases. The only exception was the US. It became the worst performing country in June and July when it saw its new cases rise by about seven times that of the world increase. Thereafter, it turned the corner in August and led the pack for a while. Unfortunately, it could not sustain its momentum and fell behind in ranking by September. France ended up being the worst performing country in August and September with number of new cases per million rising by 18 and 15 times that of the world. Japan, the only Asian country in the G7 group, stood out as an outlier. Its beta

Table 2. Interpretation of the regression coefficient beta.

Country beta value	World daily new cases rising	World daily new cases falling
$\beta < -1$	Best case scenario	Worst scenario
$-1 < \beta < 0$	Second best scenario	Third best scenario
$0 < \beta < 1$	Third best scenario	Second best scenario
$\beta > 1$	Worst scenario	Best case scenario

Table 3. Estimated β and country ranking.

	Mar 1–Apr 4	Apr5-May31	Jun1–Jul 2	Jul 3–Jul 30	Jul 31–Sep 8	Sep9–Sep30
β – new cases						
Canada	2.963	−4.220	−1.657	0.675	1.467	3.921
France	7.672	−12.156	−0.301	0.564	18.681	15.195
Germany	7.910	−11.383	0.259	0.247	−0.229	1.565
Italy	9.935	−16.6.676	−0.294	0.099	3.854	0.702
Japan	0.105	−1.053	0.048	0.519	−1.519	−0.154
UK	5.820	−13.072	−1.240	0.029	3.830	9.083
US	7.589	−8.047	7.372	6.527	−4.142	6.433
Ranking of β – New Cases						
Canada	2	6	1	6	4	4
France	5	3	3	5	7	7
Germany	6	4	6	3	3	3
Italy	7	1	4	2	6	2
Japan	1	7	5	4	2	1
UK	3	2	2	1	5	6
US	4	5	7	7	1	5

Scale: 1 to 7 implies best to worst.

values indicated that its daily new cases were aligned closely with the world throughout and had the least amount of fluctuations from one window to the next.

4.4. Analysis of rankings

For a deeper analysis of a country's beta values and its rankings, we now pay closer attention to government's policy responses. As mentioned above, we use the nine-factor stringency index developed by University of Oxford. This index is constructed as an average value of nine policy response indicators including school closures, workplace closures, stay at home orders and travel bans rescaled to a value from 0 to 100 (100 = strictest). The stringency index values changed in discrete steps as exhibited in Figure 2 below.

The stringency graphs reveal that there was a steep increase in index values for all countries from March to April except for Japan. The strictest policy response came from the Italian government where the stringency index value crossed 90. This clearly explains the sharp drop in beta values for all countries from positive to negative territory from window 1 to window 2 suggesting some success in containing the infections.[6] By May, the European countries in the group except for UK brought the stringency levels down by relaxing some of the lockdown restrictions to ease the economic hardship. France recorded the steepest drop with its stringency index hovering near 40 by June and saw its country ranking fall to 7 by August. While UK moved up in ranking in June and July by keeping most of the lockdown measures in place as reflected in higher stringency values, its ranking deteriorated in August and September despite maintaining higher stringency levels. A similar picture emerges with the North American countries in the group. They kept their stringency indexes at relatively high levels but their beta rankings in the group did not always improve in proportion. Japan, the only Asian country in the group, stands out as an outlier. It had the lowest stringency index value that was significantly below the rest and yet it performed reasonably well in beta rankings.

This suggests there is more to the story. The stringency index alone cannot explain the changes in country beta rankings over time. First, the index, by construct, is shown as the

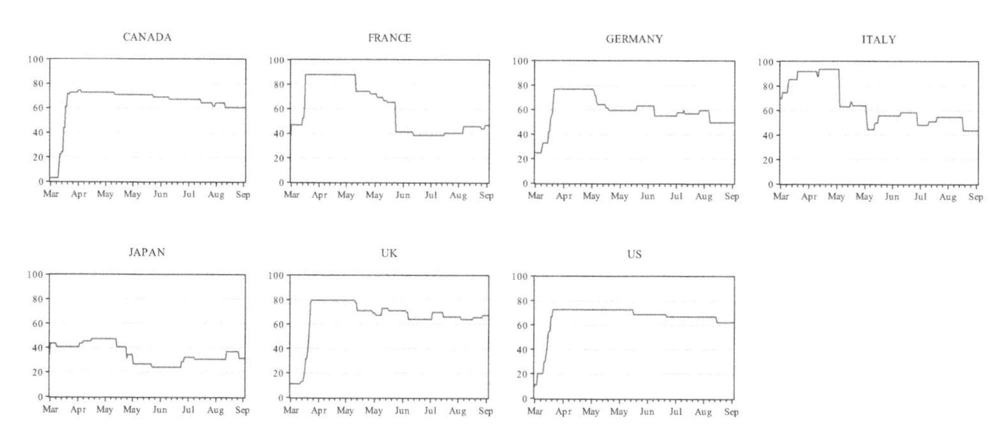

Figure 2. Stringency index of G7 countries (daily data) Source: Our World in Data: https://ourworldindata.org/coronavirus.

response level of the strictest sub-region. Hence, it overstates the strictness of policies for countries with huge sub-national variation in policy measures. This over-estimation is more likely for US and Canada in the G7 group given their size and the decentralized governance structure. For example, COVID policy responses in the US often ended up being a patchwork of state-wide or local ordinances. Similarly, in Canada, there was a lack of coordinated policy response to public health issues which were administered by the provincial governments. As mentioned above, Japan's stringency index, by contrast, was the lowest in the group throughout. This is because a forced lockdown is not possible in Japan by law (See Tashiro and Shaw 2020) Instead, what Japan instituted was a voluntary lockdown where the head of the government could only 'request' the people to follow the lockdown measures.

Furthermore, the stringency index does not reflect mask policies in place or captures testing and contact tracing. Above all, there exists wide variation in degrees of compliance with the policy rules in the G7 group highlighting the cultural and political divide across nations. First, let us take the case of the US, the UK and Canada which maintained relatively high stringency scores in the 60–70 range throughout. Yet their beta scores fluctuated a lot from one window to the next (as did their rankings) and did not show any clear pattern of improvement with time. Based on our research, the US and Canada never introduced a nationwide mask mandate in the period covered under this study. This is at least, in part, due to the decentralized governance structure in these countries making it harder to impose a federal mandate. In the UK, the mask mandate was imposed much later (on July 24) compared to its European counterparts in the group. By contrast, the remaining European countries in the group (France, Germany, and Italy) responded alike by moderately relaxing their lockdown measures by early summer as reflected in their lower stringency index values. At the same time, their masking policies stood in stark contrast with the US, Canada, and the UK. Italy introduced the mask mandate in two phases. On April 6th, masks were made mandatory in high infection areas followed by a nationwide mandate on May 4th. Germany introduced a nationwide mask mandate on April 22 and France on May 10. However, in France, the effect of mask mandate may have been compromised by a steep drop of its stringency index from 80s to 40s by end of June as restrictions on internal movement and stay at home orders were relaxed and schools and workplaces reopened. With limited opportunities to go overseas, French families packed vacation spots along the Atlantic coast and the French Riviera and young people did not always follow social distancing or wear masks.[7] As our beta rankings indicate, France was the worst performing nation in the group in the last two windows spanning July through September.

When it came to compliance with nationwide mask mandate, Italians took to wearing a mask even before there was a nationwide mask mandate. Based on a weekly survey conducted by the Imperial College London and YouGov on global face mask use, [8] Italy had the lowest non-compliance rate of all in the G7 group in the range of 1%–2% from June through September. In France, it was equally impressive, ranging between 2% and 3% while for Germany it was slightly higher, between 6% and 7%. By contrast, the non-compliance rate in the UK was significantly higher and ranged from 12% to 53% for this period. As regards contact tracing, using data and information available on https://ourworldindata.org/coronavirus, we find that the UK was behind the rest of the European countries until end of May when it had no protocol for contact tracing.

Then it went from no tracing to comprehensive tracing within a very short period which could partly explain improvement in its country rankings in window 3 and 4. On March 18, Germany eased its effort to track and trace the infections when it replaced comprehensive testing and tracking by limited testing and tracking. However, on June 16, Germany reverted back to comprehensive testing and tracking which could be part of the reason its standing in the G7 group improved from a 6th place to the 3rd place from July until September. Overall, all European countries in the group had comprehensive contact tracing in place by June. By contrast, the US settled for limited tracing throughout although Canada ramped up its efforts and moved up to comprehensive tracing by August.

Japan, the only Asian country in the group, remains an exception. Since a forced lockdown is not possible by law, the Prime Minister and governors can only appeal to the people to stay at home and request high risk facilities to close. Hence, its stringency scores were significantly lower than the rest in the G7 group. Notwithstanding, Japan's beta ranking remained relatively high from July through September suggesting that it was able to control the spread of infection even though the economy remained relatively open. Mask compliance was high from the very beginning as was the compliance with voluntary lockdown measures. This may have been due to repeated requests from governors, ministers, and the prime minister to follow stay at home orders and avoid crowded places and close contacts (see Watanabe and Yabu 2020). The willingness of Japanese people to comply with policies that required sacrificing individual freedom proved critical in containing the spread of new infections in Japan.

In short, using data from March to September 2020, we find that countries that improved their beta ranking in the G7 group overall were not the countries that maintained strict lockdown measures. Instead, countries that opened up their economies moderately while enforcing nationwide mask mandate and comprehensive contact tracing performed better between March and September. Japan proved to be an exception where the culture of compliance played a critical role in mitigating the spread of the disease.

5. Conclusions

Our key contribution to the growing literature on the pandemic lies in using time-varying beta values for new cases measured against the world to rank US with respect to its G7 counterparts in terms of COVID policy effectiveness. To estimate time-varying beta, we divide the time period covered in this study (March–September) into separate windows using the Bai-Perron structural break test that endogenizes the break dates. The advantage of tracking changes in beta values (and the associated country rankings) over time is that we can quantify the effects of policy changes. Our empirical evidence suggests that lockdown measures initially helped all countries in the group in containing the spread of infections. But as countries gradually reopened their economies, there was no clear frontrunner consistently outperforming its fellow group members. Instead, the overall pattern that emerges from our beta rankings is that countries that permitted a moderate amount of relaxation of lockdown measures combined with hefty dose of other policies such as nationwide mask mandate and comprehensive contact tracing performed better in general. Furthermore, the compliance factor proved to be critical as was clearly the case with Japan.

US had a mixed record during this period with its ranking fluctuating from one window to the next but mostly confined to the bottom half of the G7 group. Why did the US, considered one of the most-prepared countries with the greatest capacity for outbreak response, fail to respond effectively? According to Peters (2012), the normative question of how to ensure good governance remains a central concern in considering governance and at the minimum suggests the capacity to get things done. In the context of pandemic response, good governance can be interpreted as adopting and enforcing policies at national, regional, and local level in unison and convincing citizens that the effectiveness of these policies lies in its compliance. Our findings suggest that the US system of governance rooted in federalism got in the way of both a coordinated policy response and societal compliance. On the other hand, data from Japan suggest that even though its policies were less onerous (as measured by the stringency index), high compliance with mask mandate and social distancing was enough to ensure it out-performing its peer group.

Our study is limited in scope. It is important to note that the data on COVID-19 infections suffers from measurement errors. The data contains reported cases only, which are not equivalent to the total number of actual infections in a country due to testing limitations. The actual number of cases are likely to be higher than the reported cases. Furthermore, we have not factored in population density or age distribution or the state of the health care system prevalent in these countries while making cross country comparison. We have focused on containment and health measures while leaving out many other policy responses such as income support or debt relief programs.

The *beta* approach, used in this study for cross country comparison, is subject to its own limitations. *Beta* approach assumes that the numbers of cases in all G7 countries are pairwise uncorrelated thus ignoring the cross country spillover of the infection due to migration of people among G7 countries. Further, we only consider the contemporaneous relationships of the infection rate of the world and each of the G7 countries to compute beta. There may be a lag impact which is not captured in our calculation of beta. Finally, we estimate beta for each window in a linear regression framework. However, the beta coefficient for each of the G7 countries may alter with respect to increase/decrease of world new cases. Hence, our analysis can be extended further to compute a non-linear beta.

Despite such limitations, our empirical findings provide evidence that having a universal mask mandate and ensuring a high degree of compliance with policies will be critical in keeping economies to stay afloat.

Notes

1. The Gauss code for Bai-Perron test is downloaded from the website of P. Perron. Codes are available upon request.
2. Bai and Perron methodology also provide a partial structural break model where coefficients of a selected number of variables are allowed to change keeping some coefficients same throughout the sample period (See Bai and Perron (1998) for details.)
3. There is compelling scientific evidence pointing to a faster spread of the B.1.1.7 variant compared to the original SARS-CoV-2. We decided to stay away from combining different variants that will impact our calculation of beta values.

4. Note that the number of confirmed new cases is always lower than actual number of new cases on any given day primarily due to limited testing.
5. The world data is based on 207 countries on this site.
6. There is a time lag between policy implementation and its outcome of typically two weeks.
7. Coronavirus Cases Surge in France as People Return to Schools, Offices – WSJ.
8. Respondents are asked if they have worn a face mask outside their home. The response options ranged from 'Always' or 'Frequently' to 'Not at all' (i.e. complete non-compliance). https://coviddatahub.com

Disclosure statement

No potential conflict of interest was reported by the author(s).

References

Andrews, D. W. 1993. "Tests for Parameter Instability and Structural Change with Unknown Change Point." *Econometrica* 61 (4): 395–397. doi:10.2307/2951764.

Bai, J. 1997. "Estimating Multiple Breaks One at a Time." *Econometric Theory* 13 (3): 315–352. doi:10.1017/S0266466600005831.

Bai, J., and P. Perron. 1998. "Estimating and Testing Linear Models with Multiple Structural Changes." *Econometrica* 66 (1): 47–78. doi:10.2307/2998540.

Bai, J., and P. Perron. 2003a. "Computation and Analysis of Multiple Structural Change Models." *Journal of Applied Econometrics* 18 (1): 1–22. doi:10.1002/jae.659.

Bai, J., and P. Perron. 2003b. "Critical Values for Multiple Structural Change Tests." *The Econometrics Journal* 6 (1): 72–78. doi:10.1111/1368-423X.00102.

Bargain, O., and U. Aminjonov. 2020. "Trust and Compliance to Public Health Policies in Times of COVID-19." *Journal of Public Economics* 192: 104316. doi:10.1016/j.jpubeco.2020.104316.

Bonardi, J. P., Q. Gallea, D. Kalanoski, and R. Lalive. 2020. "Fast and Local: How Did Lockdown Policies Affect the Spread and Severity of the Covid-19." *Covid Economics* 23: 325–351.

Carraro, A., L. Ferrone, and M. Squarcina. 2020. "Are COVID-19 Containment Measures Equally Effective in Different World Regions?" No. wp2020_11. rdf. Universita'degli Studi di Firenze, Dipartimento di Scienze per l'Economia e l'Impresa.

Dergiades, T., C. Milas, and T. Panagiotidis. 2020. "Effectiveness of Government Policies in Response to the COVID-19 Outbreak." *Available at SSRN 3602004.*

Desson, Z., E. Weller, P. McMeekin, and M. Ammi. 2020. "An Analysis of the Policy Responses to the COVID-19 Pandemic in France, Belgium, and Canada." *Health Policy and Technology* 9 (4): 430–446. doi:10.1016/j.hlpt.2020.09.002.

Greer, S. L., E. J. King, E. M. da Fonseca, and A. Peralta-Santos. 2020. "The Comparative Politics of COVID-19: The Need to Understand Government Responses." *Global Public Health* 15 (9): 1413–1416. doi:10.1080/17441692.2020.1783340.

Hartl, T., K. Wälde, and E. Weber. 2020. "Measuring the Impact of the German Public Shutdown on the Spread of COVID19." *Covid Economics, Vetted and Real-time Papers, CEPR Press* 1: 25–32.

Kavanagh, M. M., and R. Singh. 2020. "Democracy, Capacity, and Coercion in Pandemic Response: COVID-19 in Comparative Political Perspective." *Journal of Health Politics, Policy and Law* 45 (6): 997–1012. doi:10.1215/03616878-8641530.

Kettl, D. F. 2020. "States Divided: The Implications of American Federalism for Covid-19." *Public Administration Review* 80 (4): 595–602. doi:10.1111/puar.13243.

Liu, J., S. Wu, and J. V. Zidek. 1997. "On Segmented Multivariate Regression." *Statistica Sinica* 7 (2): 497–525.

Pak, A., E. McBryde, and O. A. Adegboye. 2021. "Does High Public Trust Amplify Compliance with Stringent COVID-19 Government Health Guidelines? A Multi-country Analysis Using

Data from 102,627 Individuals." *Risk Management and Healthcare Policy* 14: 293–302. doi:10.2147/RMHP.S278774.

Perron, P., and T. Yabu. 2009. "Testing for Shifts in Trend with an Integrated or Stationary Noise Component." *Journal of Business & Economic Statistics* 27 (3): 369–396. doi:10.1198/jbes.2009.07268.

Peters, B. G. 2012. "Governance as Political Theory." In *The Oxford Handbook of Governance*, Edited by David Levi-Faur, 19.

Platteau, J. P., and V. Verardi. 2020a. "How to Exit Covid-19 Lockdowns: Culture Matters." *CEPR, Covid Economics* 23: 1–57.

Platteau, J. P., and V. Verardi. 2020b. "Because Culture Matters, There Is No One-size-fits-all Strategy for Exit from Covid-19 Lockdowns." April 3, 2021. https://voxeu.org/article/culture-and-lockdown-exit-strategies

Rothert, J., R. R. Brady, and M. Insler. 2020. "The Fragmented United States of America: The Impact of Scattered Lock-down Policies on Country-wide Infections." *COVID Economics* 43: 42–94.

Tashiro, A., and R. Shaw. 2020. "COVID-19 Pandemic Response in Japan: What Is behind the Initial Flattening of the Curve?" *Sustainability* 12 (13): 5250. doi:10.3390/su12135250.

Watanabe, T, and T. Yabu. 2020. "Japan's Voluntary Lockdown." *Covid Economics* (2020 (46): 1–31.

Welsh, D. M. 2020. "Do Masks Reduce COVID-19 Deaths? A Country-level Analysis Using IV." *COVID Economics* 57: 20–45.

Yilmazkuday, H. 2020. "Fighting against COVID-19 Requires Wearing a Face Mask by Not Some but All." *Available at SSRN 3686283.*

Index

Note: Figures are indicated by *italics*. Tables are indicated by **bold**. Endnotes are indicated by the page number followed by 'n' and the endnote number e.g., 20n1 refers to endnote 1 on page 20.

Taylor & Francis Group
an informa business